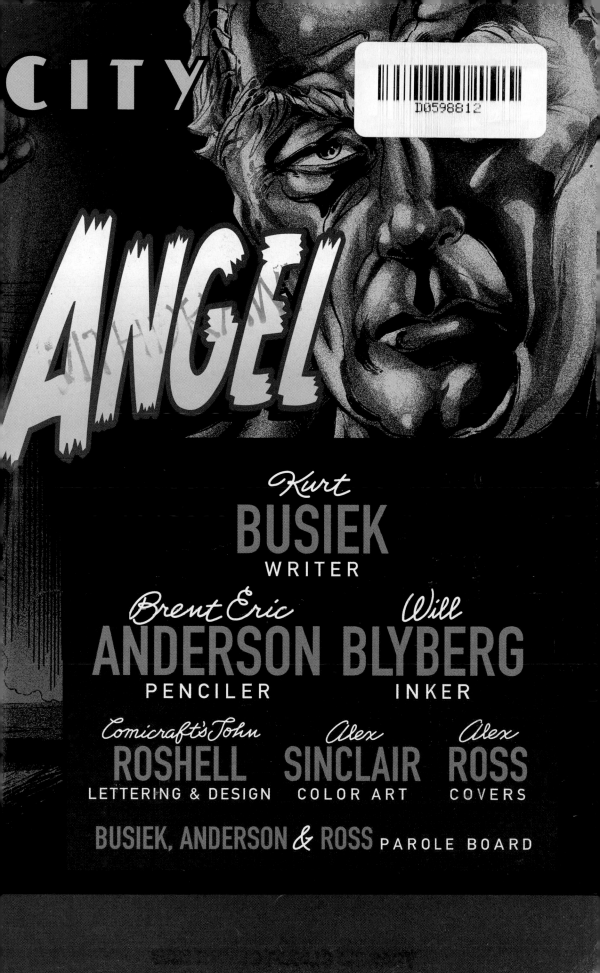

CITY

ANGEL

Kurt
BUSIEK
WRITER

Brent Eric
ANDERSON
PENCILER

Will
BLYBERG
INKER

Comicraft's John
ROSHELL
LETTERING & DESIGN

Alex
SINCLAIR
COLOR ART

Alex
ROSS
COVERS

BUSIEK, ANDERSON & ROSS PAROLE BOARD

ANN HUNTINGTON BUSIEK
Managing Editor

JOHN LAYMAN
Collection Editor

JOHN LAYMAN &
JONATHAN PETERSON
Original Series Editors

JENETTE KAHN
President & Editor-in-Chief

PAUL LEVITZ
Executive Vice President
& Publisher

JIM LEE
Editorial Director -
WildStorm

JOHN NEE
VP & General Manager -
WildStorm

RICHARD STARKINGS
Art Director

WES ABBOTT
Lettering Assistance

SCOTT DUNBIER
Group Editor

RICHARD BRUNING
VP - Creative Director

PATRICK CALDON
VP - Finance & Operations

DOROTHY CROUCH
VP - Licensed Publishing

TERRI CUNNINGHAM
VP - Managing Editor

JOEL EHRLICH
Senior VP - Advertising &
Promotions

ALISON GILL
Executive Director -
Manufacturing

LILLIAN LASERSON
VP & General Counsel

BOB WAYNE
VP - Direct Sales

ORIGINALLY PUBLISHED AS KURT BUSIEK'S ASTRO CITY VOLUME 2, #14-20

KURT BUSIEK'S ASTRO CITY: THE TARNISHED ANGEL. Published by Homage Comics, an imprint of DC Comics, 7910 Ivanhoe, Suite 438, La Jolla, CA 92037. Kurt Busiek's Astro City is ® 2000 Juke Box Productions. Compilation, sketchbook, cover and design material © Juke Box Productions. Introduction © Frank Miller. ALL RIGHTS RESERVED. Originally published as Kurt Busiek's Astro City volume 2, #14-20. Homage Comics is a trademark of DC Comics. Any similarities to persons living or dead are purely coincidental. PRINTED IN CANADA. DC Comics, a division of Warner Bros. — a Time Warner Entertainment Company

DEDICATIONS

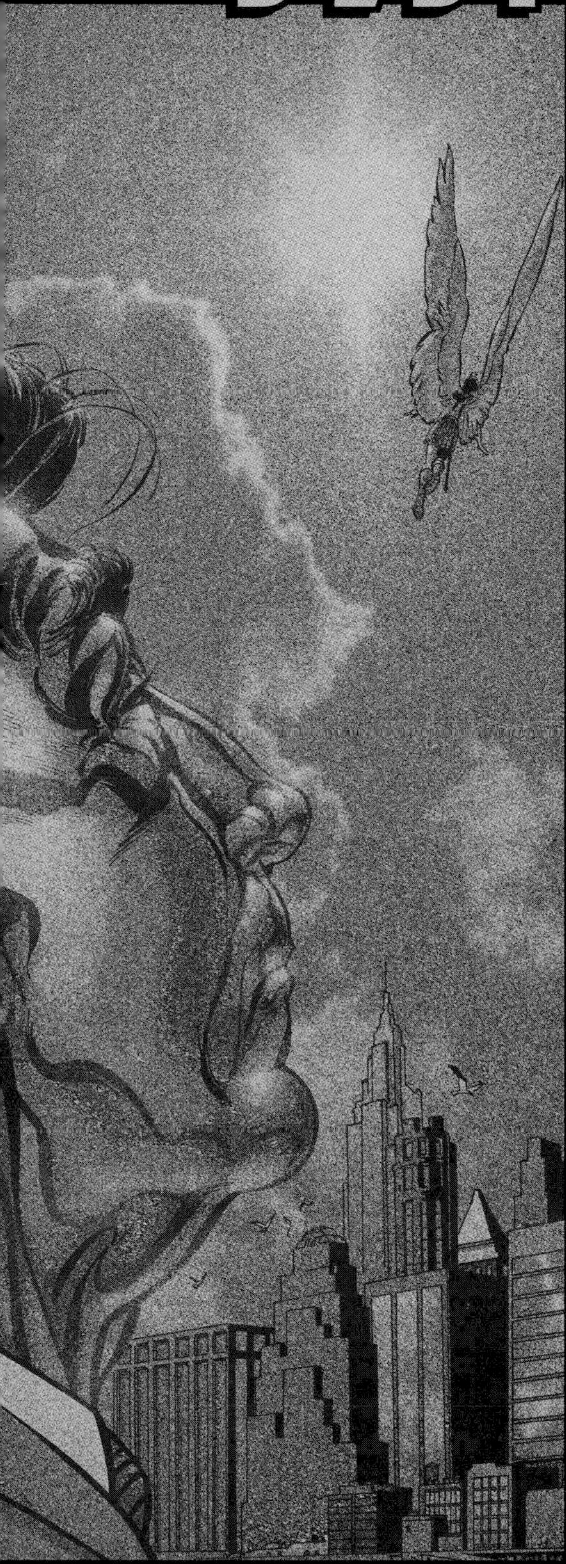

To Dashiell Hammett,
Raymond Chandler,
Donald E. Westlake,
Lawrence Block and so many
others who gave me the
vicarious pleasure of mean
streets and the tarnished,
brave souls who walk them.

-- Kurt

To the memory of Mark J.
Cohen, a cartoonist's
best friend and wiseacre,
whose bright moments of
humor lighted and smoothed
a dark and often rough
road; and to Rose Marie
McDaniel, a good sport who
complemented Mark perfectly.

-- Brent

For the late Robert Mitchum,
a great inspiration.

-- Alex

BY THE SAME CREATORS

Astro City: Life in the Big City
Astro City: Confession
Astro City: Family Album

BY KURT BUSIEK
Avengers: The Morgan Conquest (with George Pérez)
Marvels (with Alex Ross)
Untold Tales of Spider-Man (with Patrick Olliffe)
The Wizard's Tale (with David Wenzel)

BY BRENT ANDERSON
Somerset Holmes (with Bruce Jones)
X-Men: God Loves, Man Kills (with Chris Claremont)

BY ALEX ROSS
Batman: War on Crime (with Paul Dini)
Kingdom Come (with Mark Waid)
Superman: Peace on Earth (with Paul Dini)
Uncle Sam (with Steve Darnall)
Terminator: The Burning Earth (with Ron Fortier)

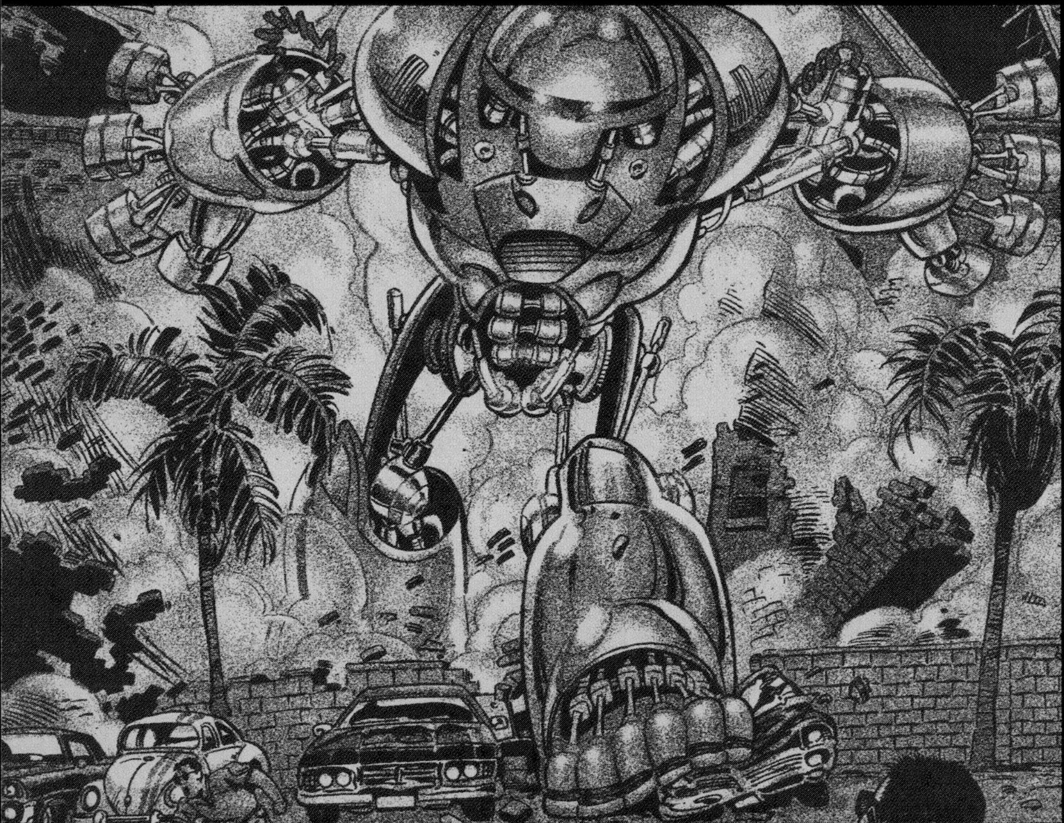

CONTENTS

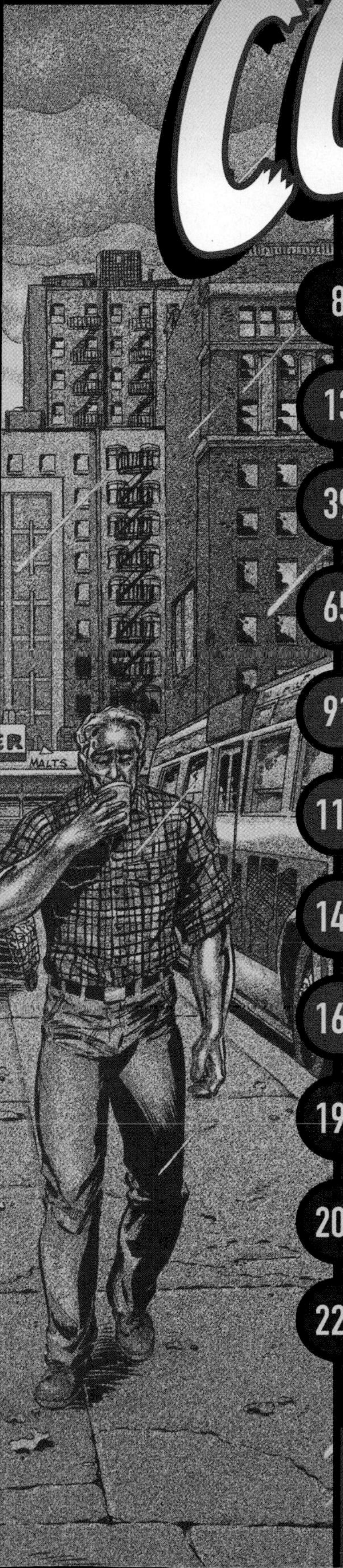
MALTS

INTRODUCTION

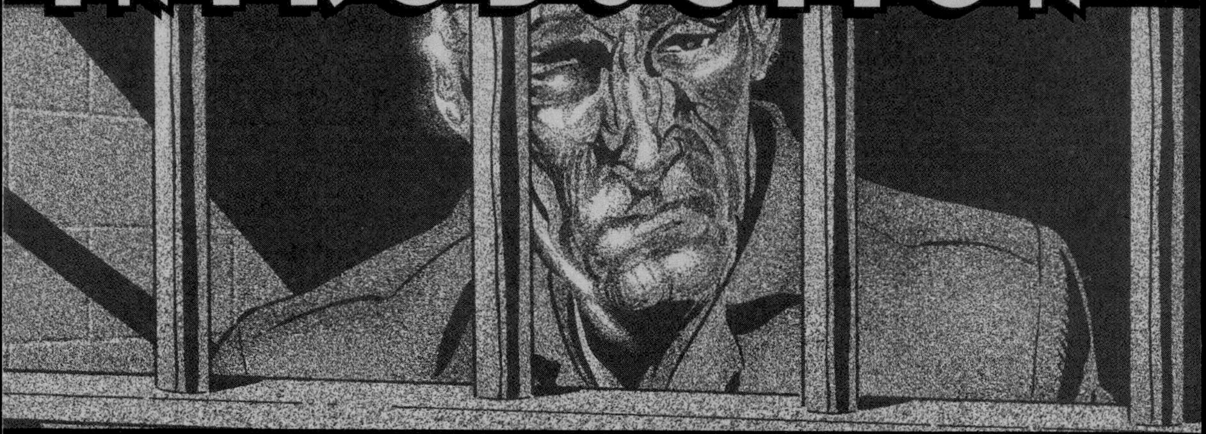

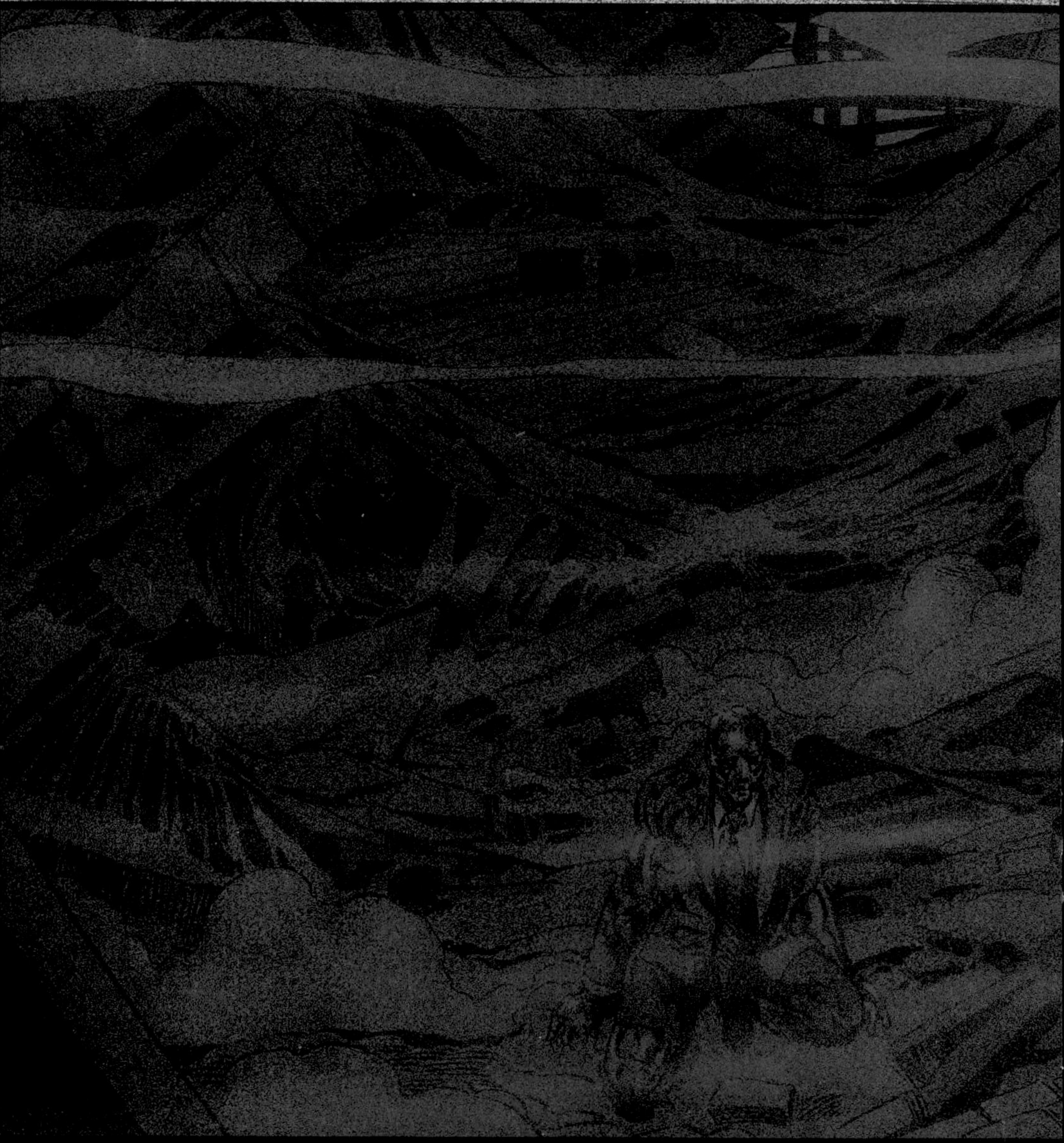

BY FRANK MILLER

They only looked dead.

They'd gotten so damned old and tired. After their violent, defiant birth in the late thirties and their full flowering in the forties, when soldiers in the field of combat would read the adventures of Captain America and Superman, the producers of superhero comics engaged in a suicide pact. They succumbed to fifties censorship pressure and turned these fighters for truth and justice into insufferable bromides. For goodness sake, they even deputized Batman.

Think of it. They deputized Batman. The guy dresses up like Dracula and hunts bad guys down like dogs and throws them through windows and they give him a badge and turn him into a walking public service announcement. He even sold Twinkies. How wrong can you be?

And don't even get me started on Superman.

It was pathetic, what happened to those dear old icons. Even the inking looked flabby.

THEY GOT A SHOT IN THE ARM in the '60s, when Jack Kirby, Stan Lee, Steve Ditko and the rest of the Marvel crew made it all seem brand new again. But the Comics Code was still making sure things couldn't get too awfully interesting, and the publishers were still stupidly submitting to its stupid rules, so

things got stale again.

It got pretty bad. The patient almost died. For the longest time, there wasn't a pulse. We're talking flatline.

But Kirby and Lee and Ditko and company, aided later in the game by talents like Neal Adams and Jim Steranko and others, applied the defibrillation pads and got the old warhorse up and at 'em again.

AND SO A NEW GENERATION OR TWO came of age, some of us madly in love with guys and gals in tights. We got to work, playing with the notion that we could amuse our fellow grownups with stories about super-heroes. A hip bunch, or at least imagining ourselves as such, we set about poking fun at the stuff that filled our childhoods with joy.

We gave it classy names, like deconstruction-ism. We added a mix of political cynicism and post-Freudian conceit and shook things up but

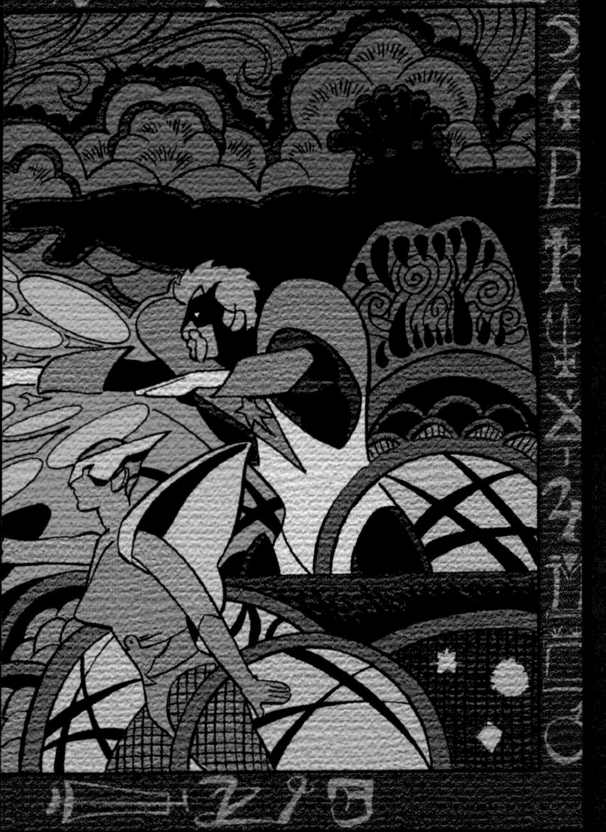

Left: The enchanted tapestry that appears in "The Only Chance," a souvenir of one of Honor Guard's earlier adventures. It never got shown clearly in the story itself, so we're displaying it here...

good — even shaking away the dumb old Comics Code and making Commissioner Gordon eat Batman's deputy badge. Underneath all our pretensions, though, we were a bunch of kids having a ball.

But we were cool. We pointed out how much of this stuff (which we just happened to be spending our professional lives writing and drawing) was goofy, silly, quirky, just plain wacky...I once joked to Alan Moore that he had (with WATCHMEN) done the autopsy on the superhero, while I (with DARK KNIGHT) had provided its brass-band funeral.

A regrettable "grim and gritty" period followed, best forgotten, that seemed to prove me right. Teeth only appeared while gritted. Good guys turned into bad guys, drunks and mass murderers. These weren't anti-heroes. They were villains. Worst, they whined incessantly. Self-pity and despair reigned supreme. It sure looked like I'd called it right.

But boy, was I wrong.

They only looked dead.

GOOD IDEAS NEVER DIE. And, though it is far from the only kind of comic book idea that, executed with skill and intelligence, can delight — far from it — the superhero remains the single genre that was created exclusively for the form.

The superhero lives on, and may yet thrive, as we get on to the business of reconstruction. Not just nostalgically revisiting the toys of our childhood, but making the concept work once again, informed by our experience and the times in which we live. Unburdened by others' prejudice or by our own, historic, undeserved shame. Building it back up and, we can only hope, making the central idea stronger than it ever was.

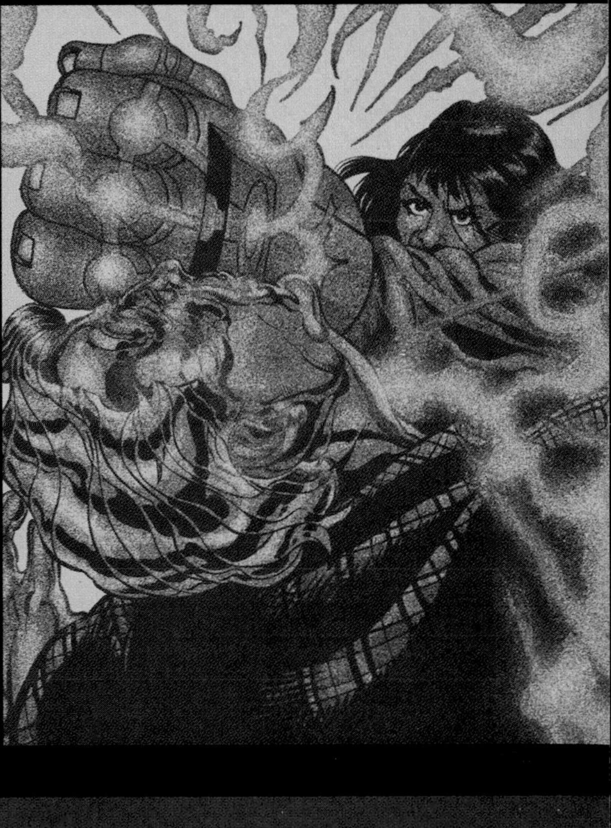

Stronger, and more versatile, no longer trapped as exclusively kid stuff. Addressing, even, adult concerns such as guilt and debt and honor, embracing the ambiguities and doubts and disappointments of real life — all the while keeping the sense of wonder that inspired us to sneak a flashlight under the bedspread and read the things when Mom wasn't watching. There's the central task facing artists who make up new superhero comics: to restore the genre's essential luster.

Busiek, Anderson and team have weighed in with their best efforts, and I'm plenty impressed. I trust you will be, as well.

Here's a very good gangster story. And a very, very good superhero story. And a sign, I hope, of things to come.

Welcome to ASTRO CITY.

FRANK MILLER
3/21/00

FRANK MILLER HAS BEEN BREAKING RULES SINCE THE LATE SEVENTIES, BOTH IN COMICS AND THE BUSINESS OF COMICS. HE FIRST CAME TO NOTORIETY ON MARVEL'S DAREDEVIL, AND REDEFINED THE SUPERHERO GENRE WITH BATMAN: THE DARK KNIGHT RETURNS. CRIME REMAINS HIS MOST FERTILE SUBJECT MATTER, EXPLORED IN CLASSIC NOIR STYLE IN HIS MANY SIN CITY STORIES FOR DARK HORSE. AN OUTSPOKEN PROPONENT OF CREATOR RIGHTS AND FREE EXPRESSION, MILLER SERVES ON THE BOARD OF DIRECTORS OF THE COMIC BOOK LEGAL DEFENSE FUND. (WWW.CBLDF.ORG)

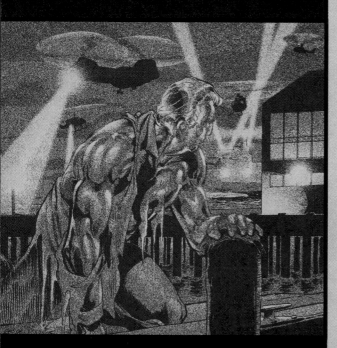

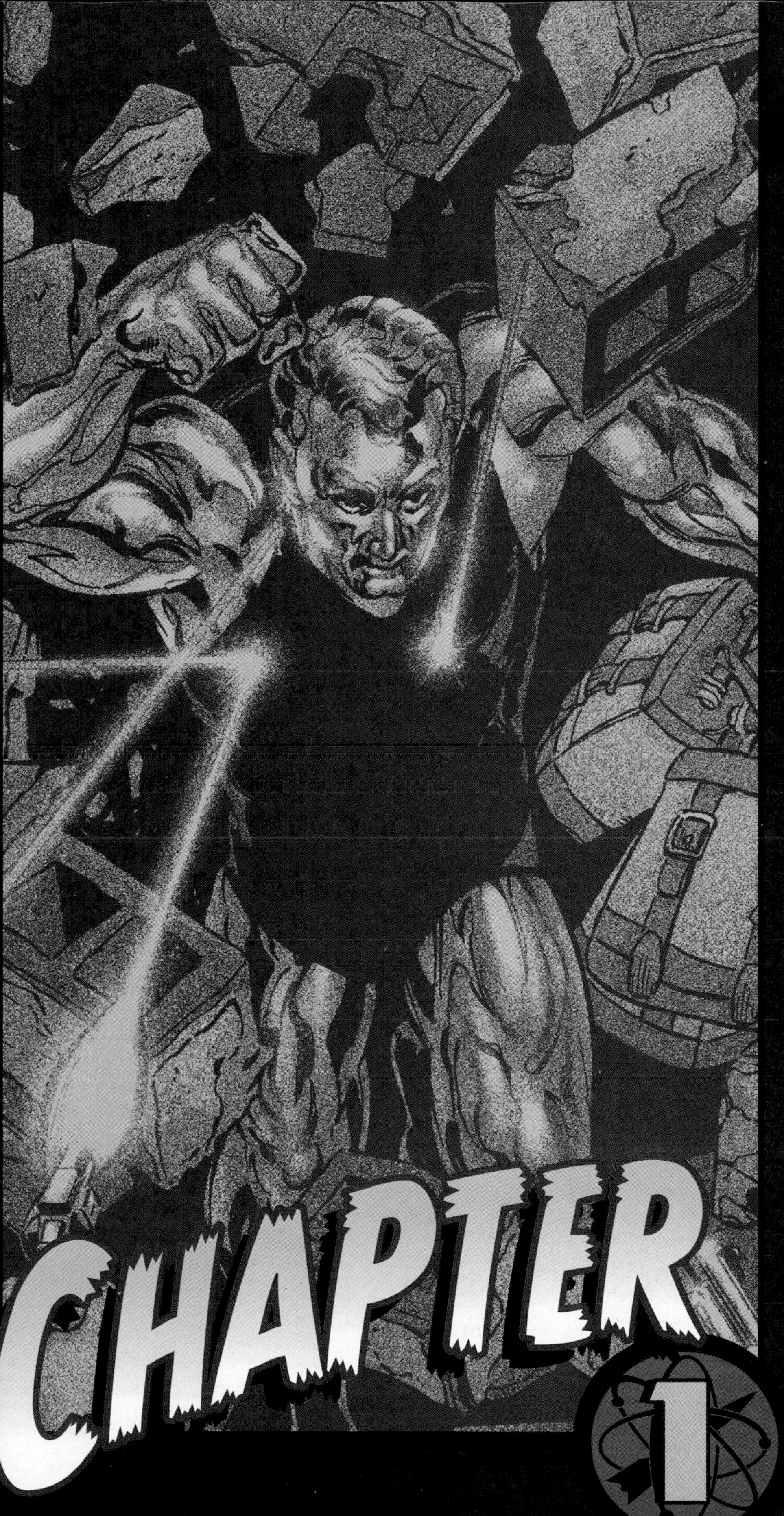
CHAPTER
1

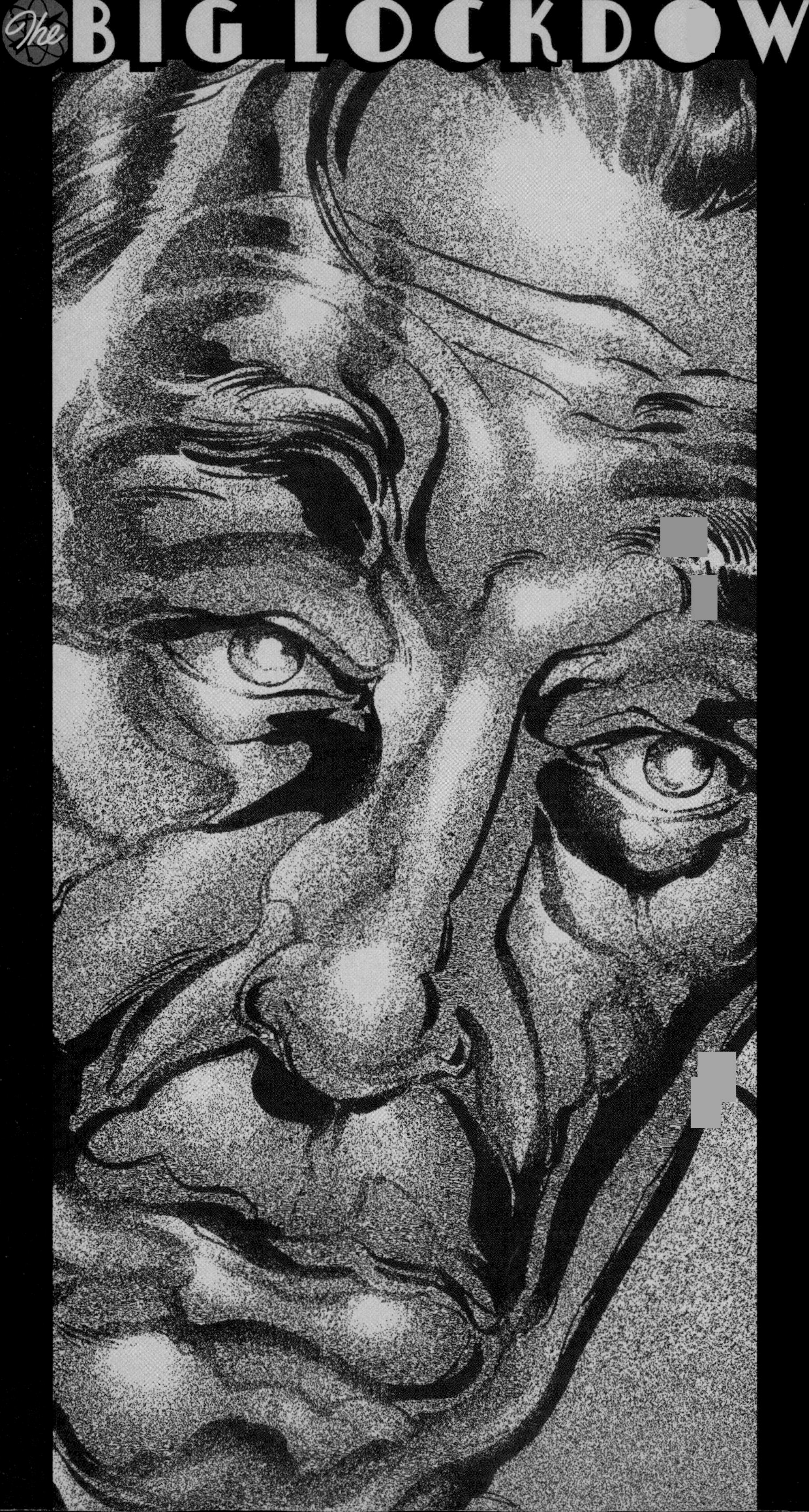
The BIG LOCKDOW

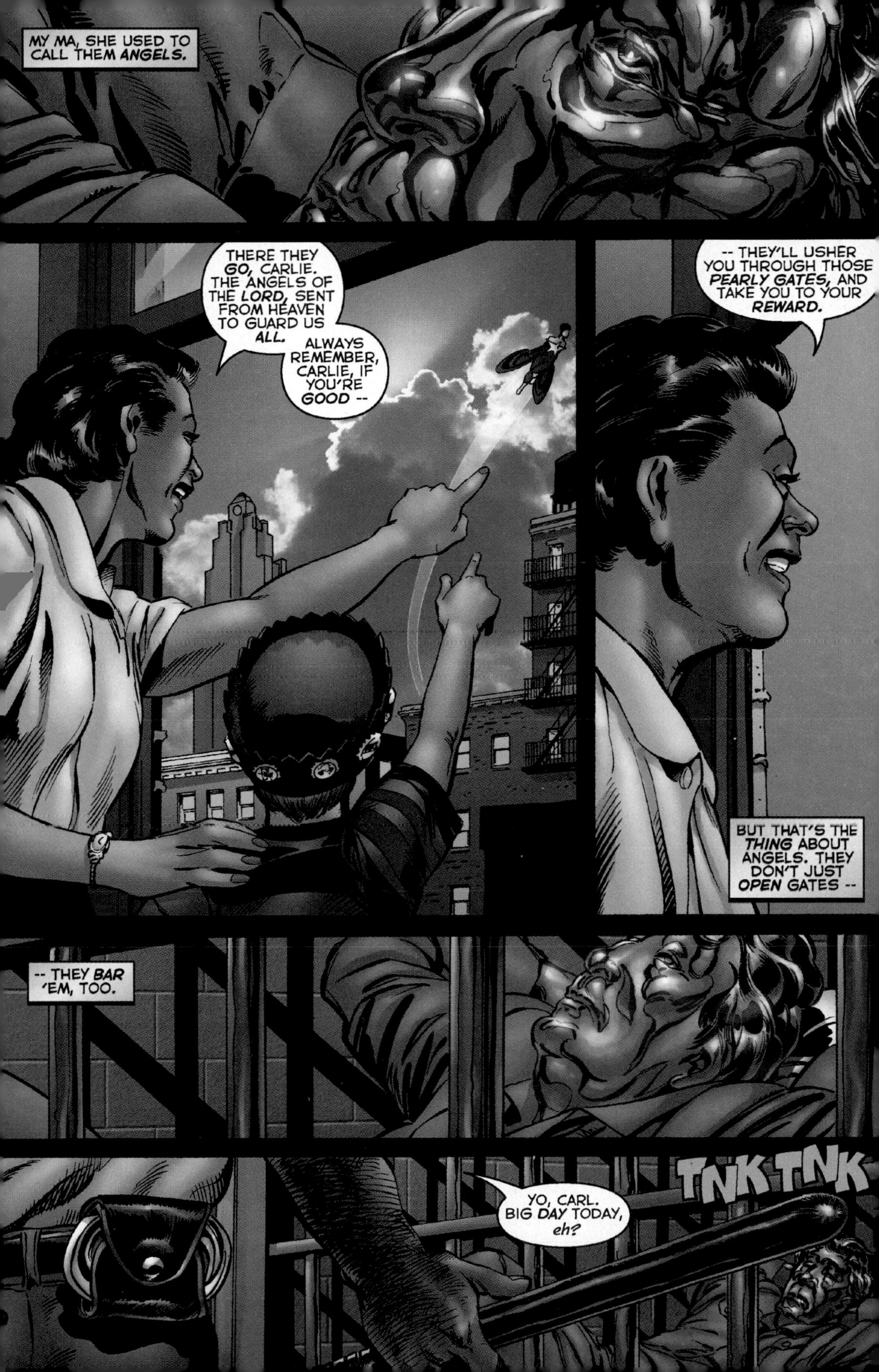
MY MA, SHE USED TO CALL THEM ANGELS.
THERE THEY GO, CARLIE. THE ANGELS OF THE LORD, SENT FROM HEAVEN TO GUARD US ALL.
ALWAYS REMEMBER, CARLIE, IF YOU'RE GOOD --
-- THEY'LL USHER YOU THROUGH THOSE PEARLY GATES, AND TAKE YOU TO YOUR REWARD.
BUT THAT'S THE THING ABOUT ANGELS. THEY DON'T JUST OPEN GATES --
-- THEY BAR 'EM, TOO.
TNK TNK
YO, CARL. BIG DAY TODAY, eh?

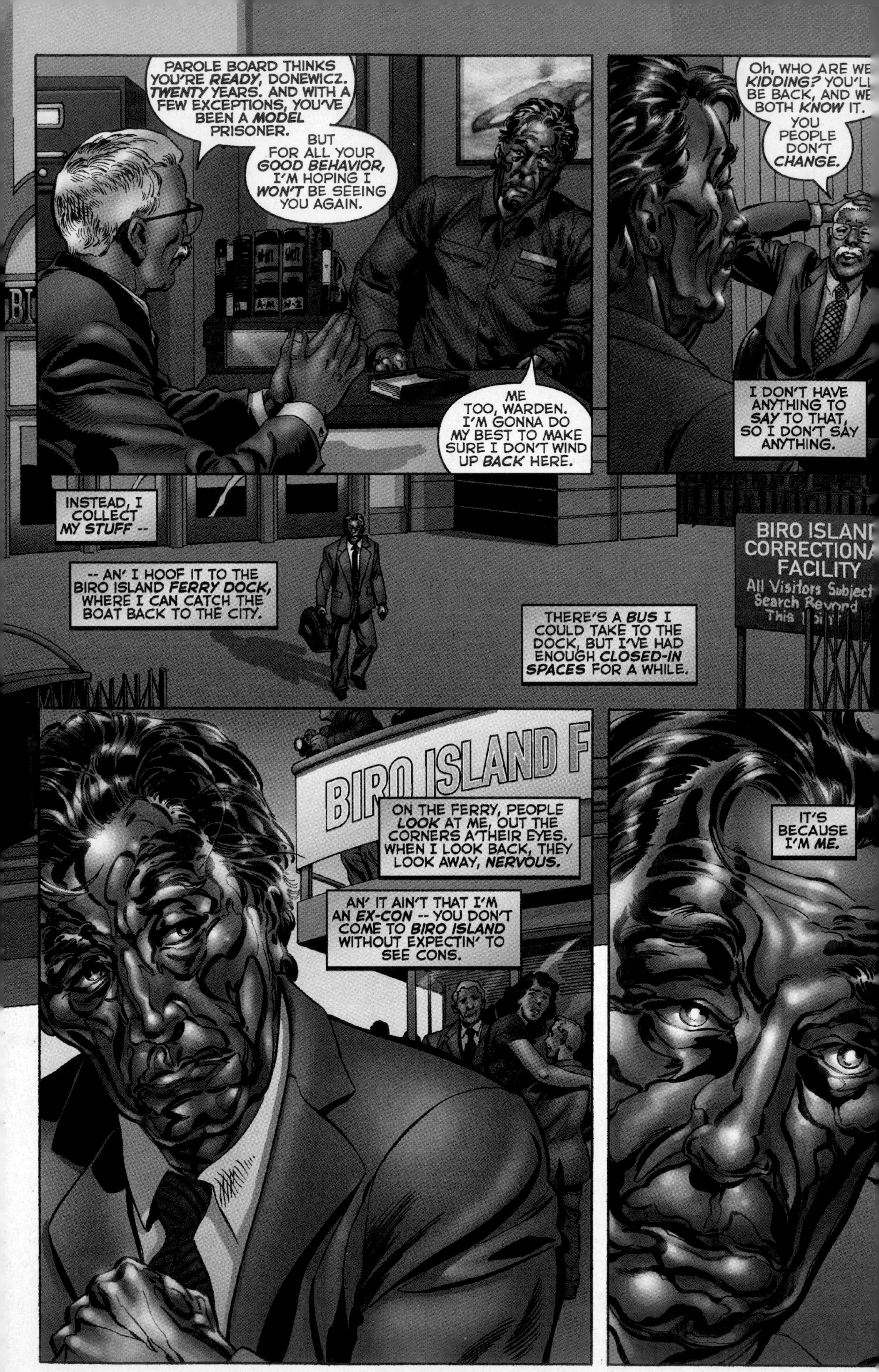
PAROLE BOARD THINKS YOU'RE READY, DONEWICZ. TWENTY YEARS. AND WITH A FEW EXCEPTIONS, YOU'VE BEEN A MODEL PRISONER.
BUT FOR ALL YOUR GOOD BEHAVIOR, I'M HOPING I WON'T BE SEEING YOU AGAIN.
ME TOO, WARDEN. I'M GONNA DO MY BEST TO MAKE SURE I DON'T WIND UP BACK HERE.
Oh, WHO ARE WE KIDDING? YOU'LL BE BACK, AND WE BOTH KNOW IT.
YOU PEOPLE DON'T CHANGE.
I DON'T HAVE ANYTHING TO SAY TO THAT, SO I DON'T SAY ANYTHING.
INSTEAD, I COLLECT MY STUFF --
-- AN' I HOOF IT TO THE BIRO ISLAND FERRY DOCK, WHERE I CAN CATCH THE BOAT BACK TO THE CITY.
BIRO ISLAND CORRECTIONAL FACILITY
All Visitors Subject Search Beyond This Point
THERE'S A BUS I COULD TAKE TO THE DOCK, BUT I'VE HAD ENOUGH CLOSED-IN SPACES FOR A WHILE.
BIRO ISLAND F
ON THE FERRY, PEOPLE LOOK AT ME, OUT THE CORNERS A'THEIR EYES. WHEN I LOOK BACK, THEY LOOK AWAY, NERVOUS.
AN' IT AIN'T THAT I'M AN EX-CON -- YOU DON'T COME TO BIRO ISLAND WITHOUT EXPECTIN' TO SEE CONS.
IT'S BECAUSE I'M ME.

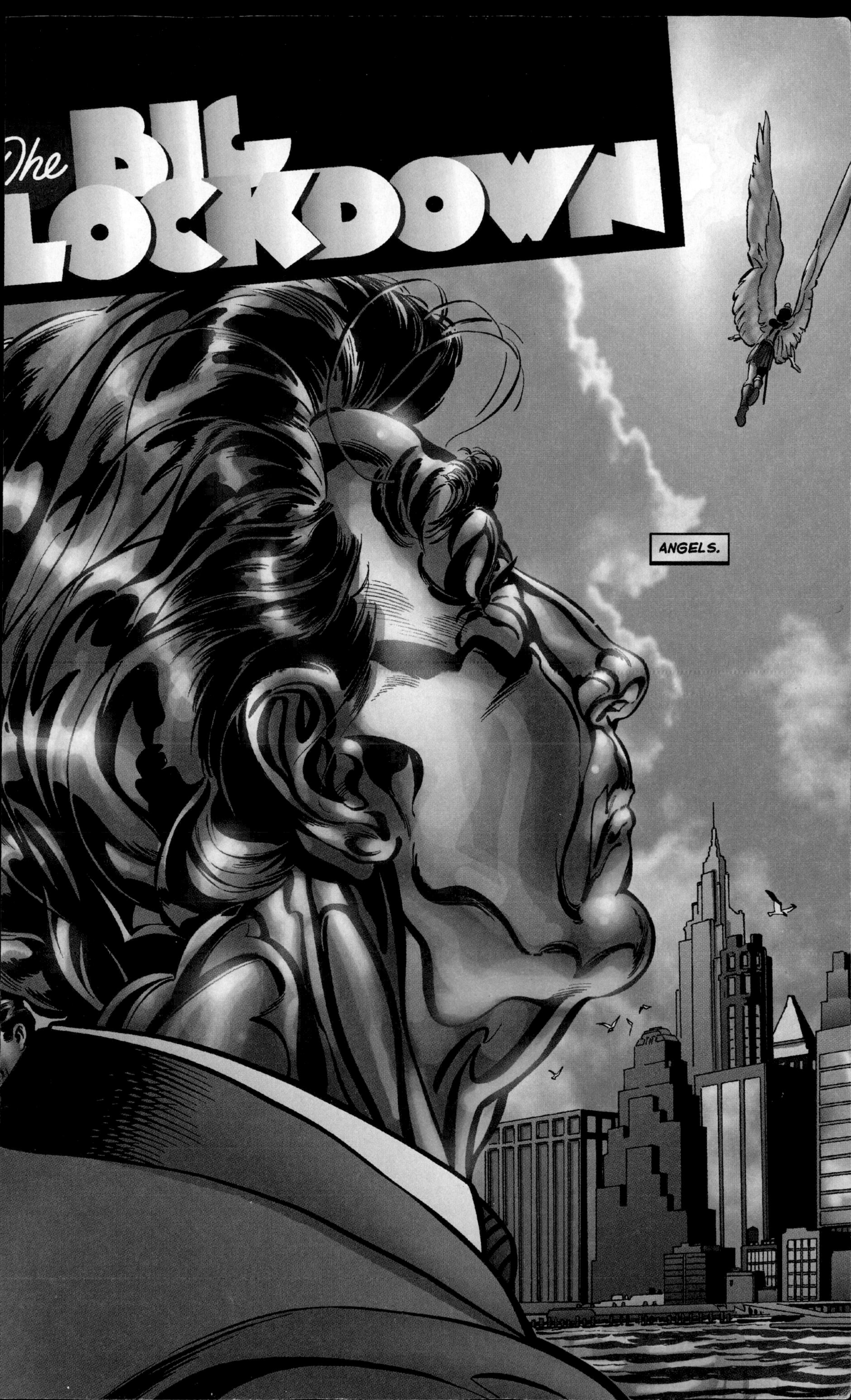

The BIG LOCKDOWN
ANGELS.

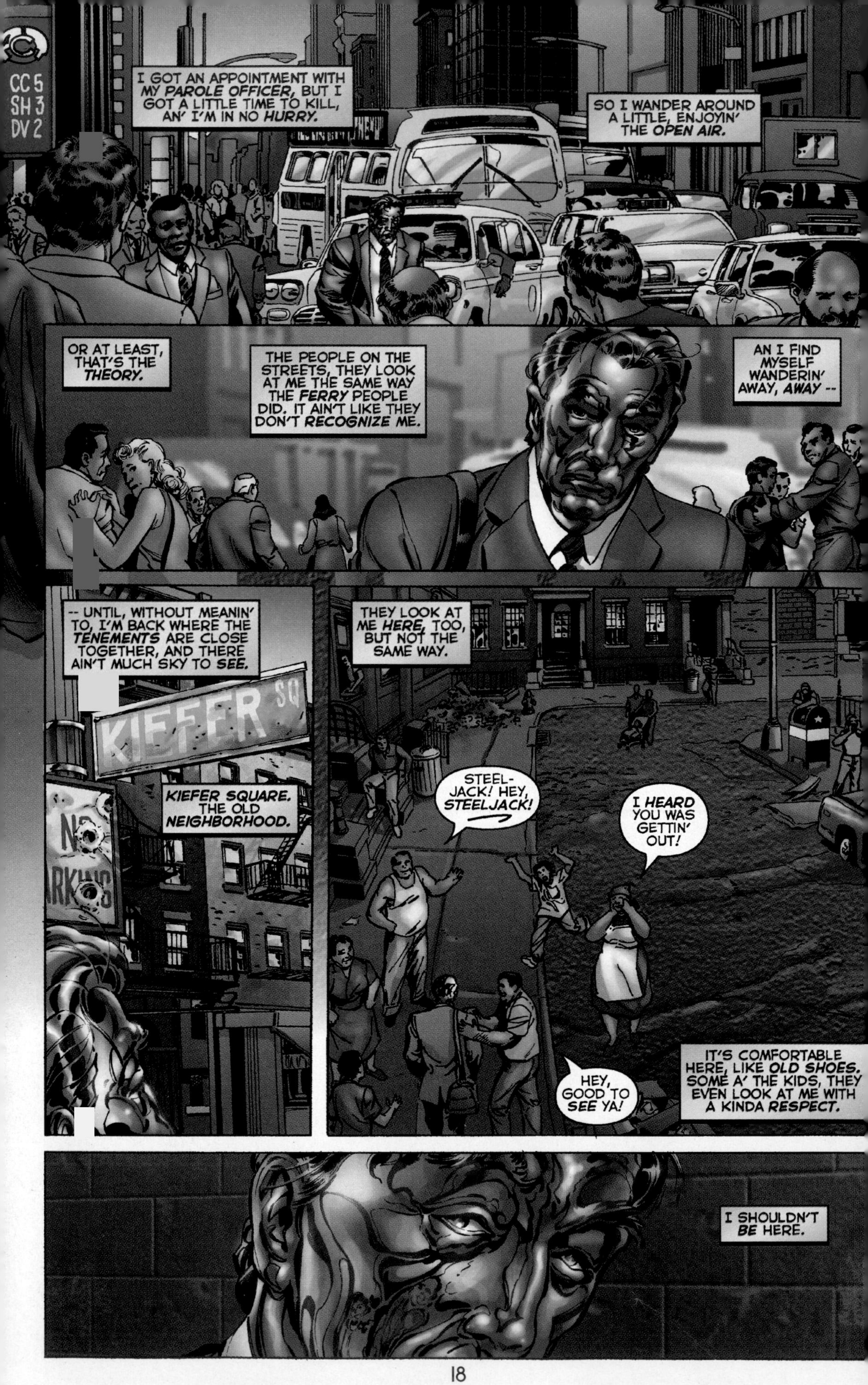
CC 5
SH 3
DV 2
I GOT AN APPOINTMENT WITH MY PAROLE OFFICER, BUT I GOT A LITTLE TIME TO KILL, AN' I'M IN NO HURRY.
SO I WANDER AROUND A LITTLE, ENJOYIN' THE OPEN AIR.
OR AT LEAST, THAT'S THE THEORY.
THE PEOPLE ON THE STREETS, THEY LOOK AT ME THE SAME WAY THE FERRY PEOPLE DID. IT AIN'T LIKE THEY DON'T RECOGNIZE ME.
AN I FIND MYSELF WANDERIN' AWAY, AWAY --
-- UNTIL, WITHOUT MEANIN' TO, I'M BACK WHERE THE TENEMENTS ARE CLOSE TOGETHER, AND THERE AIN'T MUCH SKY TO SEE.
KIEFER SQ
KIEFER SQUARE. THE OLD NEIGHBORHOOD.
THEY LOOK AT ME HERE, TOO, BUT NOT THE SAME WAY.
STEEL-JACK! HEY, STEELJACK!
I HEARD YOU WAS GETTIN' OUT!
HEY, GOOD TO SEE YA!
IT'S COMFORTABLE HERE, LIKE OLD SHOES. SOME A' THE KIDS, THEY EVEN LOOK AT ME WITH A KINDA RESPECT.
I SHOULDN'T BE HERE.

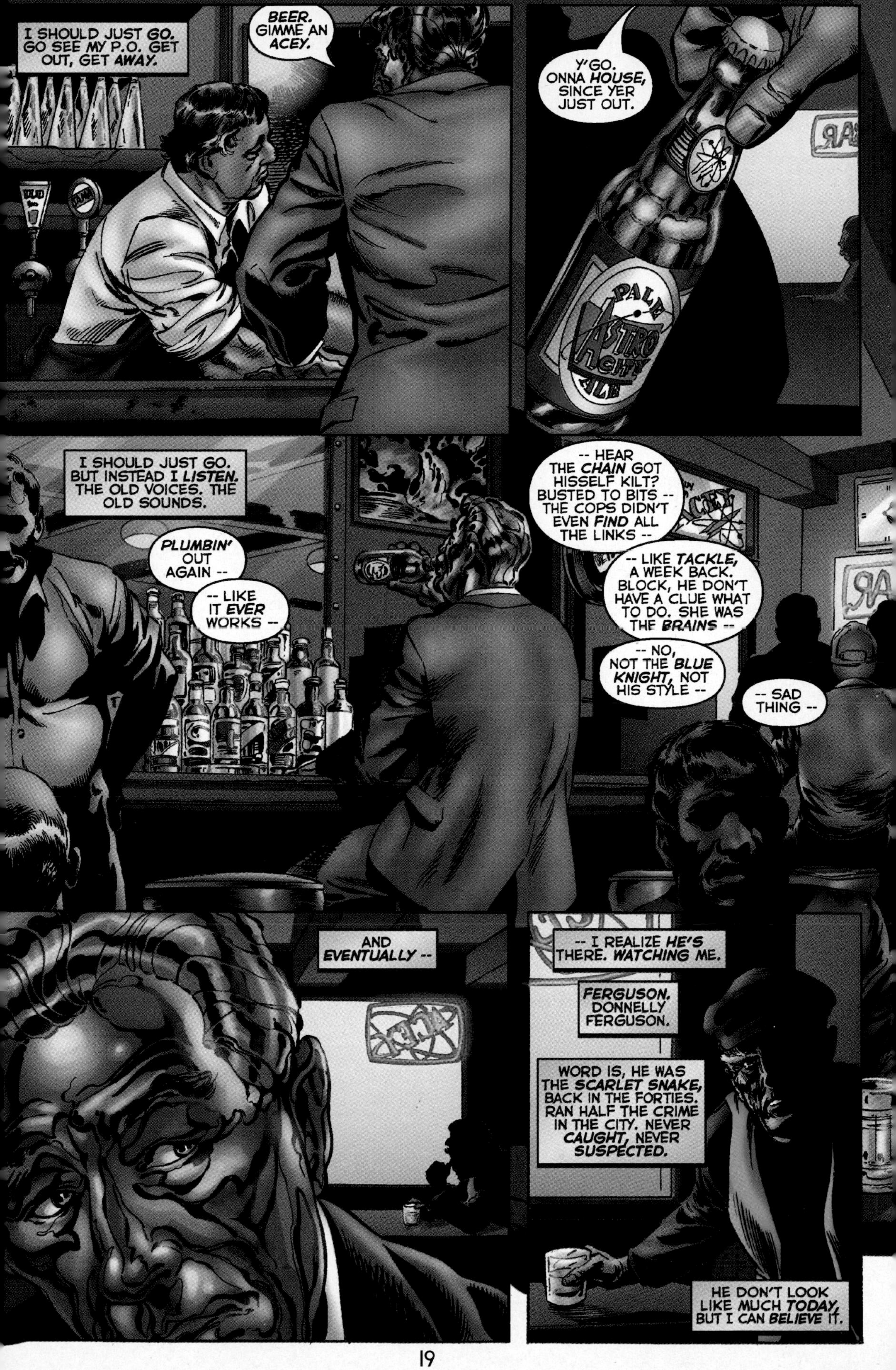

I SHOULD JUST GO. GO SEE MY P.O. GET OUT, GET AWAY.
BEER. GIMME AN ACEY.
Y'GO. ONNA HOUSE, SINCE YER JUST OUT.
PALE ASTRO CITY ALE
I SHOULD JUST GO. BUT INSTEAD I LISTEN. THE OLD VOICES. THE OLD SOUNDS.
PLUMBIN' OUT AGAIN --
-- LIKE IT EVER WORKS --
-- HEAR THE CHAIN GOT HISSELF KILT? BUSTED TO BITS -- THE COPS DIDN'T EVEN FIND ALL THE LINKS --
-- LIKE TACKLE, A WEEK BACK. BLOCK, HE DON'T HAVE A CLUE WHAT TO DO. SHE WAS THE BRAINS --
-- NO, NOT THE BLUE KNIGHT, NOT HIS STYLE --
-- SAD THING --
AND EVENTUALLY --
-- I REALIZE HE'S THERE. WATCHING ME.
FERGUSON. DONNELLY FERGUSON.
WORD IS, HE WAS THE SCARLET SNAKE, BACK IN THE FORTIES. RAN HALF THE CRIME IN THE CITY. NEVER CAUGHT, NEVER SUSPECTED.
HE DON'T LOOK LIKE MUCH TODAY, BUT I CAN BELIEVE IT.

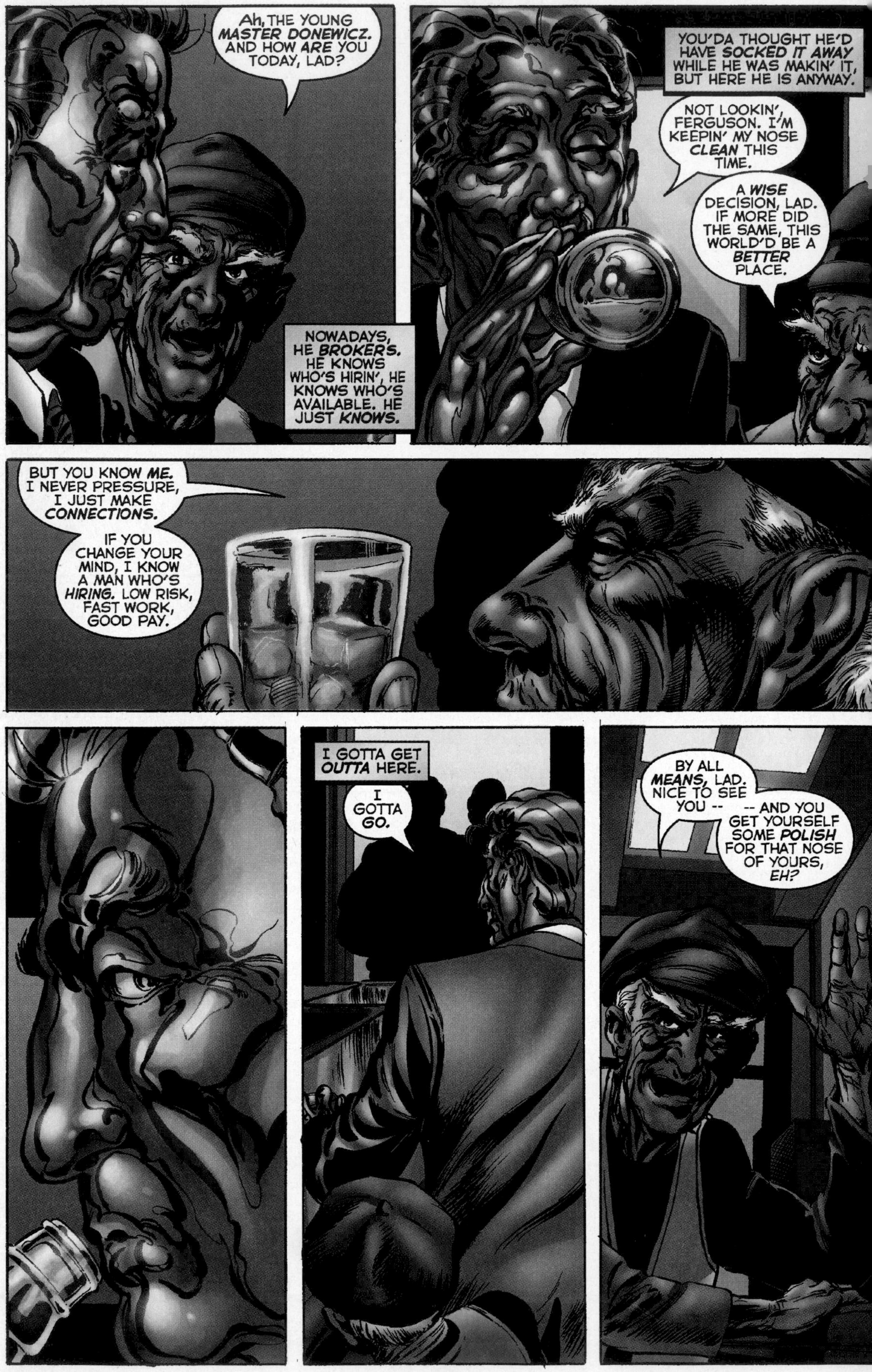

Ah, THE YOUNG MASTER DONEWICZ. AND HOW ARE YOU TODAY, LAD?
NOWADAYS, HE BROKERS. HE KNOWS WHO'S HIRIN', HE KNOWS WHO'S AVAILABLE. HE JUST KNOWS.
YOU'DA THOUGHT HE'D HAVE SOCKED IT AWAY WHILE HE WAS MAKIN' IT, BUT HERE HE IS ANYWAY.
NOT LOOKIN', FERGUSON. I'M KEEPIN' MY NOSE CLEAN THIS TIME.
A WISE DECISION, LAD. IF MORE DID THE SAME, THIS WORLD'D BE A BETTER PLACE.
BUT YOU KNOW ME. I NEVER PRESSURE, I JUST MAKE CONNECTIONS.
IF YOU CHANGE YOUR MIND, I KNOW A MAN WHO'S HIRING. LOW RISK, FAST WORK, GOOD PAY.
I GOTTA GET OUTTA HERE.
I GOTTA GO.
BY ALL MEANS, LAD. NICE TO SEE YOU --
-- AND YOU GET YOURSELF SOME POLISH FOR THAT NOSE OF YOURS, EH?

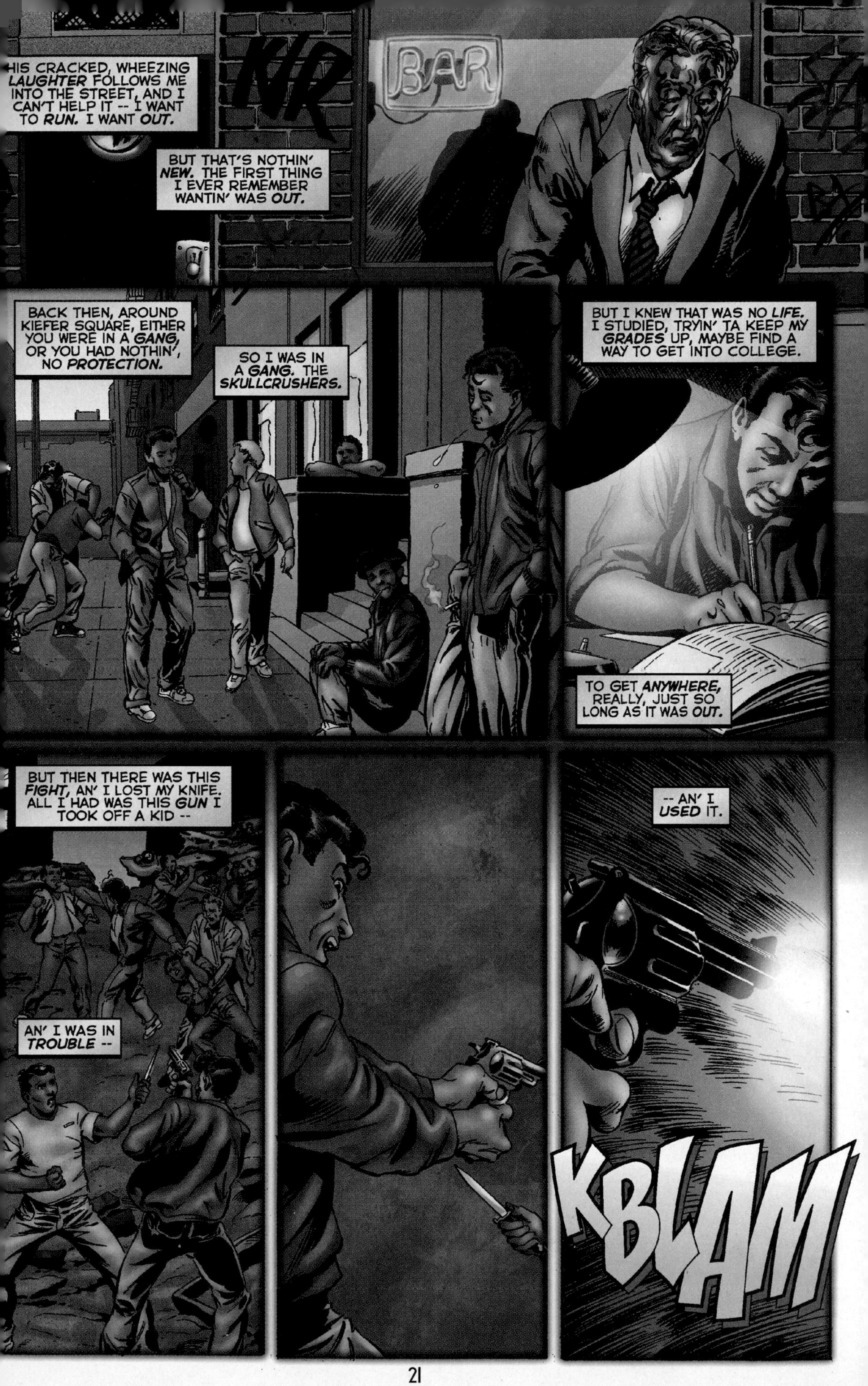
HIS CRACKED, WHEEZING LAUGHTER FOLLOWS ME INTO THE STREET, AND I CAN'T HELP IT -- I WANT TO RUN. I WANT OUT.
BUT THAT'S NOTHIN' NEW. THE FIRST THING I EVER REMEMBER WANTIN' WAS OUT.
BAR
BACK THEN, AROUND KIEFER SQUARE, EITHER YOU WERE IN A GANG, OR YOU HAD NOTHIN', NO PROTECTION.
SO I WAS IN A GANG. THE SKULLCRUSHERS.
BUT I KNEW THAT WAS NO LIFE. I STUDIED, TRYIN' TA KEEP MY GRADES UP, MAYBE FIND A WAY TO GET INTO COLLEGE.
TO GET ANYWHERE, REALLY, JUST SO LONG AS IT WAS OUT.
BUT THEN THERE WAS THIS FIGHT, AN' I LOST MY KNIFE. ALL I HAD WAS THIS GUN I TOOK OFF A KID --
AN' I WAS IN TROUBLE --
-- AN' I USED IT.
KBLAM

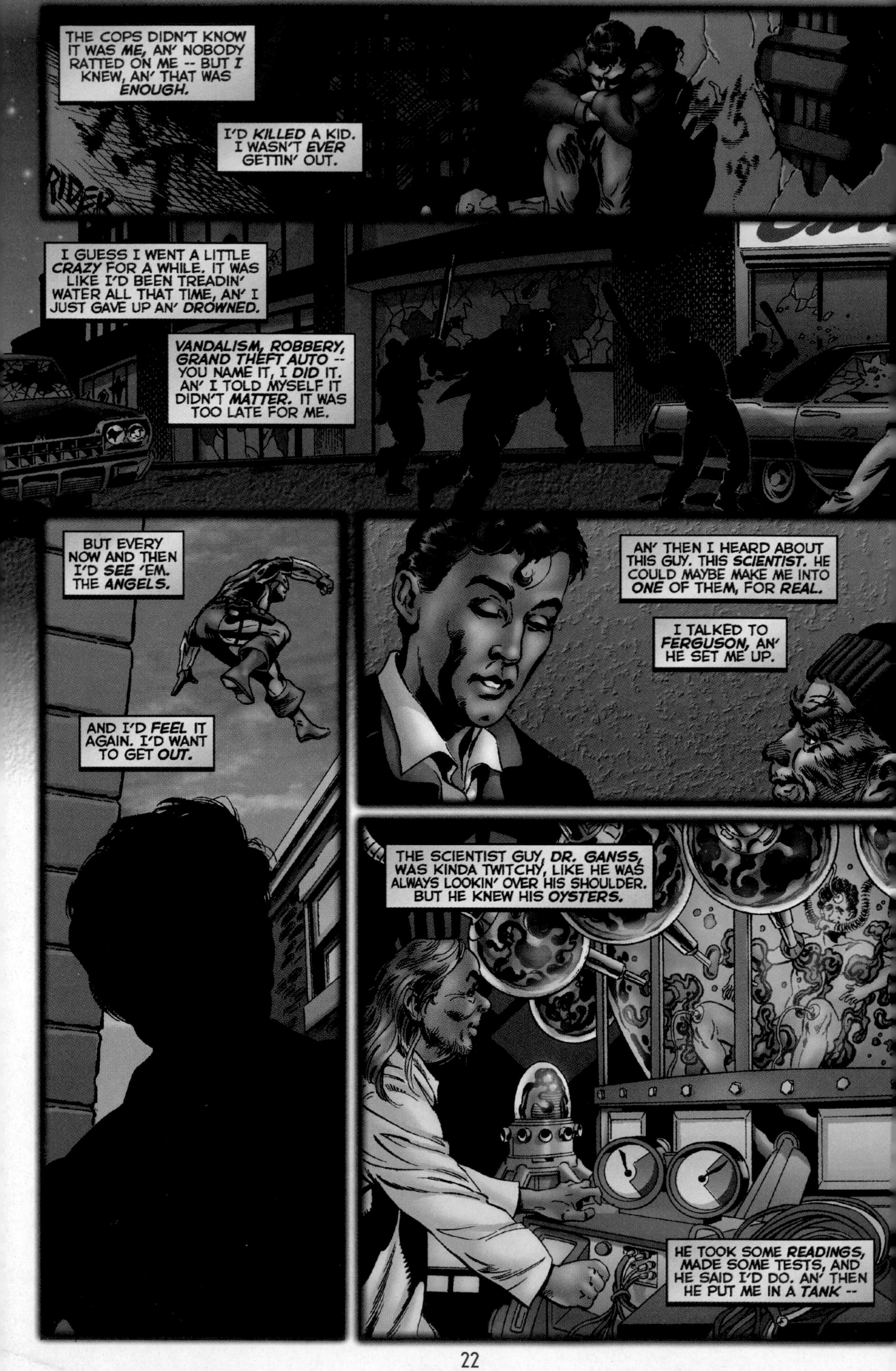
THE COPS DIDN'T KNOW IT WAS ME, AN' NOBODY RATTED ON ME -- BUT I KNEW, AN' THAT WAS ENOUGH.
I'D KILLED A KID. I WASN'T EVER GETTIN' OUT.
RIDER
I GUESS I WENT A LITTLE CRAZY FOR A WHILE. IT WAS LIKE I'D BEEN TREADIN' WATER ALL THAT TIME, AN' I JUST GAVE UP AN' DROWNED.
VANDALISM, ROBBERY, GRAND THEFT AUTO -- YOU NAME IT, I DID IT. AN' I TOLD MYSELF IT DIDN'T MATTER. IT WAS TOO LATE FOR ME.
BUT EVERY NOW AND THEN I'D SEE 'EM. THE ANGELS.
AND I'D FEEL IT AGAIN. I'D WANT TO GET OUT.
AN' THEN I HEARD ABOUT THIS GUY. THIS SCIENTIST. HE COULD MAYBE MAKE ME INTO ONE OF THEM, FOR REAL.
I TALKED TO FERGUSON, AN' HE SET ME UP.
THE SCIENTIST GUY, DR. GANSS, WAS KINDA TWITCHY, LIKE HE WAS ALWAYS LOOKIN' OVER HIS SHOULDER. BUT HE KNEW HIS OYSTERS.
HE TOOK SOME READINGS, MADE SOME TESTS, AND HE SAID I'D DO. AN' THEN HE PUT ME IN A TANK --

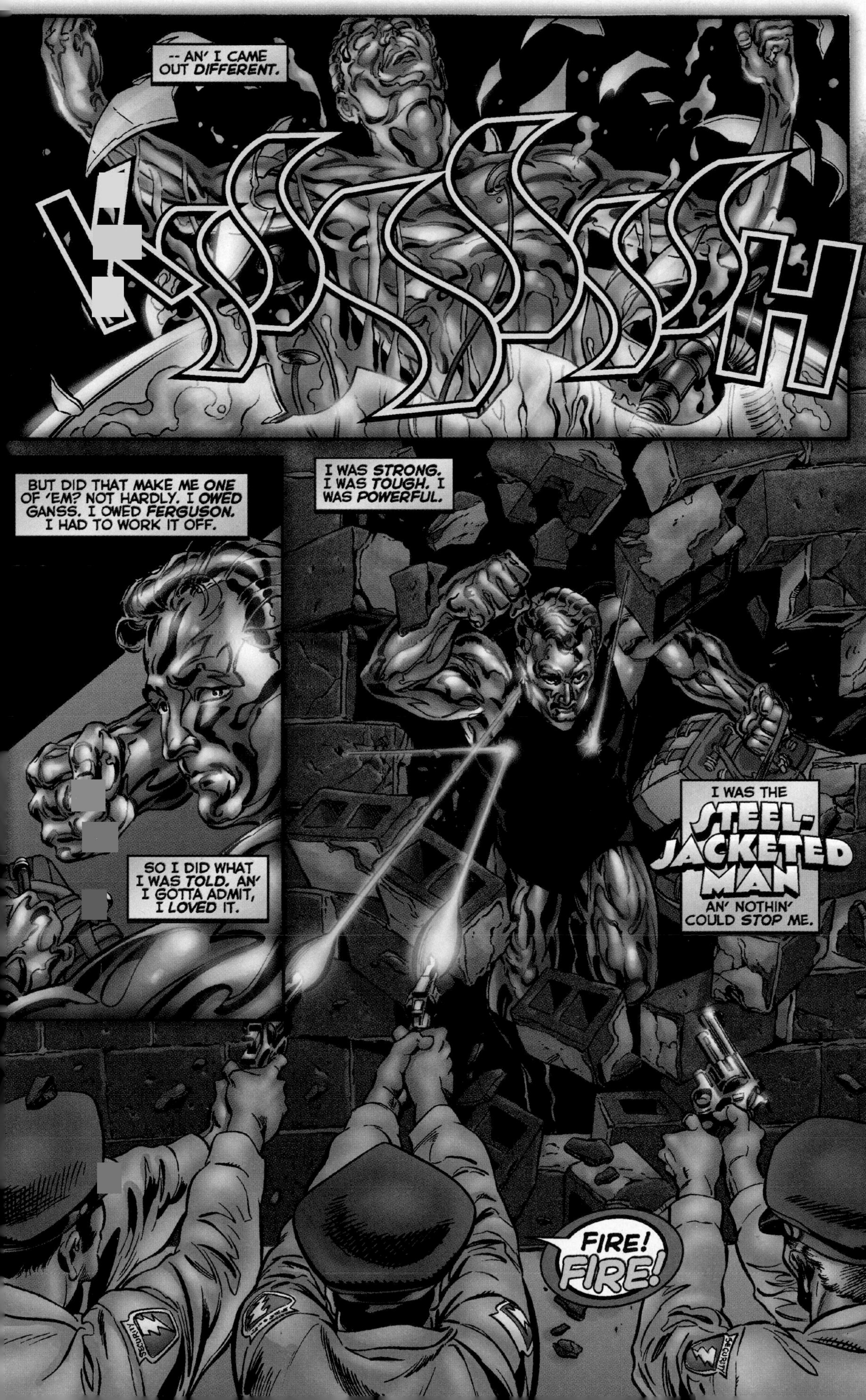
-- AN' I CAME OUT DIFFERENT.
BUT DID THAT MAKE ME ONE OF 'EM? NOT HARDLY. I OWED GANSS. I OWED FERGUSON. I HAD TO WORK IT OFF.
SO I DID WHAT I WAS TOLD. AN' I GOTTA ADMIT, I LOVED IT.
I WAS STRONG. I WAS TOUGH. I WAS POWERFUL.
I WAS THE STEEL-JACKETED MAN AN' NOTHIN' COULD STOP ME.
FIRE! FIRE!

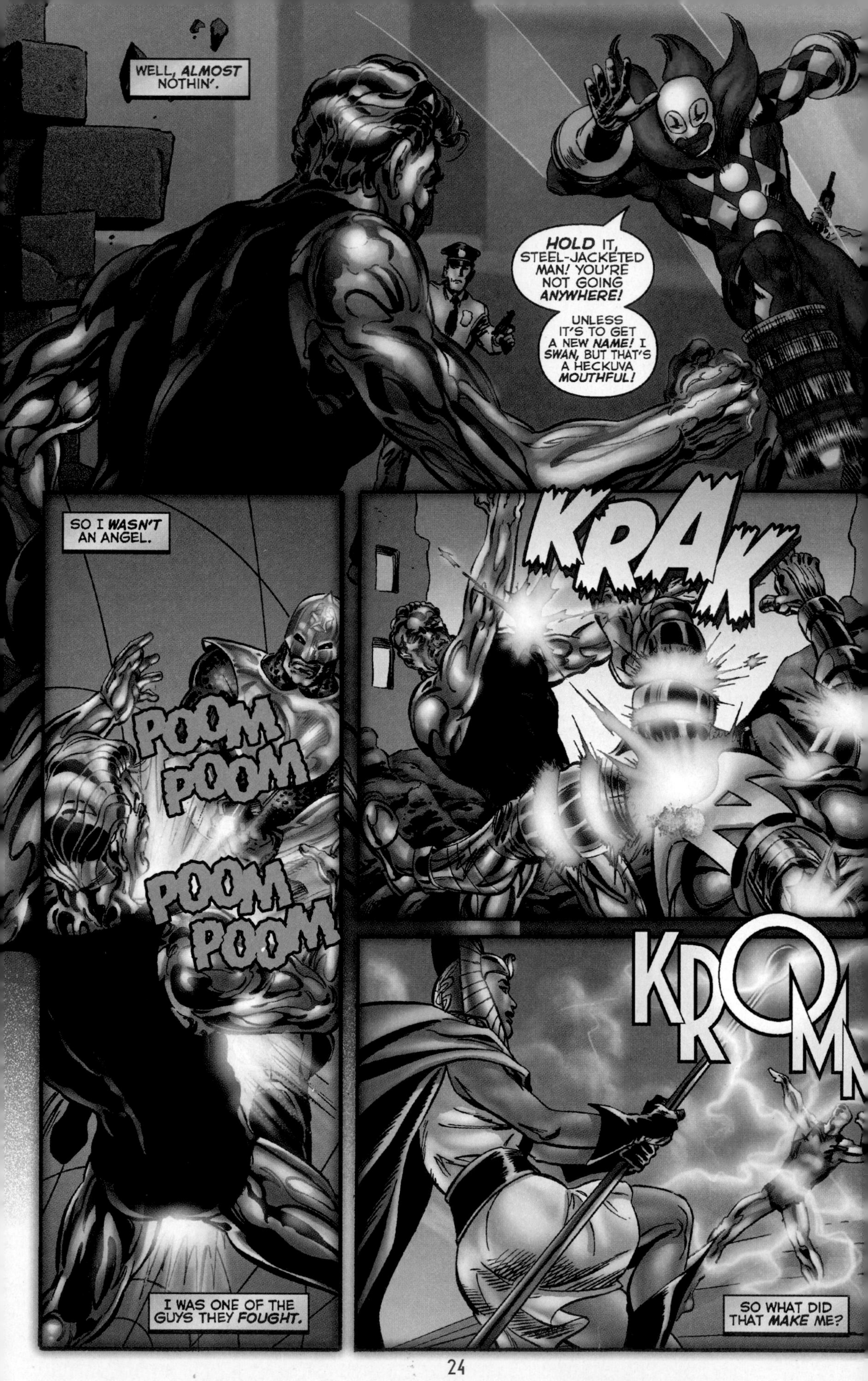

WELL, ALMOST NOTHIN'.
HOLD IT, STEEL-JACKETED MAN! YOU'RE NOT GOING ANYWHERE!
UNLESS IT'S TO GET A NEW NAME! I SWAN, BUT THAT'S A HECKUVA MOUTHFUL!
SO I WASN'T AN ANGEL.
POOM POOM
POOM POOM
I WAS ONE OF THE GUYS THEY FOUGHT.
KRAK
KROOM
SO WHAT DID THAT MAKE ME?

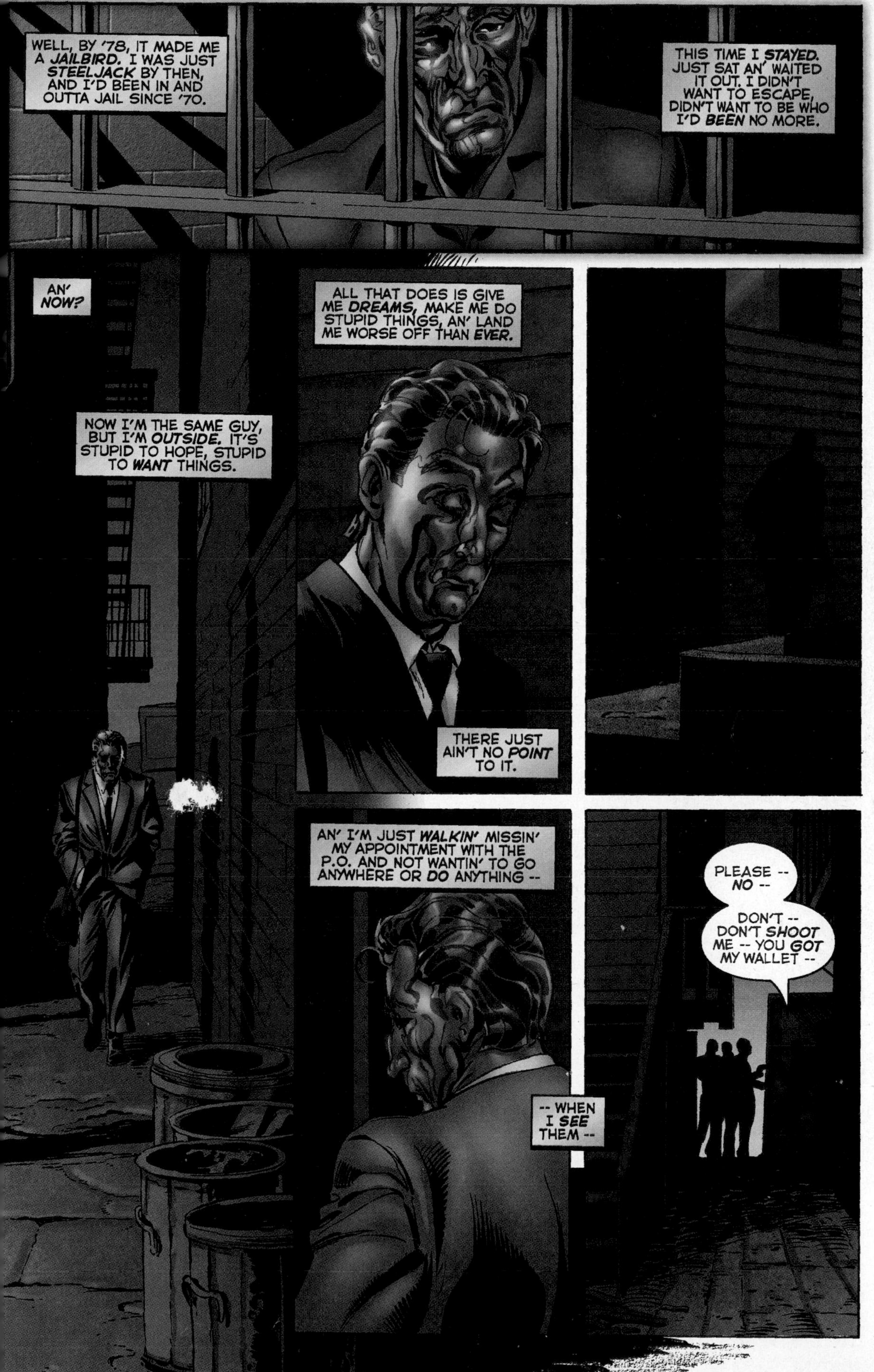
WELL, BY '78, IT MADE ME A JAILBIRD. I WAS JUST STEELJACK BY THEN, AND I'D BEEN IN AND OUTTA JAIL SINCE '70.
THIS TIME I STAYED. JUST SAT AN' WAITED IT OUT. I DIDN'T WANT TO ESCAPE, DIDN'T WANT TO BE WHO I'D BEEN NO MORE.
AN' NOW?
NOW I'M THE SAME GUY, BUT I'M OUTSIDE. IT'S STUPID TO HOPE, STUPID TO WANT THINGS.
ALL THAT DOES IS GIVE ME DREAMS, MAKE ME DO STUPID THINGS, AN' LAND ME WORSE OFF THAN EVER.
THERE JUST AIN'T NO POINT TO IT.
AN' I'M JUST WALKIN' MISSIN' MY APPOINTMENT WITH THE P.O. AND NOT WANTIN' TO GO ANYWHERE OR DO ANYTHING --
-- WHEN I SEE THEM --
PLEASE -- NO --
DON'T -- DON'T SHOOT ME -- YOU GOT MY WALLET --

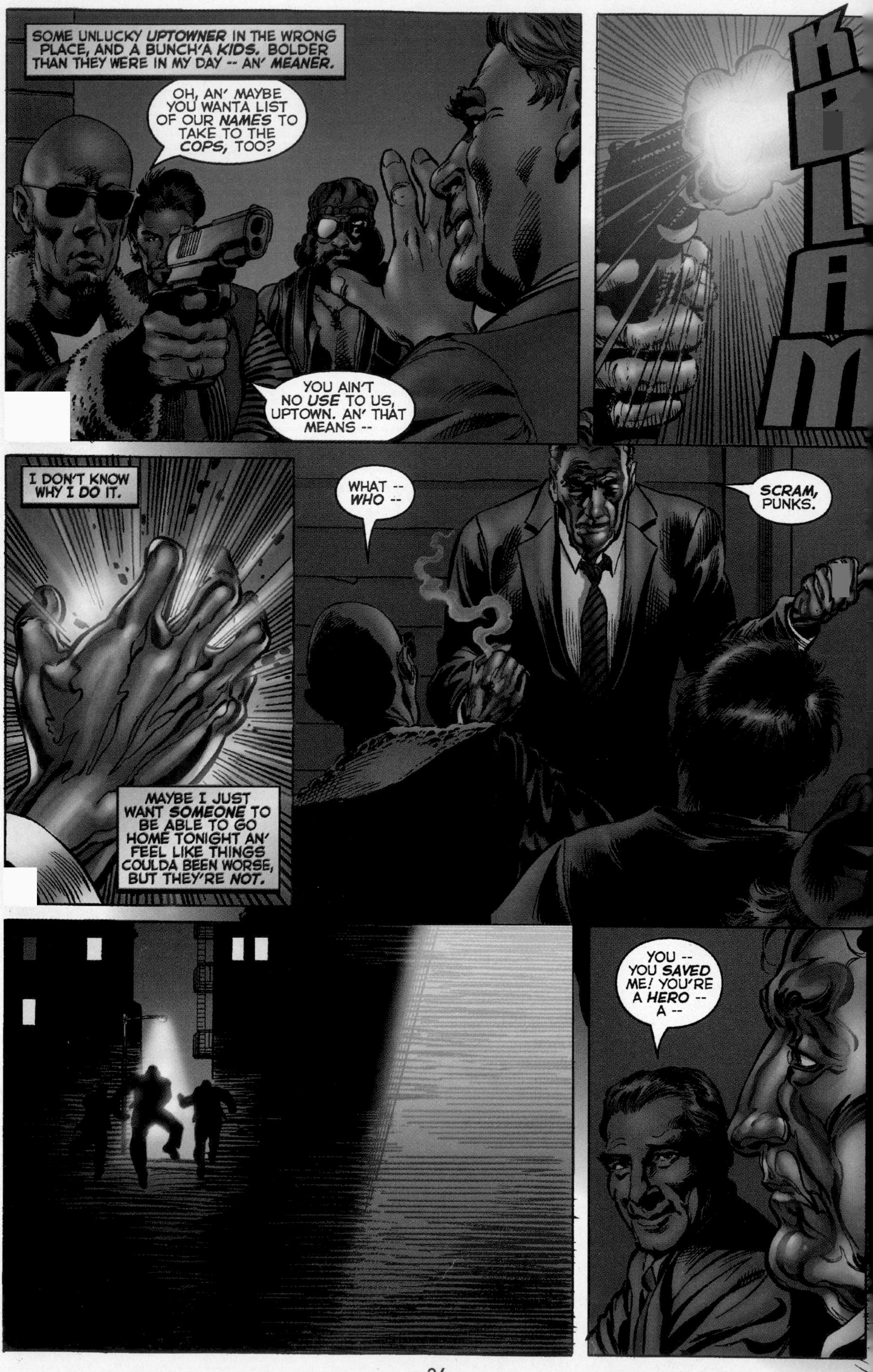
SOME UNLUCKY *UPTOWNER* IN THE WRONG PLACE, AND A BUNCH'A *KIDS*. BOLDER THAN THEY WERE IN MY DAY -- AN' *MEANER*.
OH, AN' MAYBE YOU WANTA LIST OF OUR *NAMES* TO TAKE TO THE *COPS*, TOO?
YOU AIN'T NO *USE* TO US, UPTOWN. AN' THAT MEANS --
I DON'T KNOW WHY I *DO* IT.
MAYBE I JUST WANT *SOMEONE* TO BE ABLE TO GO HOME TONIGHT AN' FEEL LIKE THINGS COULDA BEEN WORSE, BUT THEY'RE *NOT*.
WHAT -- *WHO* --
SCRAM, PUNKS.
YOU -- YOU *SAVED* ME! YOU'RE A *HERO* -- A --

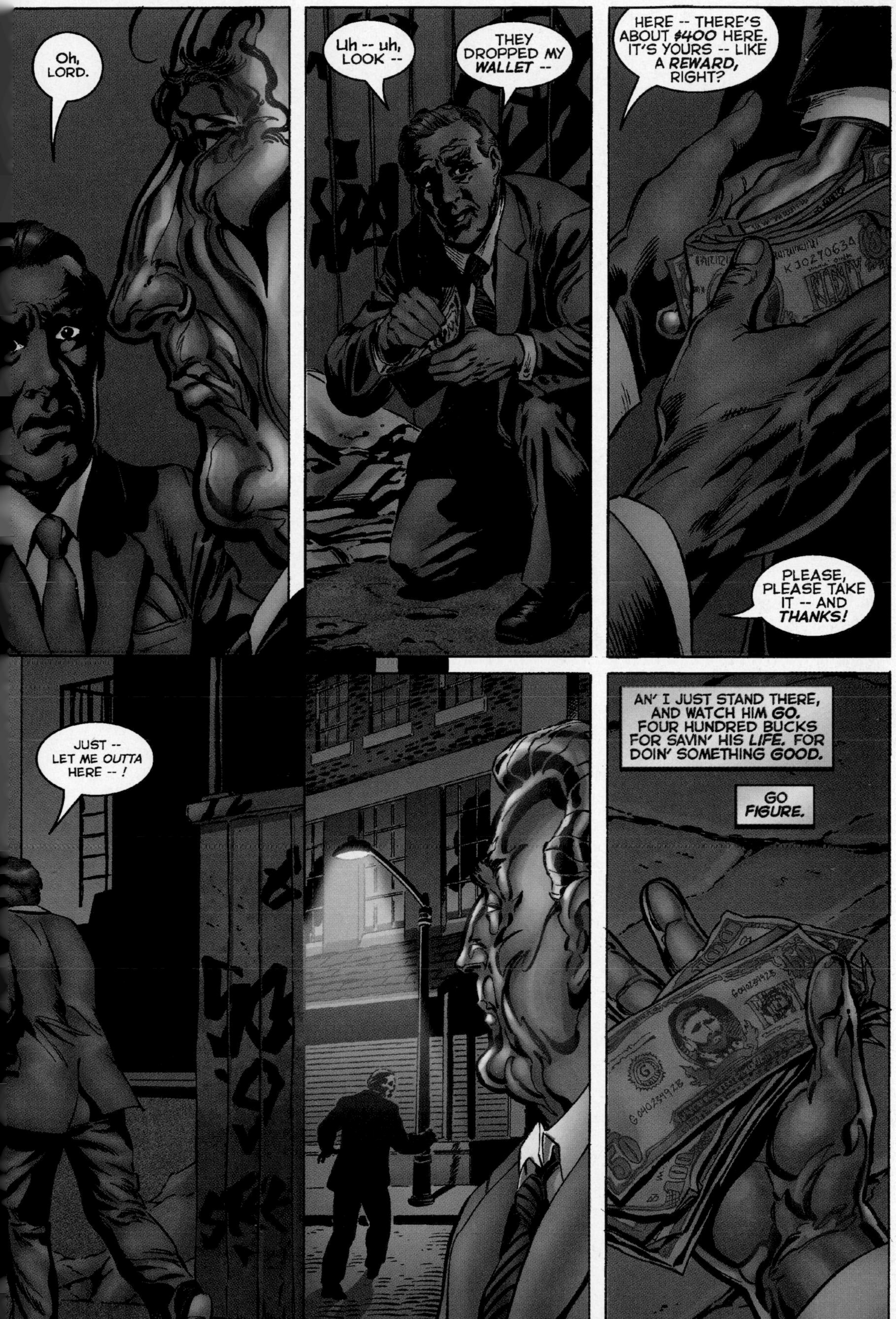

Oh, LORD.
Uh -- uh, LOOK --
THEY DROPPED MY WALLET --
HERE -- THERE'S ABOUT $400 HERE. IT'S YOURS -- LIKE A REWARD, RIGHT?
PLEASE, PLEASE TAKE IT -- AND THANKS!
JUST -- LET ME OUTTA HERE -- !
AN' I JUST STAND THERE, AND WATCH HIM GO. FOUR HUNDRED BUCKS FOR SAVIN' HIS LIFE. FOR DOIN' SOMETHING GOOD.
GO FIGURE.

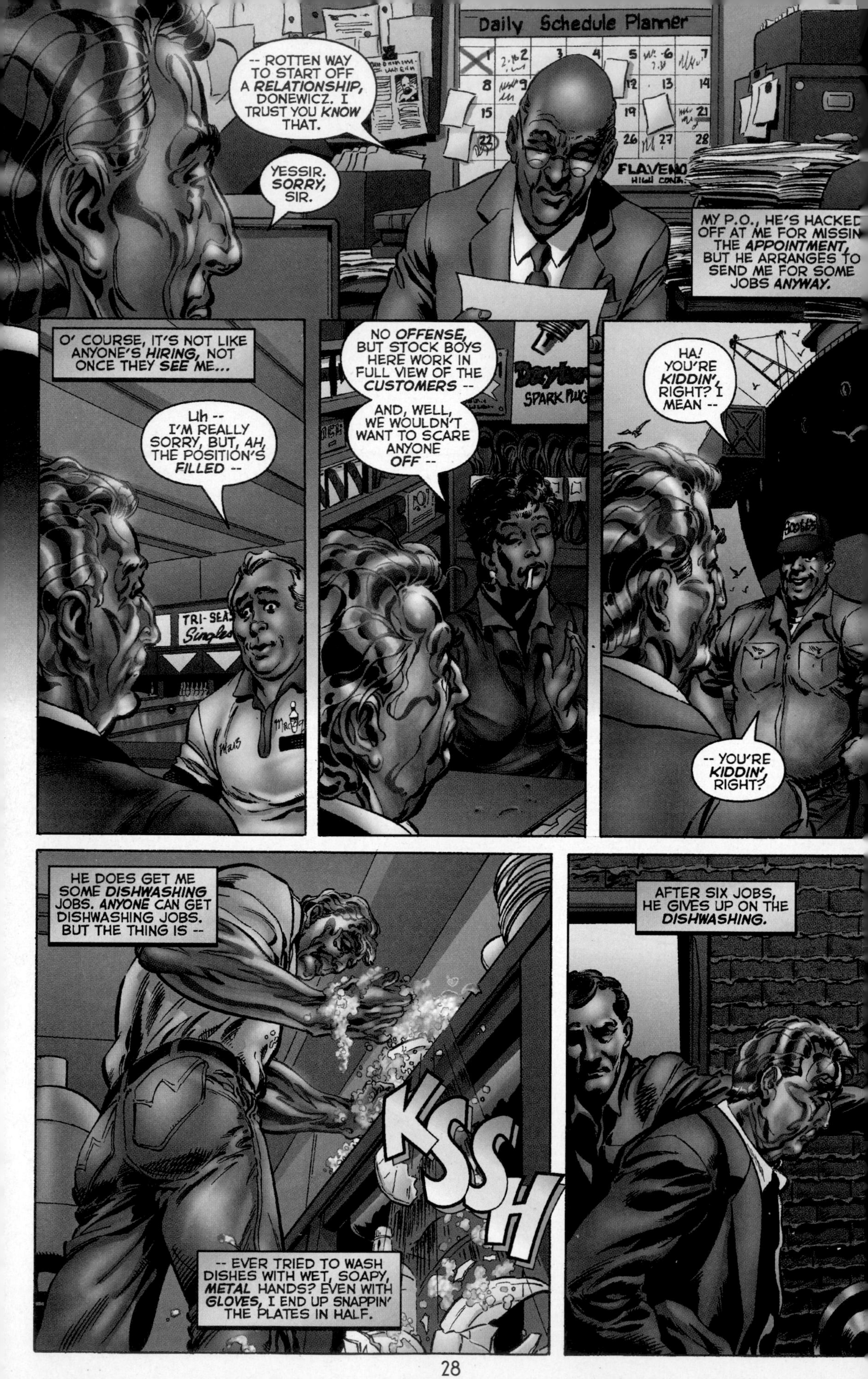
Daily Schedule Planner
-- ROTTEN WAY TO START OFF A RELATIONSHIP, DONEWICZ. I TRUST YOU KNOW THAT.
YESSIR. SORRY, SIR.
MY P.O., HE'S HACKED OFF AT ME FOR MISSIN' THE APPOINTMENT, BUT HE ARRANGES TO SEND ME FOR SOME JOBS ANYWAY.
O' COURSE, IT'S NOT LIKE ANYONE'S HIRING, NOT ONCE THEY SEE ME...
Uh -- I'M REALLY SORRY, BUT, AH, THE POSITION'S FILLED --
NO OFFENSE, BUT STOCK BOYS HERE WORK IN FULL VIEW OF THE CUSTOMERS --
AND, WELL, WE WOULDN'T WANT TO SCARE ANYONE OFF --
SPARK PLUG
HA! YOU'RE KIDDIN', RIGHT? I MEAN --
-- YOU'RE KIDDIN', RIGHT?
HE DOES GET ME SOME DISHWASHING JOBS. ANYONE CAN GET DISHWASHING JOBS. BUT THE THING IS --
KSSH
-- EVER TRIED TO WASH DISHES WITH WET, SOAPY, METAL HANDS? EVEN WITH GLOVES, I END UP SNAPPIN' THE PLATES IN HALF.
AFTER SIX JOBS, HE GIVES UP ON THE DISHWASHING.

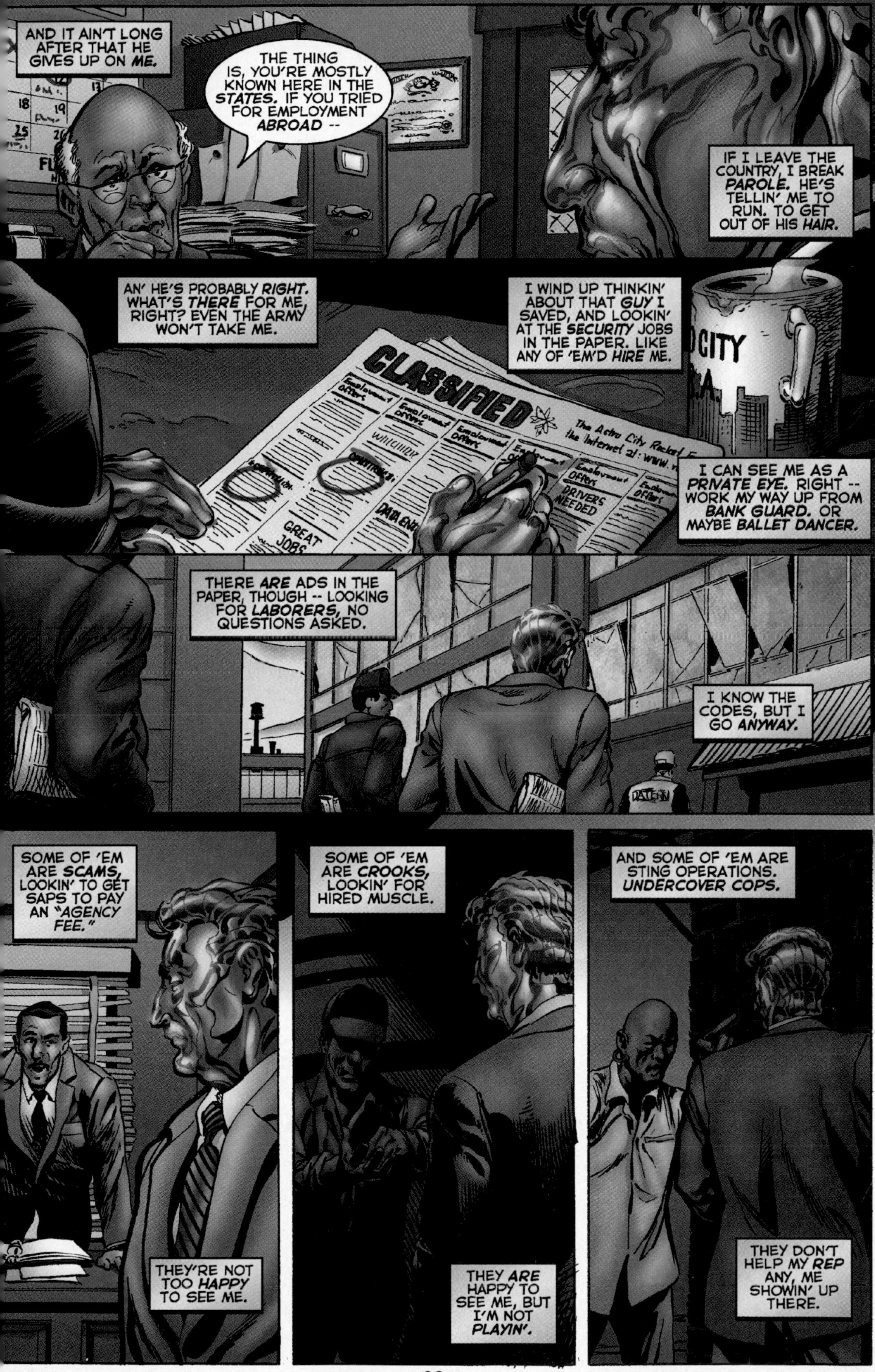

AND IT AIN'T LONG AFTER THAT HE GIVES UP ON ME.
THE THING IS, YOU'RE MOSTLY KNOWN HERE IN THE STATES. IF YOU TRIED FOR EMPLOYMENT ABROAD --
IF I LEAVE THE COUNTRY, I BREAK PAROLE. HE'S TELLIN' ME TO RUN. TO GET OUT OF HIS HAIR.
AN' HE'S PROBABLY RIGHT. WHAT'S THERE FOR ME, RIGHT? EVEN THE ARMY WON'T TAKE ME.
I WIND UP THINKIN' ABOUT THAT GUY I SAVED, AND LOOKIN' AT THE SECURITY JOBS IN THE PAPER. LIKE ANY OF 'EM'D HIRE ME.
CLASSIFIED
DRIVERS NEEDED
GREAT JOBS
I CAN SEE ME AS A PRIVATE EYE. RIGHT -- WORK MY WAY UP FROM BANK GUARD. OR MAYBE BALLET DANCER.
THERE ARE ADS IN THE PAPER, THOUGH -- LOOKING FOR LABORERS, NO QUESTIONS ASKED.
I KNOW THE CODES, BUT I GO ANYWAY.
SOME OF 'EM ARE SCAMS, LOOKIN' TO GET SAPS TO PAY AN "AGENCY FEE."
THEY'RE NOT TOO HAPPY TO SEE ME.
SOME OF 'EM ARE CROOKS, LOOKIN' FOR HIRED MUSCLE.
THEY ARE HAPPY TO SEE ME, BUT I'M NOT PLAYIN'.
AND SOME OF 'EM ARE STING OPERATIONS. UNDERCOVER COPS.
THEY DON'T HELP MY REP ANY, ME SHOWIN' UP THERE.

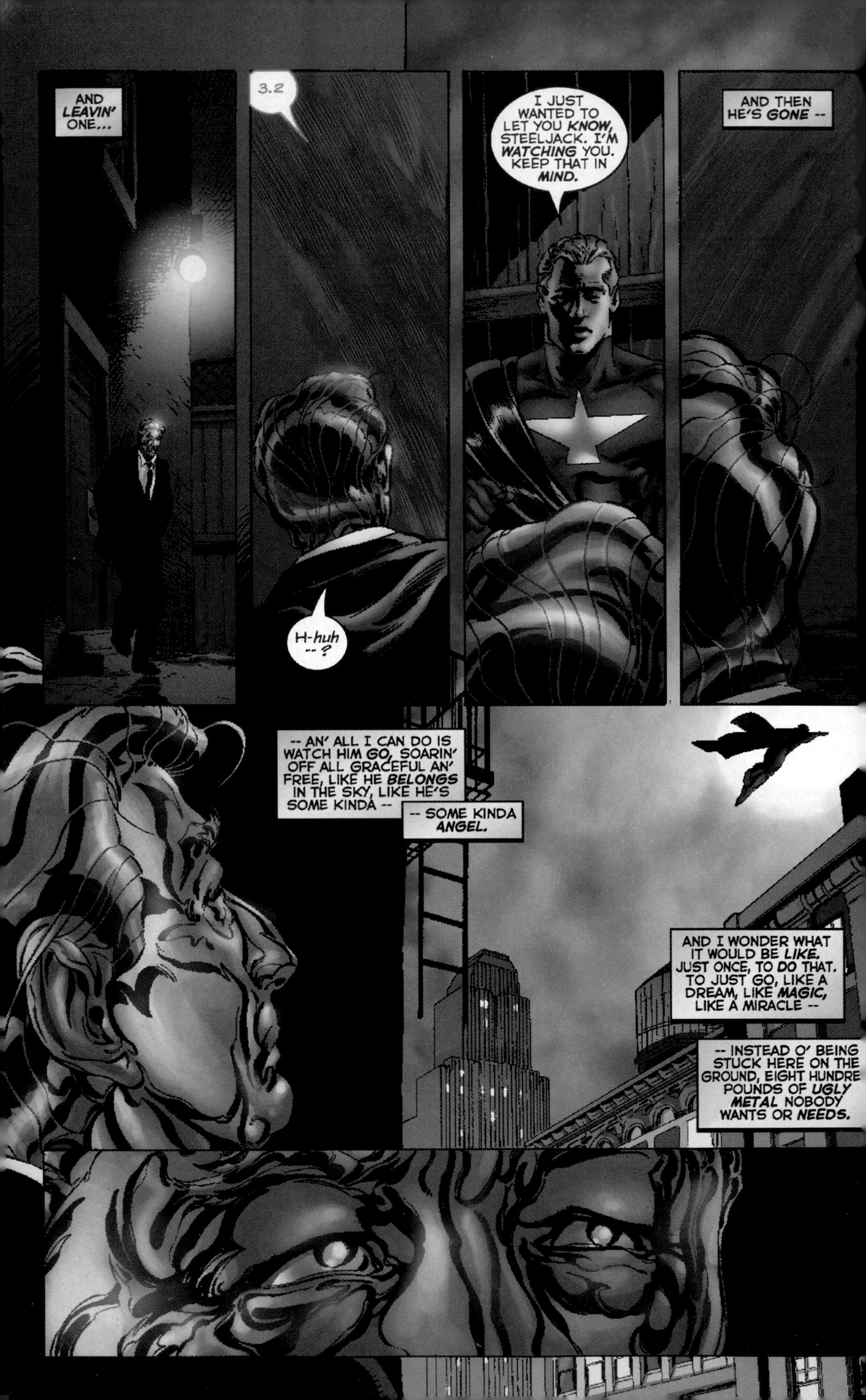
AND LEAVIN' ONE...
3.2
H-huh --?
I JUST WANTED TO LET YOU KNOW, STEELJACK. I'M WATCHING YOU. KEEP THAT IN MIND.
AND THEN HE'S GONE --
-- AN' ALL I CAN DO IS WATCH HIM GO, SOARIN' OFF ALL GRACEFUL AN' FREE, LIKE HE BELONGS IN THE SKY, LIKE HE'S SOME KINDA --
-- SOME KINDA ANGEL.
AND I WONDER WHAT IT WOULD BE LIKE. JUST ONCE, TO DO THAT. TO JUST GO, LIKE A DREAM, LIKE MAGIC, LIKE A MIRACLE --
-- INSTEAD O' BEING STUCK HERE ON THE GROUND, EIGHT HUNDRE POUNDS OF UGLY METAL NOBODY WANTS OR NEEDS.

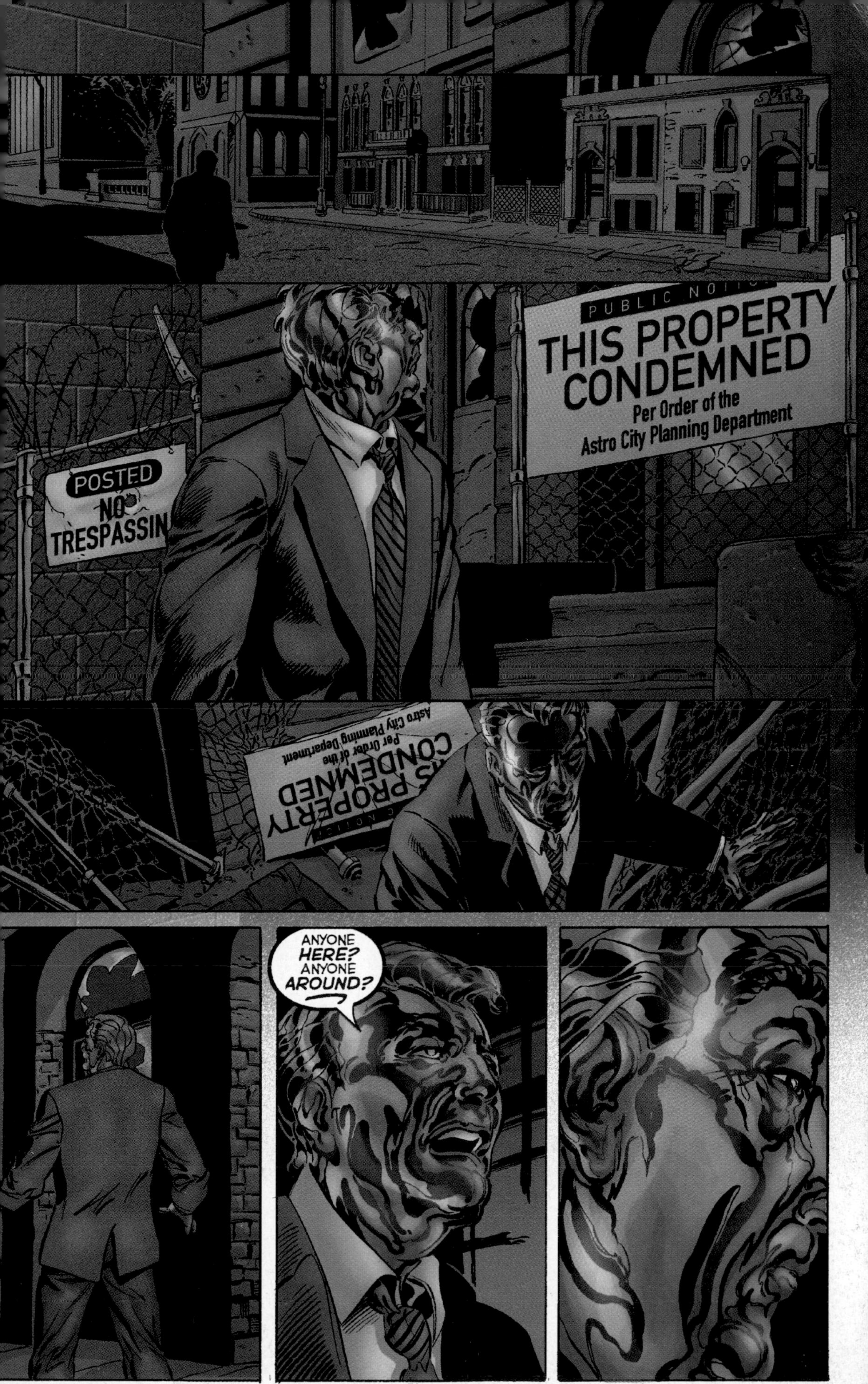
PUBLIC NOTIC
THIS PROPERTY CONDEMNED
Per Order of the
Astro City Planning Department
POSTED
NO
TRESPASSIN
PROPERTY
CONDEMNED
Per Order of the
Astro City Planning Department
ANYONE *HERE?* ANYONE *AROUND?*

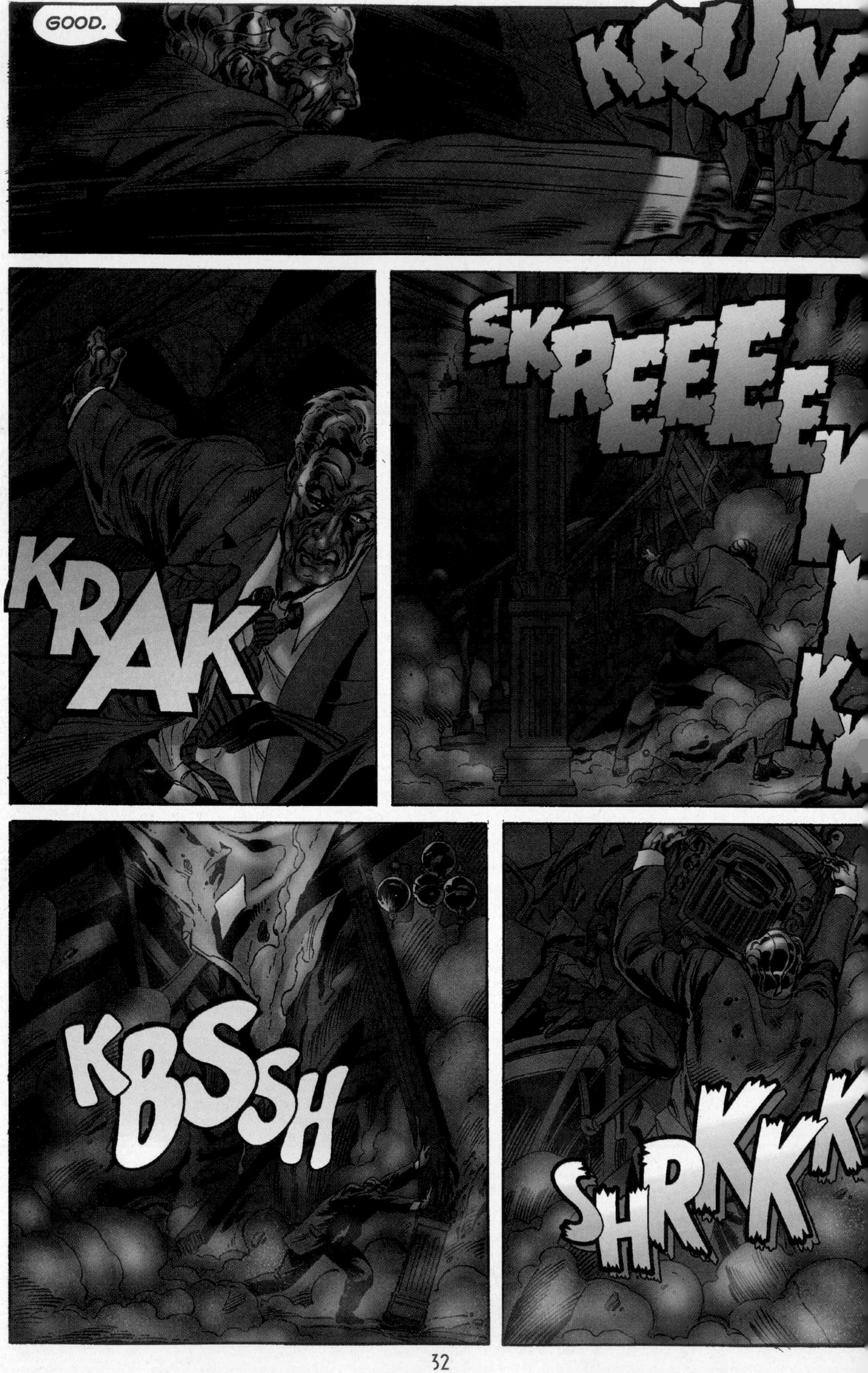
GOOD.
KRUN
KRAK
SKREEEEK
KBSSH
SHRKKK

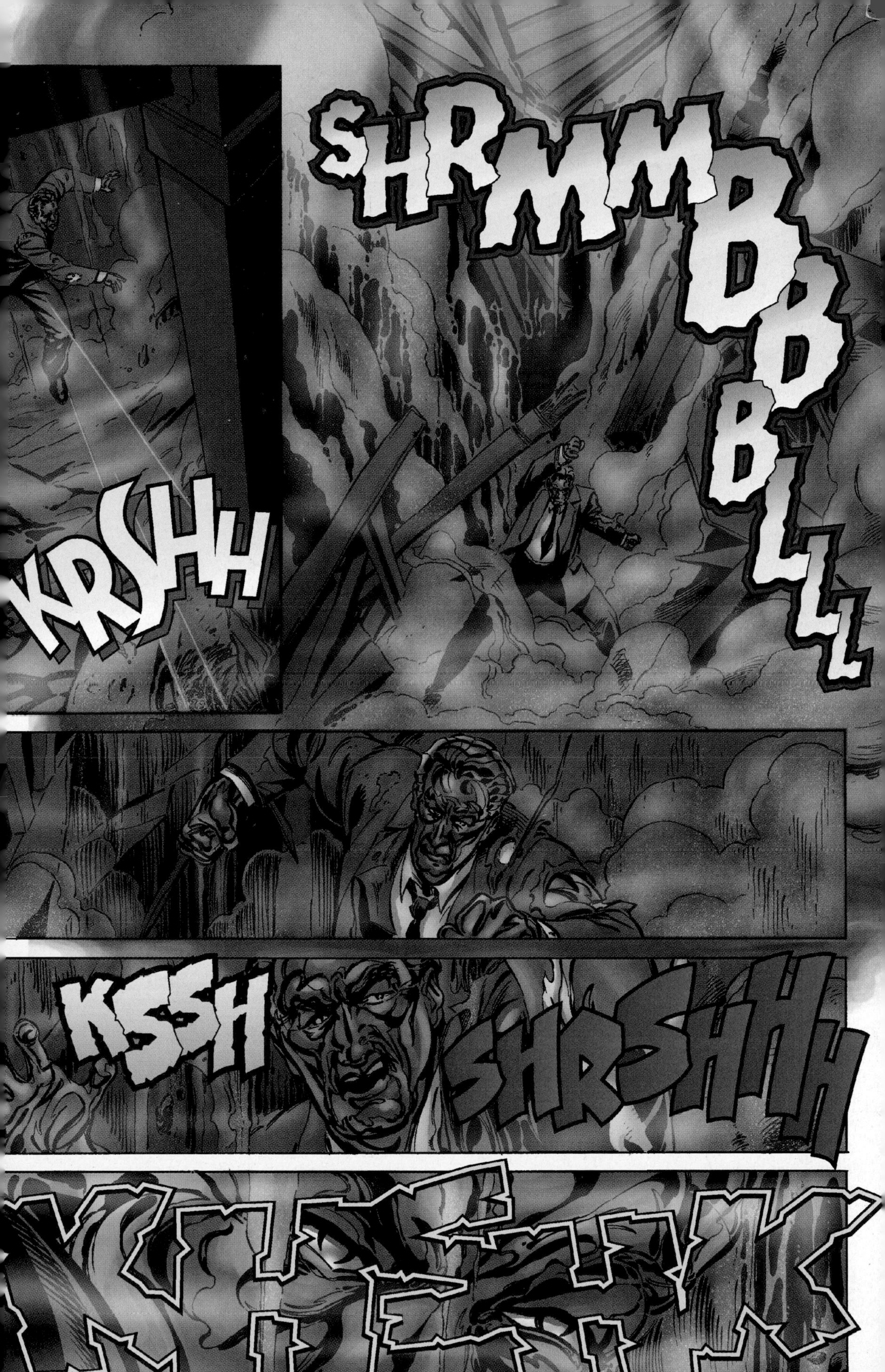
SHRMMBBBLLL
KRSHH
KSSH
SHRSHHH

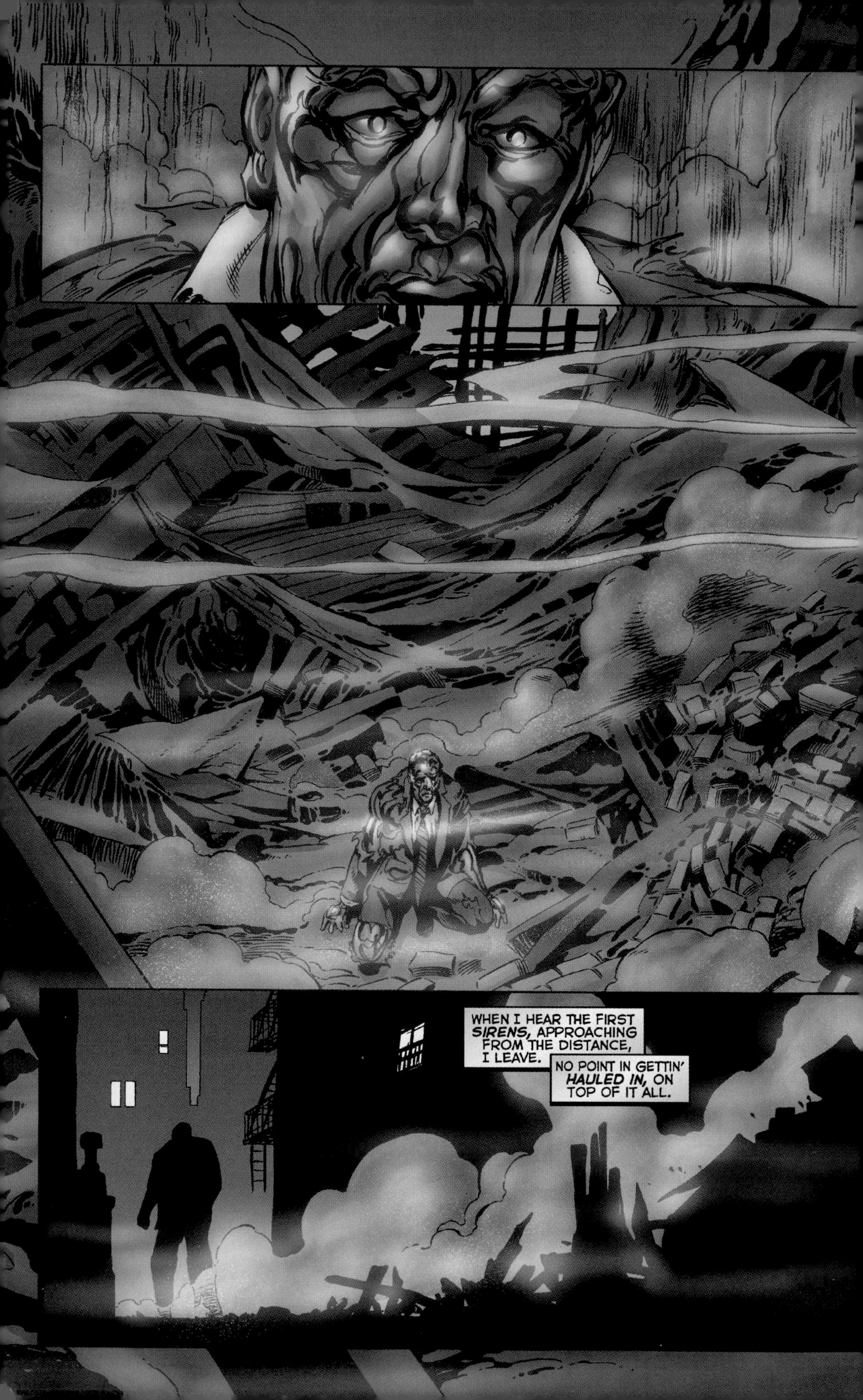
WHEN I HEAR THE FIRST SIRENS, APPROACHING FROM THE DISTANCE, I LEAVE.
NO POINT IN GETTIN' HAULED IN, ON TOP OF IT ALL.

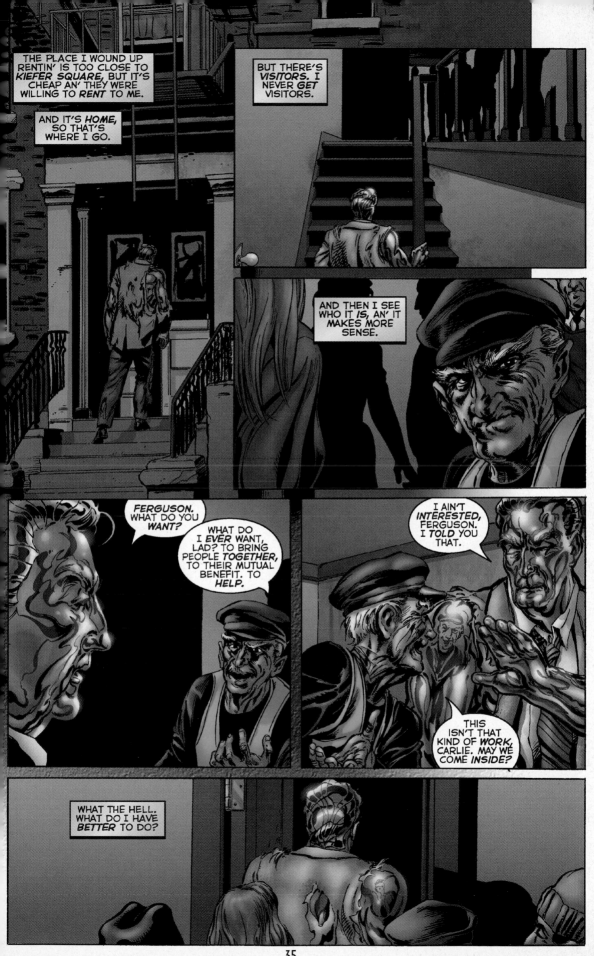

THE PLACE I WOUND UP RENTIN' IS TOO CLOSE TO *KIEFER SQUARE*, BUT IT'S CHEAP AN' THEY WERE WILLING TO *RENT* TO ME.

AND IT'S *HOME*, SO THAT'S WHERE I GO.

BUT THERE'S *VISITORS*. I NEVER *GET* VISITORS.

AND THEN I SEE WHO IT *IS*, AN' IT MAKES MORE SENSE.

FERGUSON. WHAT DO YOU *WANT*?

WHAT DO I *EVER* WANT, LAD? TO BRING PEOPLE *TOGETHER*, TO THEIR MUTUAL BENEFIT. TO *HELP*.

I AIN'T *INTERESTED*, FERGUSON. I *TOLD* YOU THAT.

THIS ISN'T THAT KIND OF *WORK*, CARLIE. MAY WE COME *INSIDE*?

WHAT THE HELL. WHAT DO I HAVE *BETTER* TO DO?

35

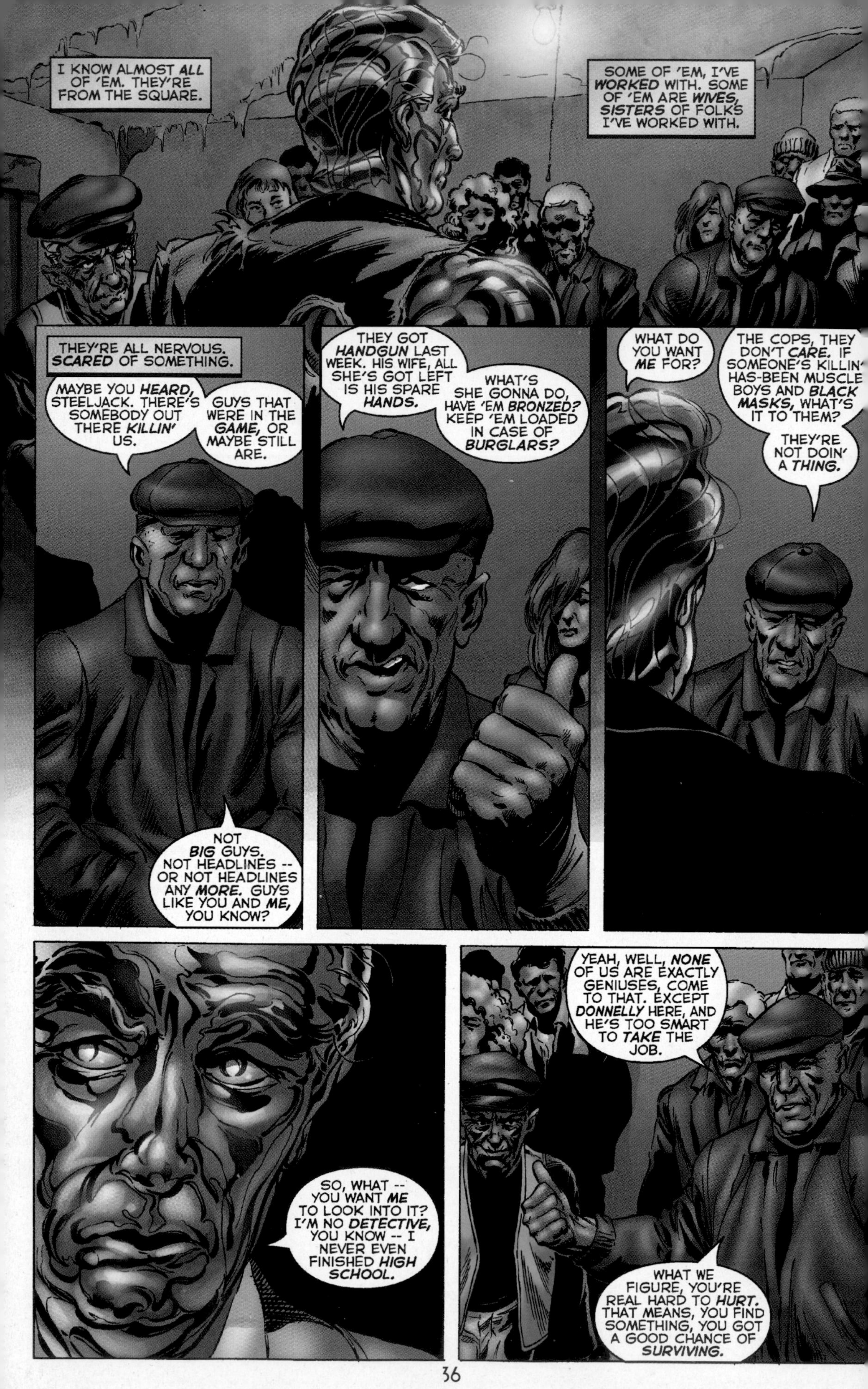

I KNOW ALMOST ALL OF 'EM. THEY'RE FROM THE SQUARE.
SOME OF 'EM, I'VE WORKED WITH. SOME OF 'EM ARE WIVES, SISTERS OF FOLKS I'VE WORKED WITH.
THEY'RE ALL NERVOUS. SCARED OF SOMETHING.
MAYBE YOU HEARD, STEELJACK. THERE'S SOMEBODY OUT THERE KILLIN' US.
GUYS THAT WERE IN THE GAME, OR MAYBE STILL ARE.
NOT BIG GUYS. NOT HEADLINES -- OR NOT HEADLINES ANY MORE. GUYS LIKE YOU AND ME, YOU KNOW?
THEY GOT HANDGUN LAST WEEK. HIS WIFE, ALL SHE'S GOT LEFT IS HIS SPARE HANDS.
WHAT'S SHE GONNA DO, HAVE 'EM BRONZED? KEEP 'EM LOADED IN CASE OF BURGLARS?
WHAT DO YOU WANT ME FOR?
THE COPS, THEY DON'T CARE. IF SOMEONE'S KILLIN' HAS-BEEN MUSCLE BOYS AND BLACK MASKS, WHAT'S IT TO THEM?
THEY'RE NOT DOIN' A THING.
SO, WHAT -- YOU WANT ME TO LOOK INTO IT? I'M NO DETECTIVE, YOU KNOW -- I NEVER EVEN FINISHED HIGH SCHOOL.
YEAH, WELL, NONE OF US ARE EXACTLY GENIUSES, COME TO THAT. EXCEPT DONNELLY HERE, AND HE'S TOO SMART TO TAKE THE JOB.
WHAT WE FIGURE, YOU'RE REAL HARD TO HURT. THAT MEANS, YOU FIND SOMETHING, YOU GOT A GOOD CHANCE OF SURVIVING.

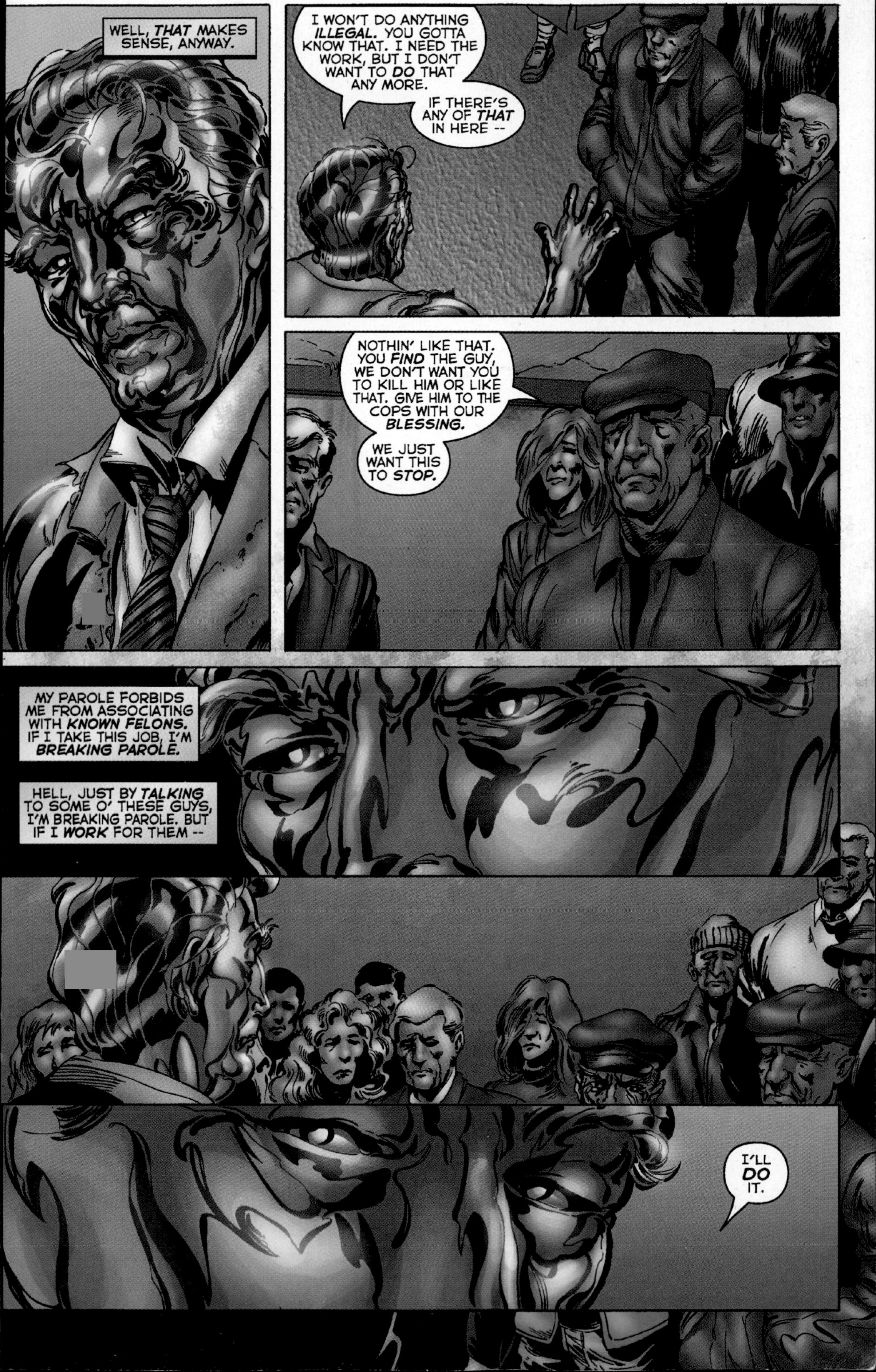
WELL, THAT MAKES SENSE, ANYWAY.
I WON'T DO ANYTHING ILLEGAL. YOU GOTTA KNOW THAT. I NEED THE WORK, BUT I DON'T WANT TO DO THAT ANY MORE.
IF THERE'S ANY OF THAT IN HERE --
NOTHIN' LIKE THAT. YOU FIND THE GUY, WE DON'T WANT YOU TO KILL HIM OR LIKE THAT. GIVE HIM TO THE COPS WITH OUR BLESSING.
WE JUST WANT THIS TO STOP.
MY PAROLE FORBIDS ME FROM ASSOCIATING WITH KNOWN FELONS. IF I TAKE THIS JOB, I'M BREAKING PAROLE.
HELL, JUST BY TALKING TO SOME O' THESE GUYS, I'M BREAKING PAROLE. BUT IF I WORK FOR THEM --
I'LL DO IT.

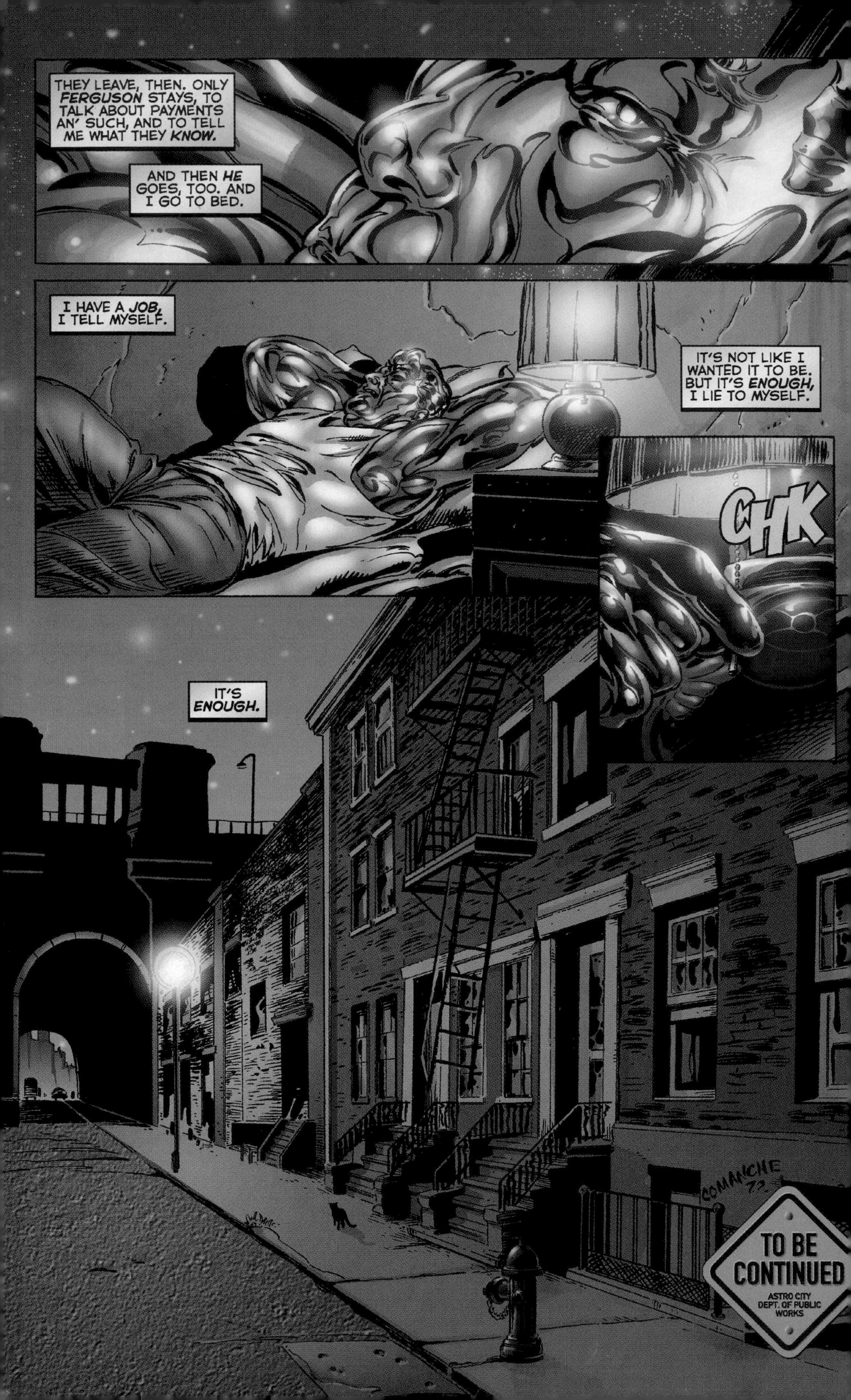
THEY LEAVE, THEN. ONLY FERGUSON STAYS, TO TALK ABOUT PAYMENTS AN' SUCH, AND TO TELL ME WHAT THEY KNOW.
AND THEN HE GOES, TOO. AND I GO TO BED.
I HAVE A JOB, I TELL MYSELF.
IT'S NOT LIKE I WANTED IT TO BE. BUT IT'S ENOUGH, I LIE TO MYSELF.
CHK
IT'S ENOUGH.
COMANCHE 72
TO BE CONTINUED
ASTRO CITY DEPT. OF PUBLIC WORKS

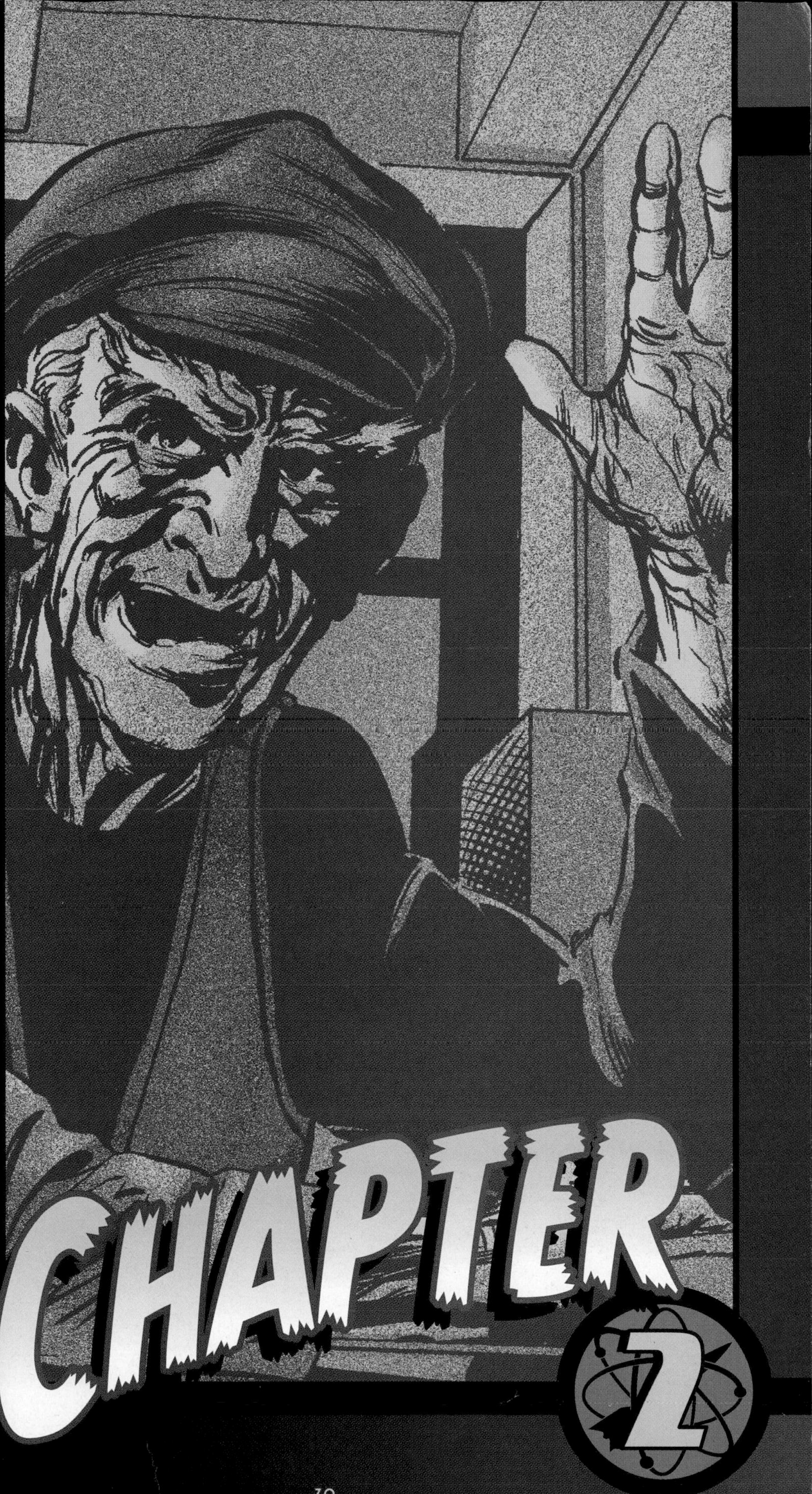
CHAPTER
2

The LONG TREADMILL

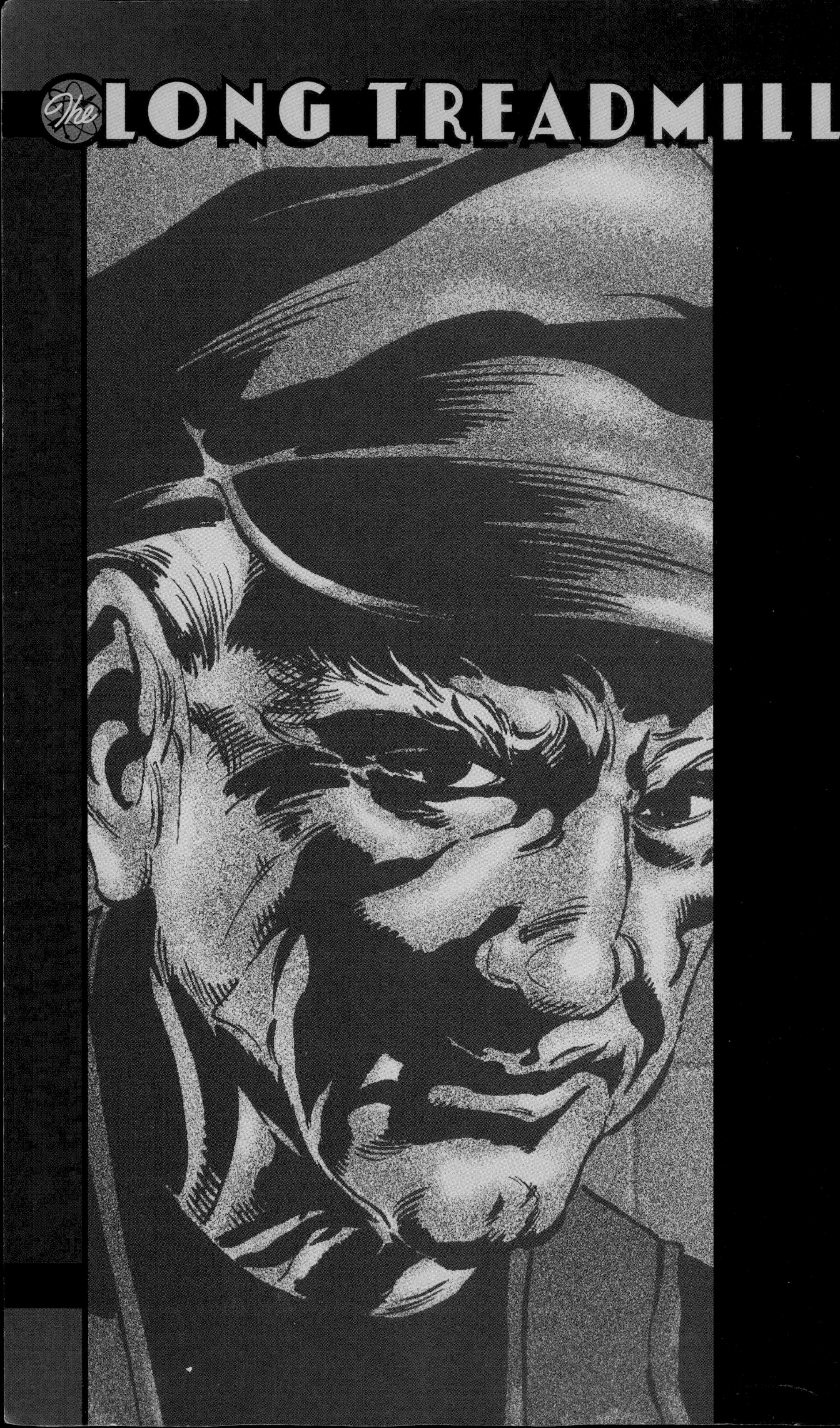

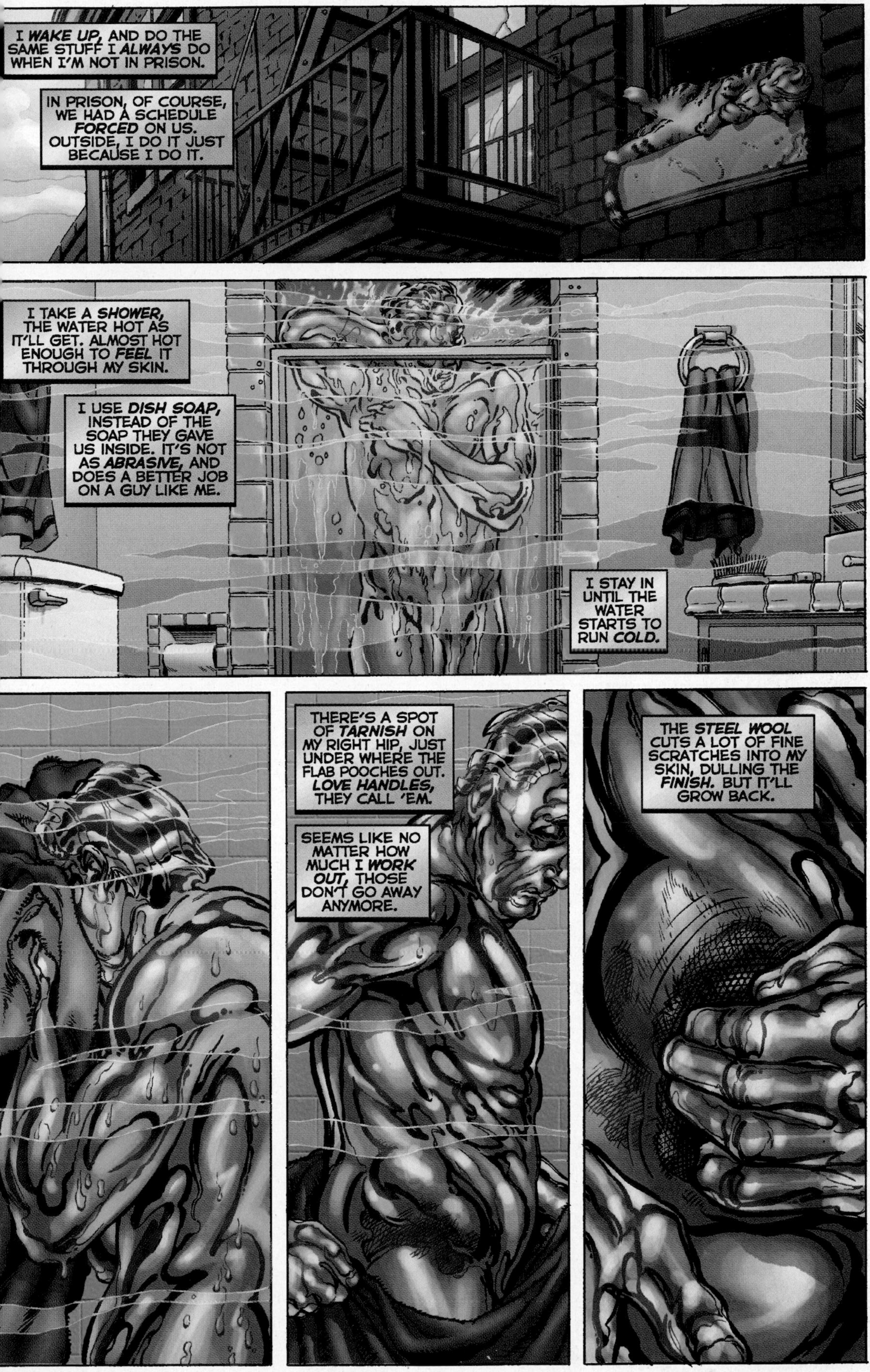

I WAKE UP, AND DO THE SAME STUFF I ALWAYS DO WHEN I'M NOT IN PRISON.
IN PRISON, OF COURSE, WE HAD A SCHEDULE FORCED ON US. OUTSIDE, I DO IT JUST BECAUSE I DO IT.
I TAKE A SHOWER, THE WATER HOT AS IT'LL GET. ALMOST HOT ENOUGH TO FEEL IT THROUGH MY SKIN.
I USE DISH SOAP, INSTEAD OF THE SOAP THEY GAVE US INSIDE. IT'S NOT AS ABRASIVE, AND DOES A BETTER JOB ON A GUY LIKE ME.
I STAY IN UNTIL THE WATER STARTS TO RUN COLD.
THERE'S A SPOT OF TARNISH ON MY RIGHT HIP, JUST UNDER WHERE THE FLAB POOCHES OUT. LOVE HANDLES, THEY CALL 'EM.
SEEMS LIKE NO MATTER HOW MUCH I WORK OUT, THOSE DON'T GO AWAY ANYMORE.
THE STEEL WOOL CUTS A LOT OF FINE SCRATCHES INTO MY SKIN, DULLING THE FINISH. BUT IT'LL GROW BACK.

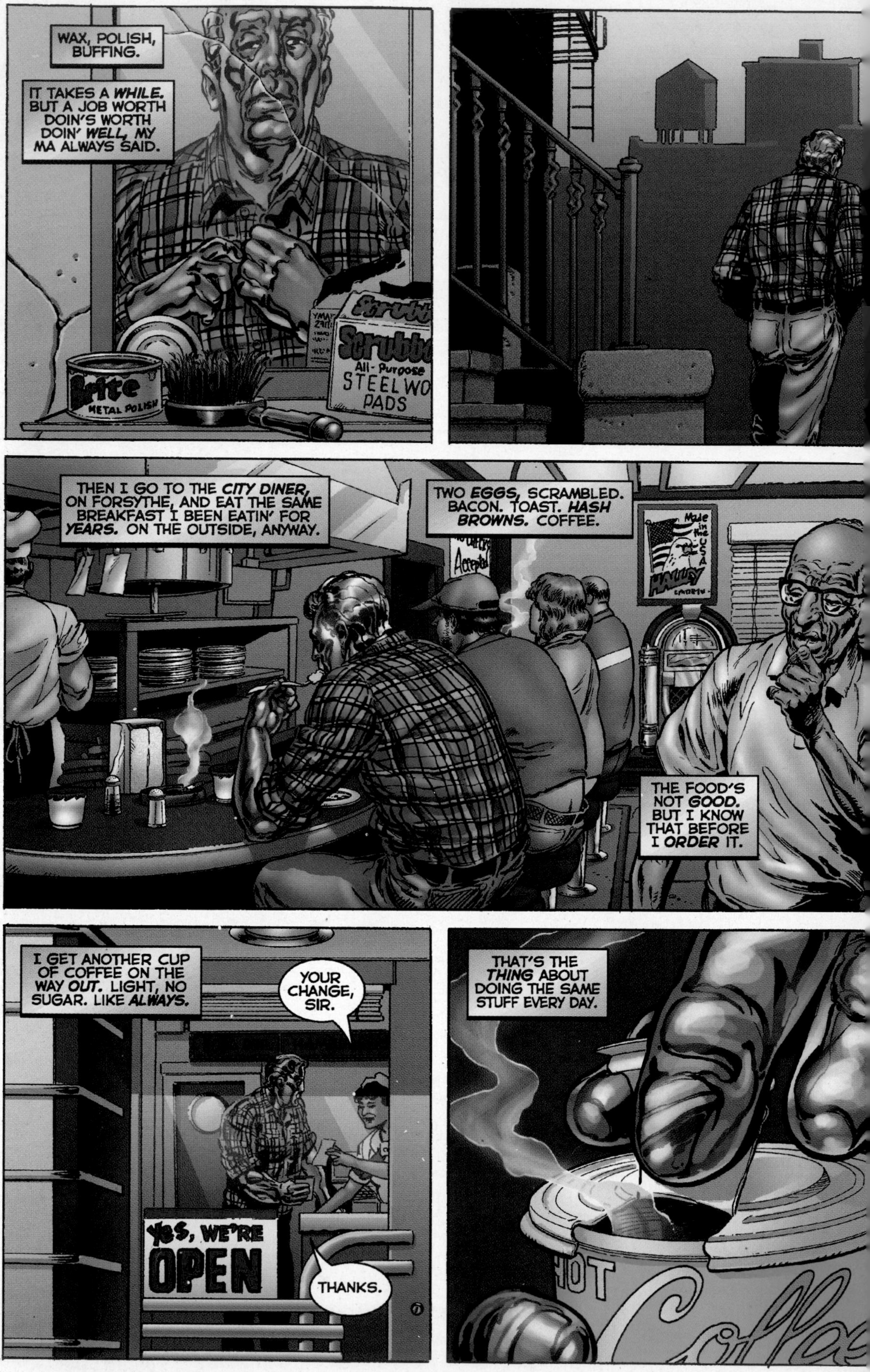
WAX, POLISH, BUFFING.
IT TAKES A WHILE. BUT A JOB WORTH DOIN'S WORTH DOIN' WELL, MY MA ALWAYS SAID.
Brite METAL POLISH
Scrubbo All-Purpose STEEL WO PADS
THEN I GO TO THE CITY DINER, ON FORSYTHE, AND EAT THE SAME BREAKFAST I BEEN EATIN' FOR YEARS. ON THE OUTSIDE, ANYWAY.
TWO EGGS, SCRAMBLED. BACON. TOAST. HASH BROWNS. COFFEE.
THE FOOD'S NOT GOOD. BUT I KNOW THAT BEFORE I ORDER IT.
I GET ANOTHER CUP OF COFFEE ON THE WAY OUT. LIGHT, NO SUGAR. LIKE ALWAYS.
YOUR CHANGE, SIR.
YES, WE'RE OPEN
THANKS.
THAT'S THE THING ABOUT DOING THE SAME STUFF EVERY DAY.
HOT

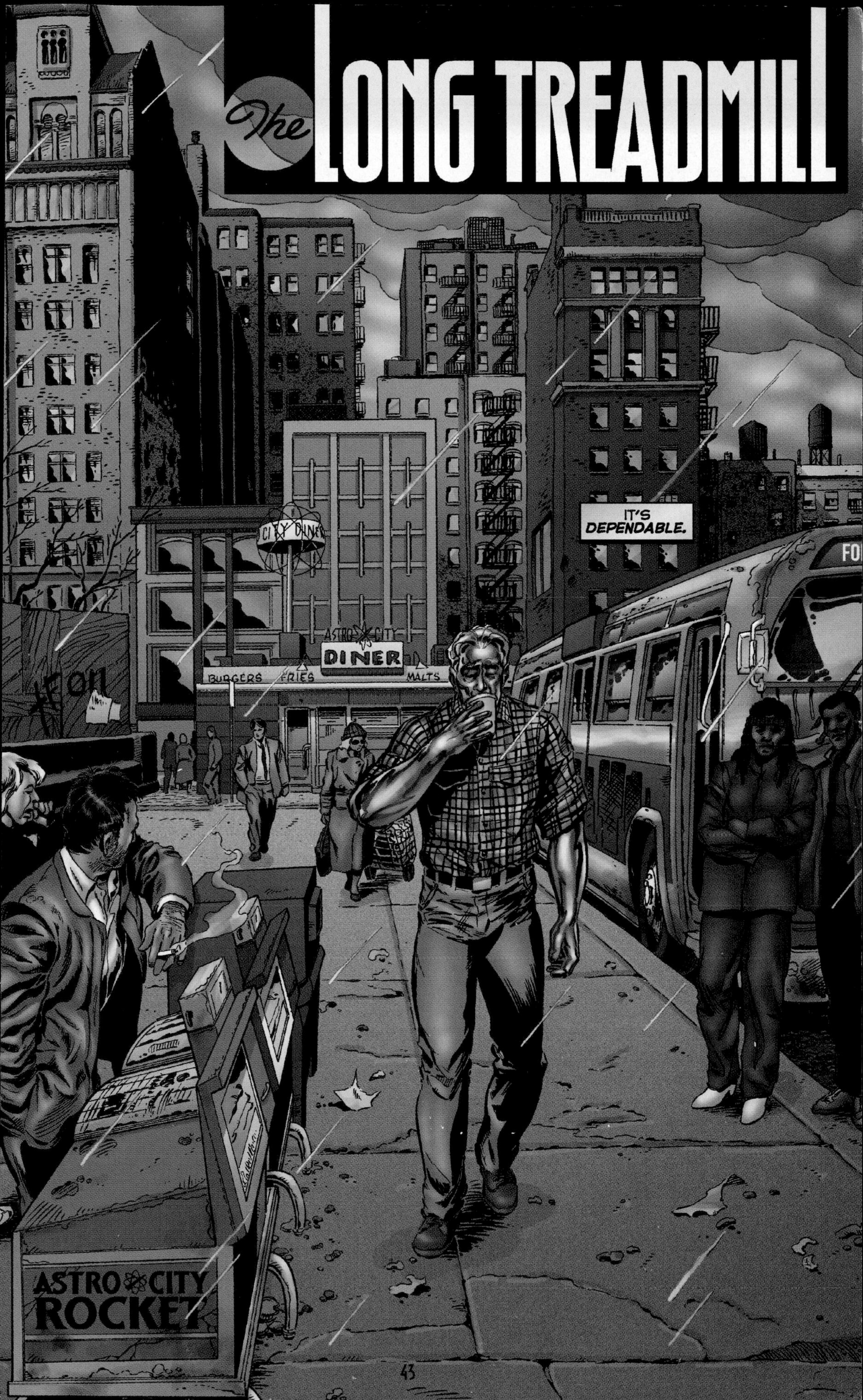

The LONG TREADMILL
IT'S DEPENDABLE.
CITY DINER
ASTRO CITY
DINER
BURGERS
FRIES
MALTS
ASTRO CITY ROCKET

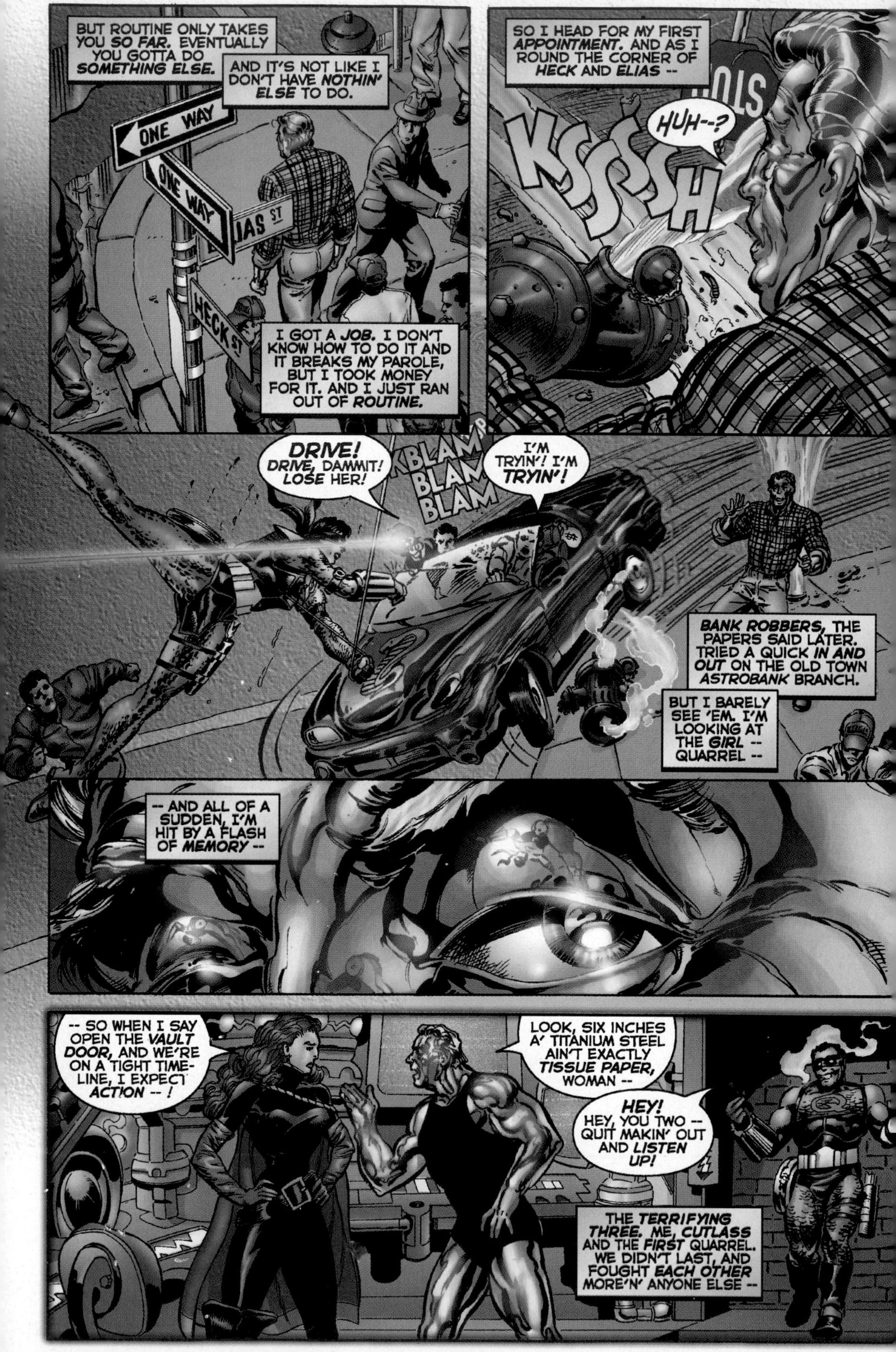
BUT ROUTINE ONLY TAKES YOU SO FAR. EVENTUALLY YOU GOTTA DO SOMETHING ELSE.
AND IT'S NOT LIKE I DON'T HAVE NOTHIN' ELSE TO DO.
ONE WAY
ONE WAY
ELIAS ST
HECK ST
I GOT A JOB. I DON'T KNOW HOW TO DO IT AND IT BREAKS MY PAROLE, BUT I TOOK MONEY FOR IT. AND I JUST RAN OUT OF ROUTINE.
SO I HEAD FOR MY FIRST APPOINTMENT. AND AS I ROUND THE CORNER OF HECK AND ELIAS --
KSSSSH
HUH--?
DRIVE! DRIVE, DAMMIT! LOSE HER!
KBLAM BLAM BLAM
I'M TRYIN'! I'M TRYIN'!
BANK ROBBERS, THE PAPERS SAID LATER. TRIED A QUICK IN AND OUT ON THE OLD TOWN ASTROBANK BRANCH.
BUT I BARELY SEE 'EM. I'M LOOKING AT THE GIRL -- QUARREL --
-- AND ALL OF A SUDDEN, I'M HIT BY A FLASH OF MEMORY --
-- SO WHEN I SAY OPEN THE VAULT DOOR, AND WE'RE ON A TIGHT TIME-LINE, I EXPECT ACTION -- !
LOOK, SIX INCHES A' TITANIUM STEEL AIN'T EXACTLY TISSUE PAPER, WOMAN --
HEY! HEY, YOU TWO -- QUIT MAKIN' OUT AND LISTEN UP!
THE TERRIFYING THREE. ME, CUTLASS AND THE FIRST QUARREL. WE DIDN'T LAST, AND FOUGHT EACH OTHER MORE'N' ANYONE ELSE --

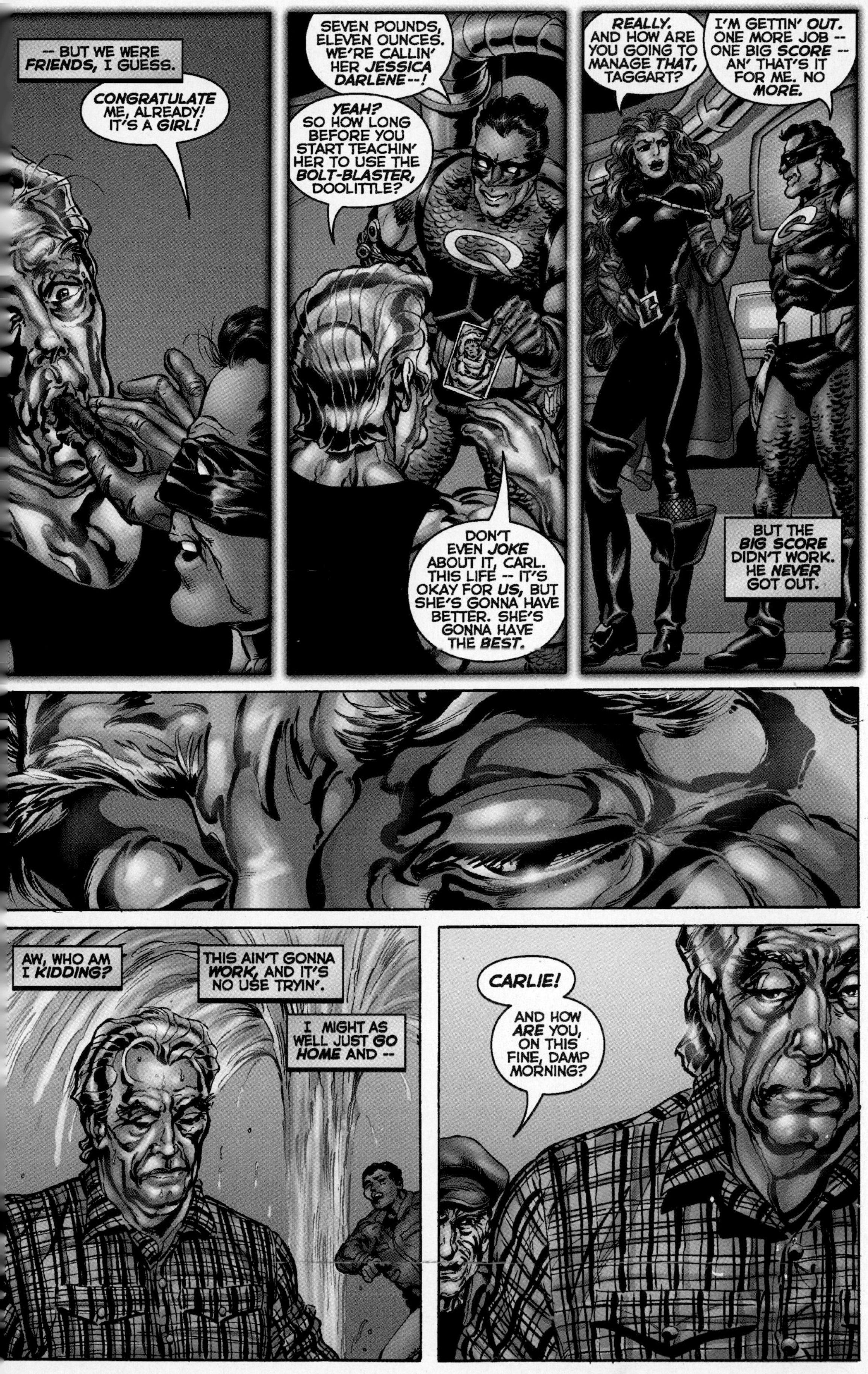
-- BUT WE WERE FRIENDS, I GUESS.
CONGRATULATE ME, ALREADY! IT'S A GIRL!
SEVEN POUNDS, ELEVEN OUNCES. WE'RE CALLIN' HER JESSICA DARLENE --!
YEAH? SO HOW LONG BEFORE YOU START TEACHIN' HER TO USE THE BOLT-BLASTER, DOOLITTLE?
DON'T EVEN JOKE ABOUT IT, CARL. THIS LIFE -- IT'S OKAY FOR US, BUT SHE'S GONNA HAVE BETTER. SHE'S GONNA HAVE THE BEST.
REALLY. AND HOW ARE YOU GOING TO MANAGE THAT, TAGGART?
I'M GETTIN' OUT. ONE MORE JOB -- ONE BIG SCORE -- AN' THAT'S IT FOR ME. NO MORE.
BUT THE BIG SCORE DIDN'T WORK. HE NEVER GOT OUT.
AW, WHO AM I KIDDING?
THIS AIN'T GONNA WORK, AND IT'S NO USE TRYIN'.
I MIGHT AS WELL JUST GO HOME AND --
CARLIE!
AND HOW ARE YOU, ON THIS FINE, DAMP MORNING?

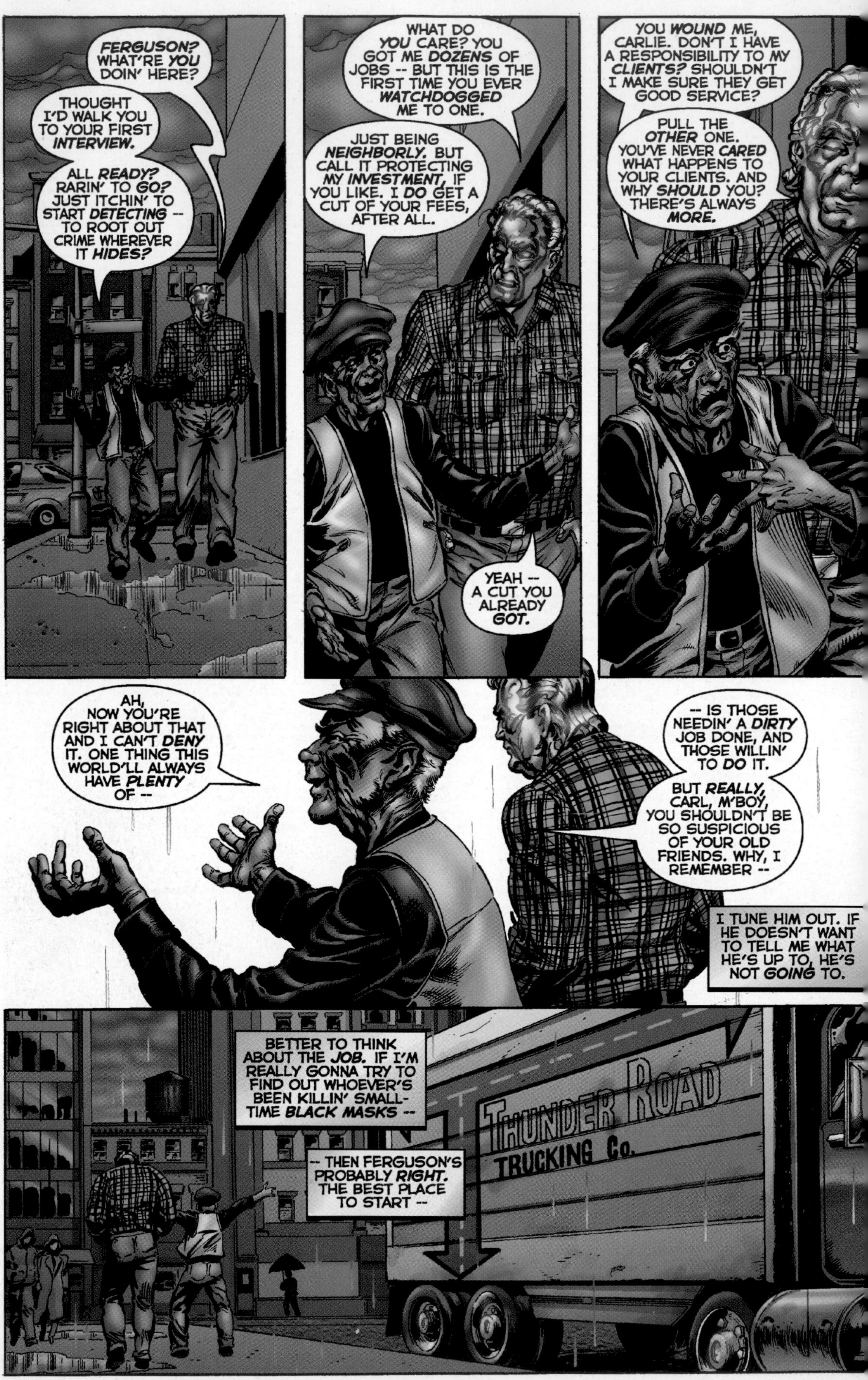
FERGUSON? WHAT'RE YOU DOIN' HERE?
THOUGHT I'D WALK YOU TO YOUR FIRST INTERVIEW.
ALL READY? RARIN' TO GO? JUST ITCHIN' TO START DETECTING -- TO ROOT OUT CRIME WHEREVER IT HIDES?
WHAT DO YOU CARE? YOU GOT ME DOZENS OF JOBS -- BUT THIS IS THE FIRST TIME YOU EVER WATCHDOGGED ME TO ONE.
JUST BEING NEIGHBORLY. BUT CALL IT PROTECTING MY INVESTMENT, IF YOU LIKE. I DO GET A CUT OF YOUR FEES, AFTER ALL.
YEAH -- A CUT YOU ALREADY GOT.
YOU WOUND ME, CARLIE. DON'T I HAVE A RESPONSIBILITY TO MY CLIENTS? SHOULDN'T I MAKE SURE THEY GET GOOD SERVICE?
PULL THE OTHER ONE. YOU'VE NEVER CARED WHAT HAPPENS TO YOUR CLIENTS. AND WHY SHOULD YOU? THERE'S ALWAYS MORE.
AH, NOW YOU'RE RIGHT ABOUT THAT AND I CAN'T DENY IT. ONE THING THIS WORLD'LL ALWAYS HAVE PLENTY OF --
-- IS THOSE NEEDIN' A DIRTY JOB DONE, AND THOSE WILLIN' TO DO IT.
BUT REALLY, CARL, M'BOY, YOU SHOULDN'T BE SO SUSPICIOUS OF YOUR OLD FRIENDS. WHY, I REMEMBER --
I TUNE HIM OUT. IF HE DOESN'T WANT TO TELL ME WHAT HE'S UP TO, HE'S NOT GOING TO.
BETTER TO THINK ABOUT THE JOB. IF I'M REALLY GONNA TRY TO FIND OUT WHOEVER'S BEEN KILLIN' SMALL-TIME BLACK MASKS --
-- THEN FERGUSON'S PROBABLY RIGHT. THE BEST PLACE TO START --
THUNDER ROAD
TRUCKING Co.

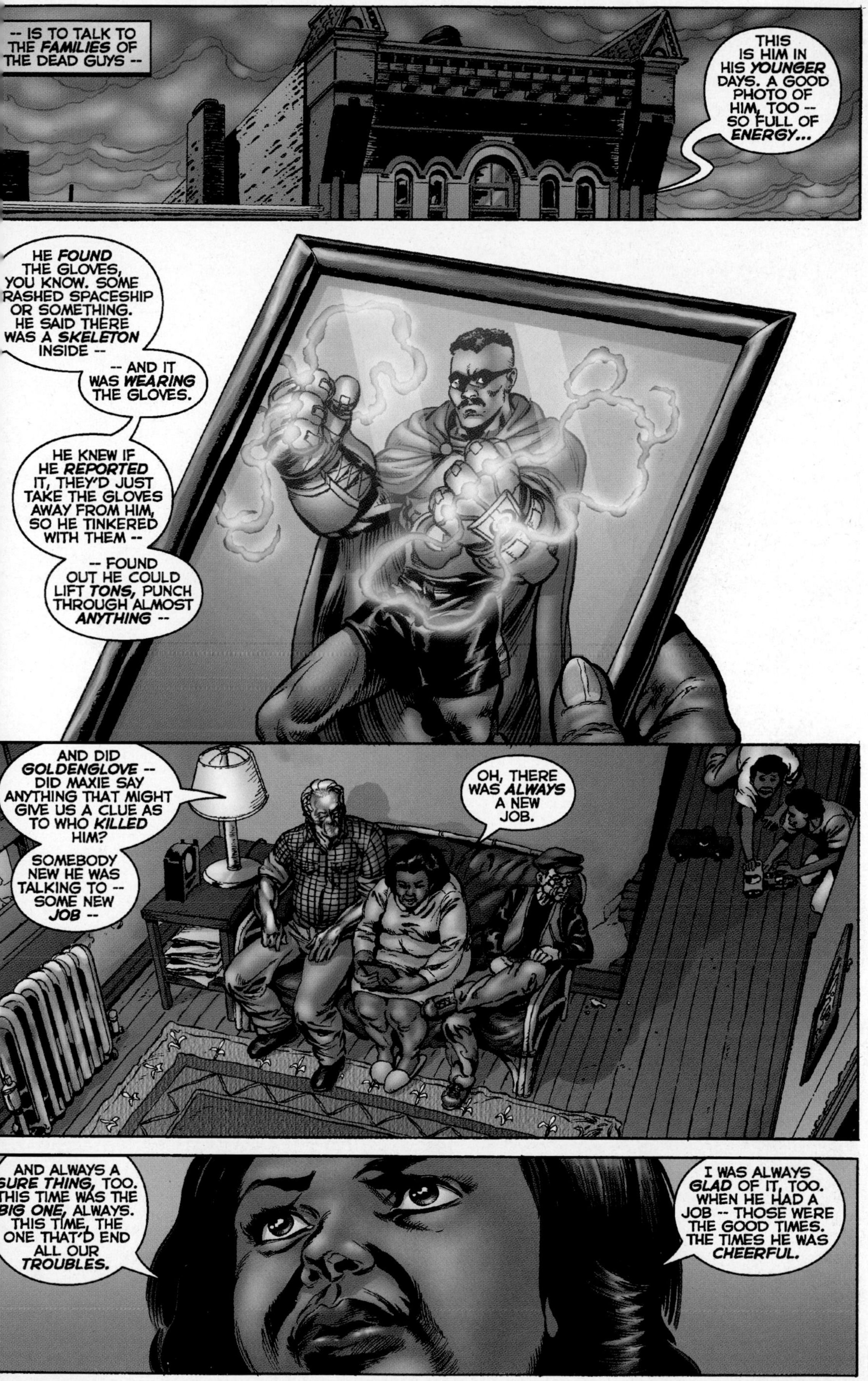
-- IS TO TALK TO THE *FAMILIES* OF THE DEAD GUYS --
THIS IS HIM IN HIS *YOUNGER* DAYS. A GOOD PHOTO OF HIM, TOO -- SO FULL OF *ENERGY...*
HE *FOUND* THE GLOVES, YOU KNOW. SOME RASHED SPACESHIP OR SOMETHING. HE SAID THERE WAS A *SKELETON* INSIDE --
-- AND IT WAS *WEARING* THE GLOVES.
HE KNEW IF HE *REPORTED* IT, THEY'D JUST TAKE THE GLOVES AWAY FROM HIM, SO HE TINKERED WITH THEM --
-- FOUND OUT HE COULD LIFT *TONS,* PUNCH THROUGH ALMOST *ANYTHING* --
AND DID *GOLDENGLOVE* -- DID MAXIE SAY ANYTHING THAT MIGHT GIVE US A CLUE AS TO WHO *KILLED* HIM?
SOMEBODY NEW HE WAS TALKING TO -- SOME NEW *JOB* --
OH, THERE WAS *ALWAYS* A NEW JOB.
AND ALWAYS A *SURE THING,* TOO. THIS TIME WAS THE *BIG ONE,* ALWAYS. THIS TIME, THE ONE THAT'D END ALL OUR *TROUBLES.*
I WAS ALWAYS *GLAD* OF IT, TOO. WHEN HE HAD A JOB -- THOSE WERE THE GOOD TIMES. THE TIMES HE WAS *CHEERFUL.*

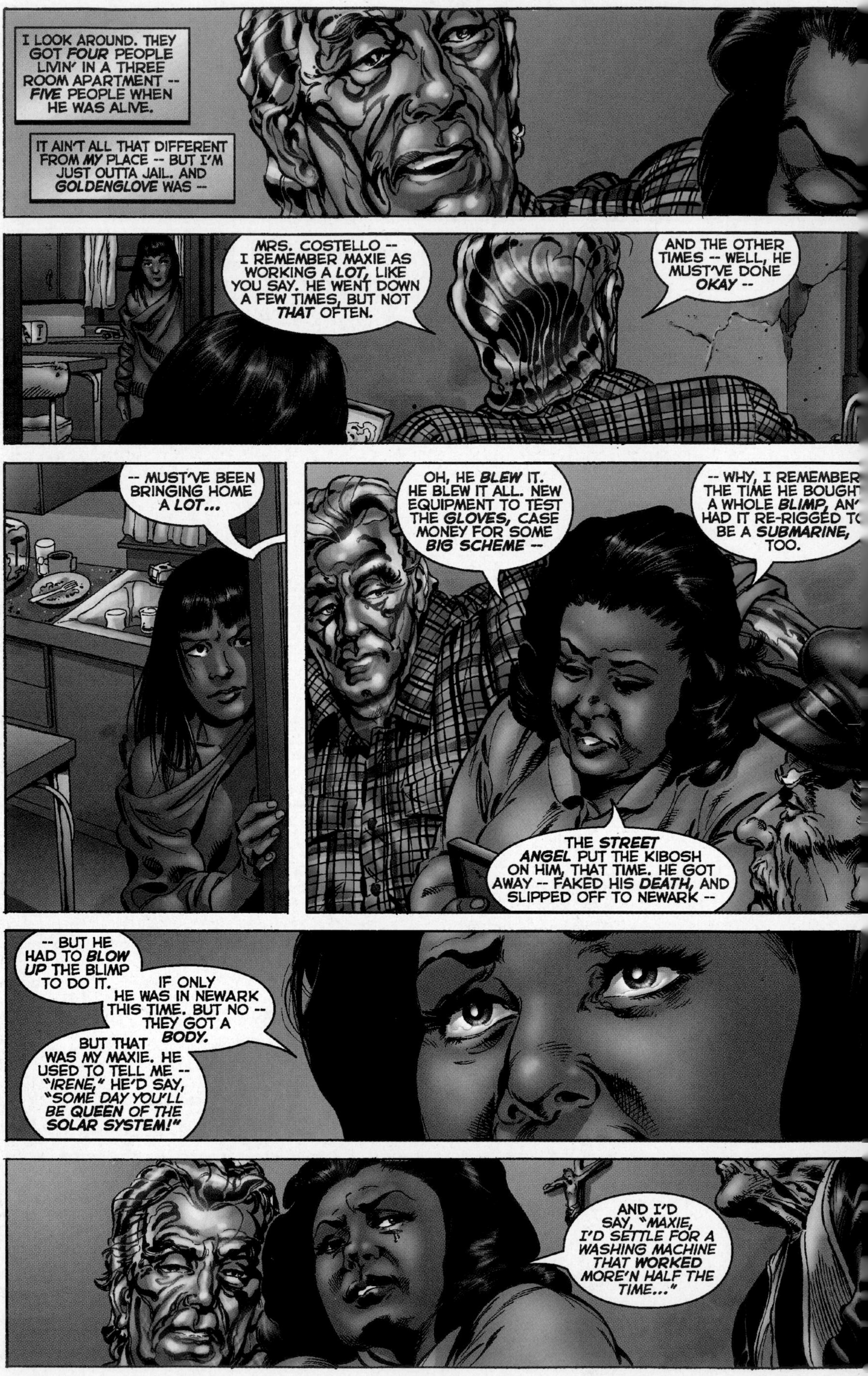
I LOOK AROUND. THEY GOT FOUR PEOPLE LIVIN' IN A THREE ROOM APARTMENT -- FIVE PEOPLE WHEN HE WAS ALIVE.
IT AIN'T ALL THAT DIFFERENT FROM MY PLACE -- BUT I'M JUST OUTTA JAIL. AND GOLDENGLOVE WAS --
MRS. COSTELLO -- I REMEMBER MAXIE AS WORKING A LOT, LIKE YOU SAY. HE WENT DOWN A FEW TIMES, BUT NOT THAT OFTEN.
AND THE OTHER TIMES -- WELL, HE MUST'VE DONE OKAY --
-- MUST'VE BEEN BRINGING HOME A LOT...
OH, HE BLEW IT. HE BLEW IT ALL. NEW EQUIPMENT TO TEST THE GLOVES, CASE MONEY FOR SOME BIG SCHEME --
-- WHY, I REMEMBER THE TIME HE BOUGHT A WHOLE BLIMP, AN' HAD IT RE-RIGGED TO BE A SUBMARINE, TOO.
THE STREET ANGEL PUT THE KIBOSH ON HIM, THAT TIME. HE GOT AWAY -- FAKED HIS DEATH, AND SLIPPED OFF TO NEWARK --
-- BUT HE HAD TO BLOW UP THE BLIMP TO DO IT. IF ONLY HE WAS IN NEWARK THIS TIME. BUT NO -- THEY GOT A BODY.
BUT THAT WAS MY MAXIE. HE USED TO TELL ME -- "IRENE," HE'D SAY, "SOME DAY YOU'LL BE QUEEN OF THE SOLAR SYSTEM!"
AND I'D SAY, "MAXIE, I'D SETTLE FOR A WASHING MACHINE THAT WORKED MORE'N HALF THE TIME..."

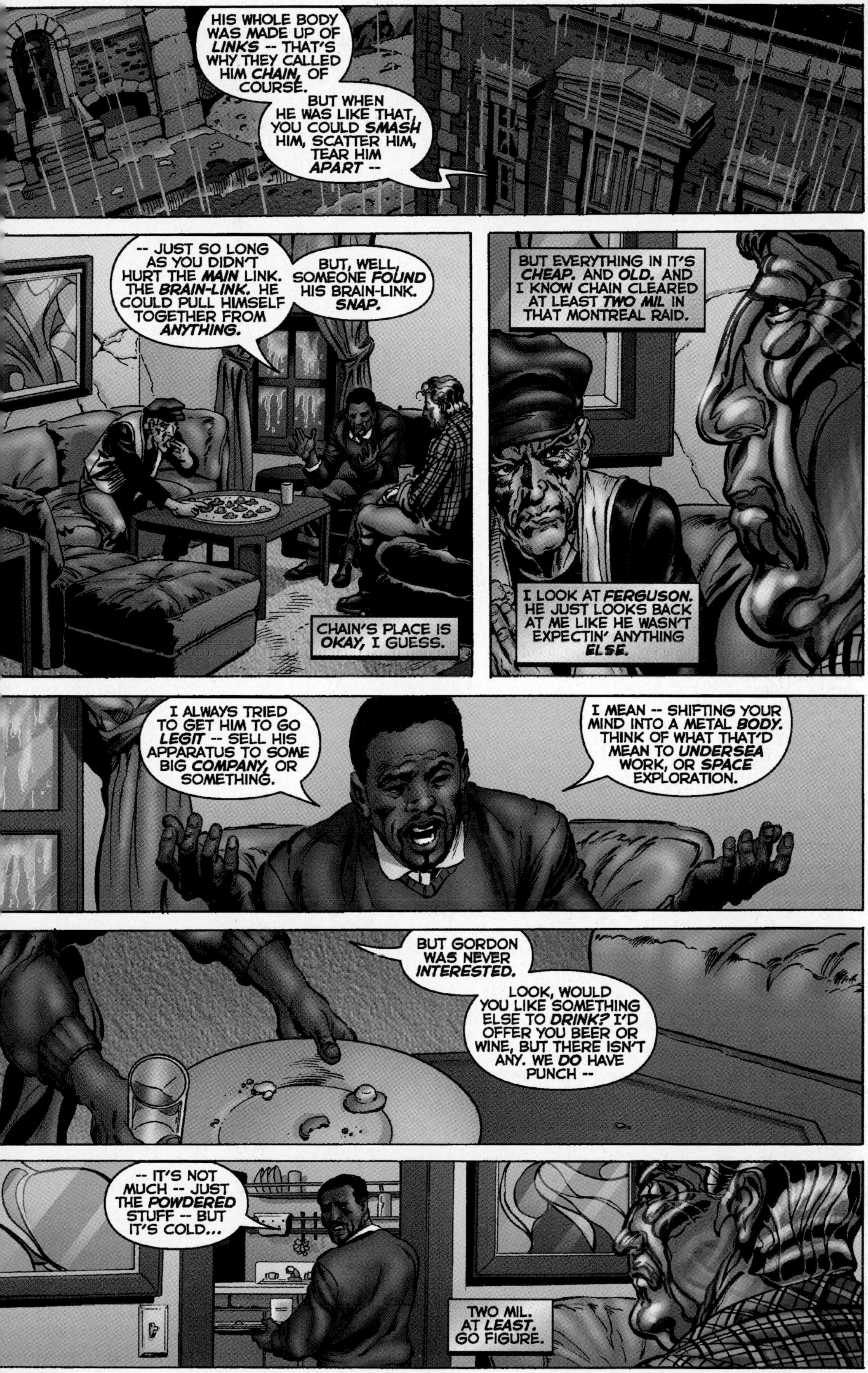

HIS WHOLE BODY WAS MADE UP OF LINKS -- THAT'S WHY THEY CALLED HIM CHAIN, OF COURSE.
BUT WHEN HE WAS LIKE THAT, YOU COULD SMASH HIM, SCATTER HIM, TEAR HIM APART --
-- JUST SO LONG AS YOU DIDN'T HURT THE MAIN LINK. THE BRAIN-LINK. HE COULD PULL HIMSELF TOGETHER FROM ANYTHING.
BUT, WELL, SOMEONE FOUND HIS BRAIN-LINK. SNAP.
CHAIN'S PLACE IS OKAY, I GUESS.
BUT EVERYTHING IN IT'S CHEAP. AND OLD. AND I KNOW CHAIN CLEARED AT LEAST TWO MIL IN THAT MONTREAL RAID.
I LOOK AT FERGUSON. HE JUST LOOKS BACK AT ME LIKE HE WASN'T EXPECTIN' ANYTHING ELSE.
I ALWAYS TRIED TO GET HIM TO GO LEGIT -- SELL HIS APPARATUS TO SOME BIG COMPANY, OR SOMETHING.
I MEAN -- SHIFTING YOUR MIND INTO A METAL BODY. THINK OF WHAT THAT'D MEAN TO UNDERSEA WORK, OR SPACE EXPLORATION.
BUT GORDON WAS NEVER INTERESTED.
LOOK, WOULD YOU LIKE SOMETHING ELSE TO DRINK? I'D OFFER YOU BEER OR WINE, BUT THERE ISN'T ANY. WE DO HAVE PUNCH --
-- IT'S NOT MUCH -- JUST THE POWDERED STUFF -- BUT IT'S COLD...
TWO MIL. AT LEAST. GO FIGURE.

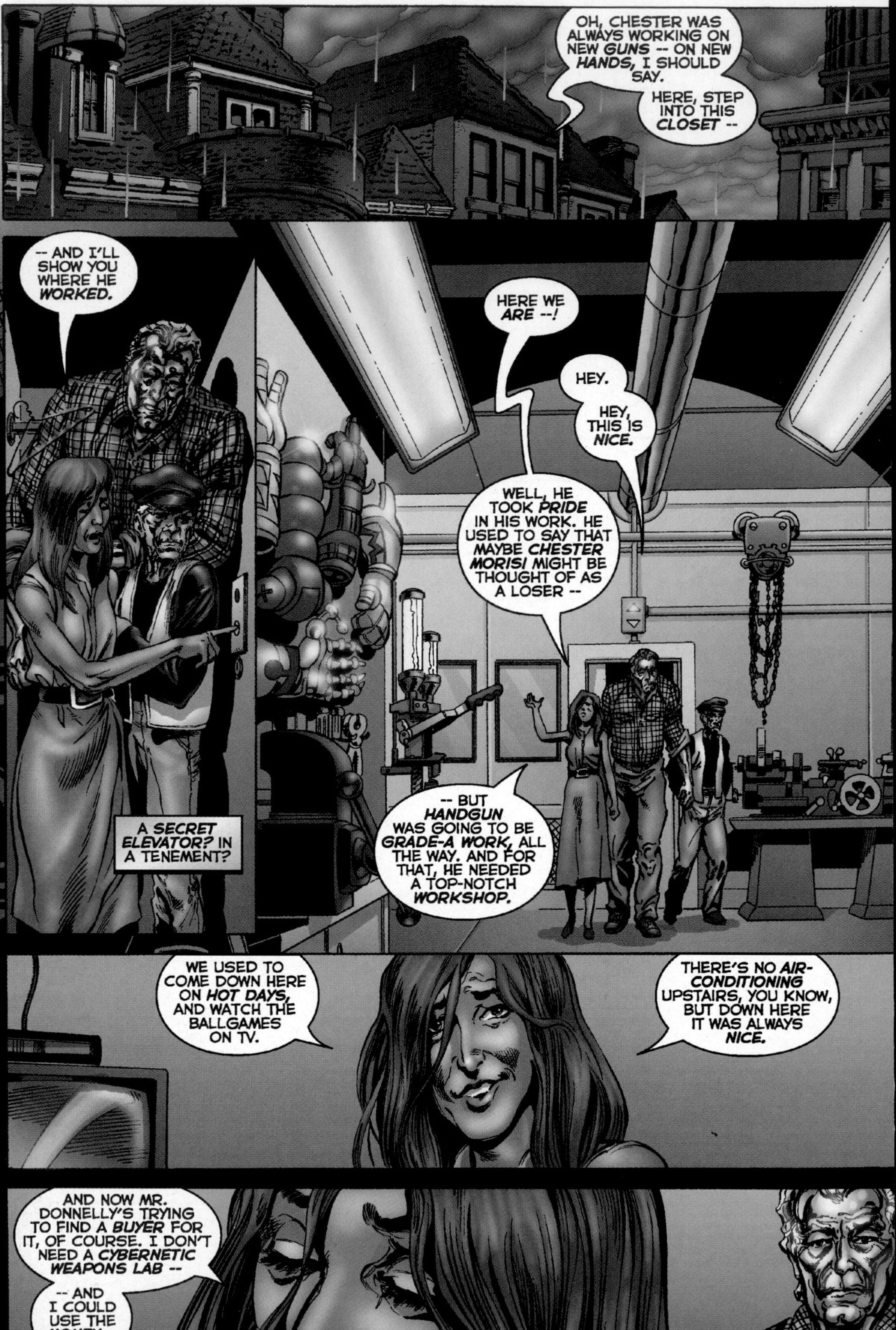
OH, CHESTER WAS ALWAYS WORKING ON NEW GUNS -- ON NEW HANDS, I SHOULD SAY.
HERE, STEP INTO THIS CLOSET --
-- AND I'LL SHOW YOU WHERE HE WORKED.
A SECRET ELEVATOR? IN A TENEMENT?
HERE WE ARE --!
HEY.
HEY, THIS IS NICE.
WELL, HE TOOK PRIDE IN HIS WORK. HE USED TO SAY THAT MAYBE CHESTER MORISI MIGHT BE THOUGHT OF AS A LOSER --
-- BUT HANDGUN WAS GOING TO BE GRADE-A WORK, ALL THE WAY. AND FOR THAT, HE NEEDED A TOP-NOTCH WORKSHOP.
WE USED TO COME DOWN HERE ON HOT DAYS, AND WATCH THE BALLGAMES ON TV.
THERE'S NO AIR-CONDITIONING UPSTAIRS, YOU KNOW, BUT DOWN HERE IT WAS ALWAYS NICE.
AND NOW MR. DONNELLY'S TRYING TO FIND A BUYER FOR IT, OF COURSE. I DON'T NEED A CYBERNETIC WEAPONS LAB --
-- AND I COULD USE THE MONEY...

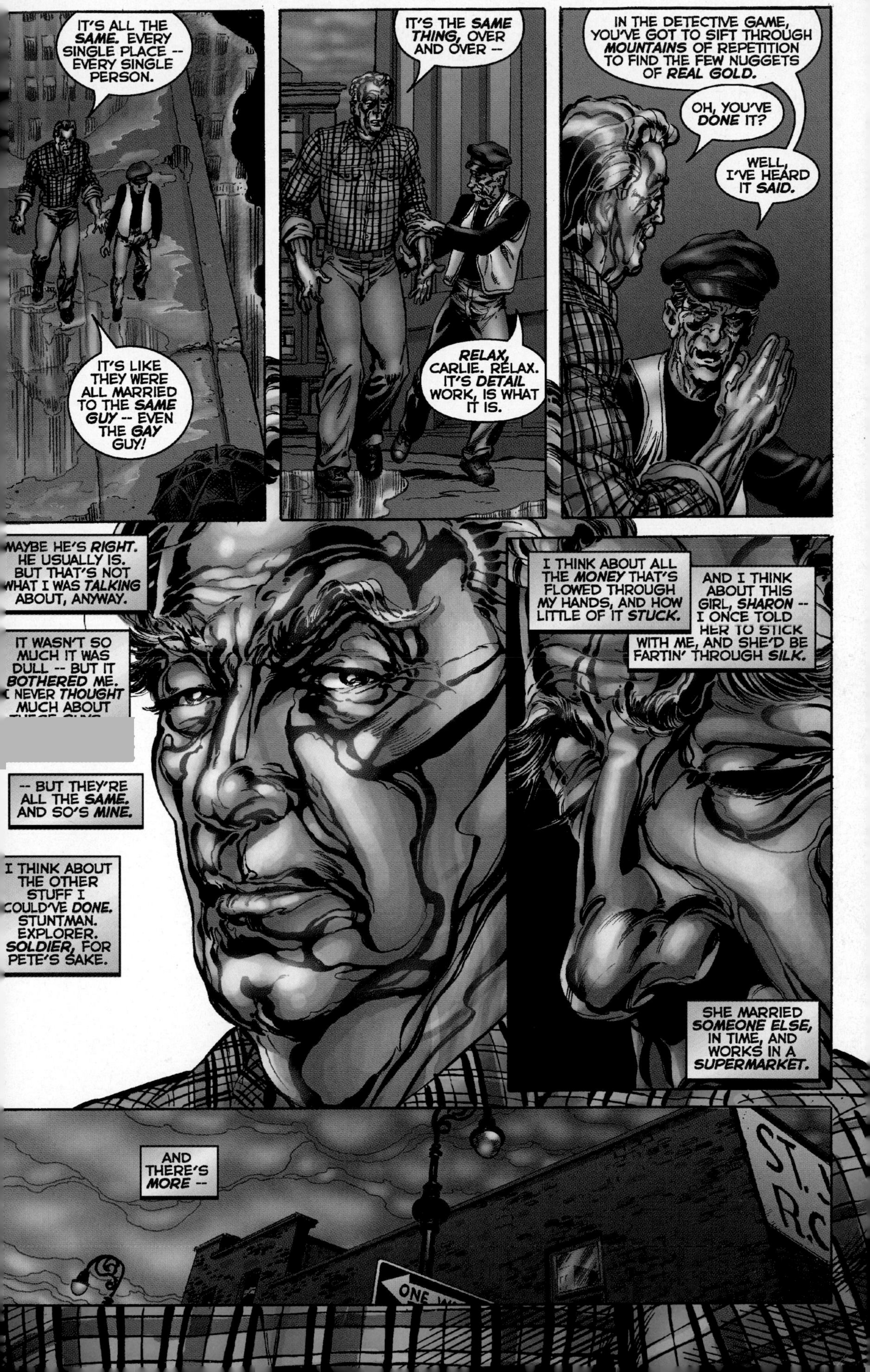

IT'S ALL THE SAME. EVERY SINGLE PLACE -- EVERY SINGLE PERSON.
IT'S LIKE THEY WERE ALL MARRIED TO THE SAME GUY -- EVEN THE GAY GUY!
IT'S THE SAME THING, OVER AND OVER --
RELAX, CARLIE. RELAX. IT'S DETAIL WORK, IS WHAT IT IS.
IN THE DETECTIVE GAME, YOU'VE GOT TO SIFT THROUGH MOUNTAINS OF REPETITION TO FIND THE FEW NUGGETS OF REAL GOLD.
OH, YOU'VE DONE IT?
WELL, I'VE HEARD IT SAID.
MAYBE HE'S RIGHT. HE USUALLY IS. BUT THAT'S NOT WHAT I WAS TALKING ABOUT, ANYWAY.
IT WASN'T SO MUCH IT WAS DULL -- BUT IT BOTHERED ME. I NEVER THOUGHT MUCH ABOUT
-- BUT THEY'RE ALL THE SAME. AND SO'S MINE.
I THINK ABOUT THE OTHER STUFF I COULD'VE DONE. STUNTMAN. EXPLORER. SOLDIER, FOR PETE'S SAKE.
I THINK ABOUT ALL THE MONEY THAT'S FLOWED THROUGH MY HANDS, AND HOW LITTLE OF IT STUCK.
AND I THINK ABOUT THIS GIRL, SHARON -- I ONCE TOLD HER TO STICK WITH ME, AND SHE'D BE FARTIN' THROUGH SILK.
SHE MARRIED SOMEONE ELSE, IN TIME, AND WORKS IN A SUPERMARKET.
AND THERE'S MORE --
ONE W
ST. J
R.C

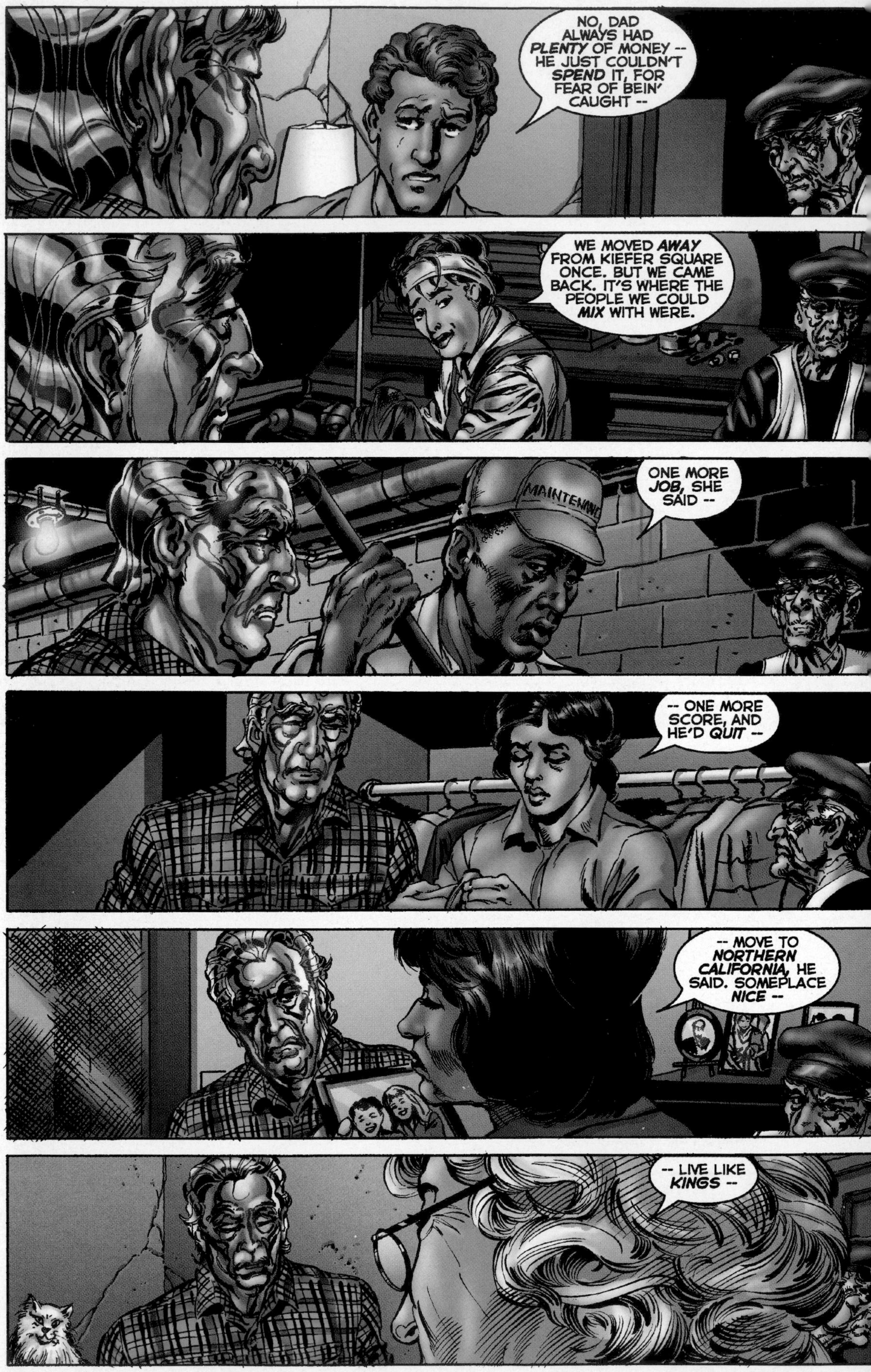
NO, DAD ALWAYS HAD PLENTY OF MONEY -- HE JUST COULDN'T SPEND IT, FOR FEAR OF BEIN' CAUGHT --
WE MOVED AWAY FROM KIEFER SQUARE ONCE. BUT WE CAME BACK. IT'S WHERE THE PEOPLE WE COULD MIX WITH WERE.
MAINTENANCE
ONE MORE JOB, SHE SAID --
-- ONE MORE SCORE, AND HE'D QUIT --
-- MOVE TO NORTHERN CALIFORNIA, HE SAID. SOMEPLACE NICE --
-- LIVE LIKE KINGS --

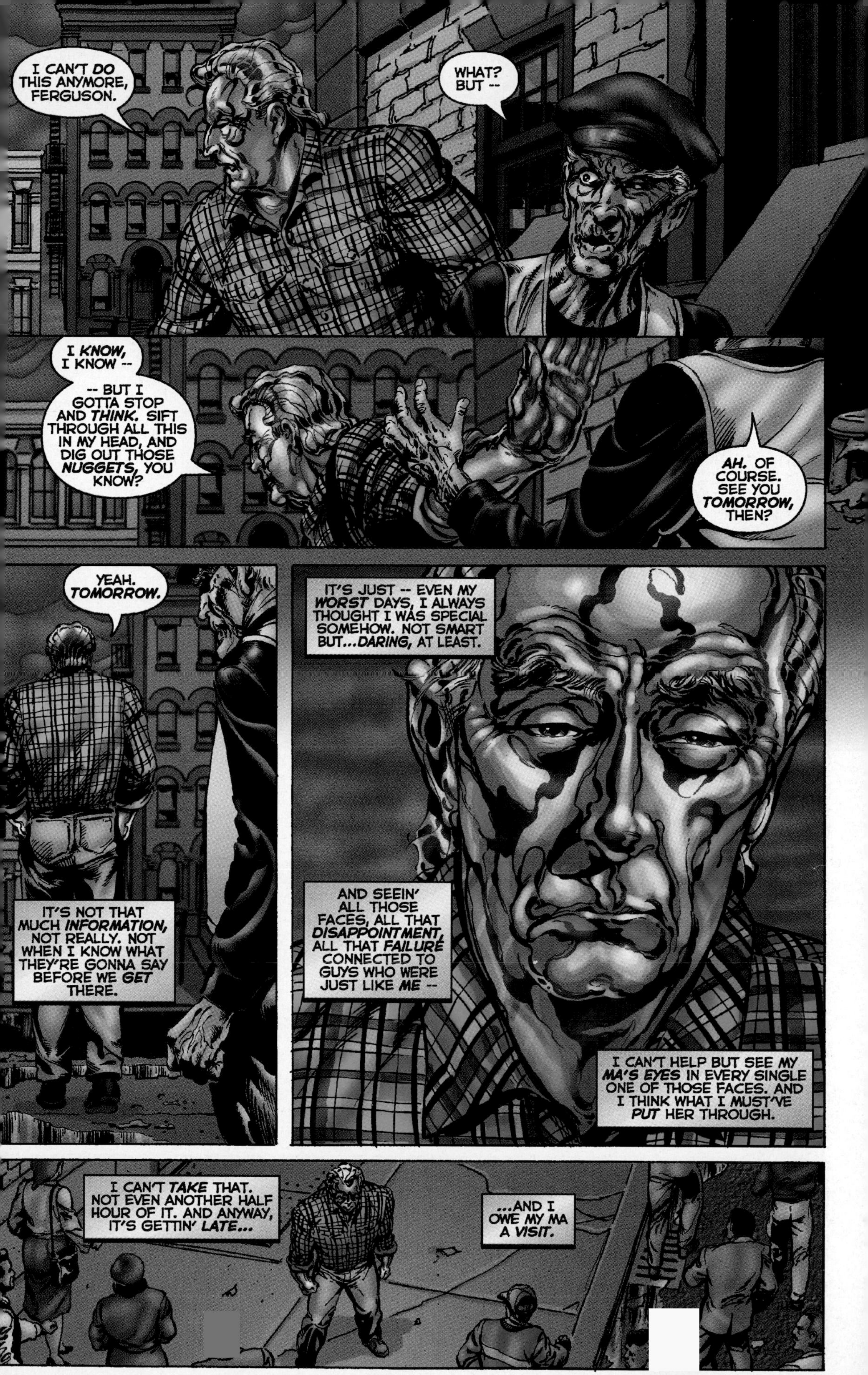
I CAN'T DO THIS ANYMORE, FERGUSON.
WHAT? BUT --
I KNOW, I KNOW --
-- BUT I GOTTA STOP AND THINK. SIFT THROUGH ALL THIS IN MY HEAD, AND DIG OUT THOSE NUGGETS, YOU KNOW?
AH. OF COURSE. SEE YOU TOMORROW, THEN?
YEAH. TOMORROW.
IT'S NOT THAT MUCH INFORMATION, NOT REALLY. NOT WHEN I KNOW WHAT THEY'RE GONNA SAY BEFORE WE GET THERE.
IT'S JUST -- EVEN MY WORST DAYS, I ALWAYS THOUGHT I WAS SPECIAL SOMEHOW. NOT SMART BUT...DARING, AT LEAST.
AND SEEIN' ALL THOSE FACES, ALL THAT DISAPPOINTMENT, ALL THAT FAILURE CONNECTED TO GUYS WHO WERE JUST LIKE ME --
I CAN'T HELP BUT SEE MY MA'S EYES IN EVERY SINGLE ONE OF THOSE FACES. AND I THINK WHAT I MUST'VE PUT HER THROUGH.
I CAN'T TAKE THAT. NOT EVEN ANOTHER HALF HOUR OF IT. AND ANYWAY, IT'S GETTIN' LATE...
...AND I OWE MY MA A VISIT.

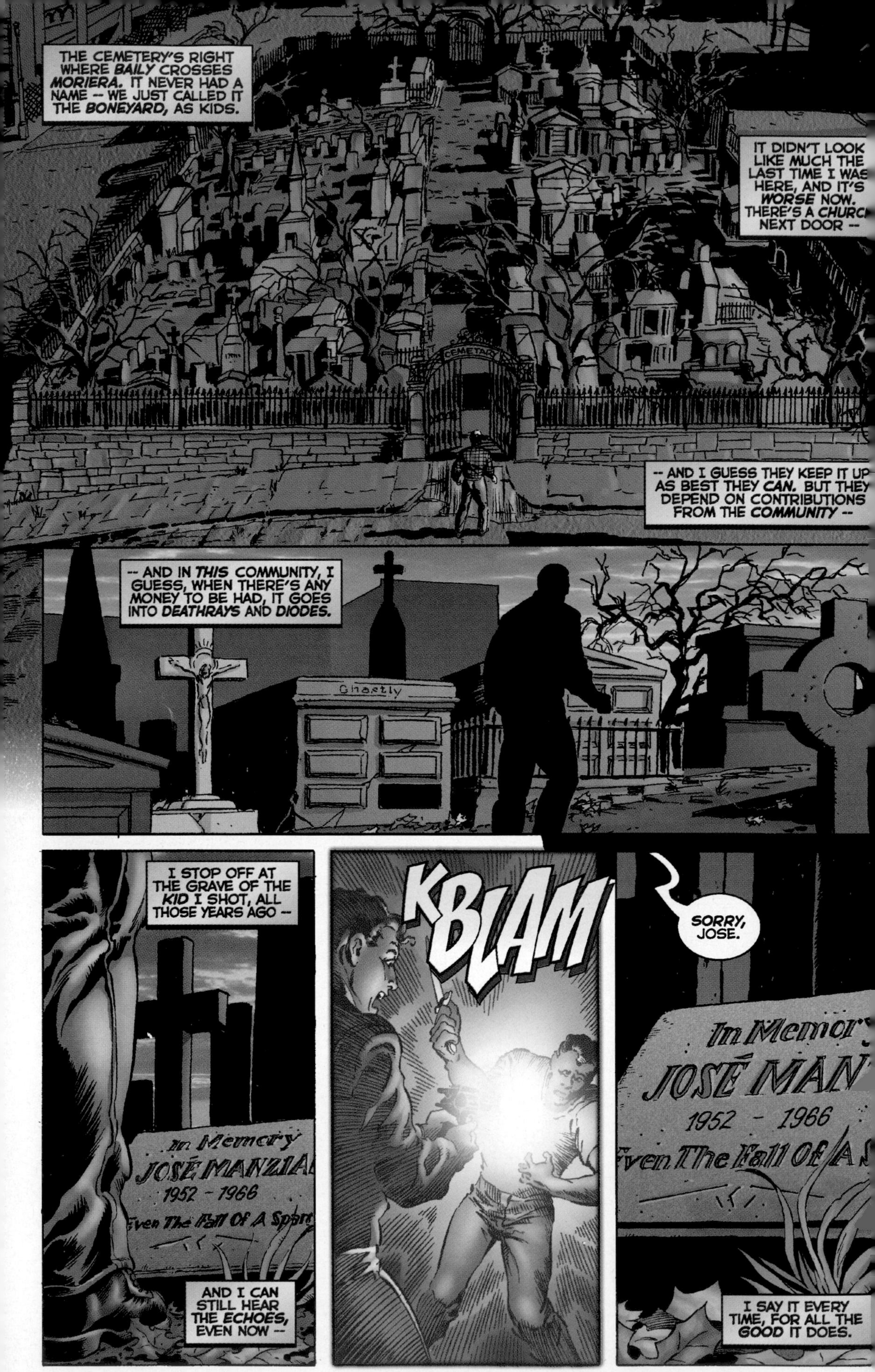
THE CEMETERY'S RIGHT WHERE BAILY CROSSES MORIERA. IT NEVER HAD A NAME -- WE JUST CALLED IT THE BONEYARD, AS KIDS.
IT DIDN'T LOOK LIKE MUCH THE LAST TIME I WAS HERE, AND IT'S WORSE NOW. THERE'S A CHURCH NEXT DOOR --
CEMETARY
-- AND I GUESS THEY KEEP IT UP AS BEST THEY CAN. BUT THEY DEPEND ON CONTRIBUTIONS FROM THE COMMUNITY --
-- AND IN THIS COMMUNITY, I GUESS, WHEN THERE'S ANY MONEY TO BE HAD, IT GOES INTO DEATHRAYS AND DIODES.
Ghastly
I STOP OFF AT THE GRAVE OF THE KID I SHOT, ALL THOSE YEARS AGO --
In Memory
1952 - 1966
AND I CAN STILL HEAR THE ECHOES, EVEN NOW --
KBLAM
SORRY, JOSE.
1952 - 1966
I SAY IT EVERY TIME, FOR ALL THE GOOD IT DOES.

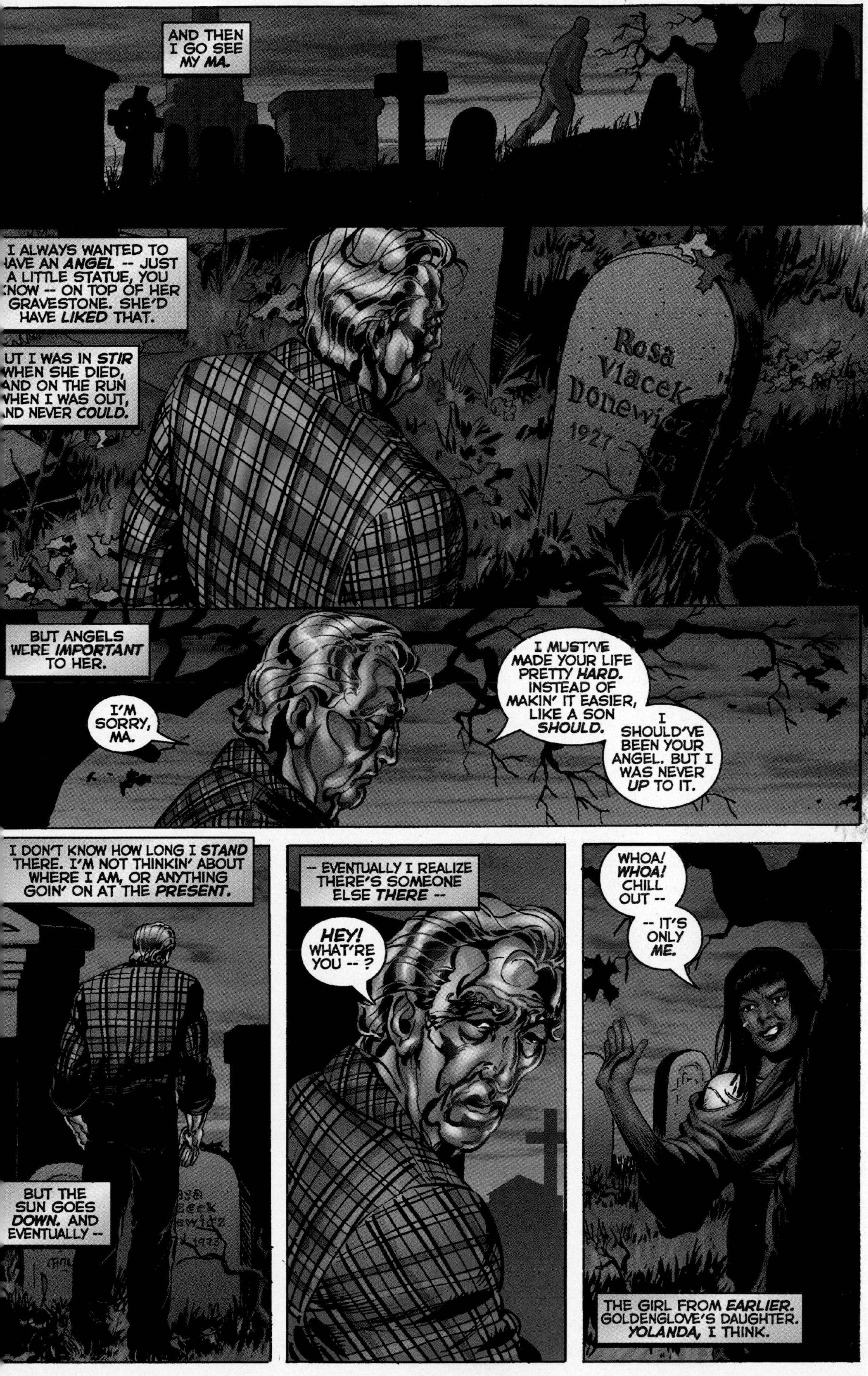
AND THEN I GO SEE MY MA.
I ALWAYS WANTED TO HAVE AN ANGEL -- JUST A LITTLE STATUE, YOU KNOW -- ON TOP OF HER GRAVESTONE. SHE'D HAVE LIKED THAT.
BUT I WAS IN STIR WHEN SHE DIED, AND ON THE RUN WHEN I WAS OUT, AND NEVER COULD.
Rosa Vlacek Donewicz 1927
BUT ANGELS WERE IMPORTANT TO HER.
I'M SORRY, MA.
I MUST'VE MADE YOUR LIFE PRETTY HARD. INSTEAD OF MAKIN' IT EASIER, LIKE A SON SHOULD.
I SHOULD'VE BEEN YOUR ANGEL. BUT I WAS NEVER UP TO IT.
I DON'T KNOW HOW LONG I STAND THERE. I'M NOT THINKIN' ABOUT WHERE I AM, OR ANYTHING GOIN' ON AT THE PRESENT.
BUT THE SUN GOES DOWN. AND EVENTUALLY --
-- EVENTUALLY I REALIZE THERE'S SOMEONE ELSE THERE --
HEY! WHAT'RE YOU -- ?
WHOA! WHOA! CHILL OUT --
-- IT'S ONLY ME.
THE GIRL FROM EARLIER. GOLDENGLOVE'S DAUGHTER. YOLANDA, I THINK.

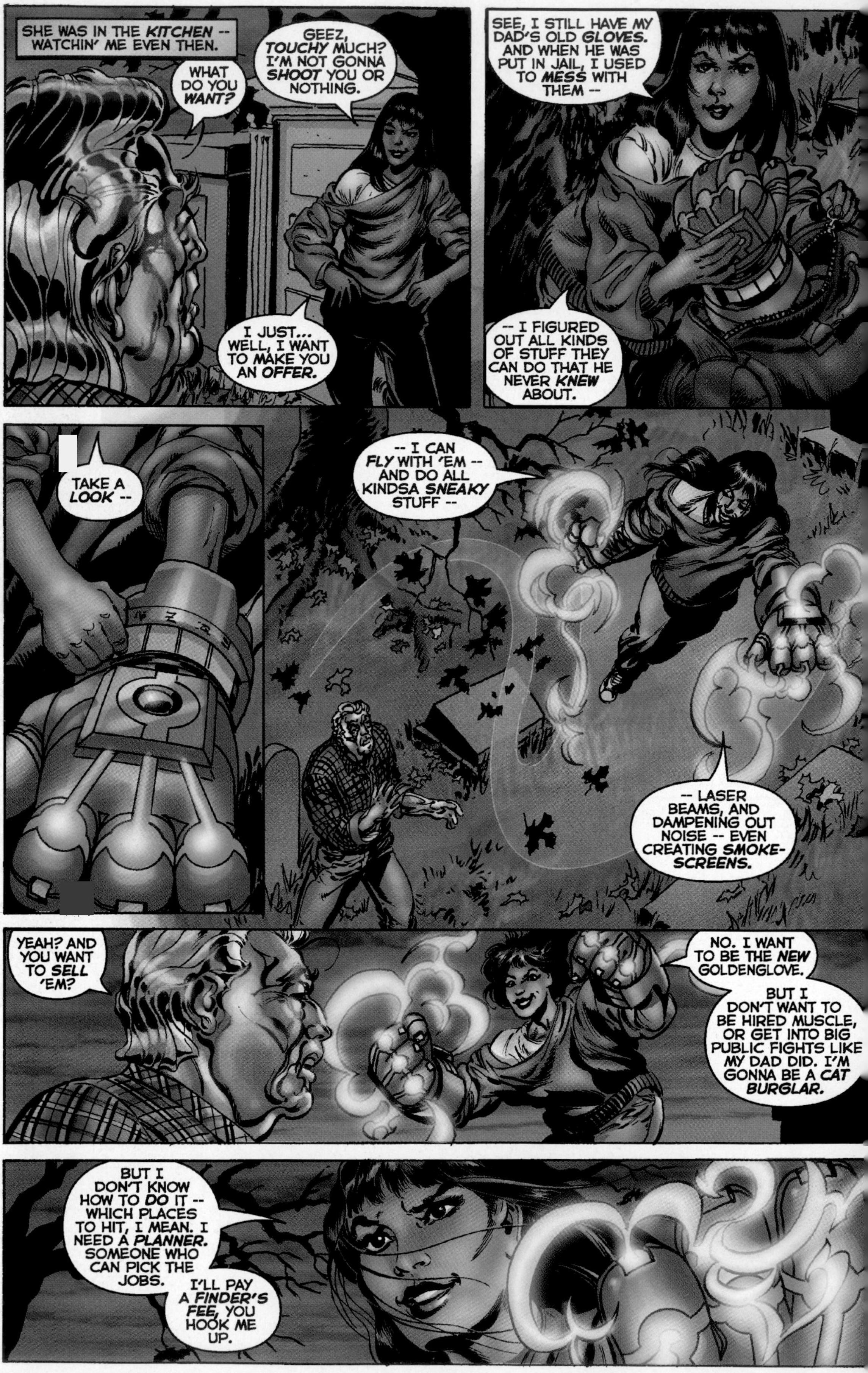
SHE WAS IN THE KITCHEN -- WATCHIN' ME EVEN THEN.
WHAT DO YOU WANT?
GEEZ, TOUCHY MUCH? I'M NOT GONNA SHOOT YOU OR NOTHING.
I JUST... WELL, I WANT TO MAKE YOU AN OFFER.
SEE, I STILL HAVE MY DAD'S OLD GLOVES. AND WHEN HE WAS PUT IN JAIL, I USED TO MESS WITH THEM --
-- I FIGURED OUT ALL KINDS OF STUFF THEY CAN DO THAT HE NEVER KNEW ABOUT.
TAKE A LOOK --
-- I CAN FLY WITH 'EM -- AND DO ALL KINDSA SNEAKY STUFF --
-- LASER BEAMS, AND DAMPENING OUT NOISE -- EVEN CREATING SMOKE-SCREENS.
YEAH? AND YOU WANT TO SELL 'EM?
NO. I WANT TO BE THE NEW GOLDENGLOVE.
BUT I DON'T WANT TO BE HIRED MUSCLE, OR GET INTO BIG PUBLIC FIGHTS LIKE MY DAD DID. I'M GONNA BE A CAT BURGLAR.
BUT I DON'T KNOW HOW TO DO IT -- WHICH PLACES TO HIT, I MEAN. I NEED A PLANNER. SOMEONE WHO CAN PICK THE JOBS.
I'LL PAY A FINDER'S FEE, YOU HOOK ME UP.

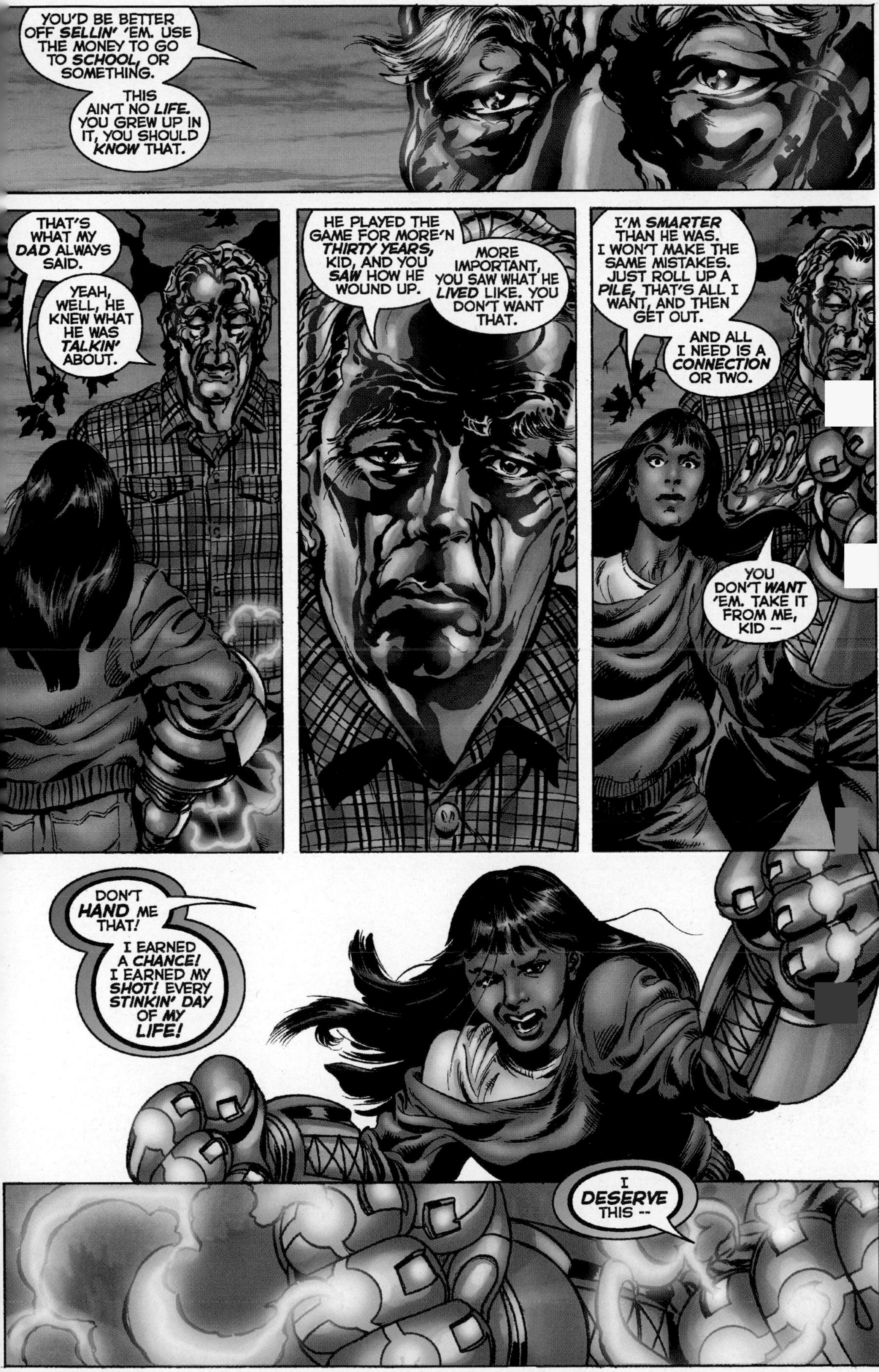

YOU'D BE BETTER OFF SELLIN' 'EM. USE THE MONEY TO GO TO SCHOOL, OR SOMETHING.
THIS AIN'T NO LIFE. YOU GREW UP IN IT, YOU SHOULD KNOW THAT.
THAT'S WHAT MY DAD ALWAYS SAID.
YEAH, WELL, HE KNEW WHAT HE WAS TALKIN' ABOUT.
HE PLAYED THE GAME FOR MORE'N THIRTY YEARS, KID, AND YOU SAW HOW HE WOUND UP.
MORE IMPORTANT, YOU SAW WHAT HE LIVED LIKE. YOU DON'T WANT THAT.
I'M SMARTER THAN HE WAS. I WON'T MAKE THE SAME MISTAKES. JUST ROLL UP A PILE, THAT'S ALL I WANT, AND THEN GET OUT.
AND ALL I NEED IS A CONNECTION OR TWO.
YOU DON'T WANT 'EM. TAKE IT FROM ME, KID --
DON'T HAND ME THAT!
I EARNED A CHANCE! I EARNED MY SHOT! EVERY STINKIN' DAY OF MY LIFE!
I DESERVE THIS --

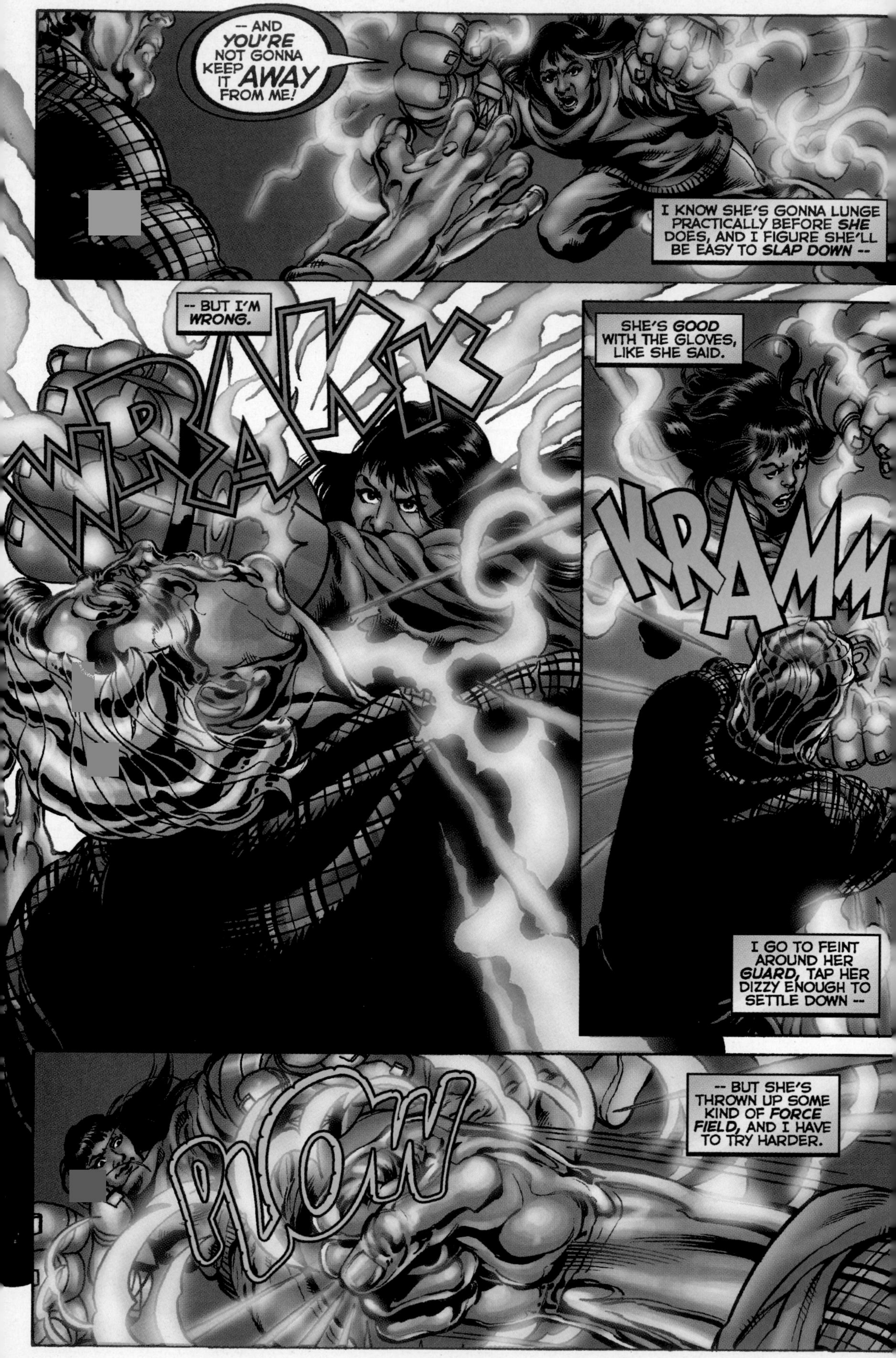
-- AND YOU'RE NOT GONNA KEEP IT AWAY FROM ME!
I KNOW SHE'S GONNA LUNGE PRACTICALLY BEFORE SHE DOES, AND I FIGURE SHE'LL BE EASY TO SLAP DOWN --
-- BUT I'M WRONG.
WRAKK
SHE'S GOOD WITH THE GLOVES, LIKE SHE SAID.
KRAMM
I GO TO FEINT AROUND HER GUARD, TAP HER DIZZY ENOUGH TO SETTLE DOWN --
-- BUT SHE'S THROWN UP SOME KIND OF FORCE FIELD, AND I HAVE TO TRY HARDER.
POW

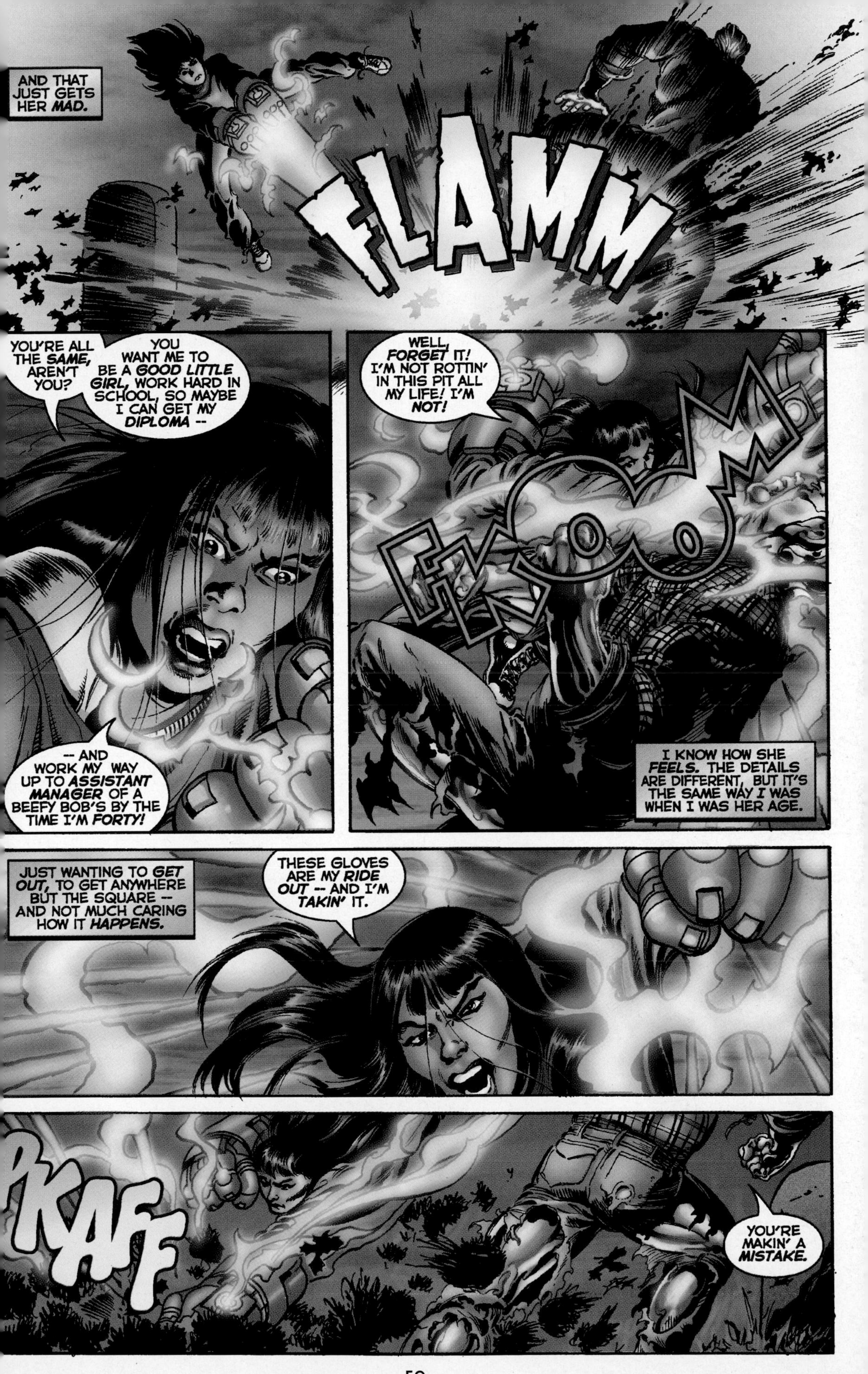
AND THAT JUST GETS HER MAD.
FLAMM
YOU'RE ALL THE SAME, AREN'T YOU?
YOU WANT ME TO BE A GOOD LITTLE GIRL, WORK HARD IN SCHOOL, SO MAYBE I CAN GET MY DIPLOMA --
-- AND WORK MY WAY UP TO ASSISTANT MANAGER OF A BEEFY BOB'S BY THE TIME I'M FORTY!
WELL, FORGET IT! I'M NOT ROTTIN' IN THIS PIT ALL MY LIFE! I'M NOT!
I KNOW HOW SHE FEELS. THE DETAILS ARE DIFFERENT, BUT IT'S THE SAME WAY I WAS WHEN I WAS HER AGE.
JUST WANTING TO GET OUT, TO GET ANYWHERE BUT THE SQUARE -- AND NOT MUCH CARING HOW IT HAPPENS.
THESE GLOVES ARE MY RIDE OUT -- AND I'M TAKIN' IT.
KAFF
YOU'RE MAKIN' A MISTAKE.

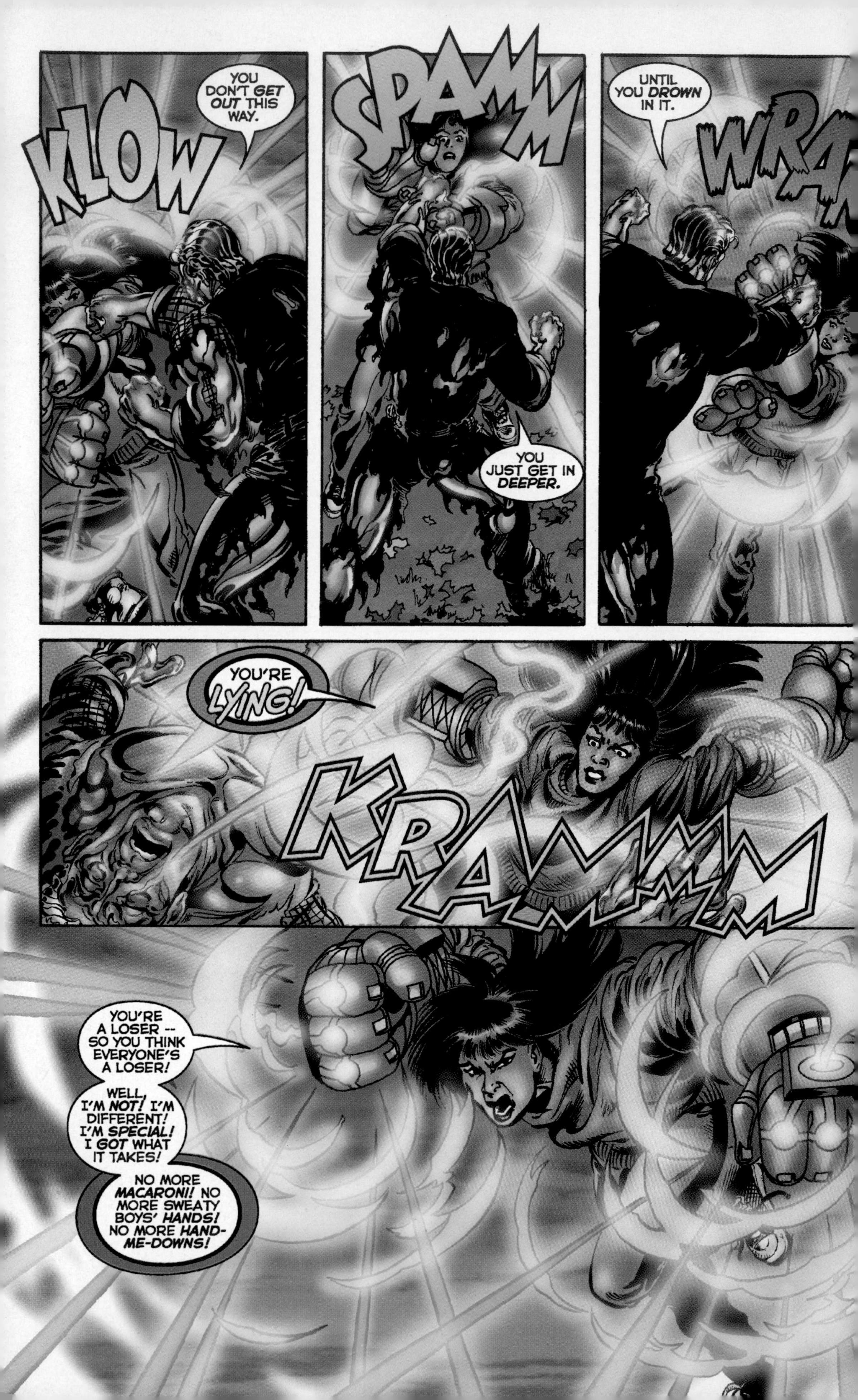
KLOW
YOU DON'T GET OUT THIS WAY.
SPAMM
YOU JUST GET IN DEEPER.
UNTIL YOU DROWN IN IT.
WRA
YOU'RE LYING!
KRAMMM
YOU'RE A LOSER -- SO YOU THINK EVERYONE'S A LOSER!
WELL, I'M NOT! I'M DIFFERENT! I'M SPECIAL! I GOT WHAT IT TAKES!
NO MORE MACARONI! NO MORE SWEATY BOYS' HANDS! NO MORE HAND-ME-DOWNS!

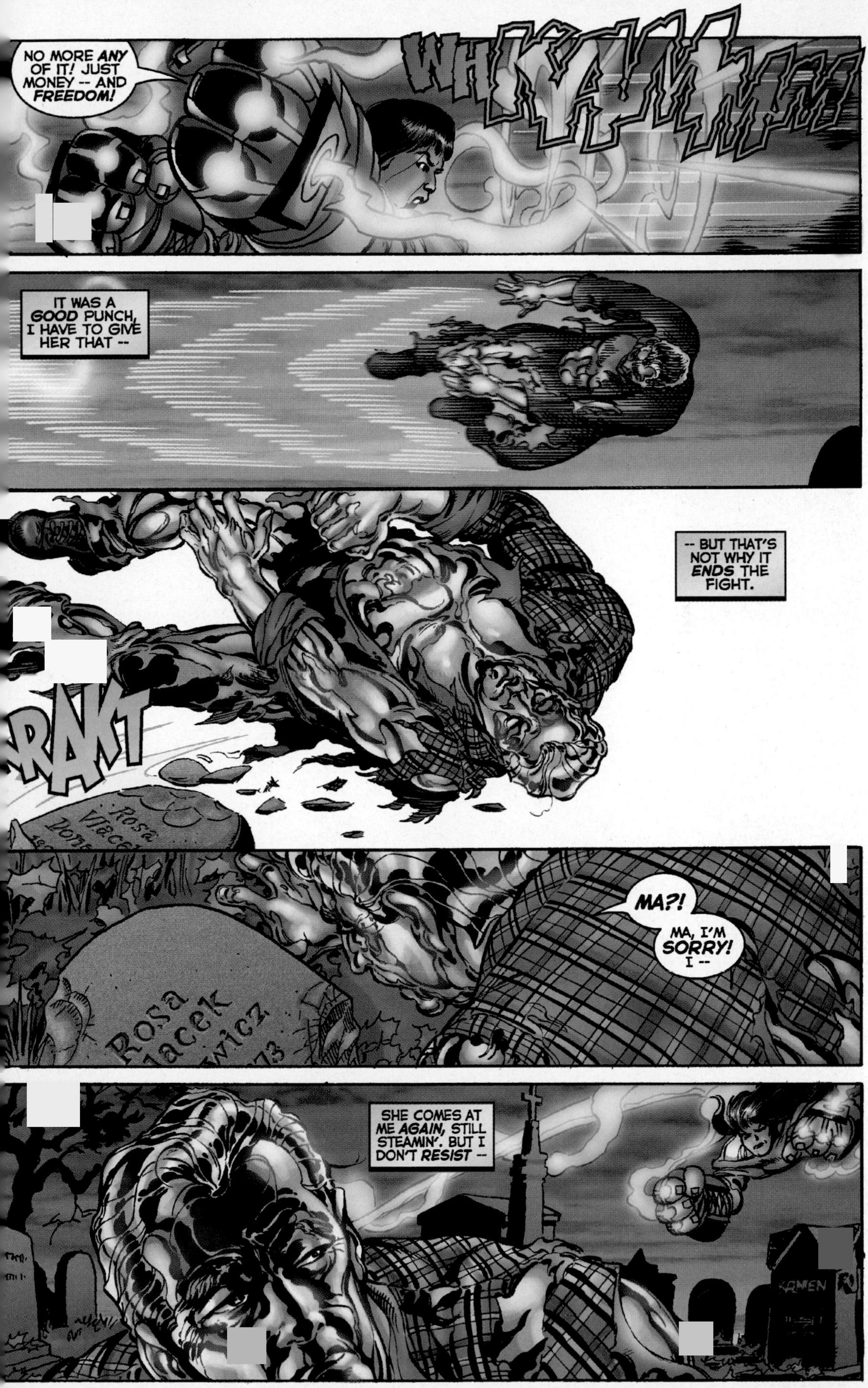
NO MORE ANY OF IT! JUST MONEY -- AND FREEDOM!
WHKAMM
IT WAS A GOOD PUNCH, I HAVE TO GIVE HER THAT --
-- BUT THAT'S NOT WHY IT ENDS THE FIGHT.
RAKT
MA?!
MA, I'M SORRY! I --
SHE COMES AT ME AGAIN, STILL STEAMIN'. BUT I DON'T RESIST --

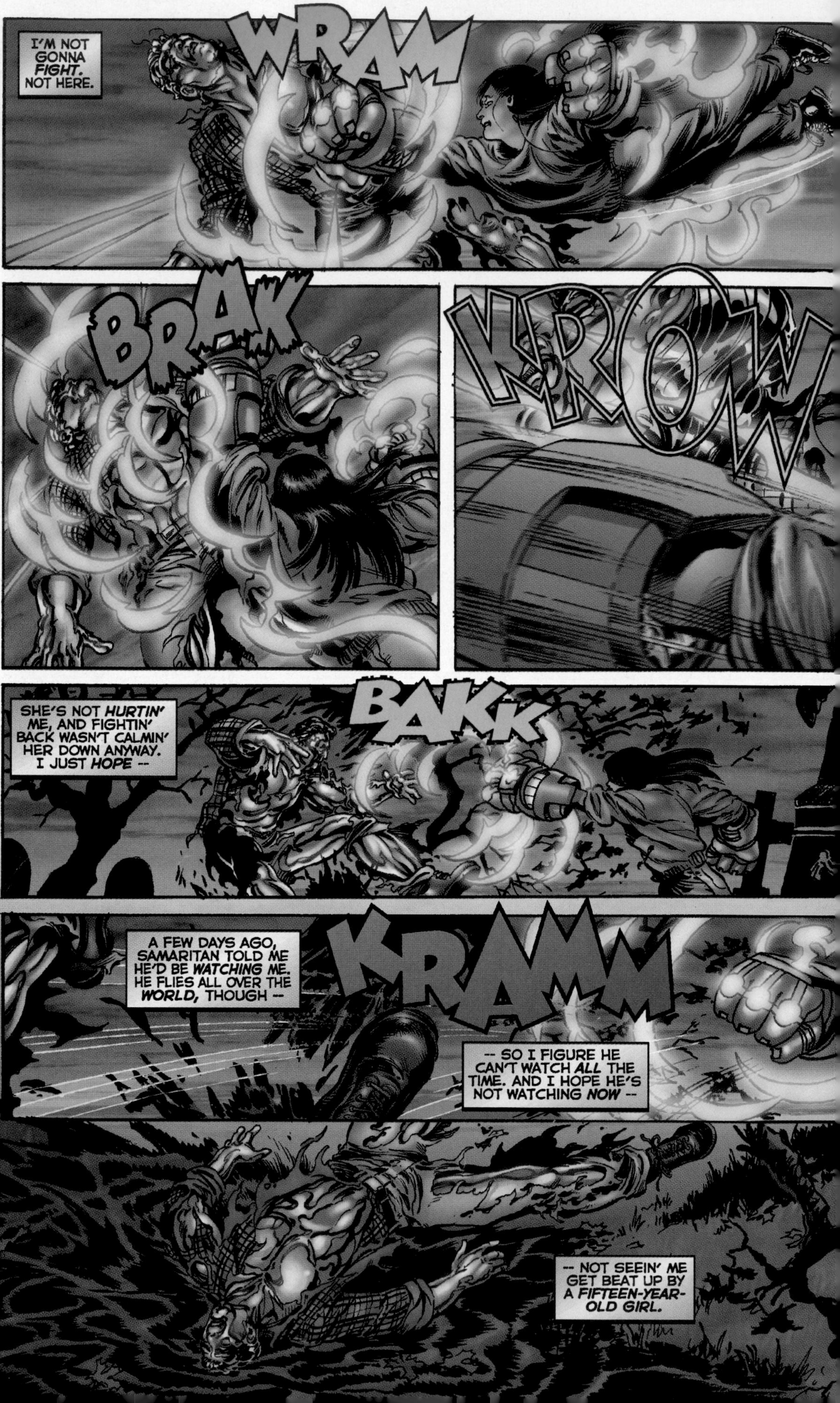
I'M NOT GONNA FIGHT. NOT HERE.
WRAM
BRAK
KRROWW
SHE'S NOT HURTIN' ME, AND FIGHTIN' BACK WASN'T CALMIN' HER DOWN ANYWAY. I JUST HOPE --
BAKK
A FEW DAYS AGO, SAMARITAN TOLD ME HE'D BE WATCHING ME. HE FLIES ALL OVER THE WORLD, THOUGH --
KRAMM
-- SO I FIGURE HE CAN'T WATCH ALL THE TIME. AND I HOPE HE'S NOT WATCHING NOW --
-- NOT SEEIN' ME GET BEAT UP BY A FIFTEEN-YEAR-OLD GIRL.

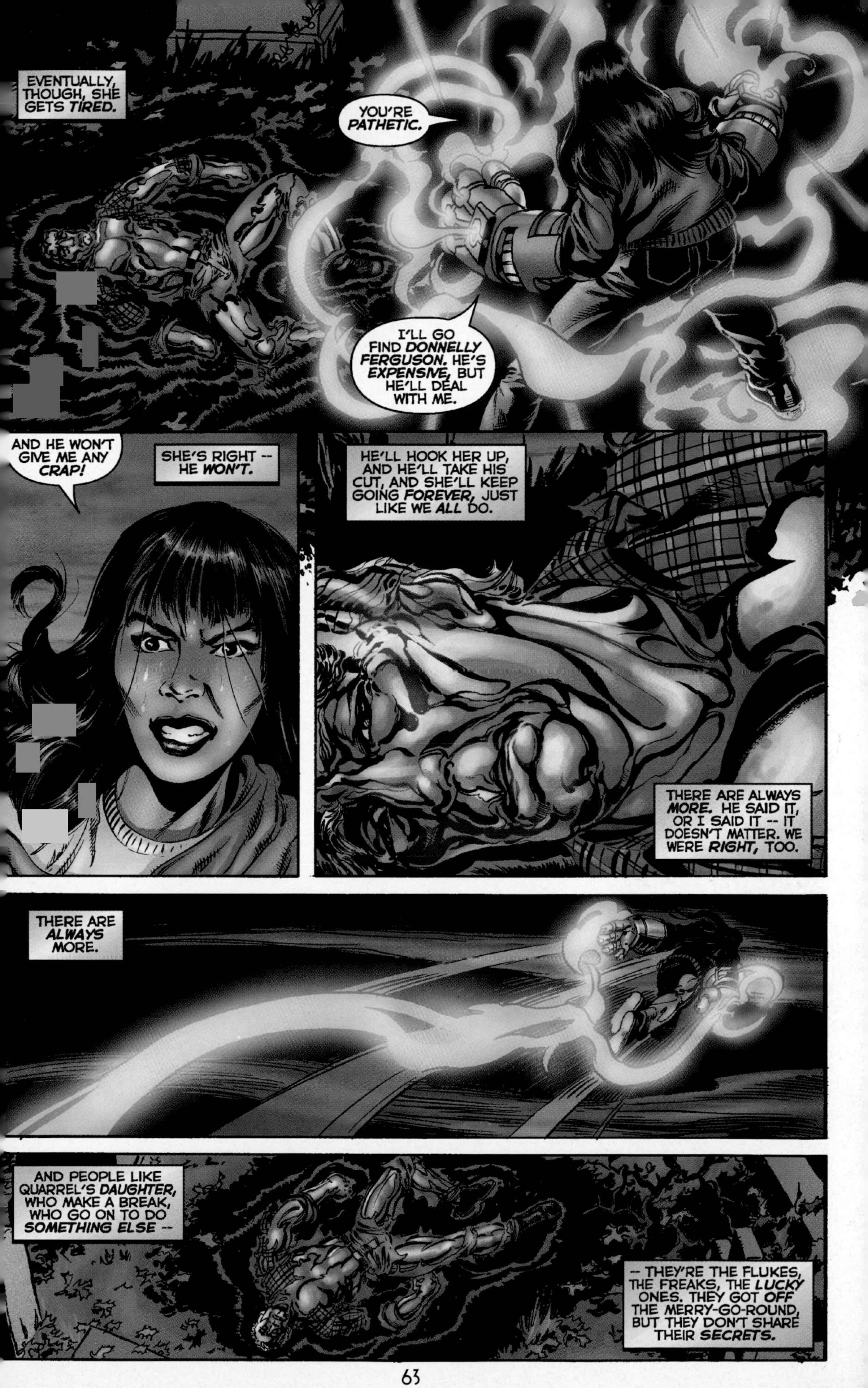
EVENTUALLY, THOUGH, SHE GETS TIRED.
YOU'RE PATHETIC.
I'LL GO FIND DONNELLY FERGUSON. HE'S EXPENSIVE, BUT HE'LL DEAL WITH ME.
AND HE WON'T GIVE ME ANY CRAP!
SHE'S RIGHT -- HE WON'T.
HE'LL HOOK HER UP, AND HE'LL TAKE HIS CUT, AND SHE'LL KEEP GOING FOREVER, JUST LIKE WE ALL DO.
THERE ARE ALWAYS MORE. HE SAID IT, OR I SAID IT -- IT DOESN'T MATTER. WE WERE RIGHT, TOO.
THERE ARE ALWAYS MORE.
AND PEOPLE LIKE QUARREL'S DAUGHTER, WHO MAKE A BREAK, WHO GO ON TO DO SOMETHING ELSE --
-- THEY'RE THE FLUKES, THE FREAKS, THE LUCKY ONES. THEY GOT OFF THE MERRY-GO-ROUND, BUT THEY DON'T SHARE THEIR SECRETS.

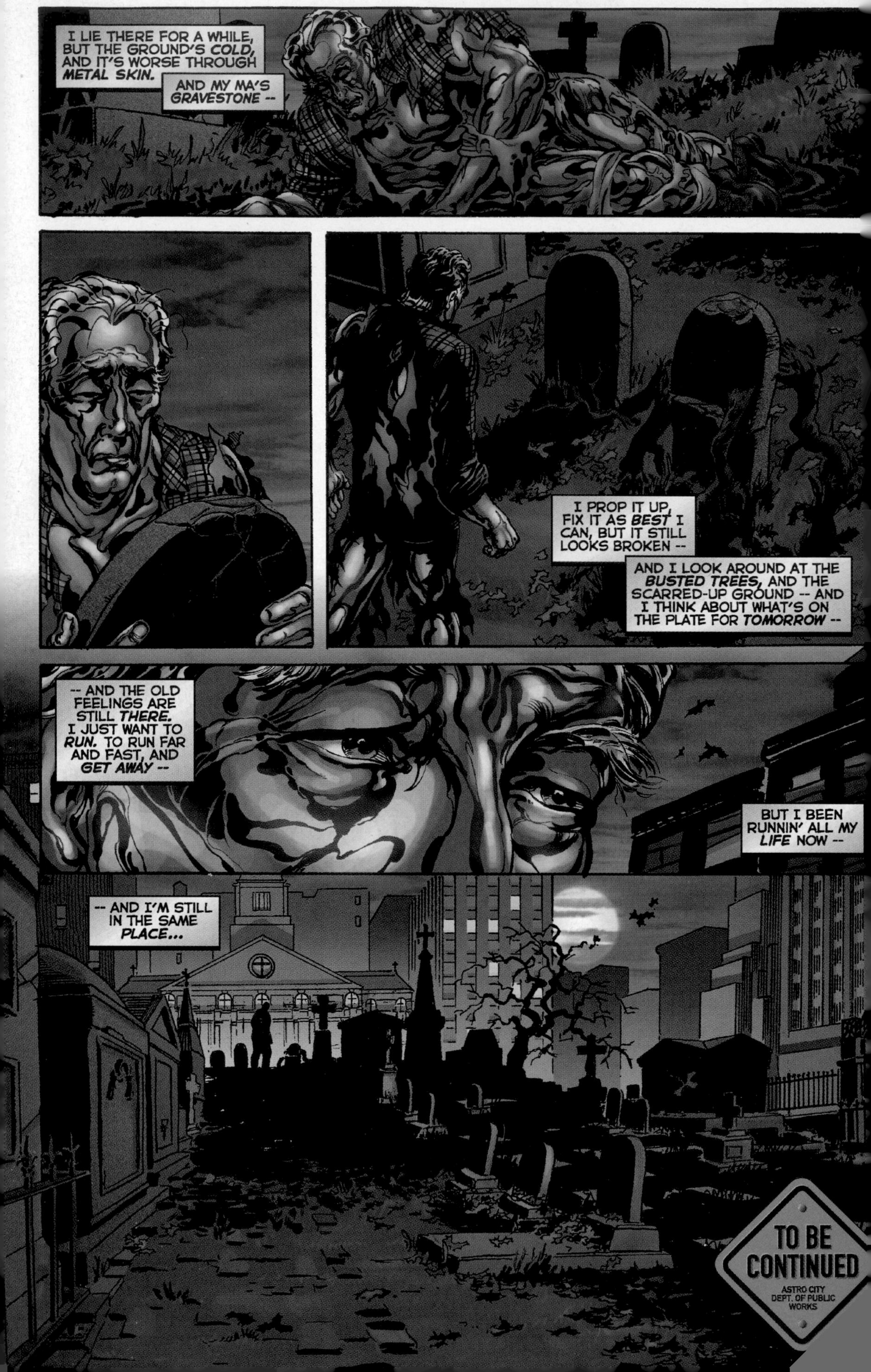
I LIE THERE FOR A WHILE, BUT THE GROUND'S COLD, AND IT'S WORSE THROUGH METAL SKIN.
AND MY MA'S GRAVESTONE --
I PROP IT UP, FIX IT AS BEST I CAN, BUT IT STILL LOOKS BROKEN --
AND I LOOK AROUND AT THE BUSTED TREES, AND THE SCARRED-UP GROUND -- AND I THINK ABOUT WHAT'S ON THE PLATE FOR TOMORROW --
-- AND THE OLD FEELINGS ARE STILL THERE. I JUST WANT TO RUN. TO RUN FAR AND FAST, AND GET AWAY --
BUT I BEEN RUNNIN' ALL MY LIFE NOW --
-- AND I'M STILL IN THE SAME PLACE...
TO BE CONTINUED
ASTRO CITY DEPT. OF PUBLIC WORKS

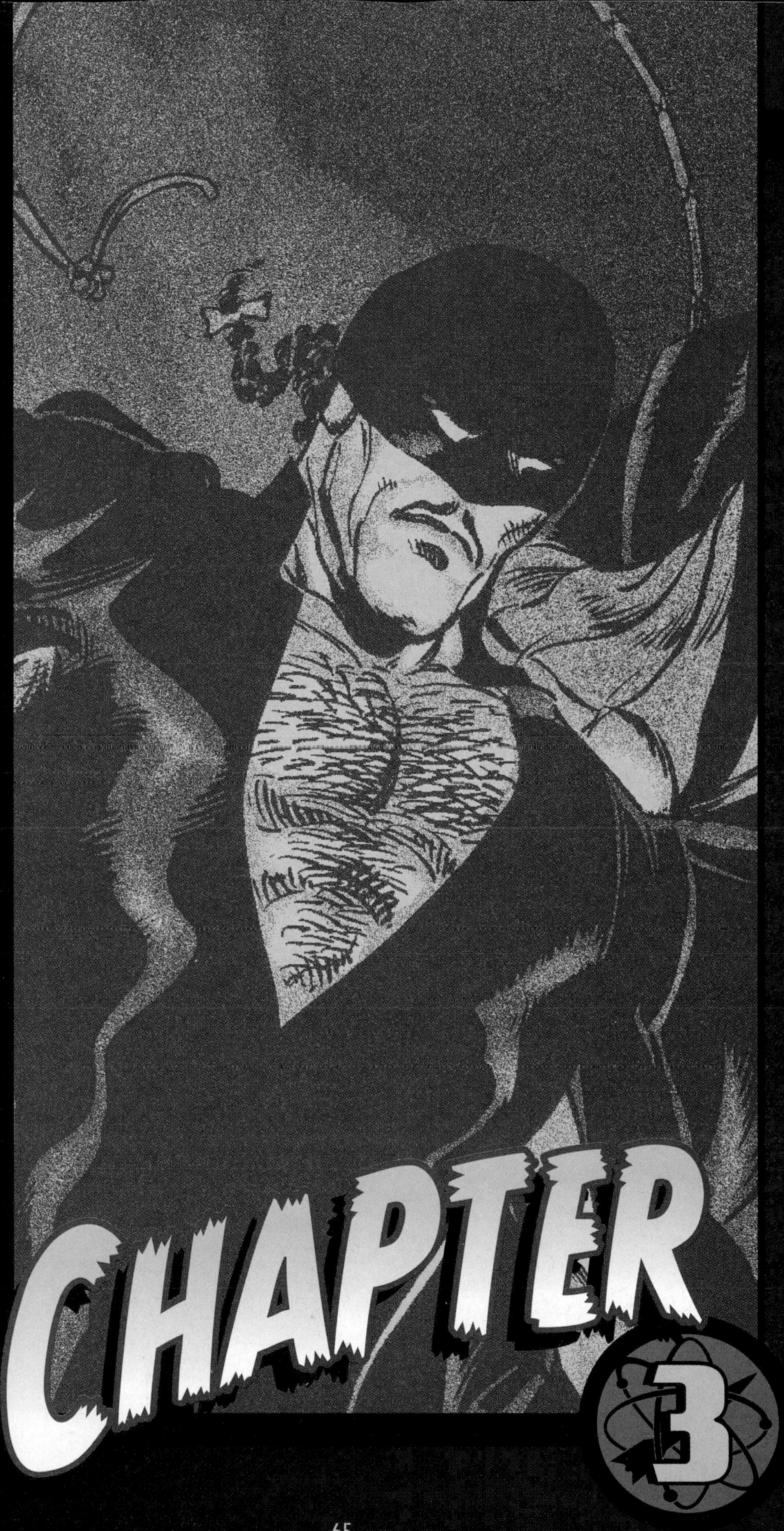
CHAPTER
3

The TARNISHED ANGEL

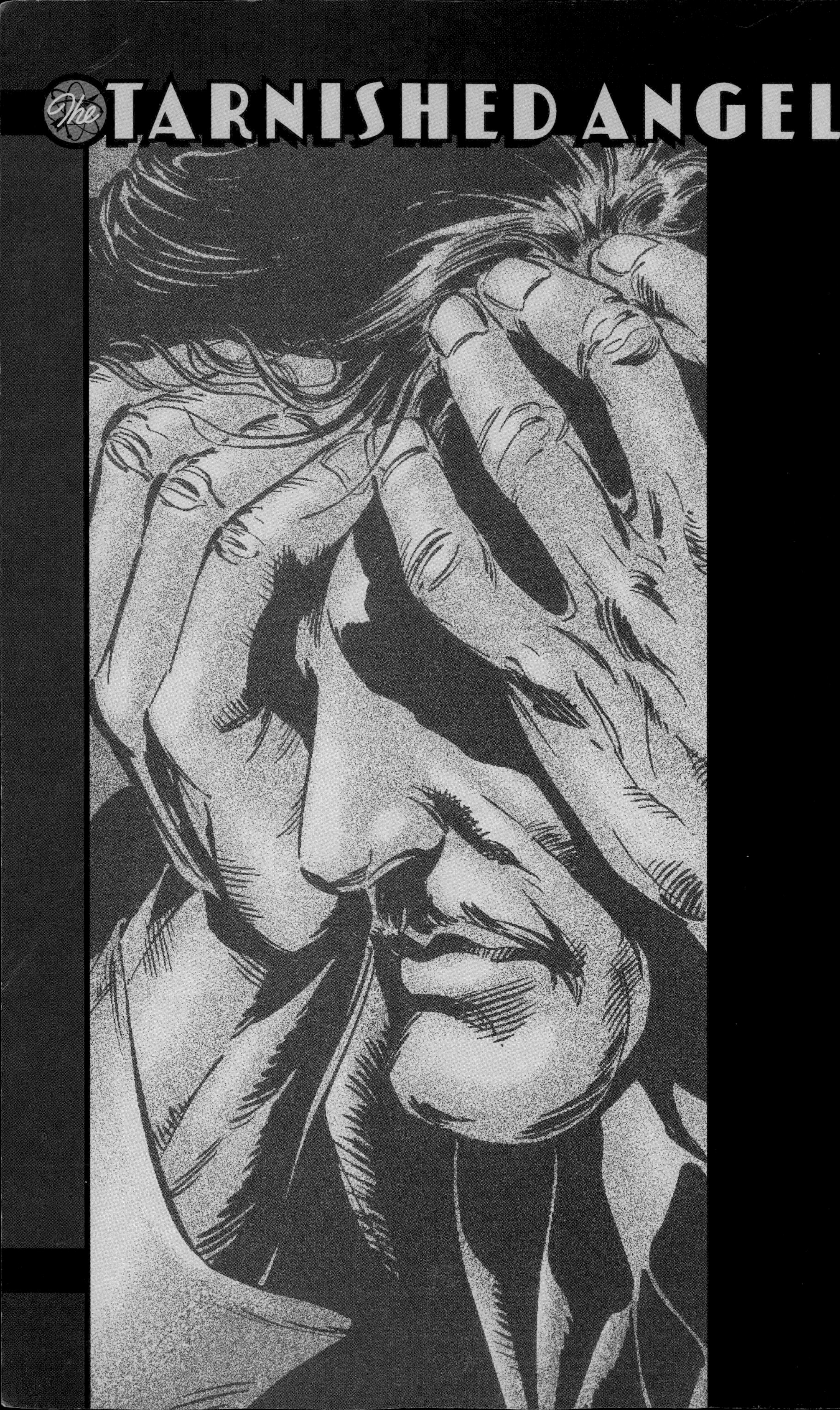

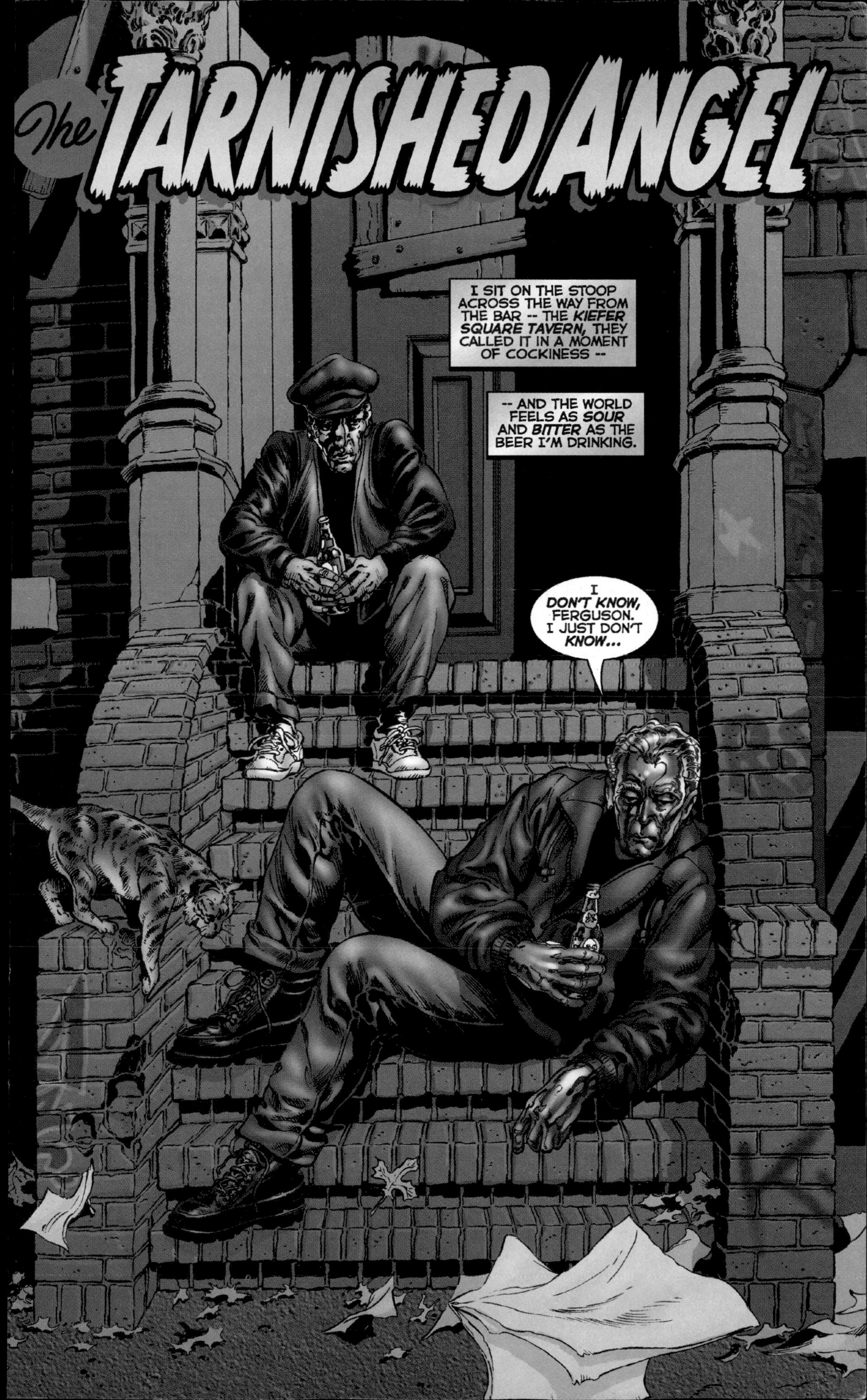
The TARNISHED ANGEL
I SIT ON THE STOOP ACROSS THE WAY FROM THE BAR -- THE KIEFER SQUARE TAVERN, THEY CALLED IT IN A MOMENT OF COCKINESS --
-- AND THE WORLD FEELS AS SOUR AND BITTER AS THE BEER I'M DRINKING.
I DON'T KNOW, FERGUSON. I JUST DON'T KNOW...

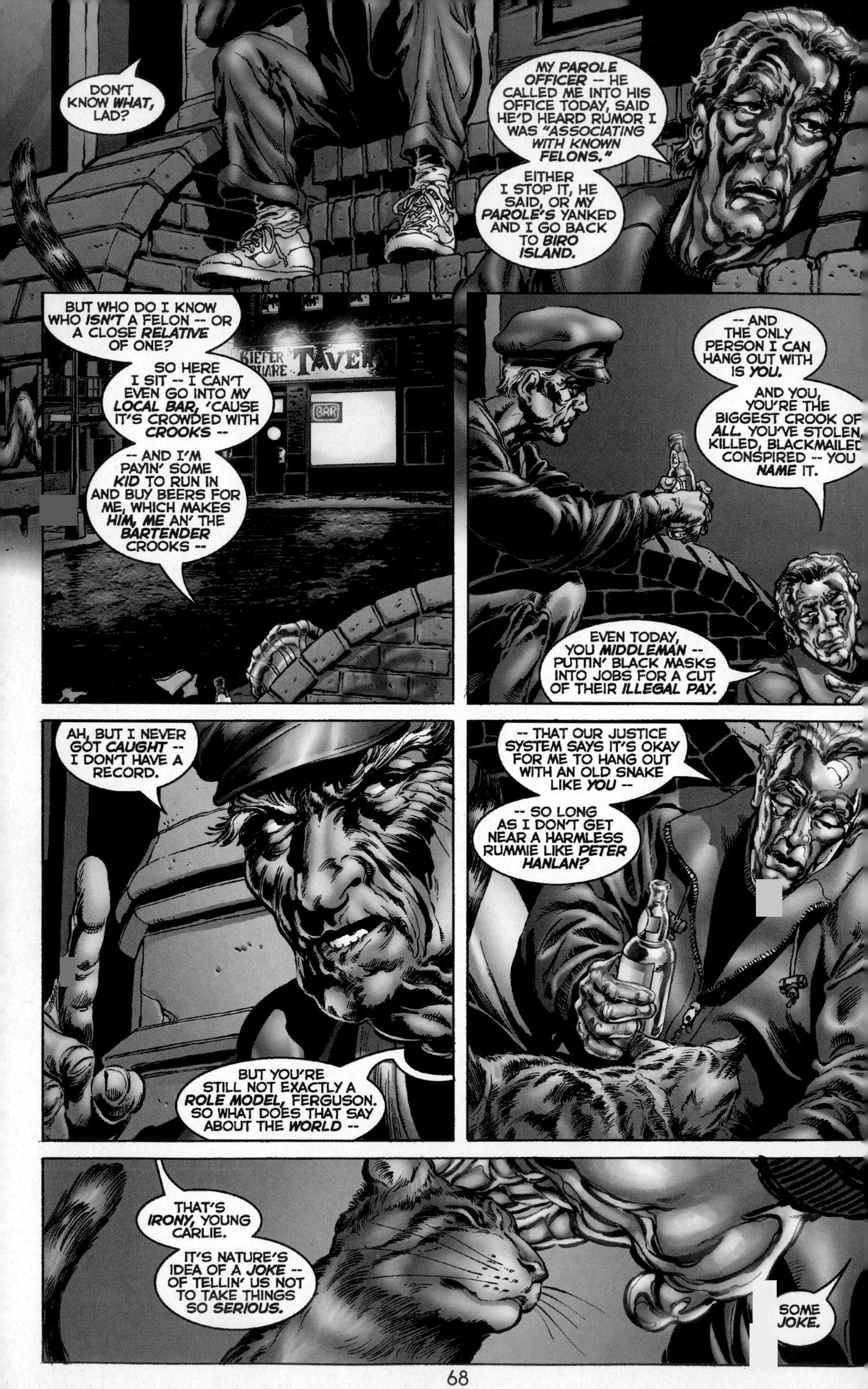
DON'T KNOW WHAT, LAD?
MY PAROLE OFFICER -- HE CALLED ME INTO HIS OFFICE TODAY, SAID HE'D HEARD RUMOR I WAS "ASSOCIATING WITH KNOWN FELONS."
EITHER I STOP IT, HE SAID, OR MY PAROLE'S YANKED AND I GO BACK TO BIRO ISLAND.
BUT WHO DO I KNOW WHO ISN'T A FELON -- OR A CLOSE RELATIVE OF ONE?
SO HERE I SIT -- I CAN'T EVEN GO INTO MY LOCAL BAR, 'CAUSE IT'S CROWDED WITH CROOKS --
-- AND I'M PAYIN' SOME KID TO RUN IN AND BUY BEERS FOR ME, WHICH MAKES HIM, ME AN' THE BARTENDER CROOKS --
KIEFER SQUARE TAVER
BAR
-- AND THE ONLY PERSON I CAN HANG OUT WITH IS YOU.
AND YOU, YOU'RE THE BIGGEST CROOK OF ALL. YOU'VE STOLEN, KILLED, BLACKMAILED, CONSPIRED -- YOU NAME IT.
EVEN TODAY, YOU MIDDLEMAN -- PUTTIN' BLACK MASKS INTO JOBS FOR A CUT OF THEIR ILLEGAL PAY.
AH, BUT I NEVER GOT CAUGHT -- I DON'T HAVE A RECORD.
BUT YOU'RE STILL NOT EXACTLY A ROLE MODEL, FERGUSON. SO WHAT DOES THAT SAY ABOUT THE WORLD --
-- THAT OUR JUSTICE SYSTEM SAYS IT'S OKAY FOR ME TO HANG OUT WITH AN OLD SNAKE LIKE YOU --
-- SO LONG AS I DON'T GET NEAR A HARMLESS RUMMIE LIKE PETER HANLAN?
THAT'S IRONY, YOUNG CARLIE.
IT'S NATURE'S IDEA OF A JOKE -- OF TELLIN' US NOT TO TAKE THINGS SO SERIOUS.
SOME JOKE.

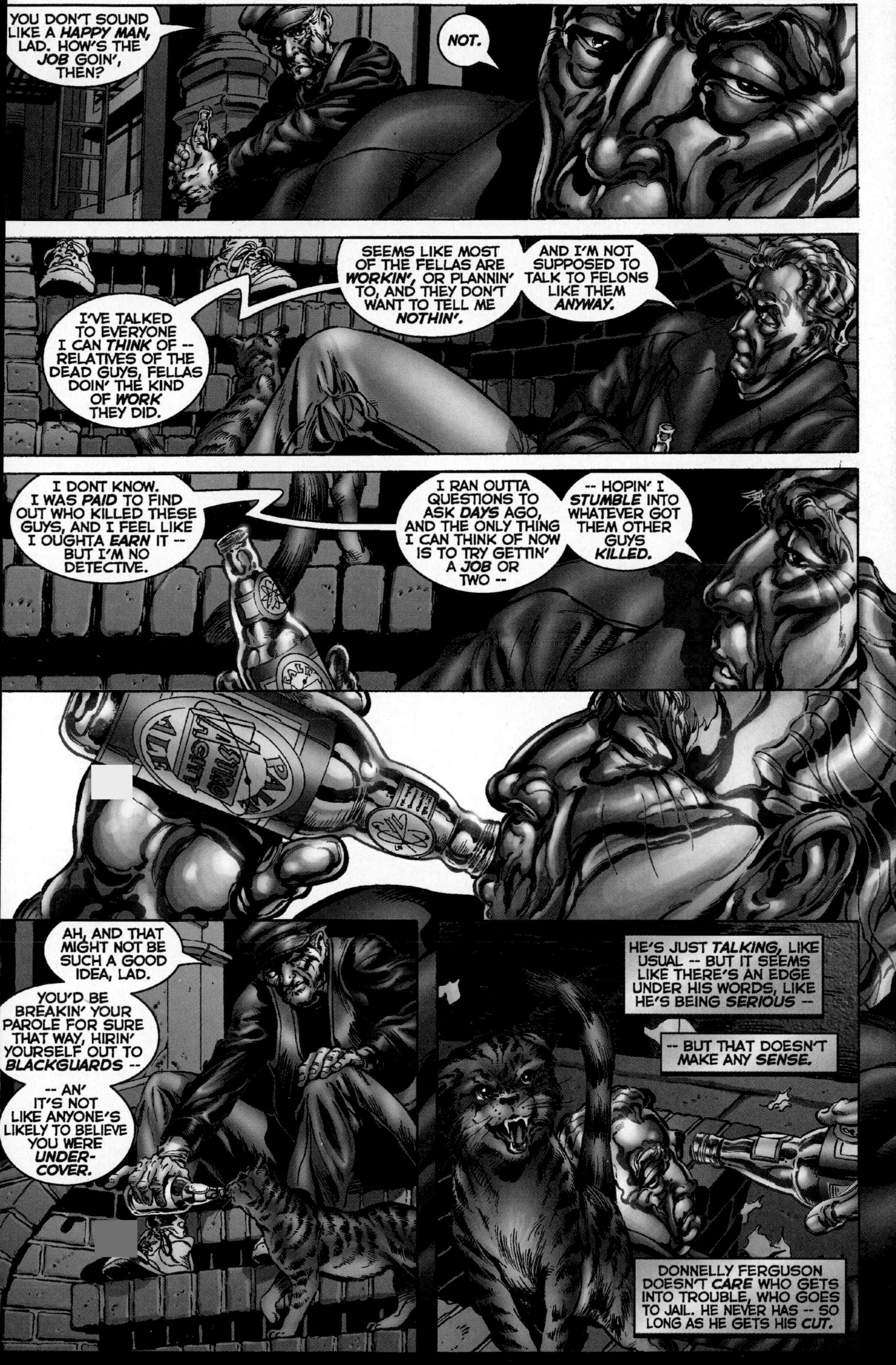
YOU DON'T SOUND LIKE A HAPPY MAN, LAD. HOW'S THE JOB GOIN', THEN?
NOT.
I'VE TALKED TO EVERYONE I CAN THINK OF -- RELATIVES OF THE DEAD GUYS, FELLAS DOIN' THE KIND OF WORK THEY DID.
SEEMS LIKE MOST OF THE FELLAS ARE WORKIN', OR PLANNIN' TO, AND THEY DON'T WANT TO TELL ME NOTHIN'.
AND I'M NOT SUPPOSED TO TALK TO FELONS LIKE THEM ANYWAY.
I DONT KNOW. I WAS PAID TO FIND OUT WHO KILLED THESE GUYS, AND I FEEL LIKE I OUGHTA EARN IT -- BUT I'M NO DETECTIVE.
I RAN OUTTA QUESTIONS TO ASK DAYS AGO, AND THE ONLY THING I CAN THINK OF NOW IS TO TRY GETTIN' A JOB OR TWO --
-- HOPIN' I STUMBLE INTO WHATEVER GOT THEM OTHER GUYS KILLED.
AH, AND THAT MIGHT NOT BE SUCH A GOOD IDEA, LAD.
YOU'D BE BREAKIN' YOUR PAROLE FOR SURE THAT WAY, HIRIN' YOURSELF OUT TO BLACKGUARDS --
-- AN' IT'S NOT LIKE ANYONE'S LIKELY TO BELIEVE YOU WERE UNDER-COVER.
HE'S JUST TALKING, LIKE USUAL -- BUT IT SEEMS LIKE THERE'S AN EDGE UNDER HIS WORDS, LIKE HE'S BEING SERIOUS --
-- BUT THAT DOESN'T MAKE ANY SENSE.
DONNELLY FERGUSON DOESN'T CARE WHO GETS INTO TROUBLE, WHO GOES TO JAIL. HE NEVER HAS -- SO LONG AS HE GETS HIS CUT.

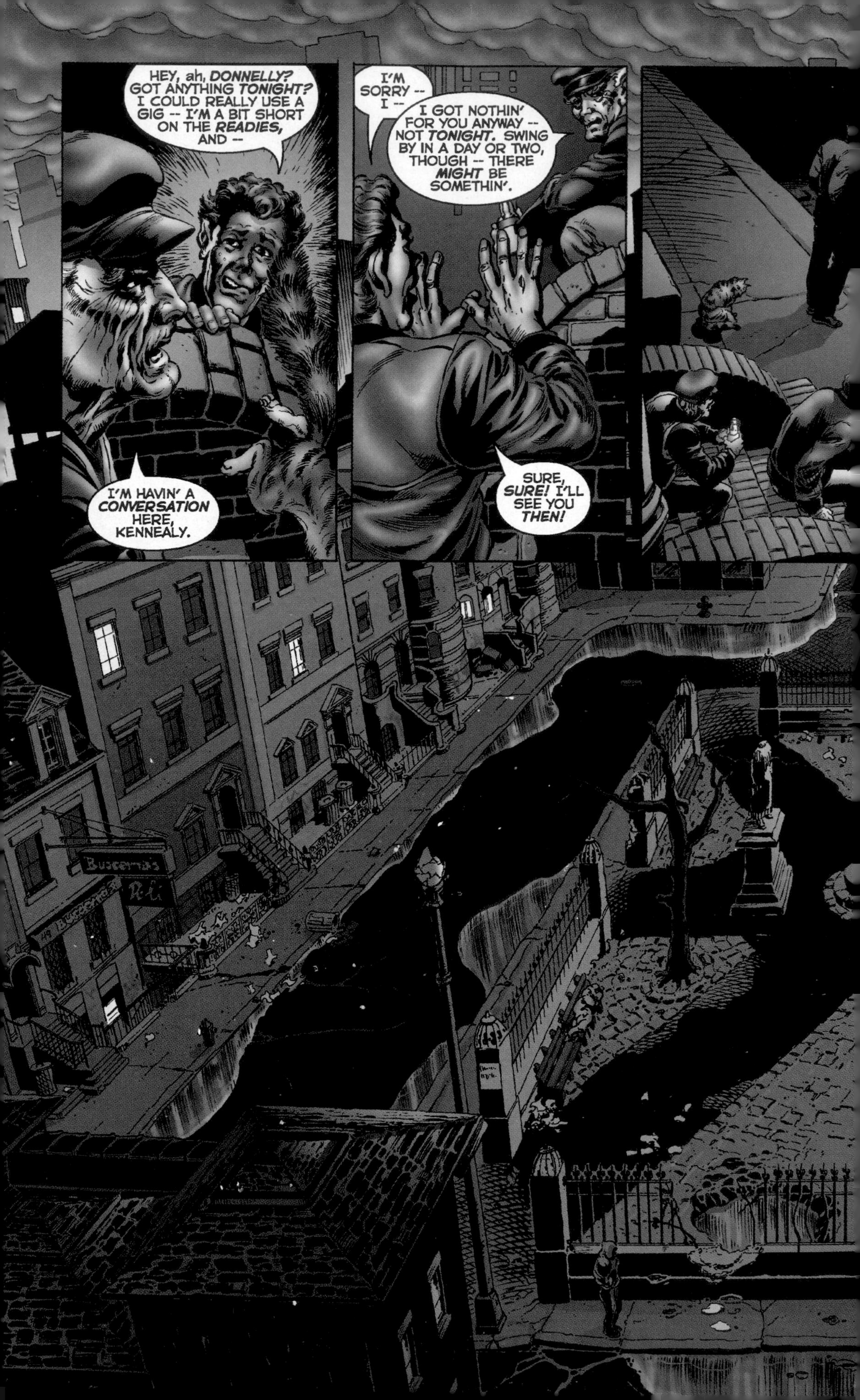
HEY, ah, DONNELLY? GOT ANYTHING TONIGHT? I COULD REALLY USE A GIG -- I'M A BIT SHORT ON THE READIES, AND --
I'M HAVIN' A CONVERSATION HERE, KENNEALY.
I'M SORRY -- I --
I GOT NOTHIN' FOR YOU ANYWAY -- NOT TONIGHT. SWING BY IN A DAY OR TWO, THOUGH -- THERE MIGHT BE SOMETHIN'.
SURE, SURE! I'LL SEE YOU THEN!
BUSCETTA'S
Deli

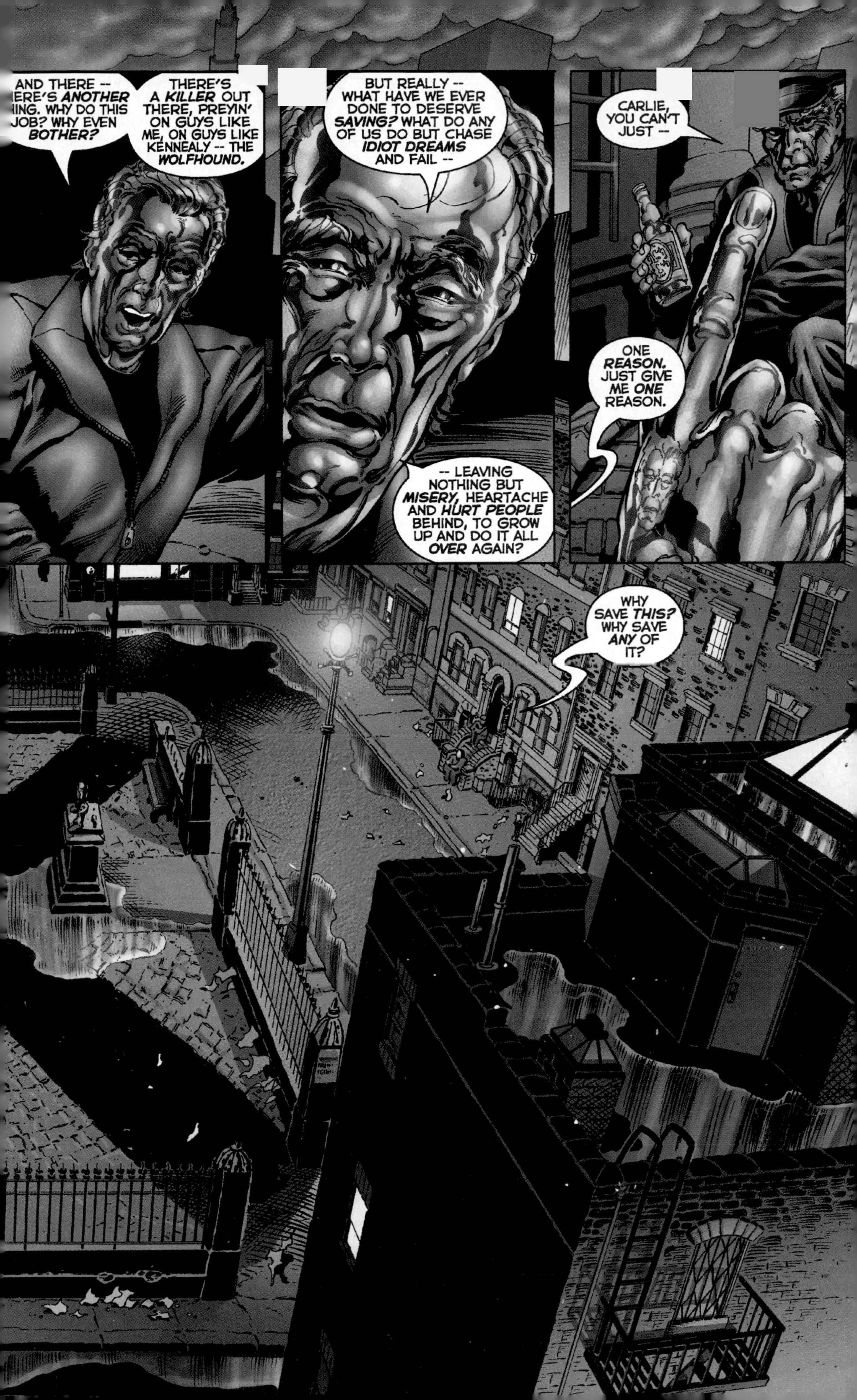
AND THERE -- ERE'S ANOTHER HING. WHY DO THIS JOB? WHY EVEN BOTHER?
THERE'S A KILLER OUT THERE, PREYIN' ON GUYS LIKE ME, ON GUYS LIKE KENNEALY -- THE WOLFHOUND.
BUT REALLY -- WHAT HAVE WE EVER DONE TO DESERVE SAVING? WHAT DO ANY OF US DO BUT CHASE IDIOT DREAMS AND FAIL --
-- LEAVING NOTHING BUT MISERY, HEARTACHE AND HURT PEOPLE BEHIND, TO GROW UP AND DO IT ALL OVER AGAIN?
CARLIE, YOU CAN'T JUST --
ONE REASON. JUST GIVE ME ONE REASON.
WHY SAVE THIS? WHY SAVE ANY OF IT?

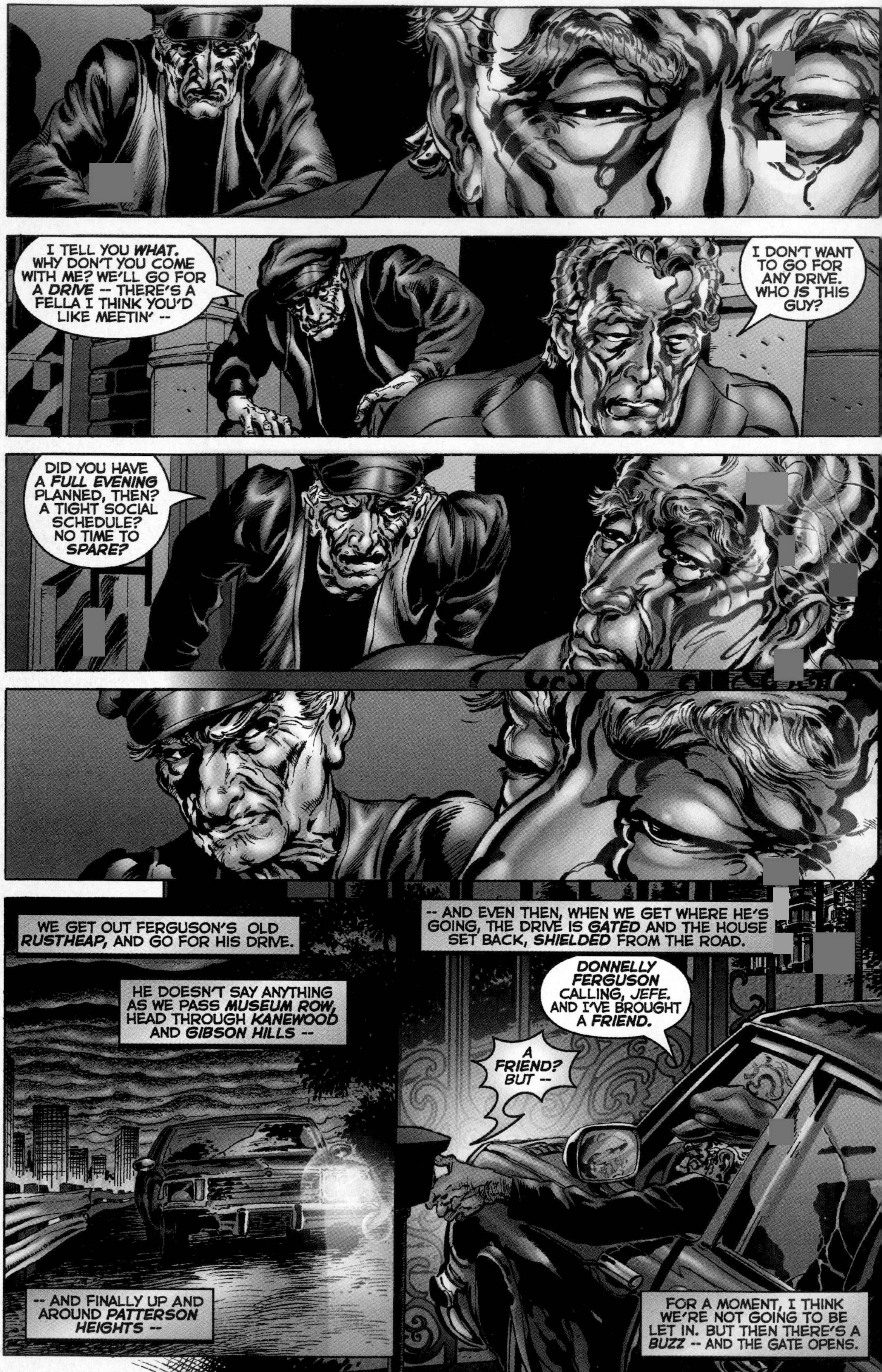
I TELL YOU WHAT. WHY DON'T YOU COME WITH ME? WE'LL GO FOR A DRIVE -- THERE'S A FELLA I THINK YOU'D LIKE MEETIN' --
I DON'T WANT TO GO FOR ANY DRIVE. WHO IS THIS GUY?
DID YOU HAVE A FULL EVENING PLANNED, THEN? A TIGHT SOCIAL SCHEDULE? NO TIME TO SPARE?
WE GET OUT FERGUSON'S OLD RUSTHEAP, AND GO FOR HIS DRIVE.
HE DOESN'T SAY ANYTHING AS WE PASS MUSEUM ROW, HEAD THROUGH KANEWOOD AND GIBSON HILLS --
-- AND FINALLY UP AND AROUND PATTERSON HEIGHTS --
-- AND EVEN THEN, WHEN WE GET WHERE HE'S GOING, THE DRIVE IS GATED AND THE HOUSE SET BACK, SHIELDED FROM THE ROAD.
DONNELLY FERGUSON CALLING, JEFE. AND I'VE BROUGHT A FRIEND.
A FRIEND? BUT --
FOR A MOMENT, I THINK WE'RE NOT GOING TO BE LET IN. BUT THEN THERE'S A BUZZ -- AND THE GATE OPENS.

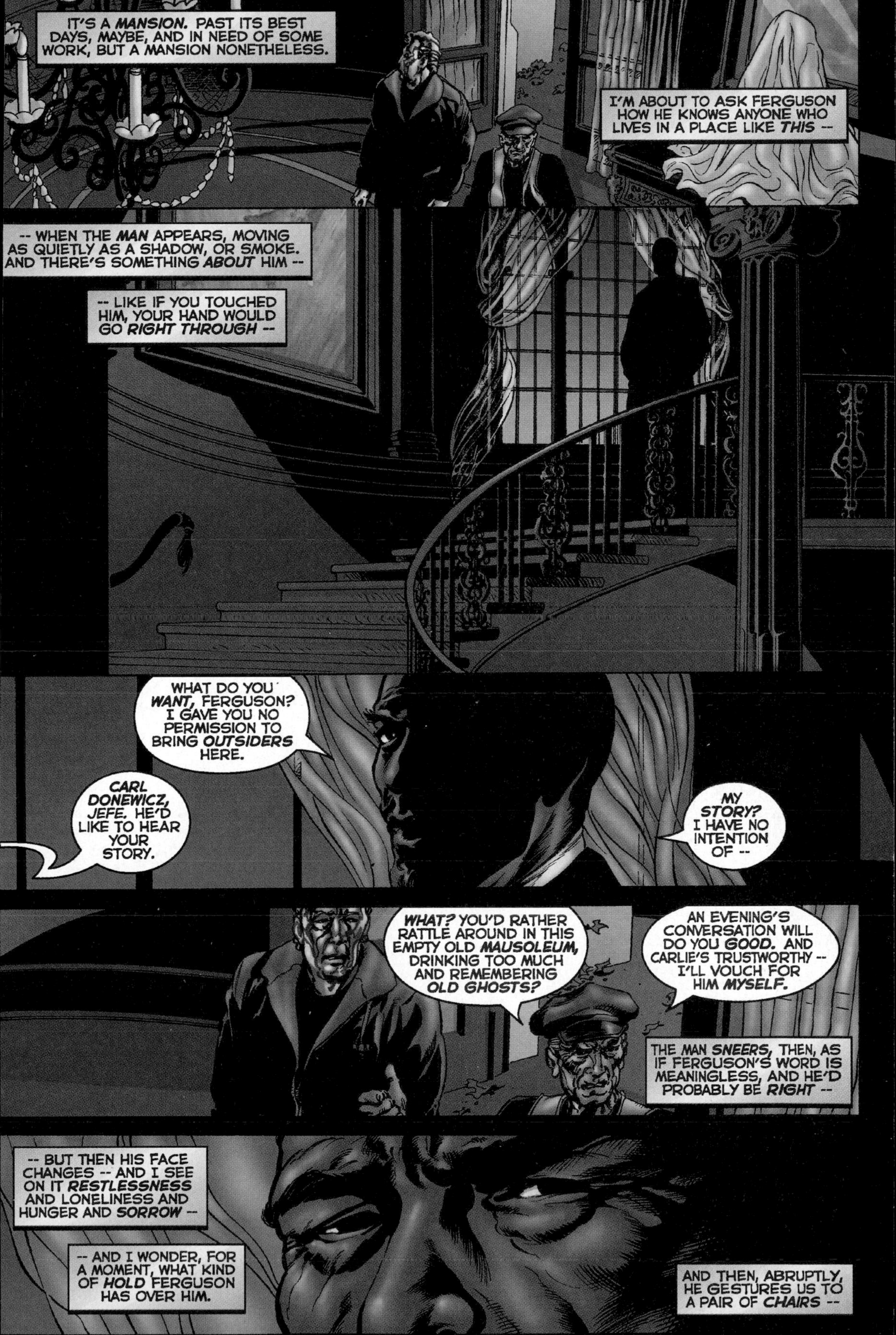
IT'S A MANSION. PAST ITS BEST DAYS, MAYBE, AND IN NEED OF SOME WORK, BUT A MANSION NONETHELESS.
I'M ABOUT TO ASK FERGUSON HOW HE KNOWS ANYONE WHO LIVES IN A PLACE LIKE THIS --
-- WHEN THE MAN APPEARS, MOVING AS QUIETLY AS A SHADOW, OR SMOKE. AND THERE'S SOMETHING ABOUT HIM --
-- LIKE IF YOU TOUCHED HIM, YOUR HAND WOULD GO RIGHT THROUGH --
WHAT DO YOU WANT, FERGUSON? I GAVE YOU NO PERMISSION TO BRING OUTSIDERS HERE.
CARL DONEWICZ, JEFE. HE'D LIKE TO HEAR YOUR STORY.
MY STORY? I HAVE NO INTENTION OF --
WHAT? YOU'D RATHER RATTLE AROUND IN THIS EMPTY OLD MAUSOLEUM, DRINKING TOO MUCH AND REMEMBERING OLD GHOSTS?
AN EVENING'S CONVERSATION WILL DO YOU GOOD. AND CARLIE'S TRUSTWORTHY -- I'LL VOUCH FOR HIM MYSELF.
THE MAN SNEERS, THEN, AS IF FERGUSON'S WORD IS MEANINGLESS, AND HE'D PROBABLY BE RIGHT --
-- BUT THEN HIS FACE CHANGES -- AND I SEE ON IT RESTLESSNESS AND LONELINESS AND HUNGER AND SORROW --
-- AND I WONDER, FOR A MOMENT, WHAT KIND OF HOLD FERGUSON HAS OVER HIM.
AND THEN, ABRUPTLY, HE GESTURES US TO A PAIR OF CHAIRS --

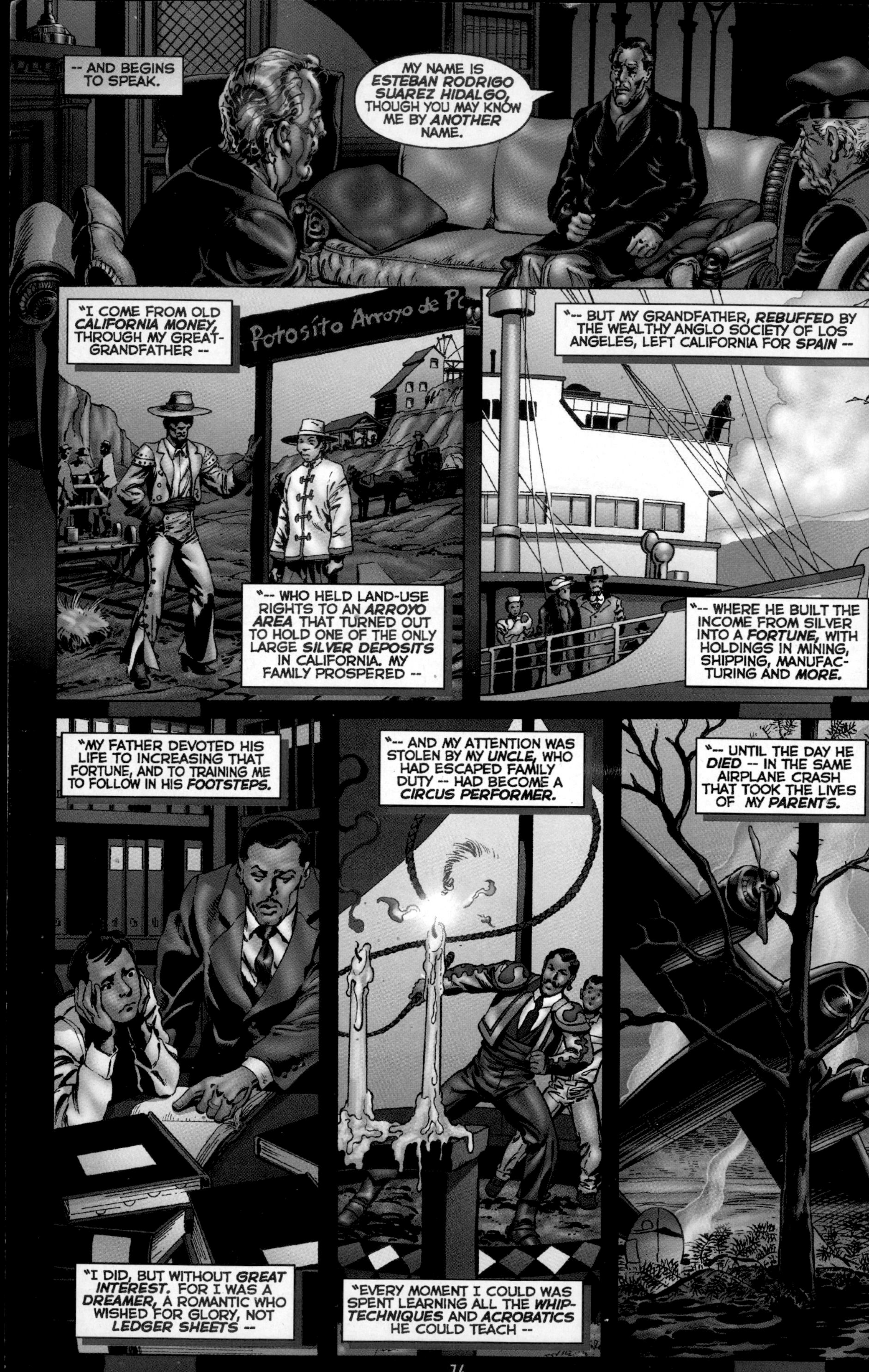
-- AND BEGINS TO SPEAK.
MY NAME IS ESTEBAN RODRIGO SUAREZ HIDALGO, THOUGH YOU MAY KNOW ME BY ANOTHER NAME.
"I COME FROM OLD CALIFORNIA MONEY, THROUGH MY GREAT-GRANDFATHER --
Potosíto Arroyo de Po
"-- WHO HELD LAND-USE RIGHTS TO AN ARROYO AREA THAT TURNED OUT TO HOLD ONE OF THE ONLY LARGE SILVER DEPOSITS IN CALIFORNIA. MY FAMILY PROSPERED --
"-- BUT MY GRANDFATHER, REBUFFED BY THE WEALTHY ANGLO SOCIETY OF LOS ANGELES, LEFT CALIFORNIA FOR SPAIN --
"-- WHERE HE BUILT THE INCOME FROM SILVER INTO A FORTUNE, WITH HOLDINGS IN MINING, SHIPPING, MANUFACTURING AND MORE.
"MY FATHER DEVOTED HIS LIFE TO INCREASING THAT FORTUNE, AND TO TRAINING ME TO FOLLOW IN HIS FOOTSTEPS.
"I DID, BUT WITHOUT GREAT INTEREST. FOR I WAS A DREAMER, A ROMANTIC WHO WISHED FOR GLORY, NOT LEDGER SHEETS --
"-- AND MY ATTENTION WAS STOLEN BY MY UNCLE, WHO HAD ESCAPED FAMILY DUTY -- HAD BECOME A CIRCUS PERFORMER.
"EVERY MOMENT I COULD WAS SPENT LEARNING ALL THE WHIP-TECHNIQUES AND ACROBATICS HE COULD TEACH --
"-- UNTIL THE DAY HE DIED -- IN THE SAME AIRPLANE CRASH THAT TOOK THE LIVES OF MY PARENTS.

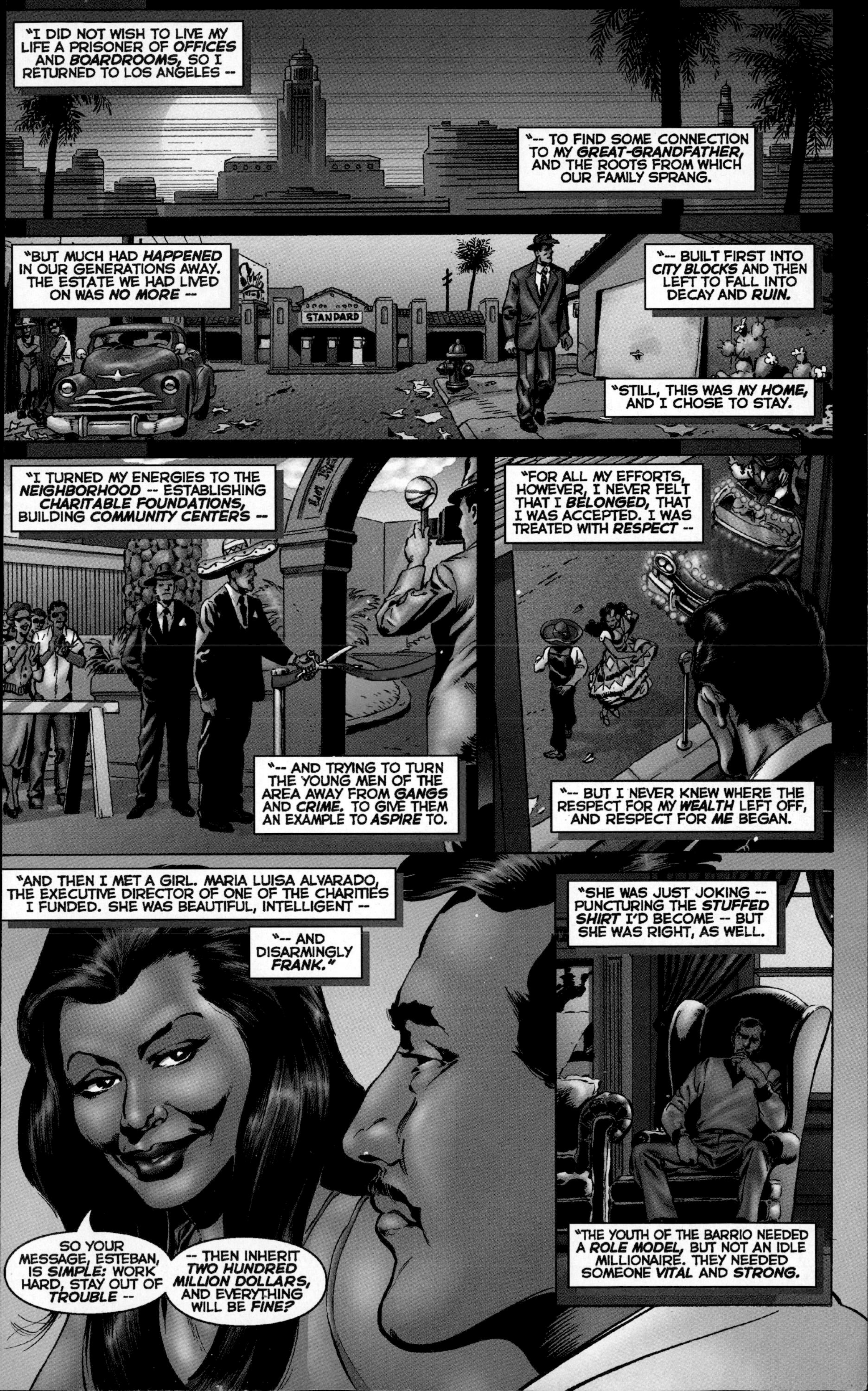

"I DID NOT WISH TO LIVE MY LIFE A PRISONER OF *OFFICES* AND *BOARDROOMS*, SO I RETURNED TO LOS ANGELES --
"-- TO FIND SOME CONNECTION TO MY *GREAT-GRANDFATHER*, AND THE ROOTS FROM WHICH OUR FAMILY SPRANG.
"BUT MUCH HAD *HAPPENED* IN OUR GENERATIONS AWAY. THE ESTATE WE HAD LIVED ON WAS *NO MORE* --
STANDARD
"-- BUILT FIRST INTO *CITY BLOCKS* AND THEN LEFT TO FALL INTO DECAY AND *RUIN*.
"STILL, THIS WAS MY *HOME*, AND I CHOSE TO STAY.
"I TURNED MY ENERGIES TO THE *NEIGHBORHOOD* -- ESTABLISHING *CHARITABLE FOUNDATIONS*, BUILDING *COMMUNITY CENTERS* --
"-- AND TRYING TO TURN THE YOUNG MEN OF THE AREA AWAY FROM *GANGS* AND *CRIME*, TO GIVE THEM AN EXAMPLE TO *ASPIRE* TO.
"FOR ALL MY EFFORTS, HOWEVER, I NEVER FELT THAT I *BELONGED*, THAT I WAS ACCEPTED. I WAS TREATED WITH *RESPECT* --
"-- BUT I NEVER KNEW WHERE THE RESPECT FOR MY *WEALTH* LEFT OFF, AND RESPECT FOR *ME* BEGAN.
"AND THEN I MET A GIRL. MARIA LUISA ALVARADO, THE EXECUTIVE DIRECTOR OF ONE OF THE CHARITIES I FUNDED. SHE WAS BEAUTIFUL, INTELLIGENT --
"-- AND DISARMINGLY *FRANK*."
SO YOUR MESSAGE, ESTEBAN, IS *SIMPLE*: WORK HARD, STAY OUT OF *TROUBLE* --
-- THEN INHERIT *TWO HUNDRED MILLION DOLLARS*, AND EVERYTHING WILL BE *FINE*?
"SHE WAS JUST JOKING -- PUNCTURING THE *STUFFED SHIRT* I'D BECOME -- BUT SHE WAS RIGHT, AS WELL.
"THE YOUTH OF THE BARRIO NEEDED A *ROLE MODEL*, BUT NOT AN IDLE MILLIONAIRE. THEY NEEDED SOMEONE *VITAL* AND *STRONG*.

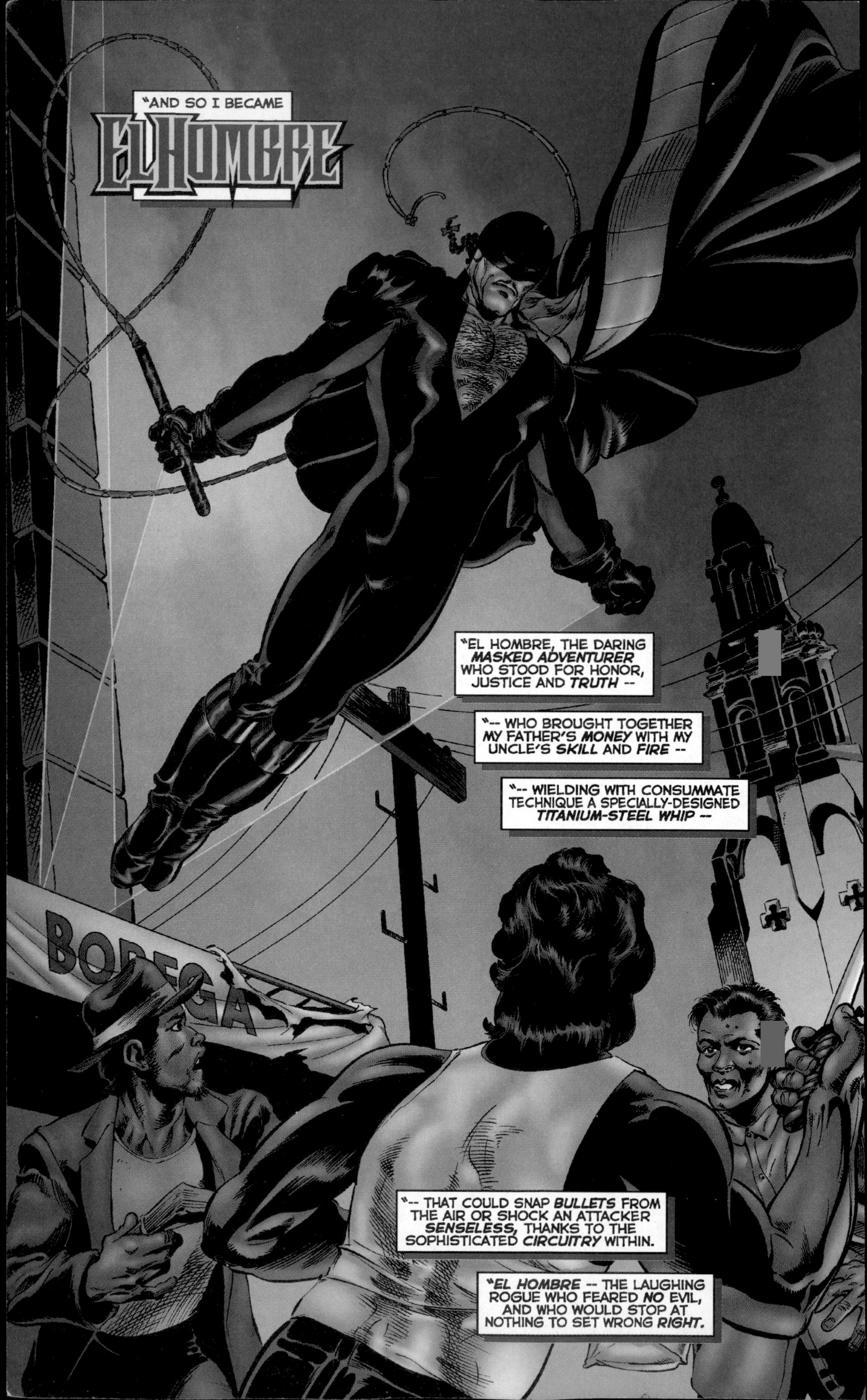
"AND SO I BECAME
EL HOMBRE
"EL HOMBRE, THE DARING MASKED ADVENTURER WHO STOOD FOR HONOR, JUSTICE AND TRUTH --
"-- WHO BROUGHT TOGETHER MY FATHER'S MONEY WITH MY UNCLE'S SKILL AND FIRE --
"-- WIELDING WITH CONSUMMATE TECHNIQUE A SPECIALLY-DESIGNED TITANIUM-STEEL WHIP --
BODEGA
"-- THAT COULD SNAP BULLETS FROM THE AIR OR SHOCK AN ATTACKER SENSELESS, THANKS TO THE SOPHISTICATED CIRCUITRY WITHIN.
"EL HOMBRE -- THE LAUGHING ROGUE WHO FEARED NO EVIL, AND WHO WOULD STOP AT NOTHING TO SET WRONG RIGHT.

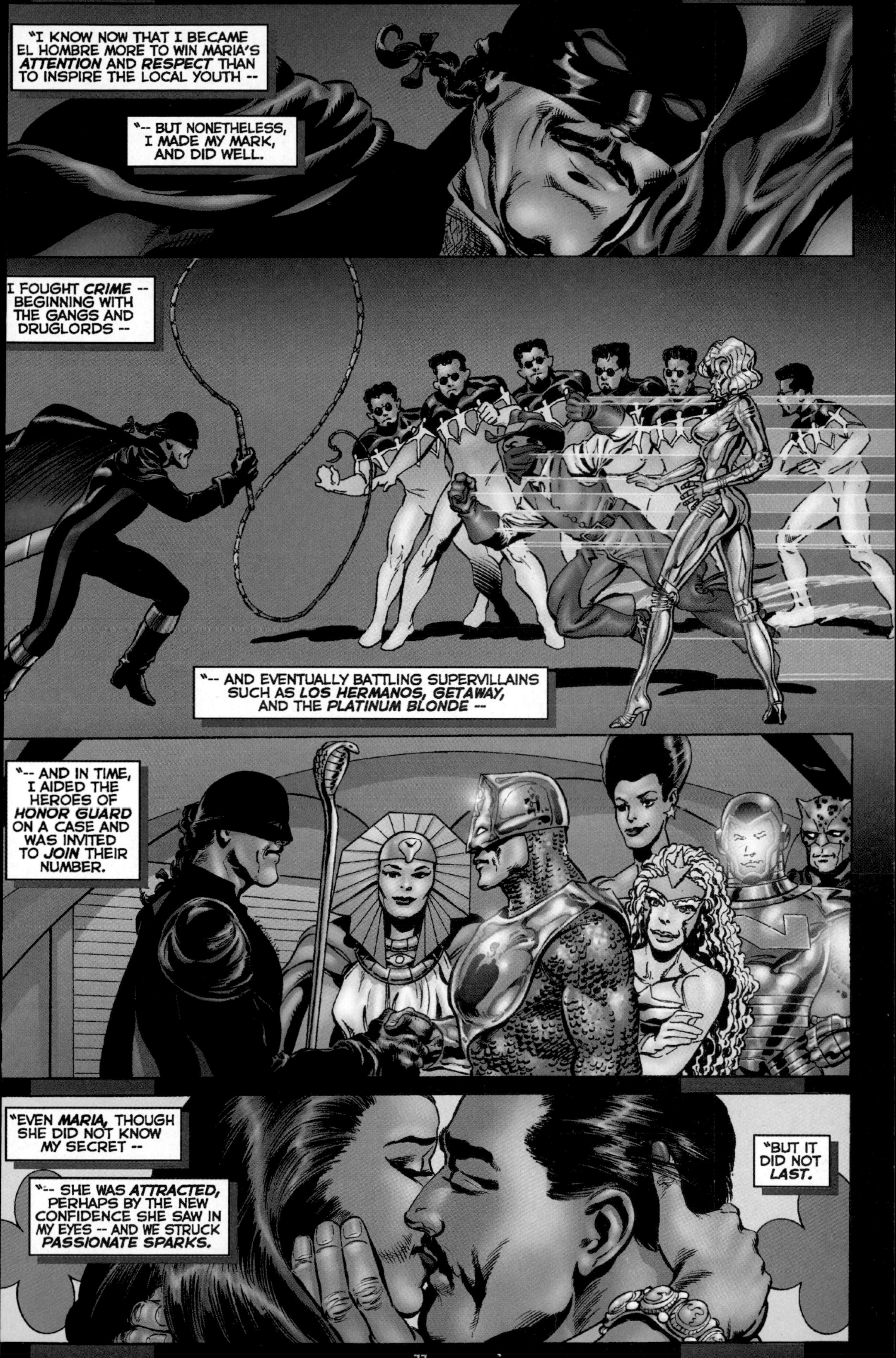

"I KNOW NOW THAT I BECAME EL HOMBRE MORE TO WIN MARIA'S ATTENTION AND RESPECT THAN TO INSPIRE THE LOCAL YOUTH --
"-- BUT NONETHELESS, I MADE MY MARK, AND DID WELL.
I FOUGHT CRIME -- BEGINNING WITH THE GANGS AND DRUGLORDS --
"-- AND EVENTUALLY BATTLING SUPERVILLAINS SUCH AS LOS HERMANOS, GETAWAY, AND THE PLATINUM BLONDE --
"-- AND IN TIME, I AIDED THE HEROES OF HONOR GUARD ON A CASE AND WAS INVITED TO JOIN THEIR NUMBER.
"EVEN MARIA, THOUGH SHE DID NOT KNOW MY SECRET --
"-- SHE WAS ATTRACTED, PERHAPS BY THE NEW CONFIDENCE SHE SAW IN MY EYES -- AND WE STRUCK PASSIONATE SPARKS.
"BUT IT DID NOT LAST.

"IT WAS A YEAR OR TWO LATER THAT *RAMON VEGA* BEGAN HIS CRUSADE.

"A YOUNG LAWYER, A *POLITICAL ACTIVIST* -- HE FOUGHT FOR THE RIGHTS OF THE PEOPLE, FOR *SOCIAL JUSTICE* MORE THAN LEGAL JUSTICE.

ENS.. MANUF.CTURING

"HE CAMPAIGNED AGAIN.. SWEATSHOPS, AND LABOR CORRUPTION..

"AND HE FOUGHT NOT MERELY FOR *EQUALITY,* BUT FOR PARITY. *ETHNIC UNITY.*

VIVA RA..

VIVA LA ..AZ..

LA RAZA ..NITA

"I'D NEVER *CONSIDERED* SUCH A THING -- HAD THOUGHT *ALL* MEN BROTHERS, AND WALLS TO BE *BREACHED,* NOT BUILT --

"-- BUT HIS MESSAGE WAS ONE WHOSE TIME HAD *COME,* AND WHILE IT SPREAD, TOOK ROOT AND GREW --

"-- I WAS TOO OFTEN *AWAY,* WITH HONOR GUARD, BATTLING *THEIR* FOES, PROTECTING THE STATUS QUO VEGA FOUGHT *AGAINST* --

"-- AND MORE AND MORE, I BEGAN TO FEEL *ISOLATED,* IRRELEVANT. *POINTLESS.*

"AND ON THOSE OCCASIONS THAT I *DID* RETURN TO THE BARRIO --"

'EY, HOMBRE -- WHY YOU HASSLIN' YOUR OWN *PEOPLE,* HUH?

THE *SILVER AGENT* TELL YOU TO KEEP US OUT OF HIS *NEIGHBORHOOD?*

"THE COMMENTS WERE *SELF-SERVING,* AND DIDN'T REFLECT THE TRUE FEELINGS OF THE COMMUNITY. OR SO I *TOLD* MYSELF.

"BUT STILL, THEY *STUNG.* THEY CAME CLOSE TO WHAT I WAS FEELING MYSELF. AND *WORSE* --

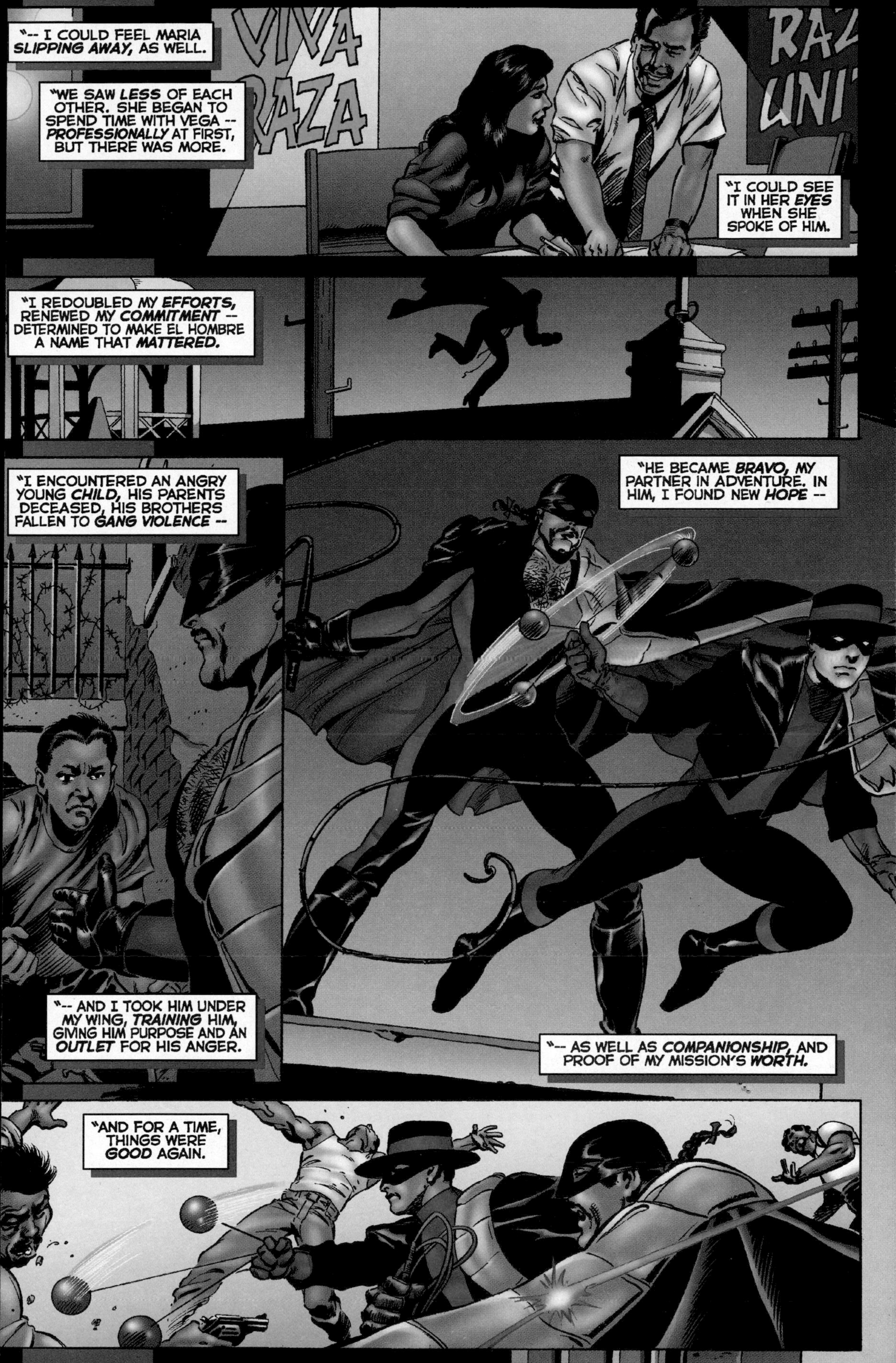

"-- I COULD FEEL MARIA SLIPPING AWAY, AS WELL.
VIVA RAZA
"WE SAW LESS OF EACH OTHER. SHE BEGAN TO SPEND TIME WITH VEGA -- PROFESSIONALLY AT FIRST, BUT THERE WAS MORE.
"I COULD SEE IT IN HER EYES WHEN SHE SPOKE OF HIM.
"I REDOUBLED MY EFFORTS, RENEWED MY COMMITMENT -- DETERMINED TO MAKE EL HOMBRE A NAME THAT MATTERED.
"I ENCOUNTERED AN ANGRY YOUNG CHILD, HIS PARENTS DECEASED, HIS BROTHERS FALLEN TO GANG VIOLENCE --
"-- AND I TOOK HIM UNDER MY WING, TRAINING HIM, GIVING HIM PURPOSE AND AN OUTLET FOR HIS ANGER.
"HE BECAME BRAVO, MY PARTNER IN ADVENTURE. IN HIM, I FOUND NEW HOPE --
"-- AS WELL AS COMPANIONSHIP, AND PROOF OF MY MISSION'S WORTH.
"AND FOR A TIME, THINGS WERE GOOD AGAIN.

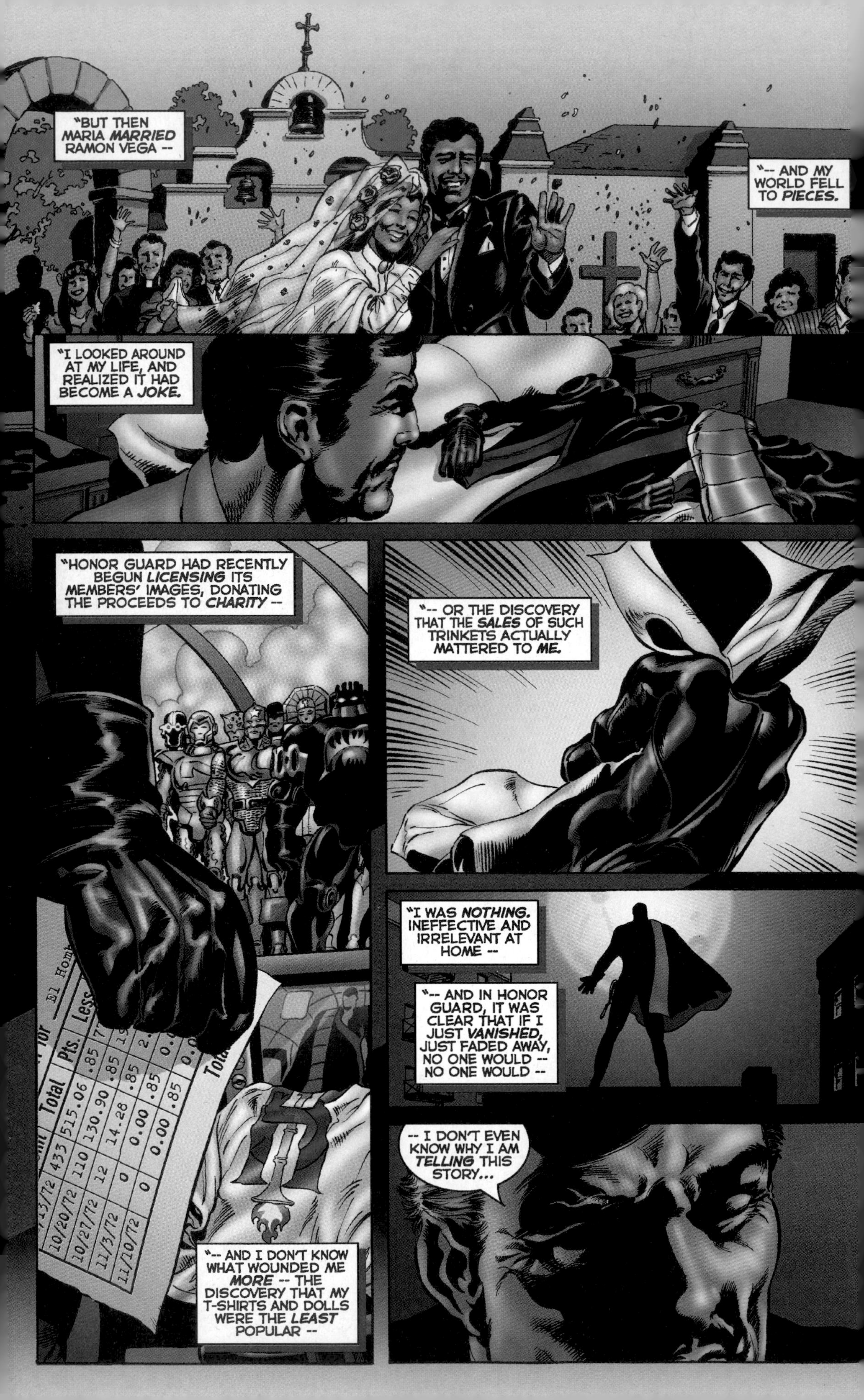
"BUT THEN MARIA MARRIED RAMON VEGA --
"-- AND MY WORLD FELL TO PIECES.
"I LOOKED AROUND AT MY LIFE, AND REALIZED IT HAD BECOME A JOKE.
"HONOR GUARD HAD RECENTLY BEGUN LICENSING ITS MEMBERS' IMAGES, DONATING THE PROCEEDS TO CHARITY --
"-- AND I DON'T KNOW WHAT WOUNDED ME MORE -- THE DISCOVERY THAT MY T-SHIRTS AND DOLLS WERE THE LEAST POPULAR --
"-- OR THE DISCOVERY THAT THE SALES OF SUCH TRINKETS ACTUALLY MATTERED TO ME.
"I WAS NOTHING. INEFFECTIVE AND IRRELEVANT AT HOME --
"-- AND IN HONOR GUARD, IT WAS CLEAR THAT IF I JUST VANISHED, JUST FADED AWAY, NO ONE WOULD -- NO ONE WOULD --
-- I DON'T EVEN KNOW WHY I AM TELLING THIS STORY...

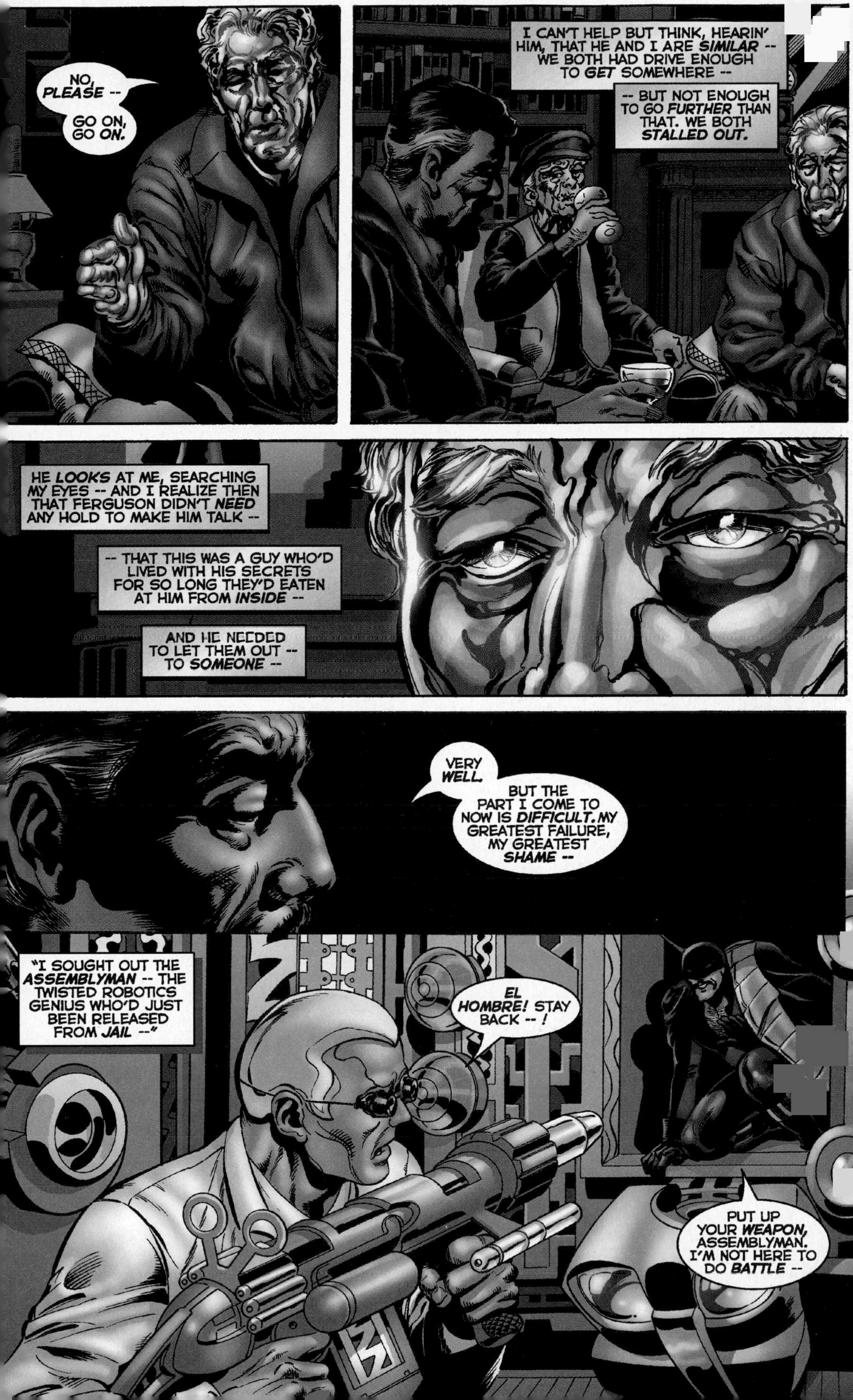
NO, PLEASE --
GO ON, GO ON.
I CAN'T HELP BUT THINK, HEARIN' HIM, THAT HE AND I ARE SIMILAR -- WE BOTH HAD DRIVE ENOUGH TO GET SOMEWHERE --
-- BUT NOT ENOUGH TO GO FURTHER THAN THAT. WE BOTH STALLED OUT.
HE LOOKS AT ME, SEARCHING MY EYES -- AND I REALIZE THEN THAT FERGUSON DIDN'T NEED ANY HOLD TO MAKE HIM TALK --
-- THAT THIS WAS A GUY WHO'D LIVED WITH HIS SECRETS FOR SO LONG THEY'D EATEN AT HIM FROM INSIDE --
AND HE NEEDED TO LET THEM OUT -- TO SOMEONE --
VERY WELL.
BUT THE PART I COME TO NOW IS DIFFICULT. MY GREATEST FAILURE, MY GREATEST SHAME --
"I SOUGHT OUT THE ASSEMBLYMAN -- THE TWISTED ROBOTICS GENIUS WHO'D JUST BEEN RELEASED FROM JAIL --"
EL HOMBRE! STAY BACK -- !
PUT UP YOUR WEAPON, ASSEMBLYMAN. I'M NOT HERE TO DO BATTLE --

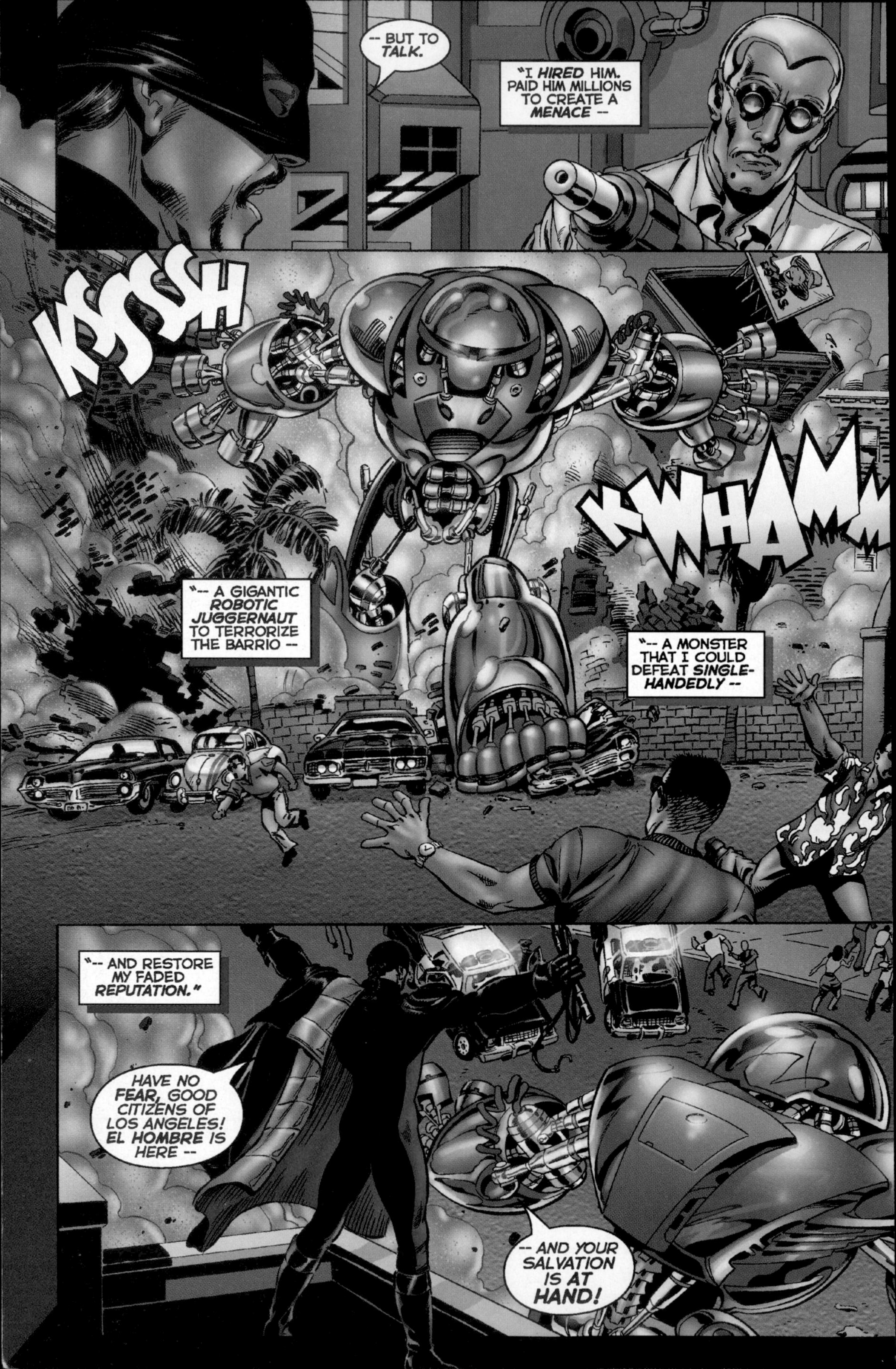
-- BUT TO TALK.
"I HIRED HIM. PAID HIM MILLIONS TO CREATE A MENACE --
KRSSH
KWHAMM
"-- A GIGANTIC ROBOTIC JUGGERNAUT TO TERRORIZE THE BARRIO --
"-- A MONSTER THAT I COULD DEFEAT SINGLE-HANDEDLY --
"-- AND RESTORE MY FADED REPUTATION."
HAVE NO FEAR, GOOD CITIZENS OF LOS ANGELES! EL HOMBRE IS HERE --
-- AND YOUR SALVATION IS AT HAND!

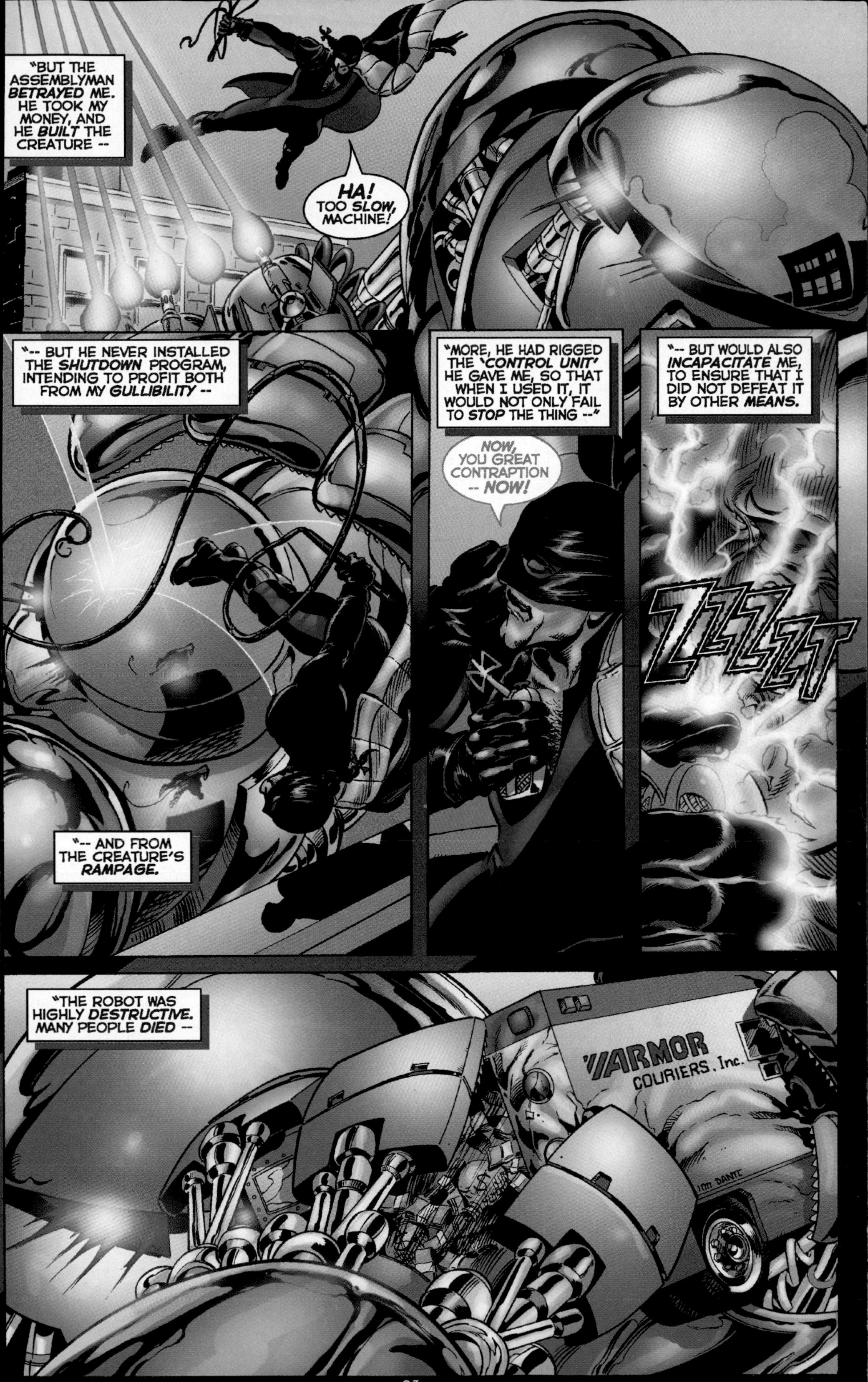
"BUT THE ASSEMBLYMAN BETRAYED ME. HE TOOK MY MONEY, AND HE BUILT THE CREATURE --
HA! TOO SLOW, MACHINE!
"-- BUT HE NEVER INSTALLED THE SHUTDOWN PROGRAM, INTENDING TO PROFIT BOTH FROM MY GULLIBILITY --
"-- AND FROM THE CREATURE'S RAMPAGE.
"MORE, HE HAD RIGGED THE 'CONTROL UNIT' HE GAVE ME, SO THAT WHEN I USED IT, IT WOULD NOT ONLY FAIL TO STOP THE THING --"
NOW, YOU GREAT CONTRAPTION -- NOW!
"-- BUT WOULD ALSO INCAPACITATE ME, TO ENSURE THAT I DID NOT DEFEAT IT BY OTHER MEANS.
ZZZZT
"THE ROBOT WAS HIGHLY DESTRUCTIVE. MANY PEOPLE DIED --
ARMOR
COURIERS, Inc.

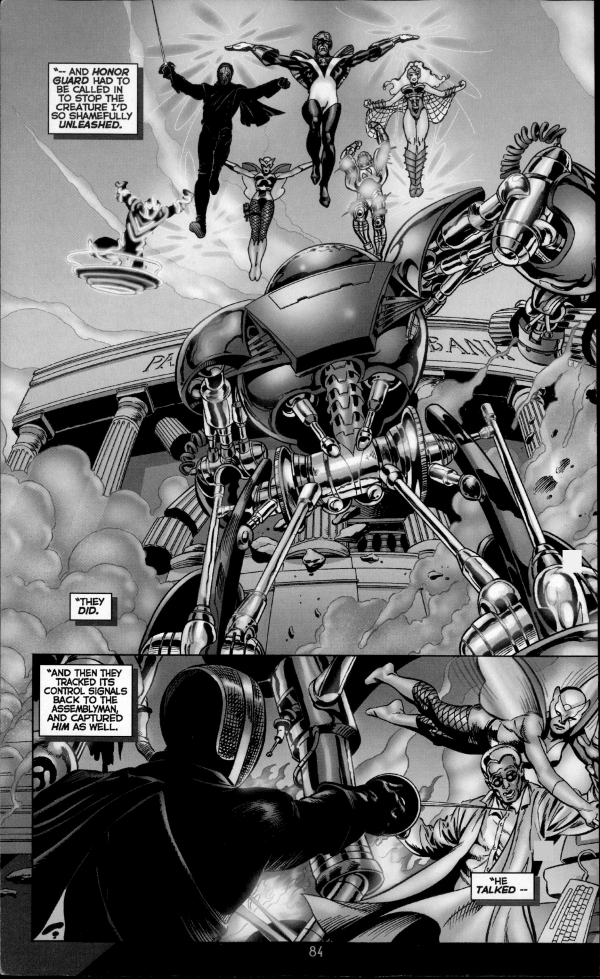

"-- AND *HONOR GUARD* HAD TO BE CALLED IN TO STOP THE CREATURE I'D SO SHAMEFULLY *UNLEASHED.*

"THEY *DID.*

"AND THEN THEY TRACKED ITS CONTROL SIGNALS BACK TO THE ASSEMBLYMAN, AND CAPTURED *HIM* AS WELL.

"HE TALKED --

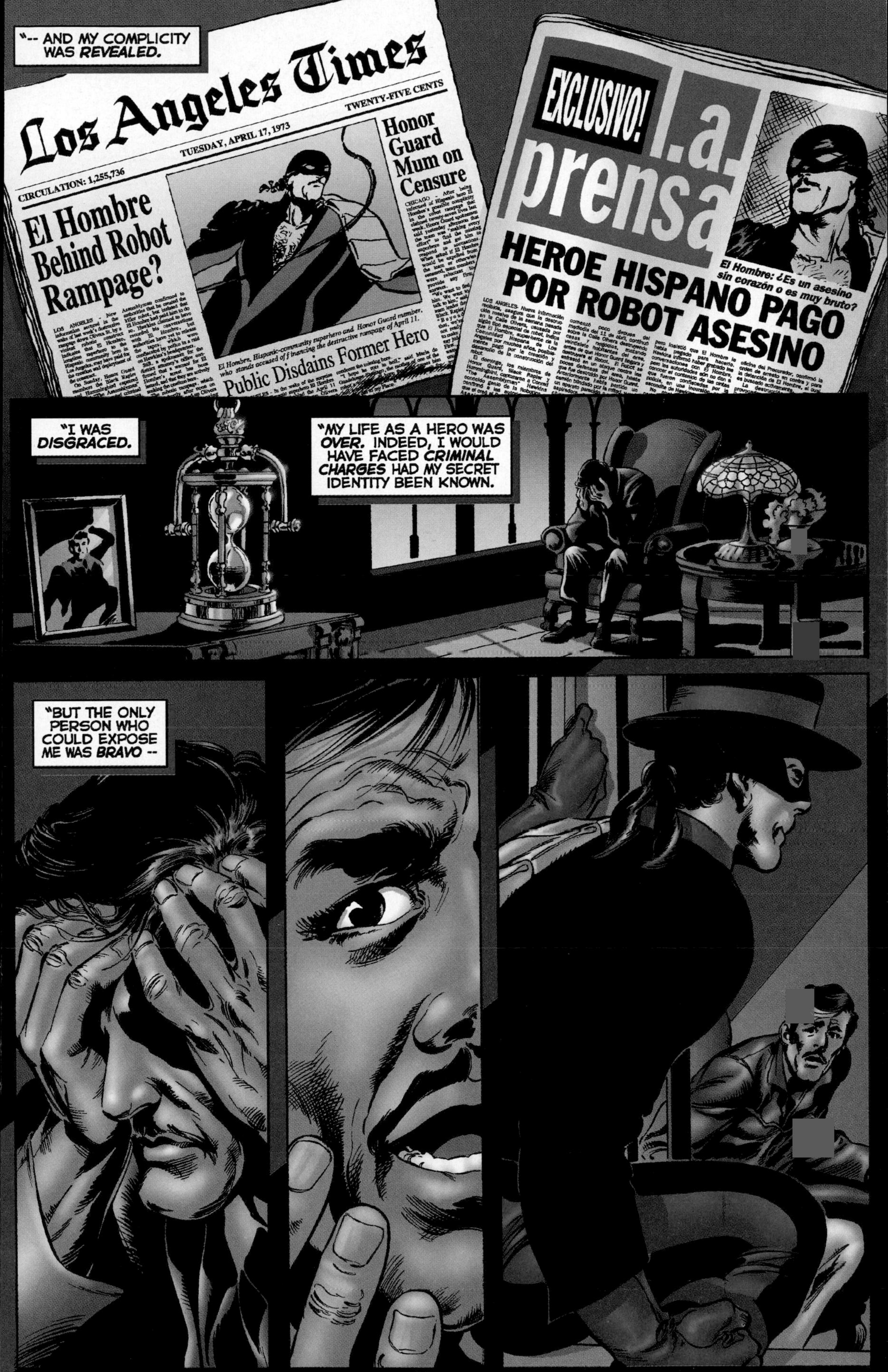
"-- AND MY COMPLICITY WAS *REVEALED.*
Los Angeles Times
TUESDAY, APRIL 17, 1973
TWENTY-FIVE CENTS
CIRCULATION: 1,255,736
El Hombre Behind Robot Rampage?
Honor Guard Mum on Censure
El Hombre, Hispanic-community superhero and Honor Guard member, who stands accused of financing the destructive rampage of April 11.
Public Disdains Former Hero
EXCLUSIVO!
La Prensa
HEROE HISPANO PAGO POR ROBOT ASESINO
El Hombre: ¿Es un asesino sin corazón o es muy bruto?
"I WAS *DISGRACED.*
"MY LIFE AS A HERO WAS *OVER.* INDEED, I WOULD HAVE FACED *CRIMINAL CHARGES* HAD MY SECRET IDENTITY BEEN KNOWN.
"BUT THE ONLY PERSON WHO COULD EXPOSE ME WAS *BRAVO* --

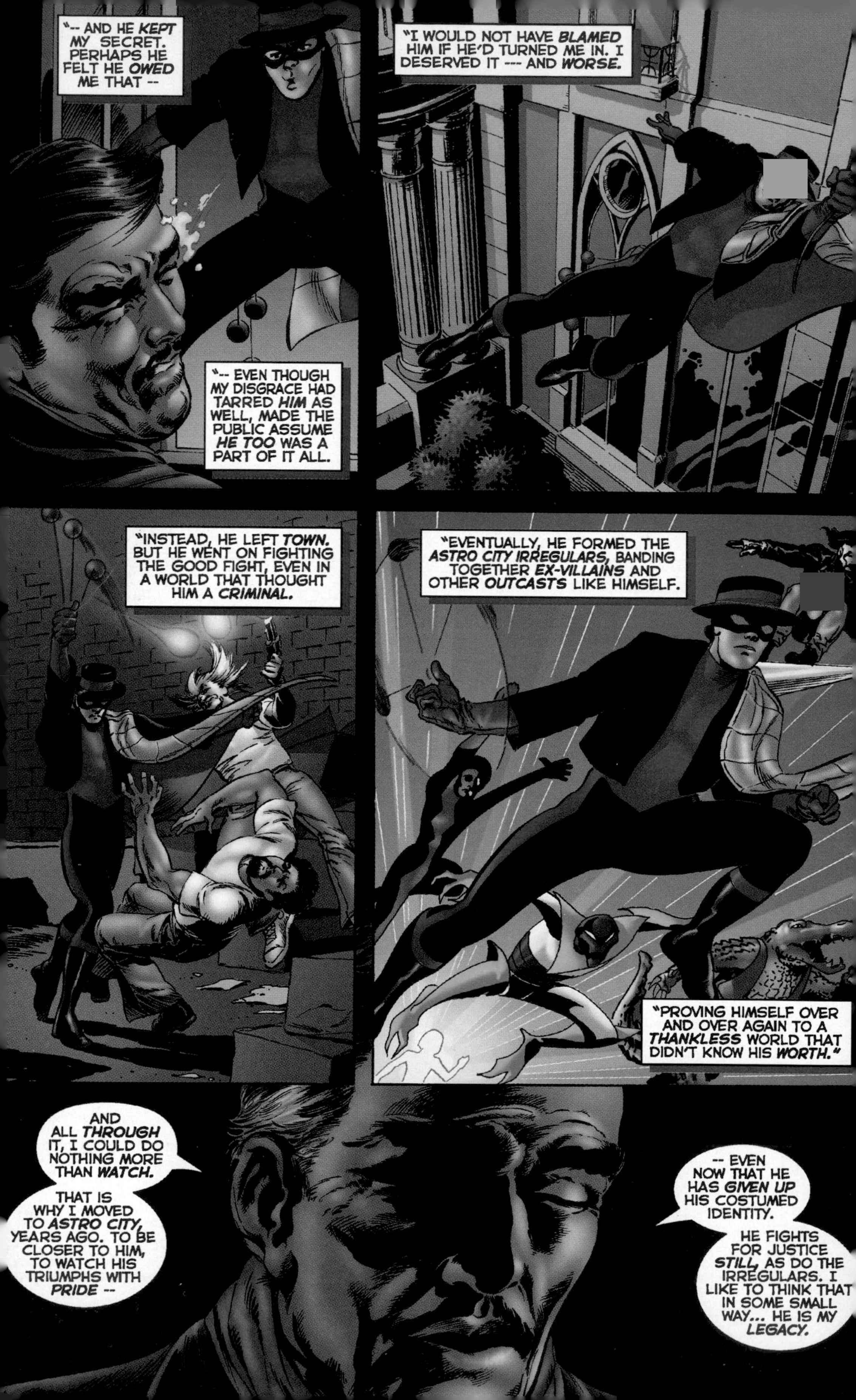
"-- AND HE KEPT MY SECRET. PERHAPS HE FELT HE OWED ME THAT --
"-- EVEN THOUGH MY DISGRACE HAD TARRED HIM AS WELL, MADE THE PUBLIC ASSUME HE TOO WAS A PART OF IT ALL.
"I WOULD NOT HAVE BLAMED HIM IF HE'D TURNED ME IN. I DESERVED IT --- AND WORSE.
"INSTEAD, HE LEFT TOWN. BUT HE WENT ON FIGHTING THE GOOD FIGHT, EVEN IN A WORLD THAT THOUGHT HIM A CRIMINAL.
"EVENTUALLY, HE FORMED THE ASTRO CITY IRREGULARS, BANDING TOGETHER EX-VILLAINS AND OTHER OUTCASTS LIKE HIMSELF.
"PROVING HIMSELF OVER AND OVER AGAIN TO A THANKLESS WORLD THAT DIDN'T KNOW HIS WORTH."
AND ALL THROUGH IT, I COULD DO NOTHING MORE THAN WATCH.
THAT IS WHY I MOVED TO ASTRO CITY, YEARS AGO. TO BE CLOSER TO HIM, TO WATCH HIS TRIUMPHS WITH PRIDE --
-- EVEN NOW THAT HE HAS GIVEN UP HIS COSTUMED IDENTITY.
HE FIGHTS FOR JUSTICE STILL, AS DO THE IRREGULARS. I LIKE TO THINK THAT IN SOME SMALL WAY... HE IS MY LEGACY.

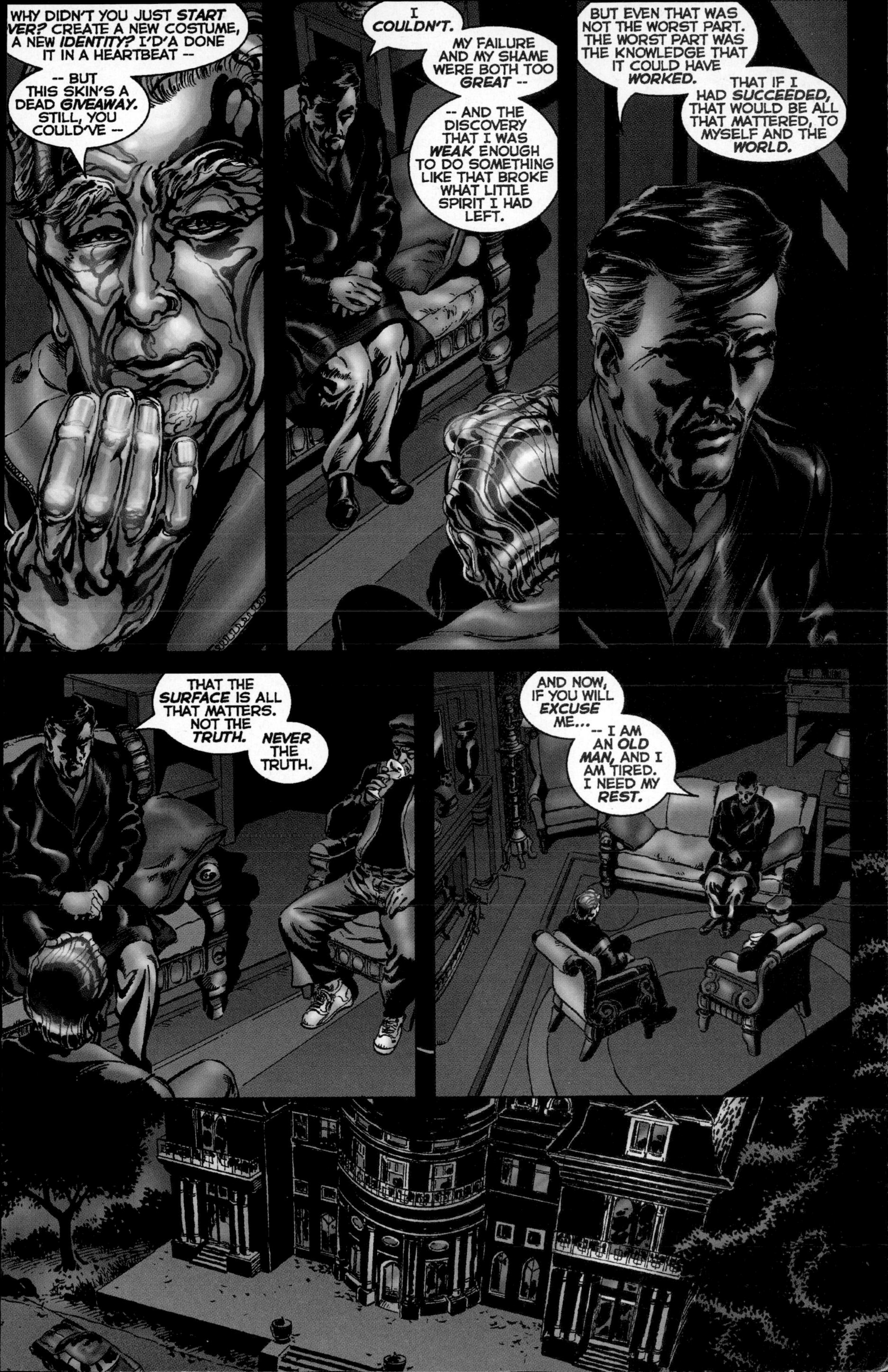
WHY DIDN'T YOU JUST START OVER? CREATE A NEW COSTUME, A NEW IDENTITY? I'D'A DONE IT IN A HEARTBEAT --
-- BUT THIS SKIN'S A DEAD GIVEAWAY. STILL, YOU COULD'VE --
I COULDN'T.
MY FAILURE AND MY SHAME WERE BOTH TOO GREAT --
-- AND THE DISCOVERY THAT I WAS WEAK ENOUGH TO DO SOMETHING LIKE THAT BROKE WHAT LITTLE SPIRIT I HAD LEFT.
BUT EVEN THAT WAS NOT THE WORST PART. THE WORST PART WAS THE KNOWLEDGE THAT IT COULD HAVE WORKED.
THAT IF I HAD SUCCEEDED, THAT WOULD BE ALL THAT MATTERED, TO MYSELF AND THE WORLD.
THAT THE SURFACE IS ALL THAT MATTERS. NOT THE TRUTH.
NEVER THE TRUTH.
AND NOW, IF YOU WILL EXCUSE ME...
-- I AM AN OLD MAN, AND I AM TIRED. I NEED MY REST.

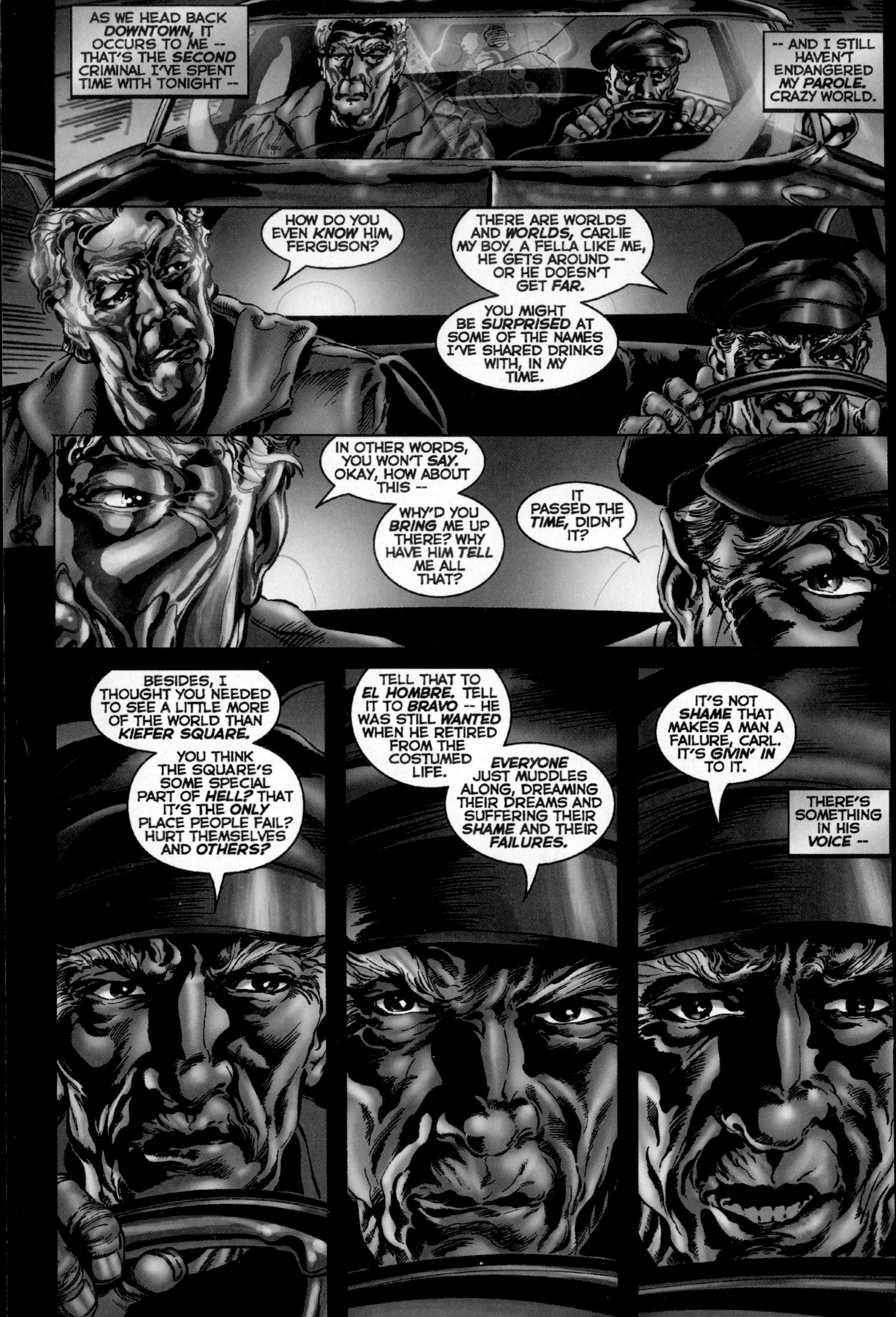
AS WE HEAD BACK DOWNTOWN, IT OCCURS TO ME -- THAT'S THE SECOND CRIMINAL I'VE SPENT TIME WITH TONIGHT --
-- AND I STILL HAVEN'T ENDANGERED MY PAROLE. CRAZY WORLD.
HOW DO YOU EVEN KNOW HIM, FERGUSON?
THERE ARE WORLDS AND WORLDS, CARLIE MY BOY. A FELLA LIKE ME, HE GETS AROUND -- OR HE DOESN'T GET FAR.
YOU MIGHT BE SURPRISED AT SOME OF THE NAMES I'VE SHARED DRINKS WITH, IN MY TIME.
IN OTHER WORDS, YOU WON'T SAY. OKAY, HOW ABOUT THIS --
WHY'D YOU BRING ME UP THERE? WHY HAVE HIM TELL ME ALL THAT?
IT PASSED THE TIME, DIDN'T IT?
BESIDES, I THOUGHT YOU NEEDED TO SEE A LITTLE MORE OF THE WORLD THAN KIEFER SQUARE.
YOU THINK THE SQUARE'S SOME SPECIAL PART OF HELL? THAT IT'S THE ONLY PLACE PEOPLE FAIL? HURT THEMSELVES AND OTHERS?
TELL THAT TO EL HOMBRE. TELL IT TO BRAVO -- HE WAS STILL WANTED WHEN HE RETIRED FROM THE COSTUMED LIFE.
EVERYONE JUST MUDDLES ALONG, DREAMING THEIR DREAMS AND SUFFERING THEIR SHAME AND THEIR FAILURES.
IT'S NOT SHAME THAT MAKES A MAN A FAILURE, CARL. IT'S GIVIN' IN TO IT.
THERE'S SOMETHING IN HIS VOICE --

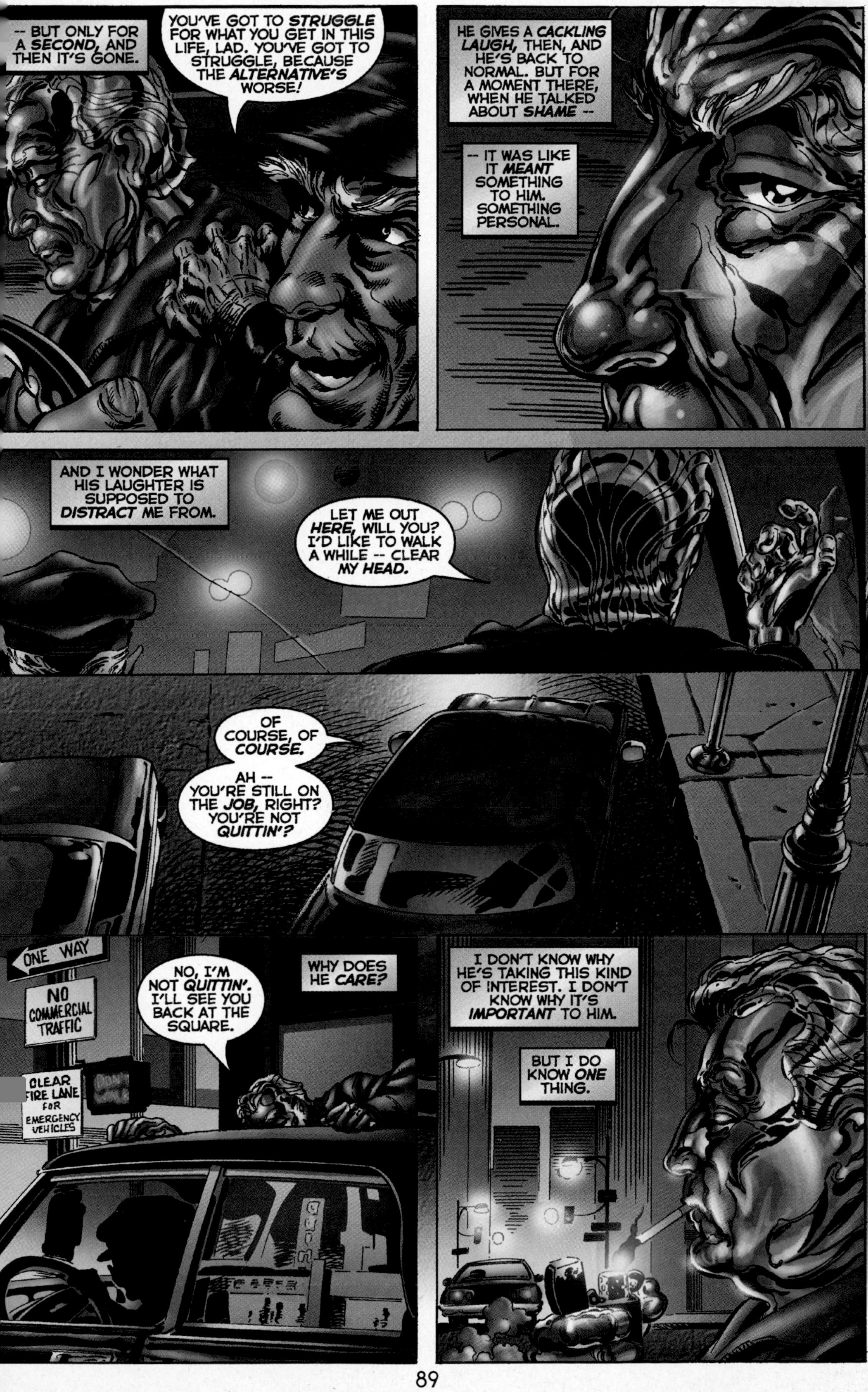
-- BUT ONLY FOR A SECOND, AND THEN IT'S GONE.
YOU'VE GOT TO STRUGGLE FOR WHAT YOU GET IN THIS LIFE, LAD. YOU'VE GOT TO STRUGGLE, BECAUSE THE ALTERNATIVE'S WORSE!
HE GIVES A CACKLING LAUGH, THEN, AND HE'S BACK TO NORMAL. BUT FOR A MOMENT THERE, WHEN HE TALKED ABOUT SHAME --
-- IT WAS LIKE IT MEANT SOMETHING TO HIM. SOMETHING PERSONAL.
AND I WONDER WHAT HIS LAUGHTER IS SUPPOSED TO DISTRACT ME FROM.
LET ME OUT HERE, WILL YOU? I'D LIKE TO WALK A WHILE -- CLEAR MY HEAD.
OF COURSE, OF COURSE.
AH -- YOU'RE STILL ON THE JOB, RIGHT? YOU'RE NOT QUITTIN'?
ONE WAY
NO COMMERCIAL TRAFFIC
CLEAR FIRE LANE FOR EMERGENCY VEHICLES
NO, I'M NOT QUITTIN'. I'LL SEE YOU BACK AT THE SQUARE.
WHY DOES HE CARE?
I DON'T KNOW WHY HE'S TAKING THIS KIND OF INTEREST. I DON'T KNOW WHY IT'S IMPORTANT TO HIM.
BUT I DO KNOW ONE THING.

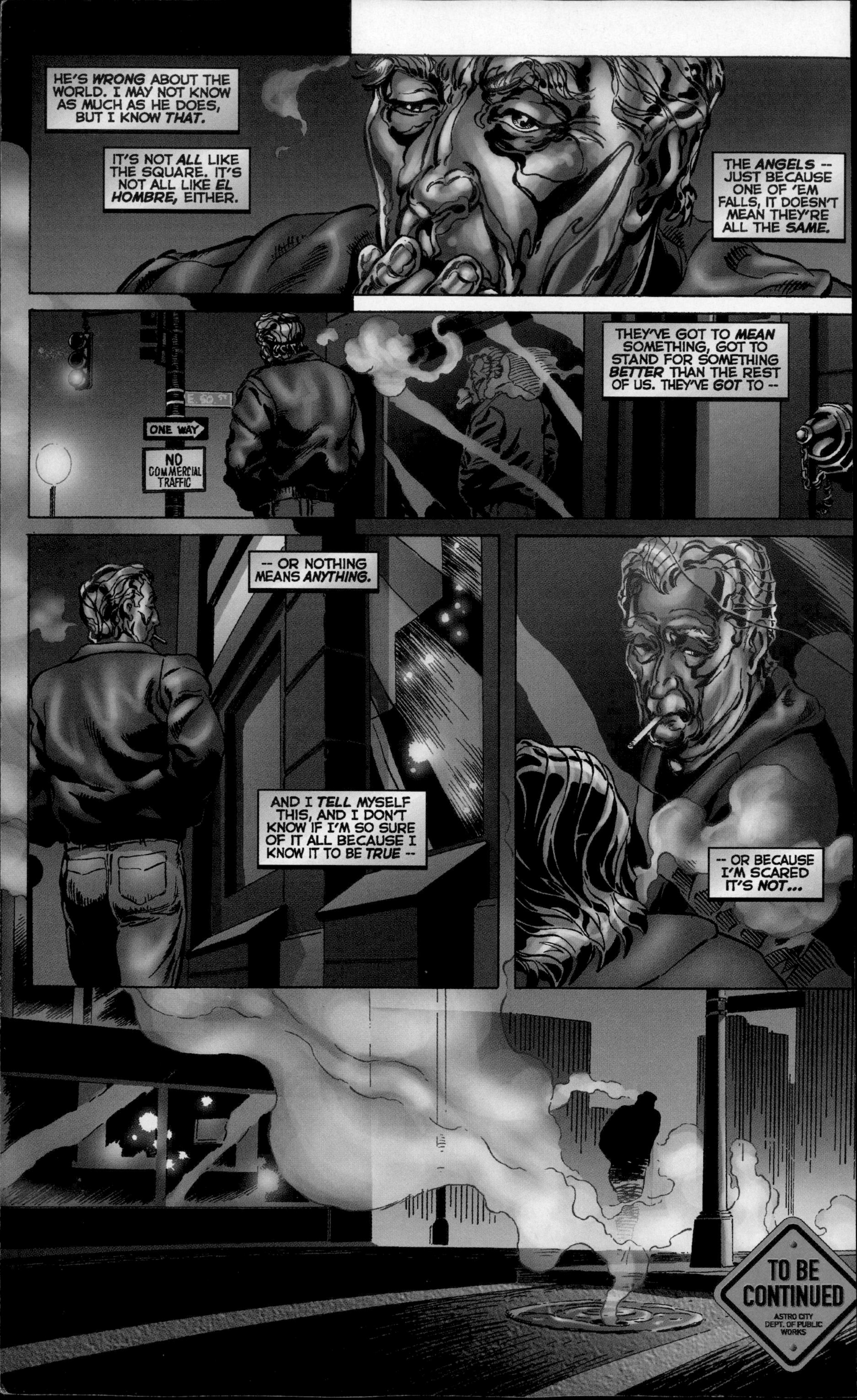

HE'S WRONG ABOUT THE WORLD. I MAY NOT KNOW AS MUCH AS HE DOES, BUT I KNOW THAT.
IT'S NOT ALL LIKE THE SQUARE. IT'S NOT ALL LIKE EL HOMBRE, EITHER.
THE ANGELS -- JUST BECAUSE ONE OF 'EM FALLS, IT DOESN'T MEAN THEY'RE ALL THE SAME.
E. 60 ST
ONE WAY
NO COMMERCIAL TRAFFIC
THEY'VE GOT TO MEAN SOMETHING, GOT TO STAND FOR SOMETHING BETTER THAN THE REST OF US. THEY'VE GOT TO --
-- OR NOTHING MEANS ANYTHING.
AND I TELL MYSELF THIS, AND I DON'T KNOW IF I'M SO SURE OF IT ALL BECAUSE I KNOW IT TO BE TRUE --
-- OR BECAUSE I'M SCARED IT'S NOT...
TO BE CONTINUED
ASTRO CITY DEPT. OF PUBLIC WORKS

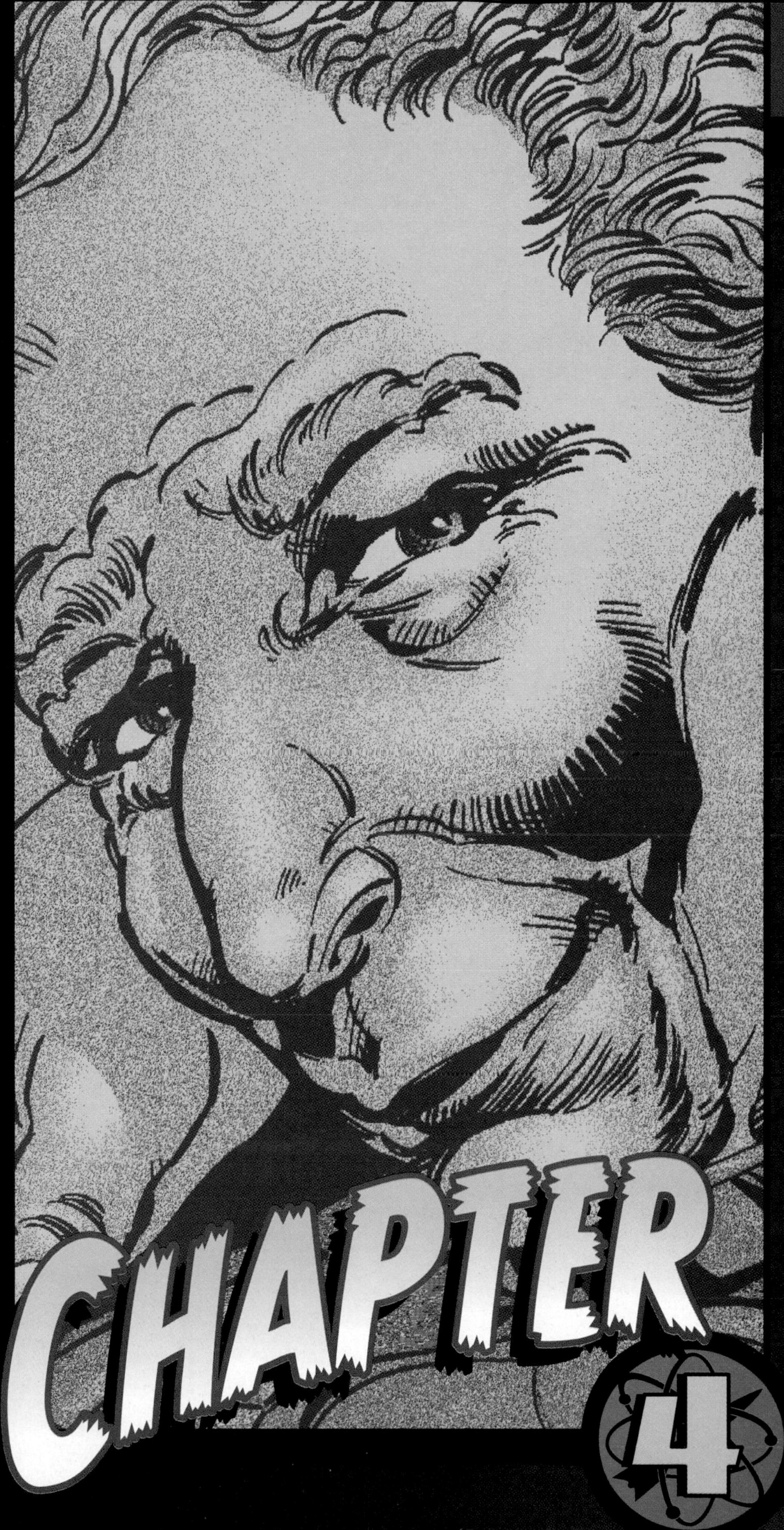
CHAPTER
4

The VOICE OF THE TURTL

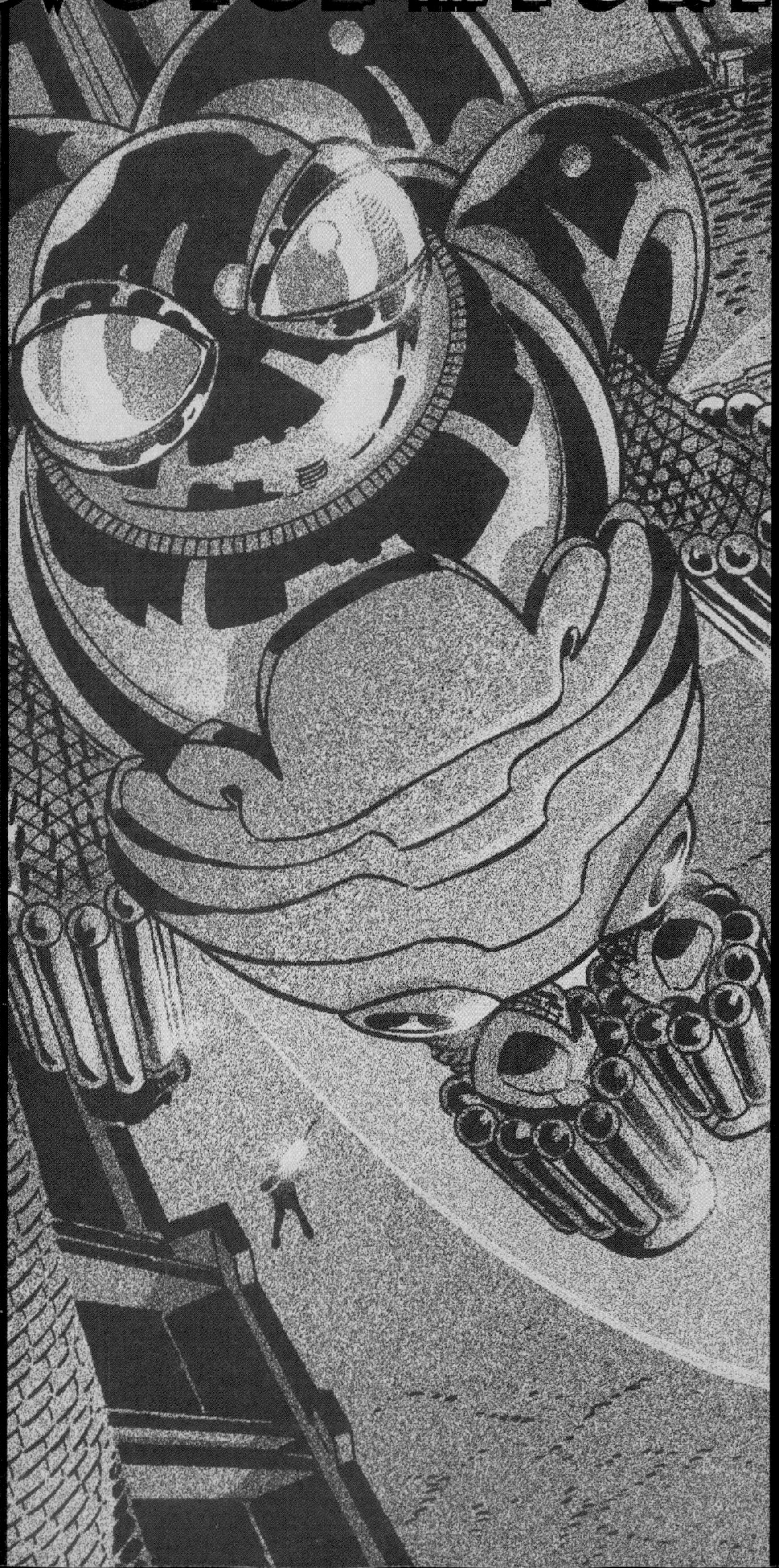

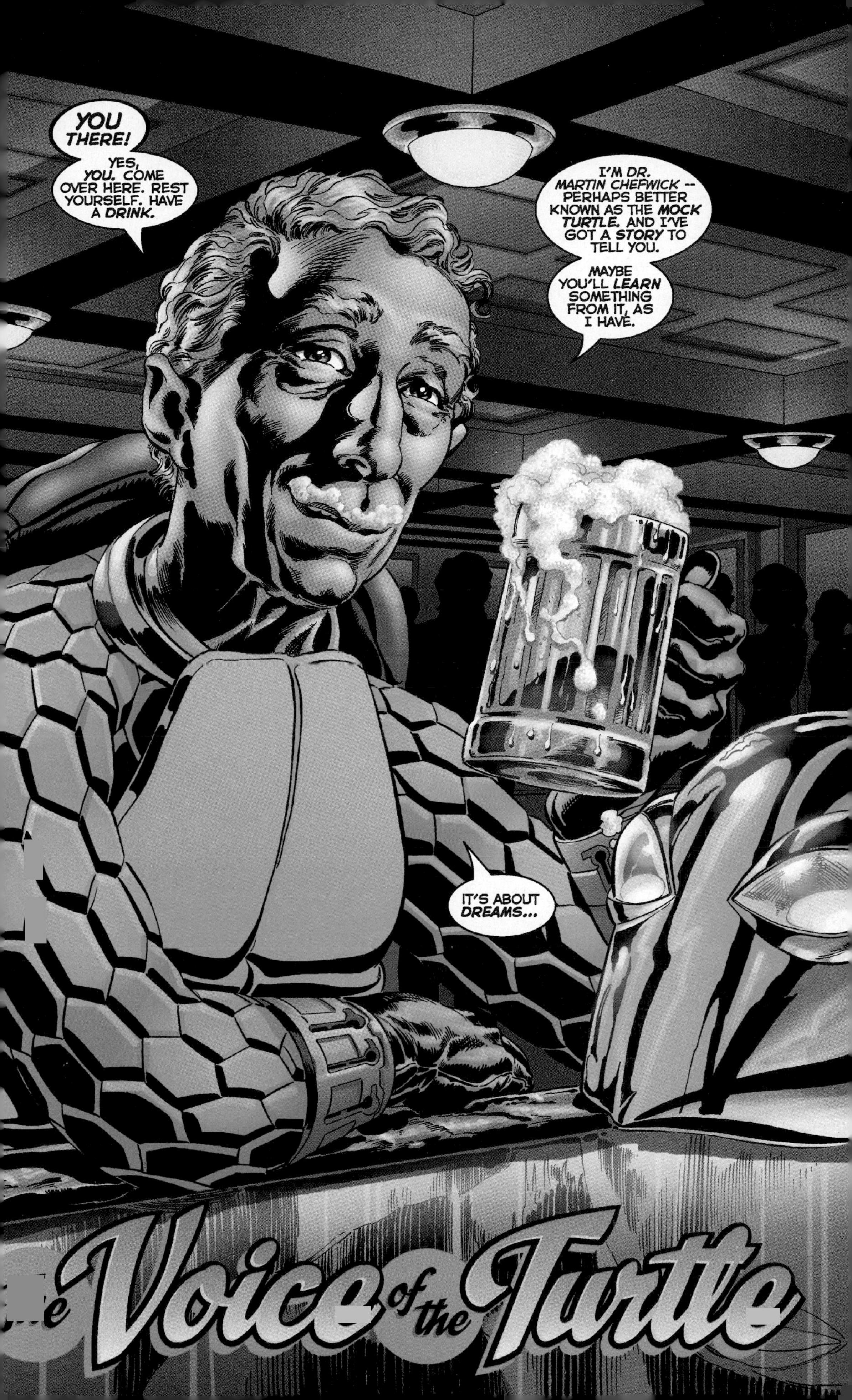
YOU THERE!
YES, YOU. COME OVER HERE. REST YOURSELF. HAVE A DRINK.
I'M DR. MARTIN CHEFWICK -- PERHAPS BETTER KNOWN AS THE MOCK TURTLE. AND I'VE GOT A STORY TO TELL YOU.
MAYBE YOU'LL LEARN SOMETHING FROM IT, AS I HAVE.
IT'S ABOUT DREAMS...
Voice of the Turtle

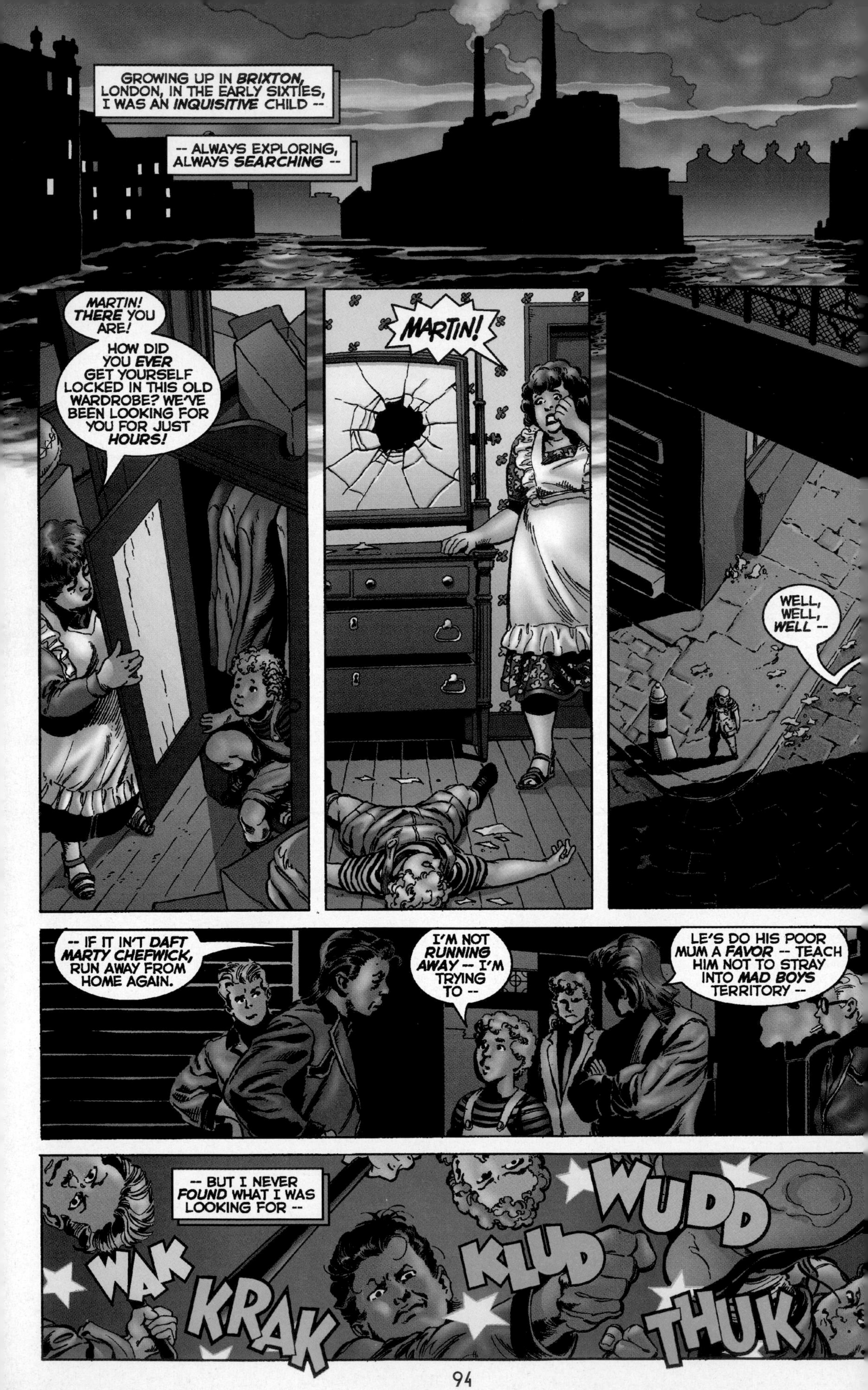
GROWING UP IN BRIXTON, LONDON, IN THE EARLY SIXTIES, I WAS AN INQUISITIVE CHILD --
-- ALWAYS EXPLORING, ALWAYS SEARCHING --
MARTIN! THERE YOU ARE!
HOW DID YOU EVER GET YOURSELF LOCKED IN THIS OLD WARDROBE? WE'VE BEEN LOOKING FOR YOU FOR JUST HOURS!
MARTIN!
WELL, WELL, WELL --
-- IF IT IN'T DAFT MARTY CHEFWICK, RUN AWAY FROM HOME AGAIN.
I'M NOT RUNNING AWAY -- I'M TRYING TO --
LE'S DO HIS POOR MUM A FAVOR -- TEACH HIM NOT TO STRAY INTO MAD BOYS TERRITORY --
-- BUT I NEVER FOUND WHAT I WAS LOOKING FOR --
WAK
KRAK
KLUD
WUDD
THUK

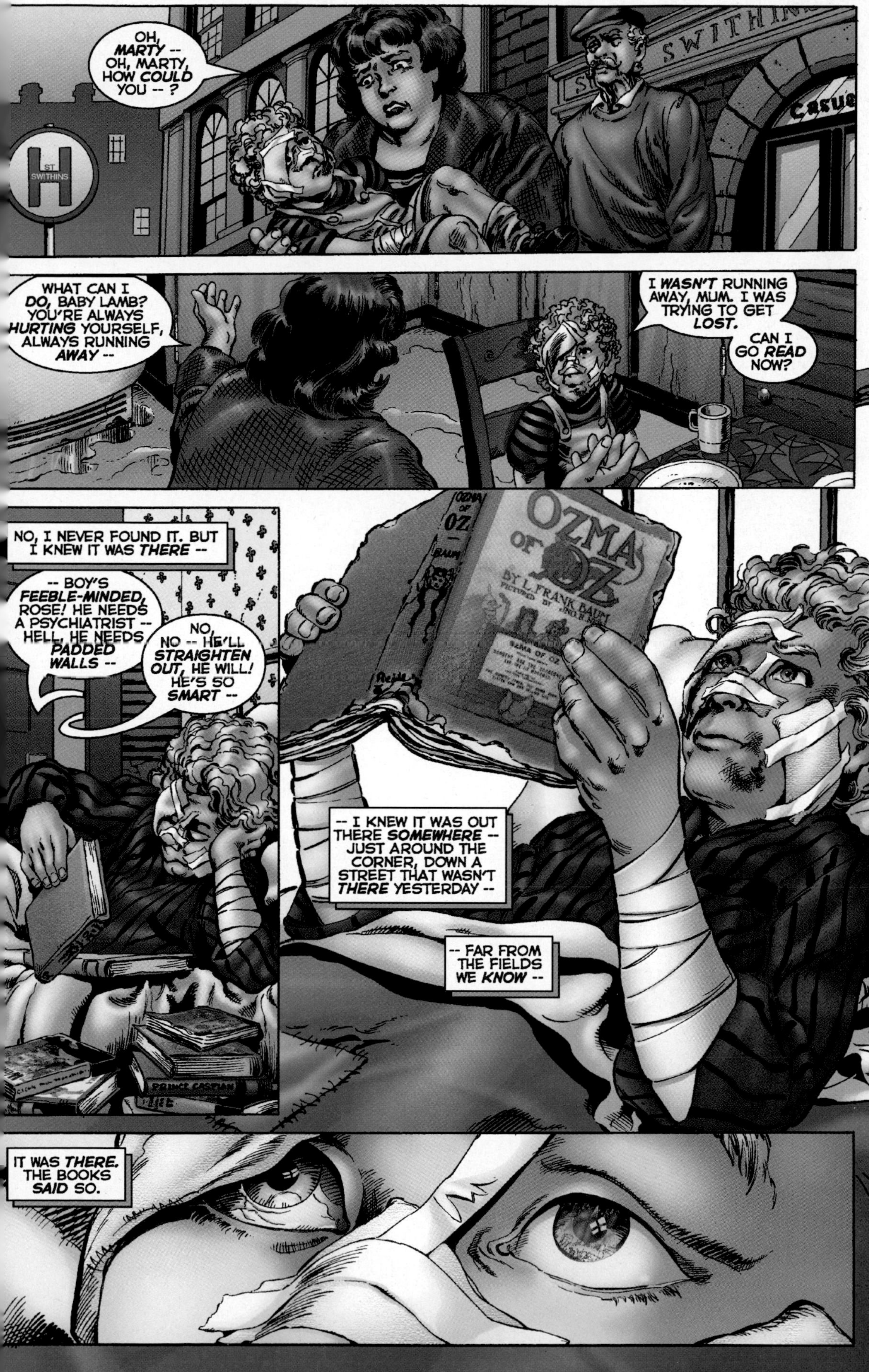
OH, MARTY -- OH, MARTY, HOW COULD YOU -- ?
ST SWITHINS
H
SWITHIN
Casua
WHAT CAN I DO, BABY LAMB? YOU'RE ALWAYS HURTING YOURSELF, ALWAYS RUNNING AWAY --
I WASN'T RUNNING AWAY, MUM. I WAS TRYING TO GET LOST.
CAN I GO READ NOW?
NO, I NEVER FOUND IT. BUT I KNEW IT WAS THERE --
-- BOY'S FEEBLE-MINDED, ROSE! HE NEEDS A PSYCHIATRIST -- HELL, HE NEEDS PADDED WALLS --
NO, NO -- HE'LL STRAIGHTEN OUT, HE WILL! HE'S SO SMART --
OZMA OF OZ
BY L. FRANK BAUM
-- I KNEW IT WAS OUT THERE SOMEWHERE -- JUST AROUND THE CORNER, DOWN A STREET THAT WASN'T THERE YESTERDAY --
-- FAR FROM THE FIELDS WE KNOW --
PRINCE CASPIAN
IT WAS THERE. THE BOOKS SAID SO.

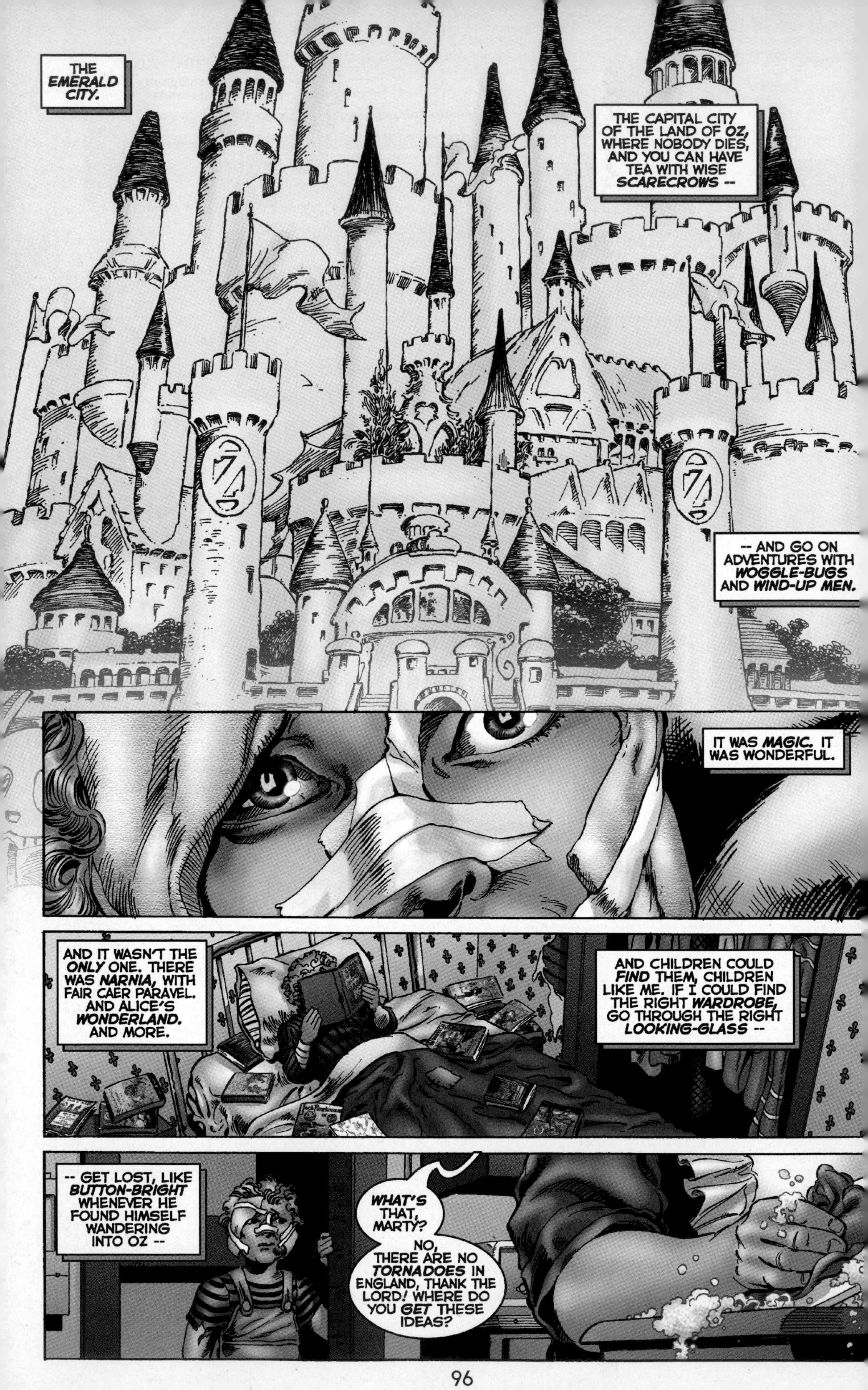
THE EMERALD CITY.
THE CAPITAL CITY OF THE LAND OF OZ, WHERE NOBODY DIES, AND YOU CAN HAVE TEA WITH WISE SCARECROWS --
-- AND GO ON ADVENTURES WITH WOGGLE-BUGS AND WIND-UP MEN.
IT WAS MAGIC. IT WAS WONDERFUL.
AND IT WASN'T THE ONLY ONE. THERE WAS NARNIA, WITH FAIR CAER PARAVEL. AND ALICE'S WONDERLAND. AND MORE.
AND CHILDREN COULD FIND THEM, CHILDREN LIKE ME. IF I COULD FIND THE RIGHT WARDROBE, GO THROUGH THE RIGHT LOOKING-GLASS --
-- GET LOST, LIKE BUTTON-BRIGHT WHENEVER HE FOUND HIMSELF WANDERING INTO OZ --
WHAT'S THAT, MARTY?
NO, THERE ARE NO TORNADOES IN ENGLAND, THANK THE LORD! WHERE DO YOU GET THESE IDEAS?

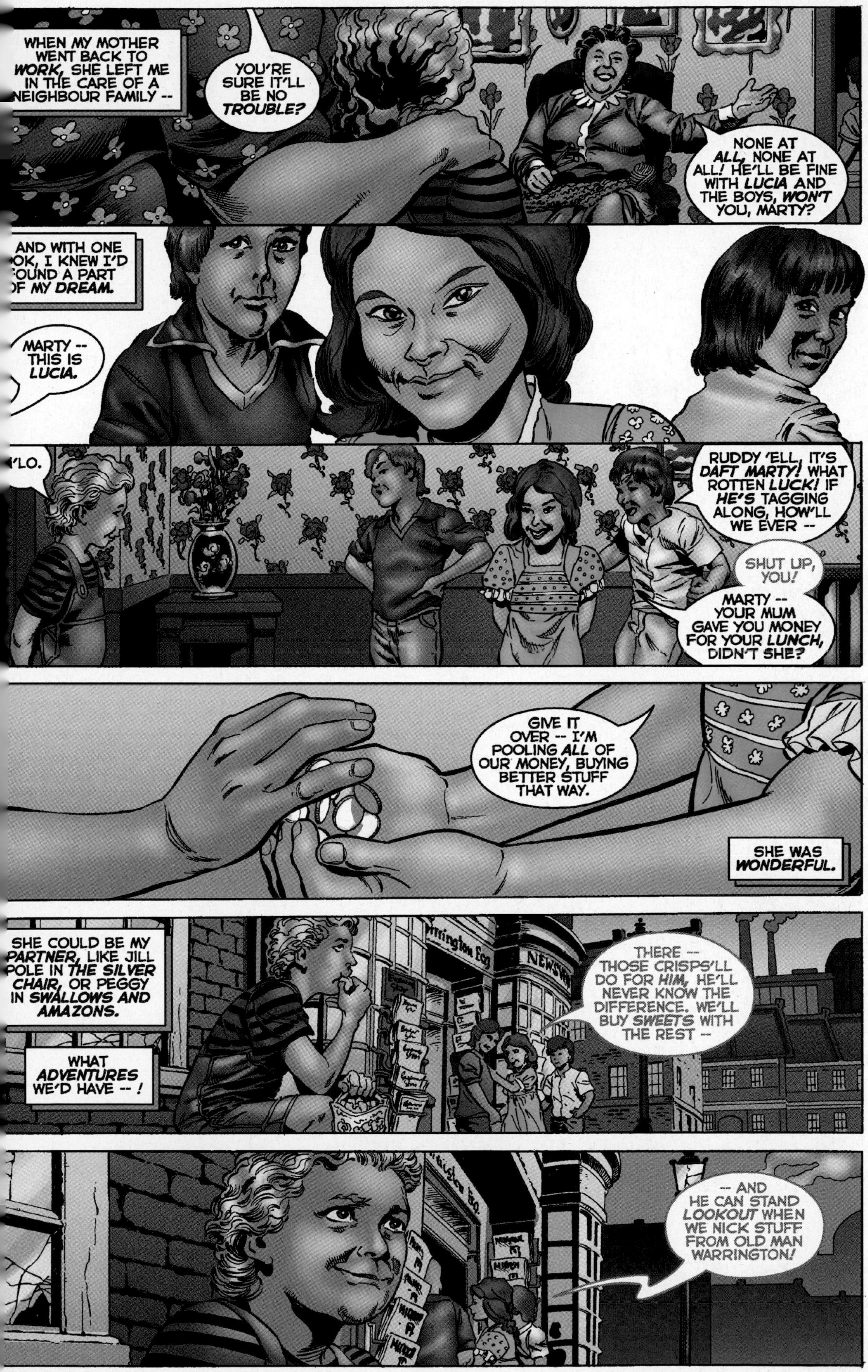

WHEN MY MOTHER WENT BACK TO WORK, SHE LEFT ME IN THE CARE OF A NEIGHBOUR FAMILY --
YOU'RE SURE IT'LL BE NO TROUBLE?
NONE AT ALL, NONE AT ALL! HE'LL BE FINE WITH LUCIA AND THE BOYS, WON'T YOU, MARTY?
AND WITH ONE LOOK, I KNEW I'D FOUND A PART OF MY DREAM.
MARTY -- THIS IS LUCIA.
'LO.
RUDDY 'ELL, IT'S DAFT MARTY! WHAT ROTTEN LUCK! IF HE'S TAGGING ALONG, HOW'LL WE EVER --
SHUT UP, YOU!
MARTY -- YOUR MUM GAVE YOU MONEY FOR YOUR LUNCH, DIDN'T SHE?
GIVE IT OVER -- I'M POOLING ALL OF OUR MONEY, BUYING BETTER STUFF THAT WAY.
SHE WAS WONDERFUL.
SHE COULD BE MY PARTNER, LIKE JILL POLE IN THE SILVER CHAIR, OR PEGGY IN SWALLOWS AND AMAZONS.
WHAT ADVENTURES WE'D HAVE -- !
THERE -- THOSE CRISPS'LL DO FOR HIM, HE'LL NEVER KNOW THE DIFFERENCE. WE'LL BUY SWEETS WITH THE REST --
-- AND HE CAN STAND LOOKOUT WHEN WE NICK STUFF FROM OLD MAN WARRINGTON!

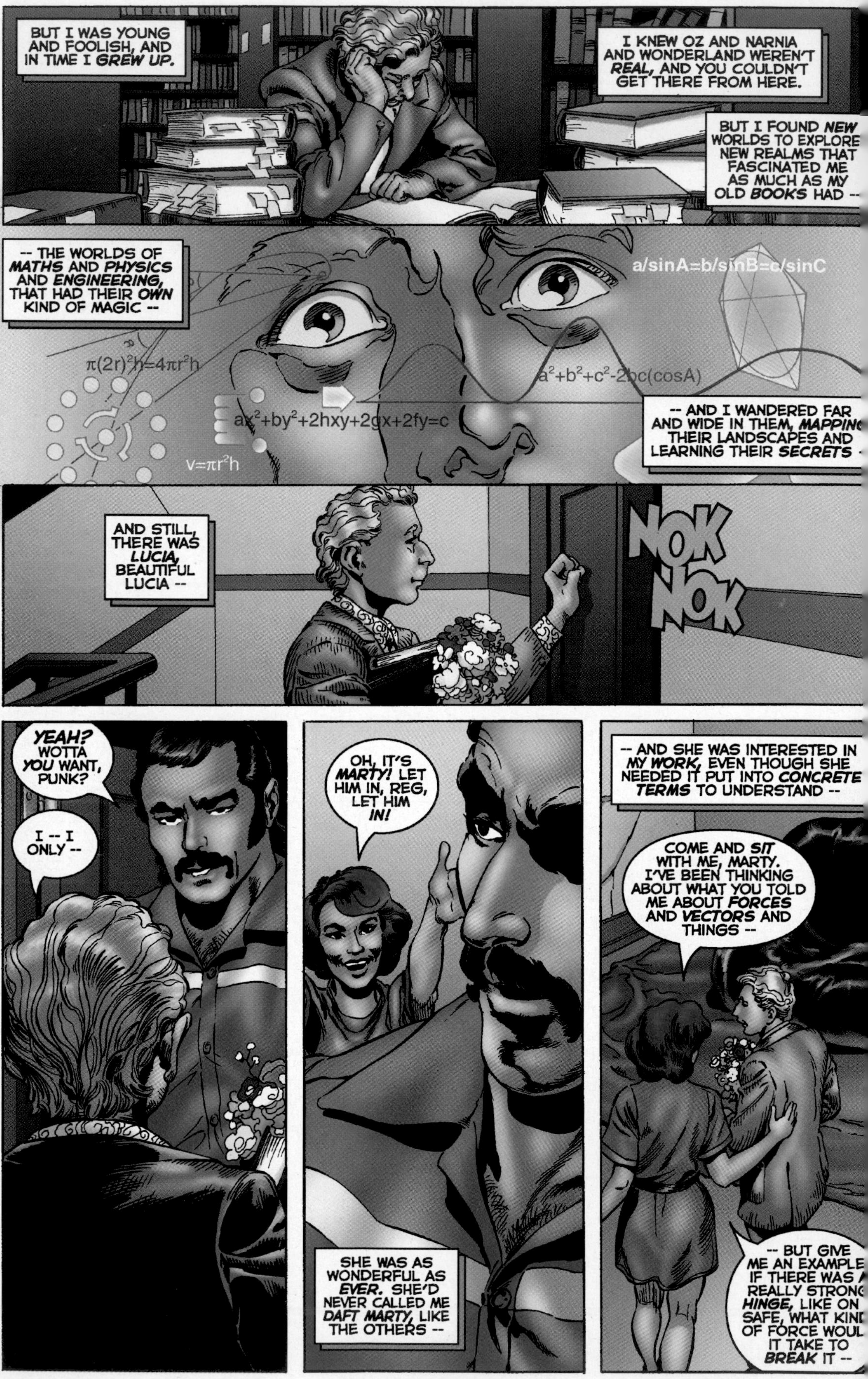
BUT I WAS YOUNG AND FOOLISH, AND IN TIME I GREW UP.
I KNEW OZ AND NARNIA AND WONDERLAND WEREN'T REAL, AND YOU COULDN'T GET THERE FROM HERE.
BUT I FOUND NEW WORLDS TO EXPLORE NEW REALMS THAT FASCINATED ME AS MUCH AS MY OLD BOOKS HAD --
-- THE WORLDS OF MATHS AND PHYSICS AND ENGINEERING, THAT HAD THEIR OWN KIND OF MAGIC --
a/sinA=b/sinB=c/sinC
π(2r)²h=4πr²h
a²+b²+c²-2bc(cosA)
ax²+by²+2hxy+2gx+2fy=c
v=πr²h
-- AND I WANDERED FAR AND WIDE IN THEM, MAPPING THEIR LANDSCAPES AND LEARNING THEIR SECRETS --
AND STILL, THERE WAS LUCIA, BEAUTIFUL LUCIA --
NOK NOK
YEAH? WOTTA YOU WANT, PUNK?
I -- I ONLY --
OH, IT'S MARTY! LET HIM IN, REG, LET HIM IN!
SHE WAS AS WONDERFUL AS EVER. SHE'D NEVER CALLED ME DAFT MARTY, LIKE THE OTHERS --
-- AND SHE WAS INTERESTED IN MY WORK, EVEN THOUGH SHE NEEDED IT PUT INTO CONCRETE TERMS TO UNDERSTAND --
COME AND SIT WITH ME, MARTY. I'VE BEEN THINKING ABOUT WHAT YOU TOLD ME ABOUT FORCES AND VECTORS AND THINGS --
-- BUT GIVE ME AN EXAMPLE. IF THERE WAS A REALLY STRONG HINGE, LIKE ON A SAFE, WHAT KIND OF FORCE WOULD IT TAKE TO BREAK IT --

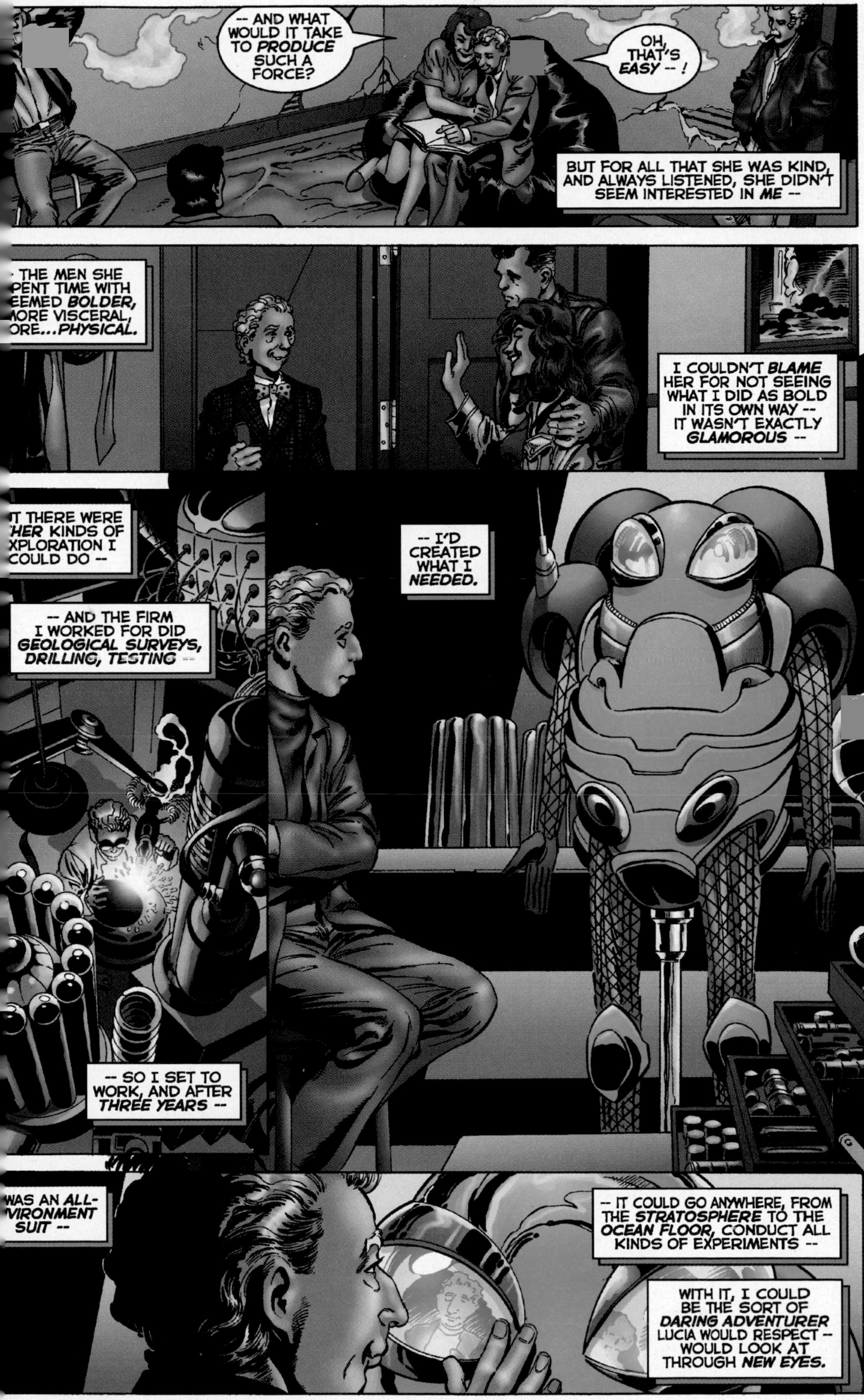
-- AND WHAT WOULD IT TAKE TO PRODUCE SUCH A FORCE?
OH, THAT'S EASY -- !
BUT FOR ALL THAT SHE WAS KIND, AND ALWAYS LISTENED, SHE DIDN'T SEEM INTERESTED IN ME --
THE MEN SHE PENT TIME WITH EEMED BOLDER, MORE VISCERAL, ORE...PHYSICAL.
I COULDN'T BLAME HER FOR NOT SEEING WHAT I DID AS BOLD IN ITS OWN WAY -- IT WASN'T EXACTLY GLAMOROUS --
T THERE WERE HER KINDS OF XPLORATION I COULD DO --
-- AND THE FIRM I WORKED FOR DID GEOLOGICAL SURVEYS, DRILLING, TESTING --
-- SO I SET TO WORK, AND AFTER THREE YEARS --
-- I'D CREATED WHAT I NEEDED.
WAS AN ALL- VIRONMENT SUIT --
-- IT COULD GO ANYWHERE, FROM THE STRATOSPHERE TO THE OCEAN FLOOR, CONDUCT ALL KINDS OF EXPERIMENTS --
WITH IT, I COULD BE THE SORT OF DARING ADVENTURER LUCIA WOULD RESPECT -- WOULD LOOK AT THROUGH NEW EYES.

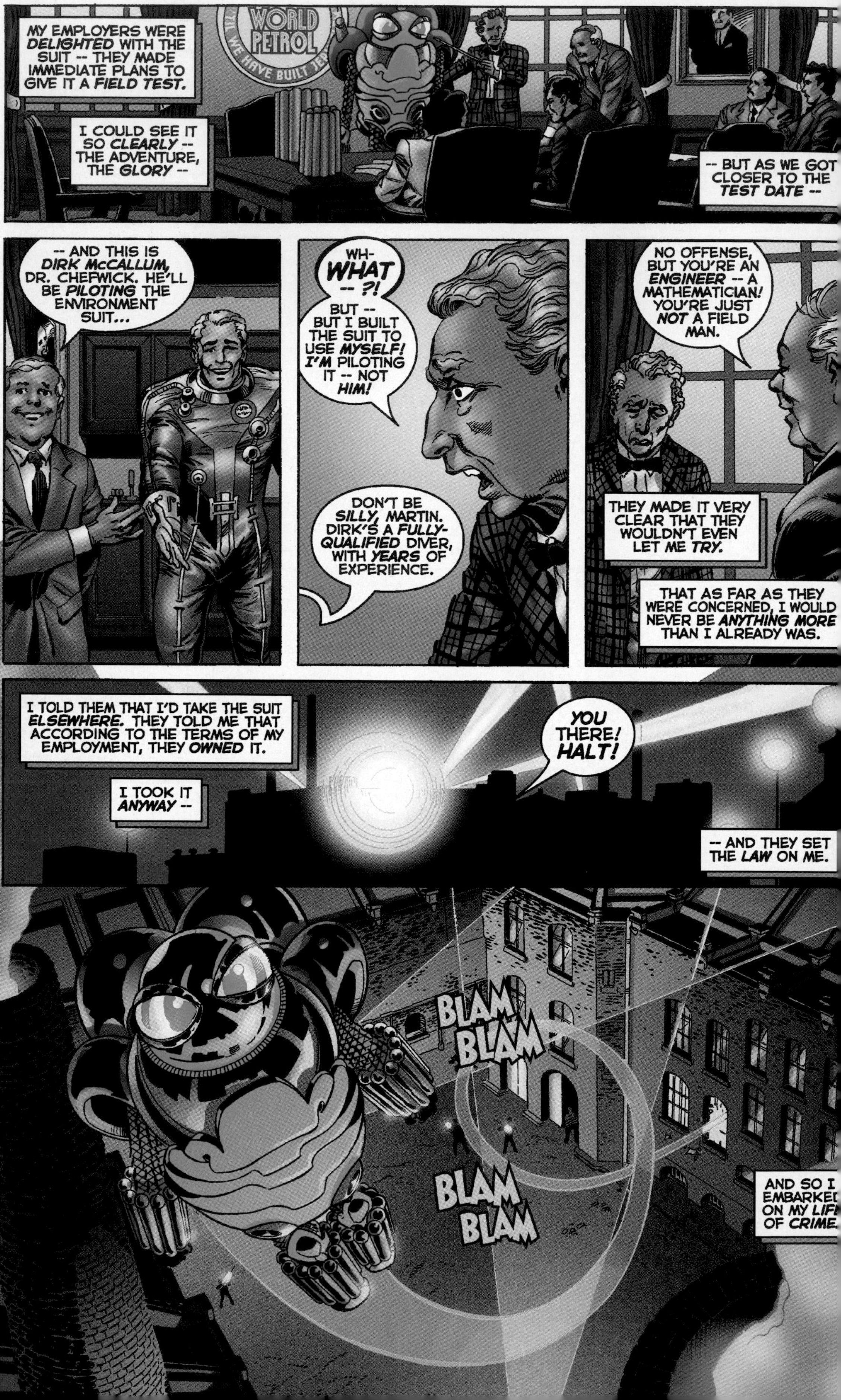

MY EMPLOYERS WERE DELIGHTED WITH THE SUIT -- THEY MADE IMMEDIATE PLANS TO GIVE IT A FIELD TEST.
WORLD PETROL
I COULD SEE IT SO CLEARLY -- THE ADVENTURE, THE GLORY --
-- BUT AS WE GOT CLOSER TO THE TEST DATE --
-- AND THIS IS DIRK McCALLUM, DR. CHEFWICK. HE'LL BE PILOTING THE ENVIRONMENT SUIT...
WH- WHAT -- ?!
BUT -- BUT I BUILT THE SUIT TO USE MYSELF! I'M PILOTING IT -- NOT HIM!
DON'T BE SILLY, MARTIN. DIRK'S A FULLY-QUALIFIED DIVER, WITH YEARS OF EXPERIENCE.
NO OFFENSE, BUT YOU'RE AN ENGINEER -- A MATHEMATICIAN! YOU'RE JUST NOT A FIELD MAN.
THEY MADE IT VERY CLEAR THAT THEY WOULDN'T EVEN LET ME TRY.
THAT AS FAR AS THEY WERE CONCERNED, I WOULD NEVER BE ANYTHING MORE THAN I ALREADY WAS.
I TOLD THEM THAT I'D TAKE THE SUIT ELSEWHERE. THEY TOLD ME THAT ACCORDING TO THE TERMS OF MY EMPLOYMENT, THEY OWNED IT.
I TOOK IT ANYWAY --
YOU THERE! HALT!
-- AND THEY SET THE LAW ON ME.
BLAM BLAM
BLAM BLAM

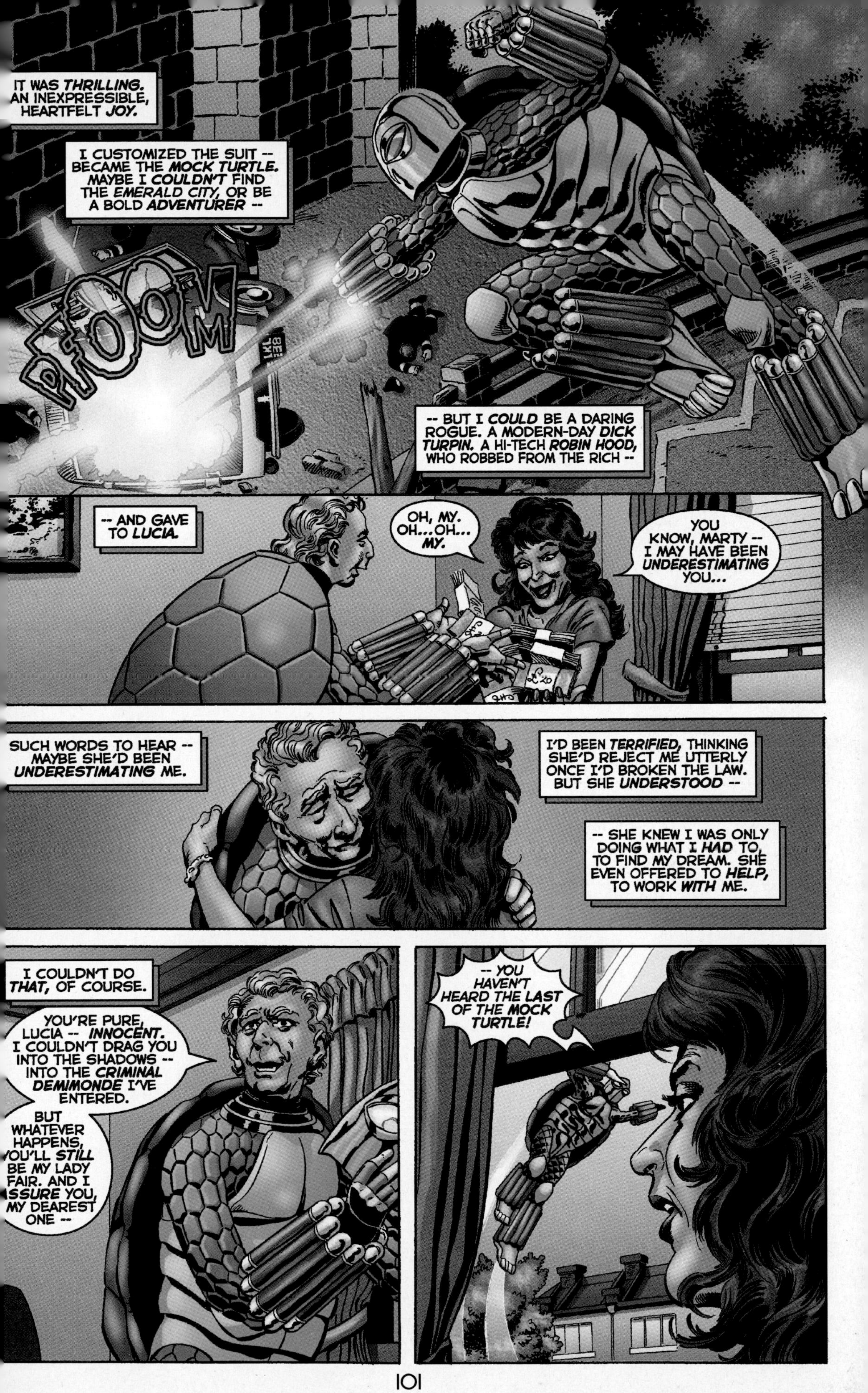
IT WAS *THRILLING.* AN INEXPRESSIBLE, HEARTFELT *JOY.*
I CUSTOMIZED THE SUIT -- BECAME THE *MOCK TURTLE.* MAYBE I *COULDN'T* FIND THE *EMERALD CITY,* OR BE A BOLD *ADVENTURER* --
PTOOOM
-- BUT I *COULD* BE A DARING ROGUE. A MODERN-DAY *DICK TURPIN.* A HI-TECH *ROBIN HOOD,* WHO ROBBED FROM THE RICH --
-- AND GAVE TO *LUCIA.*
OH, MY. OH...OH... *MY.*
YOU KNOW, MARTY -- I MAY HAVE BEEN *UNDERESTIMATING* YOU...
SUCH WORDS TO HEAR -- MAYBE SHE'D BEEN *UNDERESTIMATING* ME.
I'D BEEN *TERRIFIED,* THINKING SHE'D REJECT ME UTTERLY ONCE I'D BROKEN THE LAW. BUT SHE *UNDERSTOOD* --
-- SHE KNEW I WAS ONLY DOING WHAT I *HAD* TO, TO FIND MY DREAM. SHE EVEN OFFERED TO *HELP,* TO WORK *WITH* ME.
I COULDN'T DO *THAT,* OF COURSE.
YOU'RE PURE, LUCIA -- *INNOCENT.* I COULDN'T DRAG YOU INTO THE SHADOWS -- INTO THE *CRIMINAL DEMIMONDE* I'VE ENTERED.
BUT WHATEVER HAPPENS, YOU'LL *STILL* BE MY LADY FAIR. AND I ASSURE YOU, MY DEAREST ONE --
-- *YOU* HAVEN'T HEARD THE *LAST* OF THE *MOCK TURTLE!*

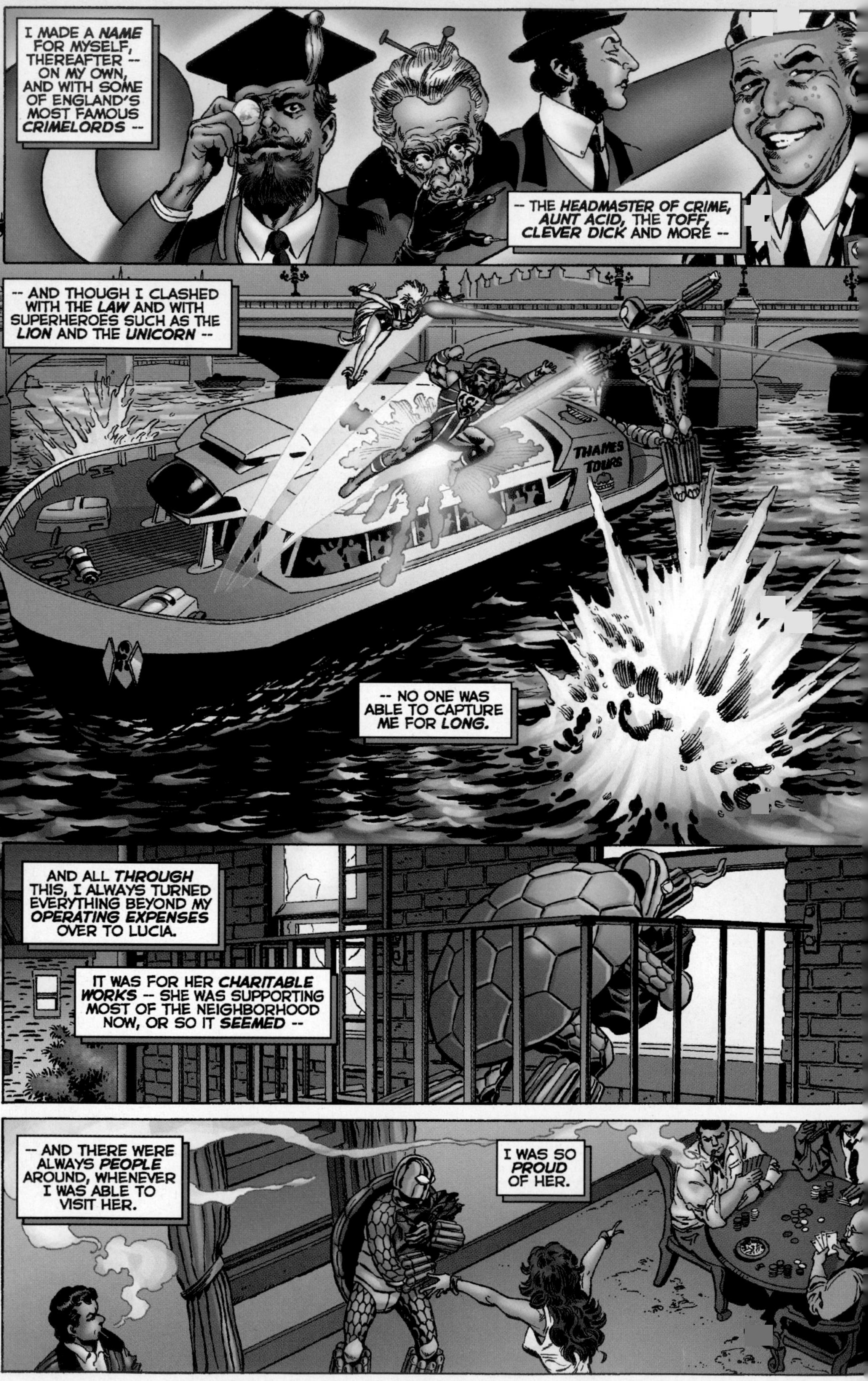
I MADE A NAME FOR MYSELF, THEREAFTER -- ON MY OWN, AND WITH SOME OF ENGLAND'S MOST FAMOUS CRIMELORDS --
-- THE HEADMASTER OF CRIME, AUNT ACID, THE TOFF, CLEVER DICK AND MORE --
-- AND THOUGH I CLASHED WITH THE LAW AND WITH SUPERHEROES SUCH AS THE LION AND THE UNICORN --
THAMES TOURS
-- NO ONE WAS ABLE TO CAPTURE ME FOR LONG.
AND ALL THROUGH THIS, I ALWAYS TURNED EVERYTHING BEYOND MY OPERATING EXPENSES OVER TO LUCIA.
IT WAS FOR HER CHARITABLE WORKS -- SHE WAS SUPPORTING MOST OF THE NEIGHBORHOOD NOW, OR SO IT SEEMED --
-- AND THERE WERE ALWAYS PEOPLE AROUND, WHENEVER I WAS ABLE TO VISIT HER.
I WAS SO PROUD OF HER.

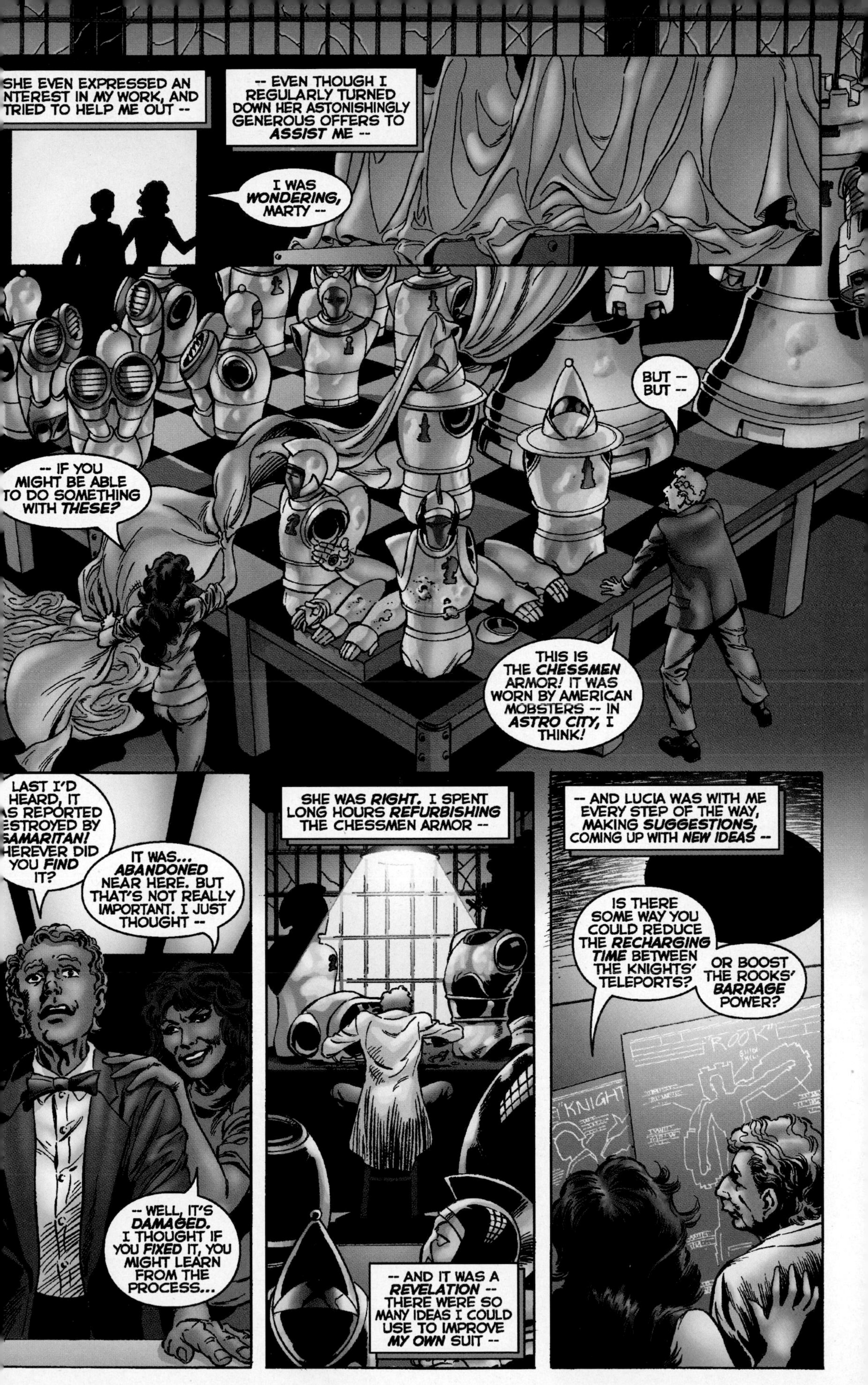
SHE EVEN EXPRESSED AN
NTEREST IN MY WORK, AND
TRIED TO HELP ME OUT --
-- EVEN THOUGH I REGULARLY TURNED DOWN HER ASTONISHINGLY GENEROUS OFFERS TO ASSIST ME --
I WAS WONDERING, MARTY --
-- IF YOU MIGHT BE ABLE TO DO SOMETHING WITH THESE?
BUT -- BUT --
THIS IS THE CHESSMEN ARMOR! IT WAS WORN BY AMERICAN MOBSTERS -- IN ASTRO CITY, I THINK!
LAST I'D HEARD, IT
AS REPORTED
ESTROYED BY
SAMARITAN!
HEREVER DID
YOU FIND
IT?
IT WAS... ABANDONED NEAR HERE. BUT THAT'S NOT REALLY IMPORTANT. I JUST THOUGHT --
-- WELL, IT'S DAMAGED. I THOUGHT IF YOU FIXED IT, YOU MIGHT LEARN FROM THE PROCESS...
SHE WAS RIGHT. I SPENT LONG HOURS REFURBISHING THE CHESSMEN ARMOR --
-- AND IT WAS A REVELATION -- THERE WERE SO MANY IDEAS I COULD USE TO IMPROVE MY OWN SUIT --
-- AND LUCIA WAS WITH ME EVERY STEP OF THE WAY, MAKING SUGGESTIONS, COMING UP WITH NEW IDEAS --
IS THERE SOME WAY YOU COULD REDUCE THE RECHARGING TIME BETWEEN THE KNIGHTS' TELEPORTS?
OR BOOST THE ROOKS' BARRAGE POWER?
"ROOK"
"KNIGHT"

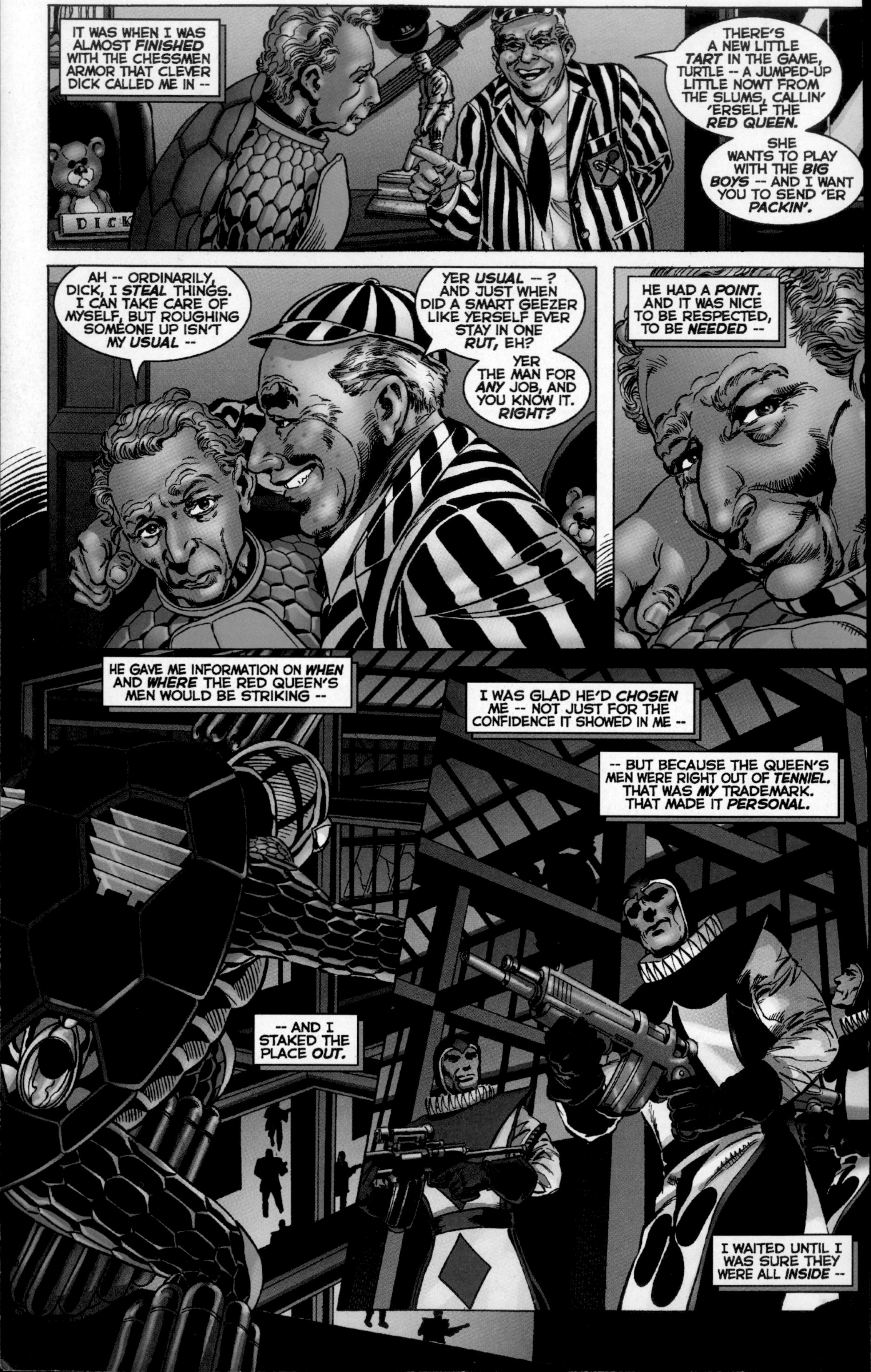

IT WAS WHEN I WAS ALMOST FINISHED WITH THE CHESSMEN ARMOR THAT CLEVER DICK CALLED ME IN --
THERE'S A NEW LITTLE TART IN THE GAME, TURTLE -- A JUMPED-UP LITTLE NOWT FROM THE SLUMS, CALLIN' 'ERSELF THE RED QUEEN.
SHE WANTS TO PLAY WITH THE BIG BOYS -- AND I WANT YOU TO SEND 'ER PACKIN'.
DICK
AH -- ORDINARILY, DICK, I STEAL THINGS. I CAN TAKE CARE OF MYSELF, BUT ROUGHING SOMEONE UP ISN'T MY USUAL --
YER USUAL -- ? AND JUST WHEN DID A SMART GEEZER LIKE YERSELF EVER STAY IN ONE RUT, EH?
YER THE MAN FOR ANY JOB, AND YOU KNOW IT. RIGHT?
HE HAD A POINT. AND IT WAS NICE TO BE RESPECTED, TO BE NEEDED --
HE GAVE ME INFORMATION ON WHEN AND WHERE THE RED QUEEN'S MEN WOULD BE STRIKING --
I WAS GLAD HE'D CHOSEN ME -- NOT JUST FOR THE CONFIDENCE IT SHOWED IN ME --
-- BUT BECAUSE THE QUEEN'S MEN WERE RIGHT OUT OF TENNIEL. THAT WAS MY TRADEMARK. THAT MADE IT PERSONAL.
-- AND I STAKED THE PLACE OUT.
I WAITED UNTIL I WAS SURE THEY WERE ALL INSIDE --

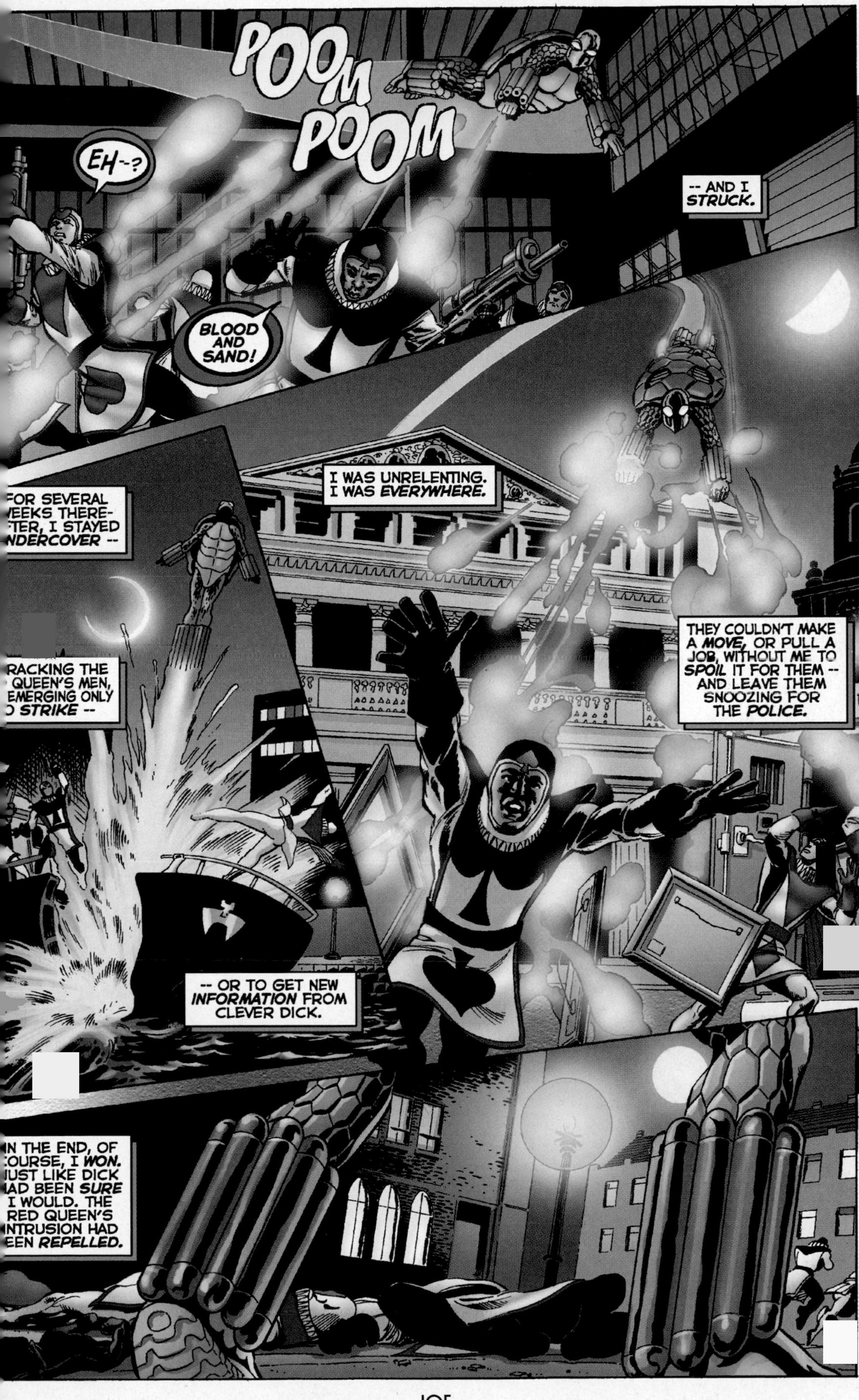
POOM POOM
EH--?
BLOOD AND SAND!
-- AND I STRUCK.
I WAS UNRELENTING. I WAS EVERYWHERE.
FOR SEVERAL WEEKS THERE-AFTER, I STAYED UNDERCOVER --
RACKING THE QUEEN'S MEN, EMERGING ONLY TO STRIKE --
-- OR TO GET NEW INFORMATION FROM CLEVER DICK.
THEY COULDN'T MAKE A MOVE, OR PULL A JOB, WITHOUT ME TO SPOIL IT FOR THEM -- AND LEAVE THEM SNOOZING FOR THE POLICE.
IN THE END, OF COURSE, I WON. JUST LIKE DICK HAD BEEN SURE I WOULD. THE RED QUEEN'S INTRUSION HAD BEEN REPELLED.

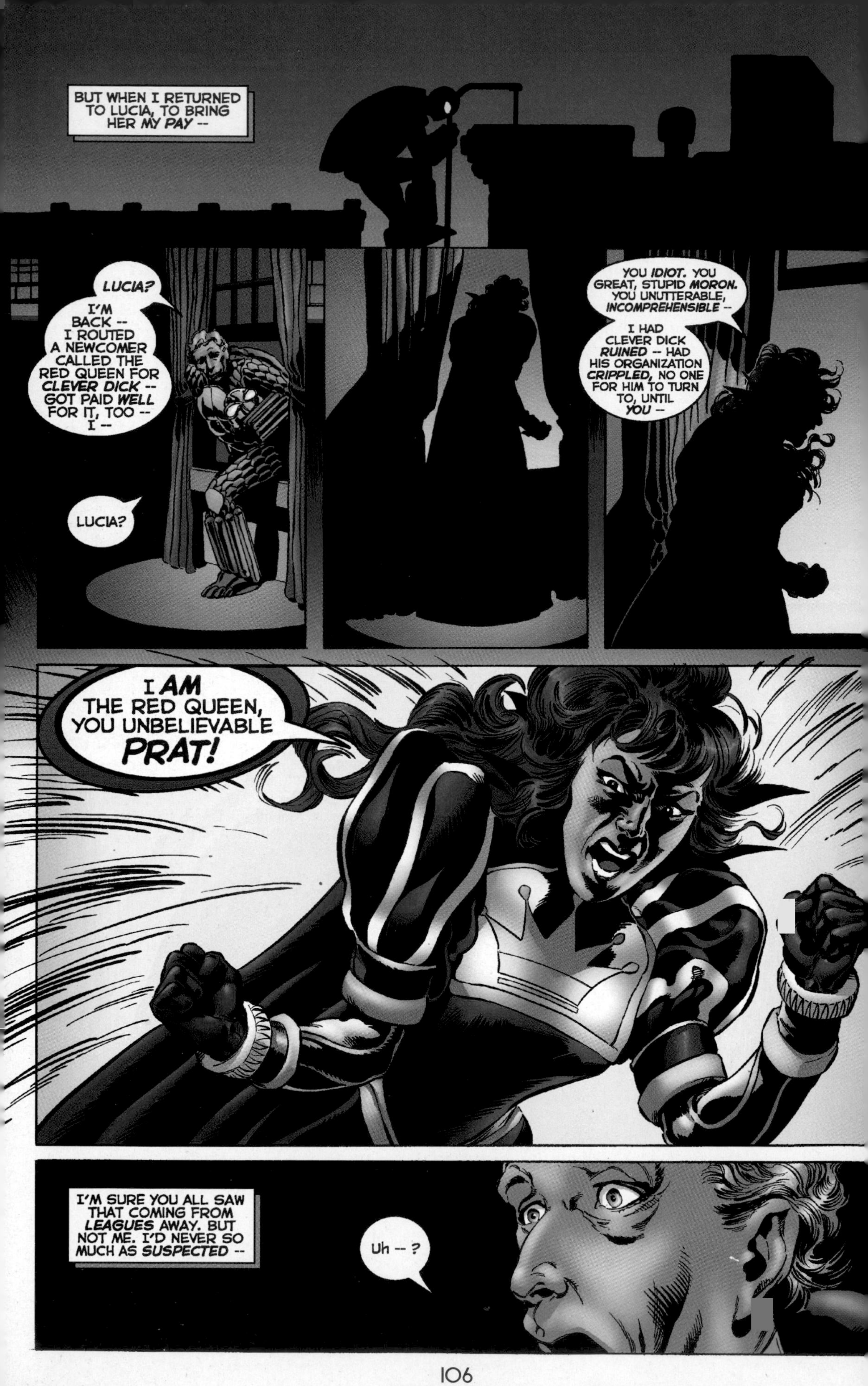
BUT WHEN I RETURNED TO LUCIA, TO BRING HER MY *PAY* --
LUCIA?
I'M BACK -- I ROUTED A NEWCOMER CALLED THE RED QUEEN FOR *CLEVER DICK* -- GOT PAID *WELL* FOR IT, TOO -- I --
LUCIA?
YOU *IDIOT.* YOU GREAT, STUPID *MORON.* YOU UNUTTERABLE, *INCOMPREHENSIBLE* --
I HAD CLEVER DICK *RUINED* -- HAD HIS ORGANIZATION *CRIPPLED,* NO ONE FOR HIM TO TURN TO, UNTIL *YOU* --
I *AM* THE RED QUEEN, YOU UNBELIEVABLE *PRAT!*
I'M SURE YOU ALL SAW THAT COMING FROM *LEAGUES* AWAY. BUT NOT ME. I'D NEVER SO MUCH AS *SUSPECTED* --
Uh -- ?

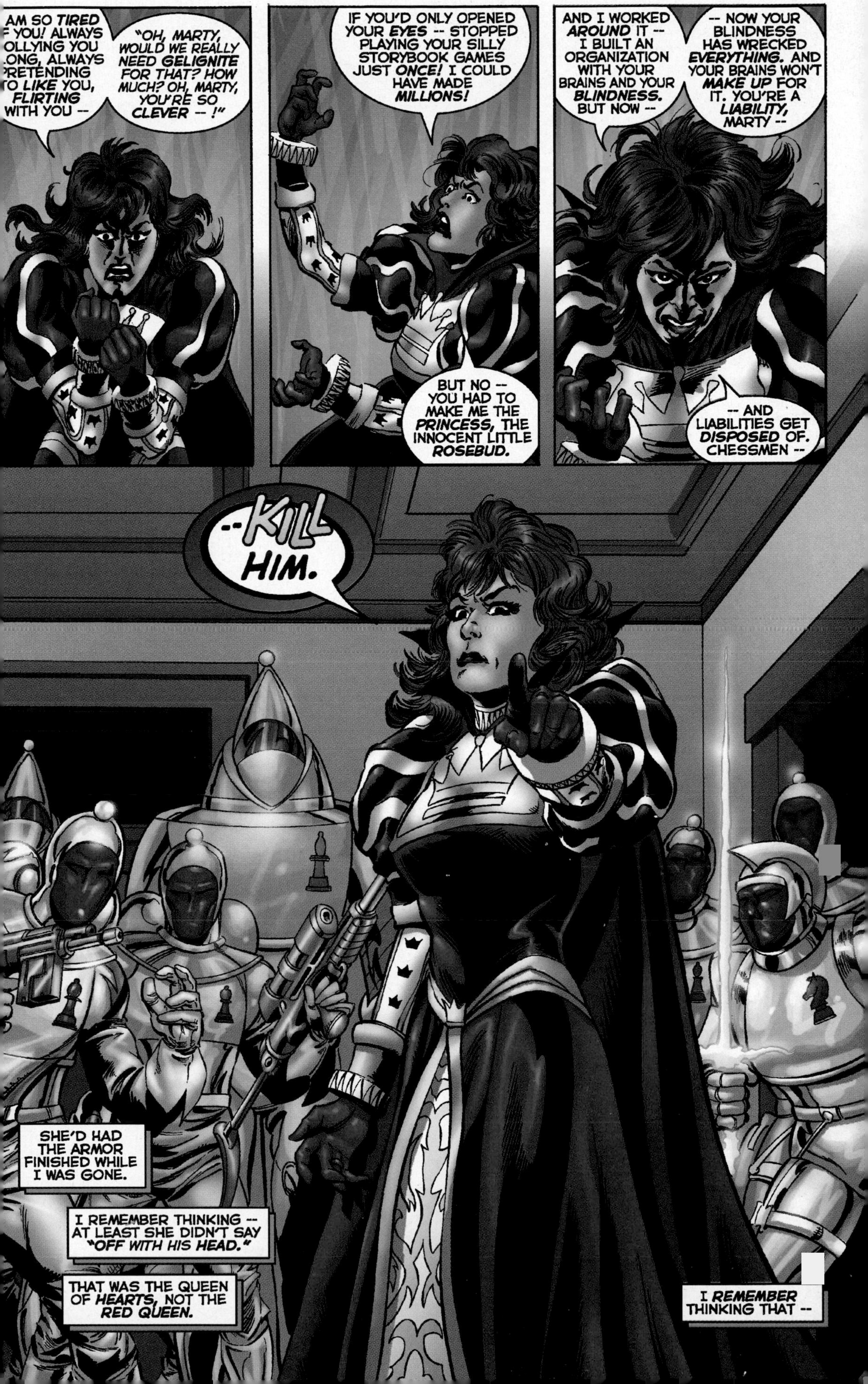
AM SO TIRED F YOU! ALWAYS OLLYING YOU ONG, ALWAYS RETENDING TO LIKE YOU, FLIRTING WITH YOU --
"OH, MARTY, WOULD WE REALLY NEED GELIGNITE FOR THAT? HOW MUCH? OH, MARTY, YOU'RE SO CLEVER -- !"
IF YOU'D ONLY OPENED YOUR EYES -- STOPPED PLAYING YOUR SILLY STORYBOOK GAMES JUST ONCE! I COULD HAVE MADE MILLIONS!
BUT NO -- YOU HAD TO MAKE ME THE PRINCESS, THE INNOCENT LITTLE ROSEBUD.
AND I WORKED AROUND IT -- I BUILT AN ORGANIZATION WITH YOUR BRAINS AND YOUR BLINDNESS. BUT NOW --
-- NOW YOUR BLINDNESS HAS WRECKED EVERYTHING. AND YOUR BRAINS WON'T MAKE UP FOR IT. YOU'RE A LIABILITY, MARTY --
-- AND LIABILITIES GET DISPOSED OF. CHESSMEN --
--KILL HIM.
SHE'D HAD THE ARMOR FINISHED WHILE I WAS GONE.
I REMEMBER THINKING -- AT LEAST SHE DIDN'T SAY "OFF WITH HIS HEAD."
THAT WAS THE QUEEN OF HEARTS, NOT THE RED QUEEN.
I REMEMBER THINKING THAT --

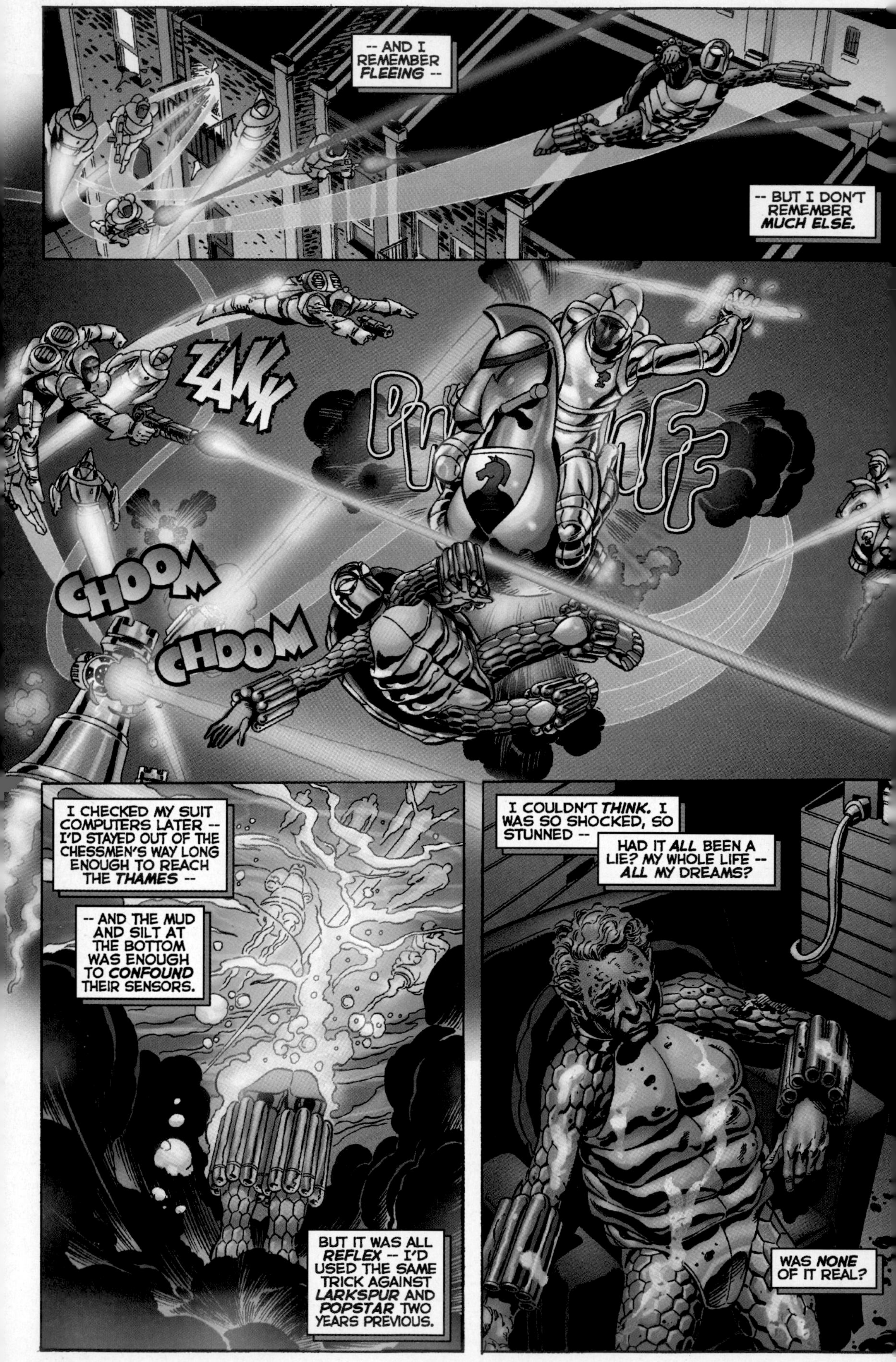
-- AND I REMEMBER FLEEING --
-- BUT I DON'T REMEMBER MUCH ELSE.
ZAKK
PWOOF
CHOOM
CHOOM
I CHECKED MY SUIT COMPUTERS LATER -- I'D STAYED OUT OF THE CHESSMEN'S WAY LONG ENOUGH TO REACH THE THAMES --
-- AND THE MUD AND SILT AT THE BOTTOM WAS ENOUGH TO CONFOUND THEIR SENSORS.
BUT IT WAS ALL REFLEX -- I'D USED THE SAME TRICK AGAINST LARKSPUR AND POPSTAR TWO YEARS PREVIOUS.
I COULDN'T THINK. I WAS SO SHOCKED, SO STUNNED --
HAD IT ALL BEEN A LIE? MY WHOLE LIFE -- ALL MY DREAMS?
WAS NONE OF IT REAL?

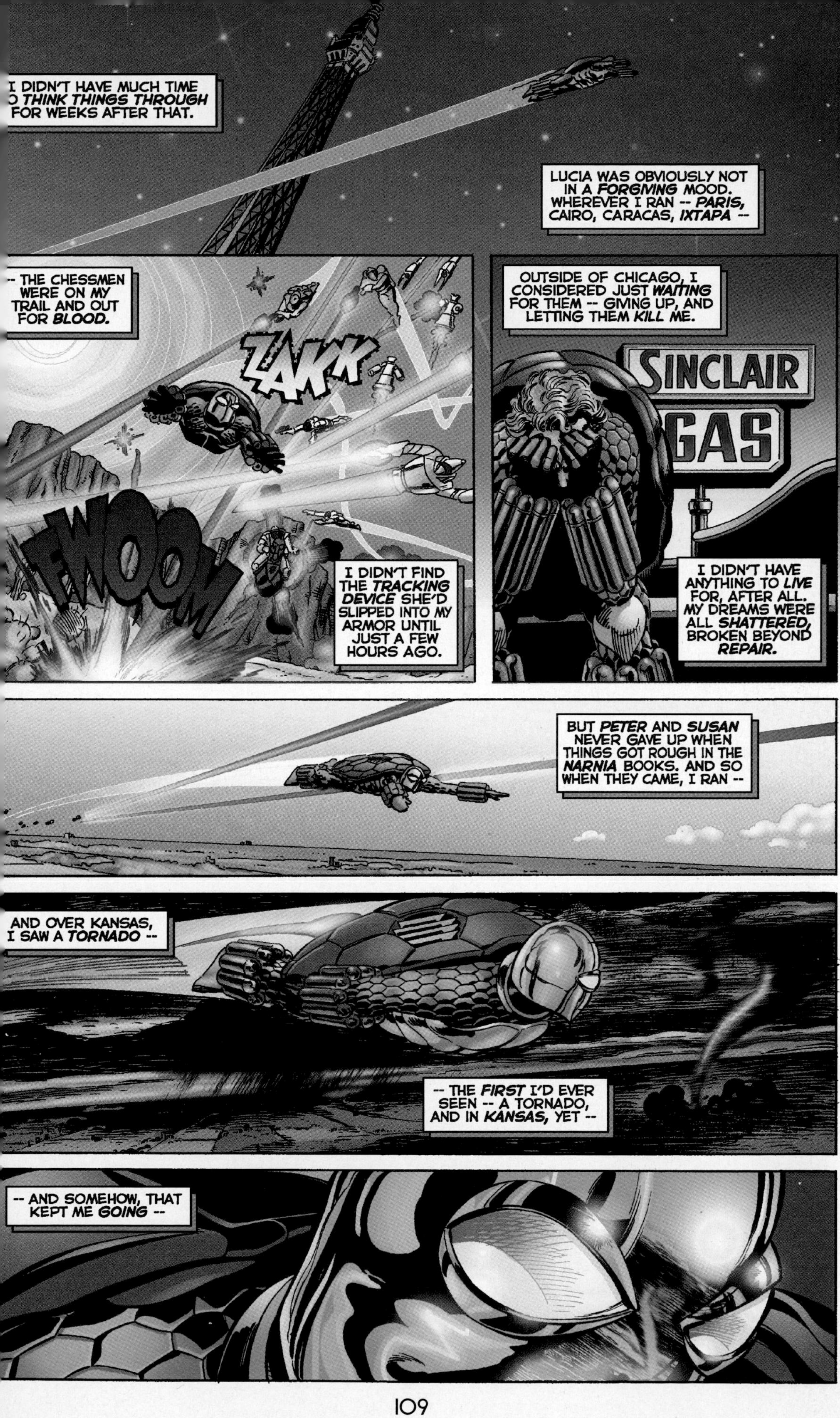
I DIDN'T HAVE MUCH TIME TO THINK THINGS THROUGH FOR WEEKS AFTER THAT.
LUCIA WAS OBVIOUSLY NOT IN A FORGIVING MOOD. WHEREVER I RAN -- PARIS, CAIRO, CARACAS, IXTAPA --
-- THE CHESSMEN WERE ON MY TRAIL AND OUT FOR BLOOD.
ZAKK
FWOOM
I DIDN'T FIND THE TRACKING DEVICE SHE'D SLIPPED INTO MY ARMOR UNTIL JUST A FEW HOURS AGO.
OUTSIDE OF CHICAGO, I CONSIDERED JUST WAITING FOR THEM -- GIVING UP, AND LETTING THEM KILL ME.
SINCLAIR
GAS
I DIDN'T HAVE ANYTHING TO LIVE FOR, AFTER ALL. MY DREAMS WERE ALL SHATTERED, BROKEN BEYOND REPAIR.
BUT PETER AND SUSAN NEVER GAVE UP WHEN THINGS GOT ROUGH IN THE NARNIA BOOKS. AND SO WHEN THEY CAME, I RAN --
AND OVER KANSAS, I SAW A TORNADO --
-- THE FIRST I'D EVER SEEN -- A TORNADO, AND IN KANSAS, YET --
-- AND SOMEHOW, THAT KEPT ME GOING --

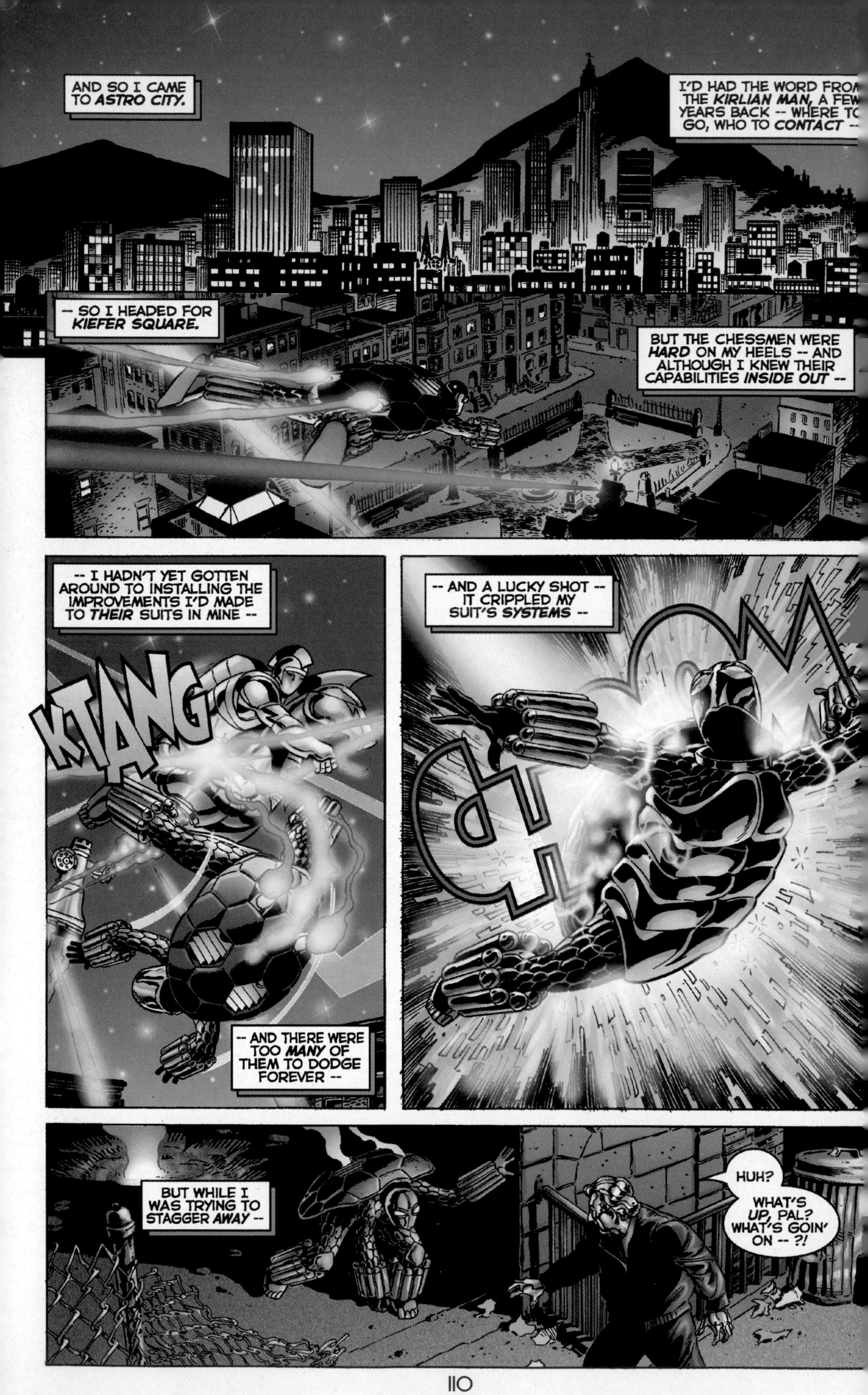
AND SO I CAME TO *ASTRO CITY.*
I'D HAD THE WORD FROM THE *KIRLIAN MAN,* A FEW YEARS BACK -- WHERE TO GO, WHO TO *CONTACT* --
-- SO I HEADED FOR *KIEFER SQUARE.*
BUT THE CHESSMEN WERE *HARD* ON MY HEELS -- AND ALTHOUGH I KNEW THEIR CAPABILITIES *INSIDE OUT* --
-- I HADN'T YET GOTTEN AROUND TO INSTALLING THE IMPROVEMENTS I'D MADE TO *THEIR* SUITS IN MINE --
KTANG
-- AND THERE WERE TOO *MANY* OF THEM TO DODGE FOREVER --
-- AND A LUCKY SHOT -- IT CRIPPLED MY SUIT'S *SYSTEMS* --
BUT WHILE I WAS TRYING TO STAGGER *AWAY* --
HUH?
WHAT'S *UP*, PAL? WHAT'S GOIN' ON -- ?!

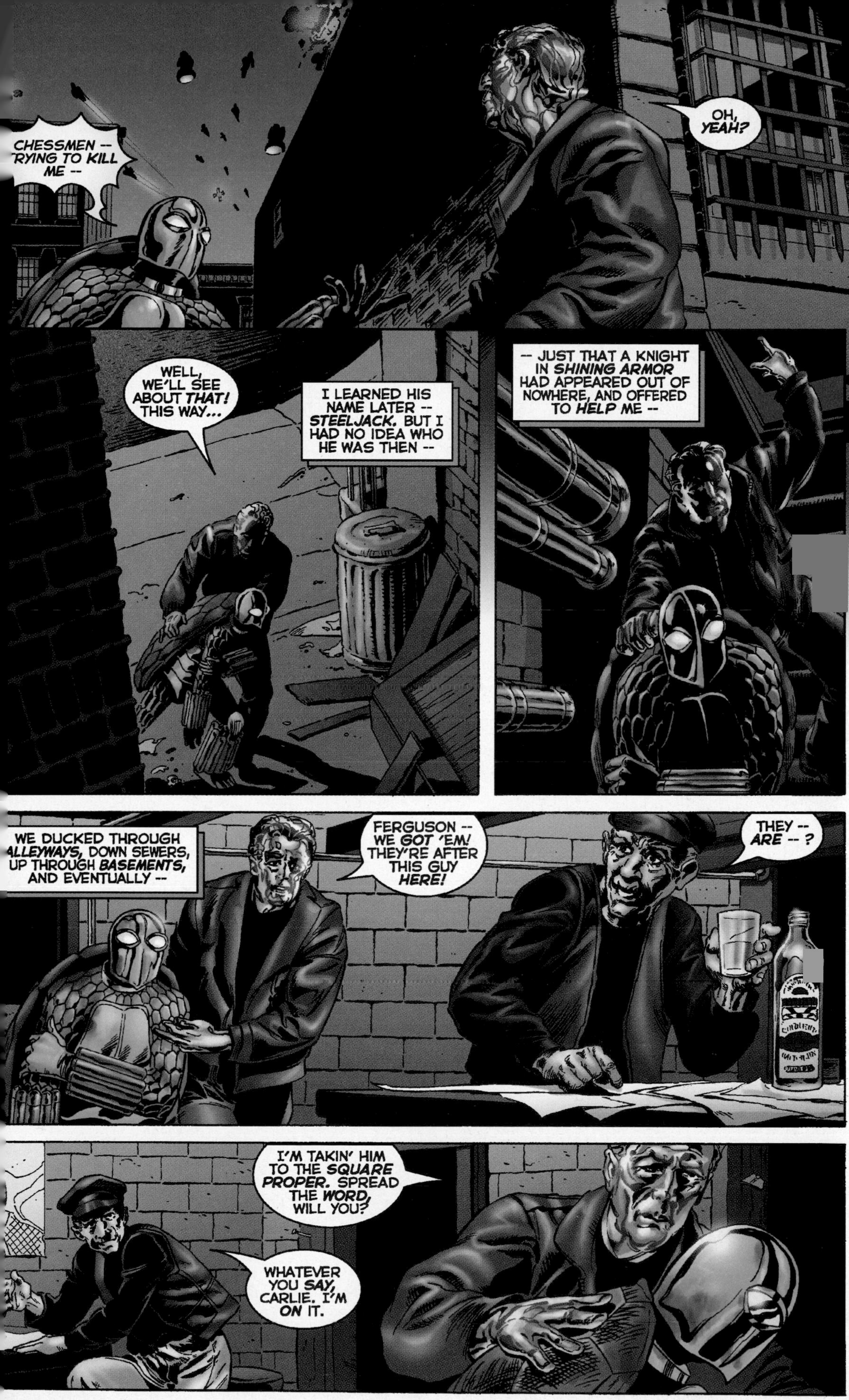
CHESSMEN -- TRYING TO KILL ME --
OH, YEAH?
WELL, WE'LL SEE ABOUT THAT! THIS WAY...
I LEARNED HIS NAME LATER -- STEELJACK. BUT I HAD NO IDEA WHO HE WAS THEN --
-- JUST THAT A KNIGHT IN SHINING ARMOR HAD APPEARED OUT OF NOWHERE, AND OFFERED TO HELP ME --
WE DUCKED THROUGH ALLEYWAYS, DOWN SEWERS, UP THROUGH BASEMENTS, AND EVENTUALLY --
FERGUSON -- WE GOT 'EM! THEY'RE AFTER THIS GUY HERE!
THEY -- ARE -- ?
I'M TAKIN' HIM TO THE SQUARE PROPER. SPREAD THE WORD, WILL YOU?
WHATEVER YOU SAY, CARLIE. I'M ON IT.

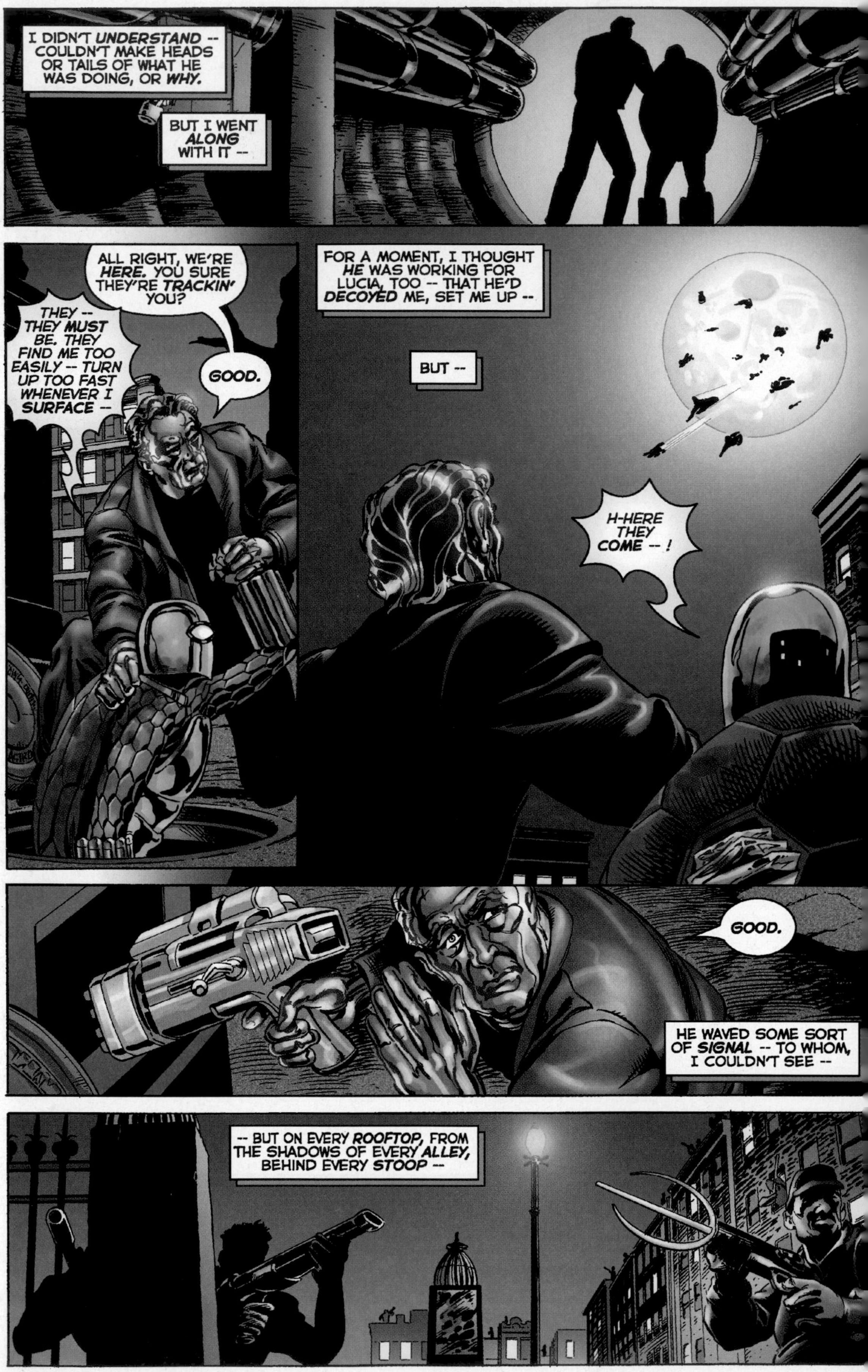
I DIDN'T UNDERSTAND -- COULDN'T MAKE HEADS OR TAILS OF WHAT HE WAS DOING, OR WHY.
BUT I WENT ALONG WITH IT --
ALL RIGHT, WE'RE HERE. YOU SURE THEY'RE TRACKIN' YOU?
THEY -- THEY MUST BE. THEY FIND ME TOO EASILY -- TURN UP TOO FAST WHENEVER I SURFACE --
GOOD.
FOR A MOMENT, I THOUGHT HE WAS WORKING FOR LUCIA, TOO -- THAT HE'D DECOYED ME, SET ME UP --
BUT --
H-HERE THEY COME -- !
GOOD.
HE WAVED SOME SORT OF SIGNAL -- TO WHOM, I COULDN'T SEE --
-- BUT ON EVERY ROOFTOP, FROM THE SHADOWS OF EVERY ALLEY, BEHIND EVERY STOOP --

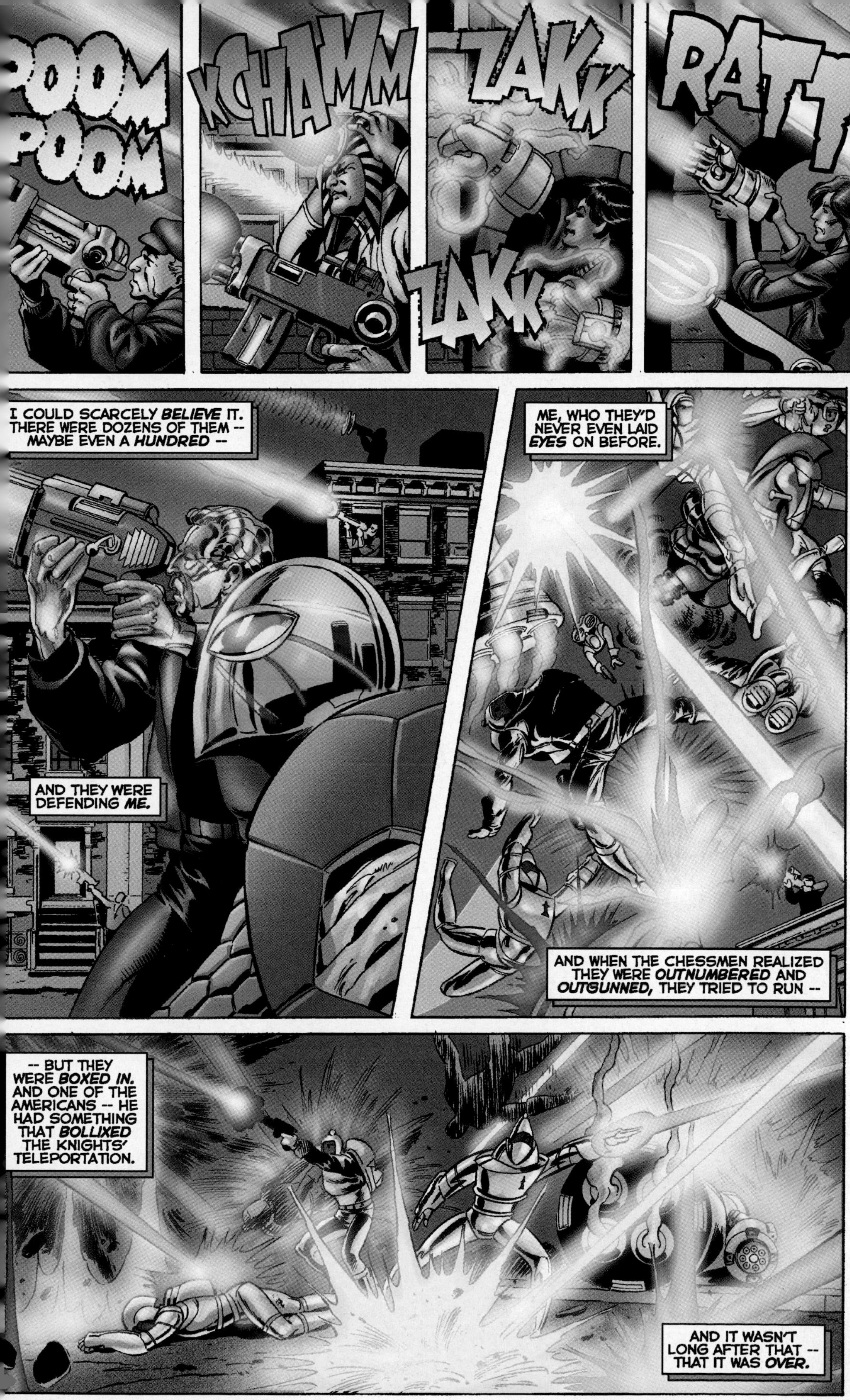
POOM POOM
KCHAMM
ZAKK
ZAKK
RATT
I COULD SCARCELY BELIEVE IT. THERE WERE DOZENS OF THEM -- MAYBE EVEN A HUNDRED --
AND THEY WERE DEFENDING ME.
ME, WHO THEY'D NEVER EVEN LAID EYES ON BEFORE.
AND WHEN THE CHESSMEN REALIZED THEY WERE OUTNUMBERED AND OUTGUNNED, THEY TRIED TO RUN --
-- BUT THEY WERE BOXED IN. AND ONE OF THE AMERICANS -- HE HAD SOMETHING THAT BOLLIXED THE KNIGHTS' TELEPORTATION.
AND IT WASN'T LONG AFTER THAT -- THAT IT WAS OVER.

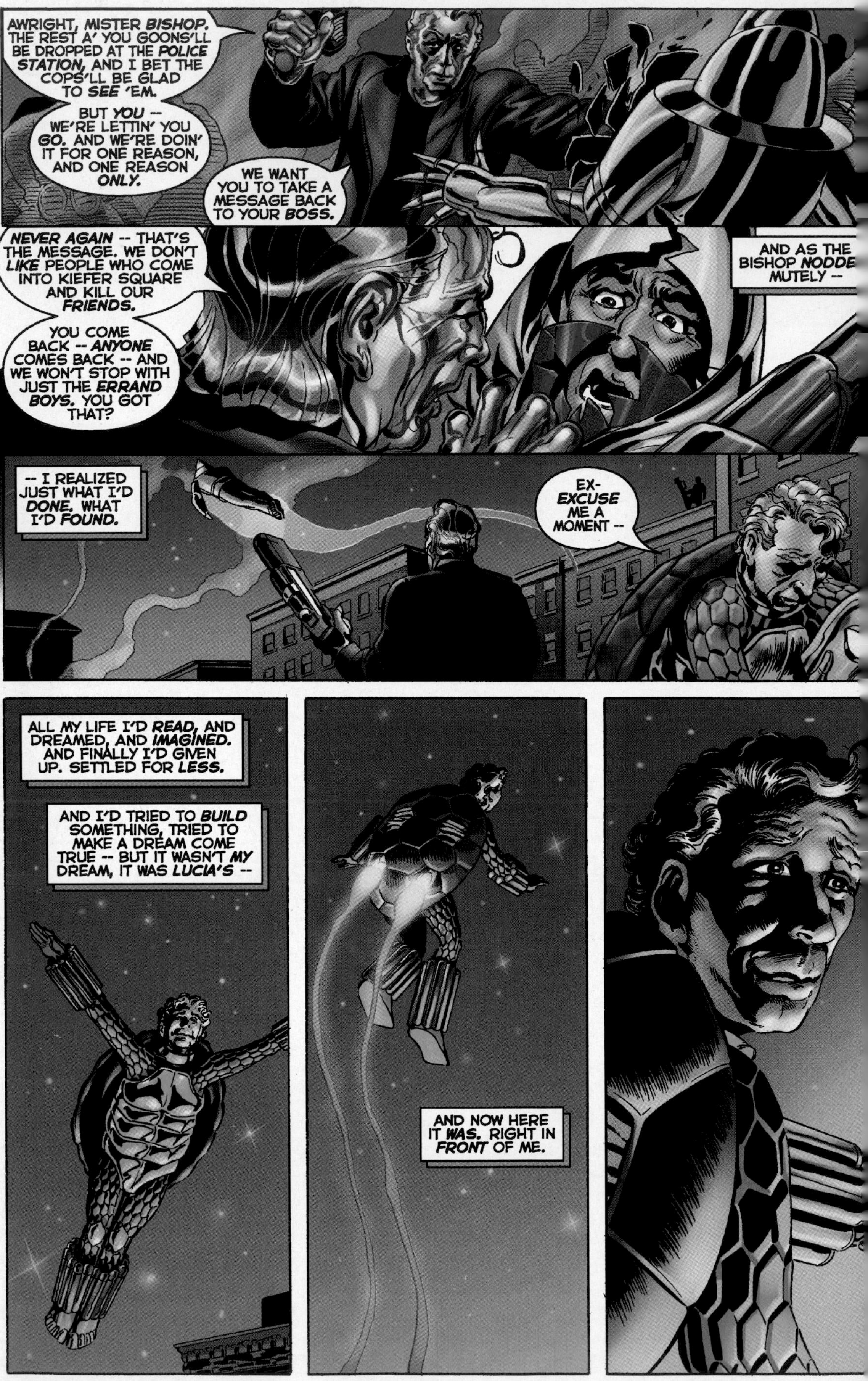

AWRIGHT, MISTER BISHOP. THE REST A' YOU GOONS'LL BE DROPPED AT THE POLICE STATION, AND I BET THE COPS'LL BE GLAD TO SEE 'EM.
BUT YOU -- WE'RE LETTIN' YOU GO. AND WE'RE DOIN' IT FOR ONE REASON, AND ONE REASON ONLY.
WE WANT YOU TO TAKE A MESSAGE BACK TO YOUR BOSS.
NEVER AGAIN -- THAT'S THE MESSAGE. WE DON'T LIKE PEOPLE WHO COME INTO KIEFER SQUARE AND KILL OUR FRIENDS.
YOU COME BACK -- ANYONE COMES BACK -- AND WE WON'T STOP WITH JUST THE ERRAND BOYS. YOU GOT THAT?
AND AS THE BISHOP NODDE MUTELY --
-- I REALIZED JUST WHAT I'D DONE. WHAT I'D FOUND.
EX- EXCUSE ME A MOMENT --
ALL MY LIFE I'D READ, AND DREAMED, AND IMAGINED. AND FINALLY I'D GIVEN UP. SETTLED FOR LESS.
AND I'D TRIED TO BUILD SOMETHING, TRIED TO MAKE A DREAM COME TRUE -- BUT IT WASN'T MY DREAM, IT WAS LUCIA'S --
AND NOW HERE IT WAS. RIGHT IN FRONT OF ME.

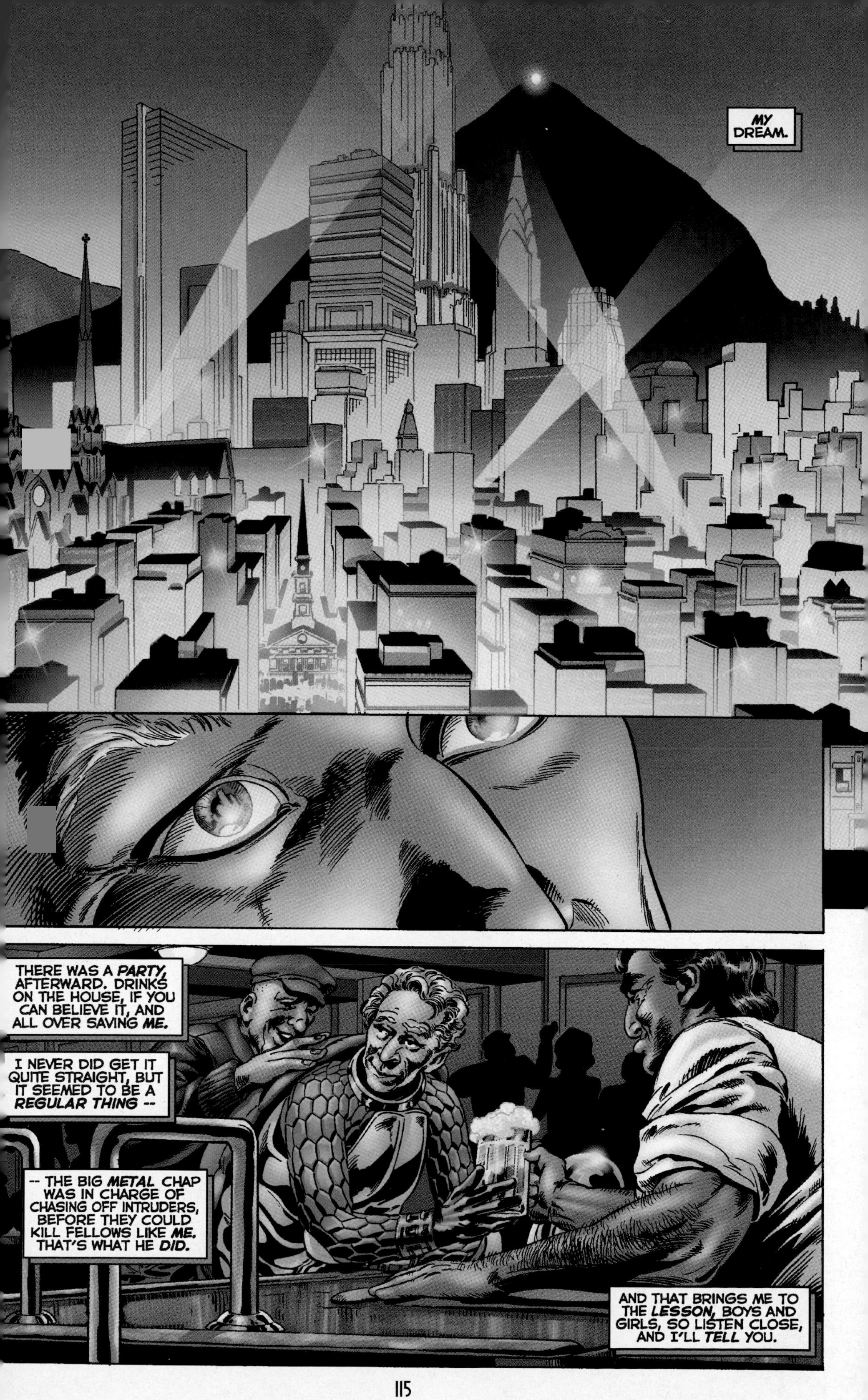
MY DREAM.
THERE WAS A PARTY, AFTERWARD. DRINKS ON THE HOUSE, IF YOU CAN BELIEVE IT, AND ALL OVER SAVING ME.
I NEVER DID GET IT QUITE STRAIGHT, BUT IT SEEMED TO BE A REGULAR THING --
-- THE BIG METAL CHAP WAS IN CHARGE OF CHASING OFF INTRUDERS, BEFORE THEY COULD KILL FELLOWS LIKE ME. THAT'S WHAT HE DID.
AND THAT BRINGS ME TO THE LESSON, BOYS AND GIRLS, SO LISTEN CLOSE, AND I'LL TELL YOU.

NEVER GIVE UP ON YOUR *DREAMS*, THAT'S THE LESSON FOR TONIGHT. *NEVER* GIVE UP ON YOUR DREAMS --

-- *WORK,* STEELJACK --

-- CHESTER'D HAVE BEEN *PROUD* --

-- KNEW YOU'D FL... 'EM OUT

-- NEVE... DOUBTE...

-- AN END TO IT ALL, *FINALLY* AN END --

YOU'RE THE *MOCK TURTLE,* AREN'T YOU? I'VE SEEN PICTURES OF YOU.

AND YOU'D BE *DONNELLY FERGUSON.* A FELLOW I KNOW TOL... ME YOU'RE THE MAN TO *SEE* IN ASTRO CITY --

-- YOU'RE THE ONE WHO KNOWS WHER... ALL THE *WOR...* IS.

I BUT *TRY,* MY FRIEND. I BUT *TRY.* AND I MIGHT HAVE SOMETHING JUST IN *YOUR* LINE, COME TO THINK OF IT.

BUT WHY DON'T WE TALK ABOUT IT *TOMORROW* -- SAY, HERE, AT *NOON?*

IT'S A *DATE,* MR. FERGUSON.

-- BECAUSE YOU NEVER *KNOW* --

-- JUST WHEN, OR *HOW,* THEY'LL COME *TRUE...*

YOU ARE NOW LEAVING **ASTRO CITY** PLEASE DRIVE CAREFULLY

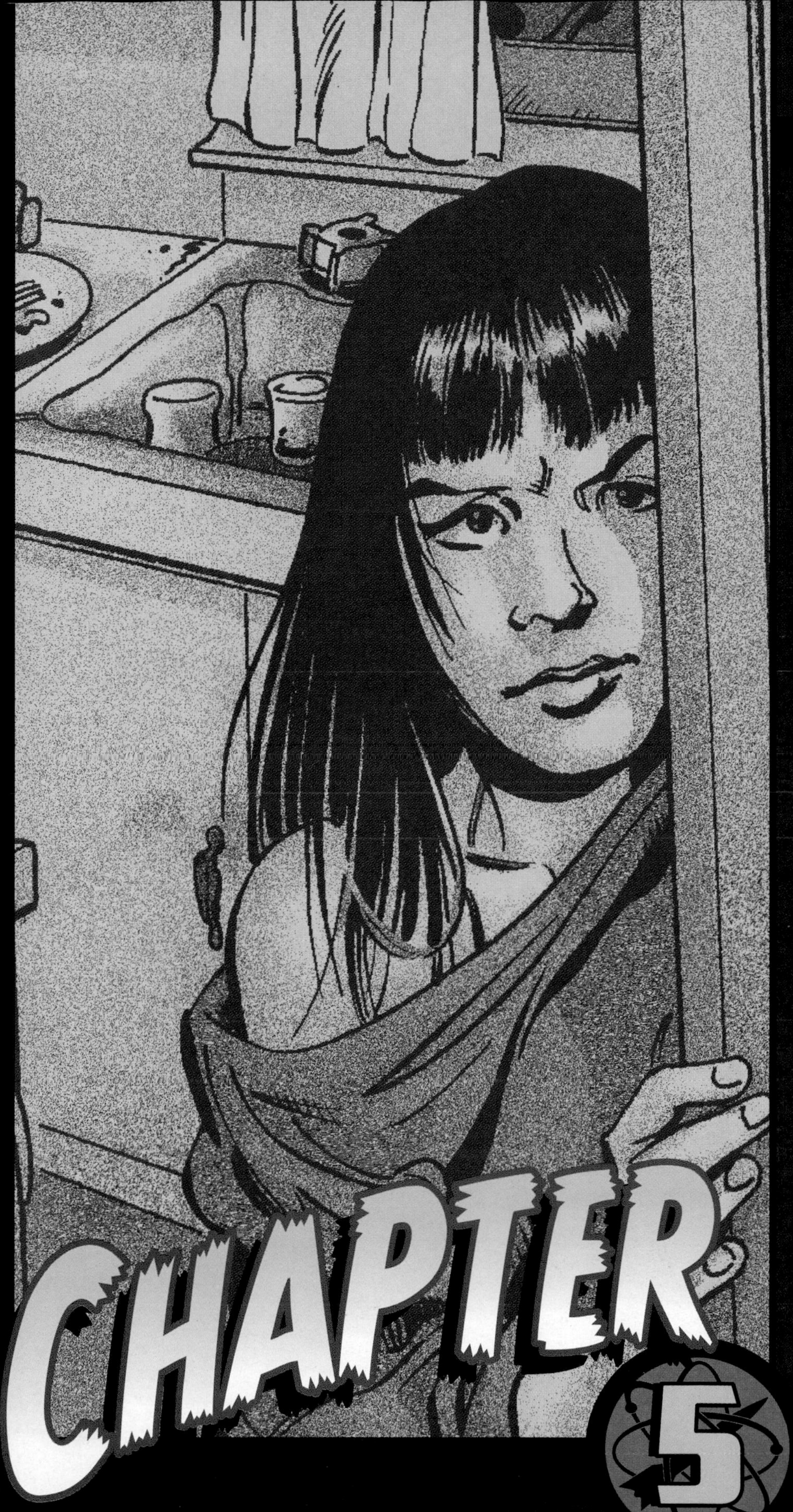
CHAPTER
5

The EMPTY SHELL

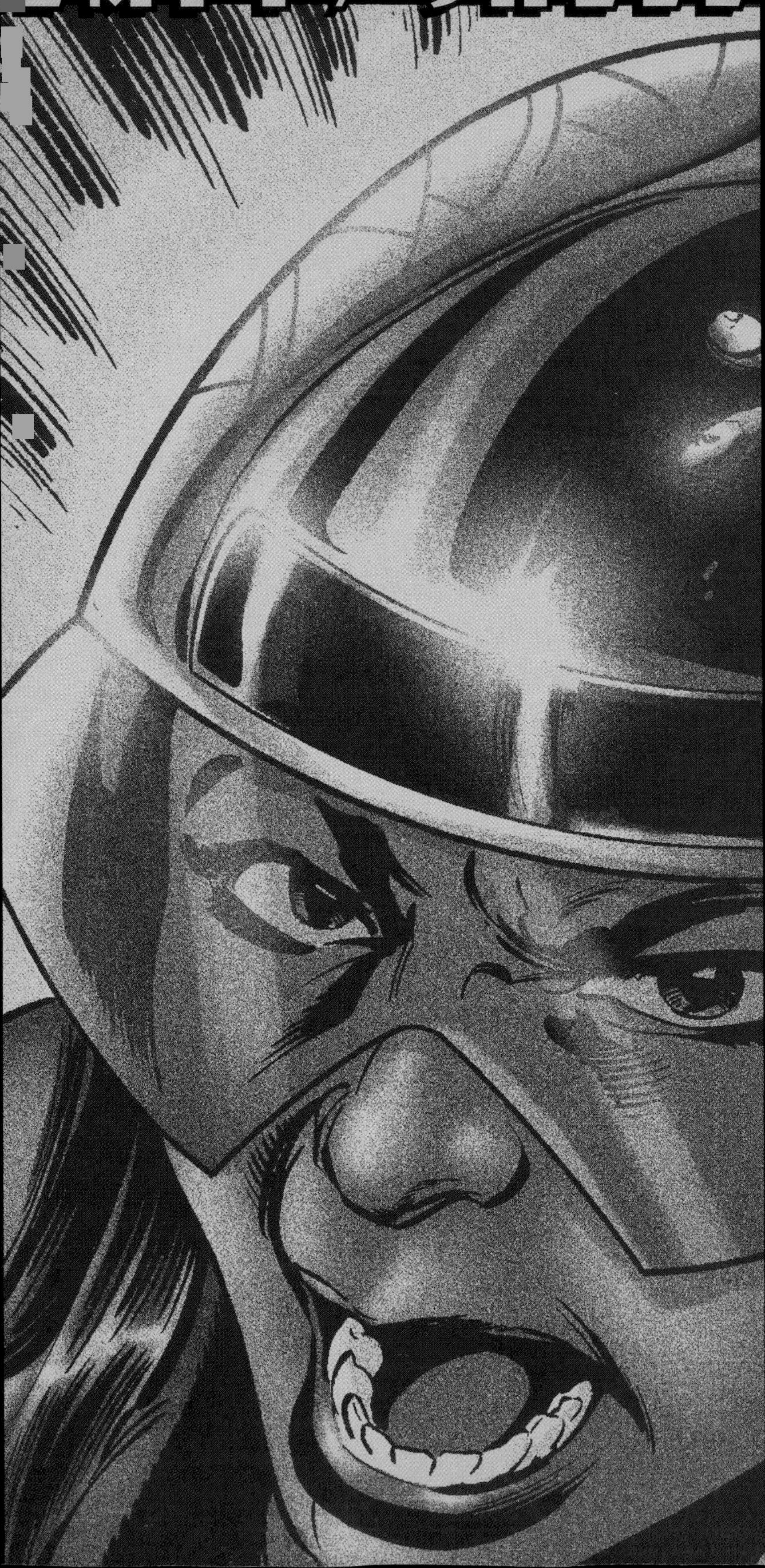

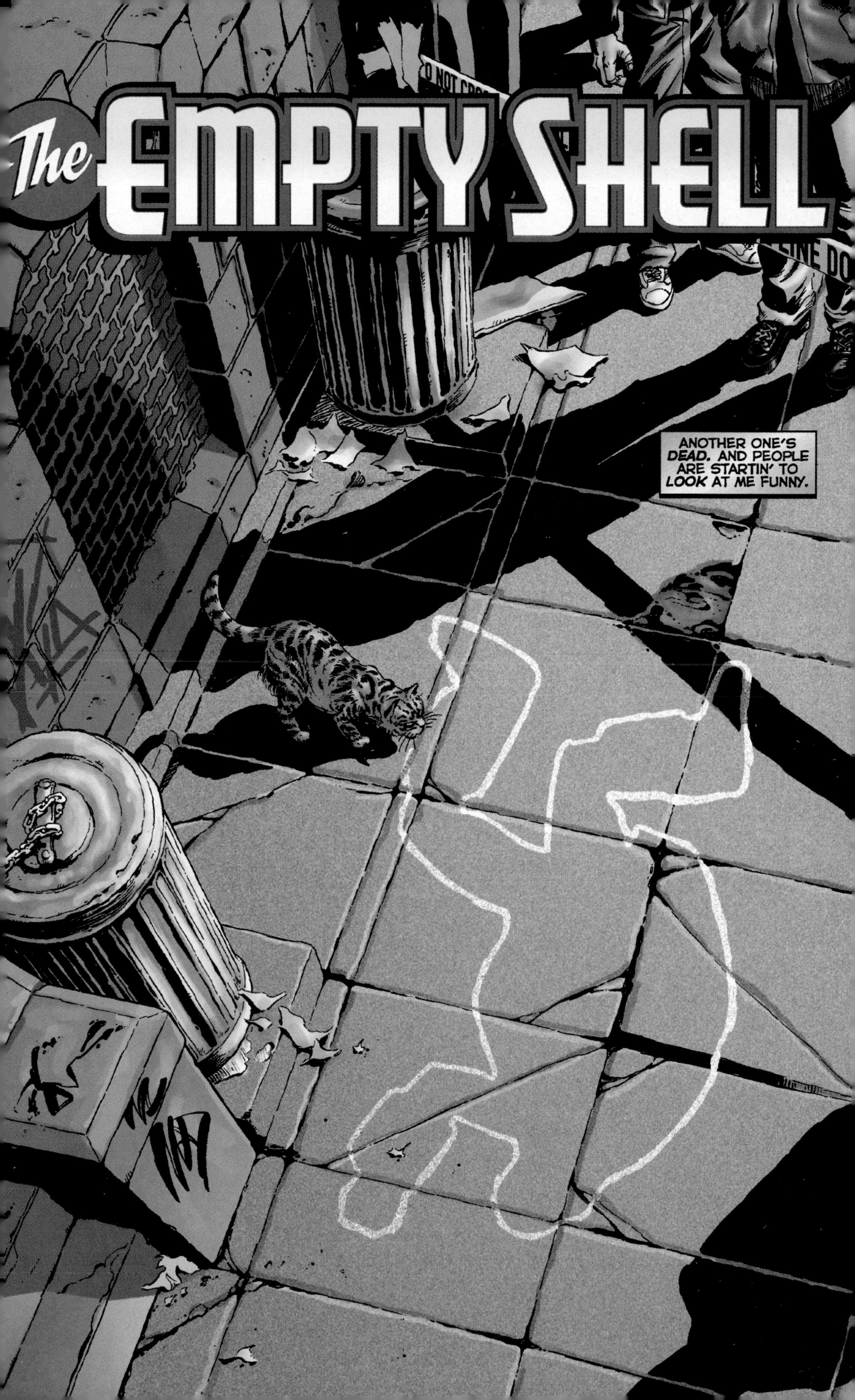

The EMPTY SHELL
ANOTHER ONE'S DEAD. AND PEOPLE ARE STARTIN' TO LOOK AT ME FUNNY.

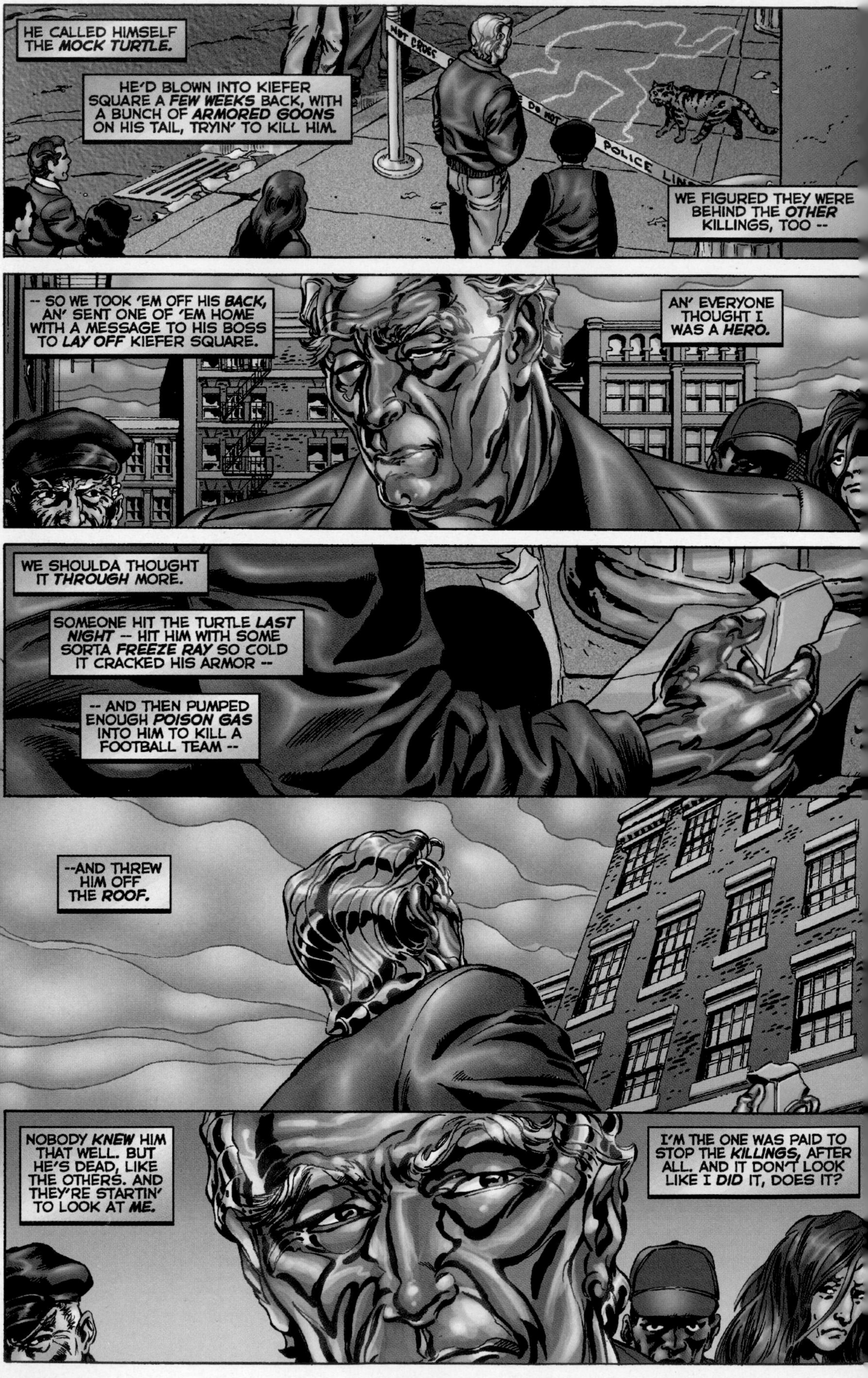
HE CALLED HIMSELF THE MOCK TURTLE.
HE'D BLOWN INTO KIEFER SQUARE A FEW WEEKS BACK, WITH A BUNCH OF ARMORED GOONS ON HIS TAIL, TRYIN' TO KILL HIM.
WE FIGURED THEY WERE BEHIND THE OTHER KILLINGS, TOO --
-- SO WE TOOK 'EM OFF HIS BACK, AN' SENT ONE OF 'EM HOME WITH A MESSAGE TO HIS BOSS TO LAY OFF KIEFER SQUARE.
AN' EVERYONE THOUGHT I WAS A HERO.
WE SHOULDA THOUGHT IT THROUGH MORE.
SOMEONE HIT THE TURTLE LAST NIGHT -- HIT HIM WITH SOME SORTA FREEZE RAY SO COLD IT CRACKED HIS ARMOR --
-- AND THEN PUMPED ENOUGH POISON GAS INTO HIM TO KILL A FOOTBALL TEAM --
--AND THREW HIM OFF THE ROOF.
NOBODY KNEW HIM THAT WELL. BUT HE'S DEAD, LIKE THE OTHERS. AND THEY'RE STARTIN' TO LOOK AT ME.
I'M THE ONE WAS PAID TO STOP THE KILLINGS, AFTER ALL. AND IT DON'T LOOK LIKE I DID IT, DOES IT?

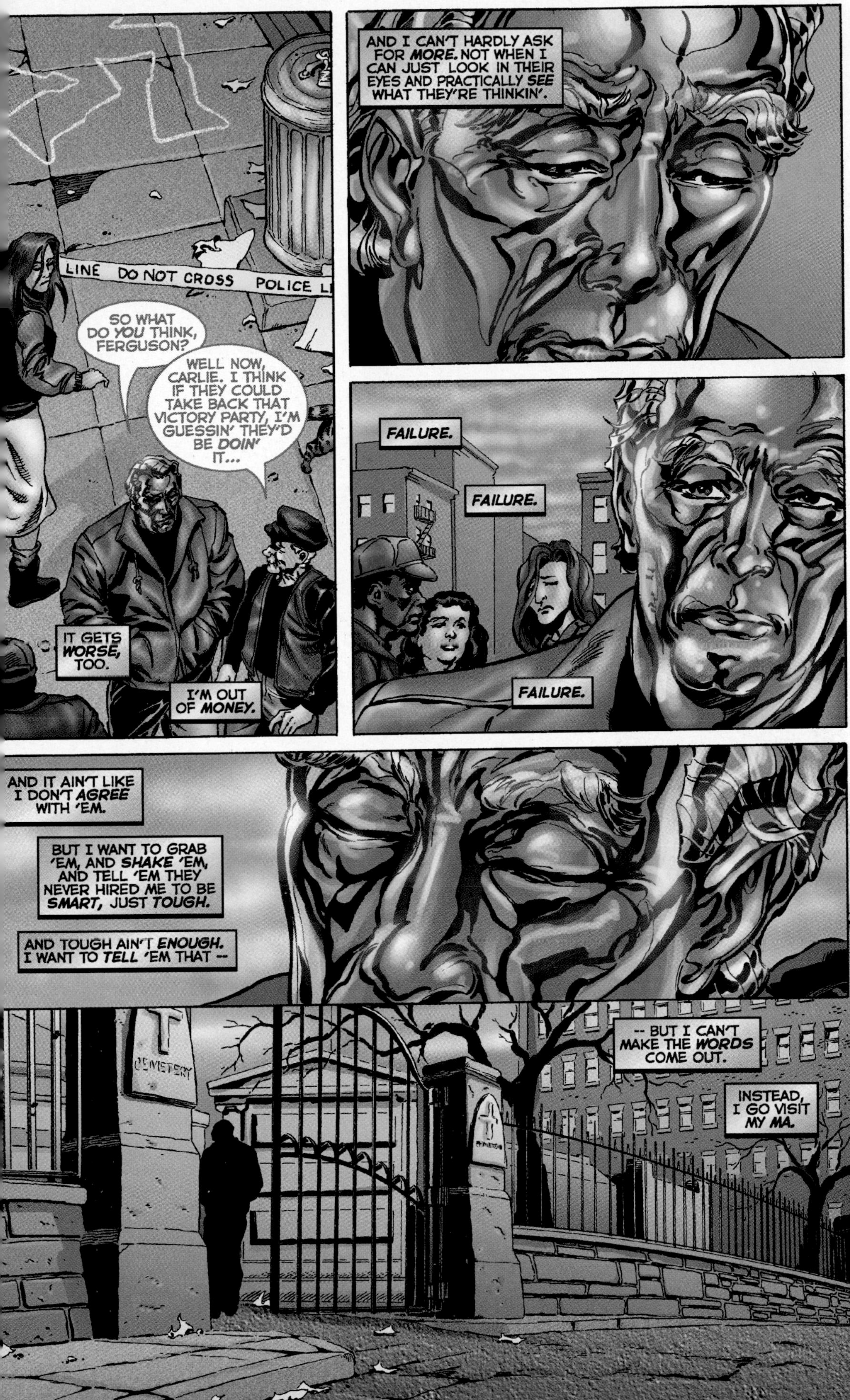
LINE DO NOT CROSS POLICE LI
SO WHAT DO YOU THINK, FERGUSON?
WELL NOW, CARLIE. I THINK IF THEY COULD TAKE BACK THAT VICTORY PARTY, I'M GUESSIN' THEY'D BE DOIN' IT...
IT GETS WORSE, TOO.
I'M OUT OF MONEY.
AND I CAN'T HARDLY ASK FOR MORE. NOT WHEN I CAN JUST LOOK IN THEIR EYES AND PRACTICALLY SEE WHAT THEY'RE THINKIN'.
FAILURE.
FAILURE.
FAILURE.
AND IT AIN'T LIKE I DON'T AGREE WITH 'EM.
BUT I WANT TO GRAB 'EM, AND SHAKE 'EM, AND TELL 'EM THEY NEVER HIRED ME TO BE SMART, JUST TOUGH.
AND TOUGH AIN'T ENOUGH. I WANT TO TELL 'EM THAT --
CEMETERY
-- BUT I CAN'T MAKE THE WORDS COME OUT.
INSTEAD, I GO VISIT MY MA.

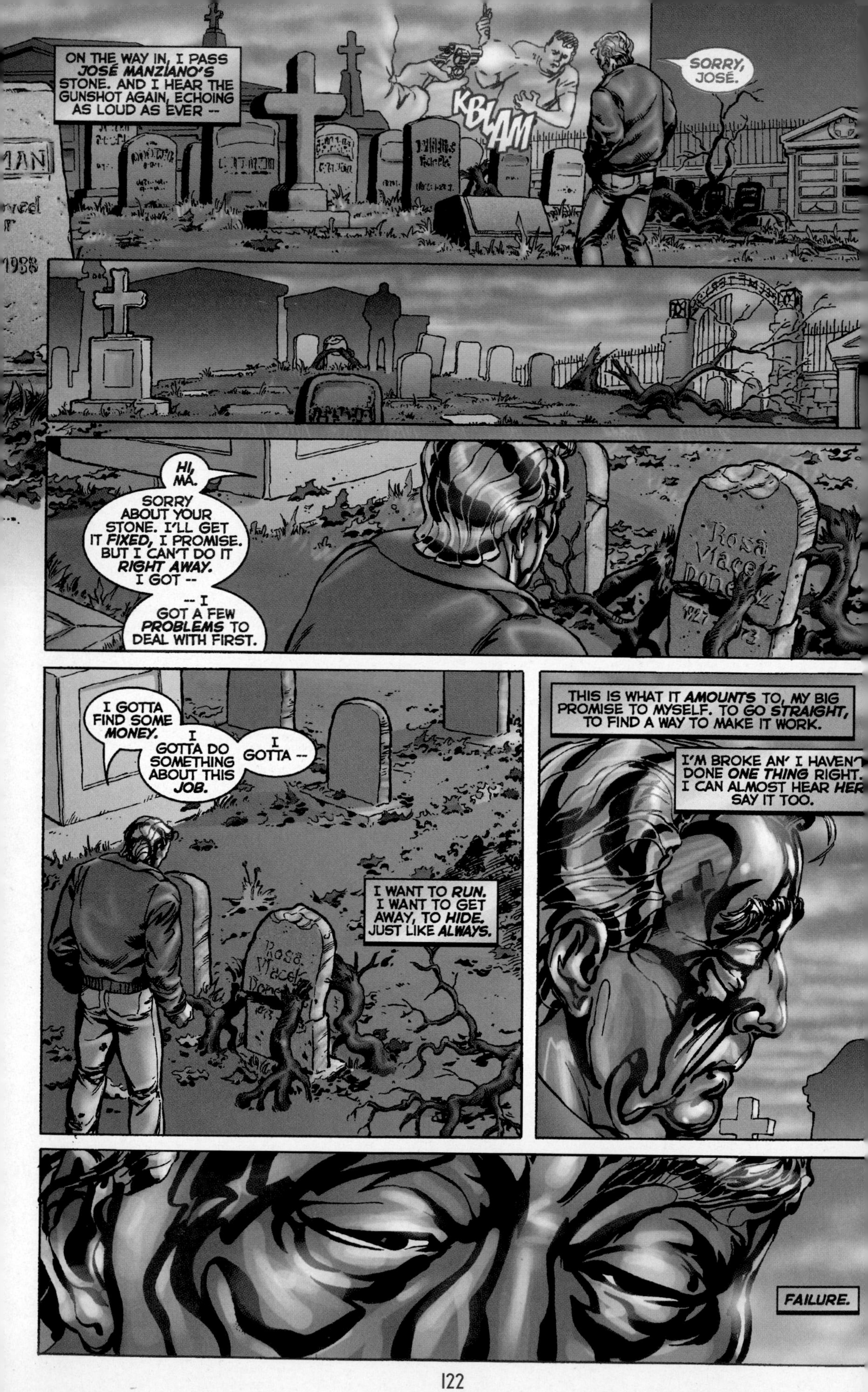

ON THE WAY IN, I PASS JOSÉ MANZIANO'S STONE. AND I HEAR THE GUNSHOT AGAIN, ECHOING AS LOUD AS EVER --
KBLAM
SORRY, JOSÉ.
HI, MA.
SORRY ABOUT YOUR STONE. I'LL GET IT FIXED, I PROMISE. BUT I CAN'T DO IT RIGHT AWAY. I GOT --
-- I GOT A FEW PROBLEMS TO DEAL WITH FIRST.
I GOTTA FIND SOME MONEY.
I GOTTA DO SOMETHING ABOUT THIS JOB.
I GOTTA --
I WANT TO RUN. I WANT TO GET AWAY, TO HIDE. JUST LIKE ALWAYS.
THIS IS WHAT IT AMOUNTS TO, MY BIG PROMISE TO MYSELF. TO GO STRAIGHT, TO FIND A WAY TO MAKE IT WORK.
I'M BROKE AN' I HAVEN' DONE ONE THING RIGHT. I CAN ALMOST HEAR HER SAY IT TOO.
FAILURE.

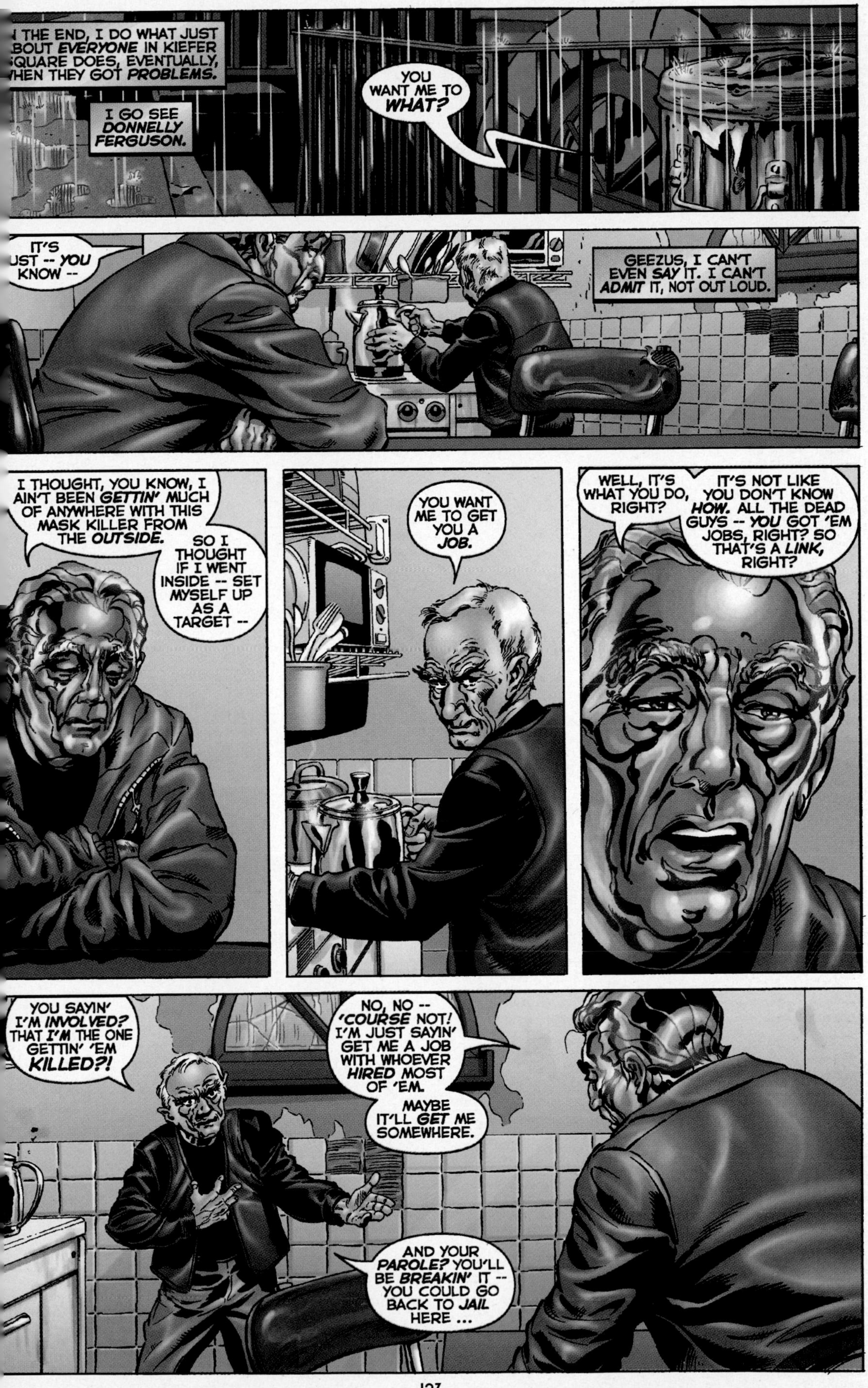

N THE END, I DO WHAT JUST
BOUT *EVERYONE* IN KIEFER
SQUARE DOES, EVENTUALLY,
WHEN THEY GOT *PROBLEMS.*
I GO SEE *DONNELLY FERGUSON.*
YOU WANT ME TO *WHAT?*
IT'S JUST -- *YOU* KNOW --
GEEZUS, I CAN'T EVEN *SAY* IT. I CAN'T *ADMIT* IT, NOT OUT LOUD.
I THOUGHT, YOU KNOW, I AIN'T BEEN *GETTIN'* MUCH OF ANYWHERE WITH THIS MASK KILLER FROM THE *OUTSIDE.*
SO I THOUGHT IF I WENT INSIDE -- SET MYSELF UP AS A TARGET --
YOU WANT ME TO GET YOU A *JOB.*
WELL, IT'S WHAT YOU DO, RIGHT?
IT'S NOT LIKE YOU DON'T KNOW *HOW.* ALL THE DEAD GUYS -- *YOU* GOT 'EM JOBS, RIGHT? SO THAT'S A *LINK,* RIGHT?
YOU SAYIN' I'M *INVOLVED?* THAT *I'M* THE ONE GETTIN' 'EM *KILLED?!*
NO, NO -- *'COURSE* NOT! I'M JUST SAYIN' GET ME A JOB WITH WHOEVER *HIRED* MOST OF 'EM.
MAYBE IT'LL *GET* ME SOMEWHERE.
AND YOUR *PAROLE?* YOU'LL BE *BREAKIN'* IT -- YOU COULD GO BACK TO *JAIL* HERE ...

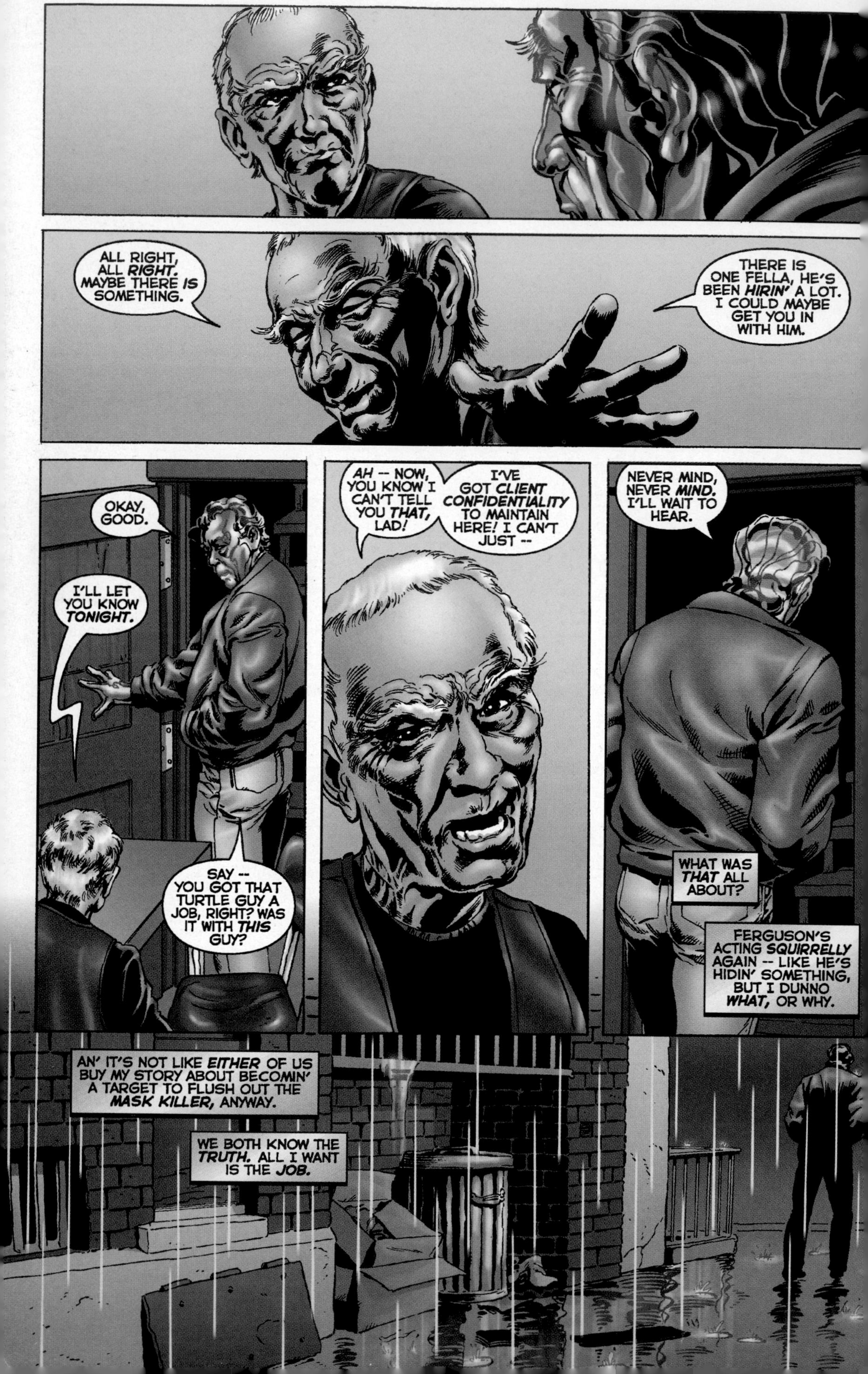
ALL RIGHT, ALL RIGHT. MAYBE THERE IS SOMETHING.
THERE IS ONE FELLA, HE'S BEEN HIRIN' A LOT. I COULD MAYBE GET YOU IN WITH HIM.
OKAY, GOOD.
I'LL LET YOU KNOW TONIGHT.
SAY -- YOU GOT THAT TURTLE GUY A JOB, RIGHT? WAS IT WITH THIS GUY?
AH -- NOW, YOU KNOW I CAN'T TELL YOU THAT, LAD!
I'VE GOT CLIENT CONFIDENTIALITY TO MAINTAIN HERE! I CAN'T JUST --
NEVER MIND, NEVER MIND. I'LL WAIT TO HEAR.
WHAT WAS THAT ALL ABOUT?
FERGUSON'S ACTING SQUIRRELLY AGAIN -- LIKE HE'S HIDIN' SOMETHING, BUT I DUNNO WHAT, OR WHY.
AN' IT'S NOT LIKE EITHER OF US BUY MY STORY ABOUT BECOMIN' A TARGET TO FLUSH OUT THE MASK KILLER, ANYWAY.
WE BOTH KNOW THE TRUTH. ALL I WANT IS THE JOB.

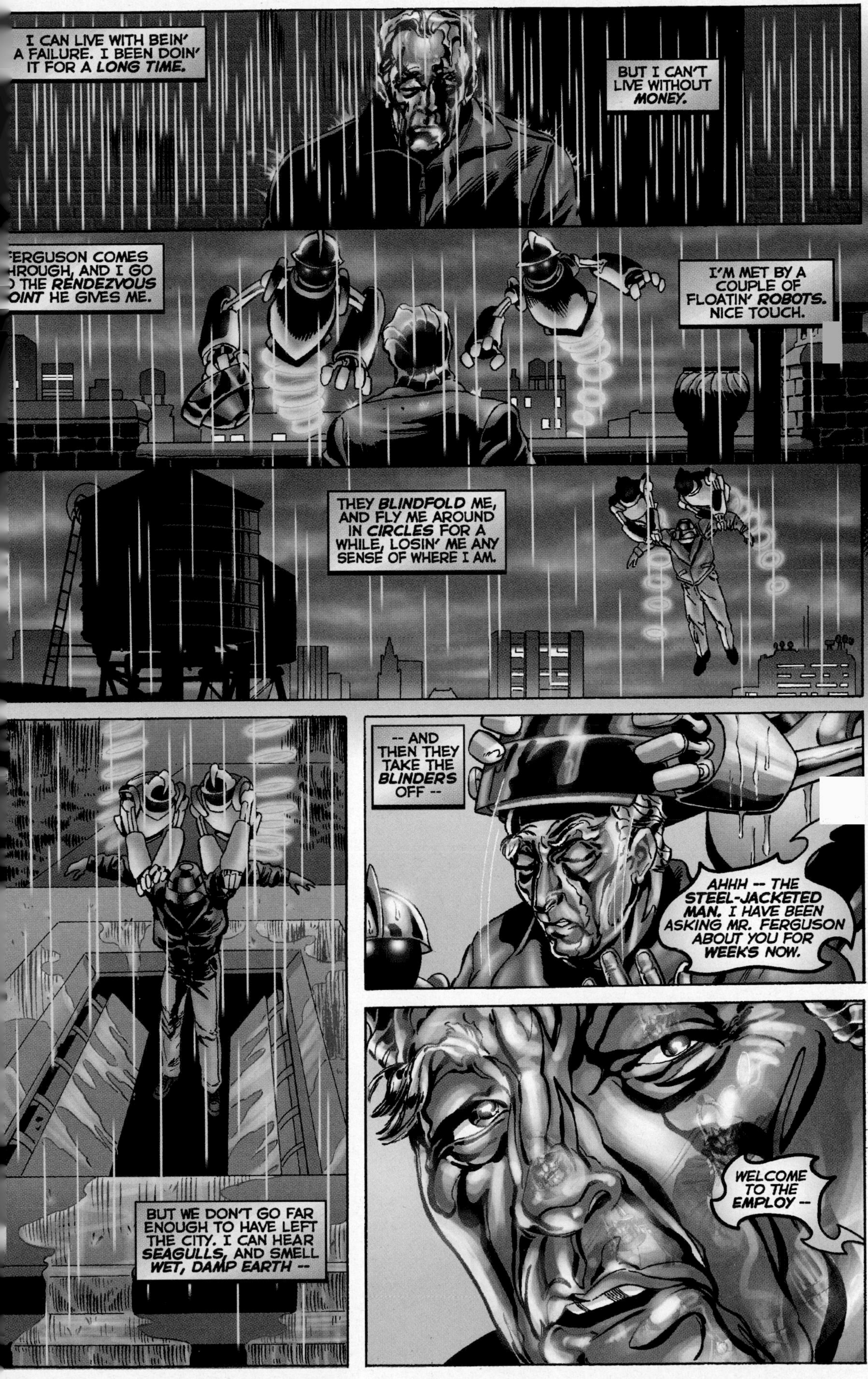
I CAN LIVE WITH BEIN' A FAILURE. I BEEN DOIN' IT FOR A LONG TIME.
BUT I CAN'T LIVE WITHOUT MONEY.
FERGUSON COMES THROUGH, AND I GO TO THE RENDEZVOUS POINT HE GIVES ME.
I'M MET BY A COUPLE OF FLOATIN' ROBOTS. NICE TOUCH.
THEY BLINDFOLD ME, AND FLY ME AROUND IN CIRCLES FOR A WHILE, LOSIN' ME ANY SENSE OF WHERE I AM.
BUT WE DON'T GO FAR ENOUGH TO HAVE LEFT THE CITY. I CAN HEAR SEAGULLS, AND SMELL WET, DAMP EARTH --
-- AND THEN THEY TAKE THE BLINDERS OFF --
AHHH -- THE STEEL-JACKETED MAN. I HAVE BEEN ASKING MR. FERGUSON ABOUT YOU FOR WEEKS NOW.
WELCOME TO THE EMPLOY --

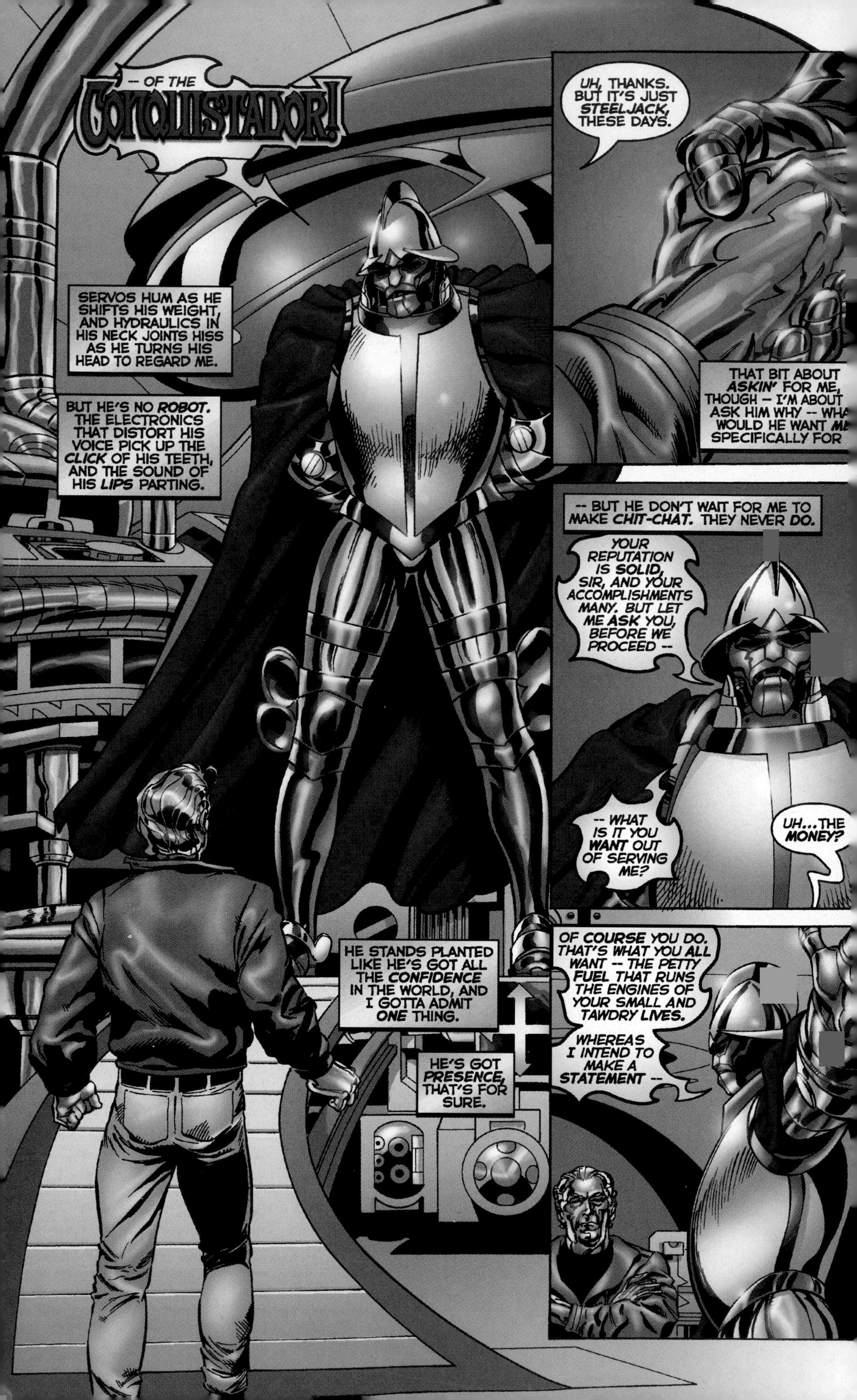
-- OF THE
CONQUISTADOR!
SERVOS HUM AS HE SHIFTS HIS WEIGHT, AND HYDRAULICS IN HIS NECK JOINTS HISS AS HE TURNS HIS HEAD TO REGARD ME.
BUT HE'S NO ROBOT. THE ELECTRONICS THAT DISTORT HIS VOICE PICK UP THE CLICK OF HIS TEETH, AND THE SOUND OF HIS LIPS PARTING.
HE STANDS PLANTED LIKE HE'S GOT ALL THE CONFIDENCE IN THE WORLD, AND I GOTTA ADMIT ONE THING.
HE'S GOT PRESENCE, THAT'S FOR SURE.
UH, THANKS. BUT IT'S JUST STEELJACK, THESE DAYS.
THAT BIT ABOUT ASKIN' FOR ME, THOUGH -- I'M ABOUT ASK HIM WHY -- WHA WOULD HE WANT M SPECIFICALLY FOR
-- BUT HE DON'T WAIT FOR ME TO MAKE CHIT-CHAT. THEY NEVER DO.
YOUR REPUTATION IS SOLID, SIR, AND YOUR ACCOMPLISHMENTS MANY. BUT LET ME ASK YOU, BEFORE WE PROCEED --
-- WHAT IS IT YOU WANT OUT OF SERVING ME?
UH...THE MONEY?
OF COURSE YOU DO. THAT'S WHAT YOU ALL WANT -- THE PETTY FUEL THAT RUNS THE ENGINES OF YOUR SMALL AND TAWDRY LIVES.
WHEREAS I INTEND TO MAKE A STATEMENT --

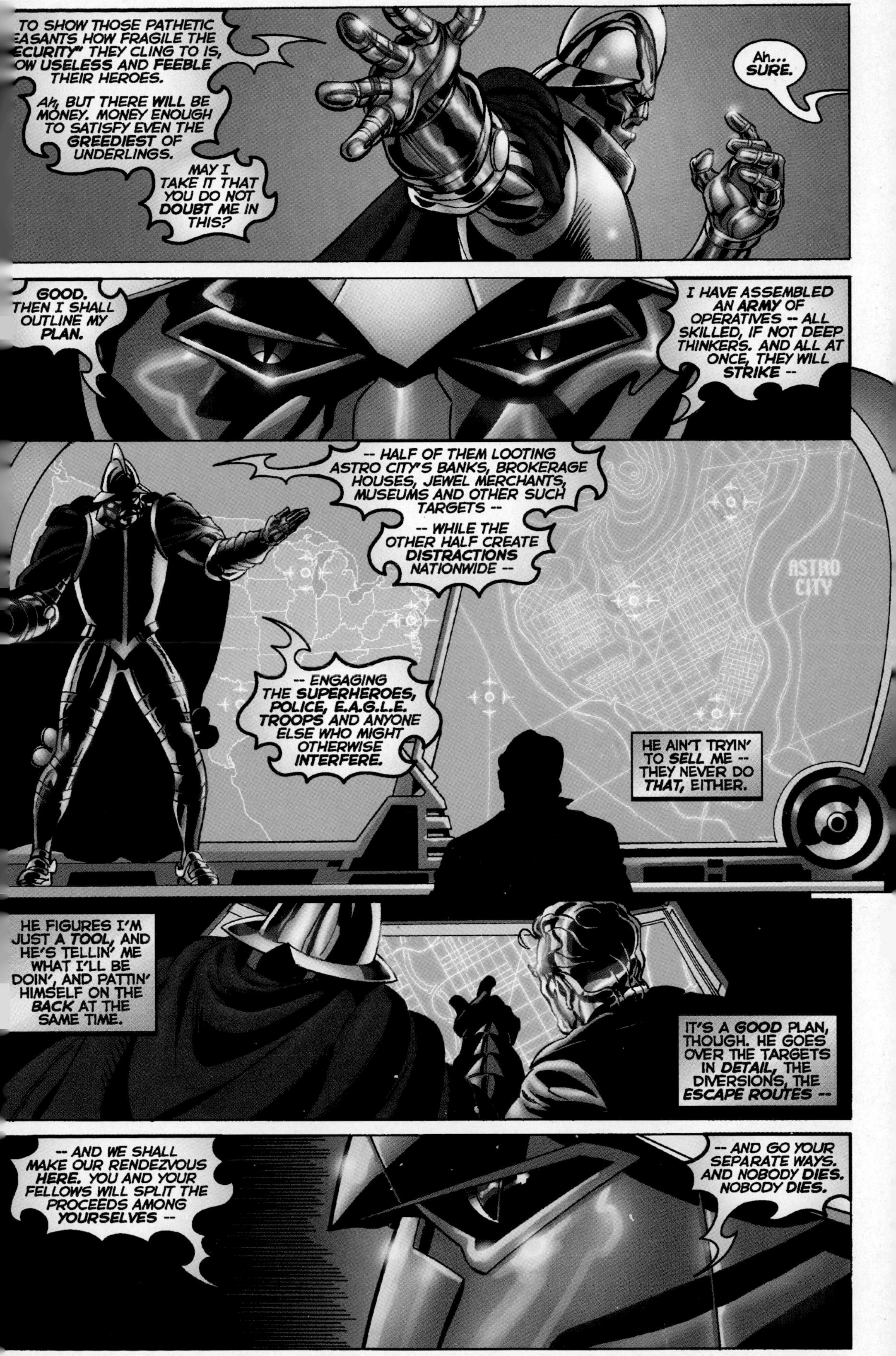
TO SHOW THOSE PATHETIC
EASANTS HOW FRAGILE THE
ECURITY" THEY CLING TO IS,
OW USELESS AND FEEBLE
THEIR HEROES.
AH, BUT THERE WILL BE MONEY. MONEY ENOUGH TO SATISFY EVEN THE GREEDIEST OF UNDERLINGS.
MAY I TAKE IT THAT YOU DO NOT DOUBT ME IN THIS?
Ah... SURE.
GOOD. THEN I SHALL OUTLINE MY PLAN.
I HAVE ASSEMBLED AN ARMY OF OPERATIVES -- ALL SKILLED, IF NOT DEEP THINKERS. AND ALL AT ONCE, THEY WILL STRIKE --
-- HALF OF THEM LOOTING ASTRO CITY'S BANKS, BROKERAGE HOUSES, JEWEL MERCHANTS, MUSEUMS AND OTHER SUCH TARGETS --
-- WHILE THE OTHER HALF CREATE DISTRACTIONS NATIONWIDE --
ASTRO CITY
-- ENGAGING THE SUPERHEROES, POLICE, E.A.G.L.E. TROOPS AND ANYONE ELSE WHO MIGHT OTHERWISE INTERFERE.
HE AIN'T TRYIN' TO SELL ME -- THEY NEVER DO THAT, EITHER.
HE FIGURES I'M JUST A TOOL, AND HE'S TELLIN' ME WHAT I'LL BE DOIN', AND PATTIN' HIMSELF ON THE BACK AT THE SAME TIME.
IT'S A GOOD PLAN, THOUGH. HE GOES OVER THE TARGETS IN DETAIL, THE DIVERSIONS, THE ESCAPE ROUTES --
-- AND WE SHALL MAKE OUR RENDEZVOUS HERE. YOU AND YOUR FELLOWS WILL SPLIT THE PROCEEDS AMONG YOURSELVES --
-- AND GO YOUR SEPARATE WAYS. AND NOBODY DIES. NOBODY DIES.

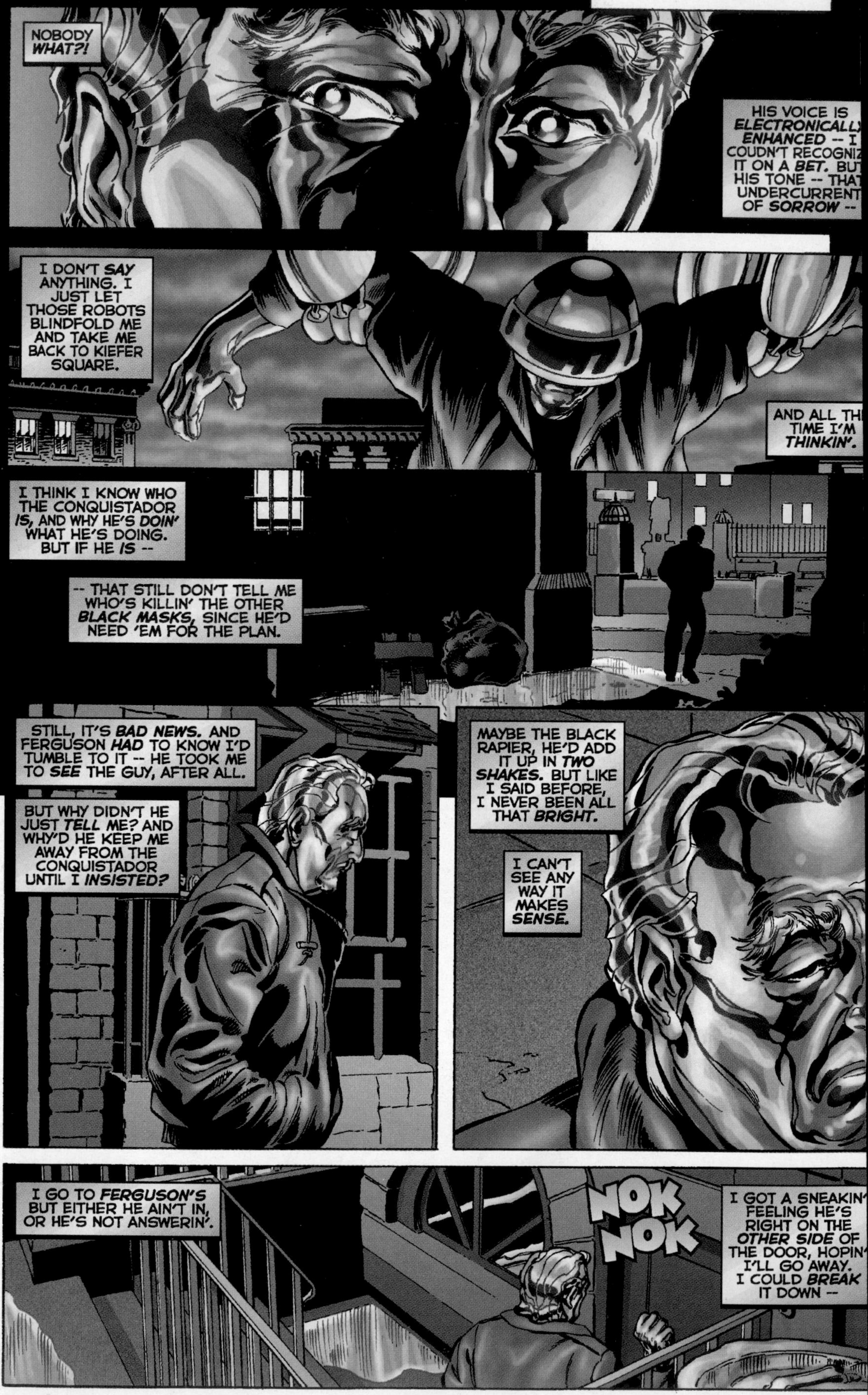
NOBODY WHAT?!
HIS VOICE IS ELECTRONICALLY ENHANCED -- I COUDN'T RECOGNIZ IT ON A BET. BUT HIS TONE -- THAT UNDERCURRENT OF SORROW --
I DON'T SAY ANYTHING. I JUST LET THOSE ROBOTS BLINDFOLD ME AND TAKE ME BACK TO KIEFER SQUARE.
AND ALL TH TIME I'M THINKIN'.
I THINK I KNOW WHO THE CONQUISTADOR IS, AND WHY HE'S DOIN' WHAT HE'S DOING. BUT IF HE IS --
-- THAT STILL DON'T TELL ME WHO'S KILLIN' THE OTHER BLACK MASKS, SINCE HE'D NEED 'EM FOR THE PLAN.
STILL, IT'S BAD NEWS. AND FERGUSON HAD TO KNOW I'D TUMBLE TO IT -- HE TOOK ME TO SEE THE GUY, AFTER ALL.
BUT WHY DIDN'T HE JUST TELL ME? AND WHY'D HE KEEP ME AWAY FROM THE CONQUISTADOR UNTIL I INSISTED?
MAYBE THE BLACK RAPIER, HE'D ADD IT UP IN TWO SHAKES. BUT LIKE I SAID BEFORE, I NEVER BEEN ALL THAT BRIGHT.
I CAN'T SEE ANY WAY IT MAKES SENSE.
I GO TO FERGUSON'S BUT EITHER HE AIN'T IN, OR HE'S NOT ANSWERIN'.
NOK NOK
I GOT A SNEAKIN' FEELING HE'S RIGHT ON THE OTHER SIDE OF THE DOOR, HOPIN' I'LL GO AWAY. I COULD BREAK IT DOWN --

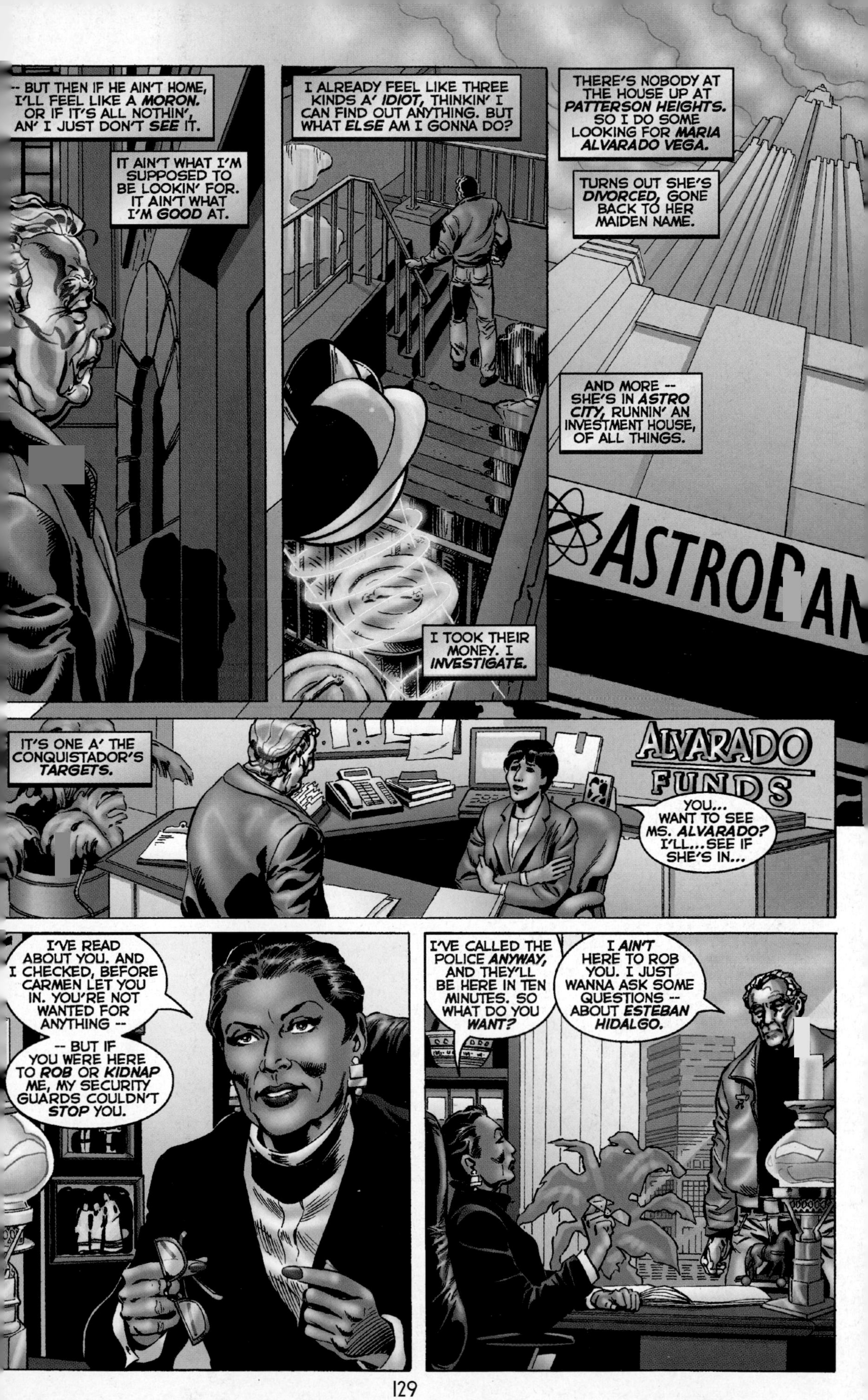
-- BUT THEN IF HE AIN'T HOME, I'LL FEEL LIKE A MORON. OR IF IT'S ALL NOTHIN', AN' I JUST DON'T SEE IT.
IT AIN'T WHAT I'M SUPPOSED TO BE LOOKIN' FOR. IT AIN'T WHAT I'M GOOD AT.
I ALREADY FEEL LIKE THREE KINDS A' IDIOT, THINKIN' I CAN FIND OUT ANYTHING. BUT WHAT ELSE AM I GONNA DO?
I TOOK THEIR MONEY. I INVESTIGATE.
THERE'S NOBODY AT THE HOUSE UP AT PATTERSON HEIGHTS. SO I DO SOME LOOKING FOR MARIA ALVARADO VEGA.
TURNS OUT SHE'S DIVORCED, GONE BACK TO HER MAIDEN NAME.
AND MORE -- SHE'S IN ASTRO CITY, RUNNIN' AN INVESTMENT HOUSE, OF ALL THINGS.
ASTROBAN
IT'S ONE A' THE CONQUISTADOR'S TARGETS.
ALVARADO FUNDS
YOU... WANT TO SEE MS. ALVARADO? I'LL...SEE IF SHE'S IN...
I'VE READ ABOUT YOU. AND I CHECKED, BEFORE CARMEN LET YOU IN. YOU'RE NOT WANTED FOR ANYTHING --
-- BUT IF YOU WERE HERE TO ROB OR KIDNAP ME, MY SECURITY GUARDS COULDN'T STOP YOU.
I'VE CALLED THE POLICE ANYWAY, AND THEY'LL BE HERE IN TEN MINUTES. SO WHAT DO YOU WANT?
I AIN'T HERE TO ROB YOU. I JUST WANNA ASK SOME QUESTIONS -- ABOUT ESTEBAN HIDALGO.

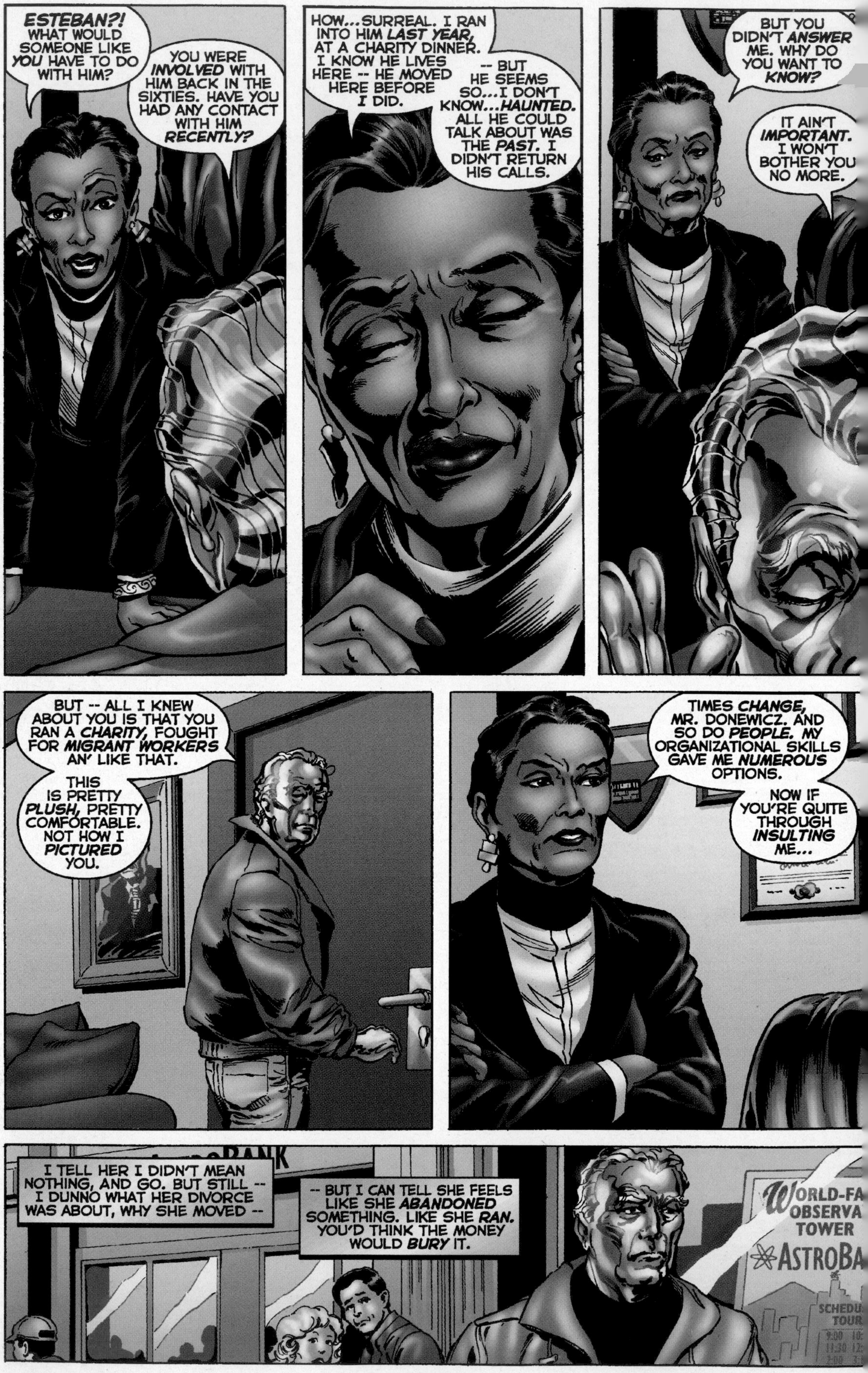
ESTEBAN?! WHAT WOULD SOMEONE LIKE YOU HAVE TO DO WITH HIM?
YOU WERE INVOLVED WITH HIM BACK IN THE SIXTIES. HAVE YOU HAD ANY CONTACT WITH HIM RECENTLY?
HOW... SURREAL. I RAN INTO HIM LAST YEAR, AT A CHARITY DINNER. I KNOW HE LIVES HERE -- HE MOVED HERE BEFORE I DID.
-- BUT HE SEEMS SO... I DON'T KNOW... HAUNTED. ALL HE COULD TALK ABOUT WAS THE PAST. I DIDN'T RETURN HIS CALLS.
BUT YOU DIDN'T ANSWER ME. WHY DO YOU WANT TO KNOW?
IT AIN'T IMPORTANT. I WON'T BOTHER YOU NO MORE.
BUT -- ALL I KNEW ABOUT YOU IS THAT YOU RAN A CHARITY, FOUGHT FOR MIGRANT WORKERS AN' LIKE THAT.
THIS IS PRETTY PLUSH, PRETTY COMFORTABLE. NOT HOW I PICTURED YOU.
TIMES CHANGE, MR. DONEWICZ. AND SO DO PEOPLE. MY ORGANIZATIONAL SKILLS GAVE ME NUMEROUS OPTIONS.
NOW IF YOU'RE QUITE THROUGH INSULTING ME...
I TELL HER I DIDN'T MEAN NOTHING, AND GO. BUT STILL -- I DUNNO WHAT HER DIVORCE WAS ABOUT, WHY SHE MOVED --
-- BUT I CAN TELL SHE FEELS LIKE SHE ABANDONED SOMETHING. LIKE SHE RAN. YOU'D THINK THE MONEY WOULD BURY IT.
TOWER

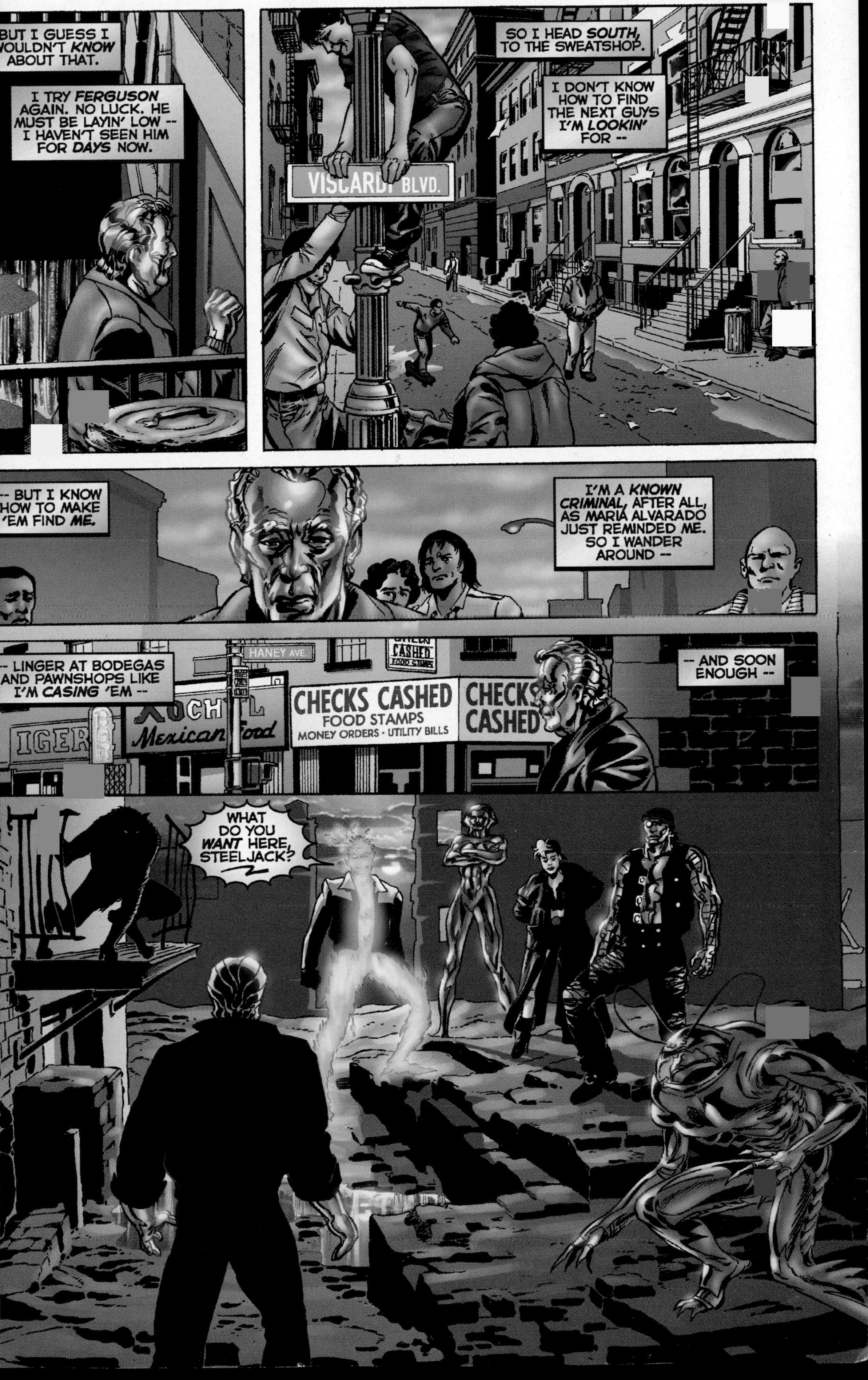

BUT I GUESS I WOULDN'T KNOW ABOUT THAT.
I TRY FERGUSON AGAIN. NO LUCK. HE MUST BE LAYIN' LOW -- I HAVEN'T SEEN HIM FOR DAYS NOW.
SO I HEAD SOUTH, TO THE SWEATSHOP.
I DON'T KNOW HOW TO FIND THE NEXT GUYS I'M LOOKIN' FOR --
VISCARDI BLVD.
-- BUT I KNOW HOW TO MAKE 'EM FIND ME.
I'M A KNOWN CRIMINAL, AFTER ALL, AS MARÍA ALVARADO JUST REMINDED ME. SO I WANDER AROUND --
-- LINGER AT BODEGAS AND PAWNSHOPS LIKE I'M CASING 'EM --
HANEY AVE.
CASHED
CHECKS CASHED
FOOD STAMPS
MONEY ORDERS · UTILITY BILLS
CHECKS CASHED
Mexican Food
-- AND SOON ENOUGH --
WHAT DO YOU WANT HERE, STEELJACK?

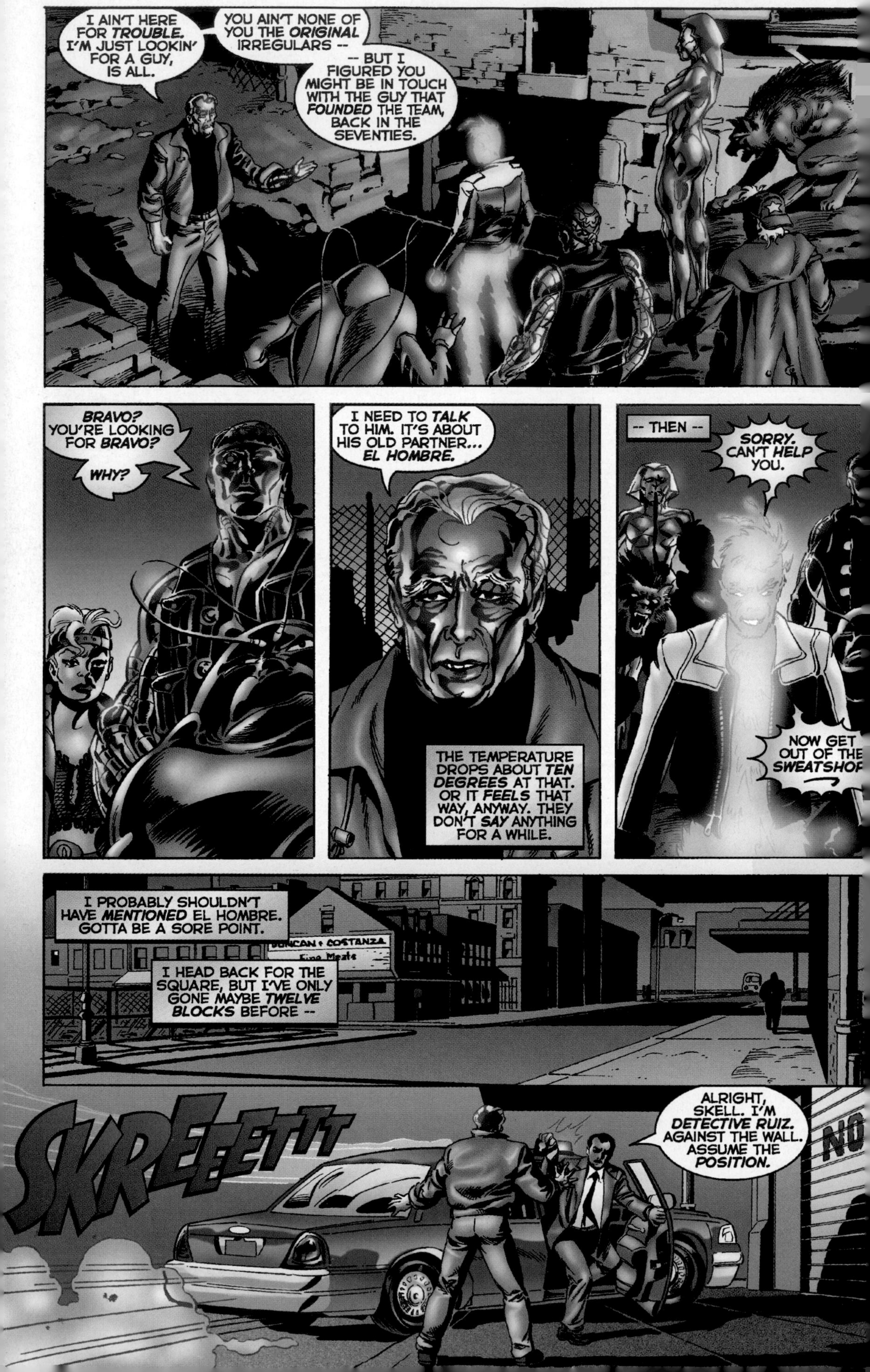

I AIN'T HERE FOR TROUBLE. I'M JUST LOOKIN' FOR A GUY, IS ALL.
YOU AIN'T NONE OF YOU THE ORIGINAL IRREGULARS --
-- BUT I FIGURED YOU MIGHT BE IN TOUCH WITH THE GUY THAT FOUNDED THE TEAM, BACK IN THE SEVENTIES.
BRAVO? YOU'RE LOOKING FOR BRAVO?
WHY?
I NEED TO TALK TO HIM. IT'S ABOUT HIS OLD PARTNER... EL HOMBRE.
THE TEMPERATURE DROPS ABOUT TEN DEGREES AT THAT. OR IT FEELS THAT WAY, ANYWAY. THEY DON'T SAY ANYTHING FOR A WHILE.
-- THEN --
SORRY. CAN'T HELP YOU.
NOW GET OUT OF THE SWEATSHOP
I PROBABLY SHOULDN'T HAVE MENTIONED EL HOMBRE. GOTTA BE A SORE POINT.
DUNCAN + COSTANZA
Fine Meats
I HEAD BACK FOR THE SQUARE, BUT I'VE ONLY GONE MAYBE TWELVE BLOCKS BEFORE --
SKREEEETTT
ALRIGHT, SKELL. I'M DETECTIVE RUIZ. AGAINST THE WALL. ASSUME THE POSITION.

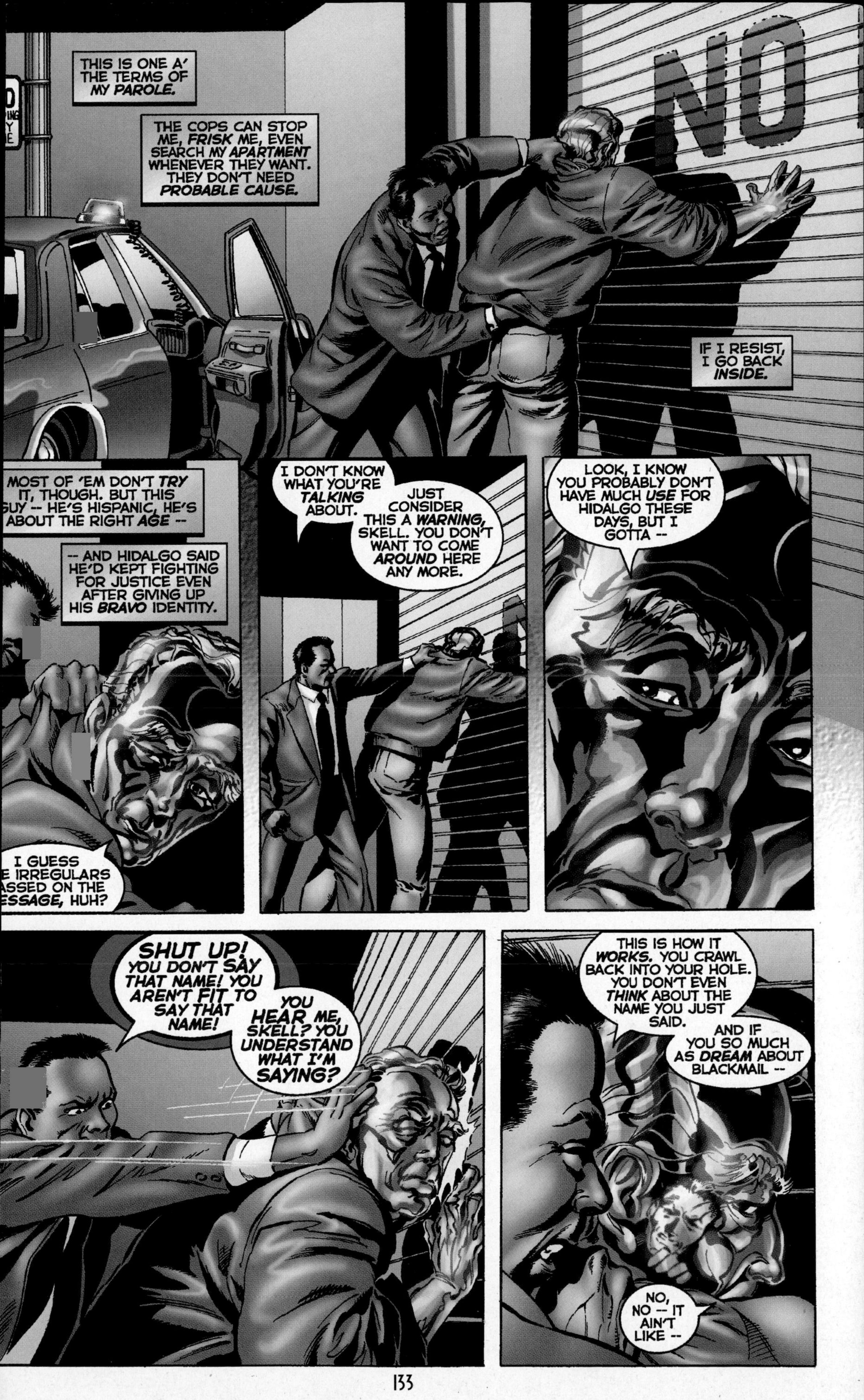
THIS IS ONE A' THE TERMS OF MY PAROLE.
THE COPS CAN STOP ME, FRISK ME, EVEN SEARCH MY APARTMENT WHENEVER THEY WANT. THEY DON'T NEED PROBABLE CAUSE.
IF I RESIST, I GO BACK INSIDE.
MOST OF 'EM DON'T TRY IT, THOUGH. BUT THIS UY -- HE'S HISPANIC, HE'S ABOUT THE RIGHT AGE --
-- AND HIDALGO SAID HE'D KEPT FIGHTING FOR JUSTICE EVEN AFTER GIVING UP HIS BRAVO IDENTITY.
I GUESS E IRREGULARS ASSED ON THE ESSAGE, HUH?
I DON'T KNOW WHAT YOU'RE TALKING ABOUT.
JUST CONSIDER THIS A WARNING, SKELL. YOU DON'T WANT TO COME AROUND HERE ANY MORE.
LOOK, I KNOW YOU PROBABLY DON'T HAVE MUCH USE FOR HIDALGO THESE DAYS, BUT I GOTTA --
SHUT UP! YOU DON'T SAY THAT NAME! YOU AREN'T FIT TO SAY THAT NAME!
YOU HEAR ME, SKELL? YOU UNDERSTAND WHAT I'M SAYING?
THIS IS HOW IT WORKS. YOU CRAWL BACK INTO YOUR HOLE. YOU DON'T EVEN THINK ABOUT THE NAME YOU JUST SAID.
AND IF YOU SO MUCH AS DREAM ABOUT BLACKMAIL --
NO, NO -- IT AIN'T LIKE --

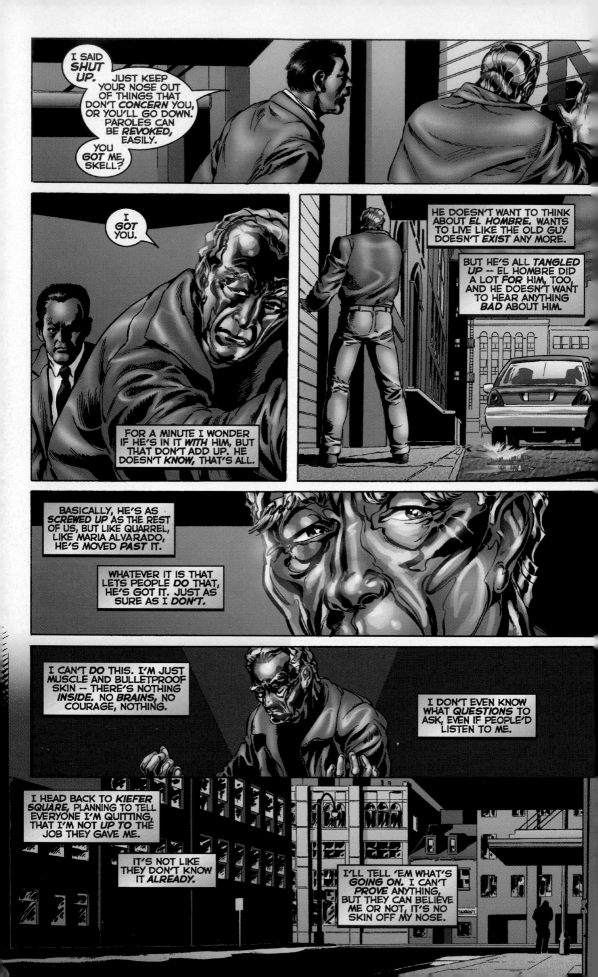

I SAID **SHUT UP.** JUST KEEP YOUR NOSE OUT OF THINGS THAT DON'T **CONCERN** YOU, OR YOU'LL GO DOWN. PAROLES CAN BE **REVOKED,** EASILY.

YOU **GOT ME, SKELL?**

I **GOT YOU.**

HE DOESN'T WANT TO THINK ABOUT **EL HOMBRE.** WANTS TO LIVE LIKE THE OLD GUY DOESN'T **EXIST** ANY MORE.

BUT HE'S ALL **TANGLED UP** -- EL HOMBRE DID A LOT **FOR** HIM, TOO, AND HE DOESN'T WANT TO HEAR ANYTHING **BAD** ABOUT HIM.

FOR A MINUTE I WONDER IF HE'S IN IT **WITH** HIM, BUT THAT DON'T ADD UP. HE DOESN'T **KNOW,** THAT'S ALL.

BASICALLY, HE'S AS **SCREWED UP** AS THE REST OF US, BUT LIKE QUARREL, LIKE MARIA ALVARADO, HE'S MOVED **PAST** IT.

WHATEVER IT IS THAT LETS PEOPLE **DO** THAT, HE'S GOT IT. JUST AS SURE AS I **DON'T.**

I CAN'T **DO** THIS. I'M JUST MUSCLE AND BULLETPROOF SKIN -- THERE'S NOTHING **INSIDE.** NO **BRAINS,** NO COURAGE, NOTHING.

I DON'T EVEN KNOW WHAT **QUESTIONS** TO ASK, EVEN IF PEOPLE'D LISTEN TO ME.

I HEAD BACK TO **KIEFER SQUARE,** PLANNING TO TELL EVERYONE I'M QUITTING, THAT I'M NOT **UP** TO THE JOB THEY GAVE ME.

IT'S NOT LIKE THEY DON'T KNOW IT **ALREADY.**

I'LL TELL 'EM WHAT'S **GOING ON.** I CAN'T **PROVE** ANYTHING, BUT THEY CAN BELIEVE ME OR NOT, IT'S NO SKIN OFF MY NOSE.

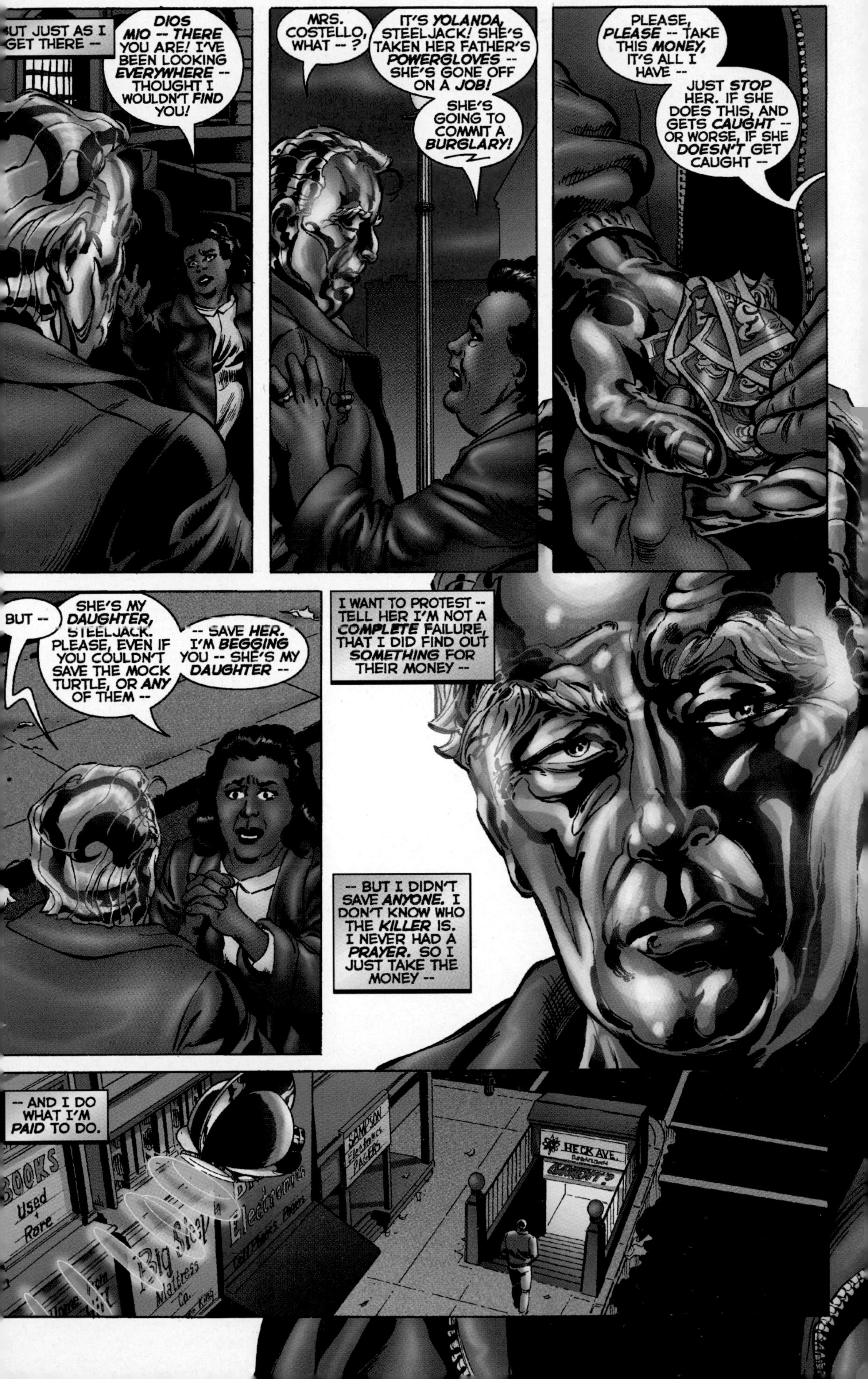
BUT JUST AS I GET THERE --
DIOS MIO -- THERE YOU ARE! I'VE BEEN LOOKING EVERYWHERE -- THOUGHT I WOULDN'T FIND YOU!
MRS. COSTELLO, WHAT -- ?
IT'S YOLANDA, STEELJACK! SHE'S TAKEN HER FATHER'S POWERGLOVES -- SHE'S GONE OFF ON A JOB!
SHE'S GOING TO COMMIT A BURGLARY!
PLEASE, PLEASE -- TAKE THIS MONEY, IT'S ALL I HAVE --
JUST STOP HER. IF SHE DOES THIS, AND GETS CAUGHT -- OR WORSE, IF SHE DOESN'T GET CAUGHT --
BUT --
SHE'S MY DAUGHTER, STEELJACK. PLEASE, EVEN IF YOU COULDN'T SAVE THE MOCK TURTLE, OR ANY OF THEM --
-- SAVE HER. I'M BEGGING YOU -- SHE'S MY DAUGHTER --
I WANT TO PROTEST -- TELL HER I'M NOT A COMPLETE FAILURE, THAT I DID FIND OUT SOMETHING FOR THEIR MONEY --
-- BUT I DIDN'T SAVE ANYONE. I DON'T KNOW WHO THE KILLER IS. I NEVER HAD A PRAYER. SO I JUST TAKE THE MONEY --
-- AND I DO WHAT I'M PAID TO DO.
BOOKS Used + Rare
SAMPSON Electronics PAGERS
HECK AVE.
Big Sleep Mattress Co.

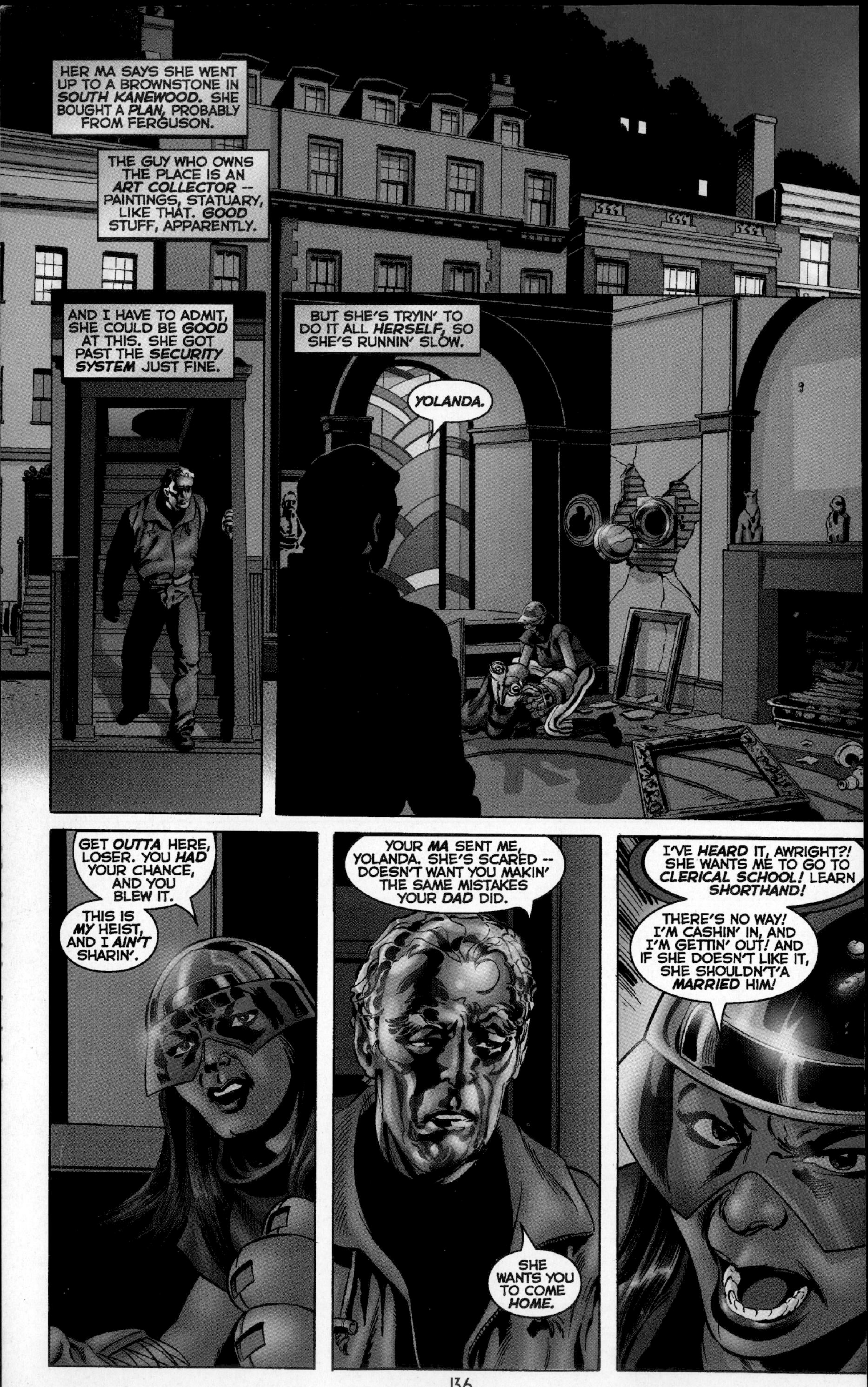
HER MA SAYS SHE WENT UP TO A BROWNSTONE IN SOUTH KANEWOOD. SHE BOUGHT A PLAN, PROBABLY FROM FERGUSON.
THE GUY WHO OWNS THE PLACE IS AN ART COLLECTOR -- PAINTINGS, STATUARY, LIKE THAT. GOOD STUFF, APPARENTLY.
AND I HAVE TO ADMIT, SHE COULD BE GOOD AT THIS. SHE GOT PAST THE SECURITY SYSTEM JUST FINE.
BUT SHE'S TRYIN' TO DO IT ALL HERSELF, SO SHE'S RUNNIN' SLOW.
YOLANDA.
GET OUTTA HERE, LOSER. YOU HAD YOUR CHANCE, AND YOU BLEW IT.
THIS IS MY HEIST, AND I AIN'T SHARIN'.
YOUR MA SENT ME, YOLANDA. SHE'S SCARED -- DOESN'T WANT YOU MAKIN' THE SAME MISTAKES YOUR DAD DID.
SHE WANTS YOU TO COME HOME.
I'VE HEARD IT, AWRIGHT?! SHE WANTS ME TO GO TO CLERICAL SCHOOL! LEARN SHORTHAND!
THERE'S NO WAY! I'M CASHIN' IN, AND I'M GETTIN' OUT! AND IF SHE DOESN'T LIKE IT, SHE SHOULDN'T'A MARRIED HIM!

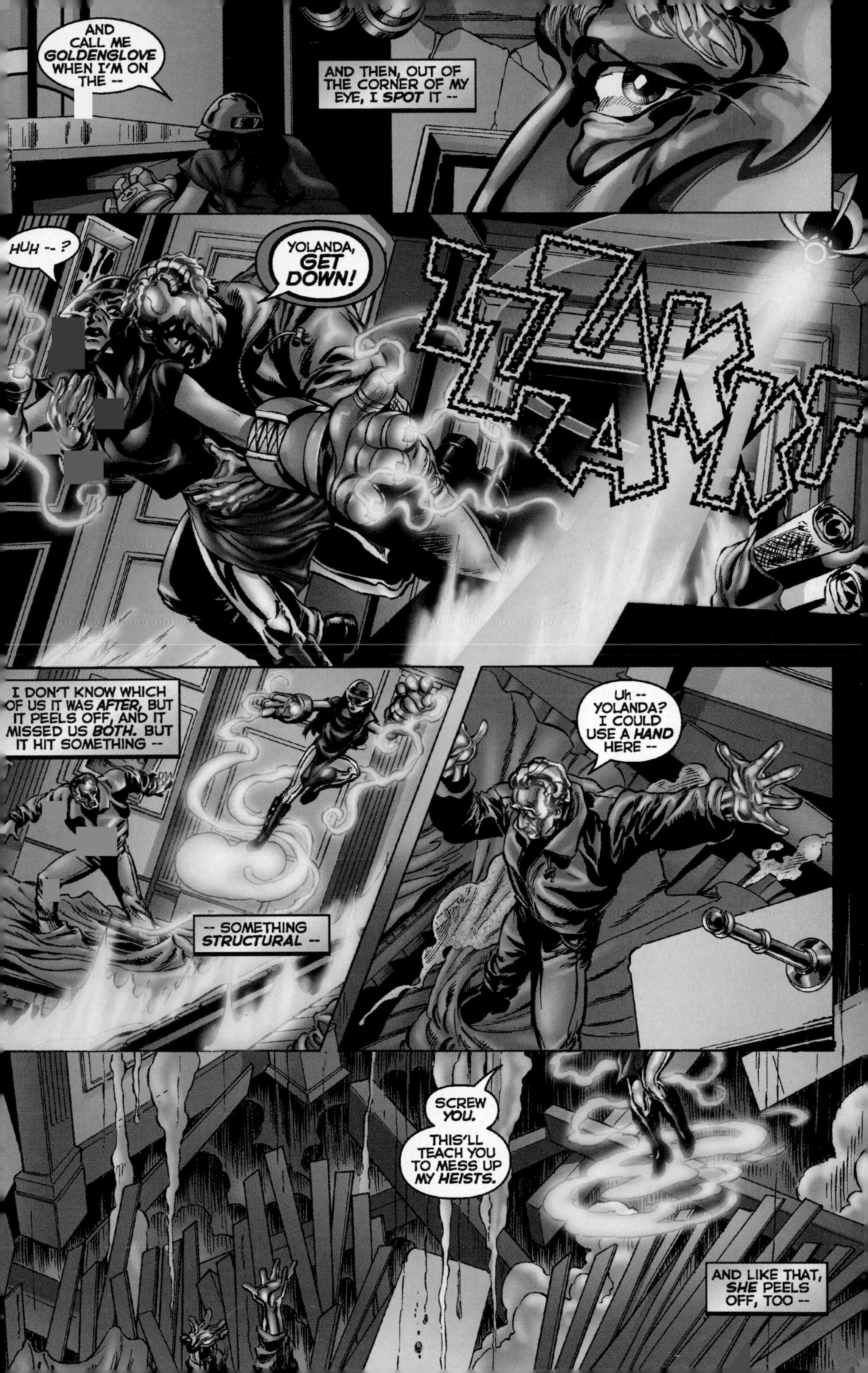
AND CALL ME GOLDENGLOVE WHEN I'M ON THE --
AND THEN, OUT OF THE CORNER OF MY EYE, I SPOT IT --
HUH -- ?
YOLANDA, GET DOWN!
I DON'T KNOW WHICH OF US IT WAS AFTER, BUT IT PEELS OFF, AND IT MISSED US BOTH. BUT IT HIT SOMETHING --
-- SOMETHING STRUCTURAL --
Uh -- YOLANDA? I COULD USE A HAND HERE --
SCREW YOU.
THIS'LL TEACH YOU TO MESS UP MY HEISTS.
AND LIKE THAT, SHE PEELS OFF, TOO --

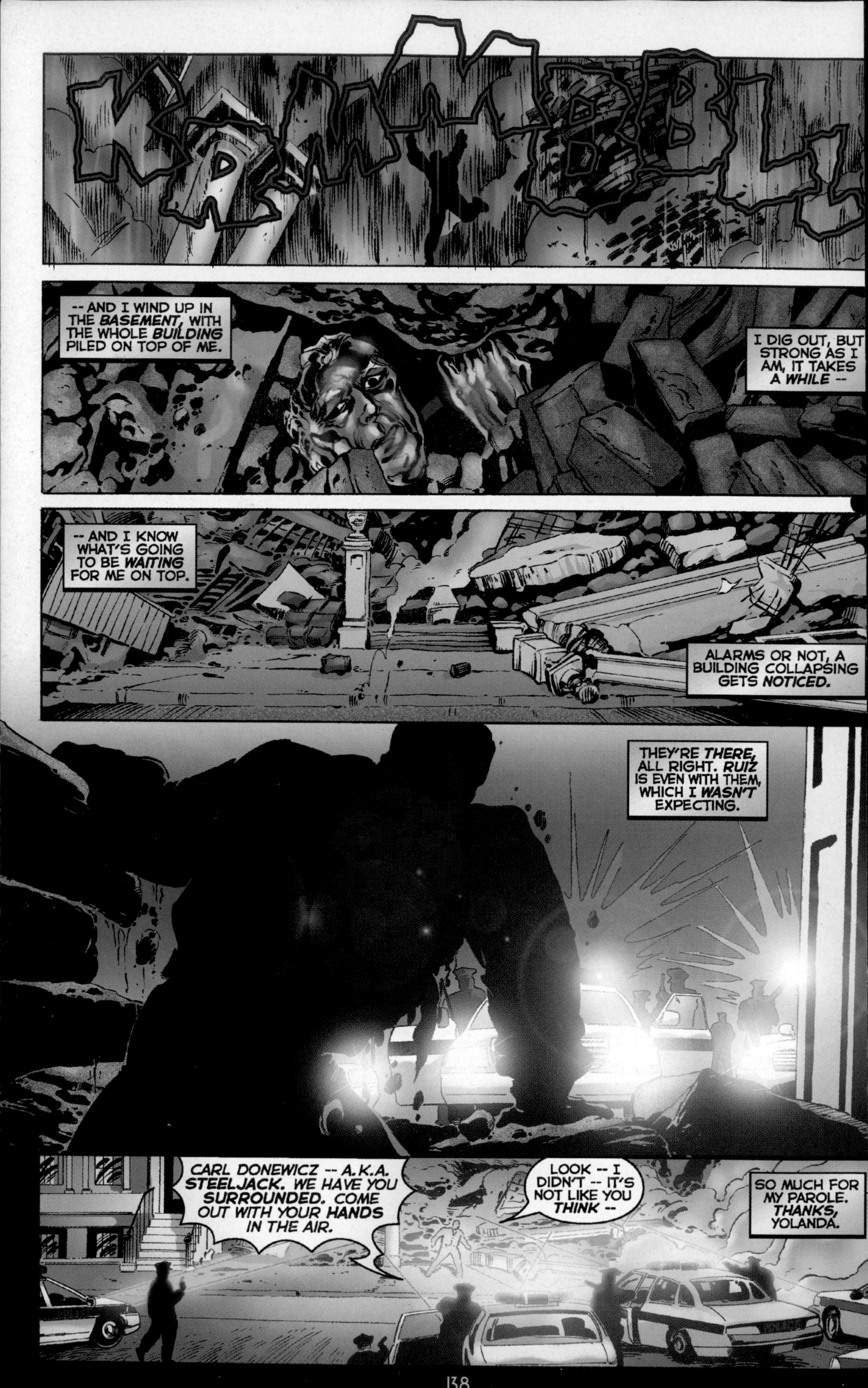
-- AND I WIND UP IN THE BASEMENT, WITH THE WHOLE BUILDING PILED ON TOP OF ME.
I DIG OUT, BUT STRONG AS I AM, IT TAKES A WHILE --
-- AND I KNOW WHAT'S GOING TO BE WAITING FOR ME ON TOP.
ALARMS OR NOT, A BUILDING COLLAPSING GETS NOTICED.
THEY'RE THERE, ALL RIGHT. RUIZ IS EVEN WITH THEM, WHICH I WASN'T EXPECTING.
CARL DONEWICZ -- A.K.A. STEELJACK. WE HAVE YOU SURROUNDED. COME OUT WITH YOUR HANDS IN THE AIR.
LOOK -- I DIDN'T -- IT'S NOT LIKE YOU THINK --
SO MUCH FOR MY PAROLE. THANKS, YOLANDA.

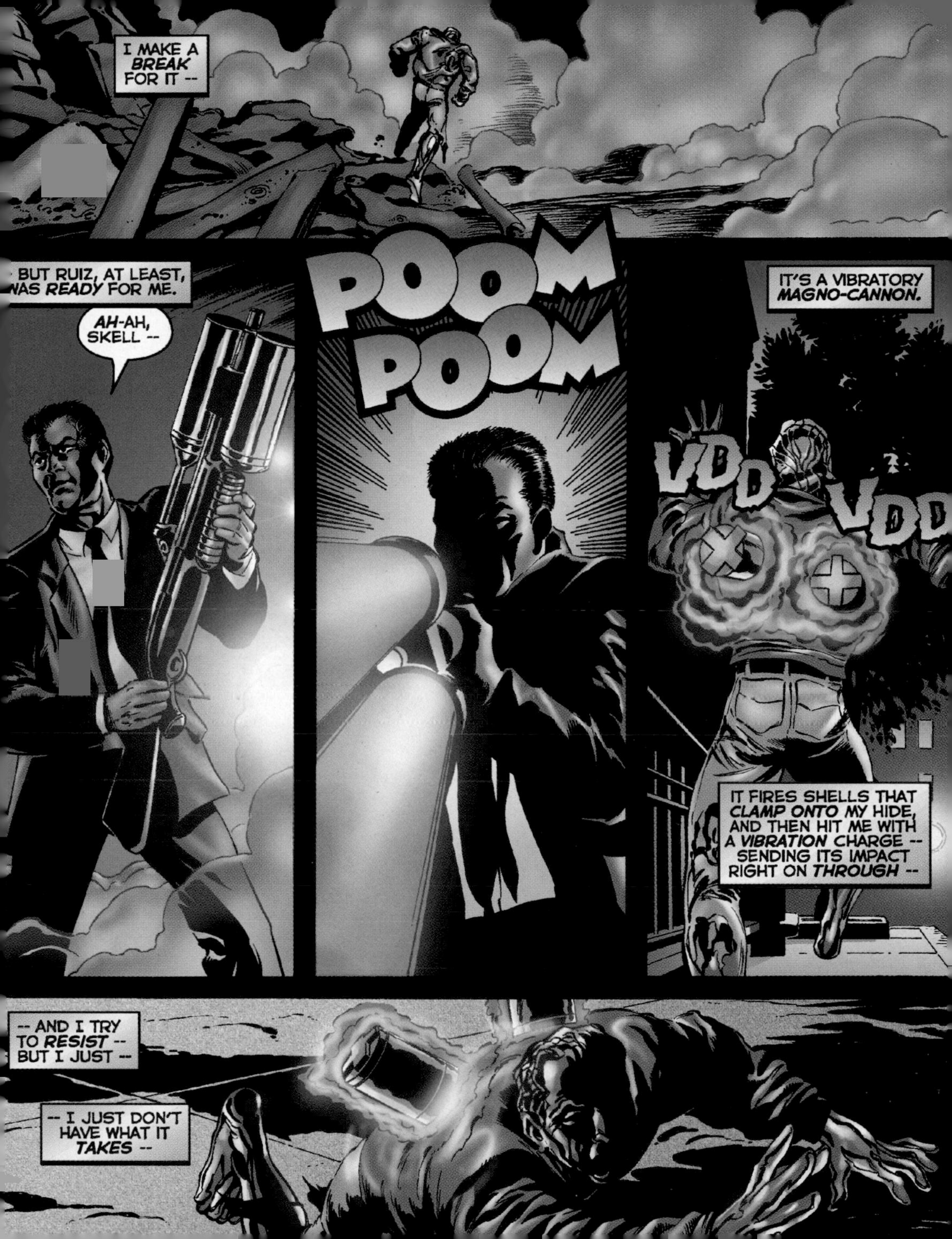
I MAKE A BREAK FOR IT --
BUT RUIZ, AT LEAST, WAS READY FOR ME.
AH-AH, SKELL --
POOM POOM
IT'S A VIBRATORY MAGNO-CANNON.
VDD VDD
IT FIRES SHELLS THAT CLAMP ONTO MY HIDE, AND THEN HIT ME WITH A VIBRATION CHARGE -- SENDING ITS IMPACT RIGHT ON THROUGH --
-- AND I TRY TO RESIST -- BUT I JUST --
-- I JUST DON'T HAVE WHAT IT TAKES --

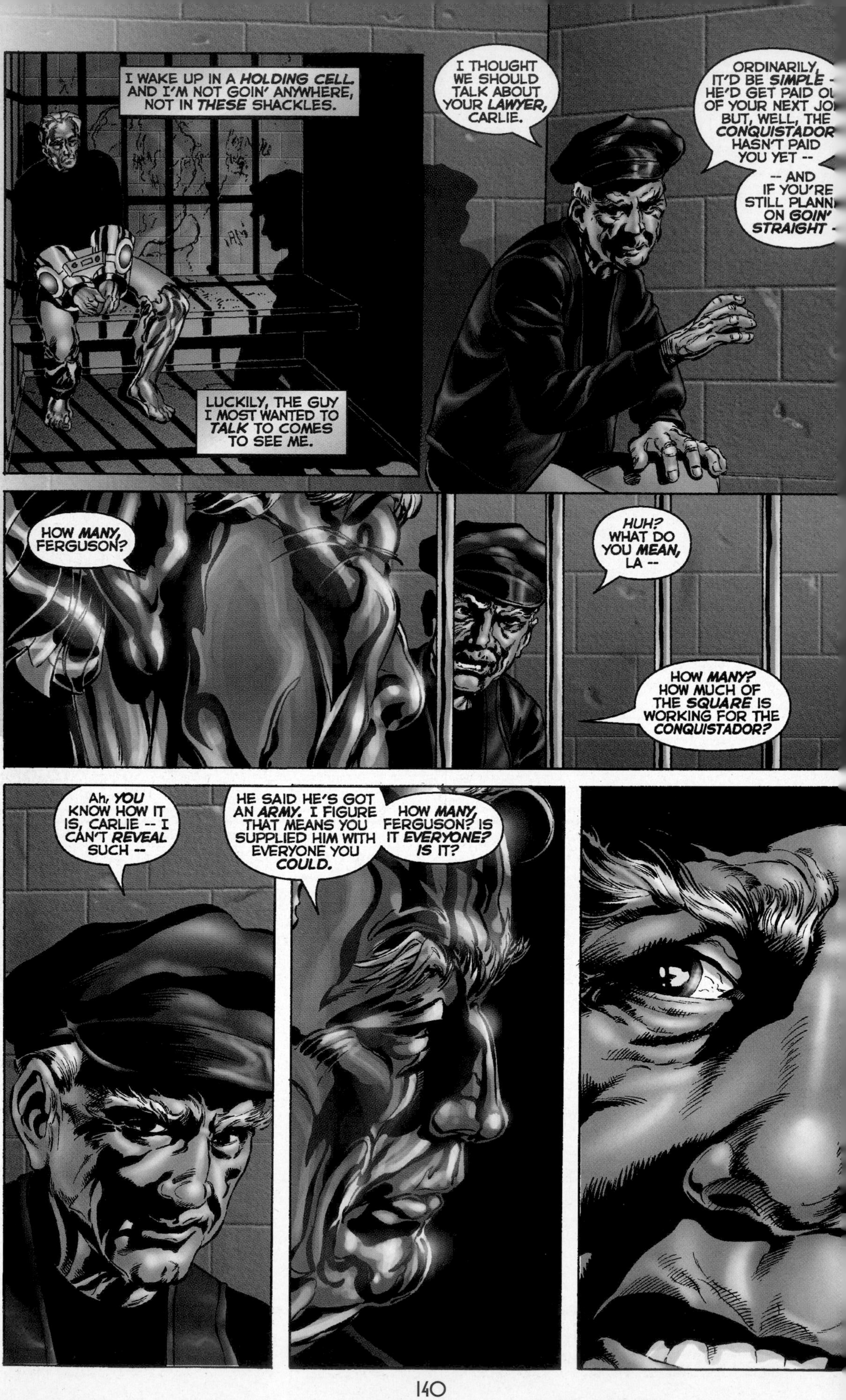

I WAKE UP IN A HOLDING CELL, AND I'M NOT GOIN' ANYWHERE, NOT IN THESE SHACKLES.
LUCKILY, THE GUY I MOST WANTED TO TALK TO COMES TO SEE ME.
I THOUGHT WE SHOULD TALK ABOUT YOUR LAWYER, CARLIE.
ORDINARILY, IT'D BE SIMPLE -- HE'D GET PAID OU OF YOUR NEXT JO BUT, WELL, THE CONQUISTADOR HASN'T PAID YOU YET --
-- AND IF YOU'RE STILL PLANN ON GOIN' STRAIGHT -
HOW MANY, FERGUSON?
HUH? WHAT DO YOU MEAN, LA --
HOW MANY? HOW MUCH OF THE SQUARE IS WORKING FOR THE CONQUISTADOR?
Ah, YOU KNOW HOW IT IS, CARLIE -- I CAN'T REVEAL SUCH --
HE SAID HE'S GOT AN ARMY. I FIGURE THAT MEANS YOU SUPPLIED HIM WITH EVERYONE YOU COULD.
HOW MANY, FERGUSON? IS IT EVERYONE? IS IT?

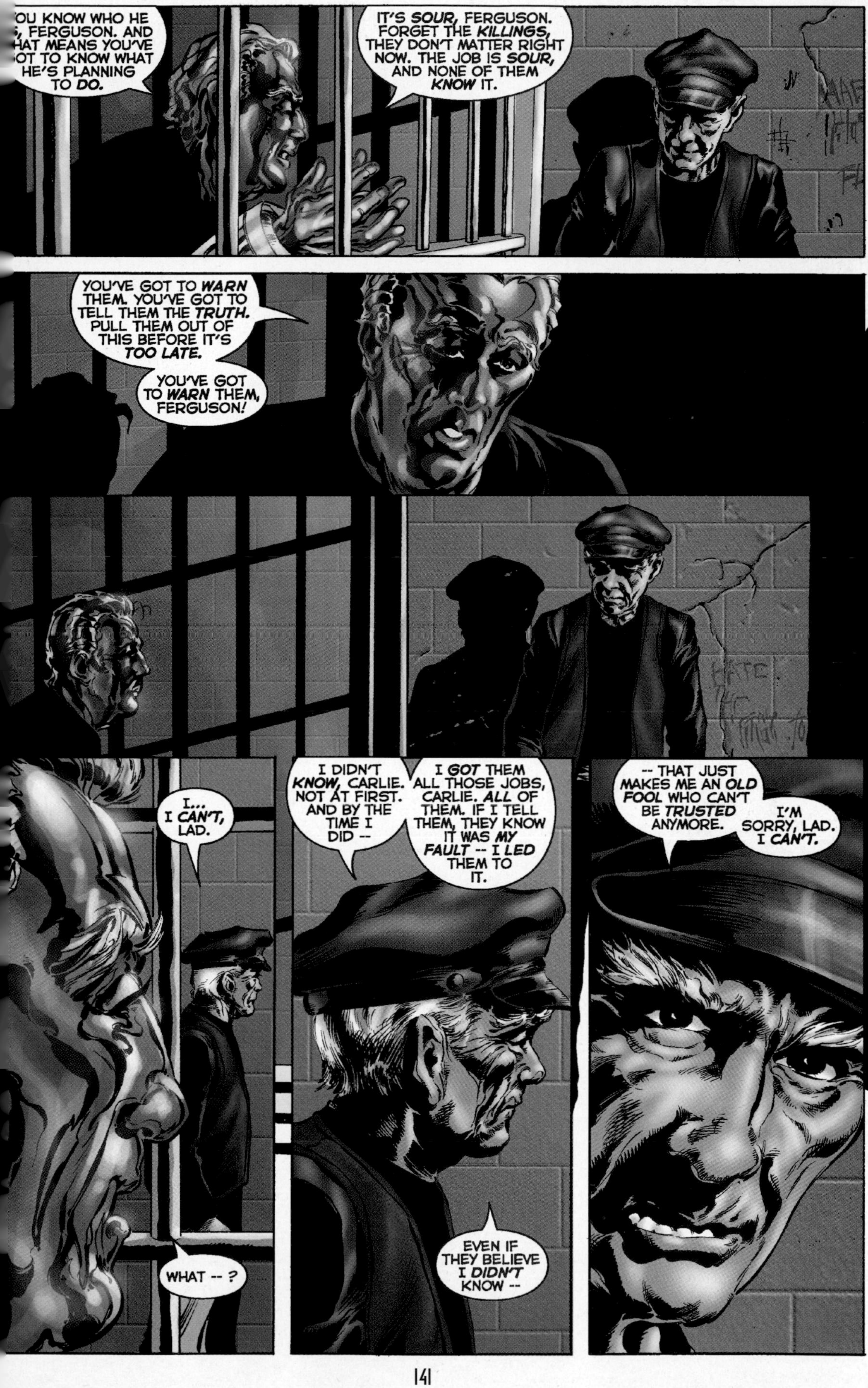
OU KNOW WHO HE , FERGUSON. AND HAT MEANS YOU'VE OT TO KNOW WHAT HE'S PLANNING TO DO.
IT'S SOUR, FERGUSON. FORGET THE KILLINGS, THEY DON'T MATTER RIGHT NOW. THE JOB IS SOUR, AND NONE OF THEM KNOW IT.
YOU'VE GOT TO WARN THEM. YOU'VE GOT TO TELL THEM THE TRUTH. PULL THEM OUT OF THIS BEFORE IT'S TOO LATE.
YOU'VE GOT TO WARN THEM, FERGUSON!
I... I CAN'T, LAD.
WHAT -- ?
I DIDN'T KNOW, CARLIE. NOT AT FIRST. AND BY THE TIME I DID --
I GOT THEM ALL THOSE JOBS, CARLIE. ALL OF THEM. IF I TELL THEM, THEY KNOW IT WAS MY FAULT -- I LED THEM TO IT.
EVEN IF THEY BELIEVE I DIDN'T KNOW --
-- THAT JUST MAKES ME AN OLD FOOL WHO CAN'T BE TRUSTED ANYMORE.
I'M SORRY, LAD. I CAN'T.

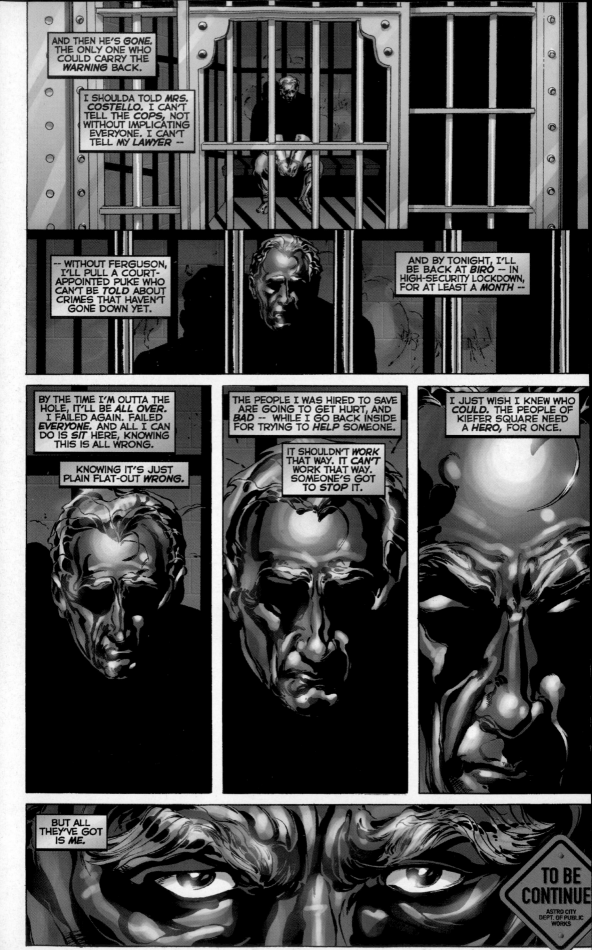

AND THEN HE'S *GONE*. THE ONLY ONE WHO COULD CARRY THE *WARNING* BACK.

I SHOULDA TOLD *MRS. COSTELLO*. I CAN'T TELL THE *COPS*, NOT WITHOUT IMPLICATING EVERYONE. I CAN'T TELL *MY LAWYER* --

-- WITHOUT FERGUSON, I'LL PULL A COURT-APPOINTED PUKE WHO CAN'T BE *TOLD* ABOUT CRIMES THAT HAVEN'T GONE DOWN YET.

AND BY TONIGHT, I'LL BE BACK AT *BIRO* -- IN HIGH-SECURITY LOCKDOWN, FOR AT LEAST A *MONTH* --

BY THE TIME I'M OUTTA THE HOLE, IT'LL BE *ALL OVER*. I FAILED AGAIN. FAILED *EVERYONE*. AND ALL I CAN DO IS *SIT* HERE, KNOWING THIS IS ALL WRONG.

KNOWING IT'S JUST PLAIN FLAT-OUT *WRONG*.

THE PEOPLE I WAS HIRED TO SAVE ARE GOING TO GET HURT, AND *BAD* -- WHILE I GO BACK INSIDE FOR TRYING TO *HELP* SOMEONE.

IT SHOULDN'T *WORK* THAT WAY. IT *CAN'T* WORK THAT WAY. SOMEONE'S GOT TO *STOP* IT.

I JUST WISH I KNEW WHO *COULD*. THE PEOPLE OF KIEFER SQUARE NEED A *HERO*, FOR ONCE.

BUT ALL THEY'VE GOT IS *ME*.

TO BE CONTINUE

ASTRO CITY DEPT. OF PUBLIC WORKS

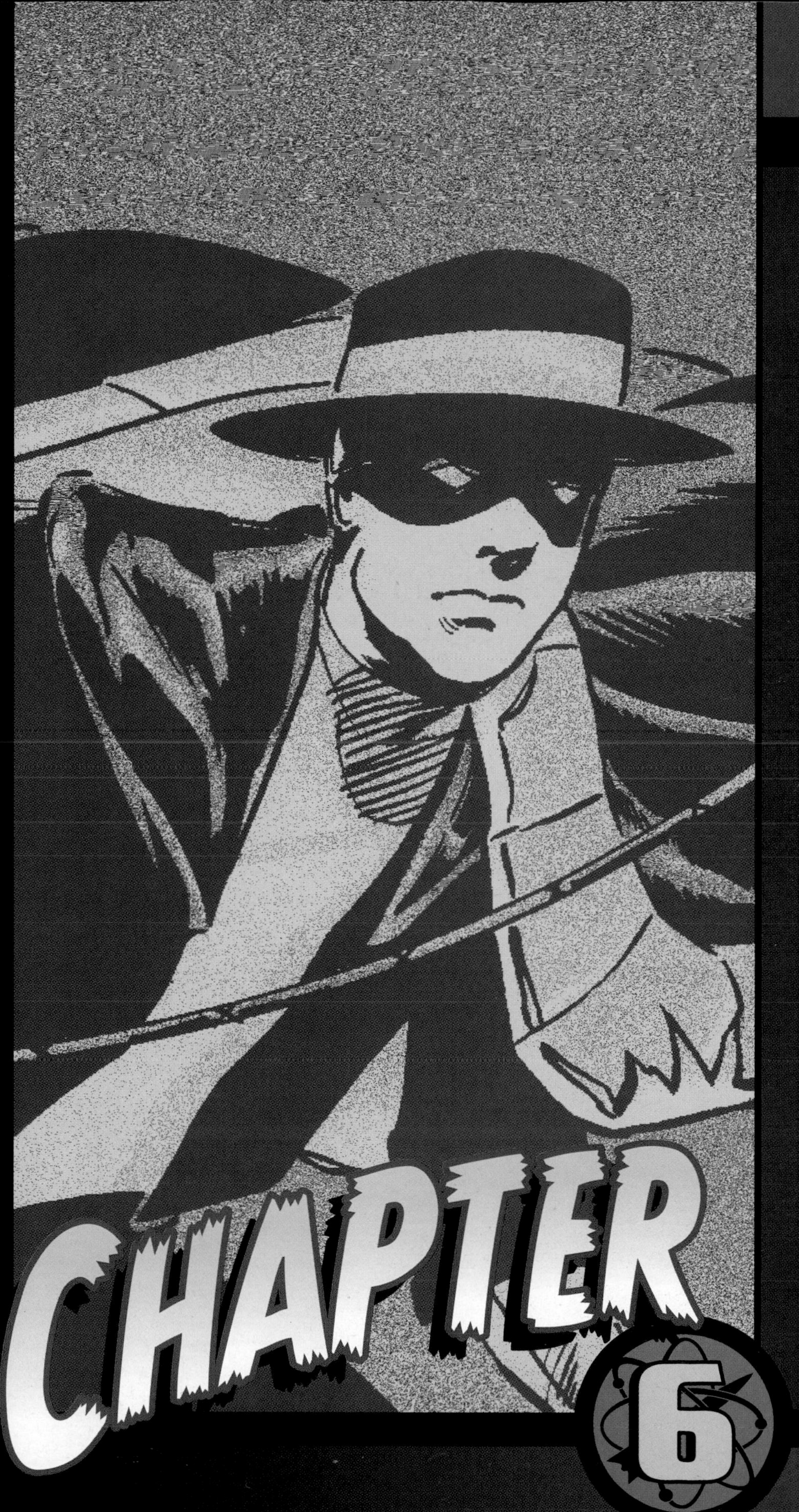

CHAPTER 6

The ONLY CHANCE

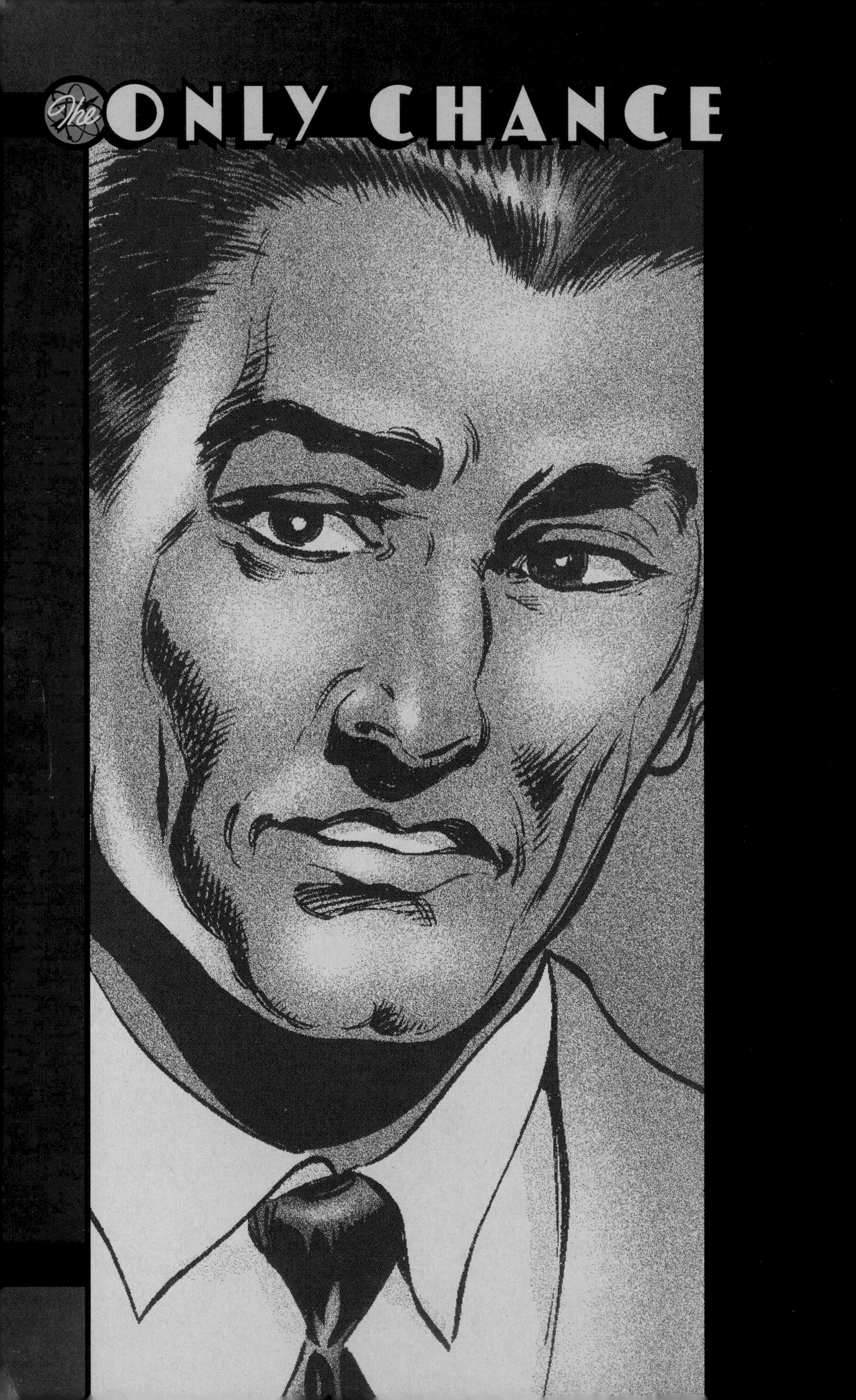

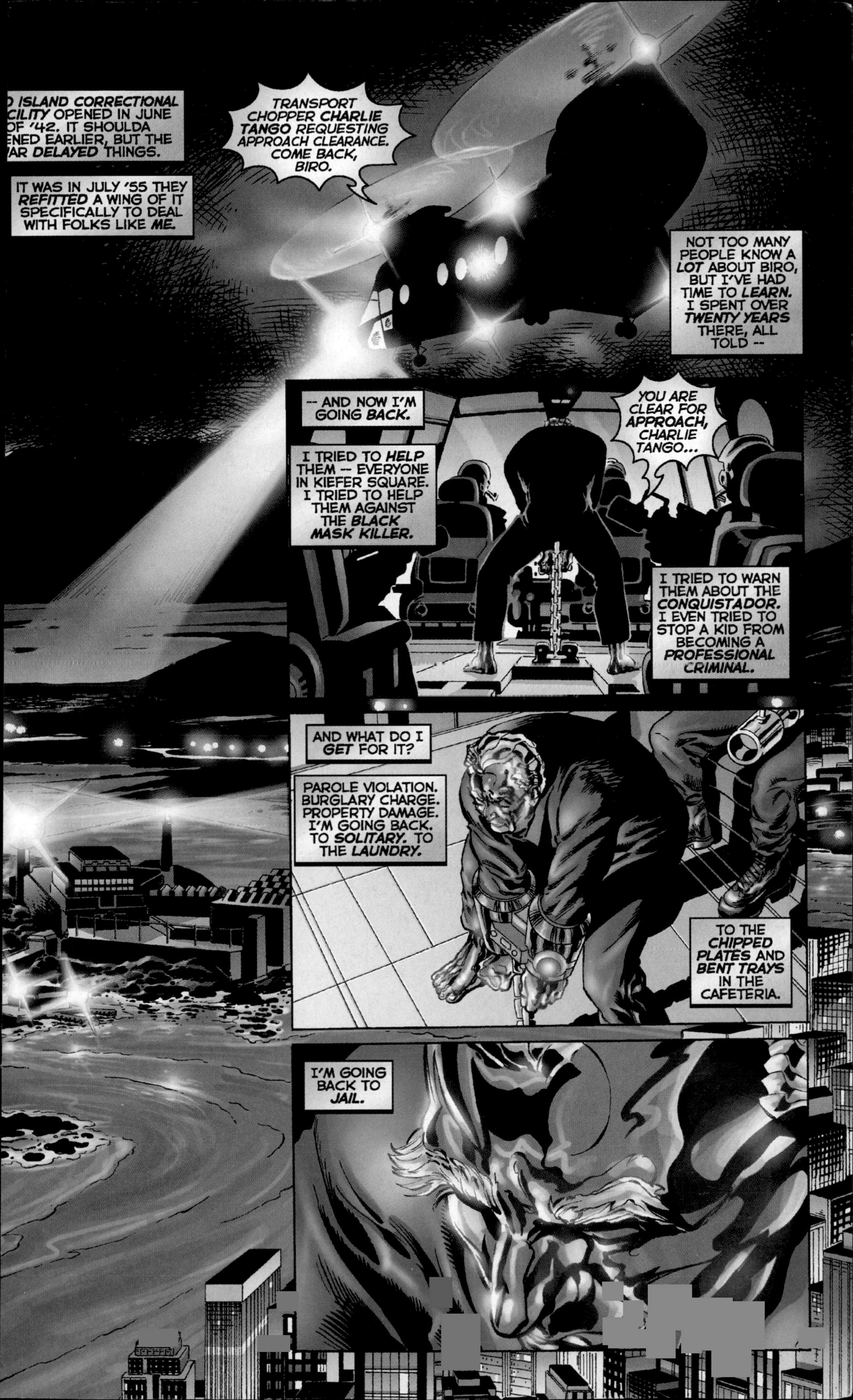
D ISLAND CORRECTIONAL CILITY OPENED IN JUNE OF '42. IT SHOULDA ENED EARLIER, BUT THE AR DELAYED THINGS.
TRANSPORT CHOPPER CHARLIE TANGO REQUESTING APPROACH CLEARANCE. COME BACK, BIRO.
IT WAS IN JULY '55 THEY REFITTED A WING OF IT SPECIFICALLY TO DEAL WITH FOLKS LIKE ME.
NOT TOO MANY PEOPLE KNOW A LOT ABOUT BIRO, BUT I'VE HAD TIME TO LEARN. I SPENT OVER TWENTY YEARS THERE, ALL TOLD --
-- AND NOW I'M GOING BACK.
YOU ARE CLEAR FOR APPROACH, CHARLIE TANGO...
I TRIED TO HELP THEM -- EVERYONE IN KIEFER SQUARE. I TRIED TO HELP THEM AGAINST THE BLACK MASK KILLER.
I TRIED TO WARN THEM ABOUT THE CONQUISTADOR. I EVEN TRIED TO STOP A KID FROM BECOMING A PROFESSIONAL CRIMINAL.
AND WHAT DO I GET FOR IT?
PAROLE VIOLATION. BURGLARY CHARGE. PROPERTY DAMAGE. I'M GOING BACK. TO SOLITARY. TO THE LAUNDRY.
TO THE CHIPPED PLATES AND BENT TRAYS IN THE CAFETERIA.
I'M GOING BACK TO JAIL.

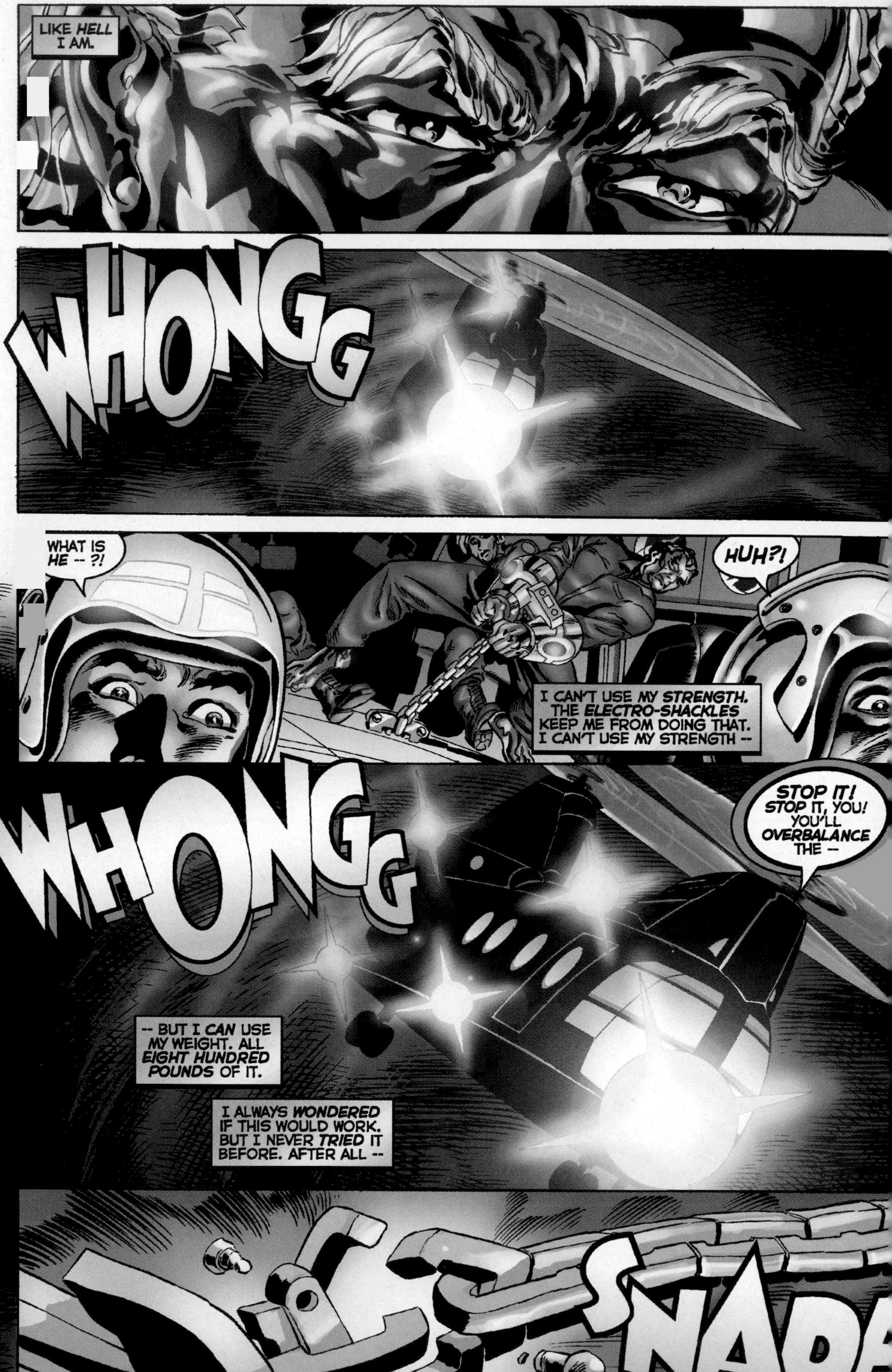

LIKE HELL I AM.
WHONGG
WHAT IS HE -- ?!
HUH?!
I CAN'T USE MY STRENGTH. THE ELECTRO-SHACKLES KEEP ME FROM DOING THAT. I CAN'T USE MY STRENGTH --
WHONGG
STOP IT! STOP IT, YOU! YOU'LL OVERBALANCE THE --
-- BUT I CAN USE MY WEIGHT. ALL EIGHT HUNDRED POUNDS OF IT.
I ALWAYS WONDERED IF THIS WOULD WORK. BUT I NEVER TRIED IT BEFORE. AFTER ALL --
SNAP

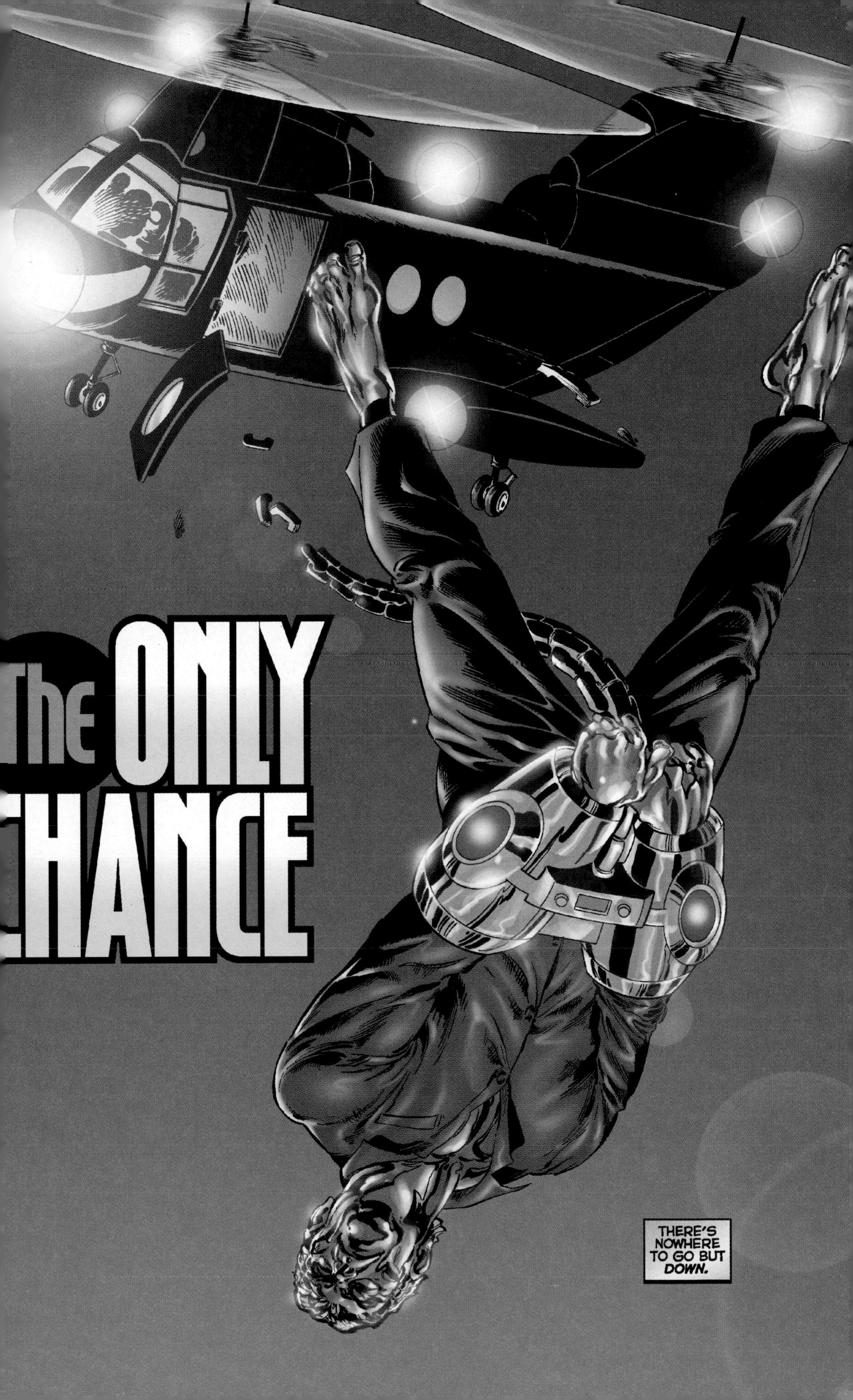

The ONLY CHANCE
THERE'S NOWHERE TO GO BUT *DOWN.*

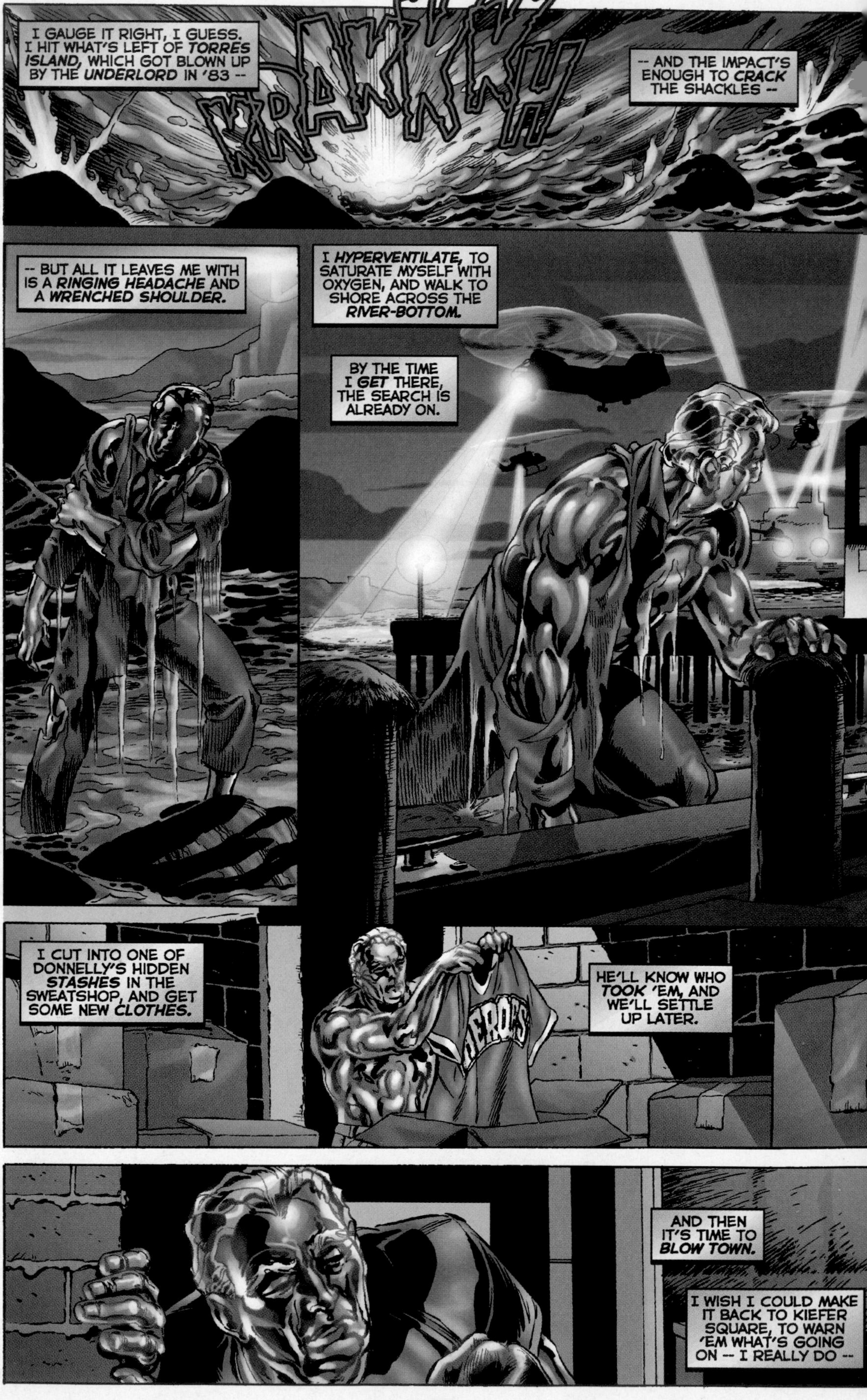
I GAUGE IT RIGHT, I GUESS. I HIT WHAT'S LEFT OF *TORRES ISLAND,* WHICH GOT BLOWN UP BY THE *UNDERLORD* IN '83 --
-- AND THE IMPACT'S ENOUGH TO *CRACK* THE SHACKLES --
-- BUT ALL IT LEAVES ME WITH IS A *RINGING HEADACHE* AND A *WRENCHED SHOULDER.*
I *HYPERVENTILATE,* TO SATURATE MYSELF WITH OXYGEN, AND WALK TO SHORE ACROSS THE *RIVER-BOTTOM.*
BY THE TIME I *GET* THERE, THE SEARCH IS ALREADY ON.
I CUT INTO ONE OF DONNELLY'S HIDDEN *STASHES* IN THE SWEATSHOP, AND GET SOME NEW *CLOTHES.*
HE'LL KNOW WHO *TOOK* 'EM, AND WE'LL SETTLE UP LATER.
AND THEN IT'S TIME TO *BLOW TOWN.*
I WISH I COULD MAKE IT BACK TO KIEFER SQUARE, TO WARN 'EM WHAT'S GOING ON -- I REALLY DO --

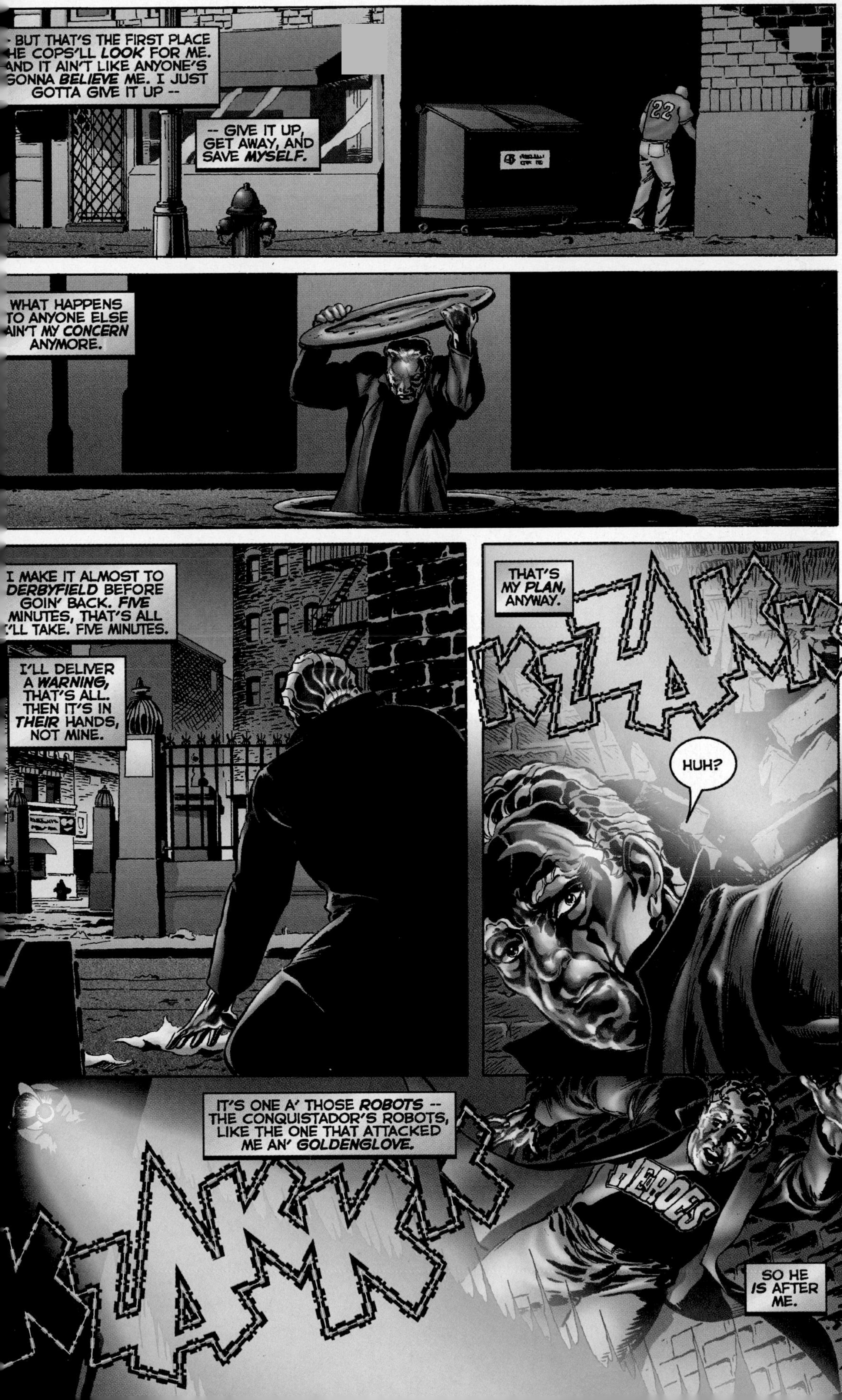
- BUT THAT'S THE FIRST PLACE HE COPS'LL LOOK FOR ME. AND IT AIN'T LIKE ANYONE'S GONNA BELIEVE ME. I JUST GOTTA GIVE IT UP --
-- GIVE IT UP, GET AWAY, AND SAVE MYSELF.
22
WHAT HAPPENS TO ANYONE ELSE AIN'T MY CONCERN ANYMORE.
I MAKE IT ALMOST TO DERBYFIELD BEFORE GOIN' BACK. FIVE MINUTES, THAT'S ALL I'LL TAKE. FIVE MINUTES.
I'LL DELIVER A WARNING, THAT'S ALL. THEN IT'S IN THEIR HANDS, NOT MINE.
THAT'S MY PLAN, ANYWAY.
KZAKK
HUH?
IT'S ONE A' THOSE ROBOTS -- THE CONQUISTADOR'S ROBOTS, LIKE THE ONE THAT ATTACKED ME AN' GOLDENGLOVE.
ZAMM
HEROES
SO HE IS AFTER ME.

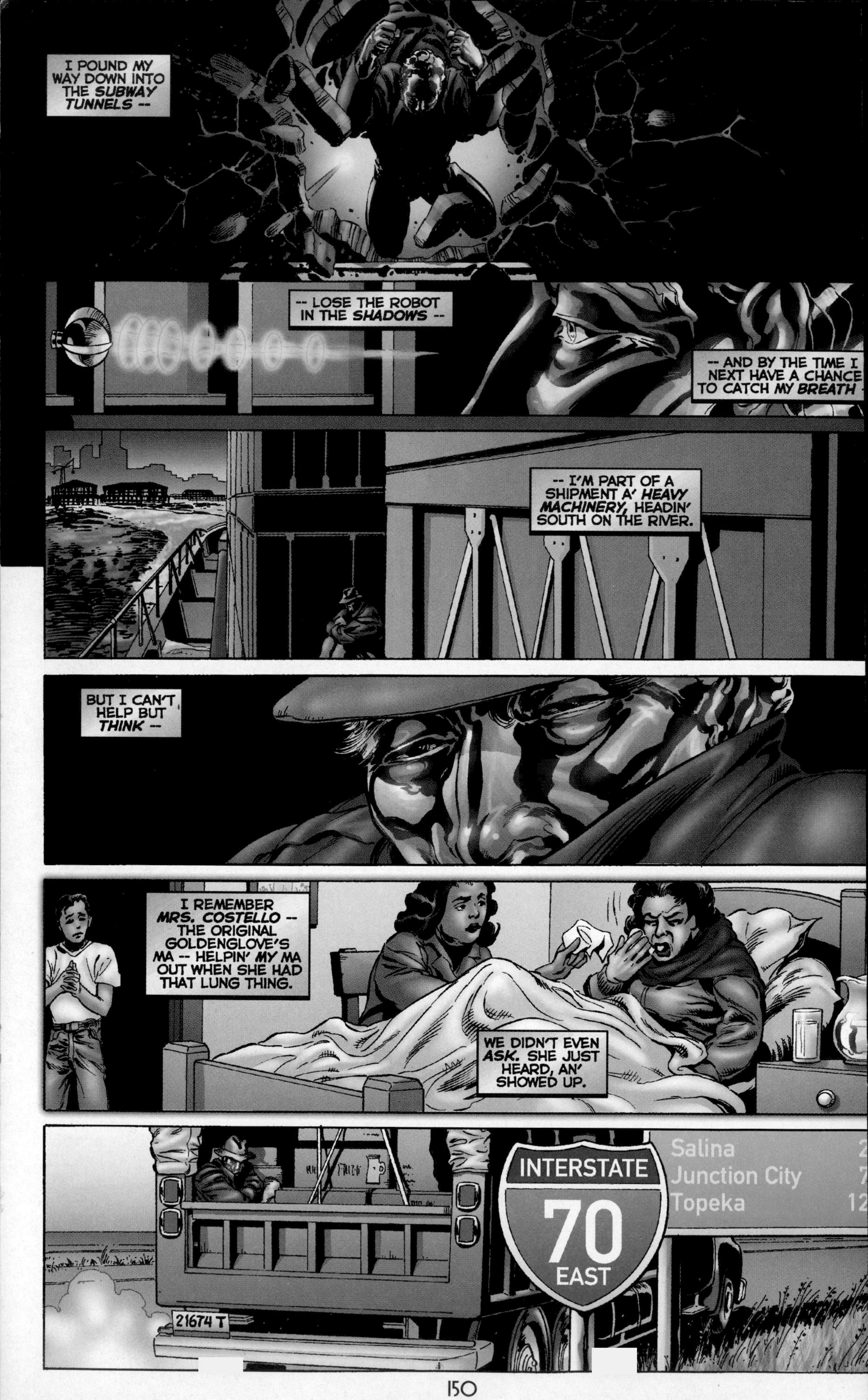

I POUND MY WAY DOWN INTO THE SUBWAY TUNNELS --
-- LOSE THE ROBOT IN THE SHADOWS --
-- AND BY THE TIME I NEXT HAVE A CHANCE TO CATCH MY BREATH --
-- I'M PART OF A SHIPMENT A' HEAVY MACHINERY, HEADIN' SOUTH ON THE RIVER.
BUT I CAN'T HELP BUT THINK --
I REMEMBER MRS. COSTELLO -- THE ORIGINAL GOLDENGLOVE'S MA -- HELPIN' MY MA OUT WHEN SHE HAD THAT LUNG THING.
WE DIDN'T EVEN ASK. SHE JUST HEARD, AN' SHOWED UP.
INTERSTATE
70
EAST
Salina
Junction City
Topeka
21674 T

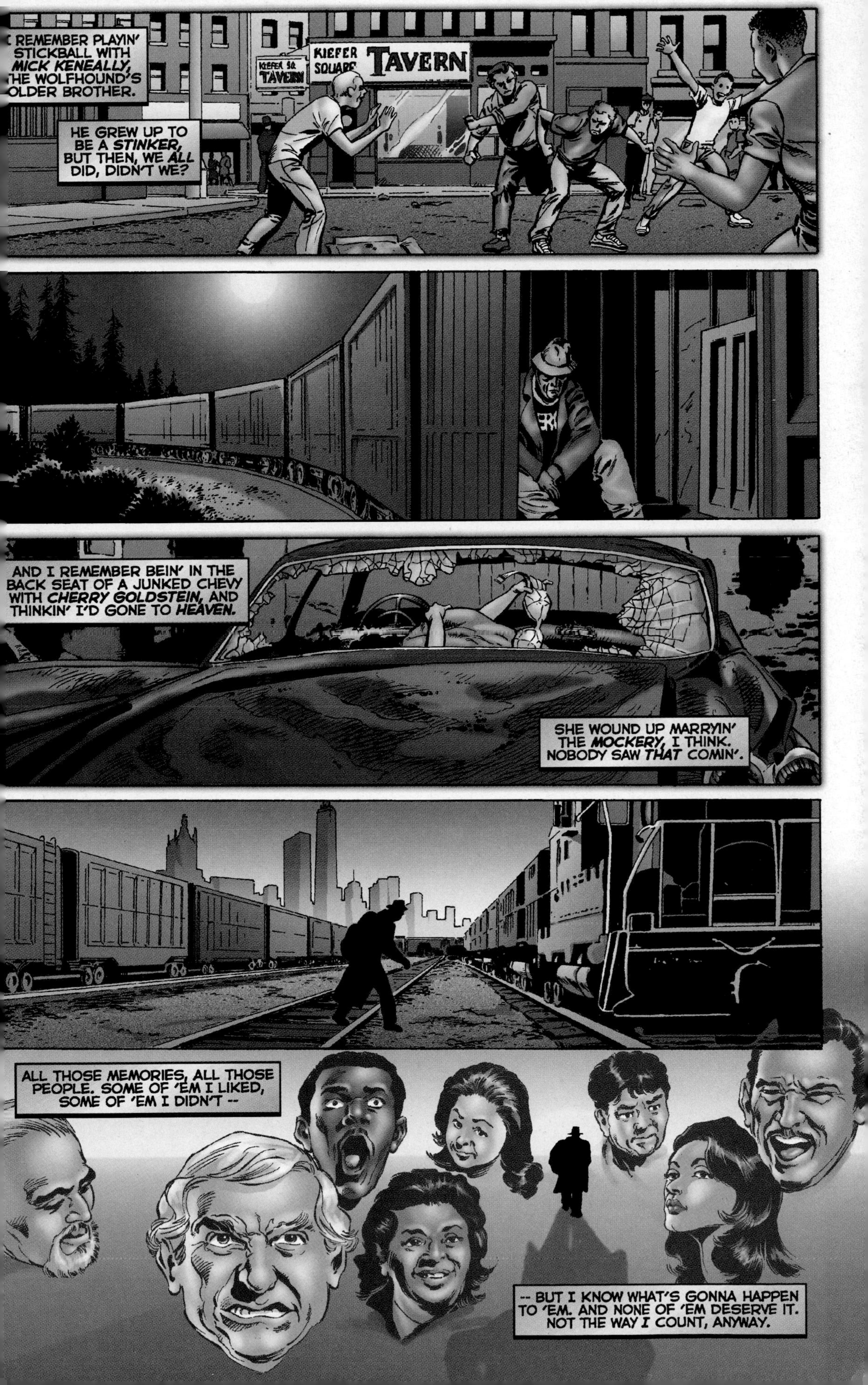
I REMEMBER PLAYIN' STICKBALL WITH MICK KENEALLY, THE WOLFHOUND'S OLDER BROTHER.
KIEFER SQ. TAVERN
KIEFER SQUARE TAVERN
HE GREW UP TO BE A STINKER, BUT THEN, WE ALL DID, DIDN'T WE?
AND I REMEMBER BEIN' IN THE BACK SEAT OF A JUNKED CHEVY WITH CHERRY GOLDSTEIN, AND THINKIN' I'D GONE TO HEAVEN.
SHE WOUND UP MARRYIN' THE MOCKERY, I THINK. NOBODY SAW THAT COMIN'.
ALL THOSE MEMORIES, ALL THOSE PEOPLE. SOME OF 'EM I LIKED, SOME OF 'EM I DIDN'T --
-- BUT I KNOW WHAT'S GONNA HAPPEN TO 'EM. AND NONE OF 'EM DESERVE IT. NOT THE WAY I COUNT, ANYWAY.

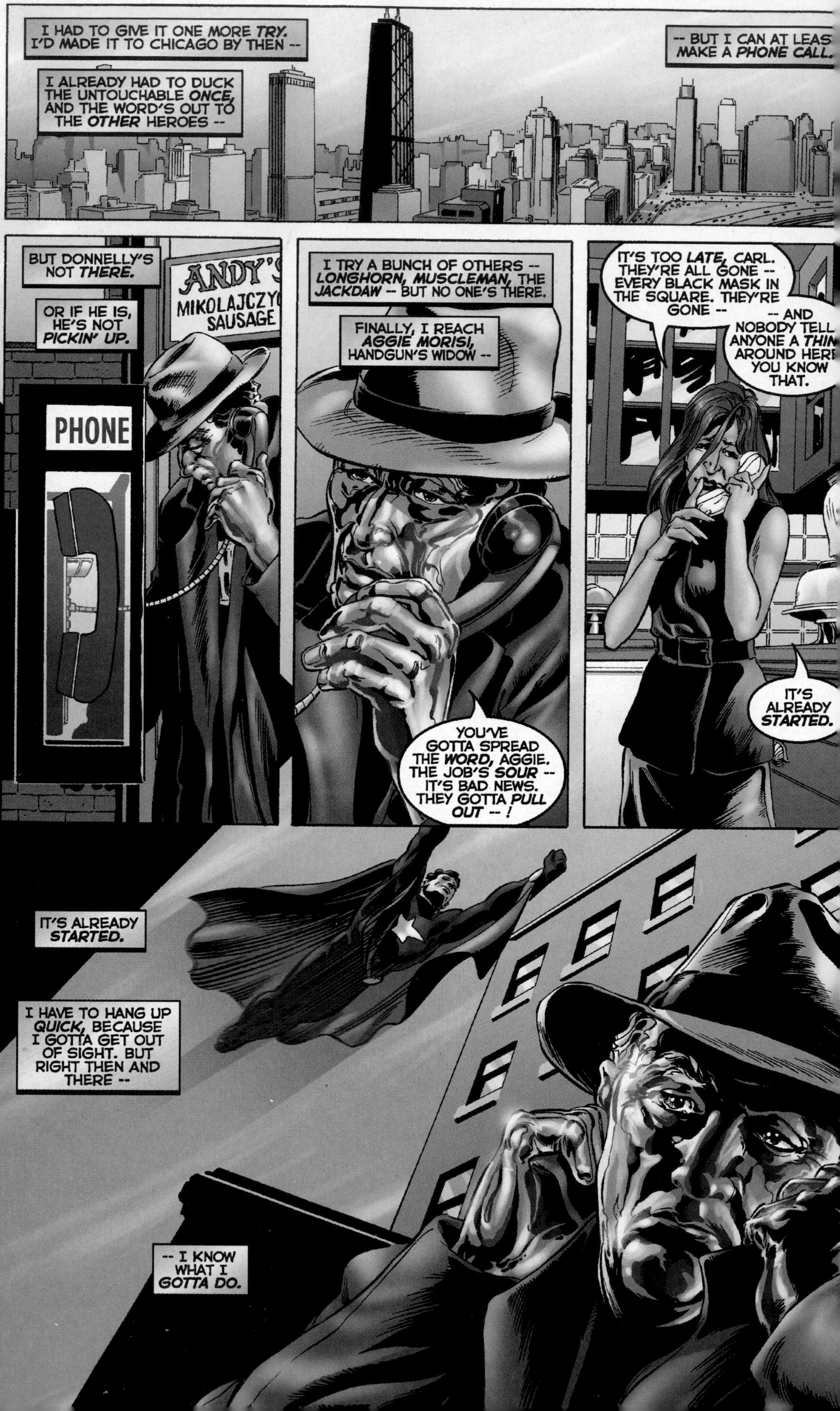
I HAD TO GIVE IT ONE MORE TRY. I'D MADE IT TO CHICAGO BY THEN --
I ALREADY HAD TO DUCK THE UNTOUCHABLE ONCE, AND THE WORD'S OUT TO THE OTHER HEROES --
-- BUT I CAN AT LEAS MAKE A PHONE CALL.
BUT DONNELLY'S NOT THERE.
OR IF HE IS, HE'S NOT PICKIN' UP.
ANDY'S
MIKOLAJCZY SAUSAGE
PHONE
I TRY A BUNCH OF OTHERS -- LONGHORN, MUSCLEMAN, THE JACKDAW -- BUT NO ONE'S THERE.
FINALLY, I REACH AGGIE MORISI, HANDGUN'S WIDOW --
YOU'VE GOTTA SPREAD THE WORD, AGGIE. THE JOB'S SOUR -- IT'S BAD NEWS. THEY GOTTA PULL OUT -- !
IT'S TOO LATE, CARL. THEY'RE ALL GONE -- EVERY BLACK MASK IN THE SQUARE. THEY'RE GONE --
-- AND NOBODY TELL ANYONE A THIN AROUND HER YOU KNOW THAT.
IT'S ALREADY STARTED.
IT'S ALREADY STARTED.
I HAVE TO HANG UP QUICK, BECAUSE I GOTTA GET OUT OF SIGHT. BUT RIGHT THEN AND THERE --
-- I KNOW WHAT I GOTTA DO.

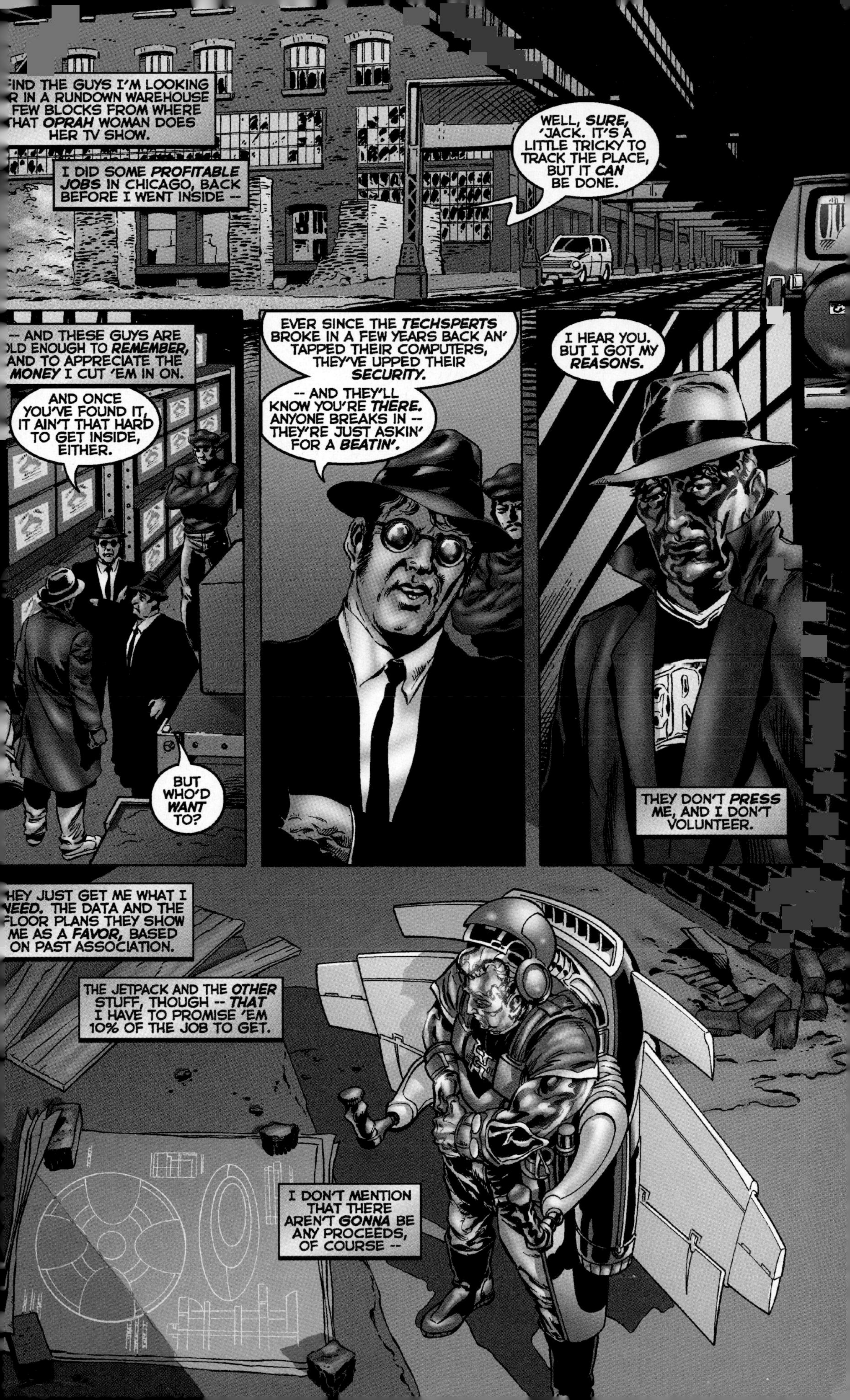

FIND THE GUYS I'M LOOKING R IN A RUNDOWN WAREHOUSE FEW BLOCKS FROM WHERE THAT OPRAH WOMAN DOES HER TV SHOW.
I DID SOME PROFITABLE JOBS IN CHICAGO, BACK BEFORE I WENT INSIDE --
WELL, SURE, 'JACK. IT'S A LITTLE TRICKY TO TRACK THE PLACE, BUT IT CAN BE DONE.
-- AND THESE GUYS ARE OLD ENOUGH TO REMEMBER, AND TO APPRECIATE THE MONEY I CUT 'EM IN ON.
AND ONCE YOU'VE FOUND IT, IT AIN'T THAT HARD TO GET INSIDE, EITHER.
BUT WHO'D WANT TO?
EVER SINCE THE TECHSPERTS BROKE IN A FEW YEARS BACK AN' TAPPED THEIR COMPUTERS, THEY'VE UPPED THEIR SECURITY.
-- AND THEY'LL KNOW YOU'RE THERE. ANYONE BREAKS IN -- THEY'RE JUST ASKIN' FOR A BEATIN'.
I HEAR YOU. BUT I GOT MY REASONS.
THEY DON'T PRESS ME, AND I DON'T VOLUNTEER.
HEY JUST GET ME WHAT I NEED. THE DATA AND THE FLOOR PLANS THEY SHOW ME AS A FAVOR, BASED ON PAST ASSOCIATION.
THE JETPACK AND THE OTHER STUFF, THOUGH -- THAT I HAVE TO PROMISE 'EM 10% OF THE JOB TO GET.
I DON'T MENTION THAT THERE AREN'T GONNA BE ANY PROCEEDS, OF COURSE --

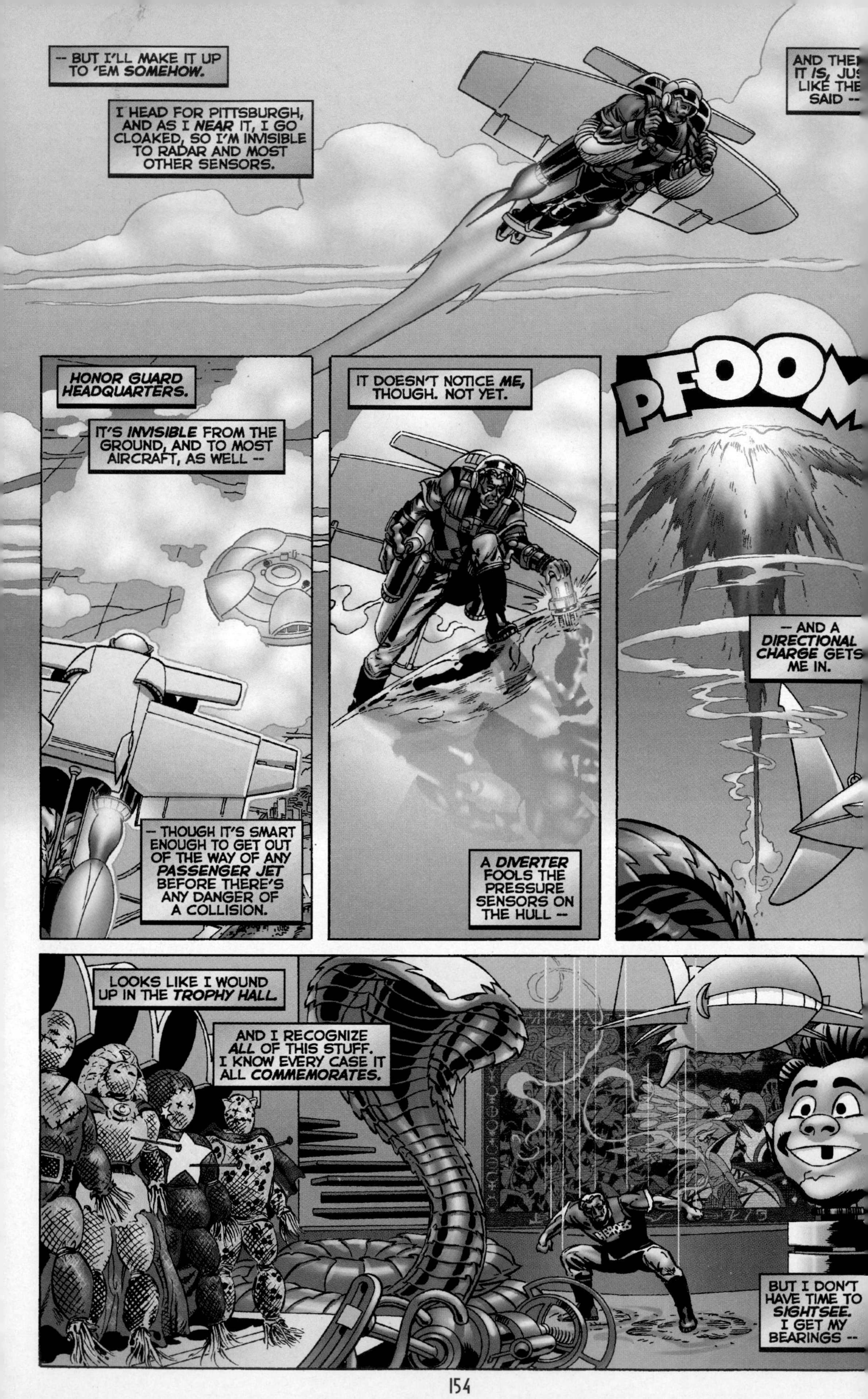
-- BUT I'LL MAKE IT UP TO 'EM SOMEHOW.
I HEAD FOR PITTSBURGH, AND AS I NEAR IT, I GO CLOAKED, SO I'M INVISIBLE TO RADAR AND MOST OTHER SENSORS.
AND THE IT IS, JUS LIKE THE SAID --
HONOR GUARD HEADQUARTERS.
IT'S INVISIBLE FROM THE GROUND, AND TO MOST AIRCRAFT, AS WELL --
-- THOUGH IT'S SMART ENOUGH TO GET OUT OF THE WAY OF ANY PASSENGER JET BEFORE THERE'S ANY DANGER OF A COLLISION.
IT DOESN'T NOTICE ME, THOUGH. NOT YET.
A DIVERTER FOOLS THE PRESSURE SENSORS ON THE HULL --
PFOO
-- AND A DIRECTIONAL CHARGE GETS ME IN.
LOOKS LIKE I WOUND UP IN THE TROPHY HALL.
AND I RECOGNIZE ALL OF THIS STUFF. I KNOW EVERY CASE IT ALL COMMEMORATES.
BUT I DON'T HAVE TIME TO SIGHTSEE. I GET MY BEARINGS --

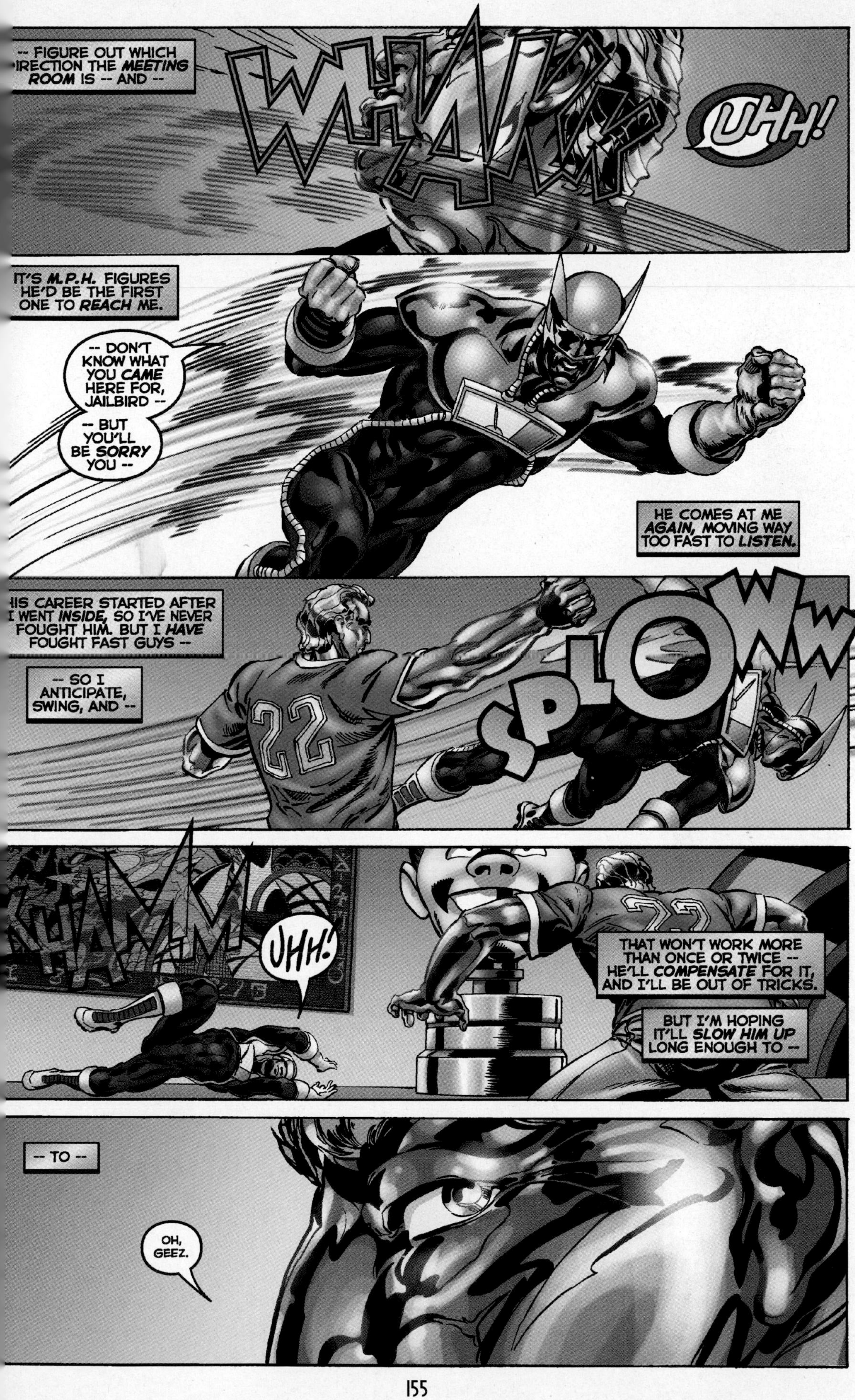

-- FIGURE OUT WHICH DIRECTION THE MEETING ROOM IS -- AND --
WHAM
UHH!
IT'S M.P.H. FIGURES HE'D BE THE FIRST ONE TO REACH ME.
-- DON'T KNOW WHAT YOU CAME HERE FOR, JAILBIRD --
-- BUT YOU'LL BE SORRY YOU --
HE COMES AT ME AGAIN, MOVING WAY TOO FAST TO LISTEN.
HIS CAREER STARTED AFTER I WENT INSIDE, SO I'VE NEVER FOUGHT HIM. BUT I HAVE FOUGHT FAST GUYS --
-- SO I ANTICIPATE, SWING, AND --
SPLOWW
KHAMM
UHH!
THAT WON'T WORK MORE THAN ONCE OR TWICE -- HE'LL COMPENSATE FOR IT, AND I'LL BE OUT OF TRICKS.
BUT I'M HOPING IT'LL SLOW HIM UP LONG ENOUGH TO --
-- TO --
OH, GEEZ.

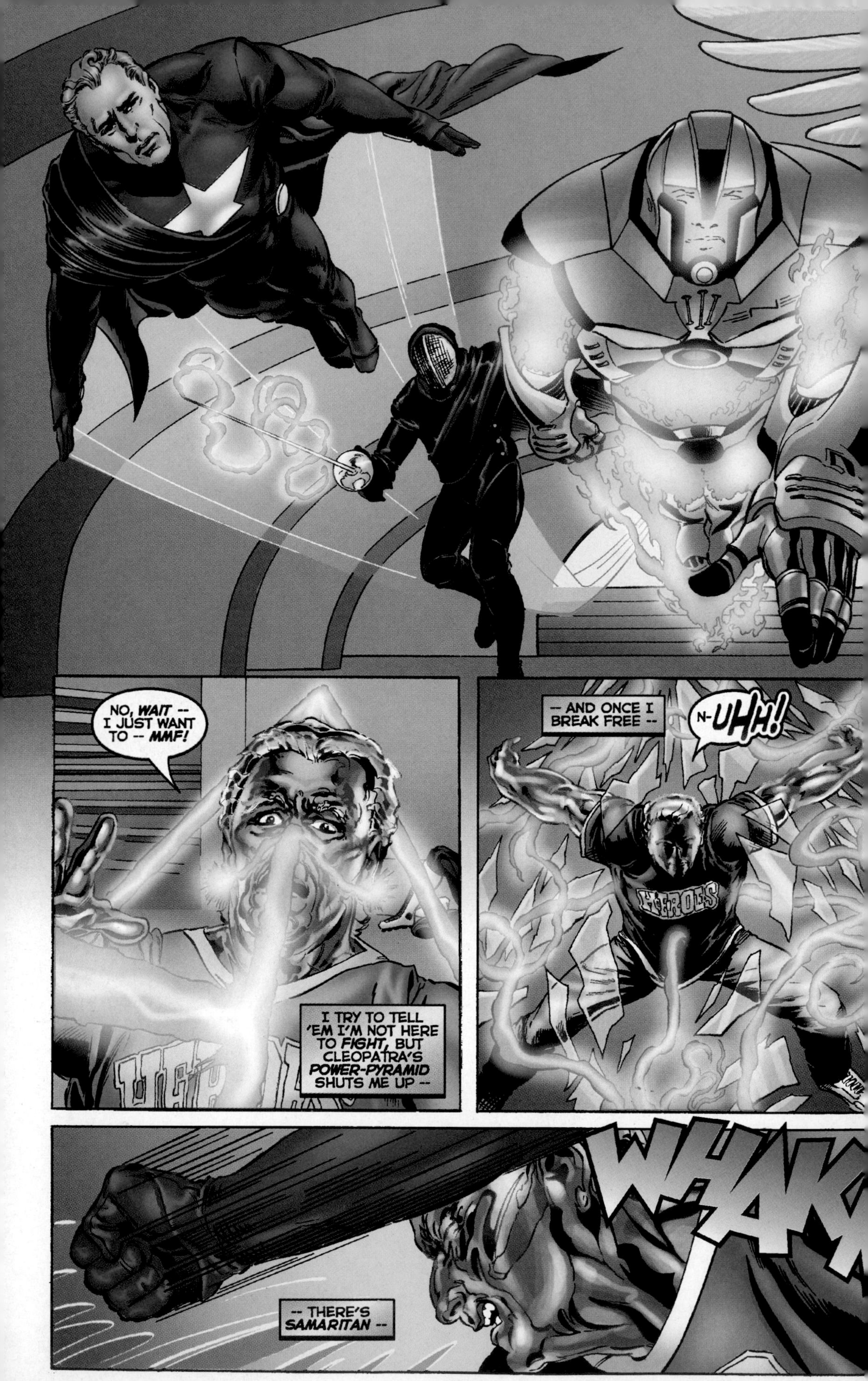
NO, WAIT -- I JUST WANT TO -- MMF!
I TRY TO TELL 'EM I'M NOT HERE TO FIGHT, BUT CLEOPATRA'S POWER-PYRAMID SHUTS ME UP --
-- AND ONCE I BREAK FREE --
N-UHH!
HEROES
-- THERE'S SAMARITAN --
WHAK

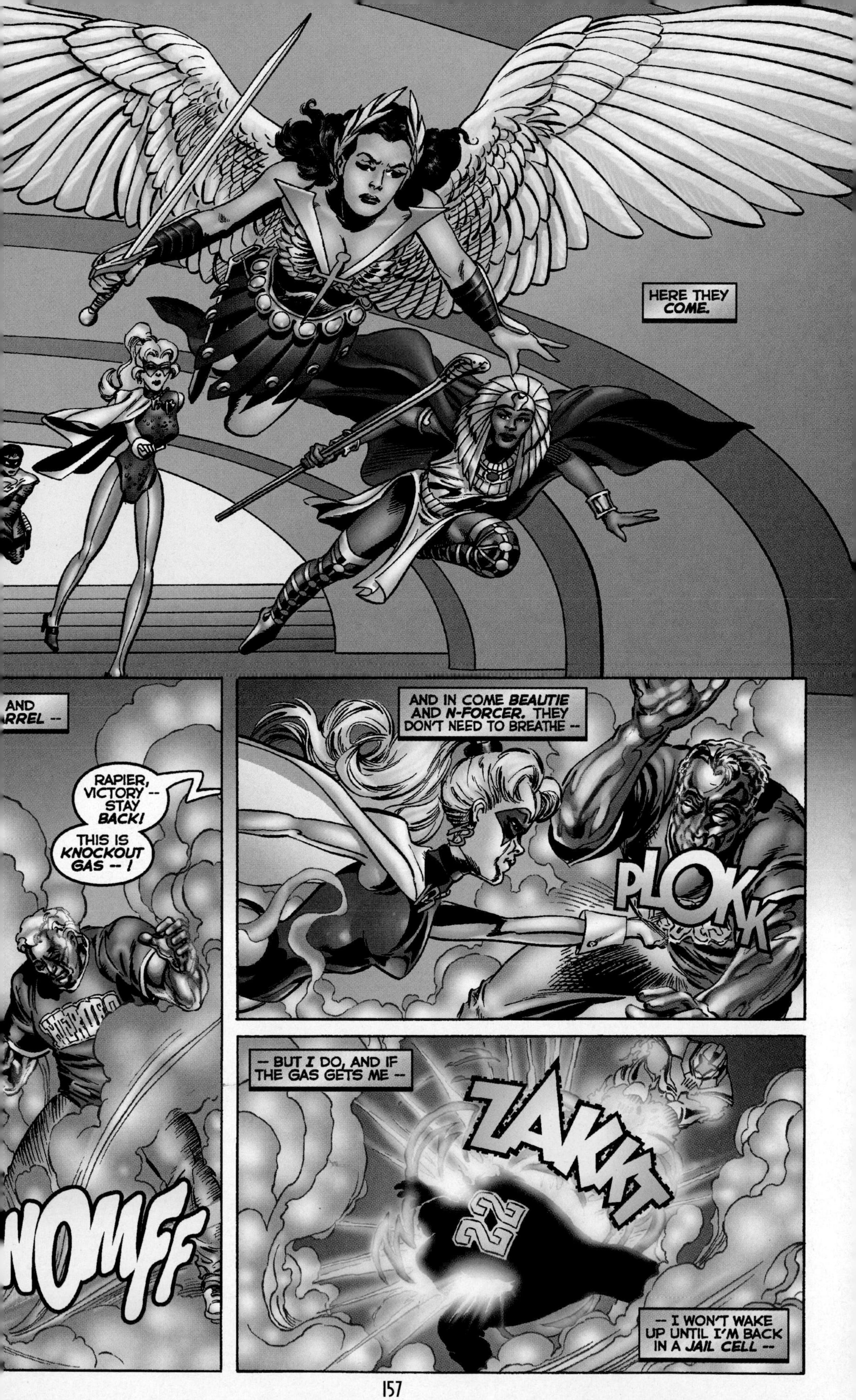
HERE THEY *COME.*
AND
RREL --
RAPIER, VICTORY -- STAY *BACK!*
THIS IS *KNOCKOUT* GAS -- !
AND IN COME *BEAUTIE* AND *N-FORCER.* THEY DON'T NEED TO BREATHE --
PLOKK
-- BUT *I* DO, AND IF THE GAS GETS ME --
ZAKKT
-- I WON'T WAKE UP UNTIL I'M BACK IN A *JAIL CELL* --

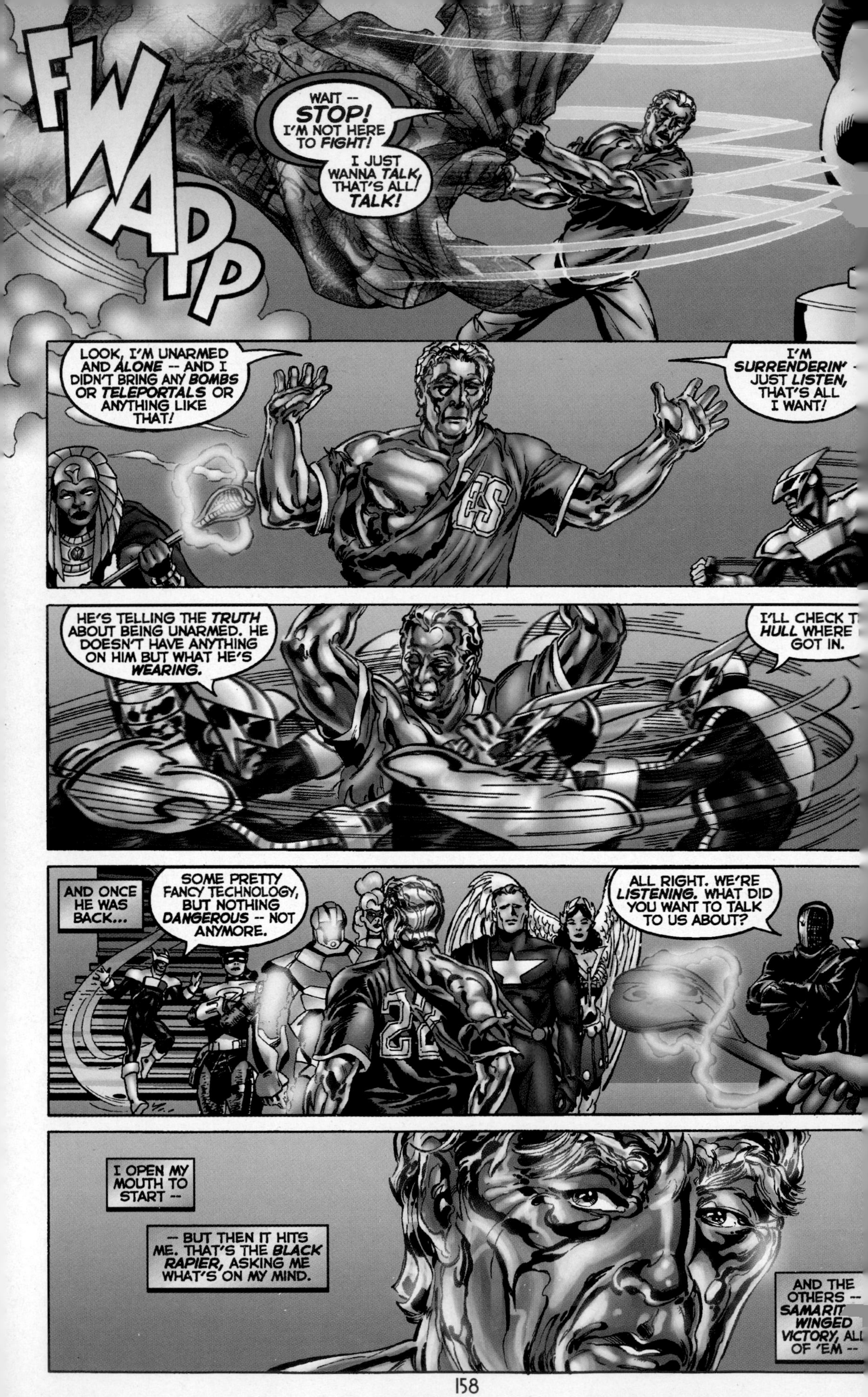
FWAPP
WAIT -- STOP! I'M NOT HERE TO FIGHT!
I JUST WANNA TALK, THAT'S ALL! TALK!
LOOK, I'M UNARMED AND ALONE -- AND I DIDN'T BRING ANY BOMBS OR TELEPORTALS OR ANYTHING LIKE THAT!
I'M SURRENDERIN' -- JUST LISTEN, THAT'S ALL I WANT!
HE'S TELLING THE TRUTH ABOUT BEING UNARMED. HE DOESN'T HAVE ANYTHING ON HIM BUT WHAT HE'S WEARING.
I'LL CHECK T HULL WHERE GOT IN.
AND ONCE HE WAS BACK...
SOME PRETTY FANCY TECHNOLOGY, BUT NOTHING DANGEROUS -- NOT ANYMORE.
ALL RIGHT. WE'RE LISTENING. WHAT DID YOU WANT TO TALK TO US ABOUT?
I OPEN MY MOUTH TO START --
-- BUT THEN IT HITS ME. THAT'S THE BLACK RAPIER, ASKING ME WHAT'S ON MY MIND.
AND THE OTHERS -- SAMARIT WINGED VICTORY, ALL OF 'EM --

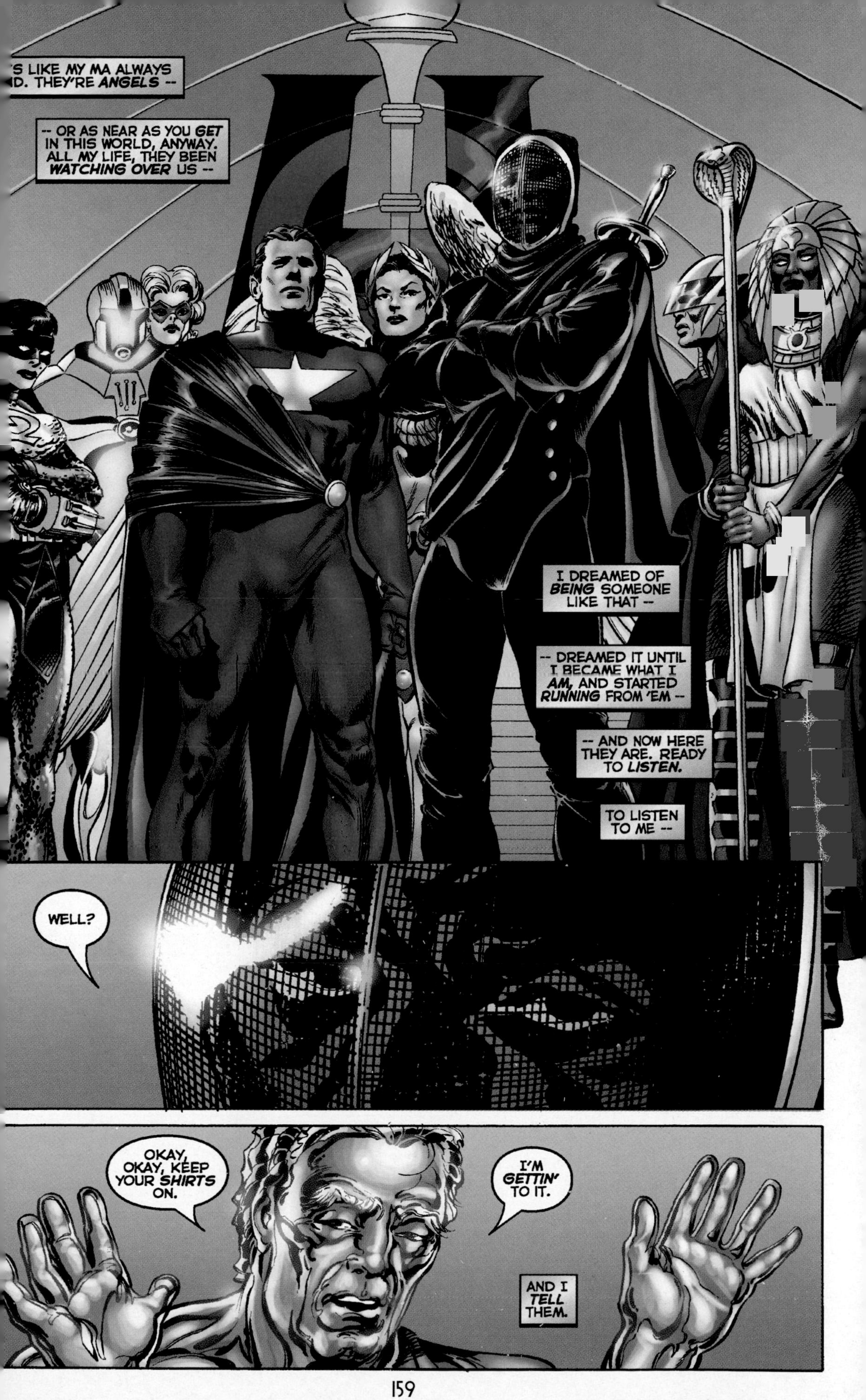

'S LIKE MY MA ALWAYS D. THEY'RE ANGELS --
-- OR AS NEAR AS YOU GET IN THIS WORLD, ANYWAY. ALL MY LIFE, THEY BEEN WATCHING OVER US --
I DREAMED OF BEING SOMEONE LIKE THAT --
-- DREAMED IT UNTIL I BECAME WHAT I AM, AND STARTED RUNNING FROM 'EM --
-- AND NOW HERE THEY ARE. READY TO LISTEN.
TO LISTEN TO ME --
WELL?
OKAY, OKAY, KEEP YOUR SHIRTS ON.
I'M GETTIN' TO IT.
AND I TELL THEM.

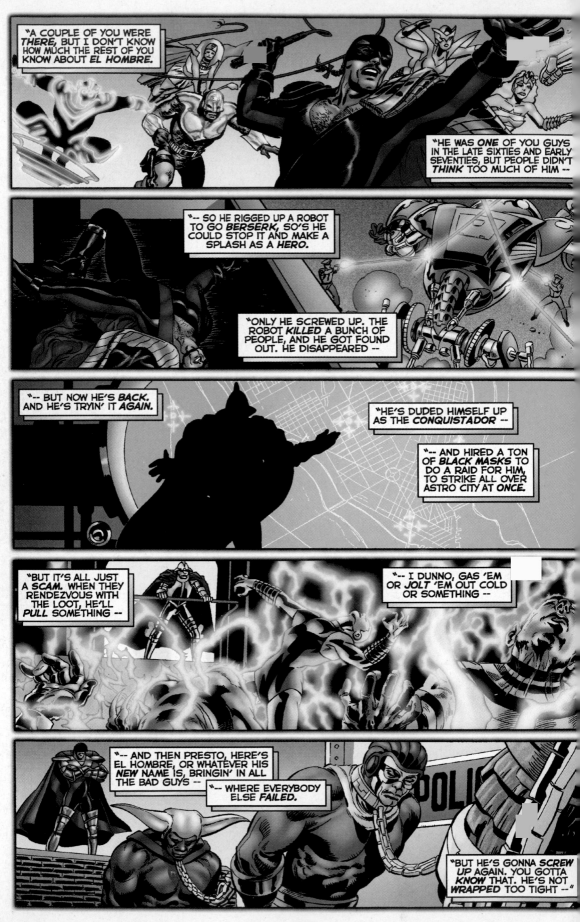

"A COUPLE OF YOU WERE *THERE*, BUT I DON'T KNOW HOW MUCH THE REST OF YOU KNOW ABOUT *EL HOMBRE*.

"HE WAS *ONE* OF YOU GUYS IN THE LATE SIXTIES AND EARLY SEVENTIES, BUT PEOPLE DIDN'T *THINK* TOO MUCH OF HIM --

"-- SO HE RIGGED UP A ROBOT TO GO *BERSERK*, SO'S HE COULD STOP IT AND MAKE A SPLASH AS A *HERO*.

"ONLY HE SCREWED UP. THE ROBOT *KILLED* A BUNCH OF PEOPLE, AND HE GOT FOUND OUT. HE DISAPPEARED --

"-- BUT NOW HE'S *BACK*. AND HE'S TRYIN' IT *AGAIN*.

"HE'S DUDED HIMSELF UP AS THE *CONQUISTADOR* --

"-- AND HIRED A TON OF *BLACK MASKS* TO DO A RAID FOR HIM, TO STRIKE ALL OVER ASTRO CITY AT *ONCE*.

"BUT IT'S ALL JUST A *SCAM*. WHEN THEY RENDEZVOUS WITH THE LOOT, HE'LL *PULL* SOMETHING --

"-- I DUNNO, GAS 'EM OR *JOLT* 'EM OUT COLD OR SOMETHING --

"-- AND THEN PRESTO, HERE'S EL HOMBRE, OR WHATEVER HIS *NEW* NAME IS, BRINGIN' IN ALL THE BAD GUYS --

"-- WHERE EVERYBODY ELSE *FAILED*.

"BUT HE'S GONNA *SCREW UP* AGAIN. YOU GOTTA *KNOW* THAT. HE'S NOT *WRAPPED* TOO TIGHT --"

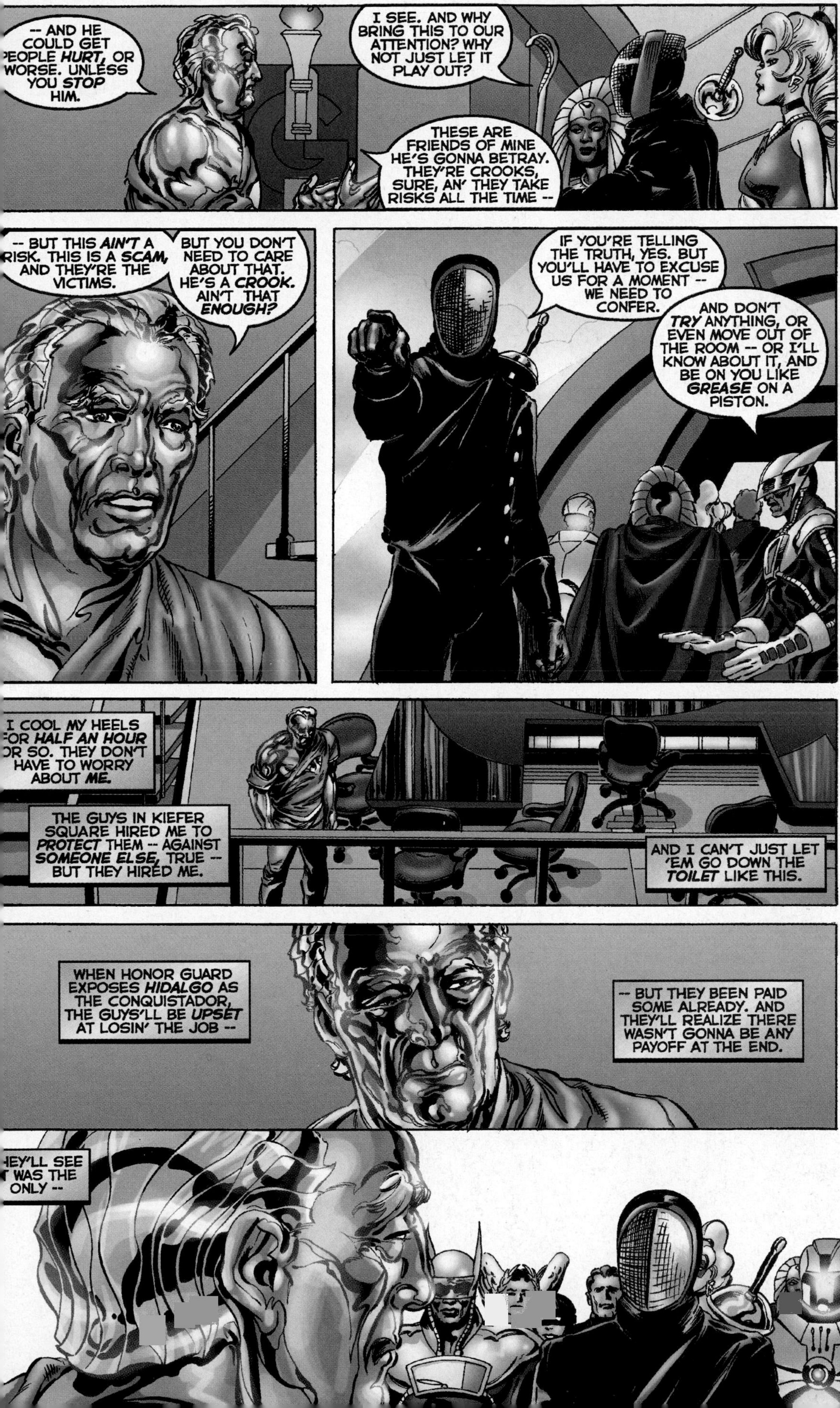

-- AND HE COULD GET PEOPLE HURT, OR WORSE. UNLESS YOU STOP HIM.
I SEE. AND WHY BRING THIS TO OUR ATTENTION? WHY NOT JUST LET IT PLAY OUT?
THESE ARE FRIENDS OF MINE HE'S GONNA BETRAY. THEY'RE CROOKS, SURE, AN' THEY TAKE RISKS ALL THE TIME --
-- BUT THIS AIN'T A RISK. THIS IS A SCAM, AND THEY'RE THE VICTIMS.
BUT YOU DON'T NEED TO CARE ABOUT THAT. HE'S A CROOK. AIN'T THAT ENOUGH?
IF YOU'RE TELLING THE TRUTH, YES. BUT YOU'LL HAVE TO EXCUSE US FOR A MOMENT -- WE NEED TO CONFER.
AND DON'T TRY ANYTHING, OR EVEN MOVE OUT OF THE ROOM -- OR I'LL KNOW ABOUT IT, AND BE ON YOU LIKE GREASE ON A PISTON.
I COOL MY HEELS FOR HALF AN HOUR OR SO. THEY DON'T HAVE TO WORRY ABOUT ME.
THE GUYS IN KIEFER SQUARE HIRED ME TO PROTECT THEM -- AGAINST SOMEONE ELSE, TRUE -- BUT THEY HIRED ME.
AND I CAN'T JUST LET 'EM GO DOWN THE TOILET LIKE THIS.
WHEN HONOR GUARD EXPOSES HIDALGO AS THE CONQUISTADOR, THE GUYS'LL BE UPSET AT LOSIN' THE JOB --
-- BUT THEY BEEN PAID SOME ALREADY. AND THEY'LL REALIZE THERE WASN'T GONNA BE ANY PAYOFF AT THE END.
HEY'LL SEE WAS THE ONLY --

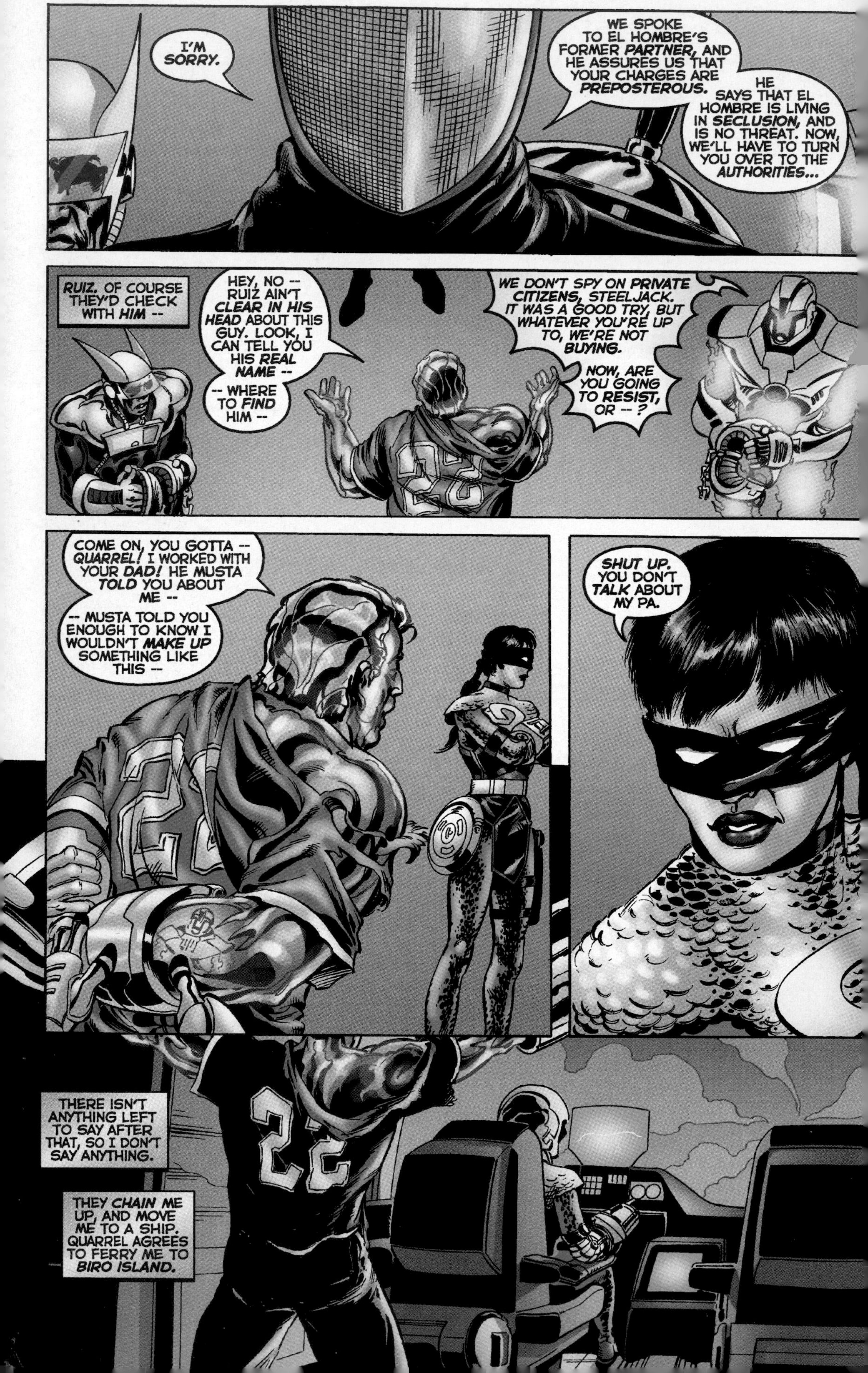
I'M SORRY.
WE SPOKE TO EL HOMBRE'S FORMER PARTNER, AND HE ASSURES US THAT YOUR CHARGES ARE PREPOSTEROUS.
HE SAYS THAT EL HOMBRE IS LIVING IN SECLUSION, AND IS NO THREAT. NOW, WE'LL HAVE TO TURN YOU OVER TO THE AUTHORITIES...
RUIZ. OF COURSE THEY'D CHECK WITH HIM --
HEY, NO -- RUIZ AIN'T CLEAR IN HIS HEAD ABOUT THIS GUY. LOOK, I CAN TELL YOU HIS REAL NAME --
-- WHERE TO FIND HIM --
WE DON'T SPY ON PRIVATE CITIZENS, STEELJACK. IT WAS A GOOD TRY, BUT WHATEVER YOU'RE UP TO, WE'RE NOT BUYING.
NOW, ARE YOU GOING TO RESIST, OR -- ?
COME ON, YOU GOTTA -- QUARREL! I WORKED WITH YOUR DAD! HE MUSTA TOLD YOU ABOUT ME --
-- MUSTA TOLD YOU ENOUGH TO KNOW I WOULDN'T MAKE UP SOMETHING LIKE THIS --
SHUT UP. YOU DON'T TALK ABOUT MY PA.
THERE ISN'T ANYTHING LEFT TO SAY AFTER THAT, SO I DON'T SAY ANYTHING.
THEY CHAIN ME UP, AND MOVE ME TO A SHIP. QUARREL AGREES TO FERRY ME TO BIRO ISLAND.

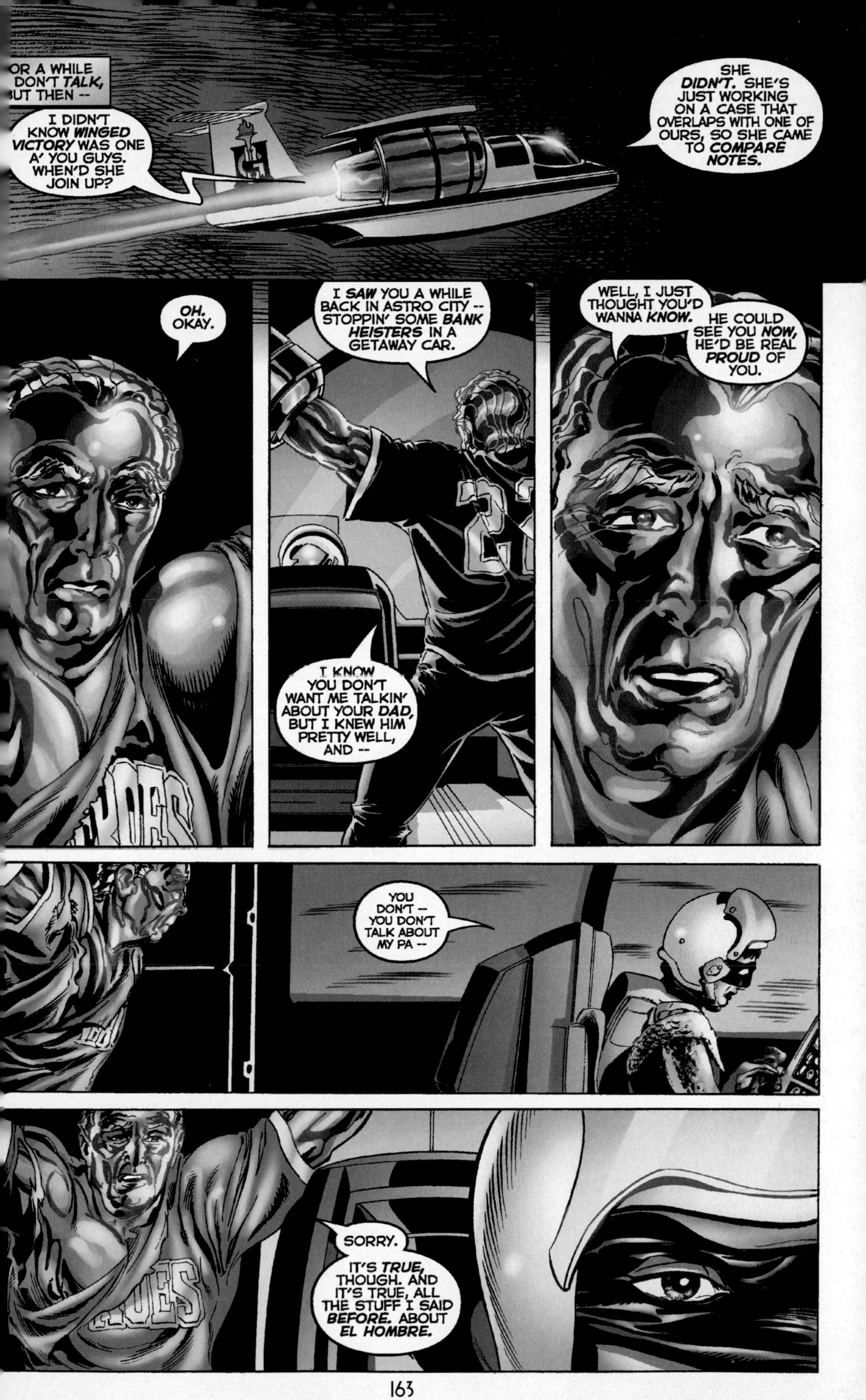

OR A WHILE DON'T *TALK*, BUT THEN --
I DIDN'T KNOW *WINGED VICTORY* WAS ONE A' YOU GUYS. WHEN'D SHE JOIN UP?
SHE *DIDN'T.* SHE'S JUST WORKING ON A CASE THAT OVERLAPS WITH ONE OF OURS, SO SHE CAME TO *COMPARE NOTES.*
OH. OKAY.
I *SAW* YOU A WHILE BACK IN ASTRO CITY -- STOPPIN' SOME *BANK HEISTERS* IN A GETAWAY CAR.
I KNOW YOU DON'T WANT ME TALKIN' ABOUT YOUR *DAD*, BUT I KNEW HIM PRETTY WELL, AND --
WELL, I JUST THOUGHT YOU'D WANNA *KNOW.*
HE COULD SEE YOU *NOW*, HE'D BE REAL *PROUD* OF YOU.
YOU DON'T -- YOU DON'T TALK ABOUT MY PA --
SORRY.
IT'S *TRUE*, THOUGH. AND IT'S TRUE, ALL THE STUFF I SAID *BEFORE.* ABOUT *EL HOMBRE.*

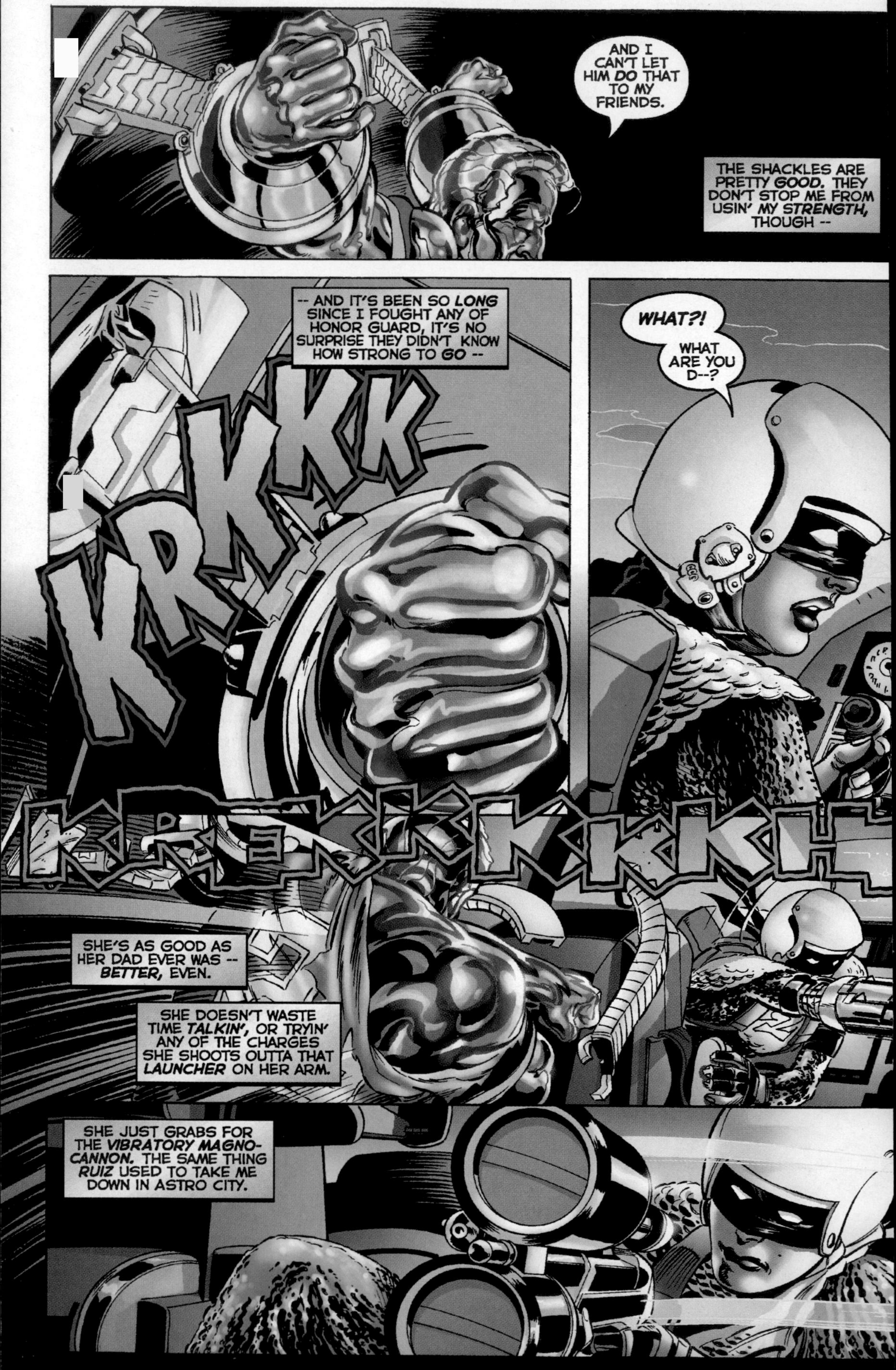
AND I CAN'T LET HIM DO THAT TO MY FRIENDS.
THE SHACKLES ARE PRETTY GOOD. THEY DON'T STOP ME FROM USIN' MY STRENGTH, THOUGH --
-- AND IT'S BEEN SO LONG SINCE I FOUGHT ANY OF HONOR GUARD, IT'S NO SURPRISE THEY DIDN'T KNOW HOW STRONG TO GO --
KRKKK
WHAT?!
WHAT ARE YOU D--?
SHE'S AS GOOD AS HER DAD EVER WAS -- BETTER, EVEN.
SHE DOESN'T WASTE TIME TALKIN', OR TRYIN' ANY OF THE CHARGES SHE SHOOTS OUTTA THAT LAUNCHER ON HER ARM.
SHE JUST GRABS FOR THE VIBRATORY MAGNO-CANNON. THE SAME THING RUIZ USED TO TAKE ME DOWN IN ASTRO CITY.

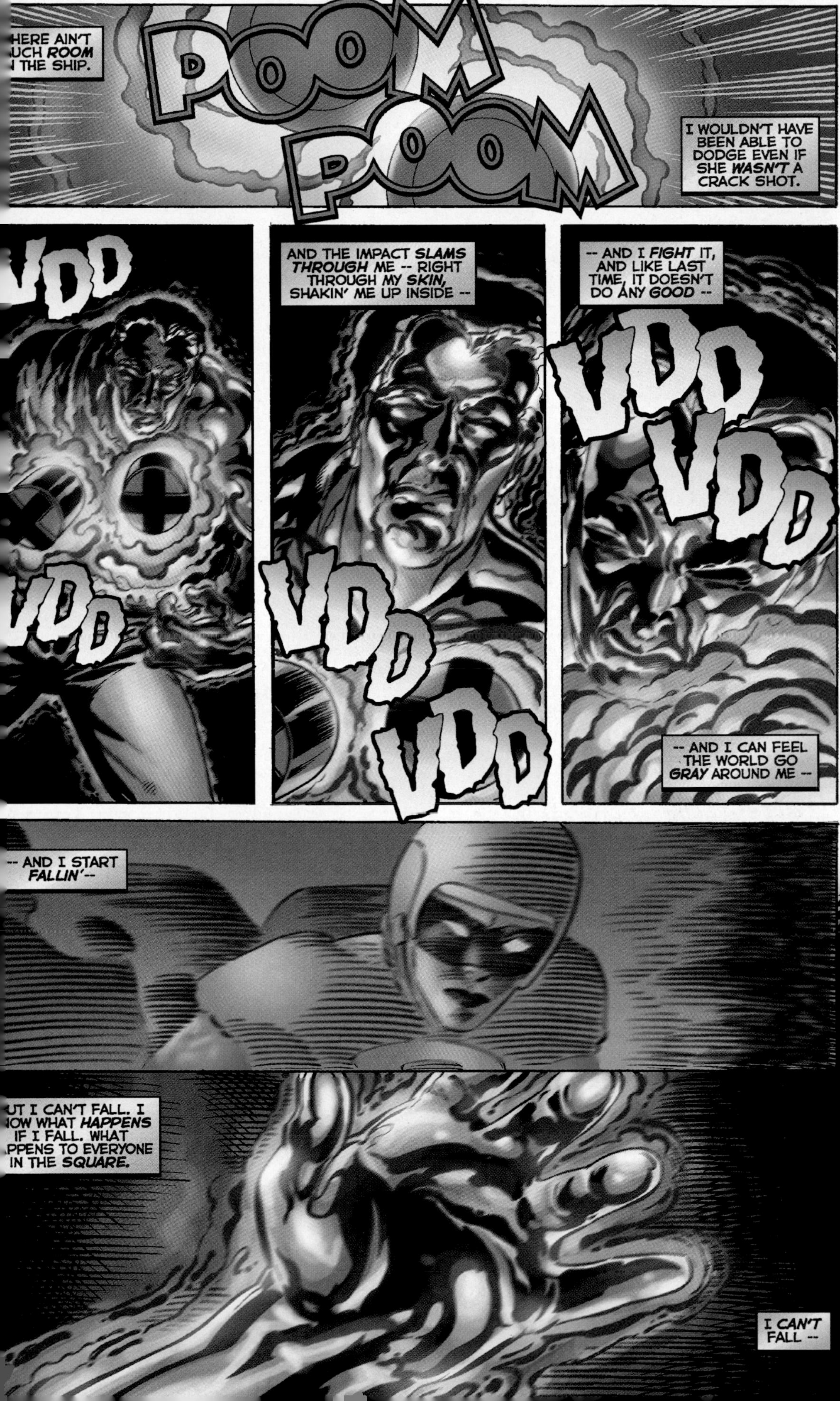
HERE AIN'T
UCH ROOM
N THE SHIP.
POOM
POOM
I WOULDN'T HAVE BEEN ABLE TO DODGE EVEN IF SHE WASN'T A CRACK SHOT.
VDD
VDD
AND THE IMPACT SLAMS THROUGH ME -- RIGHT THROUGH MY SKIN, SHAKIN' ME UP INSIDE --
VDD
VDD
-- AND I FIGHT IT, AND LIKE LAST TIME, IT DOESN'T DO ANY GOOD --
VDD
VDD
-- AND I CAN FEEL THE WORLD GO GRAY AROUND ME --
-- AND I START FALLIN'--
UT I CAN'T FALL. I
NOW WHAT HAPPENS
IF I FALL. WHAT
APPENS TO EVERYONE
IN THE SQUARE.
I CAN'T FALL --

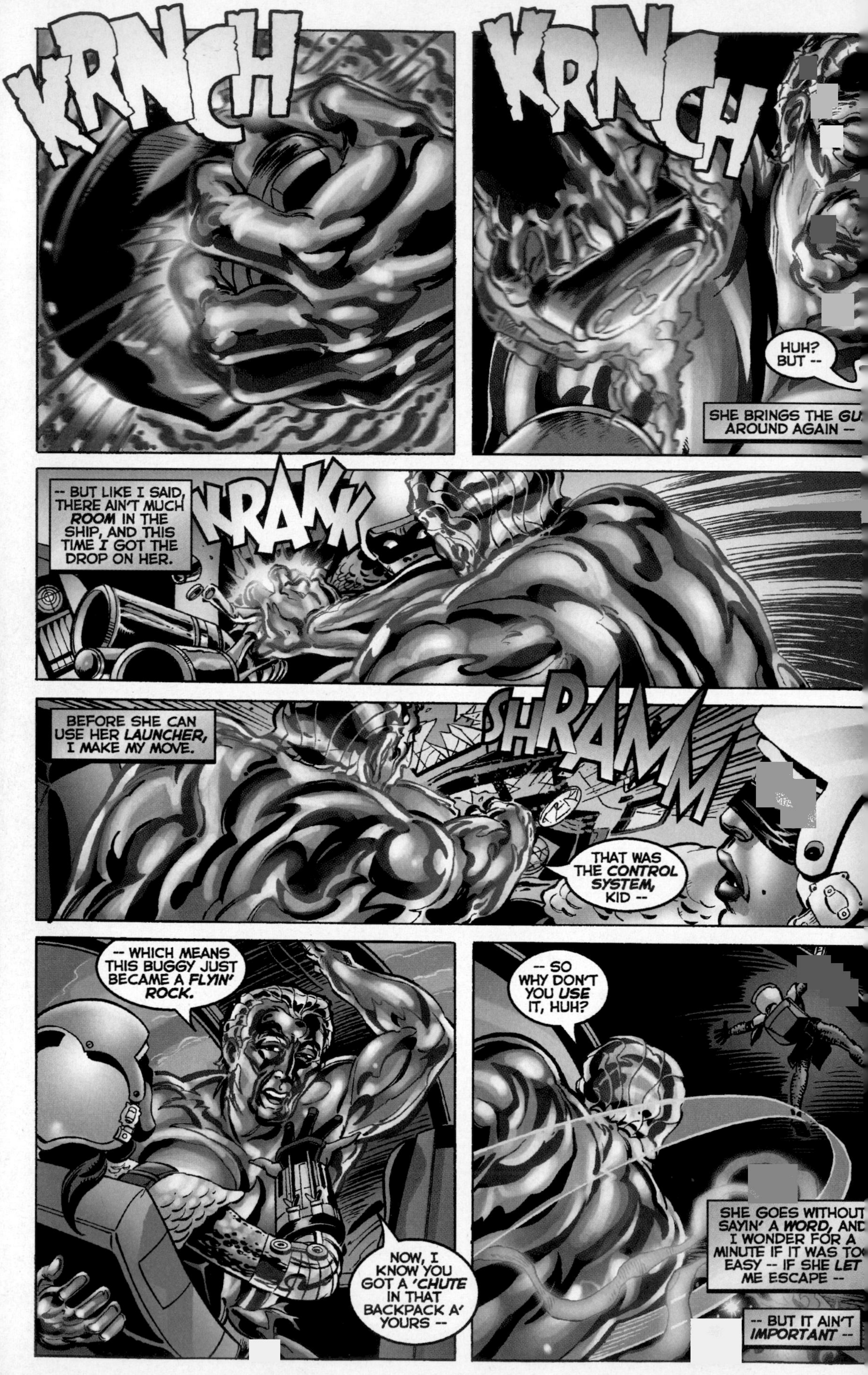
KRNCH
KRNCH
HUH? BUT --
SHE BRINGS THE GU
AROUND AGAIN --
-- BUT LIKE I SAID, THERE AIN'T MUCH ROOM IN THE SHIP, AND THIS TIME I GOT THE DROP ON HER.
KRAKK
BEFORE SHE CAN USE HER LAUNCHER, I MAKE MY MOVE.
SHRAMM
THAT WAS THE CONTROL SYSTEM, KID --
-- WHICH MEANS THIS BUGGY JUST BECAME A FLYIN' ROCK.
NOW, I KNOW YOU GOT A 'CHUTE IN THAT BACKPACK A' YOURS --
-- SO WHY DON'T YOU USE IT, HUH?
SHE GOES WITHOUT SAYIN' A WORD, AND I WONDER FOR A MINUTE IF IT WAS TO EASY -- IF SHE LET ME ESCAPE --
-- BUT IT AIN'T IMPORTANT --

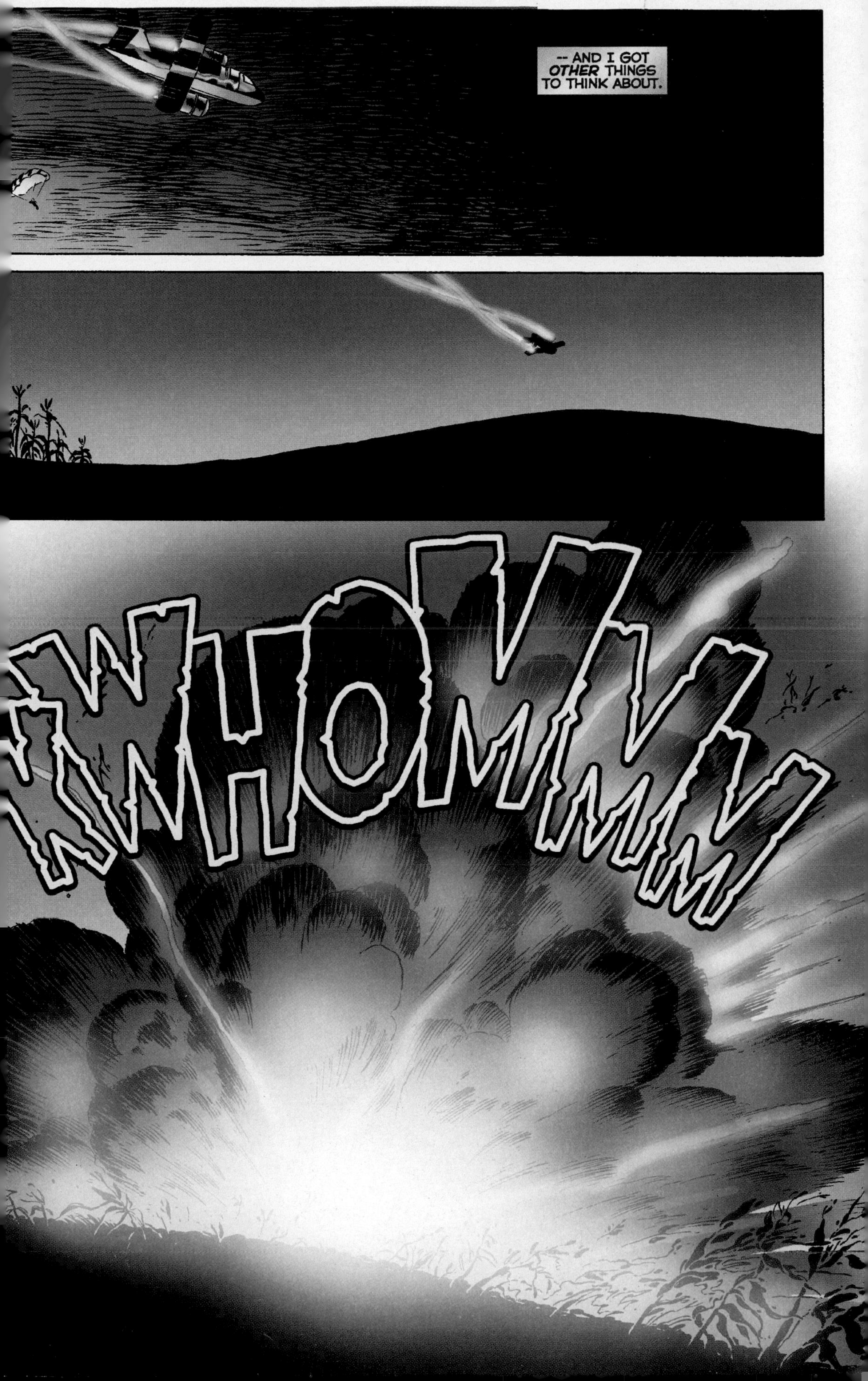
-- AND I GOT OTHER THINGS TO THINK ABOUT.
WHOMMM

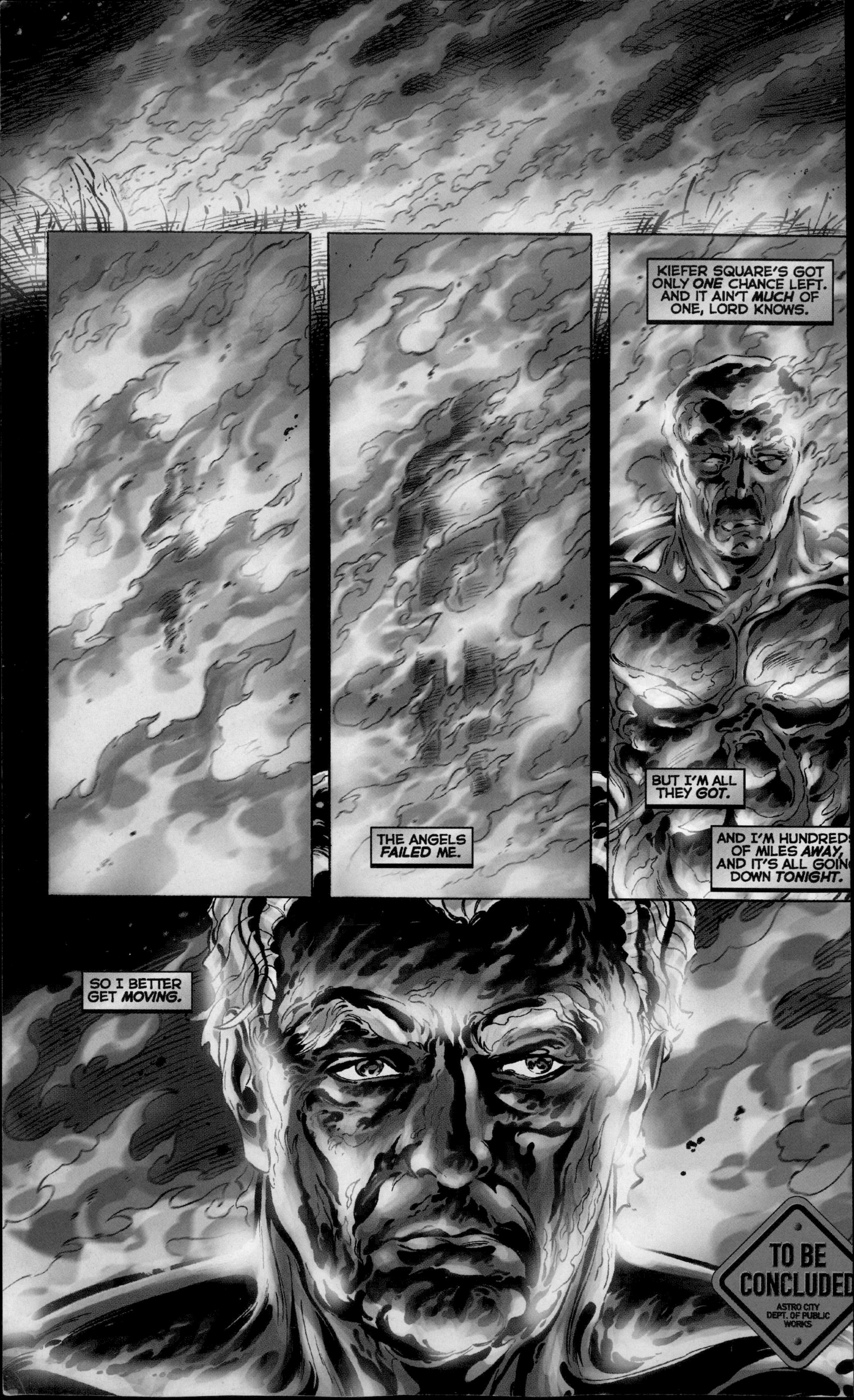
THE ANGELS FAILED ME.
KIEFER SQUARE'S GOT ONLY ONE CHANCE LEFT. AND IT AIN'T MUCH OF ONE, LORD KNOWS.
BUT I'M ALL THEY GOT.
AND I'M HUNDREDS OF MILES AWAY, AND IT'S ALL GOING DOWN TONIGHT.
SO I BETTER GET MOVING.
TO BE CONCLUDED
ASTRO CITY DEPT. OF PUBLIC WORKS

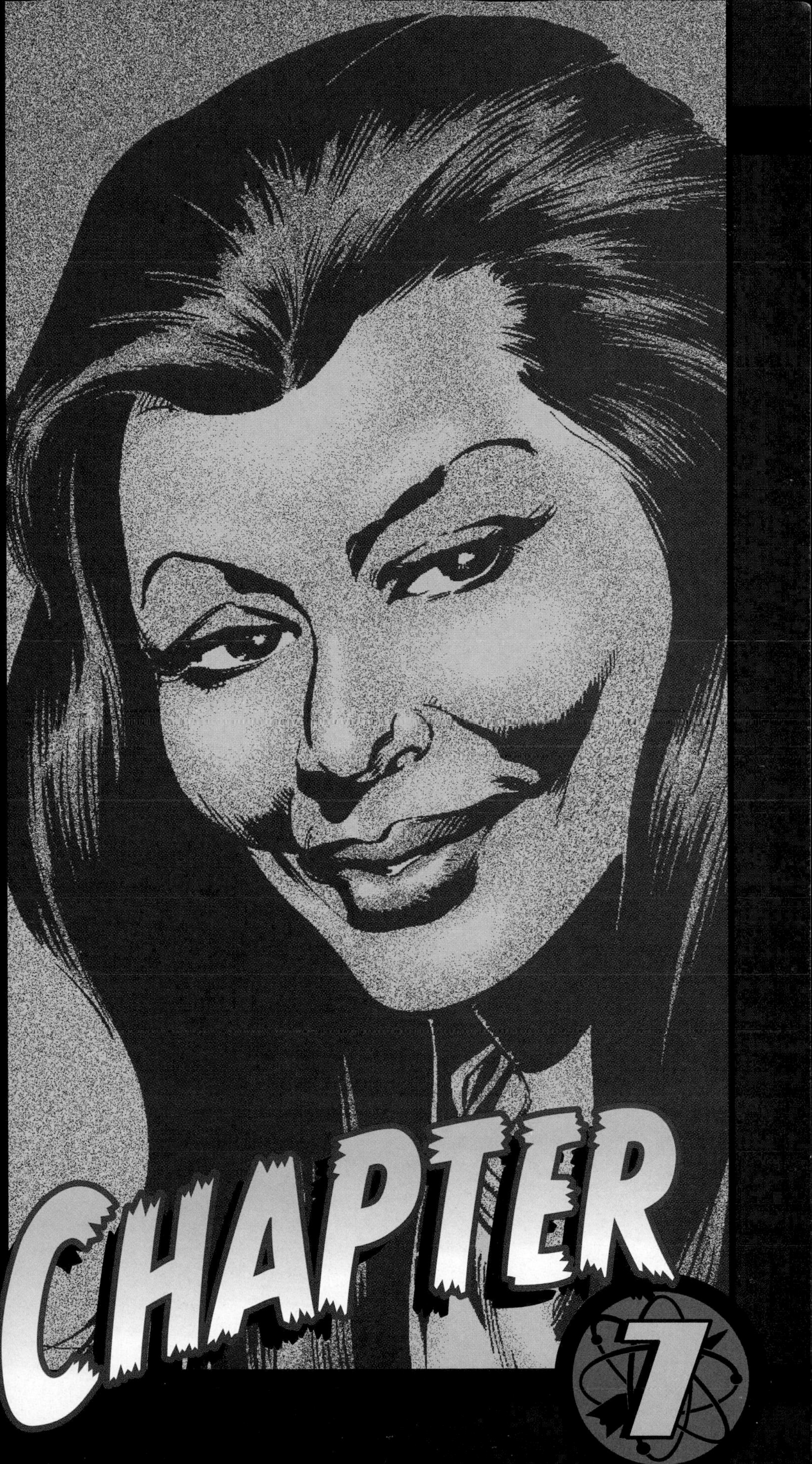
CHAPTER
7

The WOW FINISH

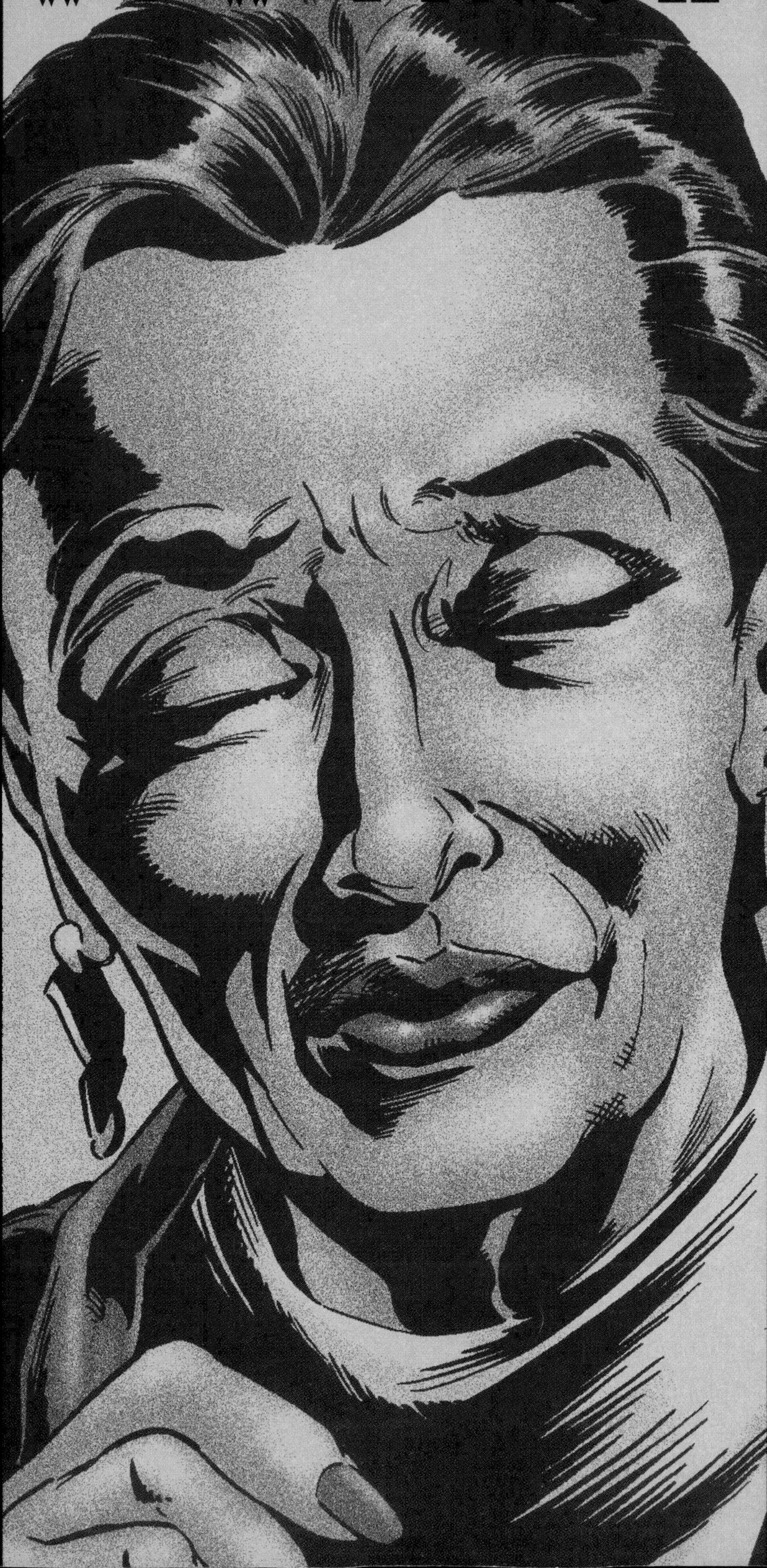

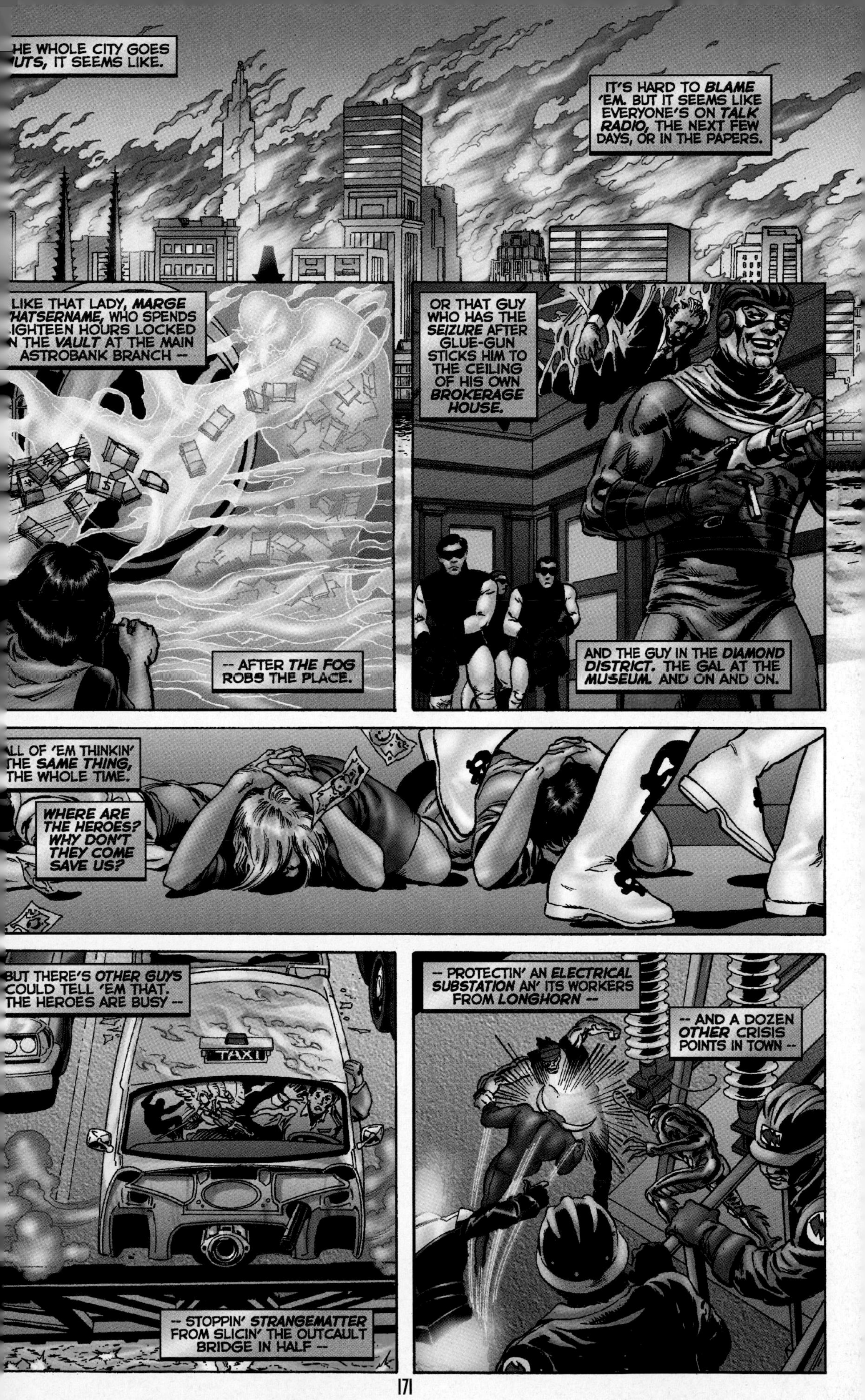
HE WHOLE CITY GOES
UTS, IT SEEMS LIKE.
IT'S HARD TO BLAME 'EM. BUT IT SEEMS LIKE EVERYONE'S ON TALK RADIO, THE NEXT FEW DAYS, OR IN THE PAPERS.
LIKE THAT LADY, MARGE HATSERNAME, WHO SPENDS IGHTEEN HOURS LOCKED N THE VAULT AT THE MAIN ASTROBANK BRANCH --
-- AFTER THE FOG ROBS THE PLACE.
OR THAT GUY WHO HAS THE SEIZURE AFTER GLUE-GUN STICKS HIM TO THE CEILING OF HIS OWN BROKERAGE HOUSE.
AND THE GUY IN THE DIAMOND DISTRICT. THE GAL AT THE MUSEUM. AND ON AND ON.
LL OF 'EM THINKIN' THE SAME THING, THE WHOLE TIME.
WHERE ARE THE HEROES? WHY DON'T THEY COME SAVE US?
BUT THERE'S OTHER GUYS COULD TELL 'EM THAT. THE HEROES ARE BUSY --
TAXI
-- STOPPIN' STRANGEMATTER FROM SLICIN' THE OUTCAULT BRIDGE IN HALF --
-- PROTECTIN' AN ELECTRICAL SUBSTATION AN' ITS WORKERS FROM LONGHORN --
-- AND A DOZEN OTHER CRISIS POINTS IN TOWN --

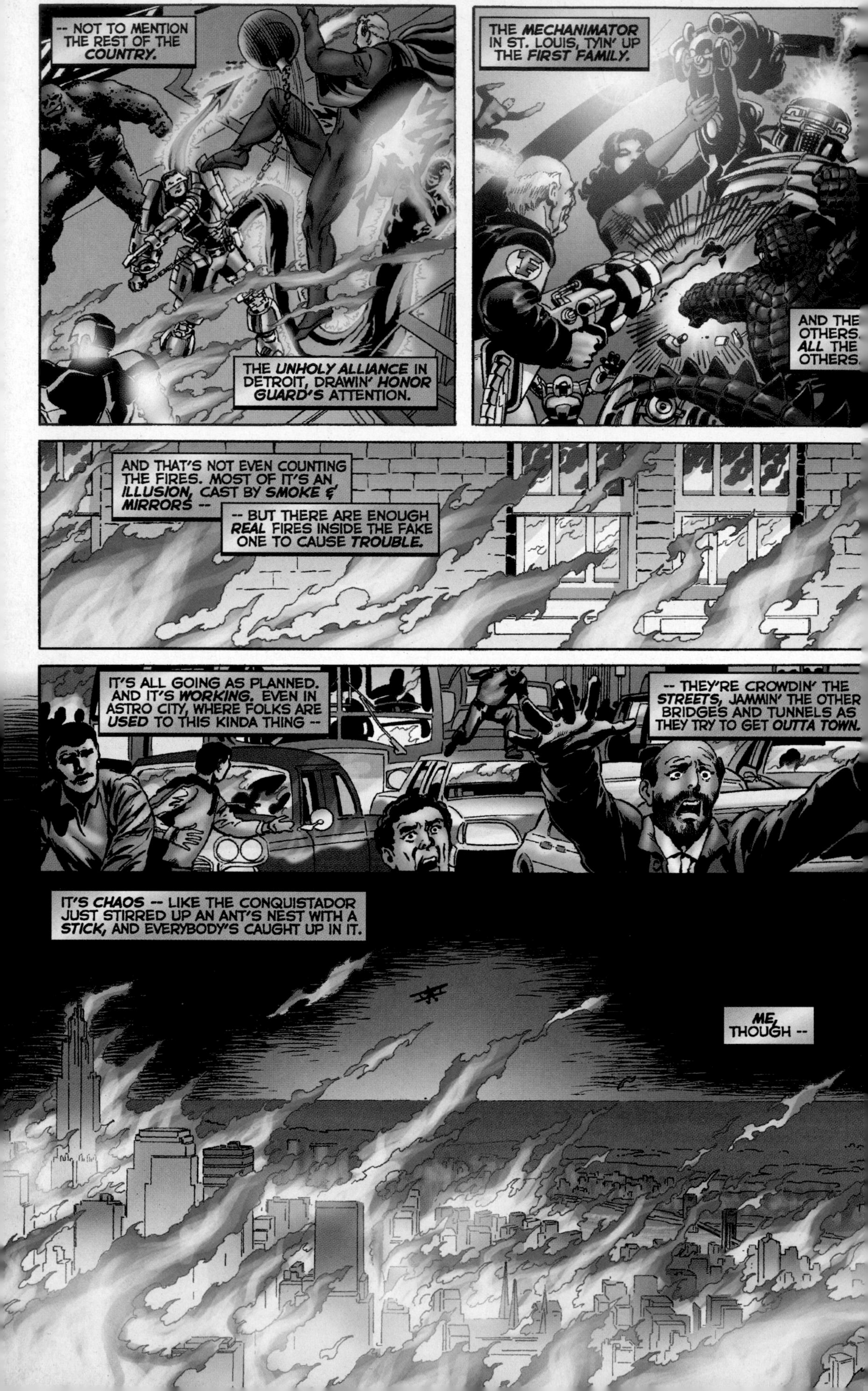
-- NOT TO MENTION THE REST OF THE COUNTRY.
THE UNHOLY ALLIANCE IN DETROIT, DRAWIN' HONOR GUARD'S ATTENTION.
THE MECHANIMATOR IN ST. LOUIS, TYIN' UP THE FIRST FAMILY.
AND THE OTHERS. ALL THE OTHERS.
AND THAT'S NOT EVEN COUNTING THE FIRES. MOST OF IT'S AN ILLUSION, CAST BY SMOKE & MIRRORS --
-- BUT THERE ARE ENOUGH REAL FIRES INSIDE THE FAKE ONE TO CAUSE TROUBLE.
IT'S ALL GOING AS PLANNED. AND IT'S WORKING. EVEN IN ASTRO CITY, WHERE FOLKS ARE USED TO THIS KINDA THING --
-- THEY'RE CROWDIN' THE STREETS, JAMMIN' THE OTHER BRIDGES AND TUNNELS AS THEY TRY TO GET OUTTA TOWN.
IT'S CHAOS -- LIKE THE CONQUISTADOR JUST STIRRED UP AN ANT'S NEST WITH A STICK, AND EVERYBODY'S CAUGHT UP IN IT.
ME, THOUGH --

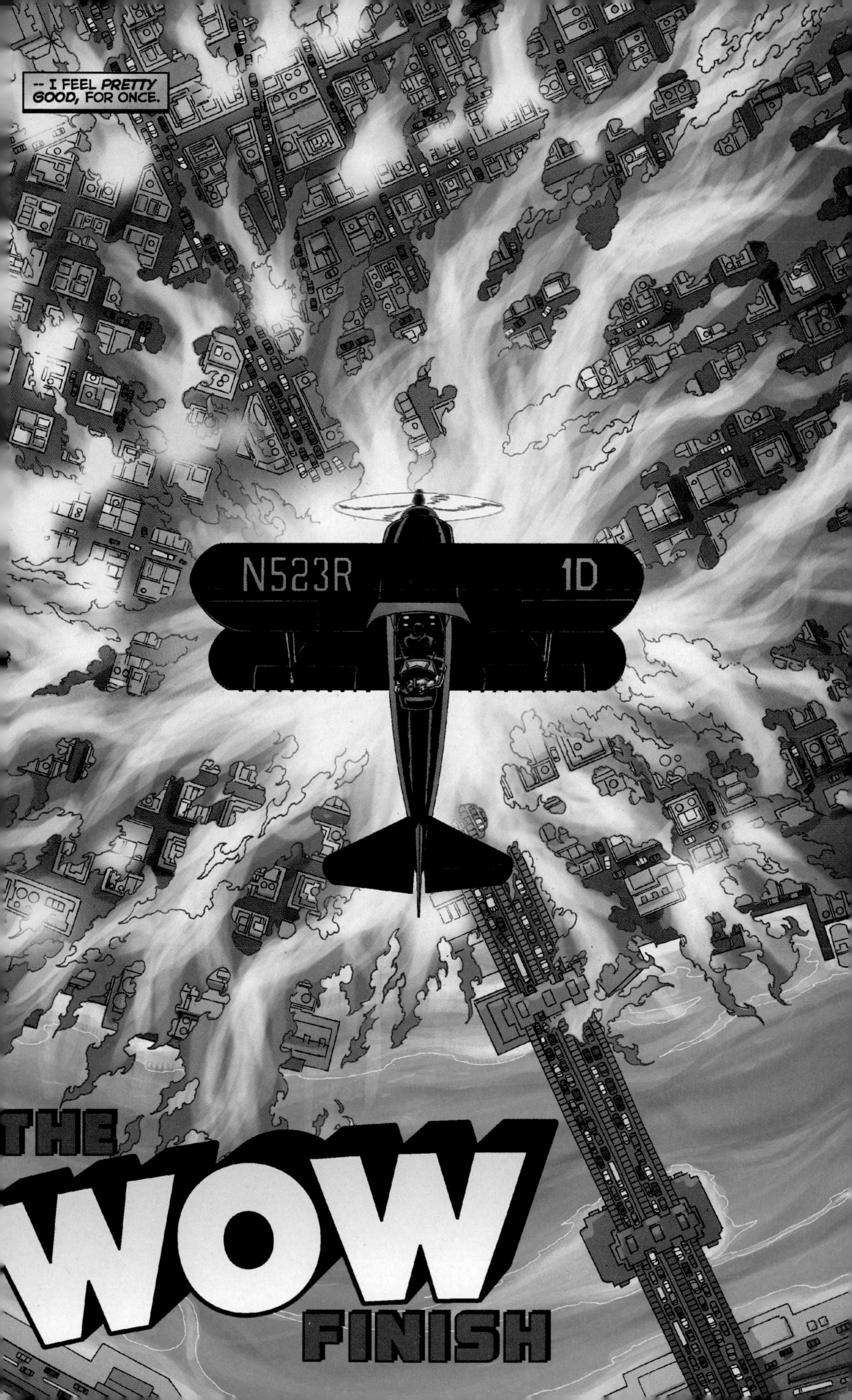
-- I FEEL *PRETTY* *GOOD*, FOR ONCE.
N523R
1D
THE WOW FINISH

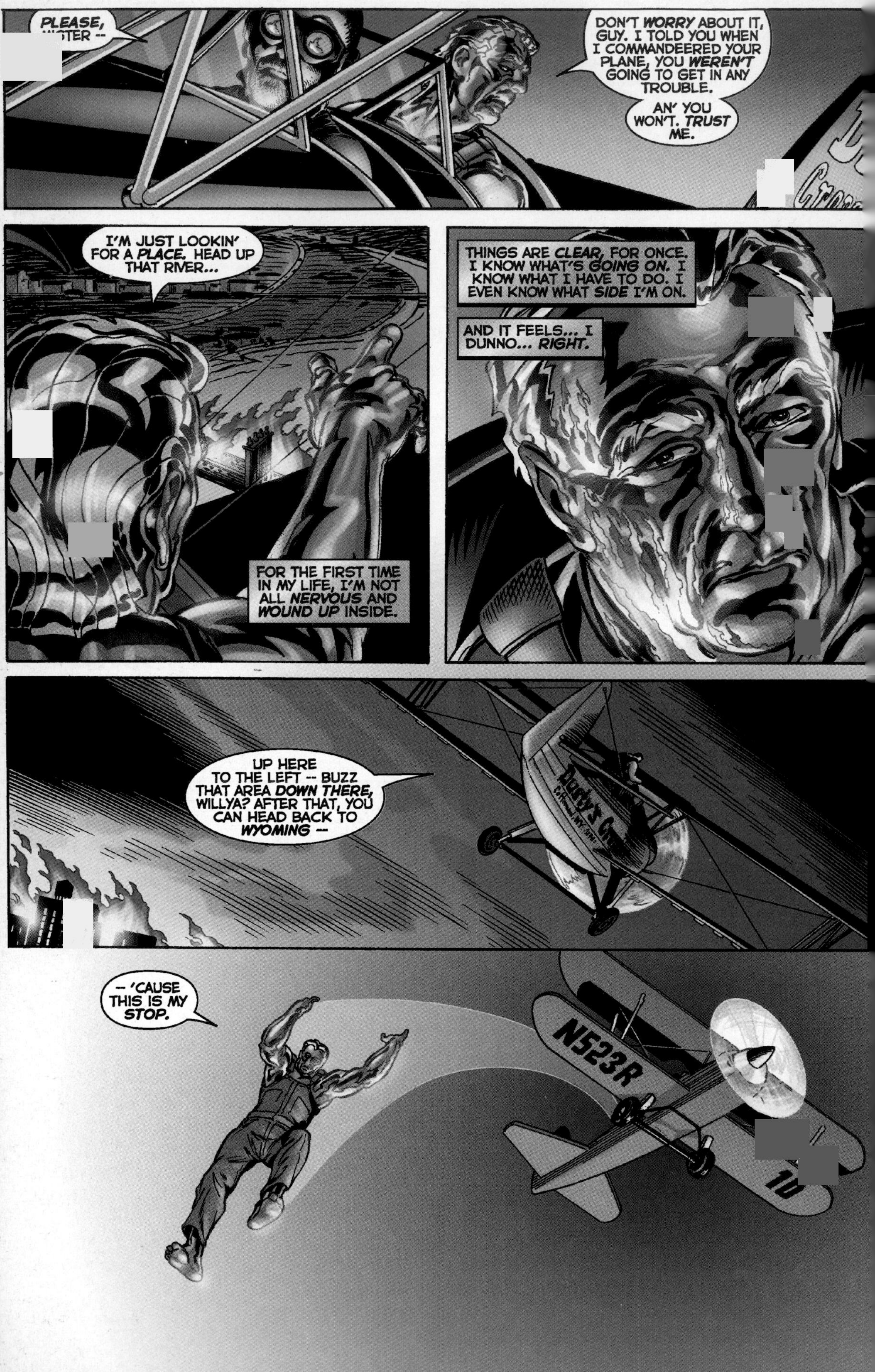
PLEASE,
DON'T WORRY ABOUT IT, GUY. I TOLD YOU WHEN I COMMANDEERED YOUR PLANE, YOU WEREN'T GOING TO GET IN ANY TROUBLE.
AN' YOU WON'T. TRUST ME.
I'M JUST LOOKIN' FOR A PLACE. HEAD UP THAT RIVER...
FOR THE FIRST TIME IN MY LIFE, I'M NOT ALL NERVOUS AND WOUND UP INSIDE.
THINGS ARE CLEAR, FOR ONCE. I KNOW WHAT'S GOING ON. I KNOW WHAT I HAVE TO DO. I EVEN KNOW WHAT SIDE I'M ON.
AND IT FEELS... I DUNNO... RIGHT.
UP HERE TO THE LEFT -- BUZZ THAT AREA DOWN THERE, WILLYA? AFTER THAT, YOU CAN HEAD BACK TO WYOMING --
-- 'CAUSE THIS IS MY STOP.
N523R

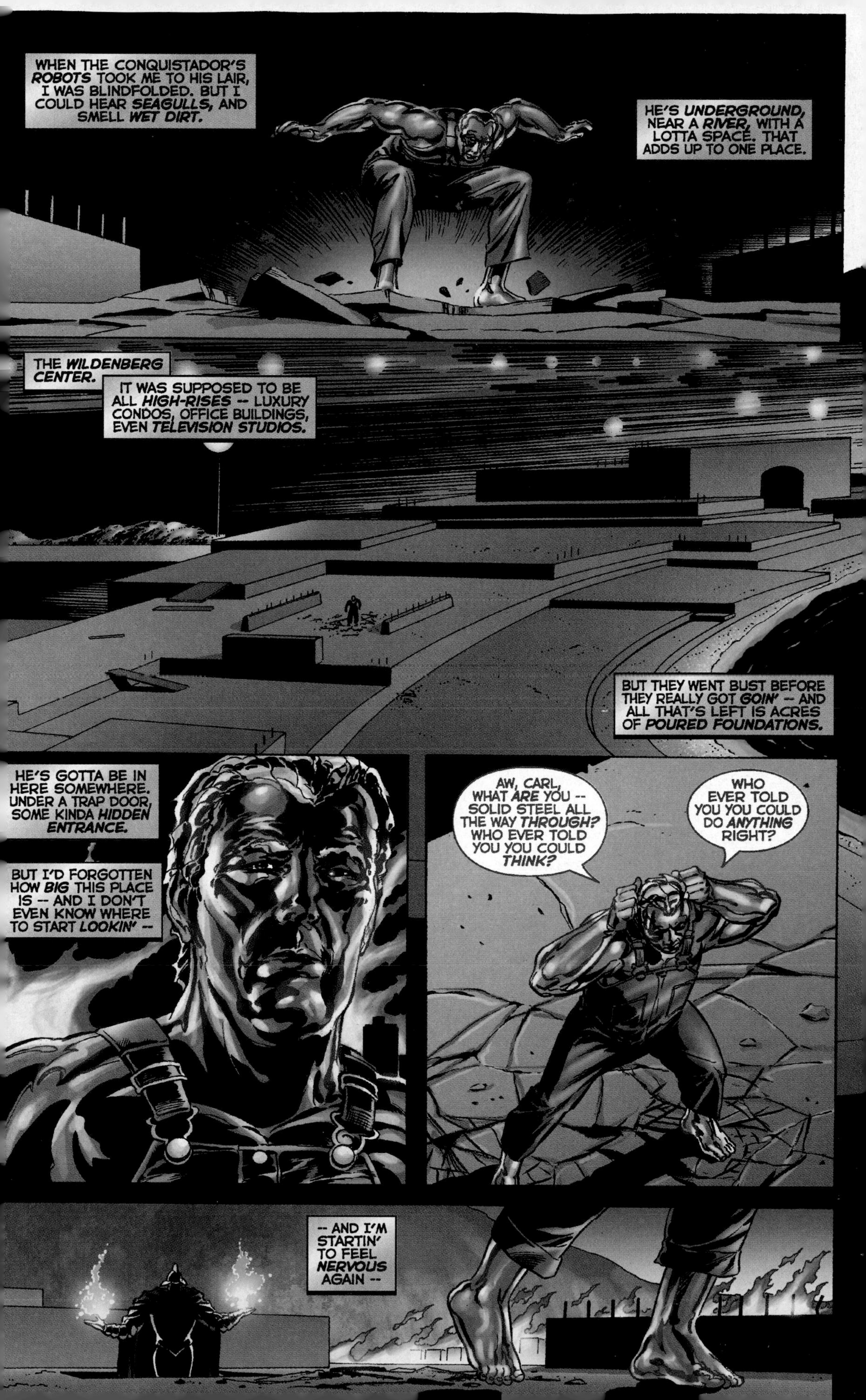
WHEN THE CONQUISTADOR'S ROBOTS TOOK ME TO HIS LAIR, I WAS BLINDFOLDED. BUT I COULD HEAR SEAGULLS, AND SMELL WET DIRT.
HE'S UNDERGROUND, NEAR A RIVER, WITH A LOTTA SPACE. THAT ADDS UP TO ONE PLACE.
THE WILDENBERG CENTER.
IT WAS SUPPOSED TO BE ALL HIGH-RISES -- LUXURY CONDOS, OFFICE BUILDINGS, EVEN TELEVISION STUDIOS.
BUT THEY WENT BUST BEFORE THEY REALLY GOT GOIN' -- AND ALL THAT'S LEFT IS ACRES OF POURED FOUNDATIONS.
HE'S GOTTA BE IN HERE SOMEWHERE. UNDER A TRAP DOOR, SOME KINDA HIDDEN ENTRANCE.
BUT I'D FORGOTTEN HOW BIG THIS PLACE IS -- AND I DON'T EVEN KNOW WHERE TO START LOOKIN' --
AW, CARL, WHAT ARE YOU -- SOLID STEEL ALL THE WAY THROUGH? WHO EVER TOLD YOU YOU COULD THINK?
WHO EVER TOLD YOU YOU COULD DO ANYTHING RIGHT?
-- AND I'M STARTIN' TO FEEL NERVOUS AGAIN --

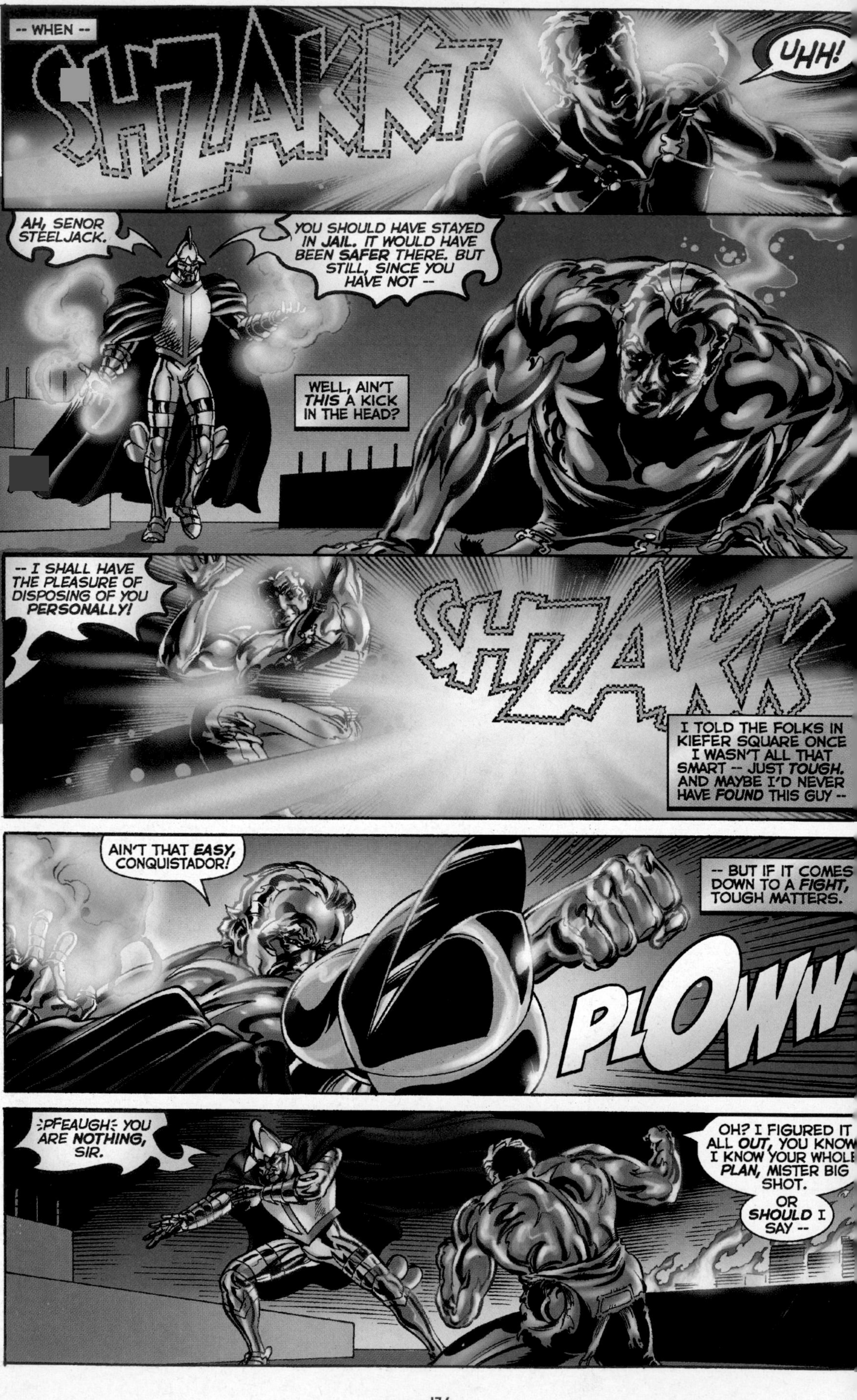
-- WHEN --
SHZAKKT
UHH!
AH, SENOR STEELJACK.
YOU SHOULD HAVE STAYED IN JAIL. IT WOULD HAVE BEEN SAFER THERE. BUT STILL, SINCE YOU HAVE NOT --
WELL, AIN'T THIS A KICK IN THE HEAD?
-- I SHALL HAVE THE PLEASURE OF DISPOSING OF YOU PERSONALLY!
SHZAKK
I TOLD THE FOLKS IN KIEFER SQUARE ONCE I WASN'T ALL THAT SMART -- JUST TOUGH. AND MAYBE I'D NEVER HAVE FOUND THIS GUY --
AIN'T THAT EASY, CONQUISTADOR!
-- BUT IF IT COMES DOWN TO A FIGHT, TOUGH MATTERS.
PLOWW
PFEAUGH YOU ARE NOTHING, SIR.
OH? I FIGURED IT ALL OUT, YOU KNOW. I KNOW YOUR WHOLE PLAN, MISTER BIG SHOT.
OR SHOULD I SAY --

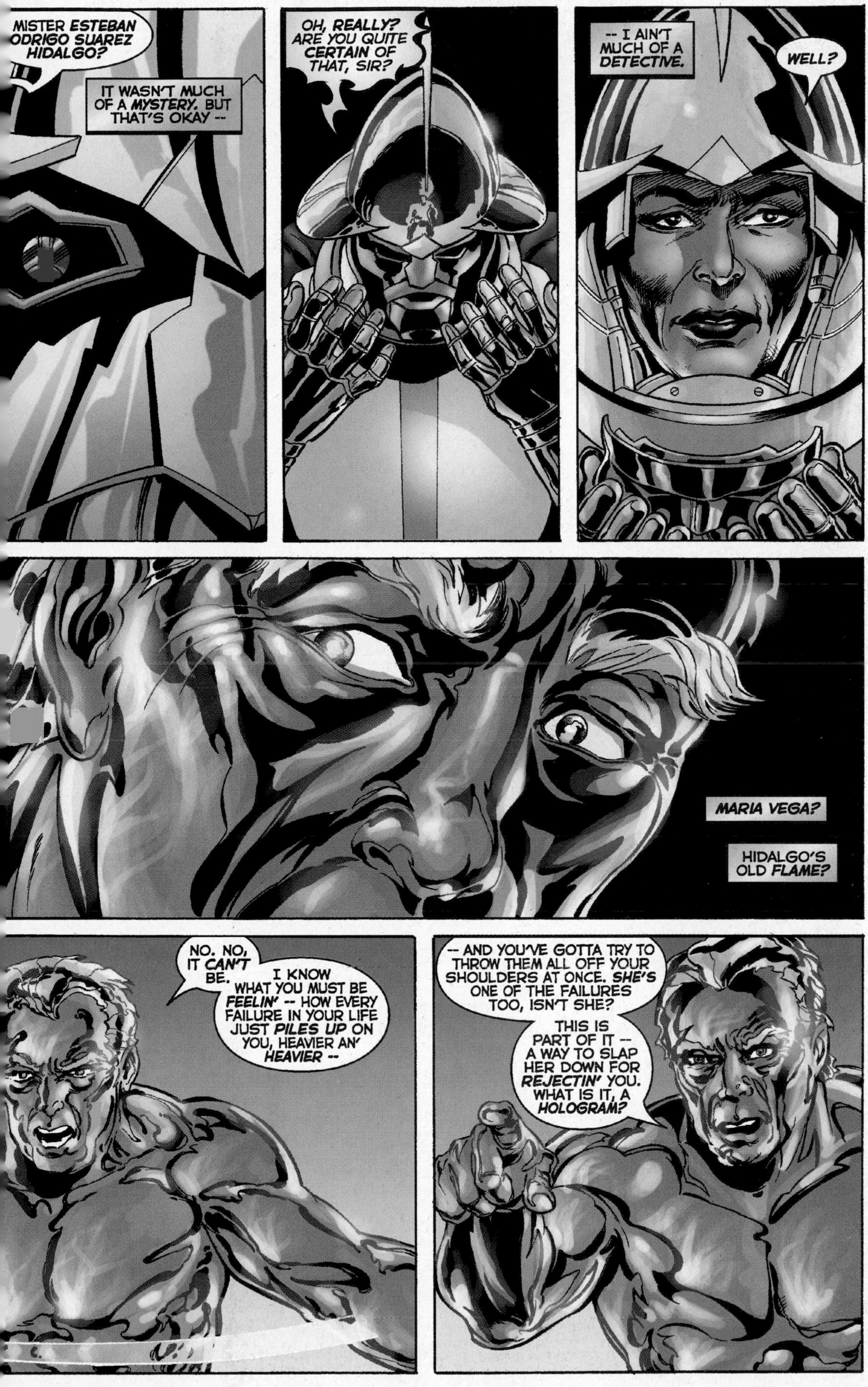

MISTER ESTEBAN ODRIGO SUAREZ HIDALGO?
IT WASN'T MUCH OF A MYSTERY. BUT THAT'S OKAY --
OH, REALLY? ARE YOU QUITE CERTAIN OF THAT, SIR?
-- I AIN'T MUCH OF A DETECTIVE.
WELL?
MARIA VEGA?
HIDALGO'S OLD FLAME?
NO. NO, IT CAN'T BE.
I KNOW WHAT YOU MUST BE FEELIN' -- HOW EVERY FAILURE IN YOUR LIFE JUST PILES UP ON YOU, HEAVIER AN' HEAVIER --
-- AND YOU'VE GOTTA TRY TO THROW THEM ALL OFF YOUR SHOULDERS AT ONCE. SHE'S ONE OF THE FAILURES TOO, ISN'T SHE?
THIS IS PART OF IT -- A WAY TO SLAP HER DOWN FOR REJECTIN' YOU. WHAT IS IT, A HOLOGRAM?

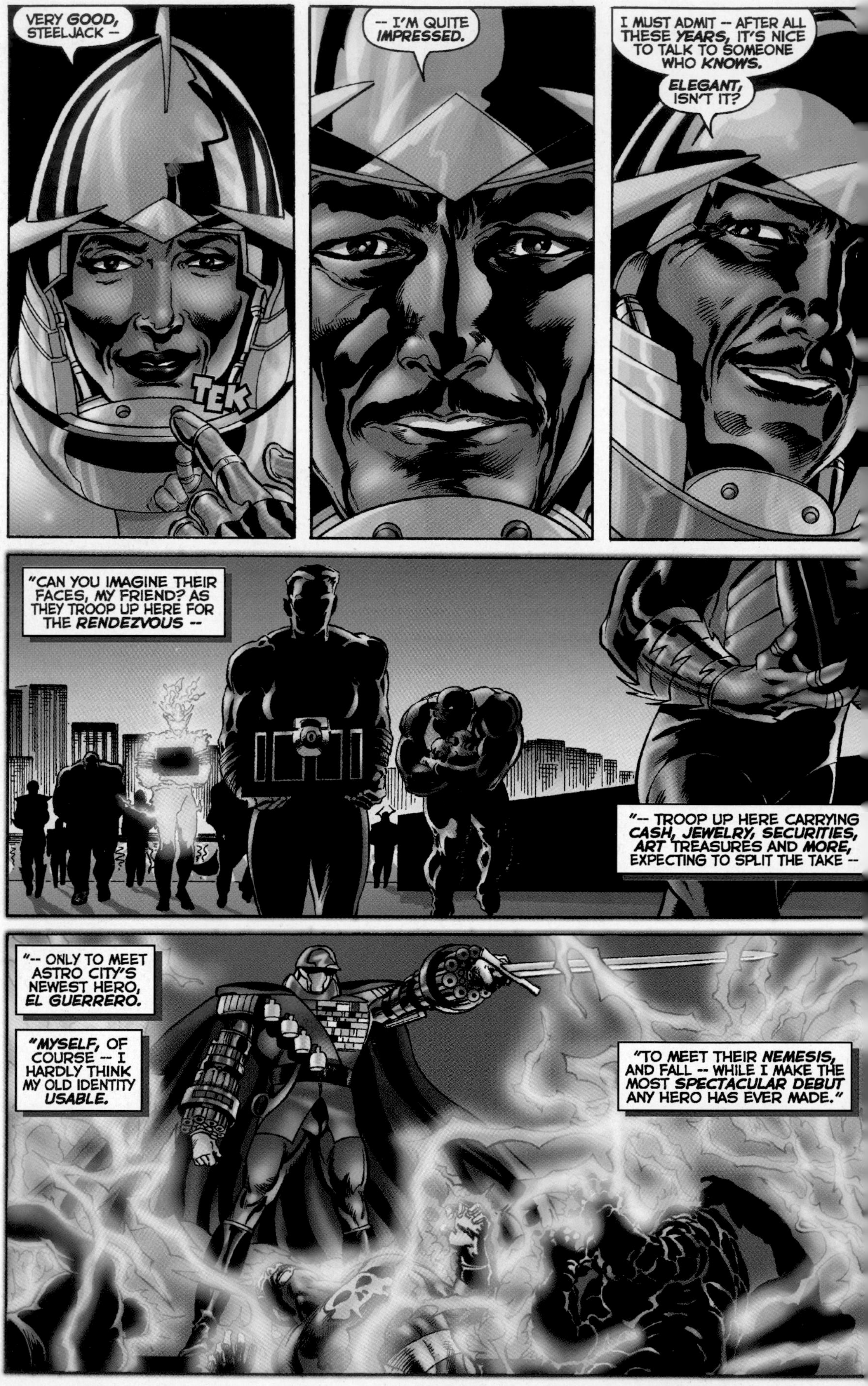
VERY GOOD, STEELJACK --
TEK
-- I'M QUITE IMPRESSED.
I MUST ADMIT -- AFTER ALL THESE YEARS, IT'S NICE TO TALK TO SOMEONE WHO KNOWS.
ELEGANT, ISN'T IT?
"CAN YOU IMAGINE THEIR FACES, MY FRIEND? AS THEY TROOP UP HERE FOR THE RENDEZVOUS --
"-- TROOP UP HERE CARRYING CASH, JEWELRY, SECURITIES, ART TREASURES AND MORE, EXPECTING TO SPLIT THE TAKE --
"-- ONLY TO MEET ASTRO CITY'S NEWEST HERO, EL GUERRERO.
"MYSELF, OF COURSE -- I HARDLY THINK MY OLD IDENTITY USABLE.
"TO MEET THEIR NEMESIS, AND FALL -- WHILE I MAKE THE MOST SPECTACULAR DEBUT ANY HERO HAS EVER MADE."

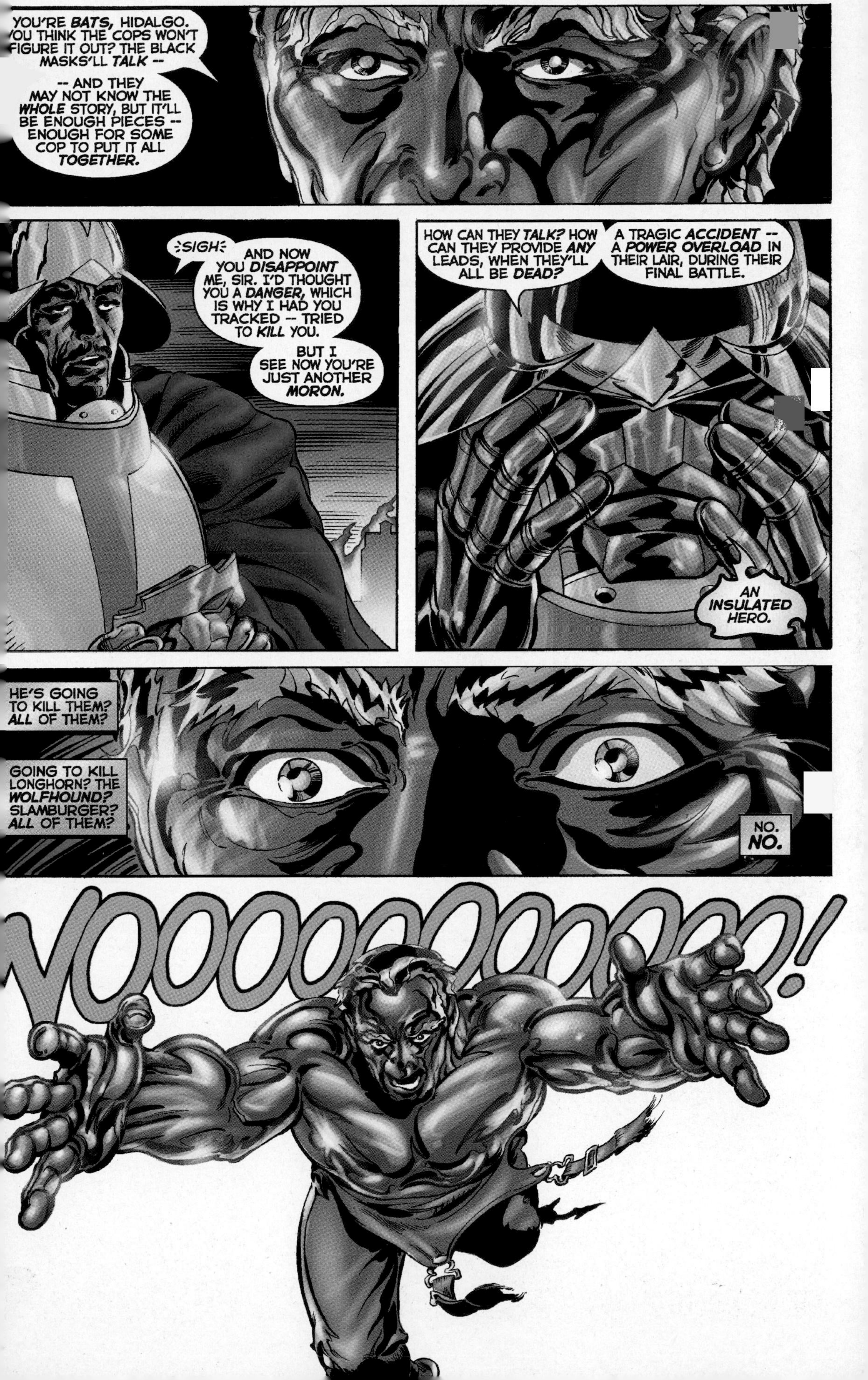
YOU'RE BATS, HIDALGO. YOU THINK THE COPS WON'T FIGURE IT OUT? THE BLACK MASKS'LL TALK --
-- AND THEY MAY NOT KNOW THE WHOLE STORY, BUT IT'LL BE ENOUGH PIECES -- ENOUGH FOR SOME COP TO PUT IT ALL TOGETHER.
SIGH
AND NOW YOU DISAPPOINT ME, SIR. I'D THOUGHT YOU A DANGER, WHICH IS WHY I HAD YOU TRACKED -- TRIED TO KILL YOU.
BUT I SEE NOW YOU'RE JUST ANOTHER MORON.
HOW CAN THEY TALK? HOW CAN THEY PROVIDE ANY LEADS, WHEN THEY'LL ALL BE DEAD?
A TRAGIC ACCIDENT -- A POWER OVERLOAD IN THEIR LAIR, DURING THEIR FINAL BATTLE.
AN INSULATED HERO.
HE'S GOING TO KILL THEM? ALL OF THEM?
GOING TO KILL LONGHORN? THE WOLFHOUND? SLAMBURGER? ALL OF THEM?
NO. NO.
NOOOOOOOOOOOO!

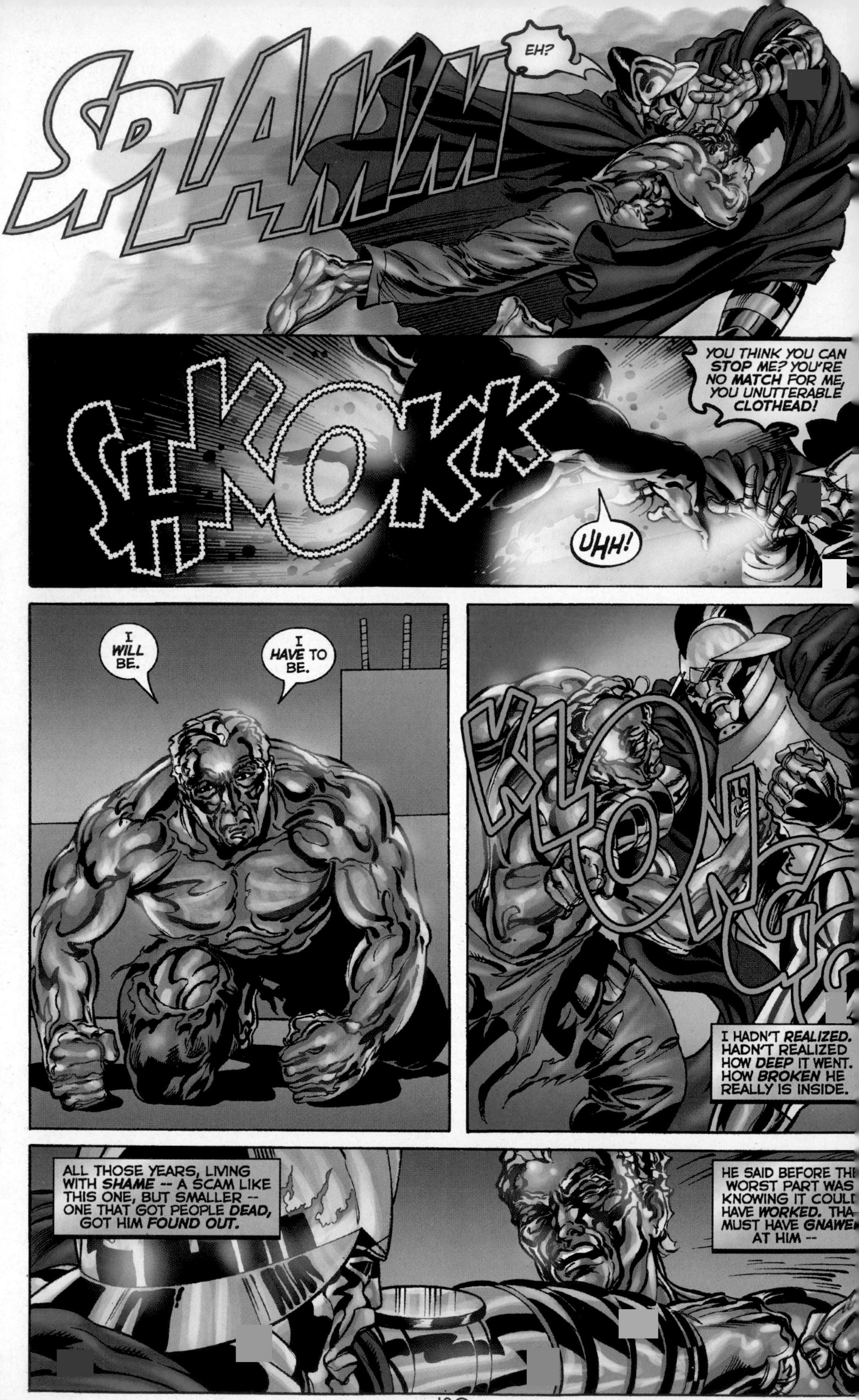
SPLAMM
EH?
YOU THINK YOU CAN STOP ME? YOU'RE NO MATCH FOR ME, YOU UNUTTERABLE CLOTHEAD!
SHKOKK
UHH!
I WILL BE.
I HAVE TO BE.
I HADN'T REALIZED. HADN'T REALIZED HOW DEEP IT WENT. HOW BROKEN HE REALLY IS INSIDE.
ALL THOSE YEARS, LIVING WITH SHAME -- A SCAM LIKE THIS ONE, BUT SMALLER -- ONE THAT GOT PEOPLE DEAD, GOT HIM FOUND OUT.
HE SAID BEFORE TH
WORST PART WAS
KNOWING IT COUL
HAVE WORKED. THA
MUST HAVE GNAWE
AT HIM --

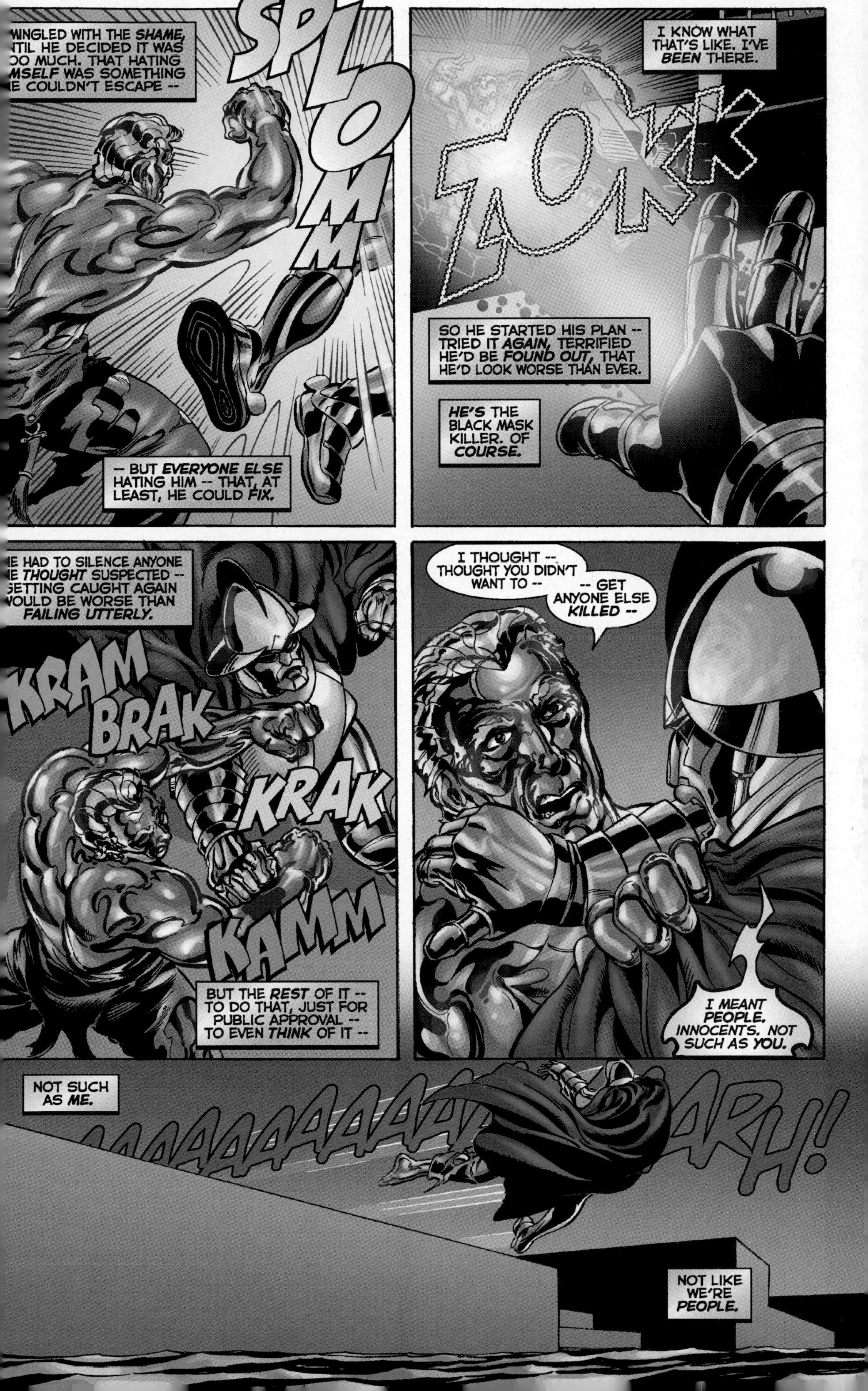

MINGLED WITH THE SHAME, UNTIL HE DECIDED IT WAS TOO MUCH. THAT HATING HIMSELF WAS SOMETHING HE COULDN'T ESCAPE --
SPLOOMMM
-- BUT EVERYONE ELSE HATING HIM -- THAT, AT LEAST, HE COULD FIX.
I KNOW WHAT THAT'S LIKE. I'VE BEEN THERE.
ZAKKK
SO HE STARTED HIS PLAN -- TRIED IT AGAIN, TERRIFIED HE'D BE FOUND OUT, THAT HE'D LOOK WORSE THAN EVER.
HE'S THE BLACK MASK KILLER. OF COURSE.
HE HAD TO SILENCE ANYONE HE THOUGHT SUSPECTED -- GETTING CAUGHT AGAIN WOULD BE WORSE THAN FAILING UTTERLY.
KRAM
BRAK
KRAK
KAMM
BUT THE REST OF IT -- TO DO THAT, JUST FOR PUBLIC APPROVAL -- TO EVEN THINK OF IT --
I THOUGHT -- THOUGHT YOU DIDN'T WANT TO --
-- GET ANYONE ELSE KILLED --
I MEANT PEOPLE. INNOCENTS. NOT SUCH AS YOU.
NOT SUCH AS ME.
AAAAAAAAAAAAARH!
NOT LIKE WE'RE PEOPLE.

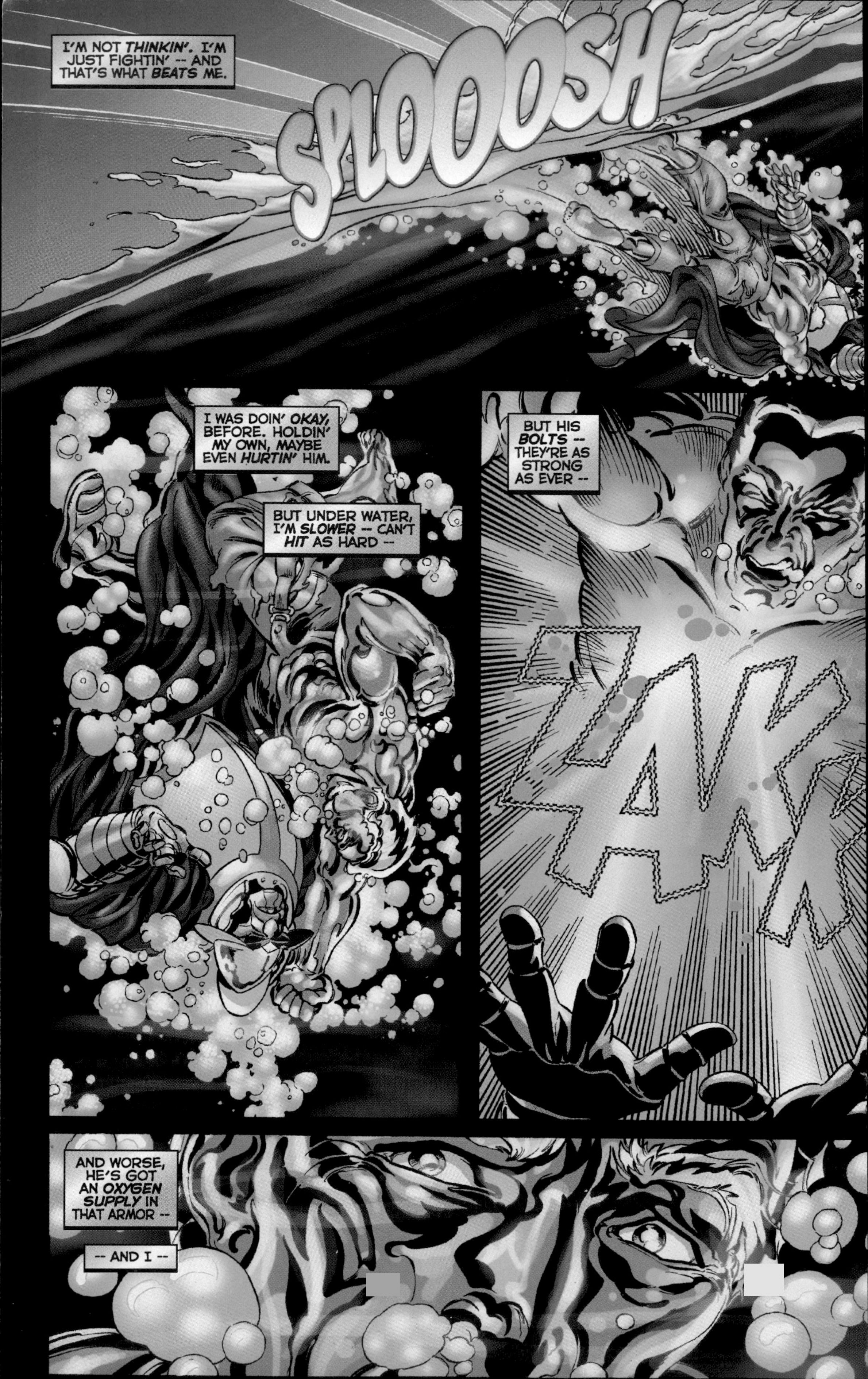

I'M NOT THINKIN'. I'M JUST FIGHTIN' -- AND THAT'S WHAT BEATS ME.
SPLOOOSH
I WAS DOIN' OKAY, BEFORE. HOLDIN' MY OWN, MAYBE EVEN HURTIN' HIM.
BUT UNDER WATER, I'M SLOWER -- CAN'T HIT AS HARD --
BUT HIS BOLTS -- THEY'RE AS STRONG AS EVER --
AND WORSE, HE'S GOT AN OXYGEN SUPPLY IN THAT ARMOR --
-- AND I --

I GOT
NOTHIN'.

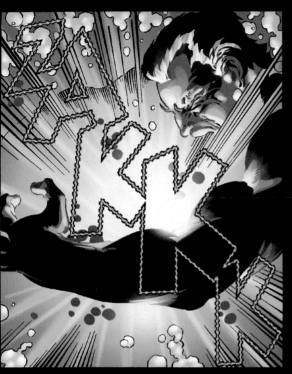

NOTHIN'.

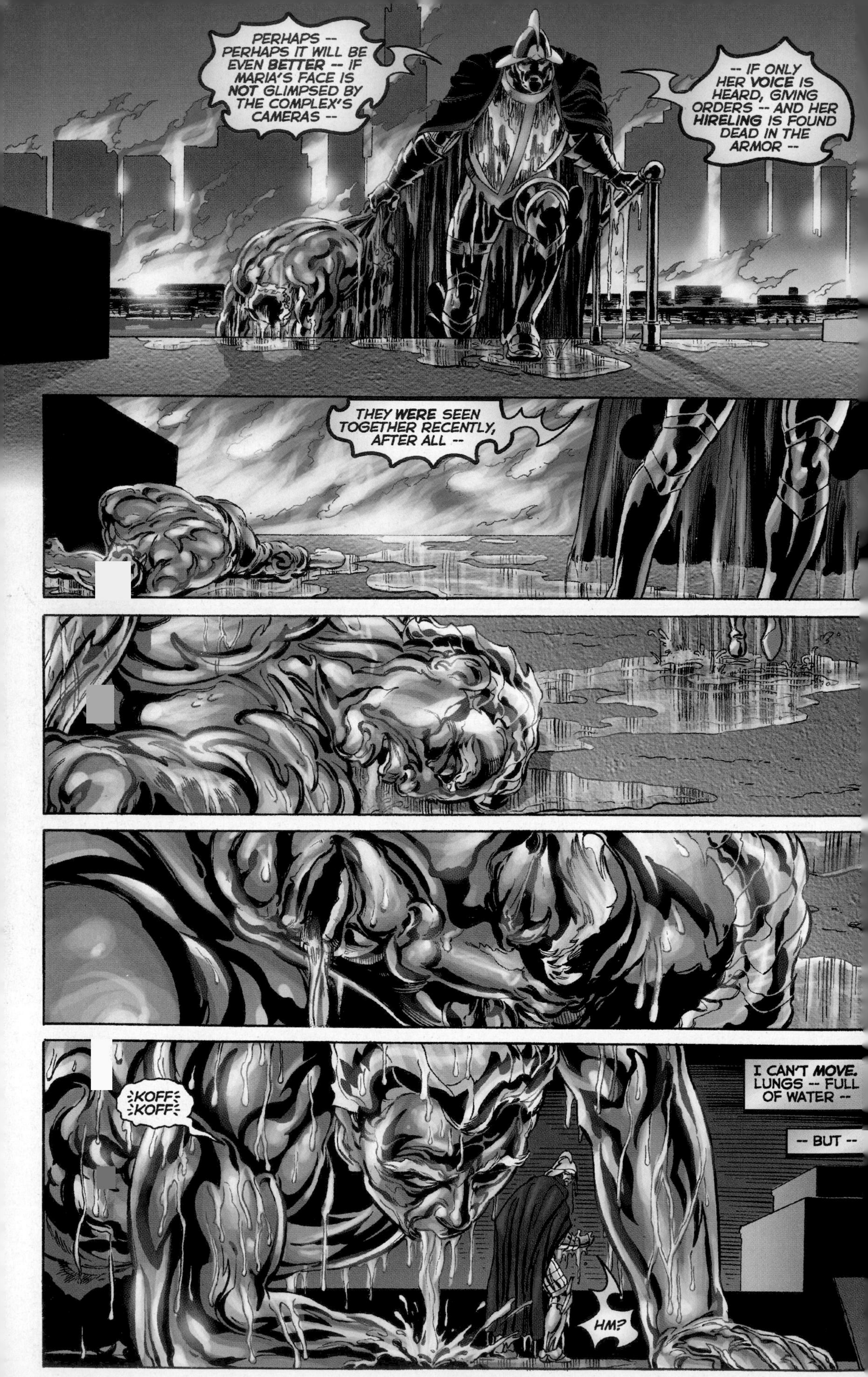
PERHAPS -- PERHAPS IT WILL BE EVEN BETTER -- IF MARIA'S FACE IS NOT GLIMPSED BY THE COMPLEX'S CAMERAS --
-- IF ONLY HER VOICE IS HEARD, GIVING ORDERS -- AND HER HIRELING IS FOUND DEAD IN THE ARMOR --
THEY WERE SEEN TOGETHER RECENTLY, AFTER ALL --
KOFF KOFF
I CAN'T MOVE. LUNGS -- FULL OF WATER --
-- BUT --
HM?

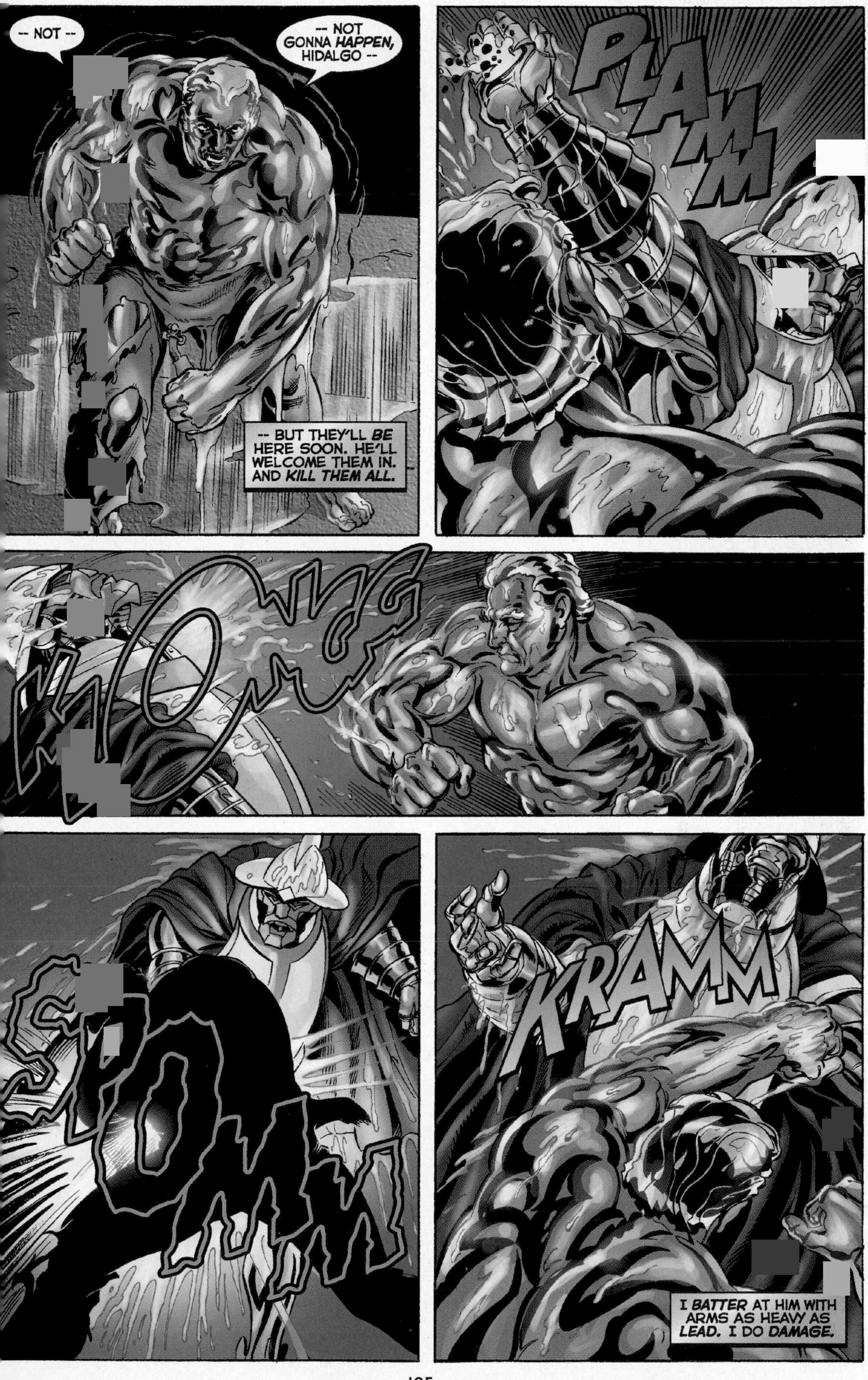
-- NOT --
-- NOT GONNA HAPPEN, HIDALGO --
-- BUT THEY'LL BE HERE SOON. HE'LL WELCOME THEM IN. AND KILL THEM ALL.
PLAMM
KRAMM
I BATTER AT HIM WITH ARMS AS HEAVY AS LEAD. I DO DAMAGE.

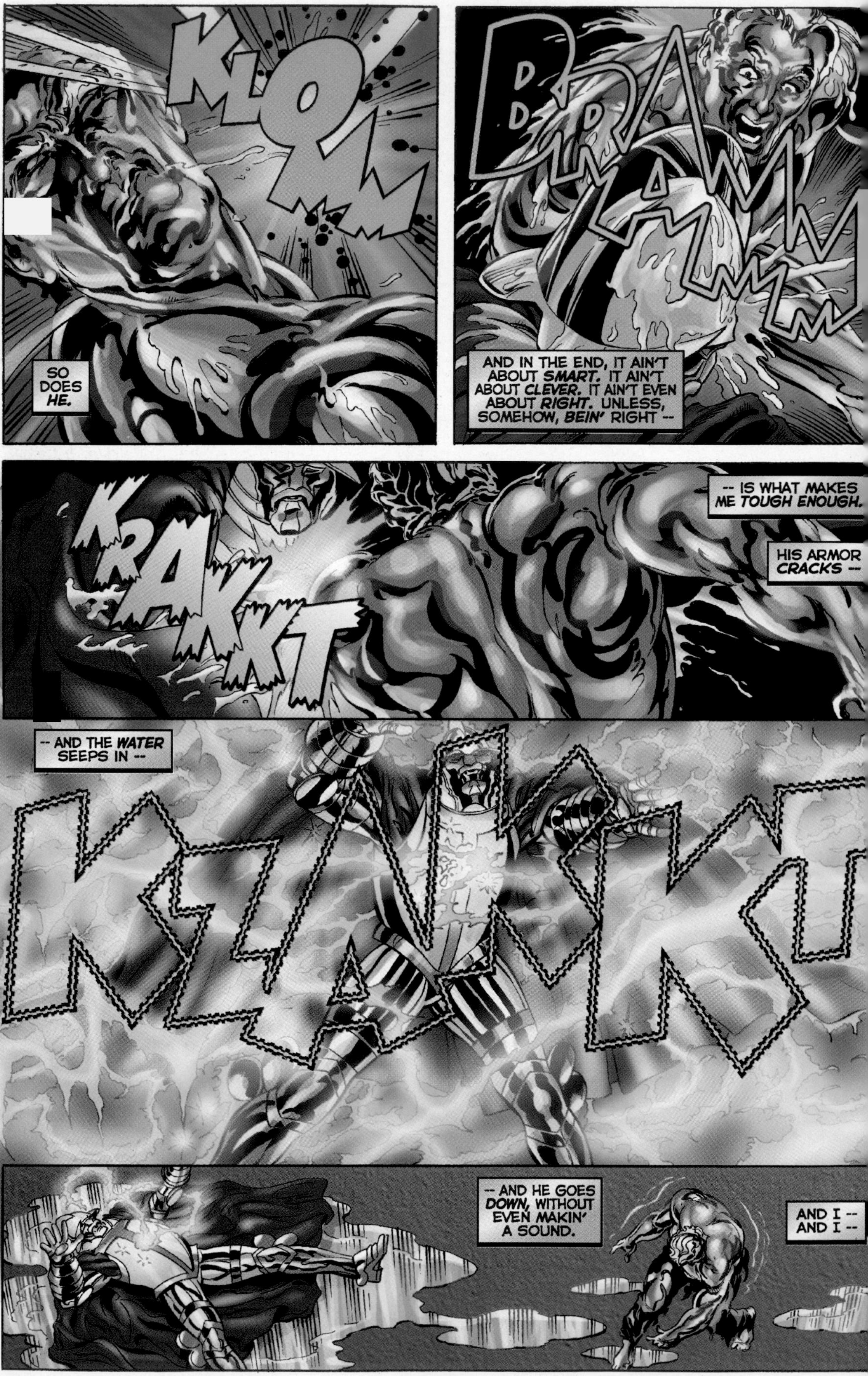

KLOOM
SO DOES HE.
BDDDRAMMM
AND IN THE END, IT AIN'T ABOUT SMART. IT AIN'T ABOUT CLEVER. IT AIN'T EVEN ABOUT RIGHT. UNLESS, SOMEHOW, BEIN' RIGHT --
KRAKKT
-- IS WHAT MAKES ME TOUGH ENOUGH.
HIS ARMOR CRACKS --
-- AND THE WATER SEEPS IN --
KZZAKKK
-- AND HE GOES DOWN, WITHOUT EVEN MAKIN' A SOUND.
AND I -- AND I --

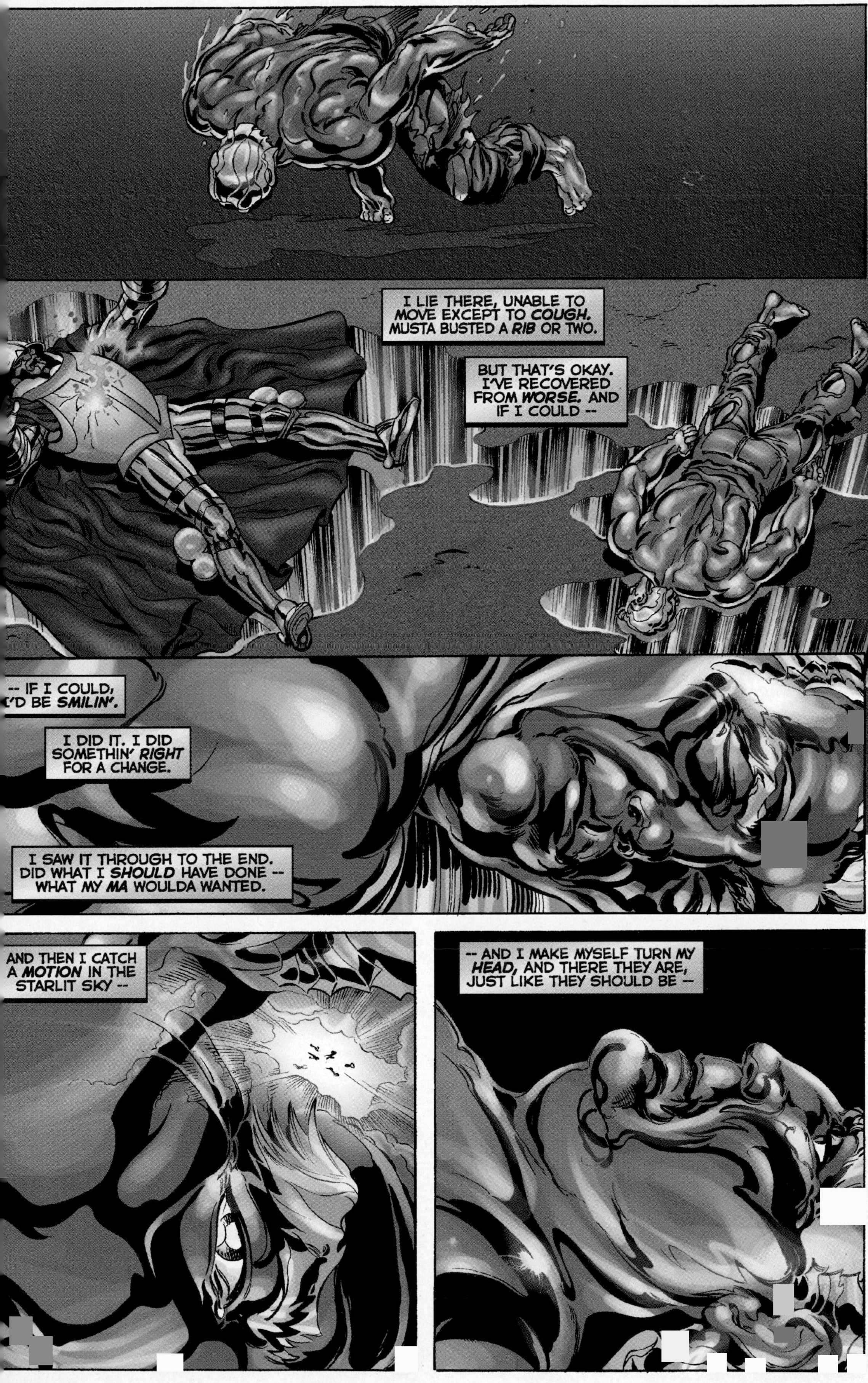
I LIE THERE, UNABLE TO MOVE EXCEPT TO COUGH. MUSTA BUSTED A RIB OR TWO.
BUT THAT'S OKAY. I'VE RECOVERED FROM WORSE. AND IF I COULD --
-- IF I COULD, I'D BE SMILIN'.
I DID IT. I DID SOMETHIN' RIGHT FOR A CHANGE.
I SAW IT THROUGH TO THE END. DID WHAT I SHOULD HAVE DONE -- WHAT MY MA WOULDA WANTED.
AND THEN I CATCH A MOTION IN THE STARLIT SKY --
-- AND I MAKE MYSELF TURN MY HEAD, AND THERE THEY ARE, JUST LIKE THEY SHOULD BE --

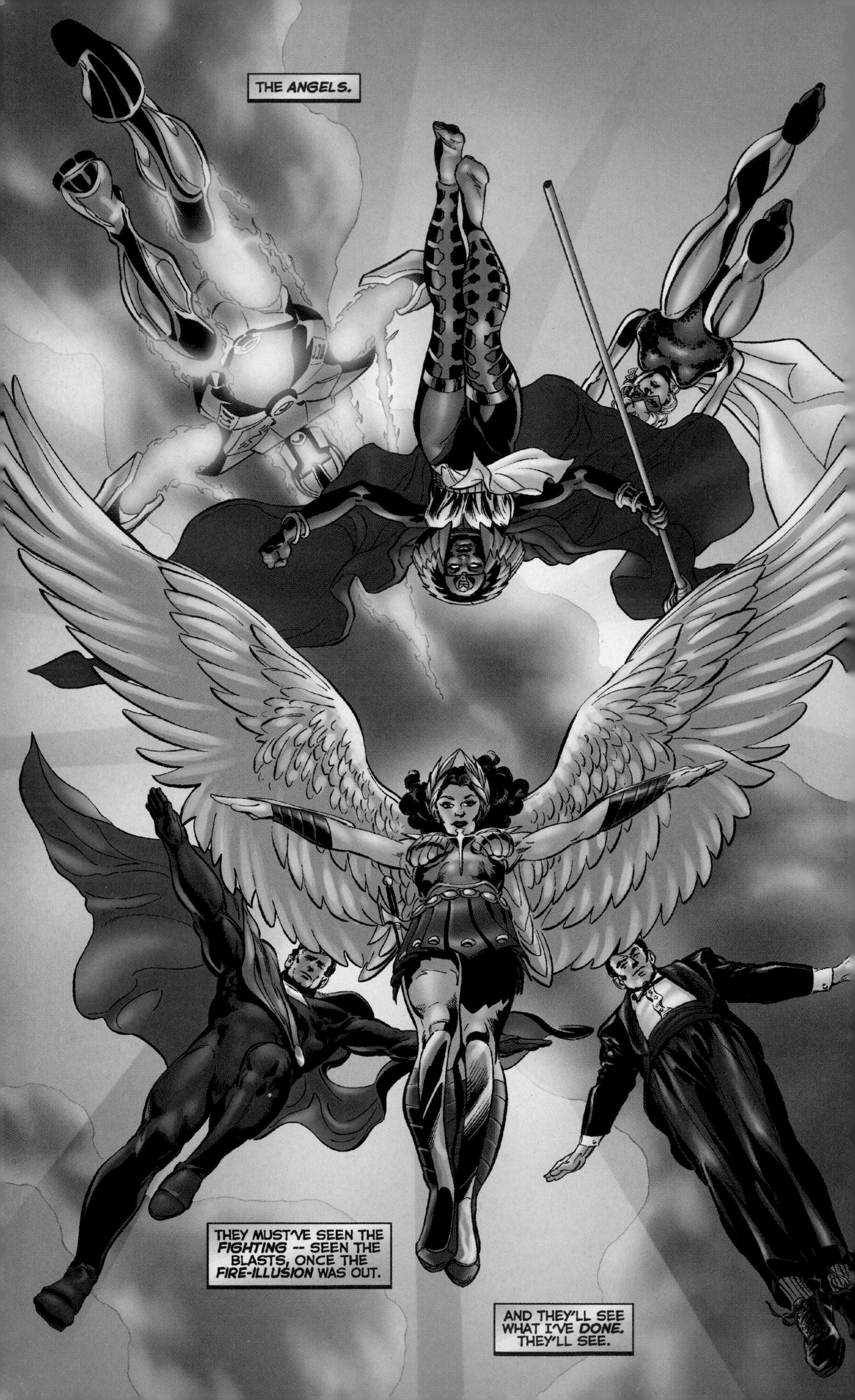
THE ANGELS.
THEY MUST'VE SEEN THE FIGHTING -- SEEN THE BLASTS, ONCE THE FIRE-ILLUSION WAS OUT.
AND THEY'LL SEE WHAT I'VE DONE. THEY'LL SEE.

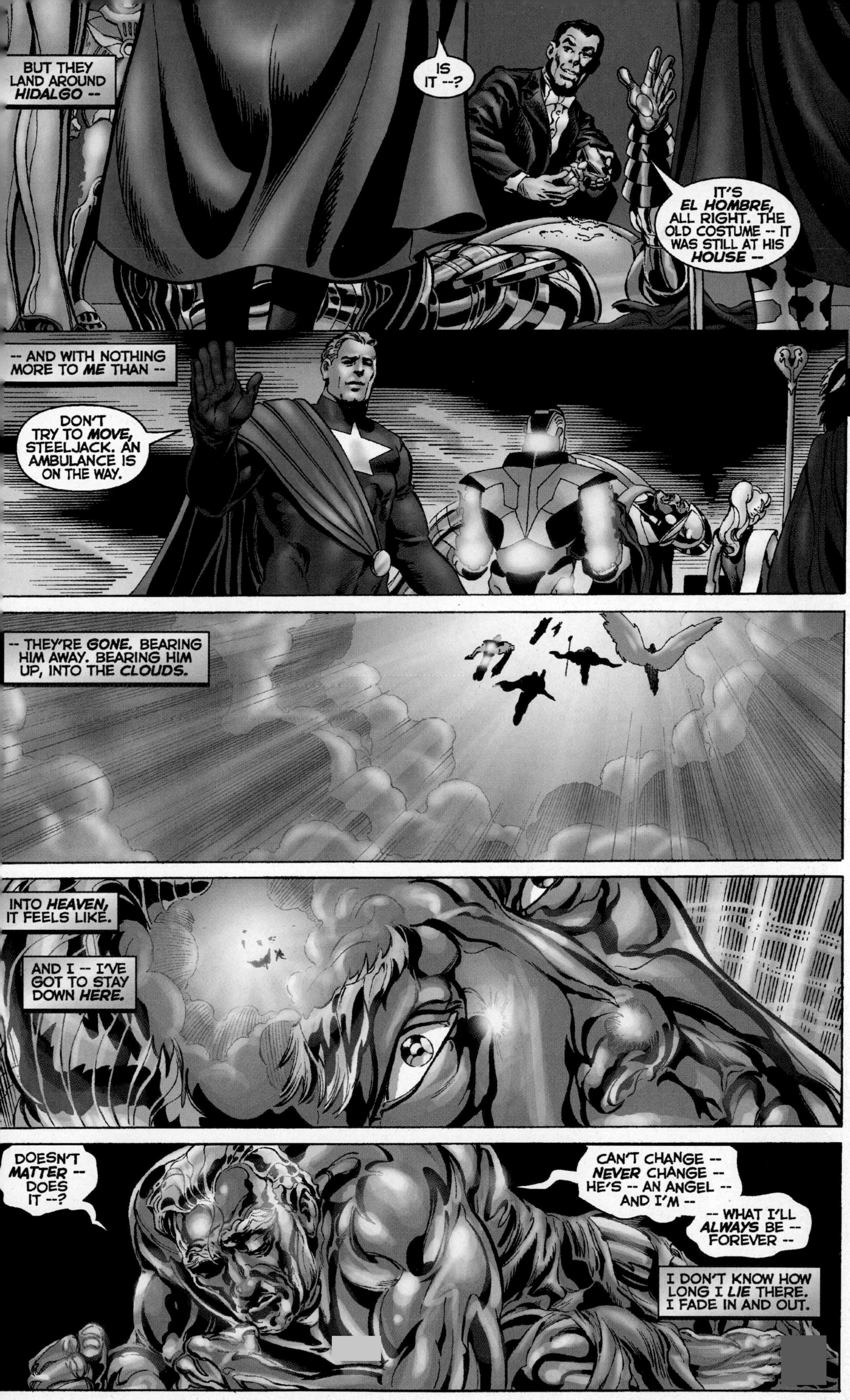
BUT THEY LAND AROUND HIDALGO --
IS IT --?
IT'S EL HOMBRE, ALL RIGHT. THE OLD COSTUME -- IT WAS STILL AT HIS HOUSE --
-- AND WITH NOTHING MORE TO ME THAN --
DON'T TRY TO MOVE, STEELJACK. AN AMBULANCE IS ON THE WAY.
-- THEY'RE GONE. BEARING HIM AWAY. BEARING HIM UP, INTO THE CLOUDS.
INTO HEAVEN, IT FEELS LIKE.
AND I -- I'VE GOT TO STAY DOWN HERE.
DOESN'T MATTER -- DOES IT --?
CAN'T CHANGE -- NEVER CHANGE -- HE'S -- AN ANGEL -- AND I'M --
-- WHAT I'LL ALWAYS BE -- FOREVER --
I DON'T KNOW HOW LONG I LIE THERE. I FADE IN AND OUT.

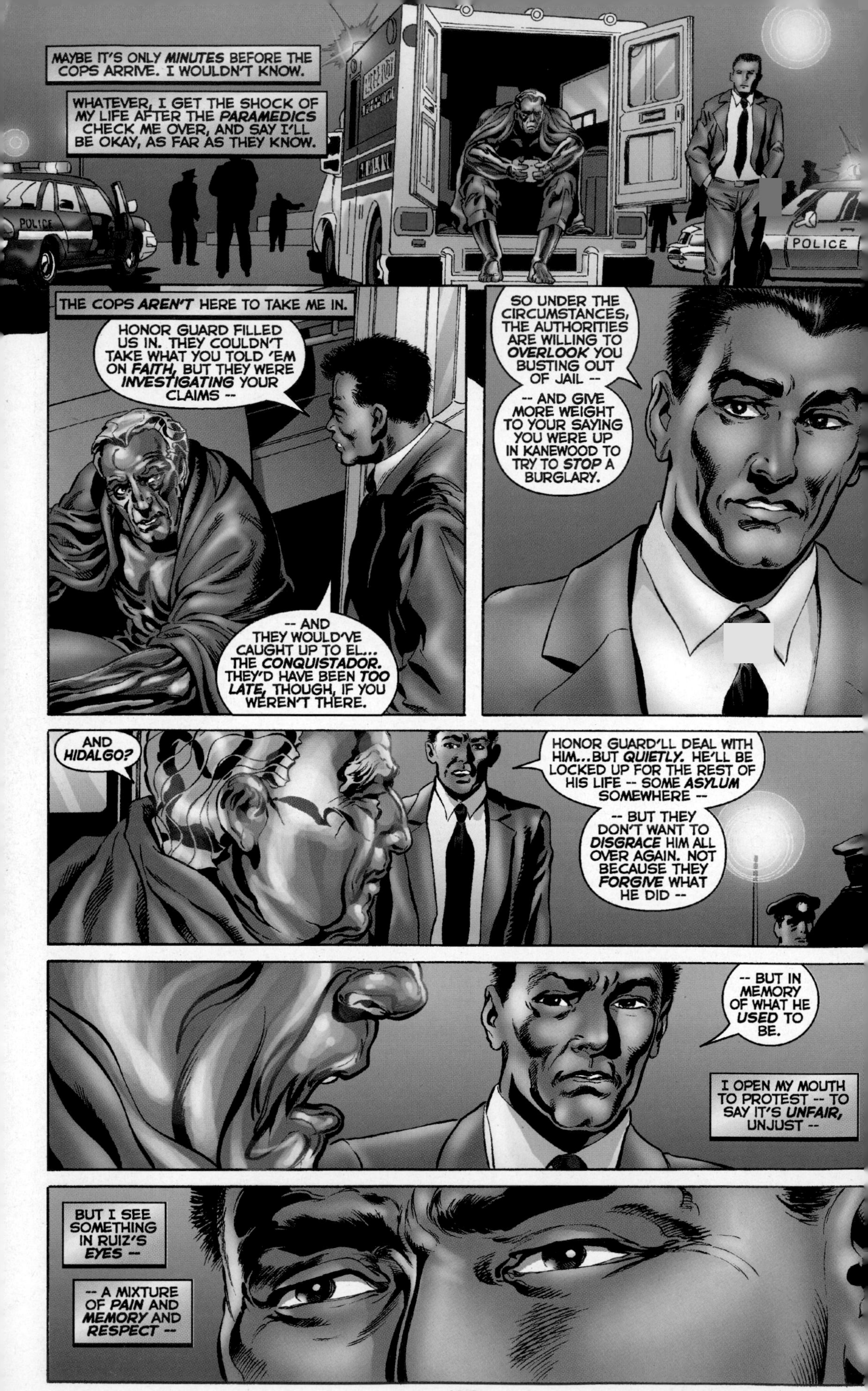
MAYBE IT'S ONLY *MINUTES* BEFORE THE COPS ARRIVE. I WOULDN'T KNOW.
WHATEVER, I GET THE SHOCK OF MY LIFE AFTER THE *PARAMEDICS* CHECK ME OVER, AND SAY I'LL BE OKAY, AS FAR AS THEY KNOW.
POLICE
POLICE
THE COPS *AREN'T* HERE TO TAKE ME IN.
HONOR GUARD FILLED US IN. THEY COULDN'T TAKE WHAT YOU TOLD 'EM ON *FAITH*, BUT THEY WERE *INVESTIGATING* YOUR CLAIMS --
-- AND THEY WOULD'VE CAUGHT UP TO EL... THE *CONQUISTADOR.* THEY'D HAVE BEEN *TOO LATE,* THOUGH, IF YOU WEREN'T THERE.
SO UNDER THE CIRCUMSTANCES, THE AUTHORITIES ARE WILLING TO *OVERLOOK* YOU BUSTING OUT OF JAIL --
-- AND GIVE MORE WEIGHT TO YOUR SAYING YOU WERE UP IN KANEWOOD TO TRY TO *STOP* A BURGLARY.
AND *HIDALGO?*
HONOR GUARD'LL DEAL WITH HIM... BUT *QUIETLY.* HE'LL BE LOCKED UP FOR THE REST OF HIS LIFE -- SOME *ASYLUM* SOMEWHERE --
-- BUT THEY DON'T WANT TO *DISGRACE* HIM ALL OVER AGAIN. NOT BECAUSE THEY *FORGIVE* WHAT HE DID --
-- BUT IN MEMORY OF WHAT HE *USED* TO BE.
I OPEN MY MOUTH TO PROTEST -- TO SAY IT'S *UNFAIR,* UNJUST --
BUT I SEE SOMETHING IN RUIZ'S *EYES* --
-- A MIXTURE OF *PAIN* AND *MEMORY* AND *RESPECT* --

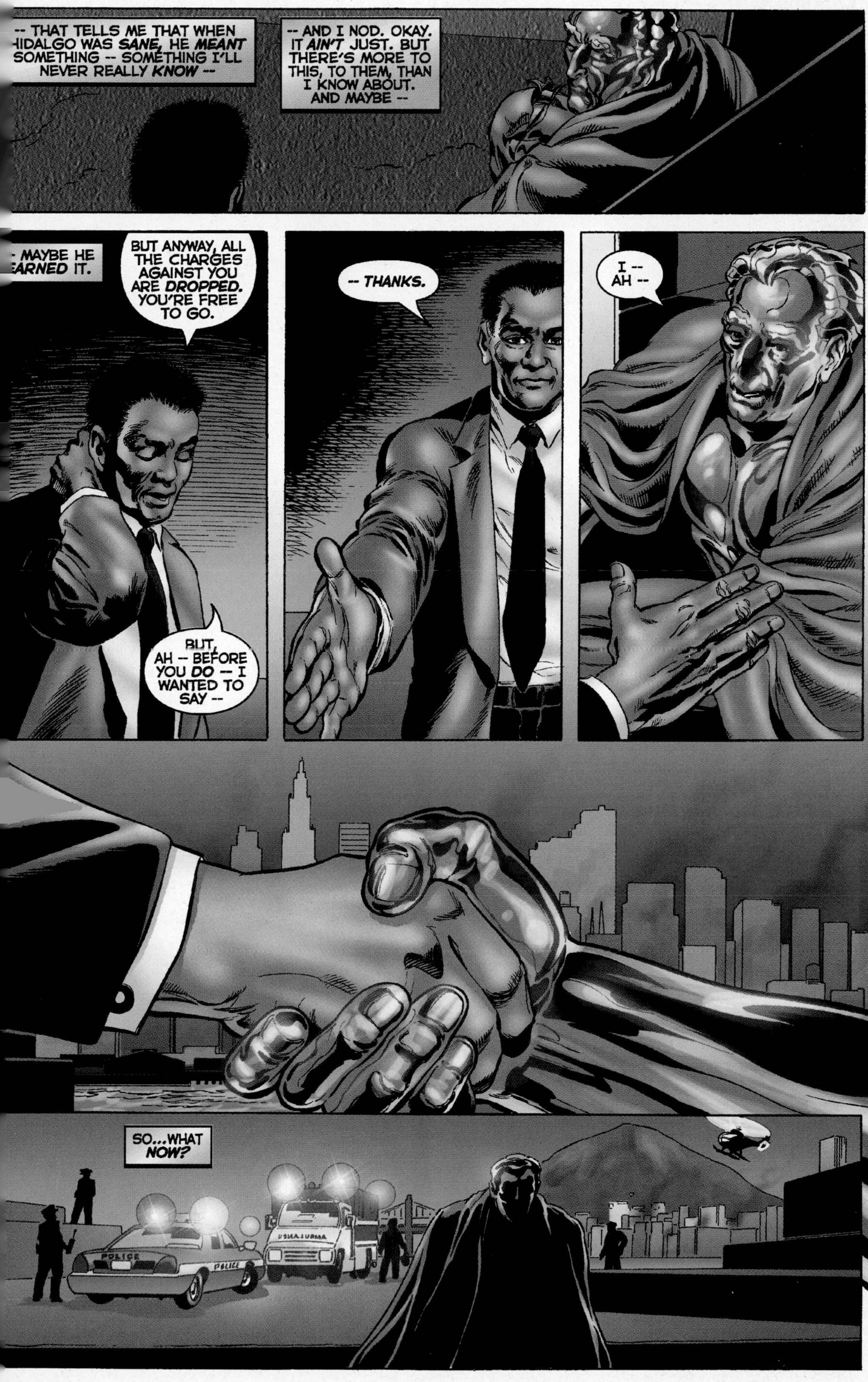
-- THAT TELLS ME THAT WHEN HIDALGO WAS SANE, HE MEANT SOMETHING -- SOMETHING I'LL NEVER REALLY KNOW --
-- AND I NOD. OKAY. IT AIN'T JUST. BUT THERE'S MORE TO THIS, TO THEM, THAN I KNOW ABOUT. AND MAYBE --
- MAYBE HE EARNED IT.
BUT ANYWAY, ALL THE CHARGES AGAINST YOU ARE DROPPED. YOU'RE FREE TO GO.
BUT, AH -- BEFORE YOU DO -- I WANTED TO SAY --
-- THANKS.
I -- AH --
SO...WHAT NOW?
POLICE
POLICE

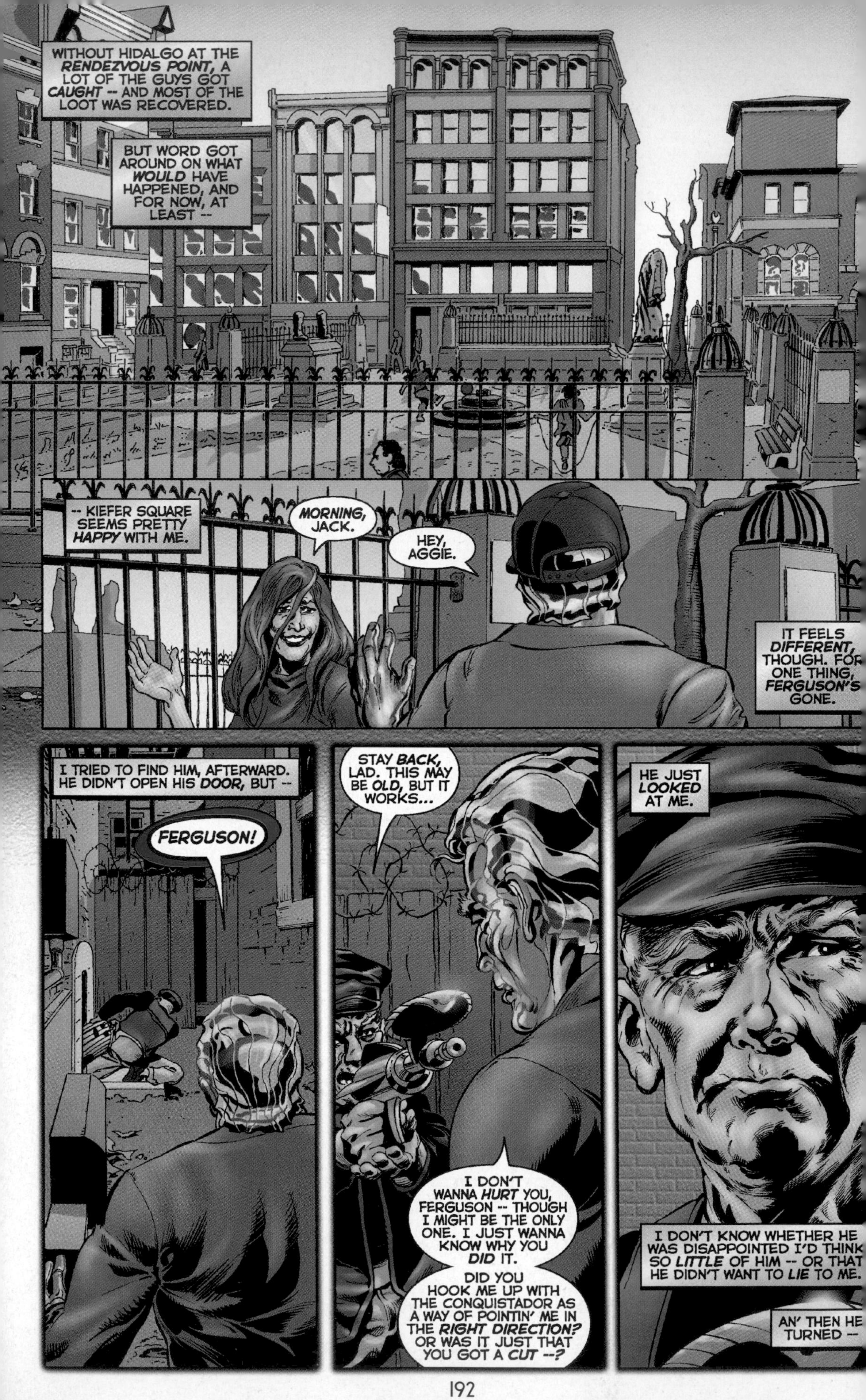

WITHOUT HIDALGO AT THE RENDEZVOUS POINT, A LOT OF THE GUYS GOT CAUGHT -- AND MOST OF THE LOOT WAS RECOVERED.
BUT WORD GOT AROUND ON WHAT WOULD HAVE HAPPENED, AND FOR NOW, AT LEAST --
-- KIEFER SQUARE SEEMS PRETTY HAPPY WITH ME.
MORNING, JACK.
HEY, AGGIE.
IT FEELS DIFFERENT, THOUGH. FOR ONE THING, FERGUSON'S GONE.
I TRIED TO FIND HIM, AFTERWARD. HE DIDN'T OPEN HIS DOOR, BUT --
FERGUSON!
STAY BACK, LAD. THIS MAY BE OLD, BUT IT WORKS...
I DON'T WANNA HURT YOU, FERGUSON -- THOUGH I MIGHT BE THE ONLY ONE. I JUST WANNA KNOW WHY YOU DID IT.
DID YOU HOOK ME UP WITH THE CONQUISTADOR AS A WAY OF POINTIN' ME IN THE RIGHT DIRECTION? OR WAS IT JUST THAT YOU GOT A CUT --?
HE JUST LOOKED AT ME.
I DON'T KNOW WHETHER HE WAS DISAPPOINTED I'D THINK SO LITTLE OF HIM -- OR THAT HE DIDN'T WANT TO LIE TO ME.
AN' THEN HE TURNED --

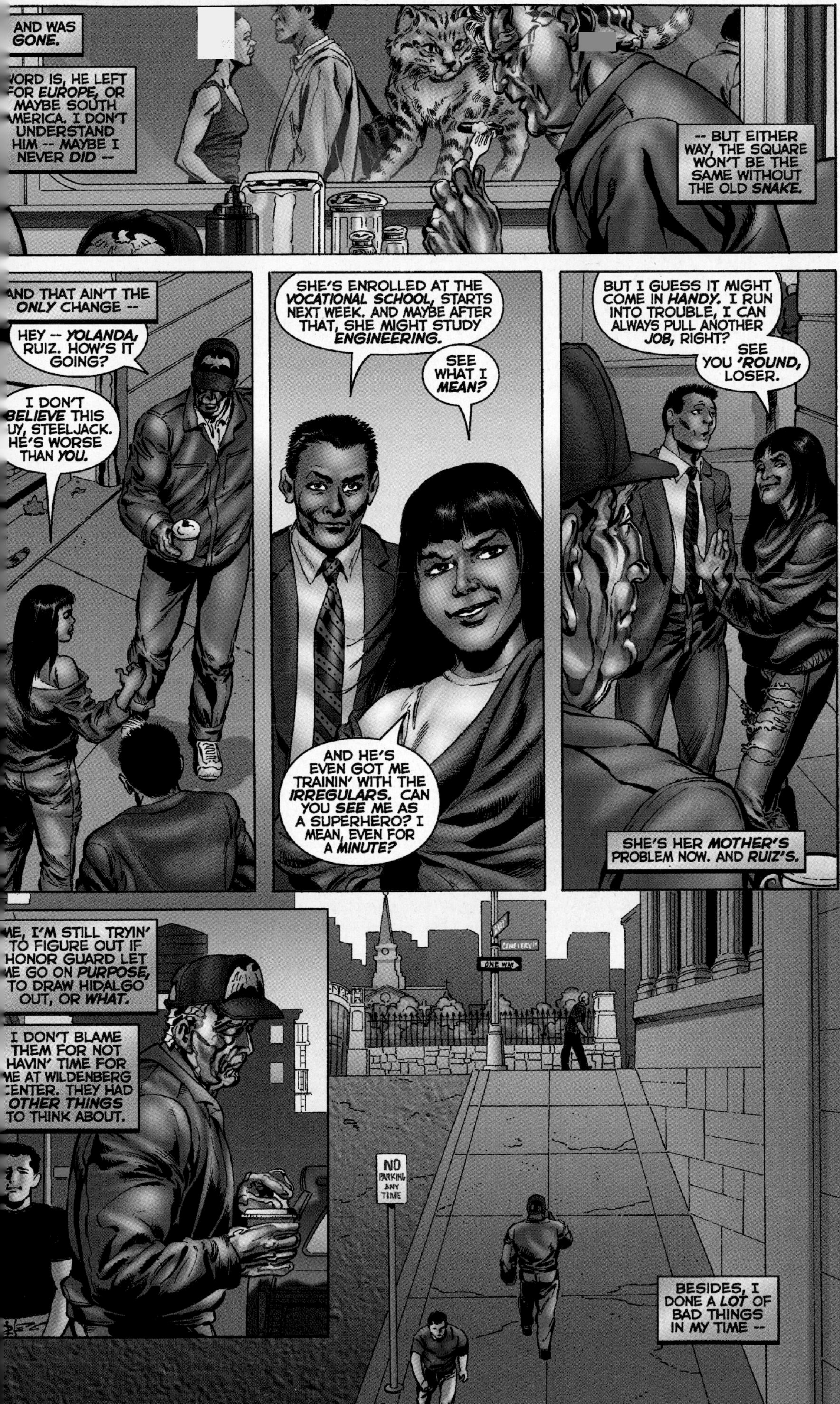
AND WAS GONE.
VORD IS, HE LEFT FOR EUROPE, OR MAYBE SOUTH MERICA. I DON'T UNDERSTAND HIM -- MAYBE I NEVER DID --
-- BUT EITHER WAY, THE SQUARE WON'T BE THE SAME WITHOUT THE OLD SNAKE.
AND THAT AIN'T THE ONLY CHANGE --
HEY -- YOLANDA, RUIZ. HOW'S IT GOING?
I DON'T BELIEVE THIS UY, STEELJACK. HE'S WORSE THAN YOU.
SHE'S ENROLLED AT THE VOCATIONAL SCHOOL, STARTS NEXT WEEK. AND MAYBE AFTER THAT, SHE MIGHT STUDY ENGINEERING.
SEE WHAT I MEAN?
AND HE'S EVEN GOT ME TRAININ' WITH THE IRREGULARS. CAN YOU SEE ME AS A SUPERHERO? I MEAN, EVEN FOR A MINUTE?
BUT I GUESS IT MIGHT COME IN HANDY. I RUN INTO TROUBLE, I CAN ALWAYS PULL ANOTHER JOB, RIGHT?
SEE YOU 'ROUND, LOSER.
SHE'S HER MOTHER'S PROBLEM NOW. AND RUIZ'S.
ME, I'M STILL TRYIN' TO FIGURE OUT IF HONOR GUARD LET ME GO ON PURPOSE, TO DRAW HIDALGO OUT, OR WHAT.
I DON'T BLAME THEM FOR NOT HAVIN' TIME FOR ME AT WILDENBERG CENTER. THEY HAD OTHER THINGS TO THINK ABOUT.
ONE WAY
NO PARKING ANY TIME
BESIDES, I DONE A LOT OF BAD THINGS IN MY TIME --

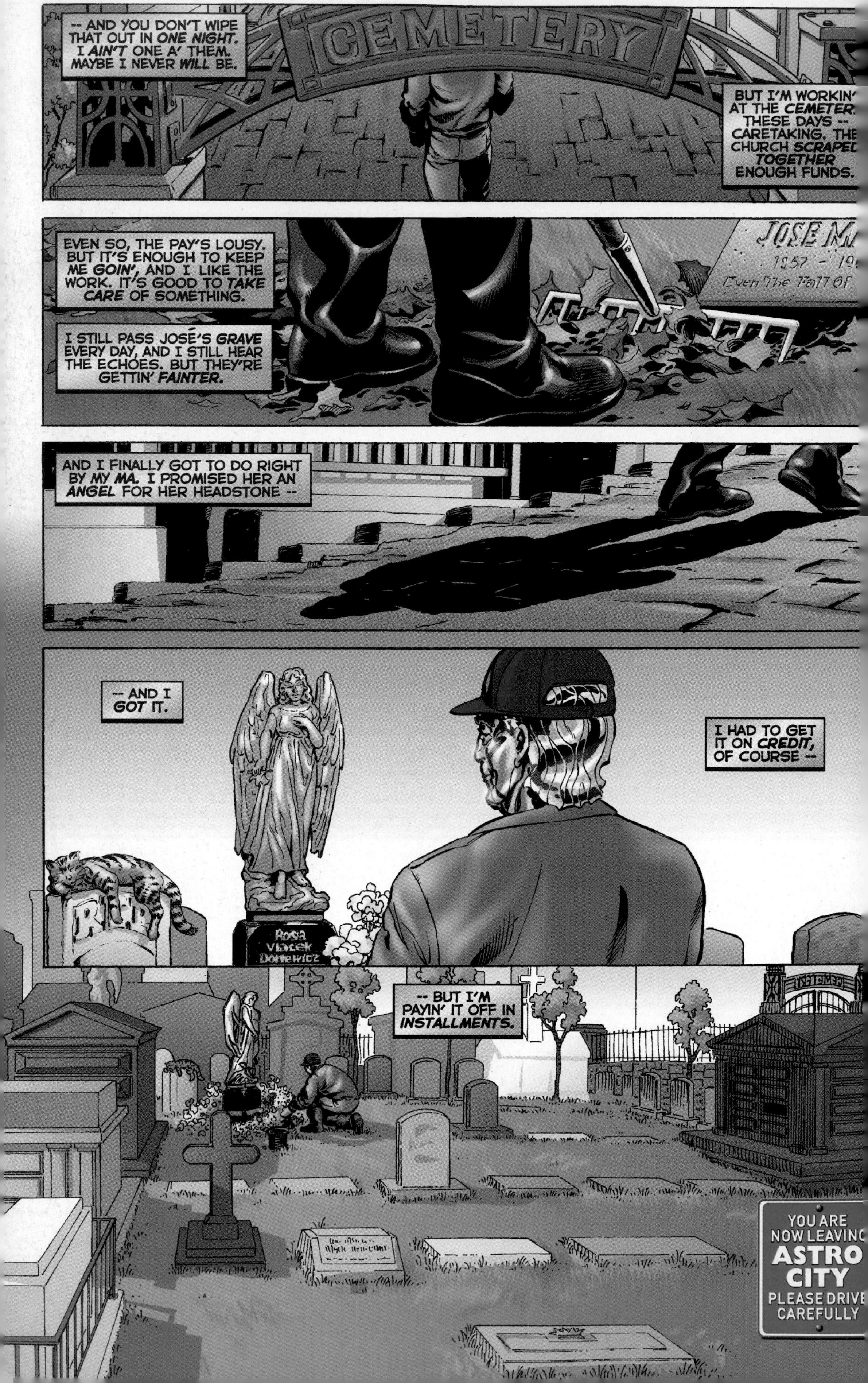
-- AND YOU DON'T WIPE THAT OUT IN ONE NIGHT. I AIN'T ONE A' THEM. MAYBE I NEVER WILL BE.
CEMETERY
BUT I'M WORKIN' AT THE CEMETER THESE DAYS -- CARETAKING. THE CHURCH SCRAPED TOGETHER ENOUGH FUNDS.
JOSE M
1957 - 19
Even The Fall Of
EVEN SO, THE PAY'S LOUSY. BUT IT'S ENOUGH TO KEEP ME GOIN', AND I LIKE THE WORK. IT'S GOOD TO TAKE CARE OF SOMETHING.
I STILL PASS JOSÉ'S GRAVE EVERY DAY, AND I STILL HEAR THE ECHOES. BUT THEY'RE GETTIN' FAINTER.
AND I FINALLY GOT TO DO RIGHT BY MY MA. I PROMISED HER AN ANGEL FOR HER HEADSTONE --
-- AND I GOT IT.
I HAD TO GET IT ON CREDIT, OF COURSE --
Rosa Vlacek Donewicz
-- BUT I'M PAYIN' IT OFF IN INSTALLMENTS.
YOU ARE NOW LEAVING ASTRO CITY PLEASE DRIVE CAREFULLY

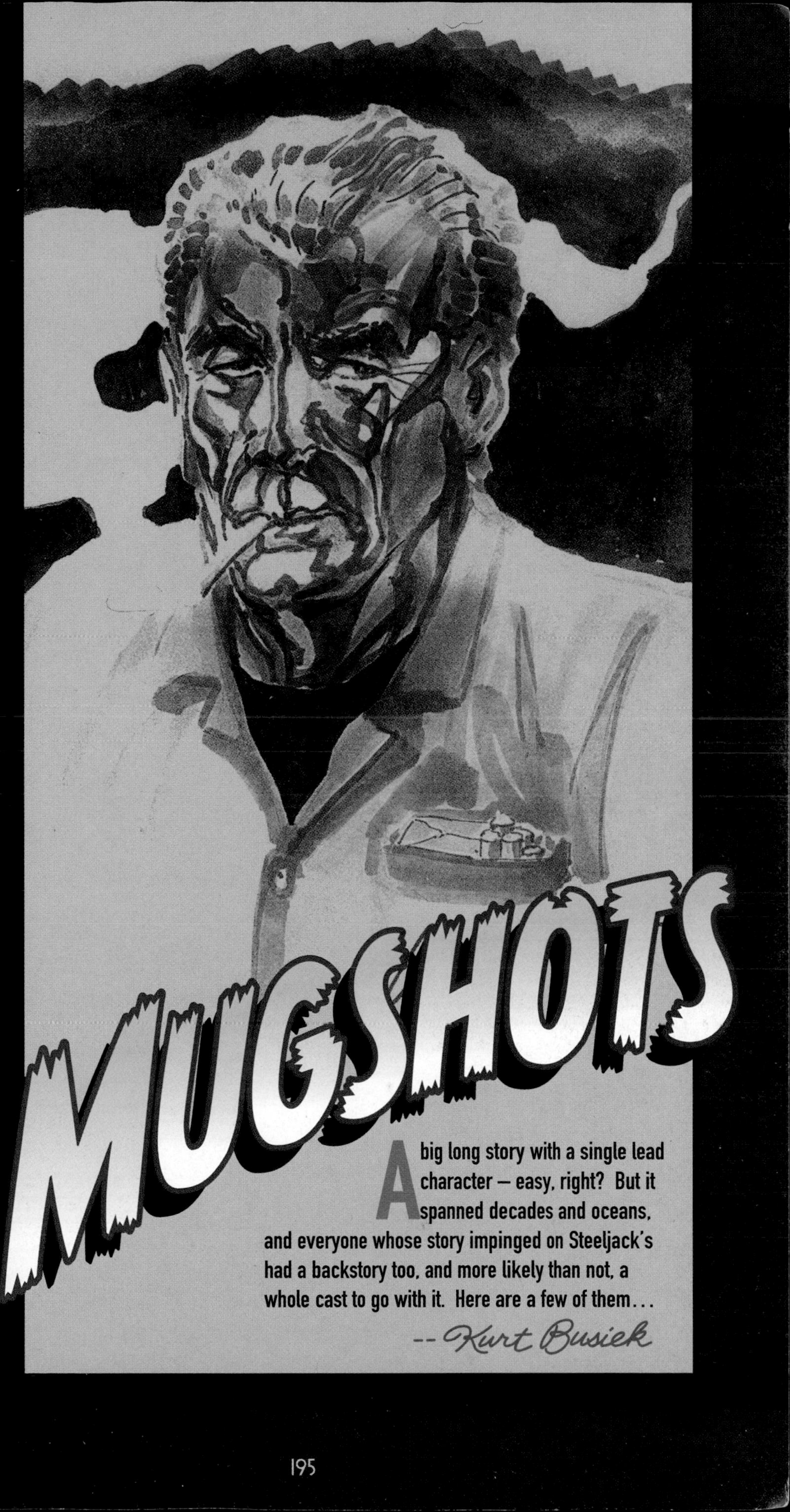

MUGSHOTS

A big long story with a single lead character — easy, right? But it spanned decades and oceans, and everyone whose story impinged on Steeljack's had a backstory too, and more likely than not, a whole cast to go with it. Here are a few of them…

-- Kurt Busiek

STEELJACK

The first thing we knew about Steeljack was that he had to look tired. We didn't want him to be a standard super-villain, all buffed and brawny, so we figured that a worn-looking guy, with some sag to his features, some flab around his waist, would contrast strongly with the shiny steel skin, giving us someone who was obviously superhuman, but even more obviously human.

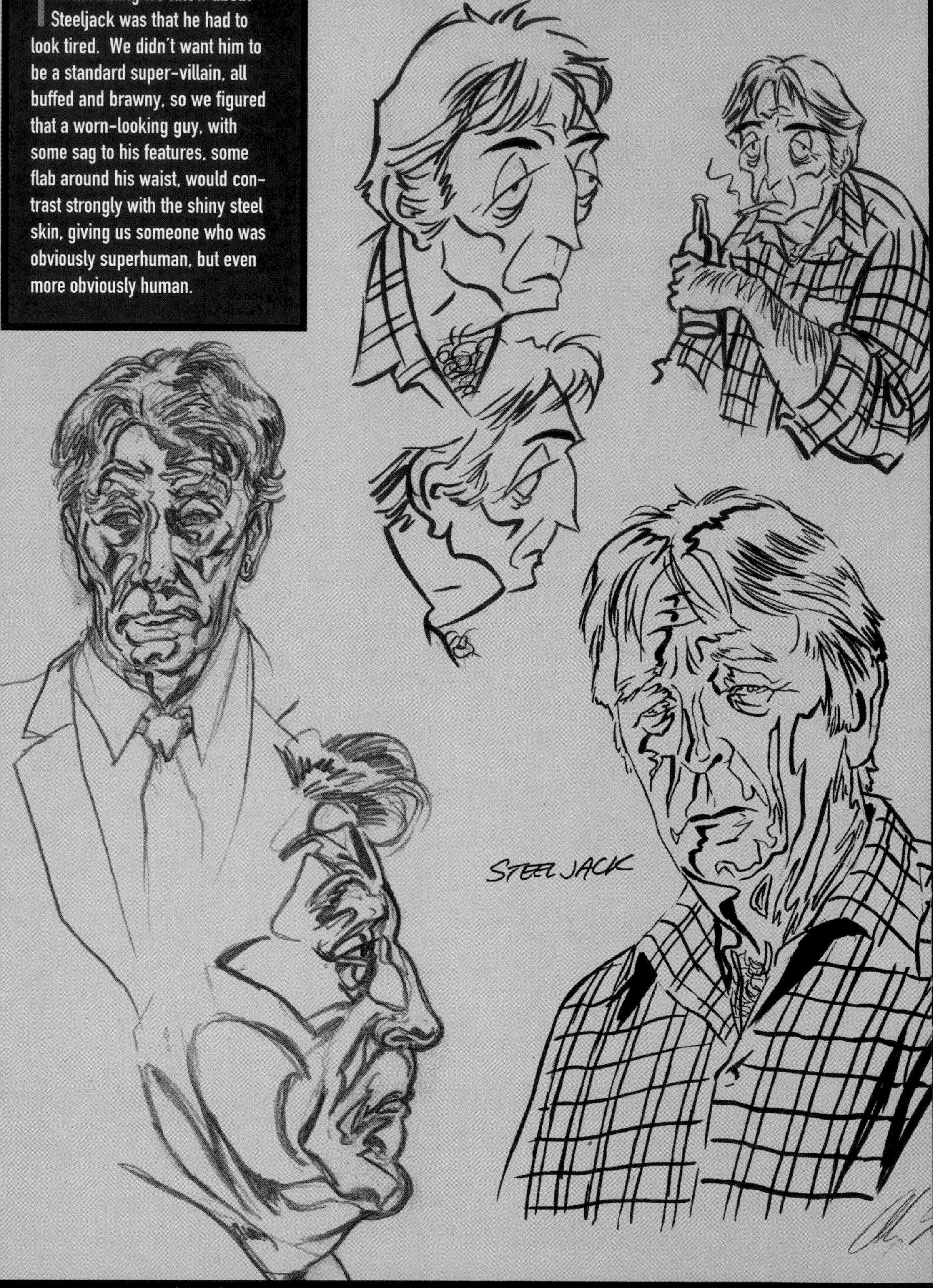
STEELJACK

KIEFER SQUARE

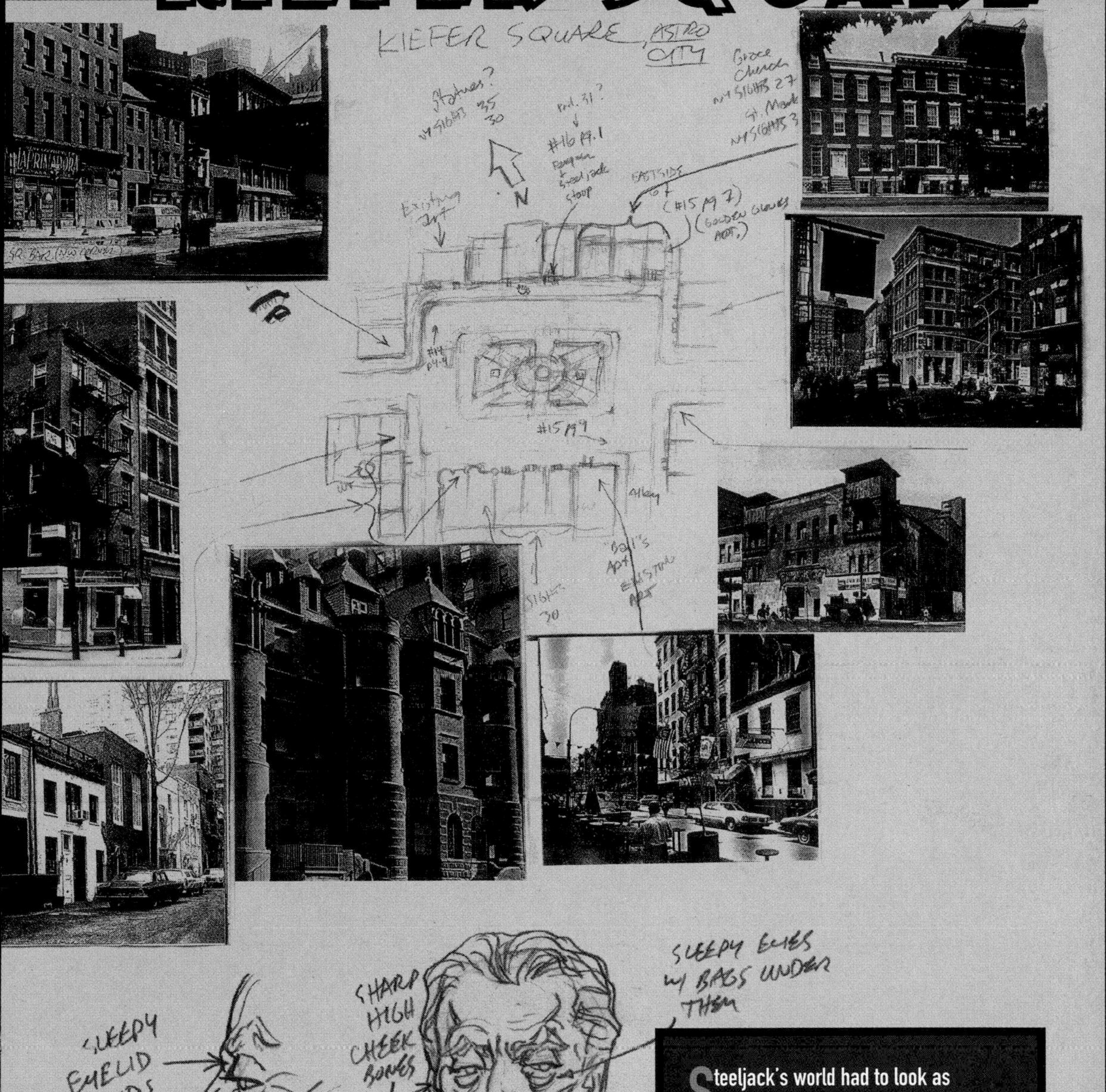

KIEFER SQUARE, ASTRO CITY
Statues?
NY SIGHTS 35 30
Grace Church
NY SIGHTS 27
St. Mark
NY SIGHTS 3
#16 Pg.1
N
Existing Art
EASTSIDE
(#15 Pg 7)
(GOLDEN GLOVES APT.)
#15 Pg 9
Alley
SIGHTS 30

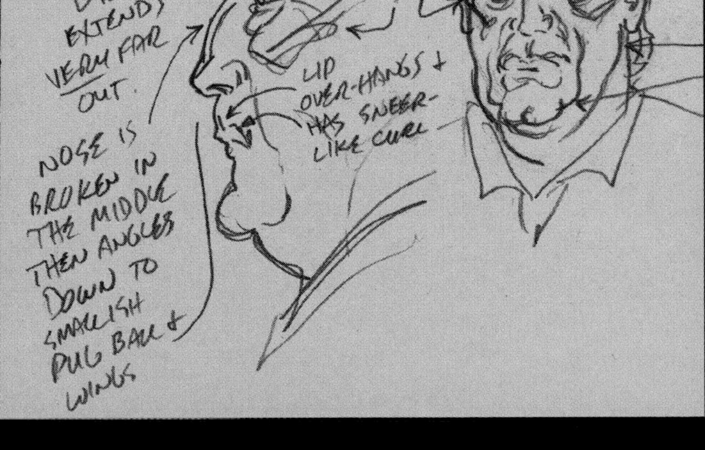

SLEEPY EYELID EXTENDS VERY FAR OUT.
NOSE IS BROKEN IN THE MIDDLE THEN ANGLES DOWN TO SMALLISH PUG BALL & WINGS
SHARP HIGH CHEEK BONES
LIP OVER-HANGS & HAS SNEER-LIKE CURL
SLEEPY EYES W/ BAGS UNDER THEM

Steeljack's world had to look as battered and run-down as he did himself, so Brent went shopping for just the right kind of buildings with which to build Kiefer Square.

Robert Mitchum's puffy, lidded eyes and world-weary attitude seemed perfect for the kind of guy we wanted, so we set out to capture that – not to duplicate Mitchum, who has sharper features than Steeljack – but to get that kind of look. Alex boiled Mitchum down to a caricature so he and Brent could build on those essential elements.

BLACK MASKS

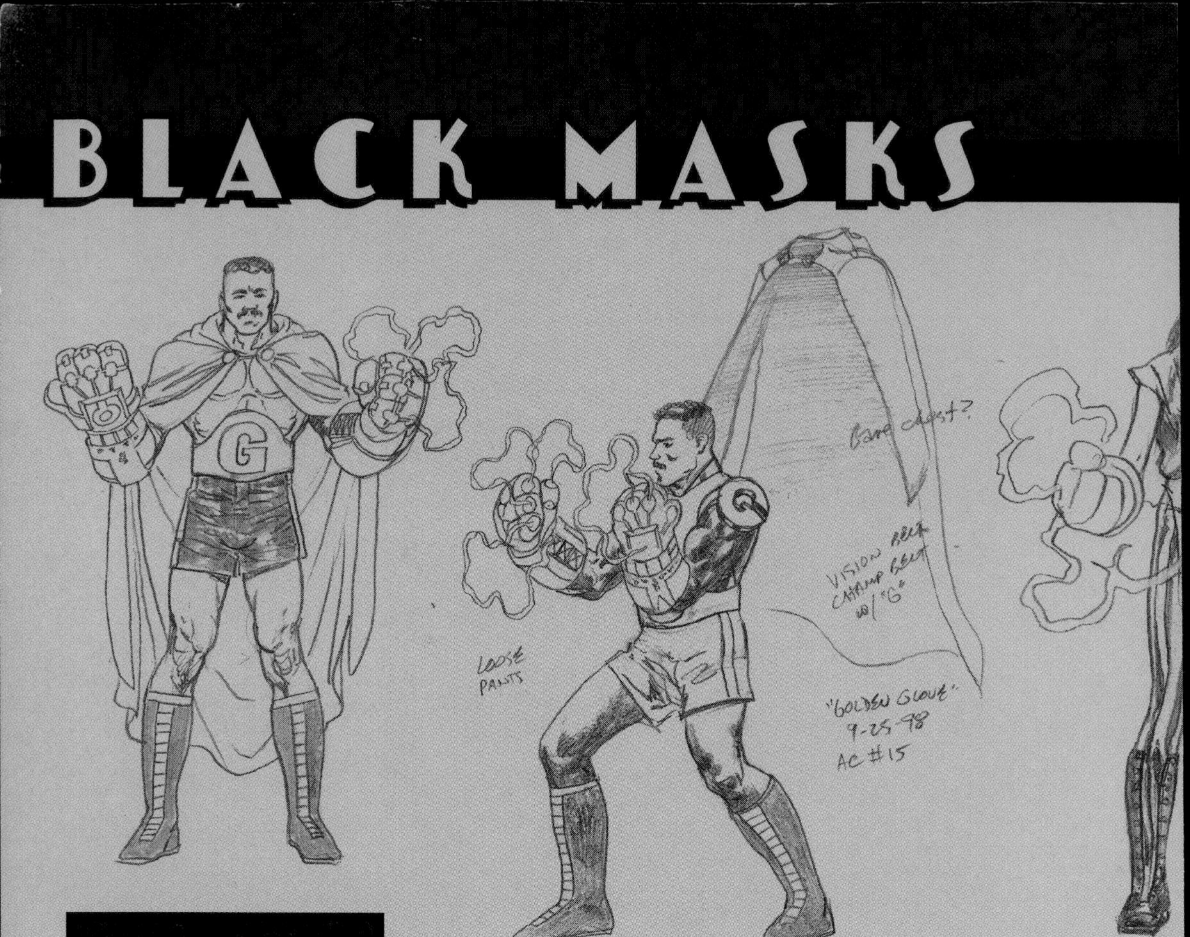
Bare chest?
VISION BELT
CHAMP BELT
w/ "G"
LOOSE
PANTS
"GOLDEN GLOVE"
9-25-98
AC #15

And of course, Steeljack had to have contemporaries. For Goldenglove, we started out with an old-style boxer, with the giant alien-tech gloves the incongruous element that made him clearly part of a superhero world.

Cutlass used pirate imagery, simplified and sleeked-down into a super-costume.

I had known from the start that the present-day Quarrel's dad had been a super-villain, and that she was wearing a variation of his costume. So for him, we worked backward from her, making him a stocky fireplug of a guy to contrast with her lithe athletic look.

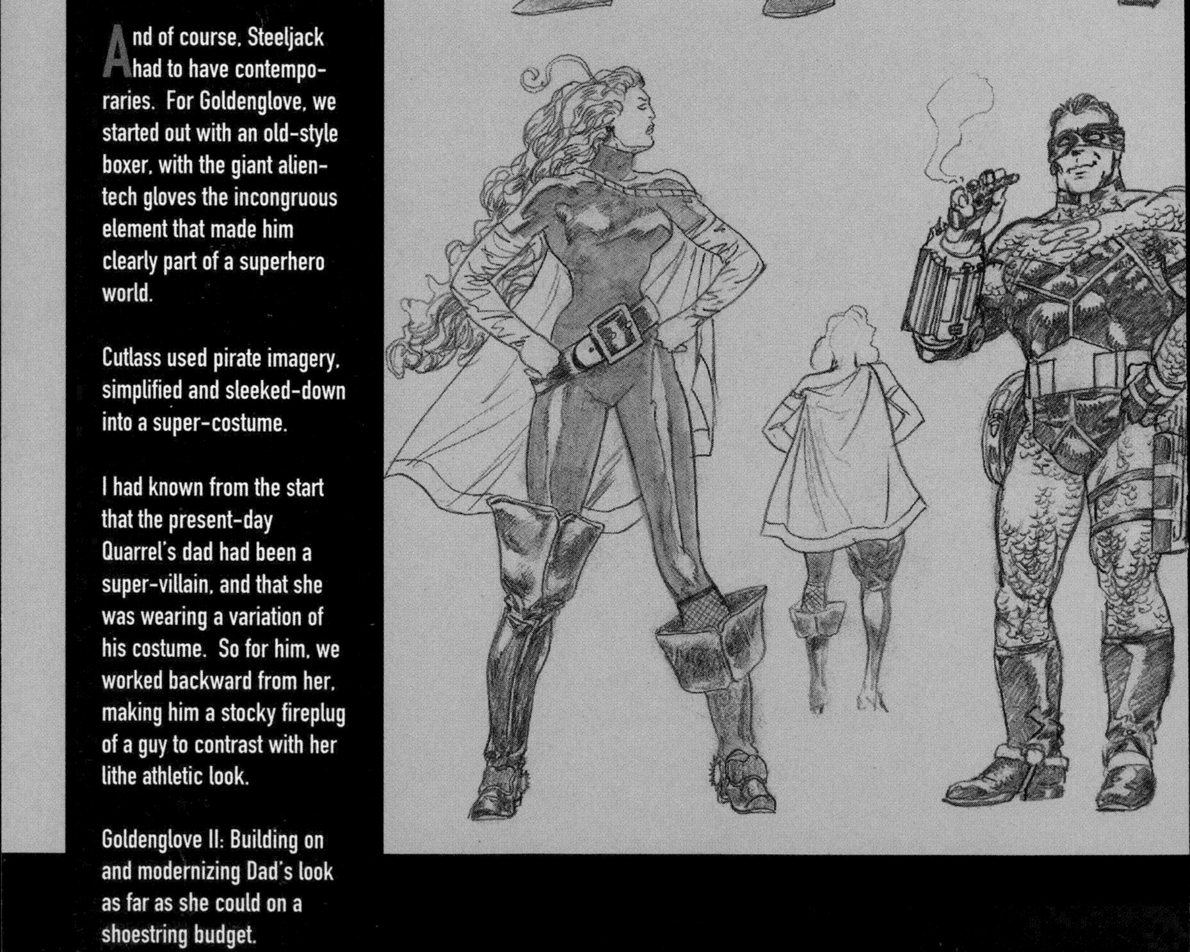

Goldenglove II: Building on and modernizing Dad's look as far as she could on a shoestring budget.

EL HOMBRE

Deep Red

Gold

Deep Red

Deep Red

Too ornate

large 'Geraldo-like' chin

leather shoulder pad

very hairy chest (& arms when you can see 'em)

El Hombre sports an 8-in long braid tied w/ a small black bow

Metal plates front + back used as a shield

shiney leather to here

El Hombre needed to be a dashing Hispanic swashbuckler with a lot of elegance and style. So we started with a matador look, but Brent's original designs were a little too real-world, a little too much like an actual matador, so we abstracted them into something that kept the cocky elegance but turned it into a bold, superheroic look.

HONOR GUARD

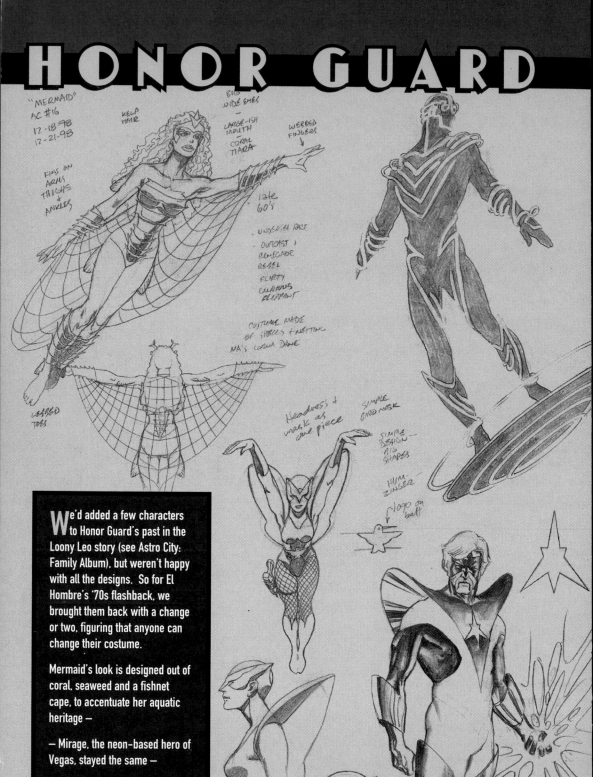

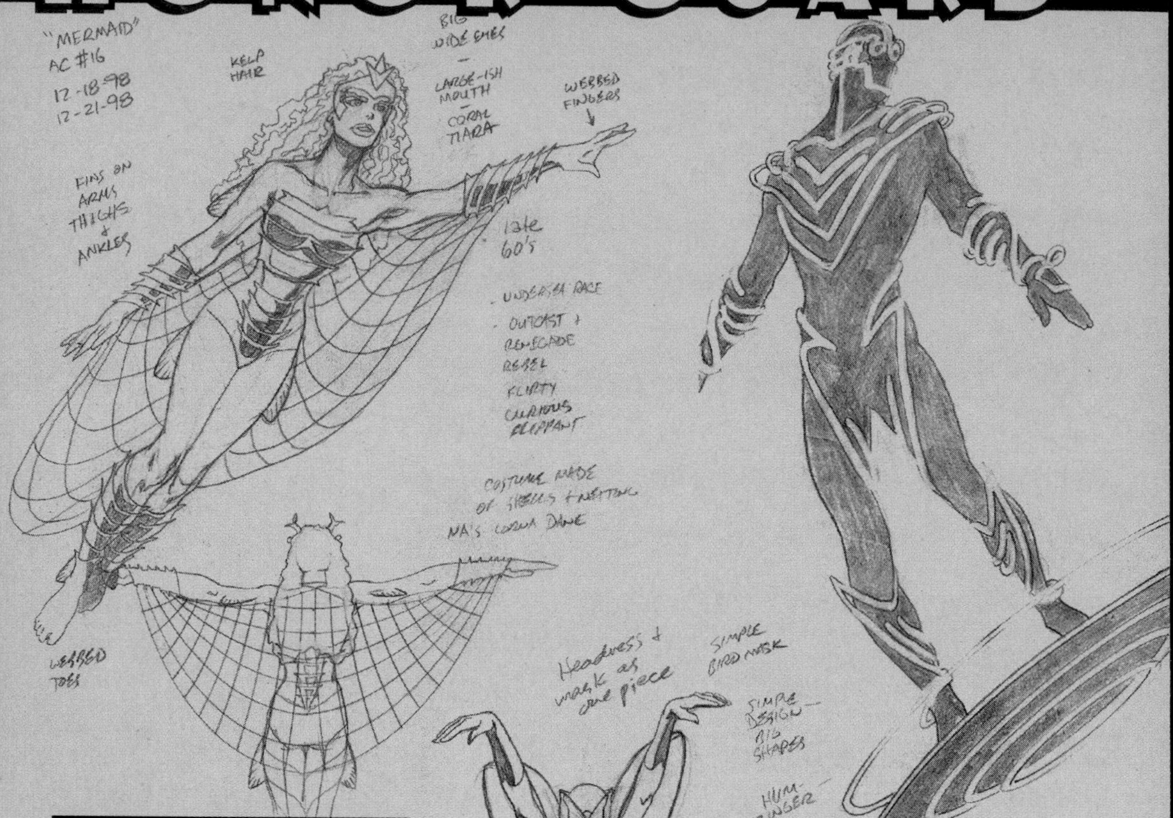
"MERMAID"
AC #16
12-18-98
12-21-98
KELP HAIR
BIG WIDE EYES
LARGE-ISH MOUTH
CORAL TIARA
WEBBED FINGERS
FINS ON ARMS THIGHS & ANKLES
late 60's
UNDERSEA RACE
OUTCAST + RENEGADE
REBEL
FLIRTY
CURIOUS
COSTUME MADE OF SHELLS + NETTING
WEBBED TOES

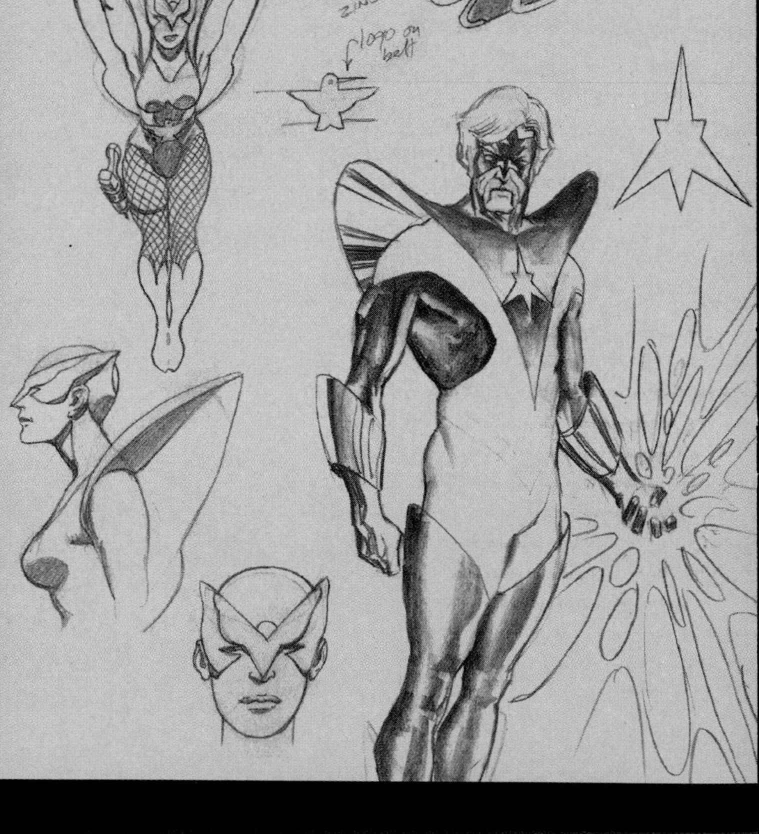
Headdress + mask as one piece
SIMPLE BIRD MASK
SIMPLE DESIGN — BIG SHAPES
HUM-ZINGER
logo on belt

We'd added a few characters to Honor Guard's past in the Loony Leo story (see Astro City: Family Album), but weren't happy with all the designs. So for El Hombre's '70s flashback, we brought them back with a change or two, figuring that anyone can change their costume.

Mermaid's look is designed out of coral, seaweed and a fishnet cape, to accentuate her aquatic heritage –

– Mirage, the neon-based hero of Vegas, stayed the same –

– while Hummingbird got fishnet stockings and flared wing-crescents, just to give her a strong early-seventies look.

We also added Starfighter, a prototypical seventies "cosmic" hero. He too had been presaged (but not seen) in the Loony Leo story, and we've got big plans for him. Someday, someday...

VILLAINS

El Hombre needed villains, too. We gave yet another look to the omnipresent PYRAMID agents and whipped up a few new malefactors.

Los Hermanos seemed like a good name for a bad guy who could split into duplicates of himself – and yes, we couldn't resist a nod to Los Hermanos Hernandez by making him look a little like Jaime…

The Platinum Blonde was simply a name I jotted down years ago, with "sultry robot" as the description. Brent did a great job realizing her. And for Getaway, we just took an Old West bandit type and gave him super-speed.

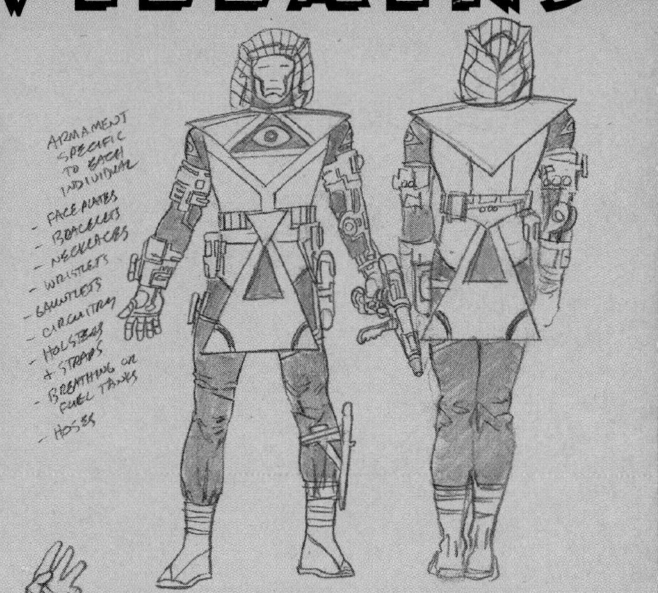
ARMAMENT SPECIFIC TO EACH INDIVIDUAL
- FACE PLATES
- BRACELETS
- NECKLACES
- WRISTLETS
- GAUNTLETS
- CIRCUITRY
- HOLSTERS + STRAPS
- BREATHING OR FUEL TANKS
- HOSES

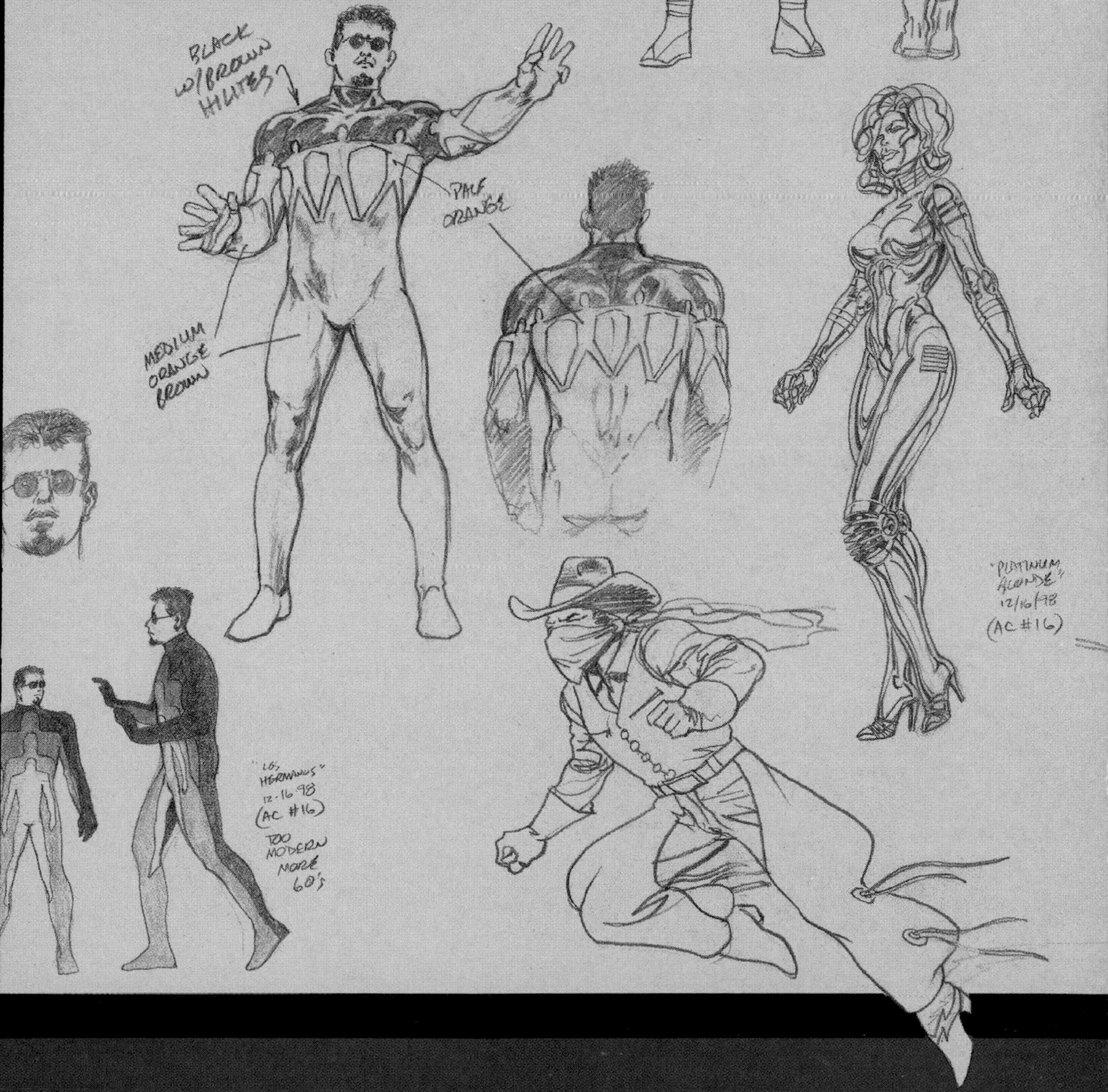
BLACK W/BROWN HILITES
PALE ORANGE
MEDIUM ORANGE BROWN
"PLATINUM BLONDE" 12/16/98 (AC #16)
"LOS HERMANOS" 12-16-98 (AC #16)
TOO MODERN MORE 60's

BRAVO

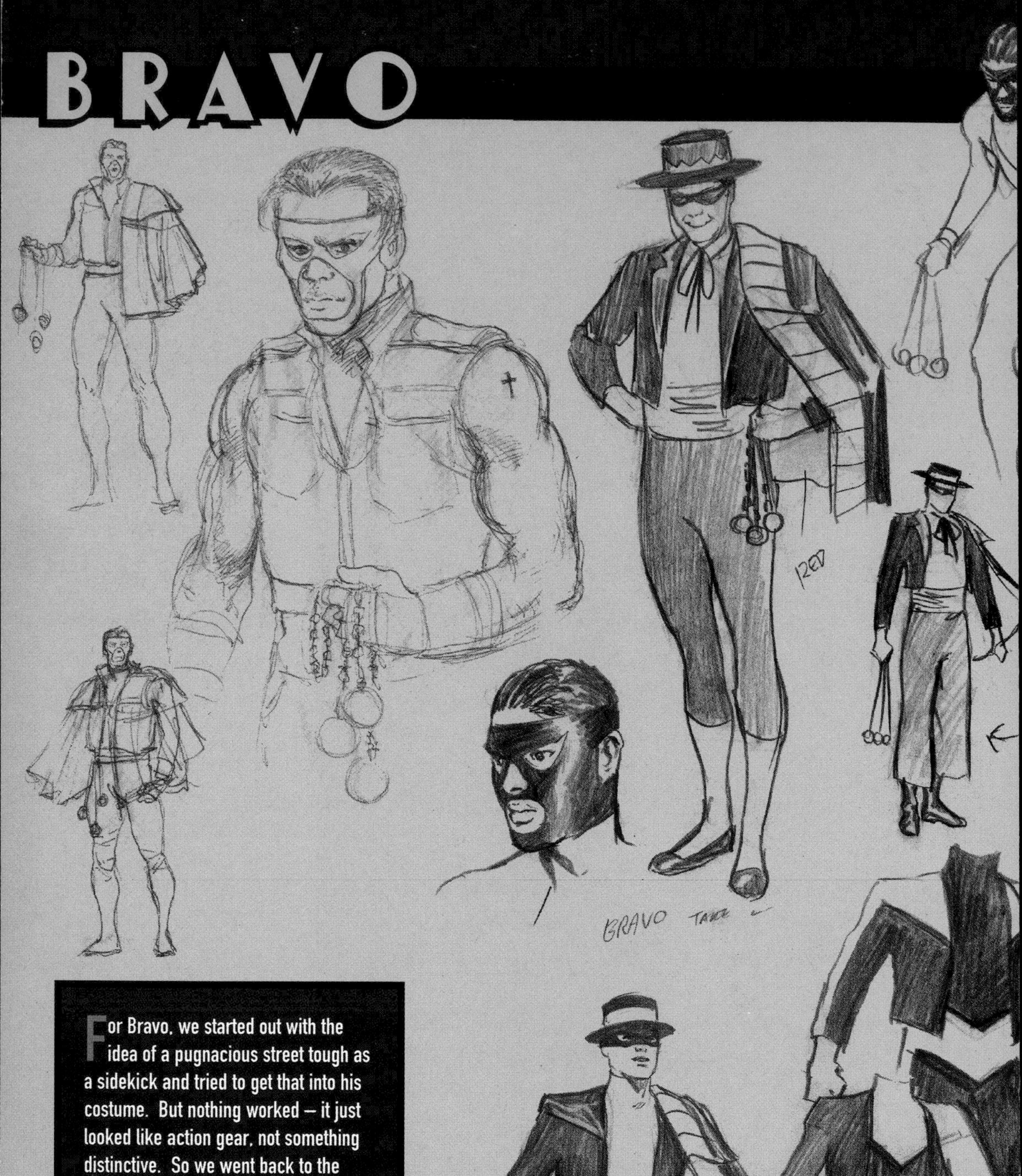
BRAVO

For Bravo, we started out with the idea of a pugnacious street tough as a sidekick and tried to get that into his costume. But nothing worked – it just looked like action gear, not something distinctive. So we went back to the bullfighter look, making him look like a junior partner to El Hombre's matador –

– and then streamlining and abstracting it into a more super-heroic look.

Still, we did manage to keep a small bit of the original intent, by changing his hat from that flat-brimmed toreador look to one of those hats you see on pugnacious Latino street toughs in movies of that era. I don't know what kind of hat that is, but it brings Bravo solidly into the sixties.

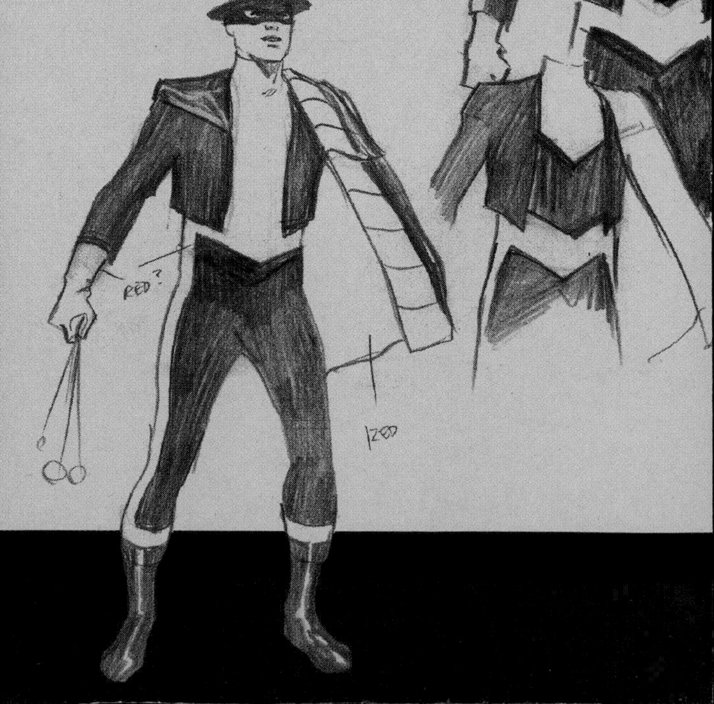
RED?

ORIGINAL IRREGULARS

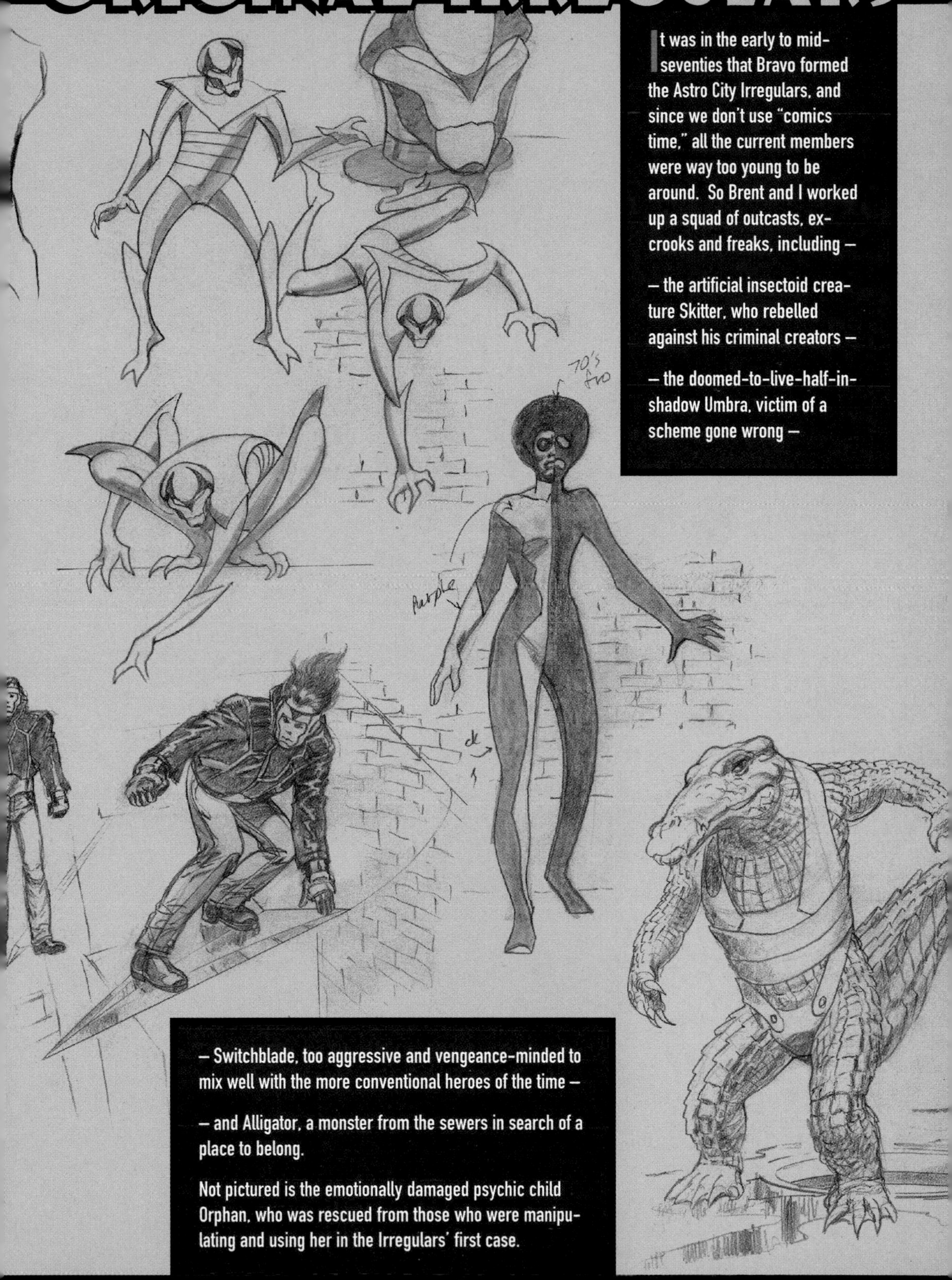
70's fro
Purple
dk

It was in the early to mid-seventies that Bravo formed the Astro City Irregulars, and since we don't use "comics time," all the current members were way too young to be around. So Brent and I worked up a squad of outcasts, ex-crooks and freaks, including –

– the artificial insectoid creature Skitter, who rebelled against his criminal creators –

– the doomed-to-live-half-in-shadow Umbra, victim of a scheme gone wrong –

– Switchblade, too aggressive and vengeance-minded to mix well with the more conventional heroes of the time –

– and Alligator, a monster from the sewers in search of a place to belong.

Not pictured is the emotionally damaged psychic child Orphan, who was rescued from those who were manipulating and using her in the Irregulars' first case.

MOCK TURTLE

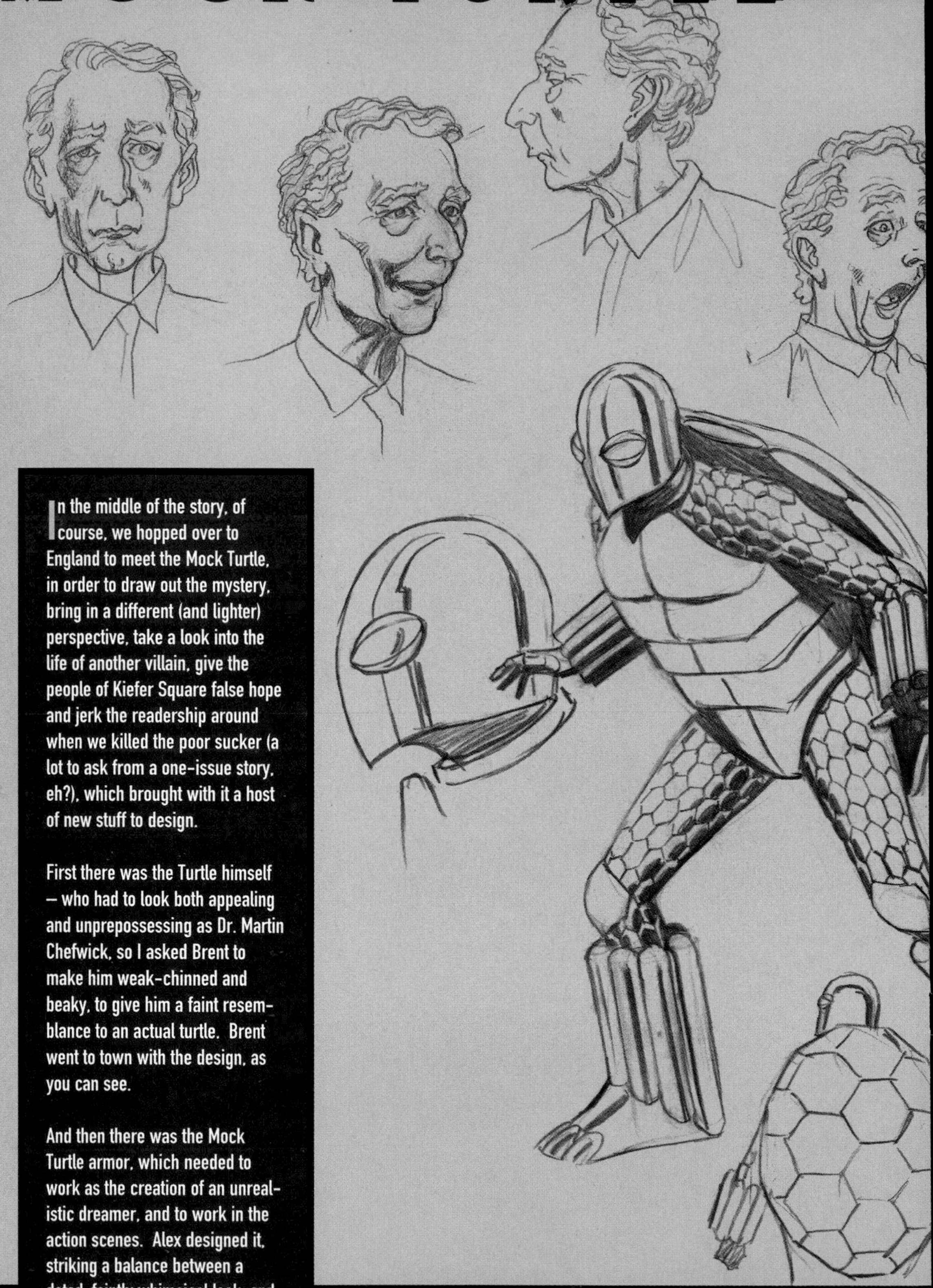

In the middle of the story, of course, we hopped over to England to meet the Mock Turtle, in order to draw out the mystery, bring in a different (and lighter) perspective, take a look into the life of another villain, give the people of Kiefer Square false hope and jerk the readership around when we killed the poor sucker (a lot to ask from a one-issue story, eh?), which brought with it a host of new stuff to design.

First there was the Turtle himself – who had to look both appealing and unprepossessing as Dr. Martin Chefwick, so I asked Brent to make him weak-chinned and beaky, to give him a faint resemblance to an actual turtle. Brent went to town with the design, as you can see.

And then there was the Mock Turtle armor, which needed to work as the creation of an unrealistic dreamer, and to work in the action scenes. Alex designed it, striking a balance between a dated, faintly whimsical look, and an armor that could be believably effective at what it did.

VILLAINS

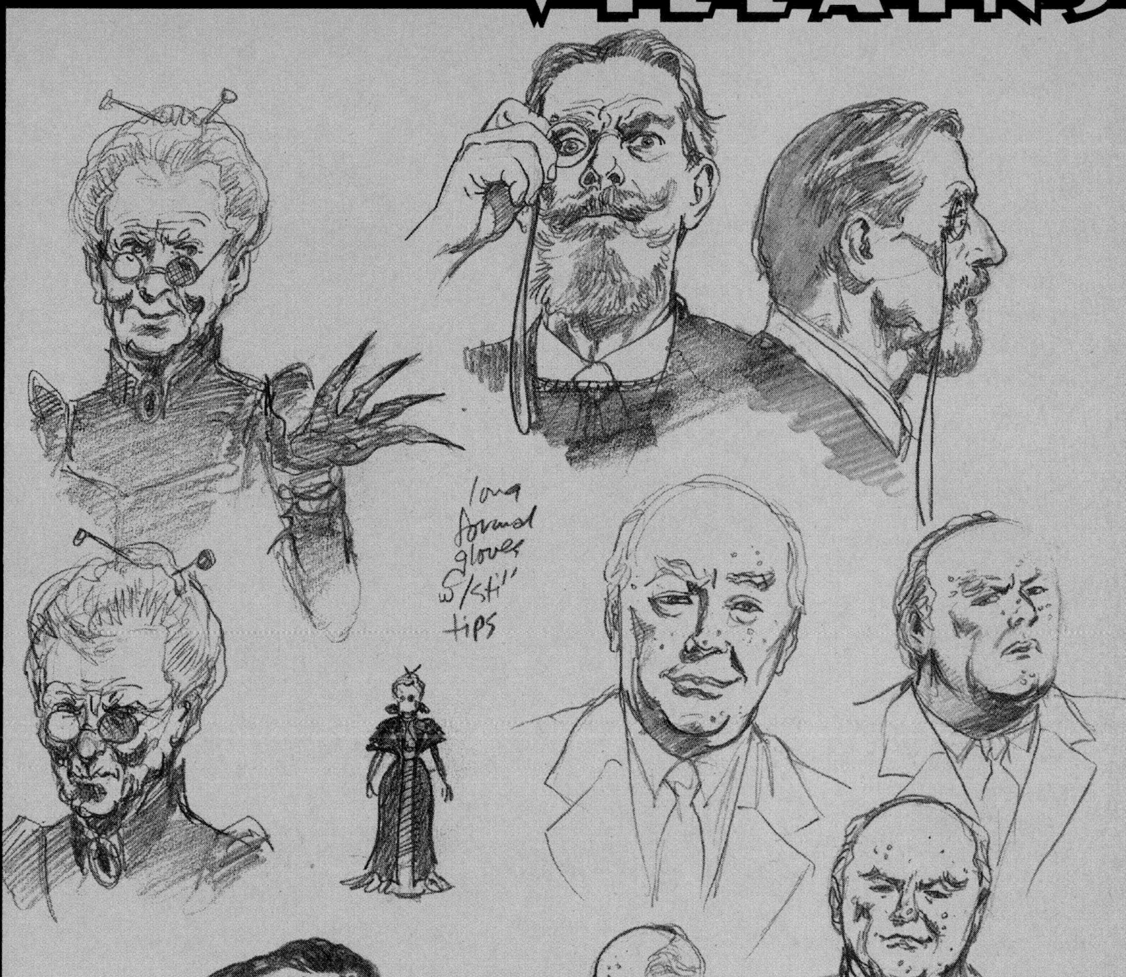
long armed gloves
tips

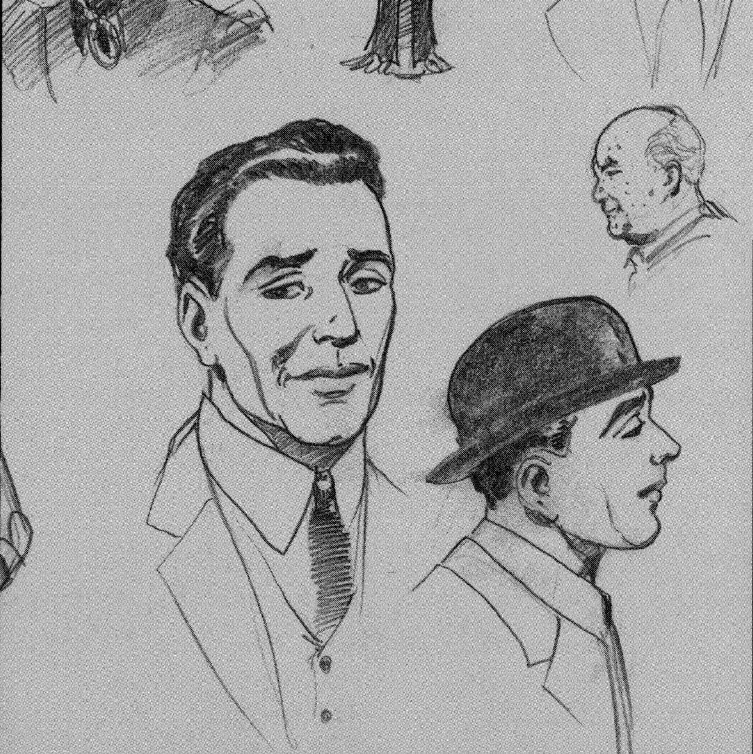

The further one gets away from Astro City itself, the more strongly tied to local culture and history the characters get. It's not realistic, but then realism isn't the point, is it? And it serves both focus and atmosphere.

The crimelords of Britain are no exception, from the stuffy, Victorian sadist Aunt Acid, to Clever Dick (who was originally called Spotted Dick, after a raisin-studded dessert, but that was too much even for us, so we changed his name and left the spots), to the Headmaster of Crime (who, underneath that beard, is based on John Cleese), to the elegant, self-satisfied Toff.

RED QUEEN

Of course, the most important crimelord in Marty Chefwick's life, even though it takes him a long time to find out, is the Red Queen. She needed to be tied more closely to the Mock Turtle than the others, so since he came out of *Alice in Wonderland*, we turned back to Carroll and Tenniel for her, too.

We briefly thought of making her the Queen of Hearts, but decided on the Red Queen (from *Through the Looking-Glass*) both because I think it's a stronger, simpler name, and because it gives her a conceptual link to the Chessmen. Brent gave her suitably overstated regal frou-frou —

— and then we hopped back to *Alice in Wonderland* and adapted her henchmen from the Queen of Hearts' loyal pack of cards. Hey, we never said she was consistent with her sources!

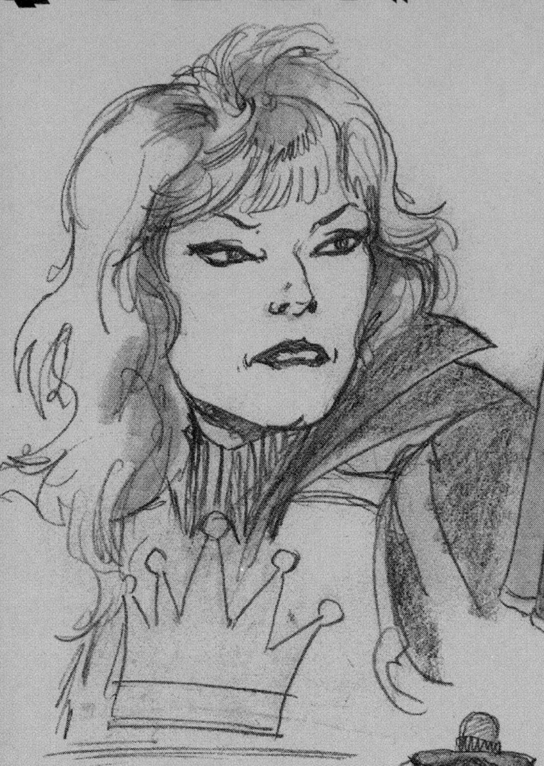

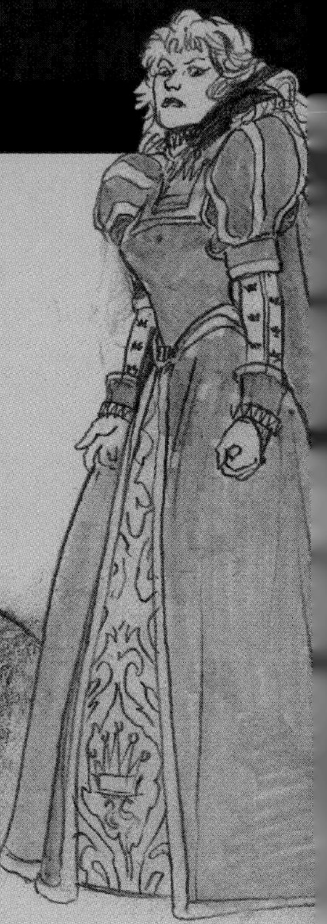

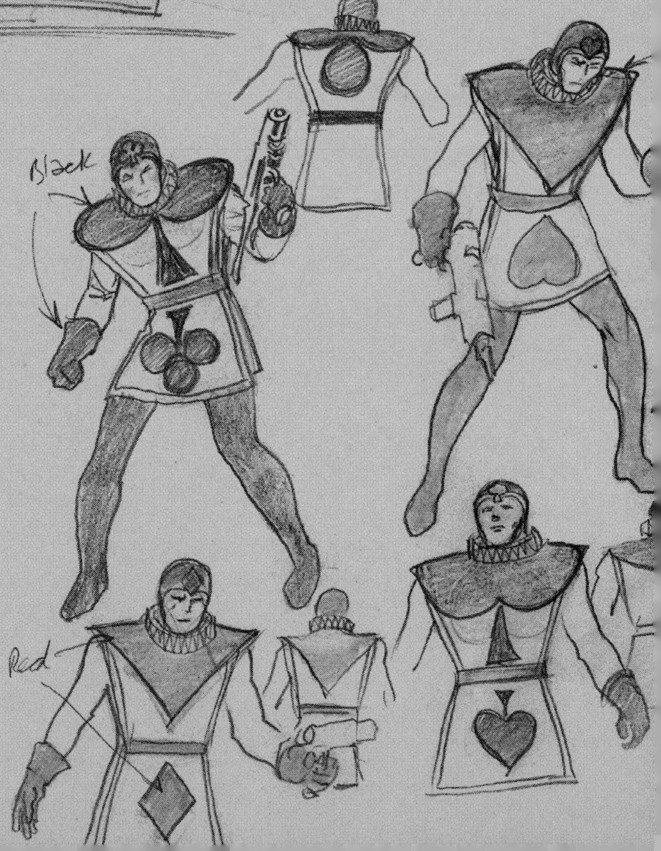
Black
Red

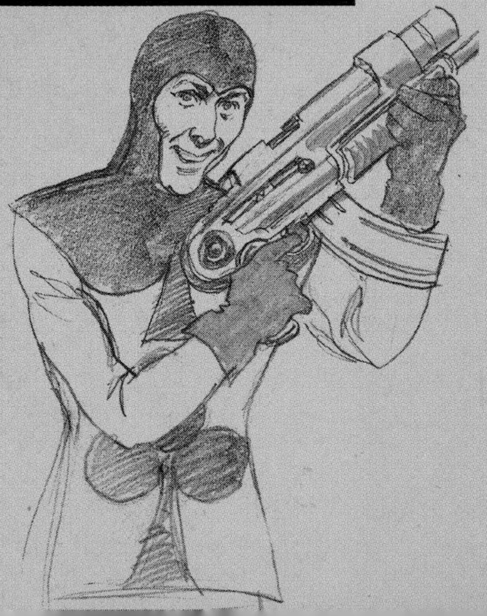

CHESSMEN

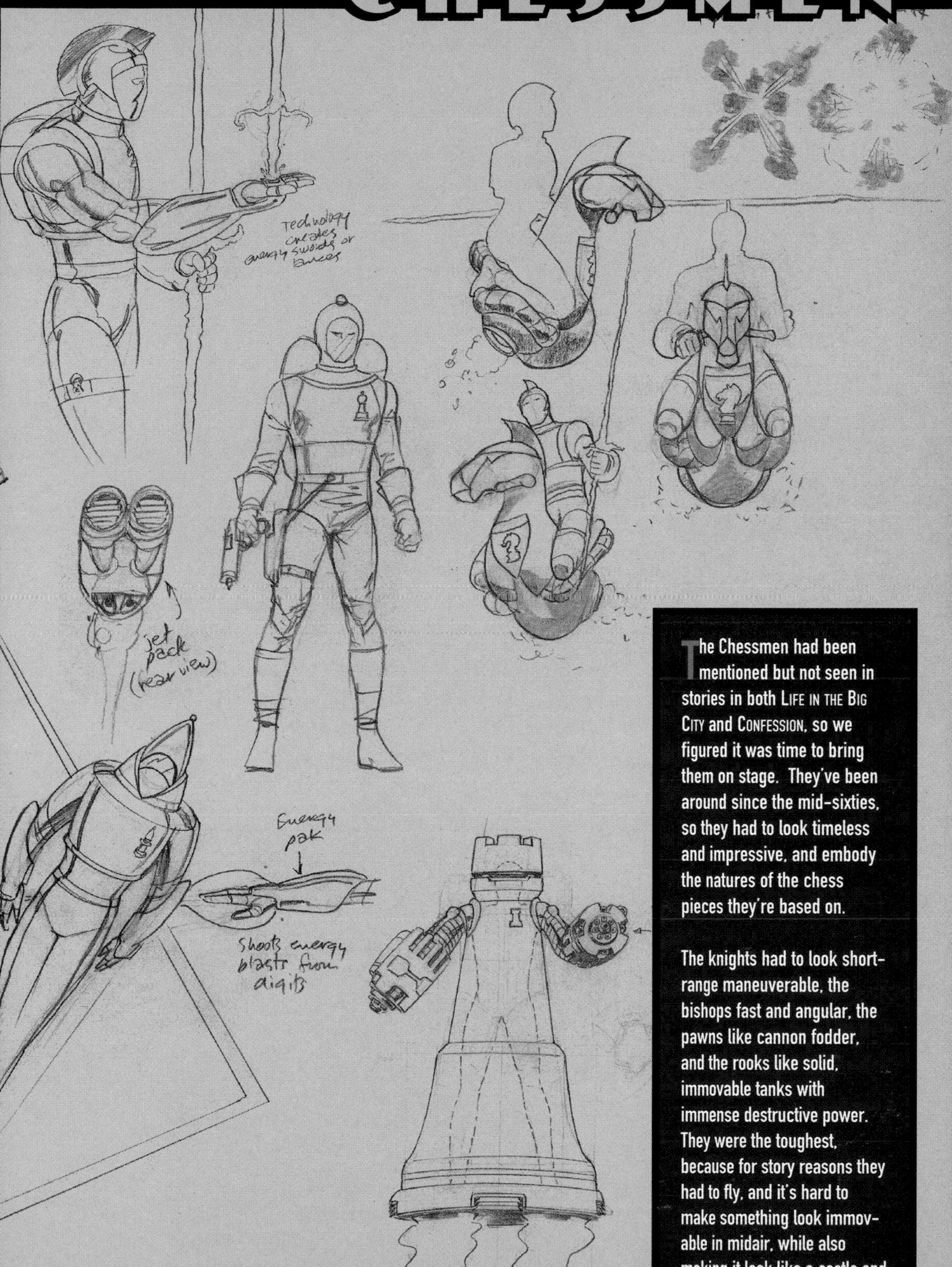
technology creates energy swords or lances
jet pack (rear view)
Energy pak
Shoots energy blasts from digits

The Chessmen had been mentioned but not seen in stories in both Life in the Big City and Confession, so we figured it was time to bring them on stage. They've been around since the mid-sixties, so they had to look timeless and impressive, and embody the natures of the chess pieces they're based on.

The knights had to look short-range maneuverable, the bishops fast and angular, the pawns like cannon fodder, and the rooks like solid, immovable tanks with immense destructive power. They were the toughest, because for story reasons they had to fly, and it's hard to make something look immovable in midair, while also making it look like a castle and more like a suit of armor than a vehicle. I'm still not sure we succeeded entirely, but it works well enough.

CONQUISTADOR

Our master villain.

We wanted someone of weight and power, and I knew he was going to be an armored villain, both to provide him with an all-concealing mask and to contrast his encasing himself in a metal shell with Steeljack's natural one.

As usual, we started with the name. Brent took elements of conquistador armor and built a design around that, but like many preliminary Astro City designs, it was too close to the source material – the conquistador elements were too much on the surface and not integrated enough into the design.

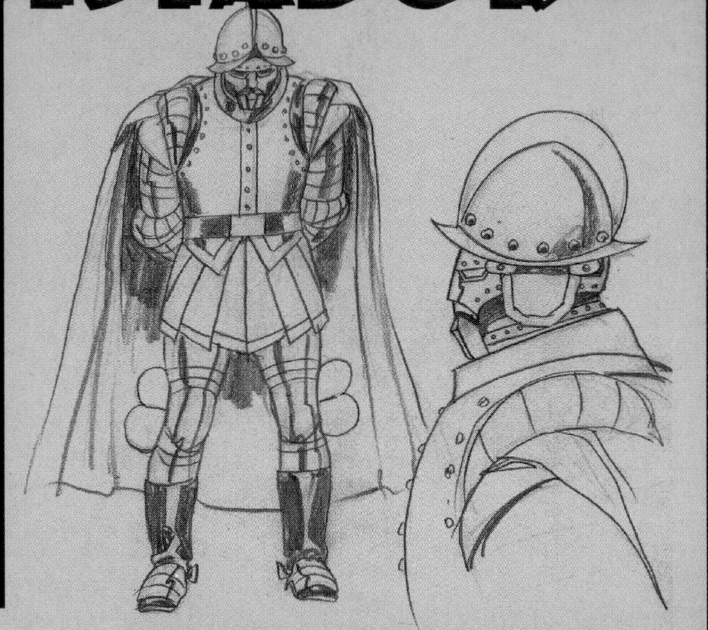

Alex took Brent's first sketches and reworked them, simplifying the design without losing the distinctive elements that said "conquistador," resulting in a more super-heroic design. Brent took it and reworked it a little –

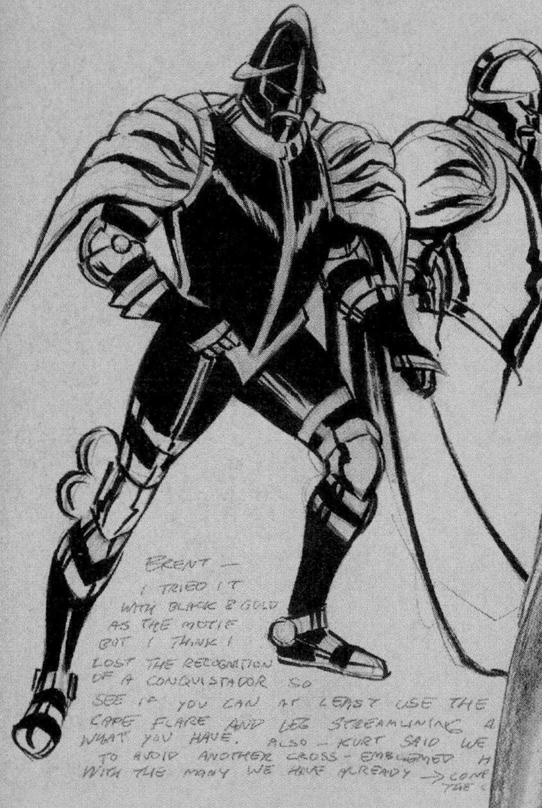

BRENT –
I TRIED IT
WITH BLACK & GOLD
AS THE MOTIF
BUT I THINK I
LOST THE RECOGNITION
OF A CONQUISTADOR SO
SEE IF YOU CAN AT LEAST USE THE
CAPE FLARE AND LEG STREAMLINING
WHAT YOU HAVE. ALSO – KURT SAID WE
TO AVOID ANOTHER CROSS-EMBLEMED
WITH THE MANY WE HAVE ALREADY → CON
THE

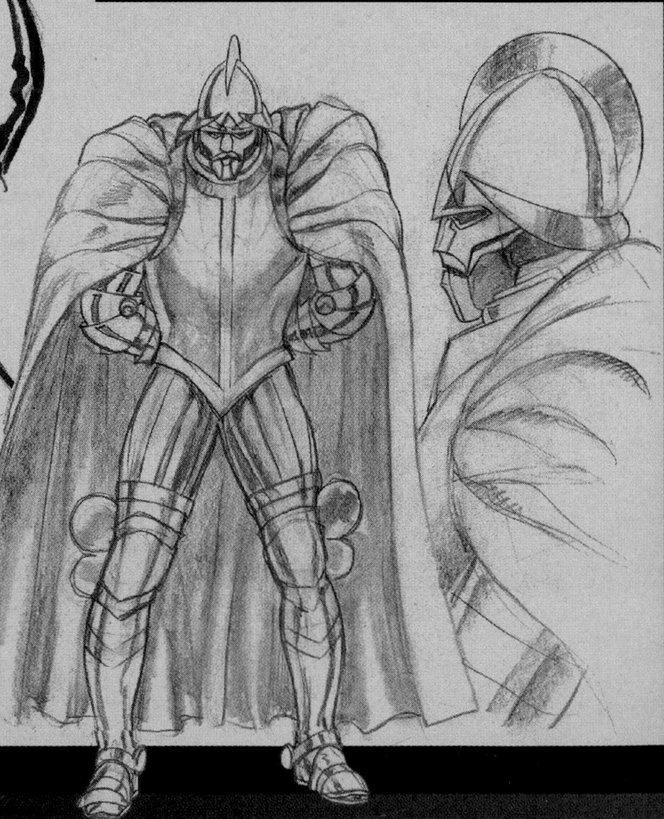

– and we had our mastermind.

Or at least, we had his exterior. Inside the armor, though, he had the same weaknesses and fears

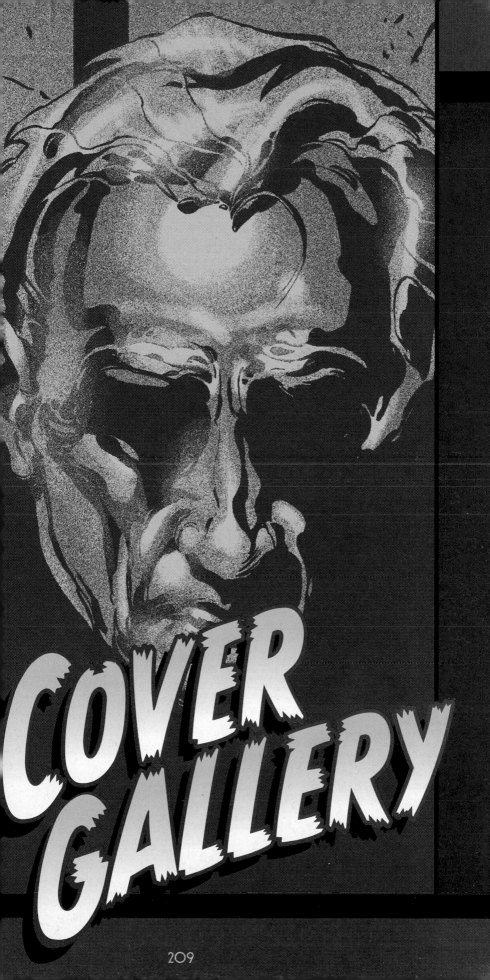

COVER GALLERY

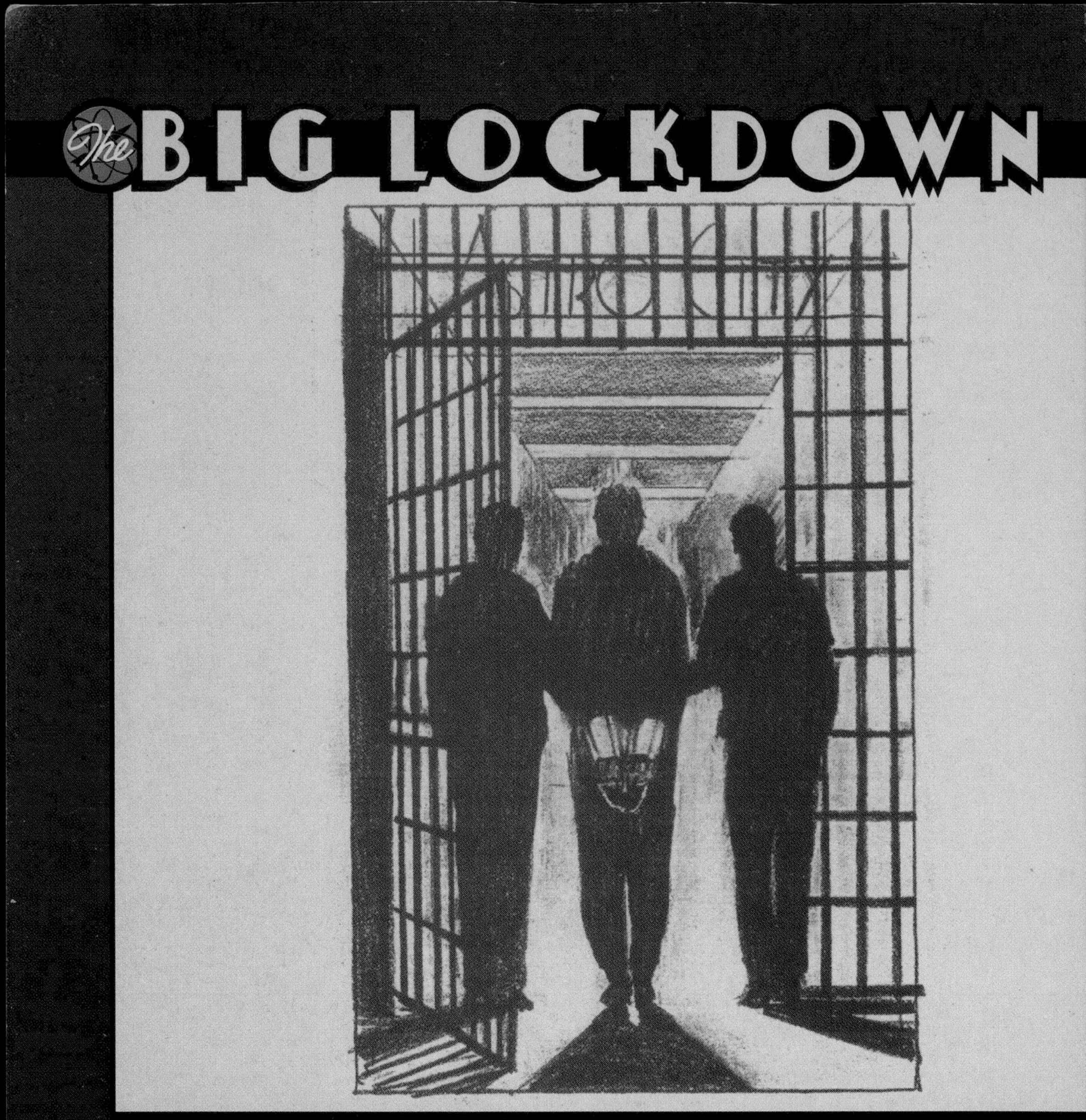

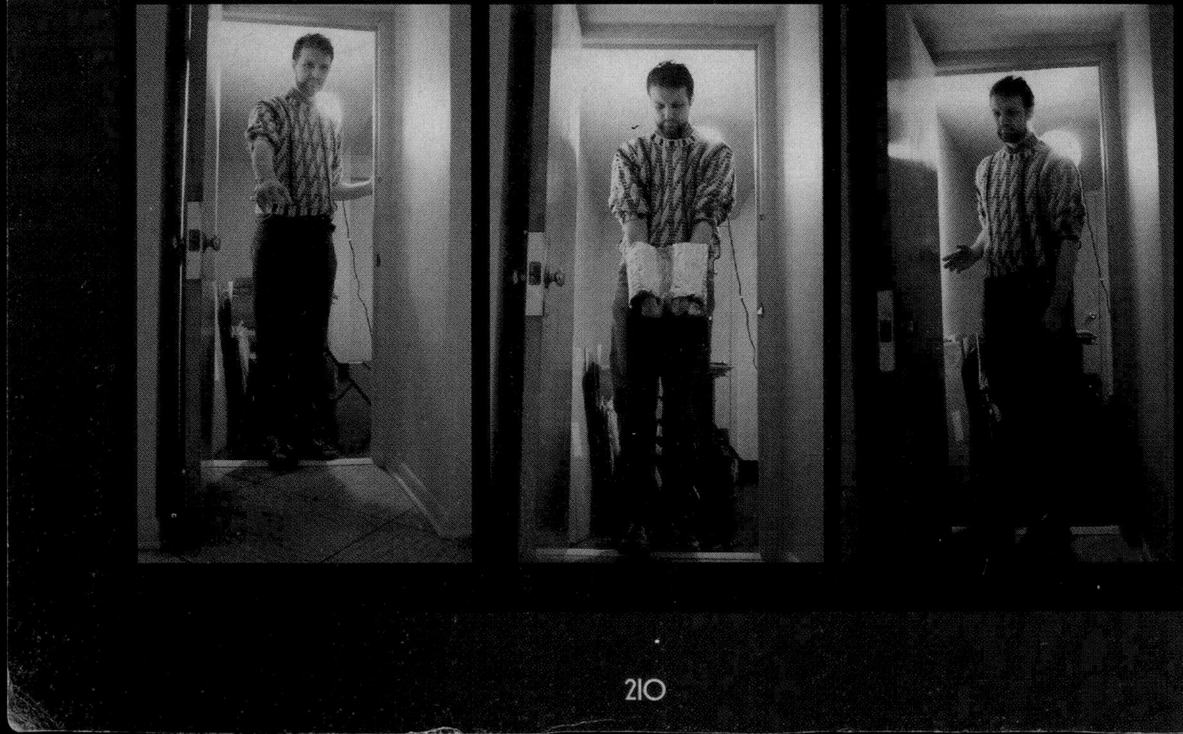

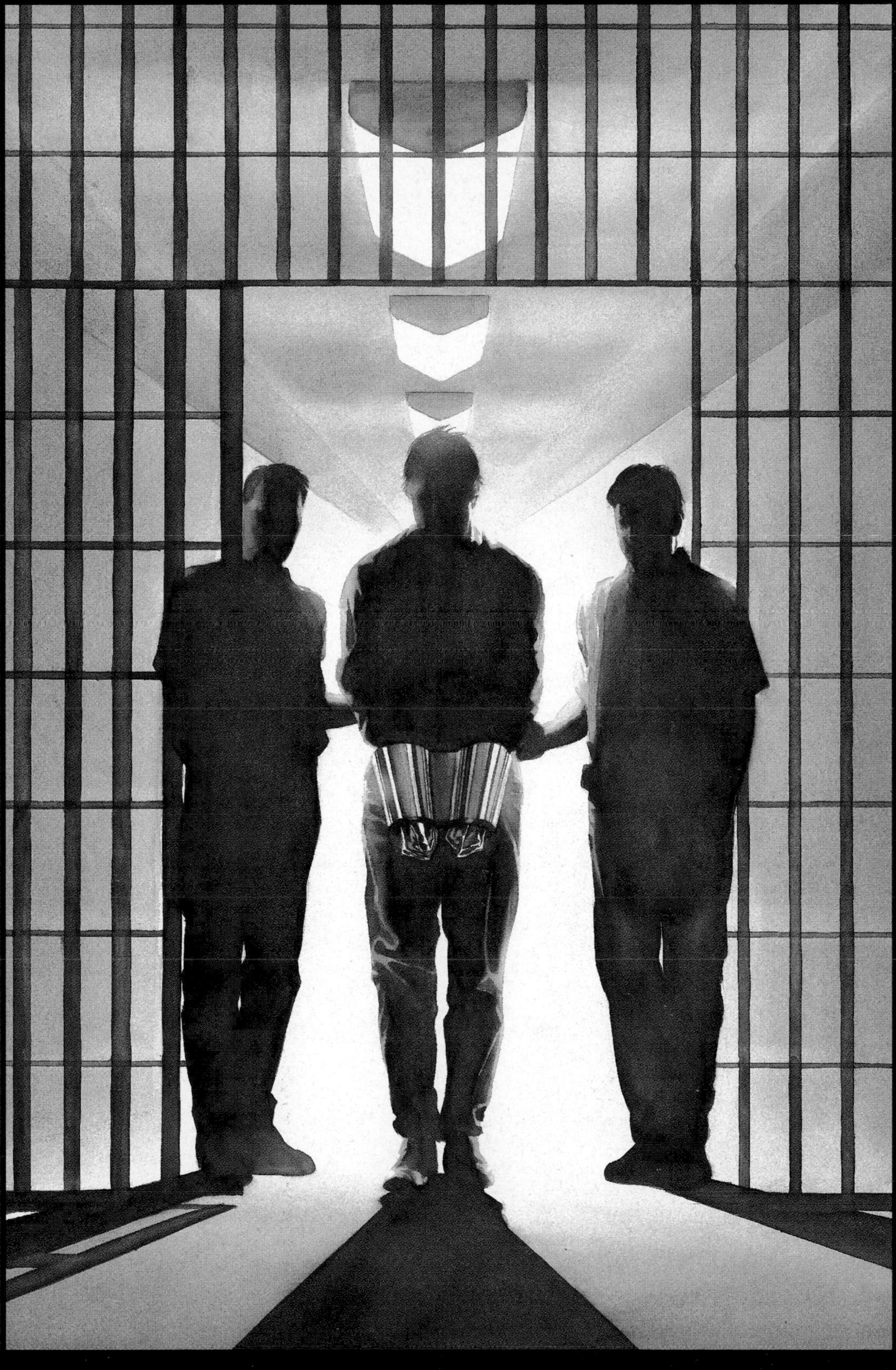

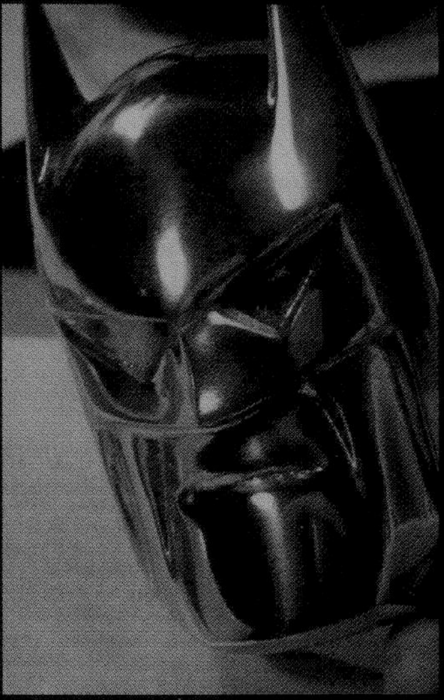

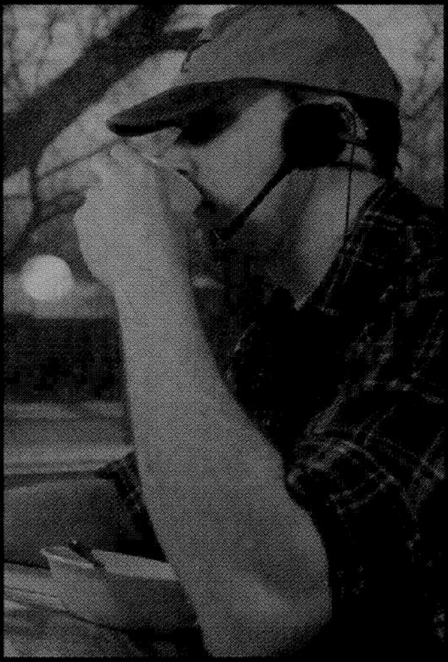

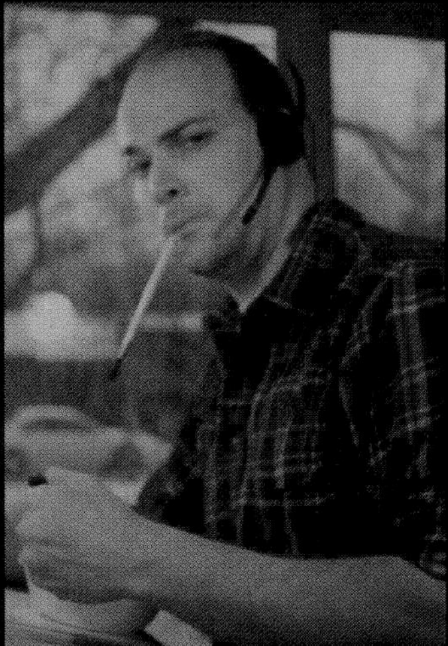

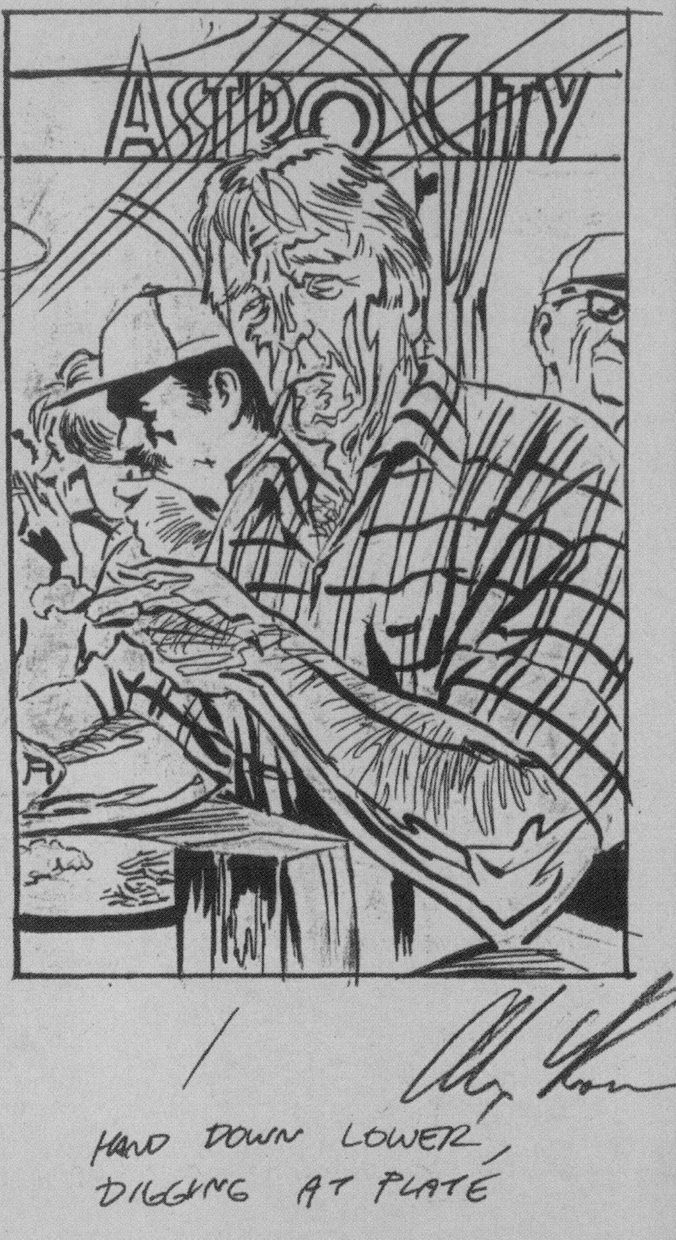
ASTRO CITY
HAND DOWN LOWER,
DIGGING AT PLATE

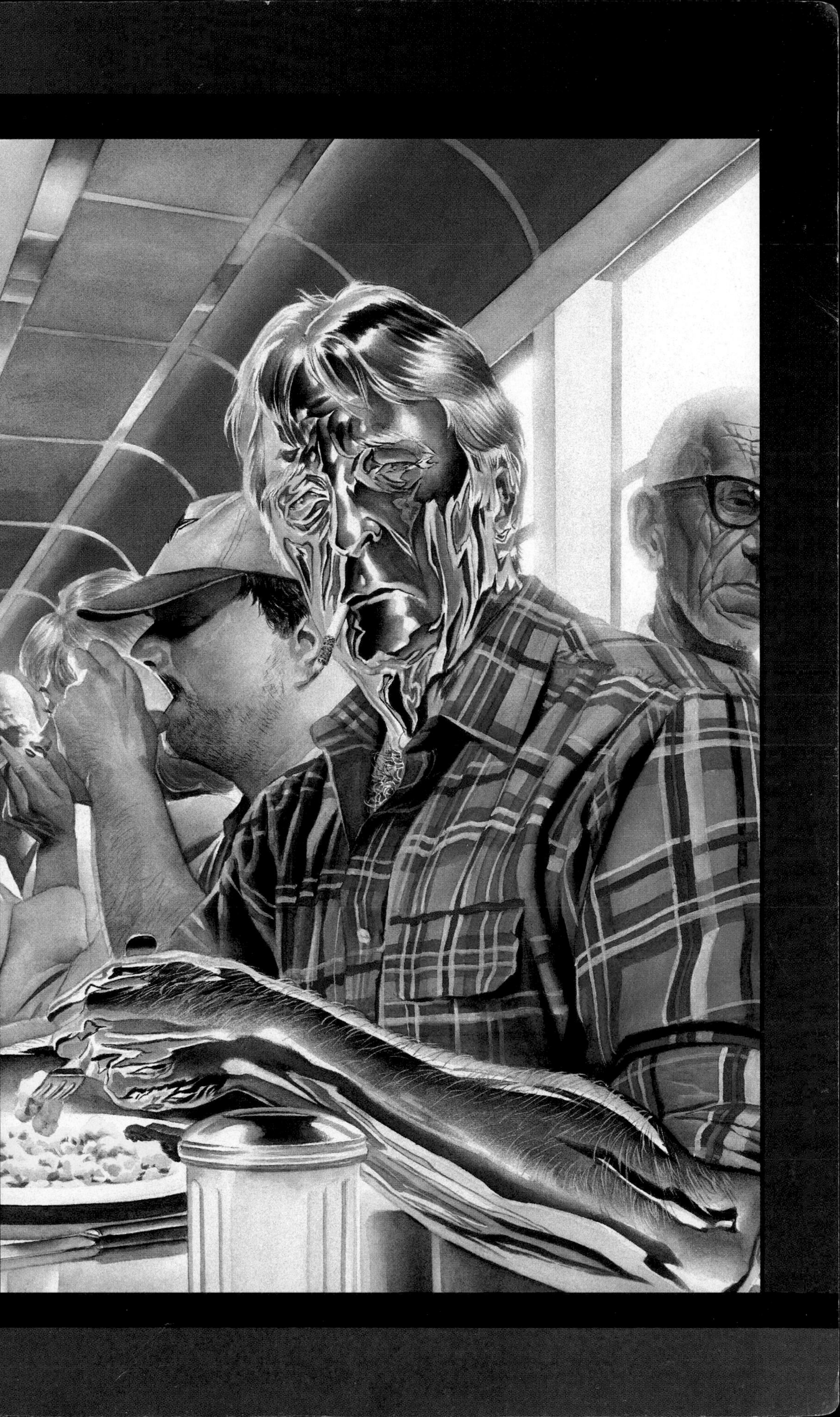

ASTRO CITY

— COSTUME LOOKING PURPLE?

RED SASH

AND RED COSTUME DETAILS. ON HOMBRE 8 BRAVO

EL HOMBRE & BRAVO

— ALL GOLDEN TONES

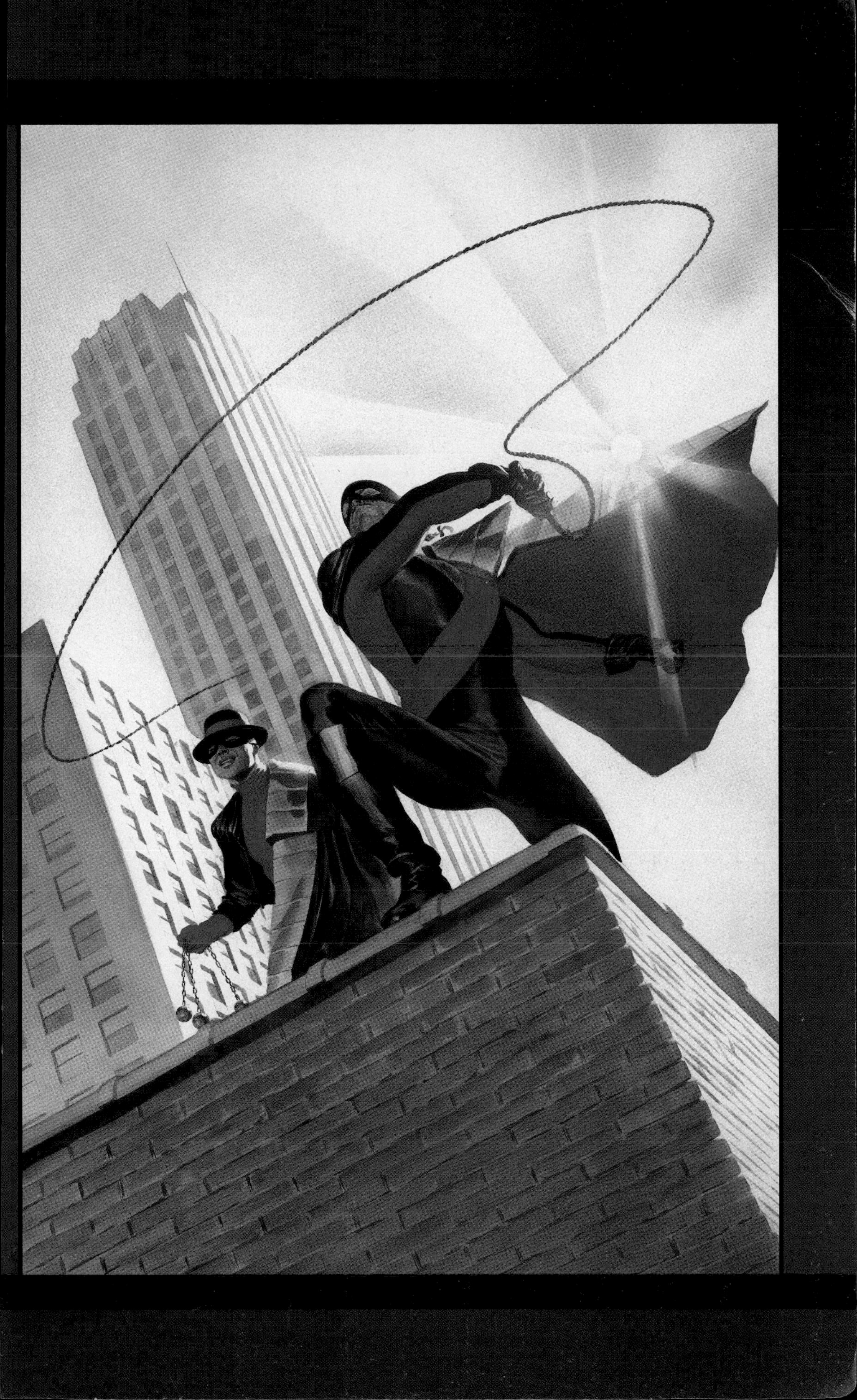

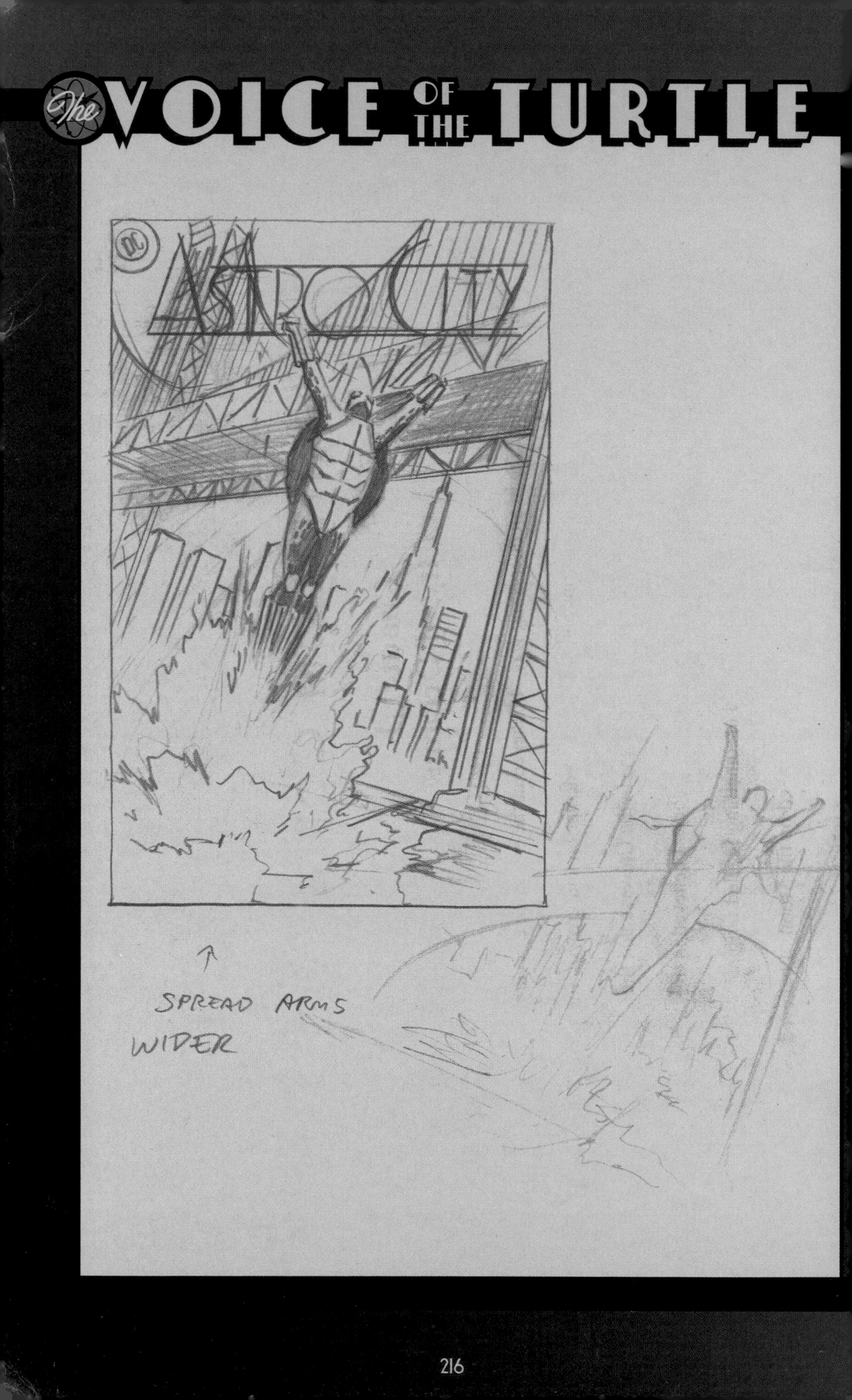
DC
ASTRO CITY
SPREAD ARMS
WIDER

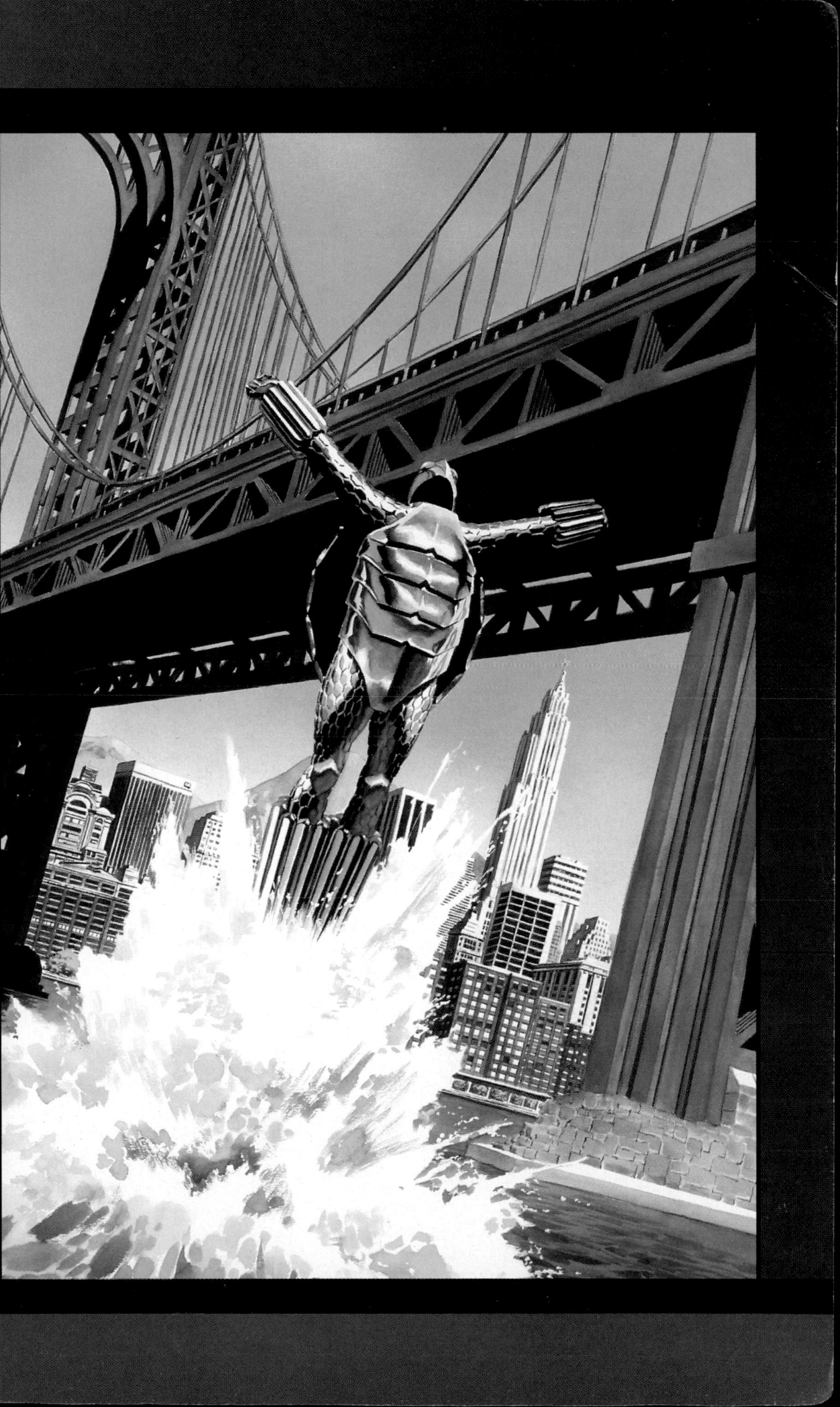

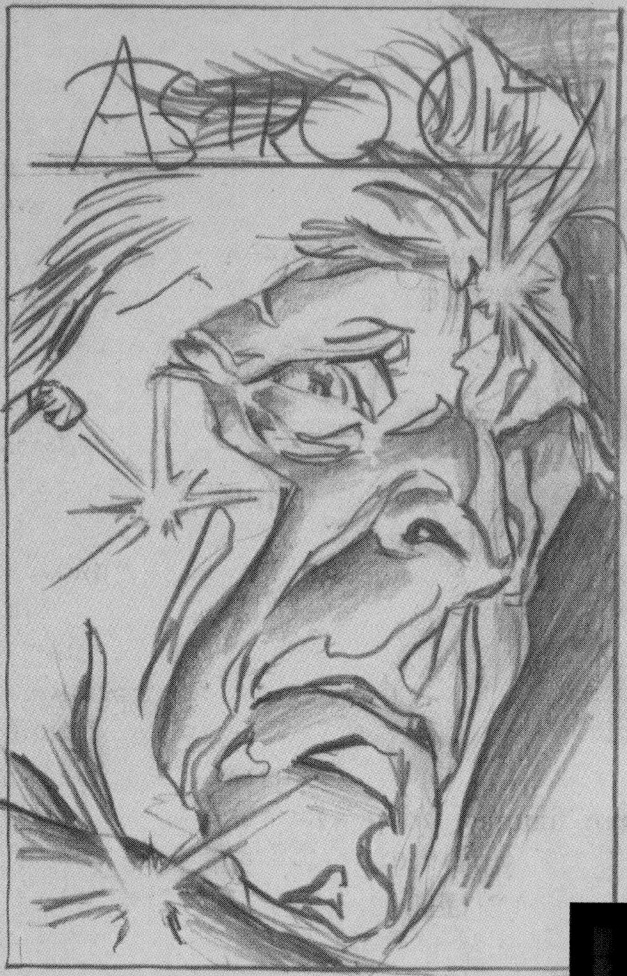
ASTRO CITY

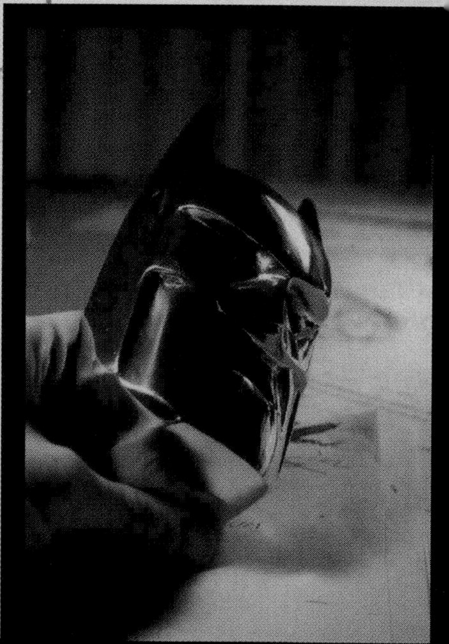

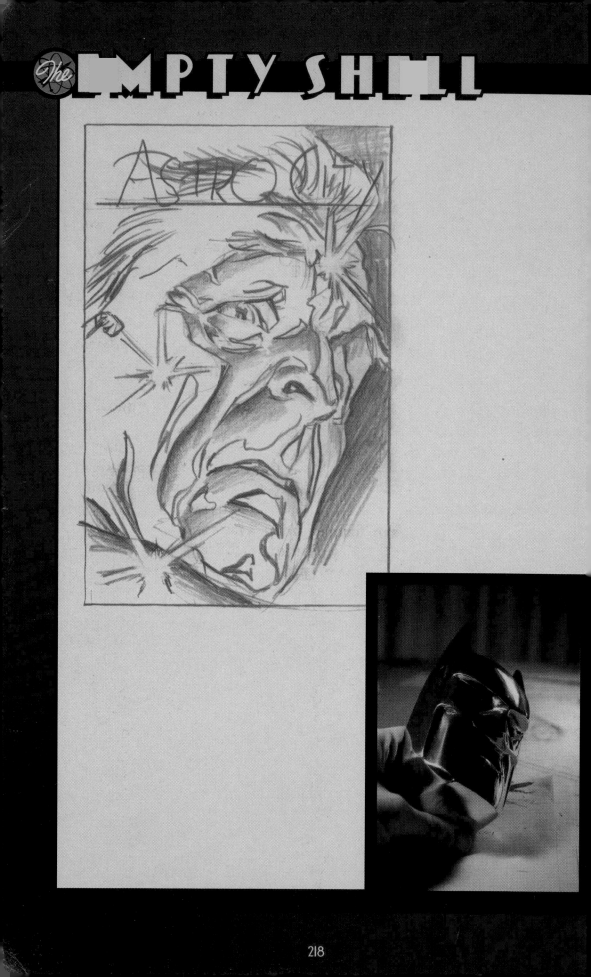

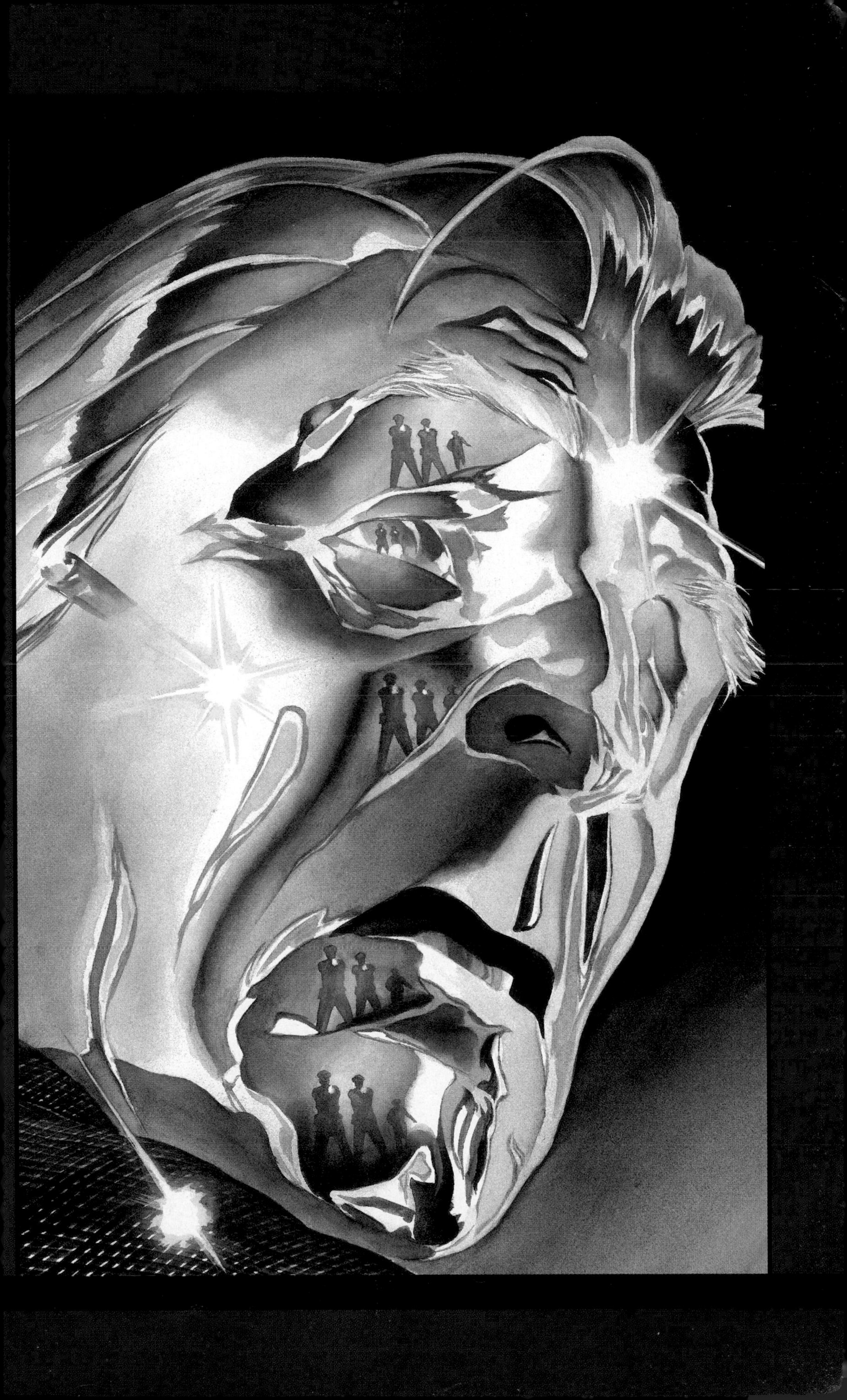

The ONLY CHANCE

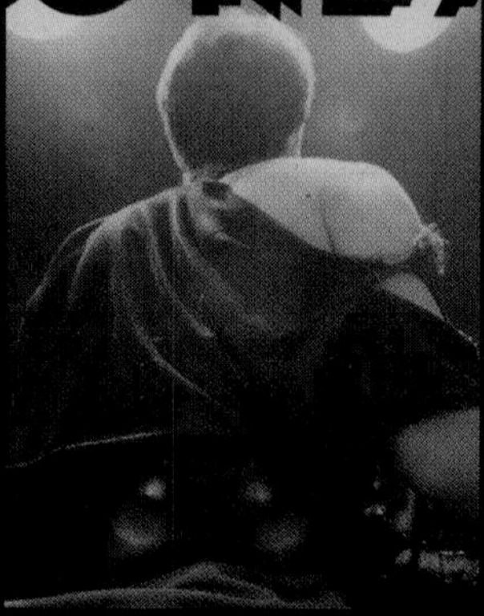

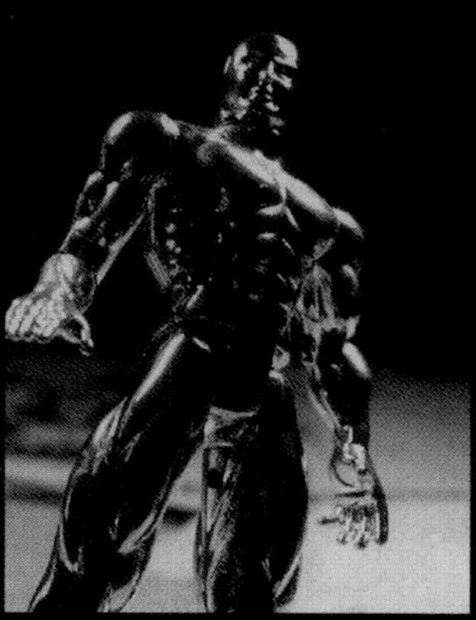

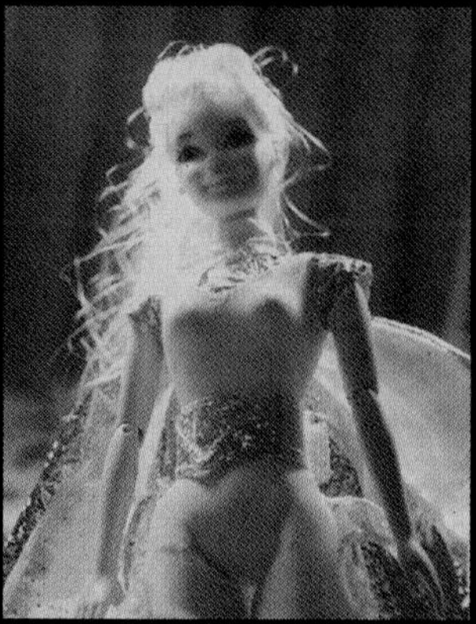

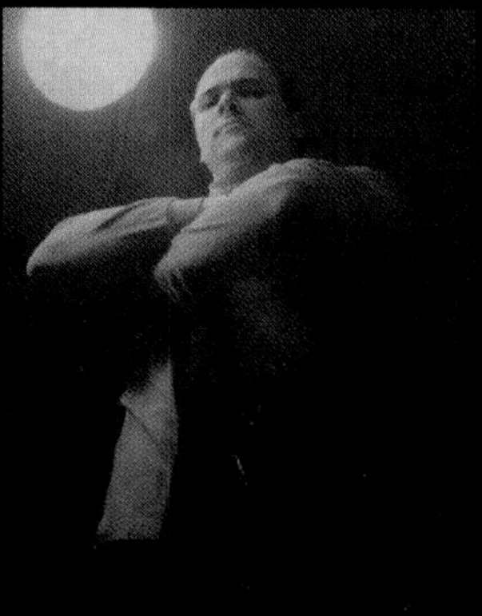

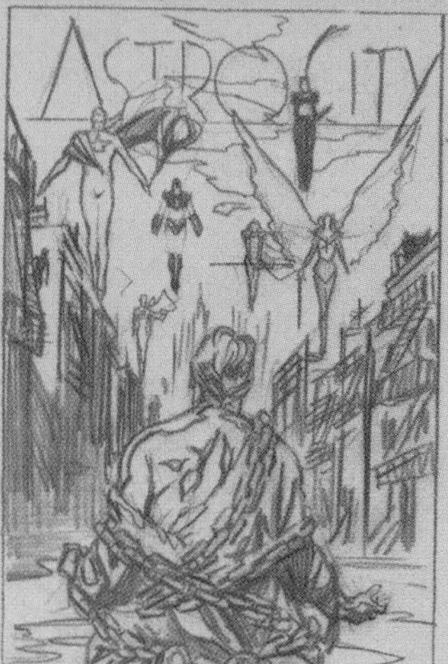
ASTRO CITY

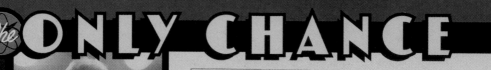

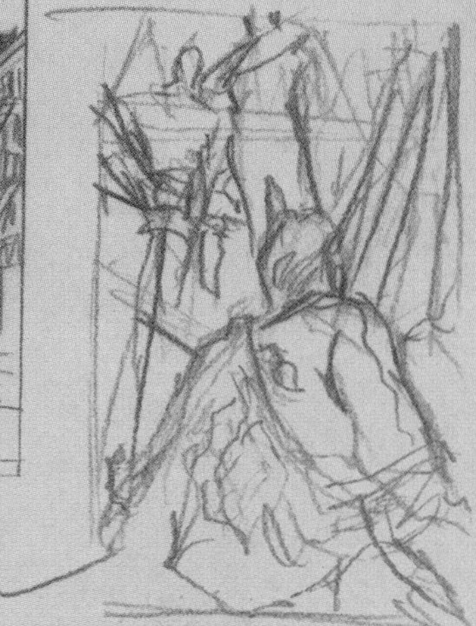
FOOTBALL SHIRT

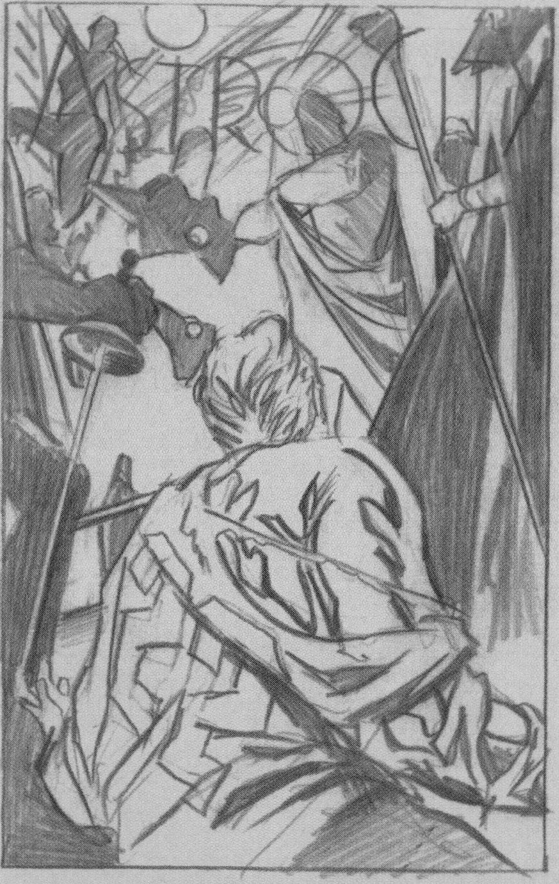

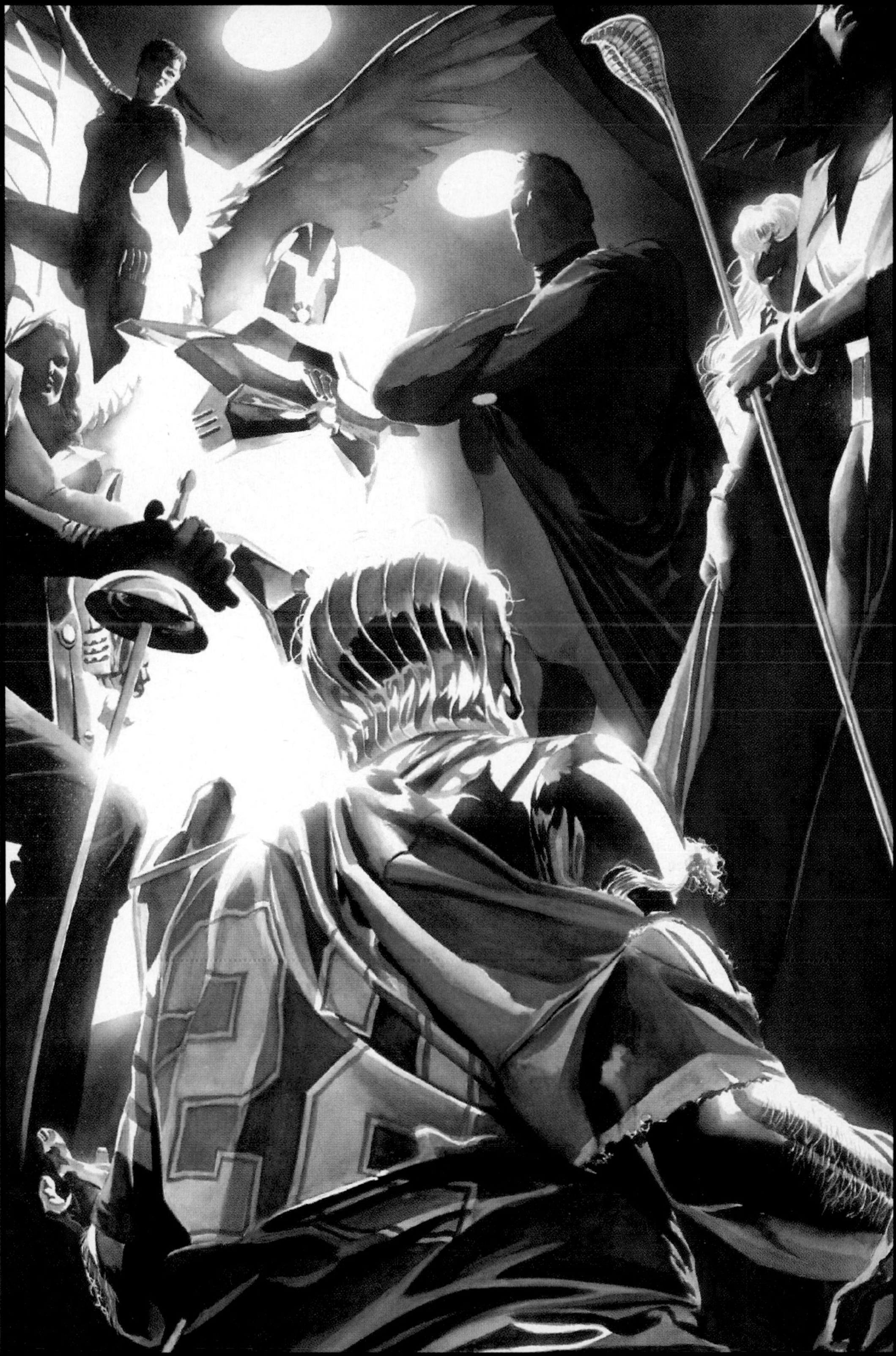

The WOW FINISH

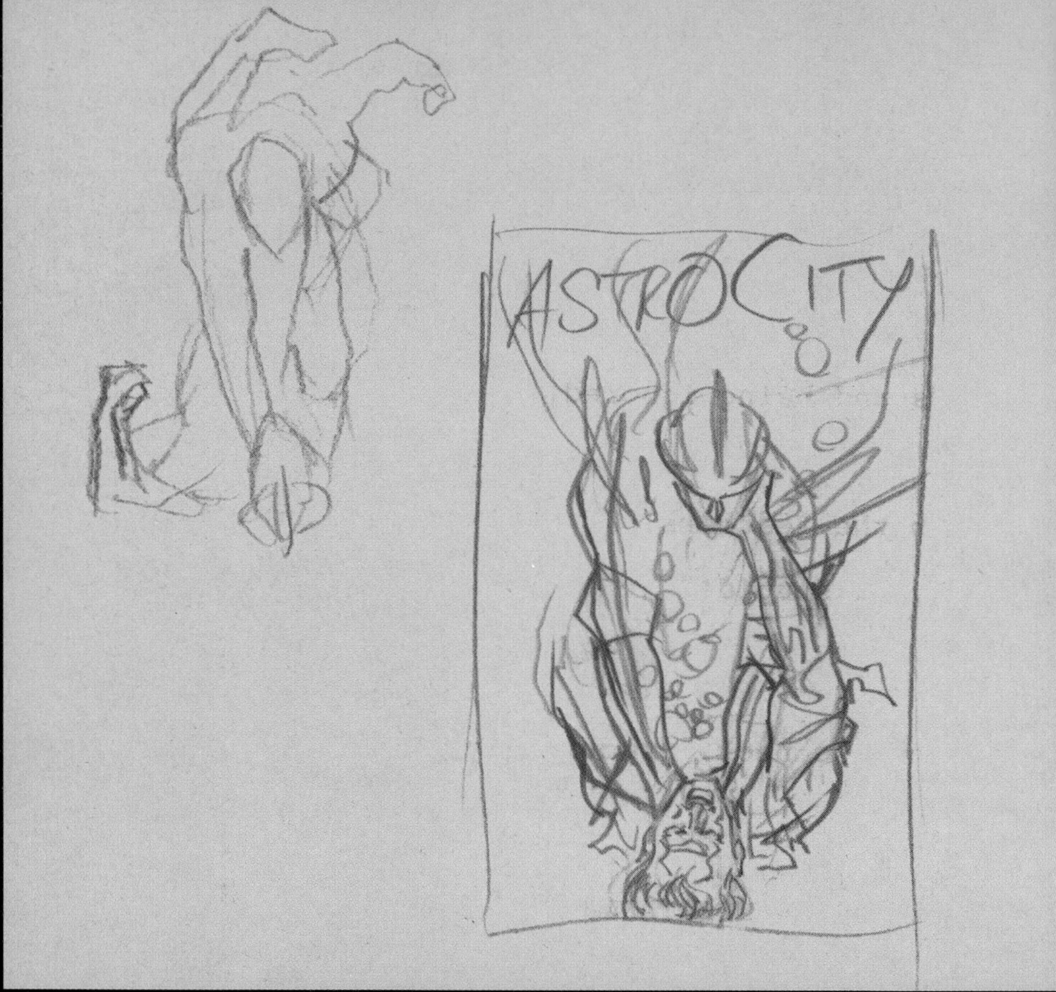
ASTRO CITY

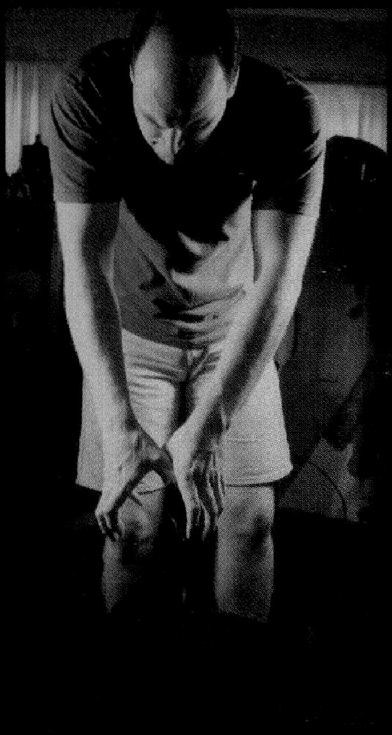

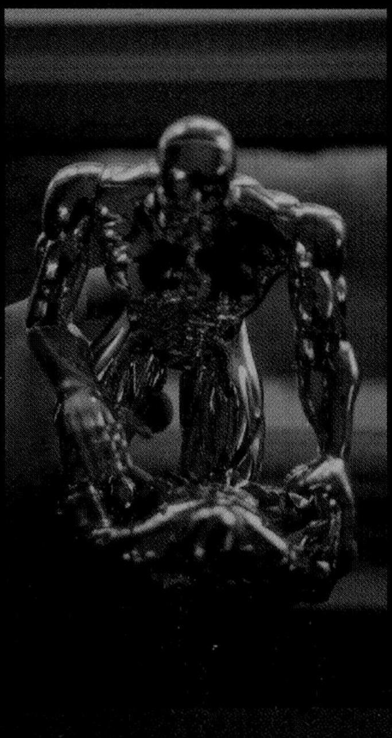

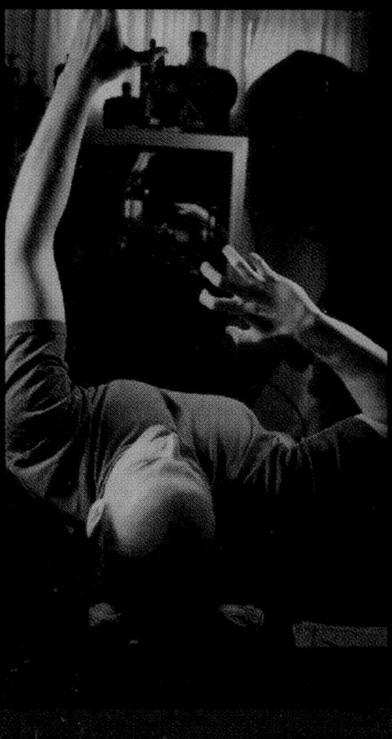

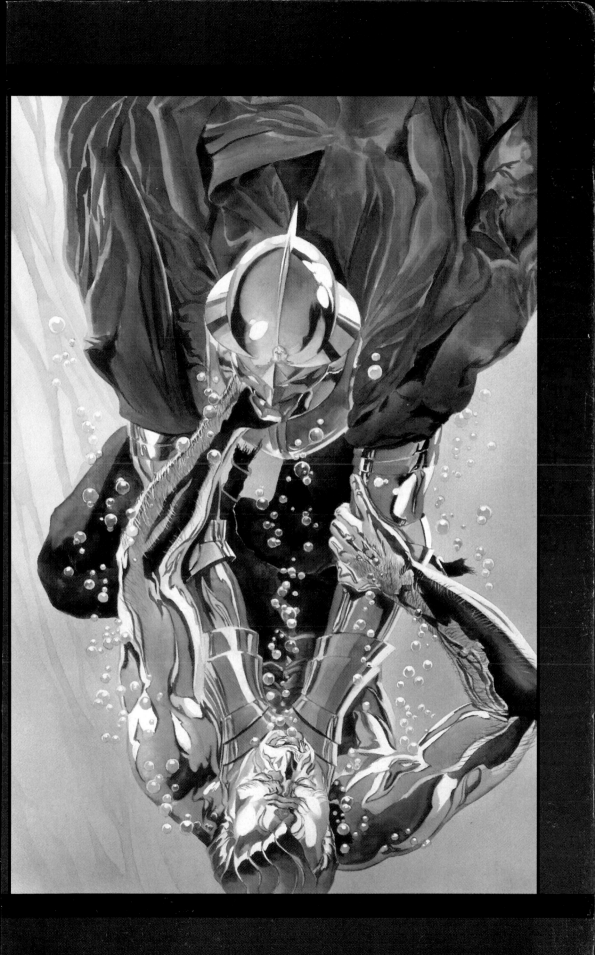

ACKNOWLEDGMENTS

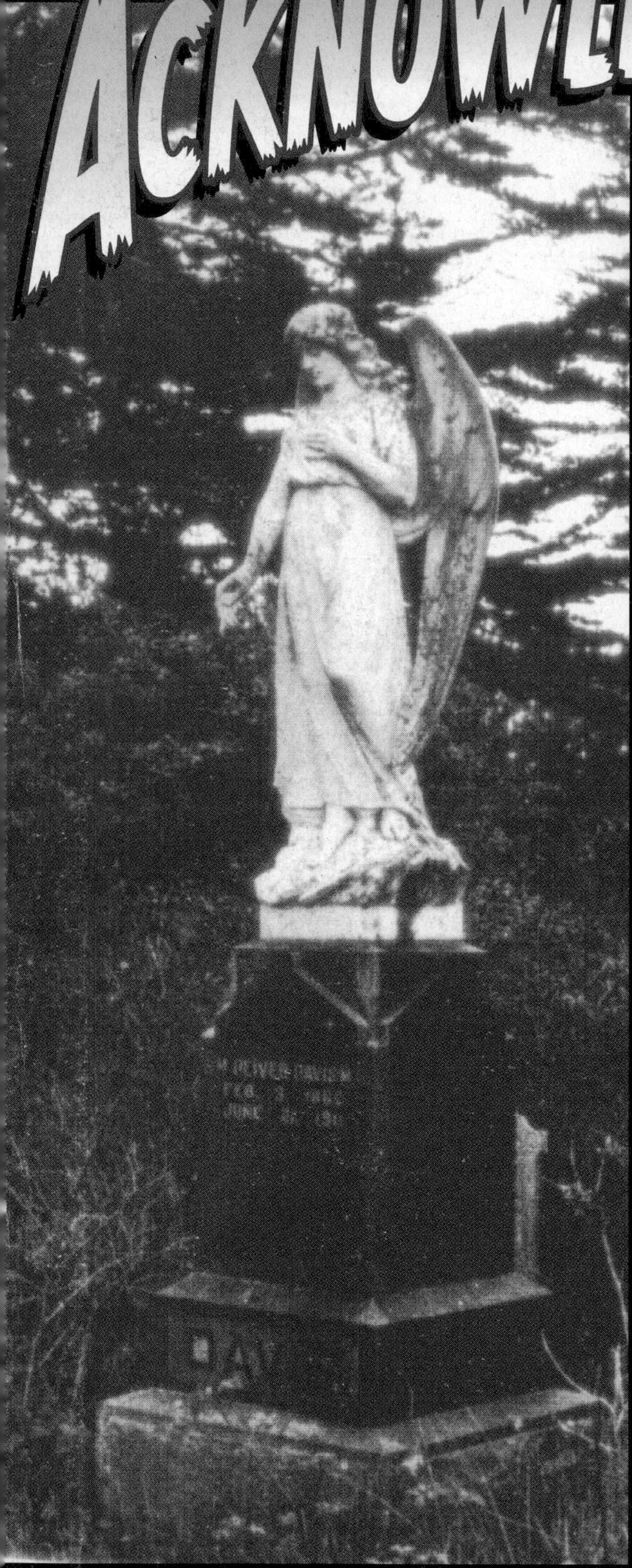

My thanks, this time around, to everyone involved with the book for their extreme patience – to the readers who kept faith with us even when the book was late, and to my collaborators, who stuck around even when the scripts appeared infrequently at best. I appreciate it, folks – and maybe I'll eventually make it through an extended storyline without getting sick for months.

Thanks also to the usual informal support network for their advice and suggestions – and specifically to Richard Starkings for vetting the "Britishisms" of "The Voice of the Turtle." And belated thanks to Gary Martin, who pitched in and inked half an issue in our last volume, and inadvertently got left out of the credits. Our sincere apologies, sir.

-- *Kurt Busiek*

Big props to all those readers who patiently awaited the next issue, and to John Layman for his tireless interest in the series; also, to my buds Ben and J.G. for their invaluable enhancement of Steeljack and his world; and to Will for our ongoing collaboration. And a final thank-you to the Davis family of Manchester, California whose beautiful angel stands against the elements in one corner of the Manchester Cemetery, and whose image now adorns the denouement of Steeljack's story.

-- *Brent Eric Anderson*

My thanks for Steve Darnall's help in modeling.

-- *Alex Ross*